OBJECT-ORIENTED DESIGN MEASUREMENT

Scott A. Whitmire
Advanced Systems Research

WILEY COMPUTER PUBLISHING

John Wiley & Sons, Inc.
New York • Chichester • Weinheim • Brisbane • Singapore • Toronto

Publisher: Robert Ipsen
Editor: Marjorie Spencer
Managing Editor: Micheline Frederick
Text Design & Composition: Pro-Image Corp.

This text is printed on acid-free paper.

Library of Congress Cataloging-in-Publication Data:
Whitmire, Scott A., 1959–
    Object-oriented design measurement / Scott A. Whitmire.
       p.   cm.
    Includes index.
    ISBN 0-471-13417-1 (cloth : alk. paper)
    1. Object-oriented programming (Computer science)   2. Computer
software—Development.   3. Computer software—Quality control.
    I. Title.
    QA76.64.W437   1997
    005.1'17—dc21
                                                              97-11380
                                                                 CIP

Printed in the United States of America
10 9 8 7 6 5 4 3 2 1

To Lisa, Stuart, and Paula, for your patience, love, and understanding.

PREFACE

Software development today is like Calvinball, from the comic strip Calvin and Hobbes: We make the rules up as we go along and we never play the game the same way twice. It is no wonder that we software people are so enamored with technology: It's the only tangible thing in this business. The intangibles, like process and people, are so chaotic that we practitioners have nothing to hold onto. So rather than learn a way of doing business, which will change with every project, we become expert at using a particular set of tools, a technology. Then, when we encounter a problem for which our tools are of no help, we are surprised, shocked . . . and stuck.

Like many endeavors, the intangibles in software development are the keys to success. Effective processes and skilled people can take you into new territory, help you learn and incorporate new tools, and do better with the tools you have. We need to get a handle on our intangibles. We need to be able to describe them, think and talk about them, and change them.

The trend towards process improvement is encouraging. Measurement is an important part of any improvement effort. Measurement is also an important part of day-to-day business. Much has been written about using measurement data to manage projects and organizations. Much, much less has been written about using measurement data to design products or processes. This book fills that gap.

Measurement has become an essential component in my design tool kit. Many of the design decisions for which I had to rely on folklore and myth can now be made using quantitative data. Design measurement and analysis have always appealed to my engineering and accounting background.

One of the great difficulties I have had applying measures to designs is the lack of design measures. This is especially true for object-oriented designs, at least until very recently. Unfortunately, even those design measures that are available do not address a specific understanding of a particular design characteristic. This means that while I can measure many characteristics of a design, I cannot always measure the characteristics I want to measure. My continual frustration at the availability and quality of existing design measures, particularly for object-oriented designs, led me to write this book.

While researching this book, I learned many things, the most surprising of which is how naive we software engineers are about measurement. I spent several months learning basic measurement theory and the mathematics behind it. I was surprised at the number of ways we can construct measures to represent some interesting characteristic. Many of the structures I learned about are very familiar in settings other than software. Euclidean geometry, for example, is a three-dimensional spatial proximity structure, which just happens to support a metric. This insight, and many others, sparks the imagination when it comes to envisioning solutions to many of the measurement problems we face in software.

I was disappointed to discover the utter lack of understanding we have about objects and object-oriented software from design and measurement perspectives. Many design characteristics, including size, complexity, coupling, and cohesion are underdefined or not defined at all. Some of these characteristics are so poorly defined as to render them useless for making design decisions. These conditions contribute to the total lack of any formal description of object-oriented software upon which we can base models of designs and measurement.

My research into object models led me through type theory, language design, and formal specification languages, none of which helped me design or measure better. The search for a suitable object model led me to metaphysics and philosophy. From there, using what I had learned about set theory and discrete mathematics, I was able to formulate an object model.

By applying both formal specification techniques and my checklists for class and method designs, I was able to add an analysis technique to the model, resulting in a complete theory of object-oriented software—not from a language perspective, but from a designer's perspective. I now had something I have wanted for years: a means to measure design characteristics and a means to test a design algebraically to determine its behavior under a given set of circumstances.

But one thing was yet missing: actual measures. Applying existing design measures to what I had learned was very disappointing. Very few current measures correctly apply measurement theory to our understanding of design characteristics. This is not too surprising, given our meager understanding of both measurement theory and most design characteristics. Things are so bad, that rather than include a set of existing measures in this book, as I had originally planned, I had to build several new measures. During this process, I "discovered" ("stumbled across" is more accurate) a way to examine a characteristic, explain it empirically in terms of my formal model, map that explanation to one of the many structures from measurement theory, then construct a theoretically valid measure for the precise characteristic I want to measure.

This book, then, contains the results of over two years of research, learning, and hard work, which were preceded by over 15 years of software development experience. It is the culmination of my work to date in both software measurement and software development.

HOW THE BOOK IS ORGANIZED

The book is organized into three parts. In the Prologue, I define software engineering, discuss the very important concept of the design as hypothesis, with everything that implies, and measurement as a design tool. Part I puts measurement into the overall context of software engineering. Chapter 1 provides a framework for measurement, including various views of measurement, objects of measurement, roles of measurement in design, and the three dimensions from which software can be measured.

In Chapter 2, I describe the front end of the design process I have evolved over the years. I use the *crash and burn* approach to process development. I borrowed this approach from aviation. After a project crashes, which may range from a minor delay in delivery to a major event which prohibits completion, I try as best as I can to figure out what went wrong. When I determine the probable cause, I modify my process to prevent the problem from recurring. At least, that's the idea.

Chapter 3 presents the Goal Question Metric approach to selecting measures. It also includes my technique for constructing a measure from an empirical understanding of some design characteristic, a model, and measurement theory. A key part of this process is what I believe to be the only listing of measurement structure by scale type. The measure construction technique and this cross-reference listing proved to be invaluable tools for writing the chapters in Part III.

Part II contains the technical information I needed to write Part III. Chapter 4 contains brief introductions to several structures from discrete mathematics. These structures are used in measurement theory, object theory, or are required to understand some other structure that is used.

Chapter 5 contains what I learned about measurement theory. Some of this material is familiar in that we've seen it before in the software engineering literature. The vast majority of this material will be new to you. I guarantee it.

Chapters 4 and 5 may be skipped upon your initial reading. They contain reference material to allow the book to stand on its own. As you use the techniques in this book, you will need to refer to these chapters. Including them makes such reference more convenient. Your only risk in skipping them is that some of the terms and constructs in Chapter 6 through 15 will be unfamiliar and confusing.

Chapter 6 presents my theory of objects. The theory includes a formal model and a means of manipulating that model. The model forms the basis for expressing an empirical understanding of some design characteristic, including many not included in Part III. The analytical techniques allow you to seed a design with an event, propagate a series of messages through the design, and determine its final state, all without having to execute code. You can also describe design changes in terms of nine operations you can apply to the design. Combining these, and with the support of a tool, you can test a design by executing it directly. Or, you can modify it, then test the changes, all without writing code or even modifying the current design models.

Part III applies all that comes before to a set of nine design characteristics, each of which is covered in a separate chapter. In the chapters of Part III, I define nine new, unnamed measures—one for each design characteristic. This part includes 12 measures, but three of them are too obvious to be considered new.

Size (Chapter 7) is an important characteristic with many uses, including estimating and normalizing. Complexity (Chapter 8) is also an important input into the estimating process and gives clues about where the defects are most likely to reside. Complexity is suspected to contribute to increased maintenance costs, but we can't yet prove anything. Coupling (Chapter 9) is the best understood design characteristic I cover. It is straightforward, fairly simple, and easy to measure. Many people believe coupling to be a form of complexity. Coupling most certainly influences the scope of many types of modifications and contributes to exposure to change, a form of volatility.

Sufficiency (Chapter 10), Completeness (Chapter 11), and Cohesion (Chapter 12) together measure the quality of an abstraction in the analysis model or of a design component in the design. These three concepts are closely related, and can be used to assess the degree to which we have met our requirements and the degree to which we can reuse domain-level abstractions and design components. In this book, we take a view of cohesion that is different than that taken by nearly every person researching the topic. You'll have to read Chapter 12 to see why.

Primitiveness (Chapter 13) describes the extent to which an object's methods do not depend on other methods of the object. Ideally, the methods in the public interface should represent coherent operations relevant to the abstraction the object represents. These operations should use private atomic methods that in turn access the internal structure of the object. This stratification allows us to separate, both logically and physically, an object's interface from its implementation.

Similarity (Chapter 14) is a characteristic that I use very often when I consider creating superclasses to contain common properties of two or more classes in my design. I have identified four kinds of similarity and developed a measure for three of them.

Volatility (Chapter 15) has two faces: The likelihood an object will be changed due to changes in the domain and the risk of change due to a change in some other object. We have long known that highly volatile parts of the design should be isolated into as few components as possible. We have also known to isolate these components as much as possible from the rest of the design. Until now, only one other attempt has been made to measure this characteristic (Martin 1994). That attempt was based on a weak empirical understanding of the problem and had no underlying model.

Volatility, size, and probably complexity have a major influence on the staffing requirements for maintenance efforts. Those few people who actually estimate maintenance effort do so based solely on size. These people are a step ahead of the vast majority, but they have one major problem: One person can maintain an infinite amount of code or function points if that code or those functions never change. On the other hand, the faster the code or functions change, the less one person is able to handle. In other words, maintenance effort is a function of both size and volatility, and probably complexity. Until now, we haven't been able to model the effects of volatility.

ACKNOWLEDGMENTS

Writing this book has been an interesting exercise. Like all such efforts, it would not have been possible without the support and assistance of many people. First of all, I want to thank Diane Cerra for convincing me to start this project and for getting John Wiley & Sons to accept it. Majorie Spencer took over when Diane moved on. Marjorie has been absolutely amazing to work with, from gentle prodding to encouragement and advice. She has listened, talked, and guided the final form of this book with a patience very uncharacteristic of an editor.

Then, there are the many colleagues, coworkers, and strangers on the Internet who have contributed to, challenged, and honed my understanding of measurement and software. Several of these people deserve special mention. Howard Rubin started me down the road of writing about software measurement. Brian Henderson-Sellers provided a forum to introduce my object theory. People like David Card, Capers Jones, Allan Albrecht, and Tom DeMarco have listened to and answered annoying questions, and offered advice and encouragement.

Chas Dowd, while he did not actively participate in the development of this book, taught me more about how to write than any other single person. Chas not only taught me the skill, but also gave me the confidence in my writing to even think of tackling a project such as this. So, Chas, thank you.

I am especially grateful for the assistance of Nicole Bianco, who reviewed every word, discussed every topic over and over, challenged every assertion, and helped out in many other ways. Through this process, Nikki and I have become friends.

I gratefully thank my family, Lisa, Stuart, and Paula, who gave up a lot to let me indulge myself in this effort. Stuart was very patient while I worked, even when he really wanted to play with his daddy, or with daddy's computer. Paula came along just as the book was nearing completion. For those of you who develop software, this was like getting a new set of requirements during integration testing. Writing a book and having a baby are similar, but different, in many ways. Having a baby is more painful, but not much, and takes much less time.

Lastly, I want to thank you, the reader. If you are reading this, you have either bought the book or have been standing in a book store for a long time. I hope you find the rest of the book as useful as I do.

Scott A. Whitmire
Kent, Washington
September, 1997

CONTENTS

2

AN OBJECT-ORIENTED DESIGN PROCESS   24

3

SELECTING A SET OF MEASURES   55

PART II   TECHNICAL FOUNDATIONS   73

4

MATHEMATICAL STRUCTURES   75

5

MEASUREMENT THEORY   140

6

A THEORY OF OBJECTS   235

15

VOLATILITY   414

FOREWORD

Once in a while a potentially classic book comes along—one that is built not only to last but also to have a lasting impact on its field. In this case, Scott Whitmire's text is likely to offer significant influences on the very foundational ideas underpinning object technology.

Starting with a desire to improve measurement techniques and processes, Scott's research then led him into much more fundamental questions. This necessitated that he learn measurement theory, category theory, and a whole lot of other mathematically and formally focused disciplines that he says he would rather not have had to do. However, in doing so, he uncovered a number of fallacies or miscomprehensions. Whilst applauding the pioneer work in measurement theory by eminent figures such as Horst Zuse and Norman Fenton, he also uncovers a whole other part of measurement theory that has been dormant (at least from an object-oriented context) for very many years.

Scott also dares to attempt to create a formal object model based on category theory. Whilst we have all known that this would be a fruitful path to follow, no one until Scott has dared to accept this challenge in what I know is a difficult area for many of us not trained as pure mathematicians and logicians.

Not until he has undertaken this tour de force does Scott turn to his original aim: Of formally describing many of the object-oriented measures that have been proposed in the literature and are in use in industry today. He summarizes and transcends the empirical, theoretical, and mathematical work done before, integrating it into a whole that is both satisfying and valuable. At the same time, this is not a dry, theoretical treatise with no obvious utility. Scott is an industry user driven to investigate these areas from his industry needs.

Whether the ideas presented here are correct in their detail or not, only time will tell—in their totality, they will open many new avenues of exploration and understanding. Scott Whitmire's text takes a large stride forward into our object-oriented future.

Brian Henderson-Sellers
Director, Centre for Object Technology
Applications and Research (Victoria)

SOFTWARE ENGINEERING IS A VERB

It is pretty clear today that the practice of software development has not quite reached the status of an engineering discipline. When this will happen, and whether it ever will, is a matter of considerable debate. It is my strong belief that not only is it possible to truly engineer software, but we are close to making it reality. Notice that I use the word "engineer" as a verb here. More than a discipline or body of knowledge, engineering is fundamentally a verb, an action word, a way of approaching a problem. Software development *can* become software engineering. This book is part of my contribution towards that end.

Software developers are moving from relying on testing to identify defects to relying on inspections. This does not mean that testing is no longer important. Certain kinds of defects, such as completely missing the point of the requirements (building the wrong system), can best be caught by testing the system as a single entity. We hear, however, of teams and organizations making tremendous progress on reducing their defects through the use of inspections. The goal is to catch defects as early in the process as possible. There is no longer any doubt that inspections are an effective means for detecting defects. Still, something doesn't seem quite right. Let's explore this for a moment.

I'll be the first to point out that manufacturing is a bad analogy for software development. There are many reasons for this, some of which we will discuss later. Even so, manufacturing has some important lessons that we in software should learn. I bring up one here, so bear with me. About 70 years ago, manufacturers began inspecting the finished product before it was shipped from the factory. Even today, manufacturing concerns inspect and/or test both their finished products and the raw materials or components they purchase from their suppliers. This activity evolved into the quality control function. Over time, the quality control function moved into the manufacturing process, eventually inspecting a part after every process sequence or step. Quality Control became the gatekeeper between steps in the manufacturing process. At any point, a part could fail an inspection and be pulled off the line. As time moved on, the pace of business picked up speed. The quality control process became a necessary evil, then an obstacle to be overcome by force or circumvention.

During the 1950s, the Japanese began to listen to people like W. Edwards Demming, who said that quality could not be inspected into a product—it had to be built into it. They began to examine their processes to determine where defects crept into the product. When such a point was found, they worked to modify their process to prevent further defects. They kept this up for over 20 years, until they finally overtook the rest of the world as the leaders in producing quality products. Yet even in Japan, they still exhaustively test and inspect their products, just to be sure. U.S. manufacturers caught on, a bit late, in the 1980s. In the last 15 years, we have made significant progress in improving the quality of our own products.

One of the basic tenets of manufacturing for quality is that testing and inspections can only determine the absence of quality. Yet, we in the software business are just beginning to embrace inspections as a way to detect defects. Some of us even doubt the value of inspections, and the debate rages on. Why is that?

Manufacturing is by definition the repeated creation of a product from a relatively stable design. Thus, it is not a good analogy for the one-of-a-kind-from-scratch world software developers inhabit. We know, of course, that one-of-a-kind-from-scratch is not the best way to do things. So what is the best way? Is there another field that is similar enough to software to give us some valuable lessons? I believe that structural engineering is such a field. There is little doubt that structural engineering is a true engineering discipline. Yet structural engineers never build more than one identical structure either. Before you start throwing things, think about it. No matter how similar two structures are—I'm thinking buildings and bridges—they have one fundamental difference: They occupy different space in a different location. They sit on different soils, the land has different topographies, they are subject to different climates, and the list goes on. All of these things are mostly outside the influence of the engineer. The engineer must adapt the design to the environment in which the structure will reside. In the final analysis, every structure is unique. Still, structures very rarely fail.

In software, we build a system only once. Even if we reuse substantial parts from some other system, we build each system only once. Like structures, each application resides in a slightly different environment. The problem faced by software designers sounds very similar to that faced by structural designers. While things have improved over the years, a much larger portion of software projects are considered failures than are building projects. Why is that?

Despite the similarities, software and structural engineering have two very important differences. Neither of these differences is inherent to either discipline, and in my opinion, neither difference is necessary.

First, structural engineering and most other engineering fields have a process for capturing knowledge and experience that works. They are able to learn from past failures—although not as much as they should, according to some (Petroski 1985). Each major engineering field has a well-defined body of knowledge, some of which is formally captured in codes, standards, and regulations, while some is passed along informally through mentor relationships. Given a canyon, an experienced civil engineer will have a pretty good idea of the sorts of bridges that can be built economically. In any particular case, only a small number of the many possible types of bridges will apply. The length of the span, the depth of the canyon, the condition of the anchors on each end, and the types and amounts of traffic it must bear all play a role in deciding the type of bridge to build. The choices are further constrained by the available funds and time. Sometimes, only one option will satisfy all of the constraints, but there is still a lot of creative work to be done and a lot of choices to make.

We have nothing like this body of knowledge in software. It is starting to form—the work in design patterns is a good start—but there is no widespread acceptance of the conditions under which certain types and classes of software work better than others. However important this work is, and it is important, it is beyond the scope of this book.

The second major difference between structural and software engineering is that the structural engineer has a very good understanding of the behavior of the product, including its response to certain loads, its expected life, and the most likely points of failure *while the product is still on paper*. In engineering, this understanding is gained through mathematical analysis of the design. A structural design consists of a set of drawings and specifications, and a set of calculations. The calculations describe and predict the behavior of the structure built according to the drawings and specifications. A design is not complete until the calculations are done. Further, the drawings and specifications, and the calculations, are checked by another engineer (at least) before they are released for construction. When the design is complete, the engineer knows pretty much whether and how well the structure will perform, at least on paper, and how much it will cost to build.

Most software developers don't know if their product will even work until it is built and run the first time. Even then, most of us don't know how well we've solved the problem until our customer gets his or her hands on it the first time. Very few of us (relatively) design our software. Almost nobody analyzes their designs. Inspecting a design is not the same thing as analyzing it. Looking at a design, most developers couldn't say, with any degree of confidence, how the software will respond to an external event, or how it will hold up under stress, or how it will handle modifications over time. We lack a method for performing the calculations on a design which are so important to other engineering disciplines.

I hope that this book helps remedy the situation. Over my development career, I have begun to realize the amount of time I waste for the lack of good design practices. It is substantial. In every case where it was necessary to recode a substantial part of an application, sometimes costing weeks of development time, the cause would have been discovered by a few hours of additional design. This statement is based on my own project records, some going back over 15 years. This may not be true for everyone, but I am not unique; most of the people I've talked to, numbering in the hundreds now, agree that this is true for them as well.

This book presents measurement and analysis techniques to help determine the behavior of object-oriented software, *while the design is still on paper*, before any code exists. It provides methods and techniques for making design decisions based on measurement data and calculations. In the process, it provides the mathematical means to simulate not only the behavior of a design under execution, but the behavior of a design after a set of simulated changes have been applied—before the design is actually modified and before any code exists. All of these techniques are built upon a theory of objects developed in Chapter 6.

It is always a good thing to start at the beginning. In keeping with this practice, we begin by defining software engineering as a process, with measurement as an essential tool. I hope to convince you that software engineering cannot be engineering without measurement. Measurement is a necessary, but not sufficient, condition for software development practices to become true engineering.

First we develop a working definition of software engineering. This definition is borrowed from the discipline of structural engineering, and takes certain liberties with the intent of the original. The definition is not presented for debate, although debate is welcomed. It is presented so that you know and understand my view of software engineering. It provides the context, assumptions, and motivations for the rest of the book. I encourage active discussion about the definition of software engineering. It is an evolving discipline, make up of practitioners who are also evolving. Continued discussion can help lead to consensus. One day, we may be able to define the discipline, including the body of knowledge and skills required to become a member of the profession.

Next, we introduce, at least for software, the notion that a design is an hypothesis. This is an important notion, and has major implications for how we approach and think about designs. Finally, we discuss measurement as an essential design tool, at least as important for good design as idioms and design patterns.

A WORKING DEFINITION

Software engineering is a slippery term. To most practitioners, it seems to mean a specific set of practices that can be applied only to large projects. To others, it is simply a figment of our collective imaginations. In 48 states, in fact, it is illegal to describe yourself as a software engineer unless you are a licensed professional engineer, *in some other discipline*.

I propose the following as a working definition of software engineering. This definition is borrowed from the definition of structural engineering used by the British Institution of Structural Engineers (Petroski 1985):

> *Software engineering is the science and art of designing and building, with economy and elegance, software systems and applications so they can safely fill the uses to which they may be subjected.*

The discussion which follows was inspired by the wonderful book by Henry Petroski, *To Engineer is Human* (1985). While the book focuses on the role of failure in the improvement of engineering designs, his discussions on the nature of engineering should be very enlightening for those of us who develop software. Petroski's book should be required reading for engineers of all kinds.

This definition, as simple as it is, carries a lot of information. First, it recognizes that engineering is both science and art. It is art applied to a practical purpose, tempered by the knowledge and methods of science. It recognizes the need for creativity, while also recognizing the need for technical knowledge. The conception of a design requires all of the tools and talents of the artist. The analysis of the design requires all of the tools and rigor of the scientist. To some software developers, the use of formal processes, often characteristics of engineering practices, stifles the personal creativity which is so important to innovation. This definition argues against this view, saying that science and creativity are both essential.

Second, the definition covers both the design and construction of software. This implies that engineers must bring to bear on each and every problem everything they know about requirements, data structures, algorithms, design structures, design methods, tools, programming practices, and languages. The best practices, techniques, and tools available to engineers are to be applied to the problem, unless there is a compelling reason not to do so. Software engineering covers the code development and maintenance processes as much as it covers the analysis and design processes. Thus, coding and modification decisions are to be made with all of the care and deliberation of the initial design. Everything done, or not done, must have a deliberate, rational decision behind it. The rationale for all of these decisions should be documented as part of the project history, for the benefit of those on the project as well as those who follow behind.

Third, the phrase "with economy and elegance" recognizes both practical and artistic needs. Economy and elegance are both defined by the problem at hand. If the nature of the problem is such that it doesn't make sense to use a highly formal process, then the definition permits not using one, provided that the decision was reached deliberately, using objective analysis, which incidentally, implies the use of measurement. On the other hand, if some aspect of the problem, such as a requirement for extremely high reliability, forces the use of a more formal process, this definition requires the use of that process, again provided the decision was made deliberately using objective analysis.

The inclusion of elegance in the definition carries several meanings. First, simple is better than complex. It follows an axiom: "Keep a design as simple as possible, but no simpler" (attributed to Albert Einstein). The solution must first solve the problem, then must strive to be as simple as possible. Second, efficiency is a desired attribute. Both the design process and the solution must be as efficient in their use of resources as possible. Waste is to be avoided, which also relates to economy. It places upon the engineer the burden of being reasonably certain—through whatever means are available—that the provided solution is the best he or she can produce given the constraints of the problem. Engineers should be able to defend their choices using rational, objective analysis—assuming, of course, that the audience is rational and objective, which is rarely the case.

Finally, this definition states that software systems must "safely fill the uses to which they may be subjected." This phrase includes both the notion of safety and the implication that a software application may be used for purposes for which it was not designed. In fact, it carries a much stronger notion—that software should be able to be used for unintended purposes, or it should safely resist such use, while informing the user in some way that the use is inappropriate without compromising the safety of people, property, or information. This notion has major implications for the design of areas like exceptions and error handling, user interface design, and data integrity concerns. Put another way, this definition declares that a software application should either be able to fulfill a purpose, intended or not, or fail to fill that purpose without hurting anyone or anything. Very little software I use on a daily basis meets even this basic requirement.

DESIGN AS HYPOTHESIS

Petroski says that "the object of a science can be said to construct theories about the behavior of whatever it is the science studies" (Petroski 1985, 42). The object of computer science, then, might be to construct theories about various aspects of computing—including how software behaves under various conditions. Theories originate in the ether. They are usually half-baked ideas born around the dinner table and developed into a coherent, unambiguous statement of the way things work. From there, a theory's life is much more difficult. It is subject to testing through experimentation, which is very much a form of torture whose primary goal is to prove the theory wrong. A theory can never be proven correct, but it can be conclusively proven wrong. Any number of experiments in which the results support the theory do not guarantee that the next experiment will also support it. A single experiment where the results disagree with the theory can prove the theory wrong, provided the experiment rigorously followed the scientific method, and can be repeated.

Experiments must follow strict rules so that cheating, biases, and points of view do not color the results. These tests have to be repeatable, for it is through repeated experiments that get the same or similar results that we begin to draw clear conclusions. The scientific method requires that an experimenter first develop an hypothesis—a statement about the behavior of a thing which will be tested. The test itself and the analysis of the results have strict rules and protocols to prevent intended or unintended influences of the results.

A design is also an hypothesis. Instead of an hypothesis about the way things behave in the natural world, the design is an hypothesis about how a particular arrangement of components will behave in a world of the designer's own making (Petroski 1985). The design states, implicitly or explicitly, the hypothesis that the structure or software application which is built to a given set of specifications, using the specified materials and methods, and used within the specified guidelines, will fill the specified function, for the specified period of time, *without fail*. A design can only be proven correct when all of these conditions are met, including the passage of the specified period of time. A design can be proven wrong, however, by a single exception to the intended behavior, provided that all of the other conditions have been met.

Engineering is a process which consists of a succession of hypotheses. Each design is sketched (or built), figuratively or literally, then analyzed (or tested). This analysis (or testing) seeks to understand the behavior of the design under a series of imagined (or simulated) conditions. Some of the analysis requires the use of calculations, which in turn require the use of measurement. If any of the components of the design fail the analysis (or test), the entire design is said to have failed. The weak components are redesigned, possibly changing the whole design, and the analysis is performed again. This process repeats until the engineer can think of no possible way for the design to fail, within a set of specified conditions and uses and for a specified period of time.

MEASUREMENT AS A DESIGN TOOL

Basili, Caldiera, and Rombach (1994a) write that an engineering discipline requires a measurement mechanism to provide feedback and assist in evaluation. It helps create corporate memory and assists in answering a variety of questions. These two sentences contain many of the motivations for measurement. Process measures are fed back into the process management mechanism to allow for the evaluation of past process changes and to see where future process changes might be made. Product measures are tracked over time to see the effects of processes on product characteristics and to determine which measures available early in the development cycle are reliable predictors of important measures available only much later in the development cycle.

Engineering isn't just about finding a solution to a problem. It's about finding the best solution given the goals and constraints of the current situation. These goals and constraints may originate within the problem itself or they may be externally imposed in the form of management goals, professional or legal standards, or resource constraints. Sometimes—often, really—these goals are in conflict with each other. Engineering, then, is an optimization problem consisting of a sequence of tradeoff decisions. Solutions to the same problem may differ due to dissimilar sets of goals and constraints. Tradeoff decisions select one solution from among many, with the goal of selecting the alternative which best fits all of the goals and constraints, and which still solves the problem.

Each of these tradeoff decisions may use a variety of criteria. These criteria are dependent on the goals and constraints of the situation. The criteria, or how they are used, may change given another set of goals or constraints. The criteria must be as objective as possible to give us confidence in the decisions we make while using them. Objective criteria depend upon data gathered through measurement.

Measurement is not an optional tool in design; it is an essential tool. The current state of software engineering is as it is, in large part, due to the current state of software measurement. Part of the problem, to be sure, is that we as a discipline do not know how to measure some of the characteristics of software we need to measure. More often, the problem is that software professionals choose not to measure. Measurement is often done after-the-fact and for the sole benefit of management. Measurement for management is often viewed with suspicion, usually rightfully so. But managers need information in order to run the business and we practitioners are their only source. However, measurement is most useful when you as designer use it during the course of designing an application. As a design tool, measurement can create tremendous payoffs, especially when coupled with a design analysis technique such as the one presented in Chapter 6.

I am very interested in measures which can be used during the design of object-oriented software, for two reasons. One, I only build object-oriented software, and two, I have experienced first hand the power available to me as a designer as a result of measurement-based information. In "The Object-Oriented Brewery," Sharble and Cohen (1993) use a set of object-oriented design measures to compare designs developed using different design approaches. They designed the same application using each approach and compared the results. Their purpose was to determine the relative effectiveness of the two design approaches. This could not have been done without design measurement data.

Measurement is an essential part of every engineering discipline except software; this is *the* reason software engineering is not a true engineering discipline. I hope this book helps change that. You will find no management measures in this volume. All of the information, and especially the measures, is intended to help you, the designer, create better designs.

Part I

PUTTING MEASUREMENT INTO CONTEXT

Like any technical activity, measurement requires a context. You need to define the environment in which you expect to perform your measurement. This environment, or context, provides boundaries around your measurement activities.

In Part I, the context for measurement is set in terms of who you measure for and why (Chapter 1), what you measure and when you measure it (Chapter 2), and what measures to use (Chapter 3). The three dimensions from which software can be measured and why they are true dimensions and not just points of view are also discussed.

The section entitled "Measure Construction" in Chapter 3 introduces a technique for constructing measures from an empirical understanding of a concept, a formal model in which to express that understanding, and a set of ready-made empirical relational structures from measurement theory. I applied this technique to develop every measure included in the chapters in Part III. With this technique, the requirements for each structure in Chapter 5, and the formal object model from Chapter 6, you can build a measure for any characteristic you can describe in terms of the object model. When you do, you can be sure that it is theoretically correct. The empirical test for your new measure is covered by your description of the characteristic—the more care with which you describe your characteristic, the more likely you are to have an empirically valid measure. The technique works, trust me.

1

A SOFTWARE MEASUREMENT FRAMEWORK

Collecting data without a context in which to use it is as useful as collecting dust under the bed. Data randomly collected is just that: data. There is no informational content. To turn data into information, you need a context—a purpose and a set of goals. You need to know why you are collecting the data, how you plan to use the data, and have some idea of where you are trying to go through the use of the data. A context must be supplied by those who are collecting the data—that is, you. Without either a purpose or destination, you will not gain by collecting data. This is as true of software measurement data as it is any other kind of data. Measurement data costs money to collect. Without some reason for collecting it, and without some end in mind, there will be only costs, no benefits. However, if you have a purpose and a destination, such as improving the quality of your software from some perspective, you will find software measurement data indispensable.

In every software development organization, there are at least three points of view: strategic, tactical, and technical. A valid measurement context can be built from any of these points of view. Ideally, all three points of view will be included in any measurement effort, but only the technical view is required for such an effort to succeed. These points of view form one basis of a framework for measurement. This framework is one of many possible measurement frameworks, but it is one I have seen succeed in many companies over the past few years, in a variety of forms. The purpose of this framework is to give the measurement practitioner a starting point from which to build a measurement program. By selecting one or more points of view, and one or more objects (discussed later), you have gone a long way towards building the context for your organization. The purpose for measurement is determined by looking at each of the selected objects from each of the selected points of view and asking what you need to know about these objects in order to achieve your goals. This chapter describes the framework; goal selection is covered in Chapter 3.

The other basis for the framework is a set of four basic objects for which measurement data can be collected: processes, products, resources, and projects. Fenton (1991) and others believe that only three objects exist and that projects are really included in processes. I disagree; this issue is discussed more fully in the section titled "Objects of Measurement" in this chapter. A representation of the framework is presented in Figure 1.1. A more technical view is presented in Figure 1.4, which is discussed later. The framework is used to organize and co-ordinate your measurement activities. An entire measurement program can be built on the framework. A complete measurement program will include all aspects of the framework. It is permissible to use only those portions of the framework relevant to your purposes, which is what we will do. The concentration will be on the technical measurement of products, specifically, design products.

The generic measurement process is modeled in Figure 1.2. There is an intelligence barrier between observed relationships between objects of interest and the interpretation of those relationships into relevant results. The ongoing debate about how to measure software size is a perfect example.

To illustrate the importance of measurement, two lines are shown in Figure 1.3. Without measurement, that is, by empirical observation alone, it is difficult to tell

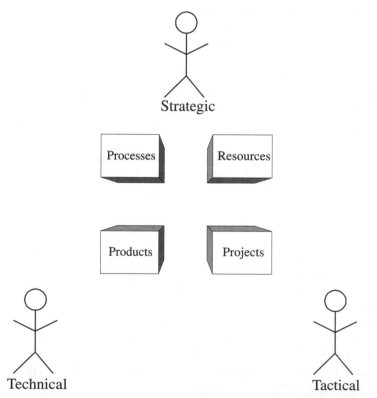

Figure 1.1 *The views and objects in the measurement framework.*

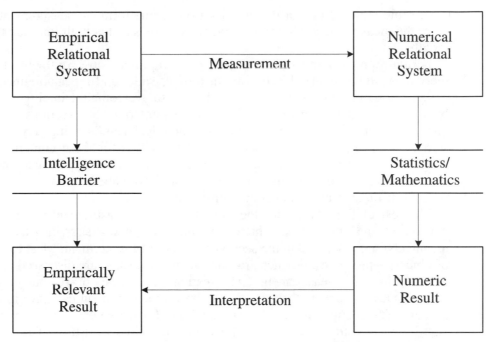

Figure 1.2 *The "intelligence" barrier to understanding. Reprinted, by permission of John Wiley & Sons, Inc., from J. Marciniak, ed.,* Encyclopedia of Software Engineering. *© 1994 by John Wiley & Sons, Inc.*

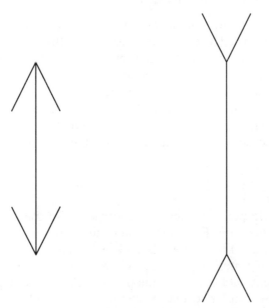

Figure 1.3 *Are both lines the same length?*

which line is the longer of the two. By using some form of measurement, in this case, the measurement of distance, you can readily see that both lines are the same length.

Formally, measurement is a mapping of empirical (observed) objects to numerical (mathematical) objects using a formal, valid, and repeatable mechanism, called a homomorphism. Measurement is used to overcome the intelligence barrier by converting the empirical observations to numerical observations. These numerical observations are converted into numerical results using any of several statistical and mathematical techniques. The intent is for these numerical results to be easier to interpret than the original empirical relationships. Once interpreted into empirically valid results, we can use this information for whatever purpose we had in mind, subject to certain constraints.

The rest of Part I provides the tools to build a measurement process upon a portion of the framework. The three points of view—strategic, tactical, and technical—are discussed in the section "Views of Measurement." The four classes of objects—processes, products, resources, and projects—are discussed in the section "Objects of Measurement." The section "The Roles of Technical Measurement in Design" covers the roles that technical measurement can have in a design process. The section titled "Design and Code Measurement" discusses why design-based measures are more useful than code-based measures. The section on object-oriented software discusses why object-oriented software requires different measures from other forms of software. Finally, the last section covers the three dimensions of software: structure, function, and behavior, first proposed by DeMarco (1982)—he called them data, function, and control.

VIEWS OF MEASUREMENT

In every software development organization, there are three distinct points of view. Each is concerned with different aspects of the organization. Each has a different time span. Each has different uses, and therefore different needs, for software measurement data. These different viewpoints are not mutually exclusive, nor are they necessarily held by different people. A single person may hold more than one viewpoint at any moment. My point is that the information requirements and the uses for that information are very different for each viewpoint. The three points of view are strategic, tactical, and technical and were introduced by Whitmire (1994).

Strategic View

The strategic point of view is concerned with the long-term performance of the entire organization. For large organizations, this may include many projects using many different kinds of tools and techniques. Also, as practices and processes change over time, the strategic view needs to be able to compare and contrast measurement data between time periods. For the strategic view, measurement data plays a role similar to that of summary financial data. It helps people to assess the performance of the organization over long periods of time and to spot trends which need management attention. Also like summary financial data, it is sometimes risky to draw detailed conclusions from the data, as the complete story may not be fully represented in the data.

The emphasis of the strategic view tends to be on the processes used, with project, product, and resource data being reduced to summary trends. This emphasis is necessitated by two things. First, the strategic view is responsible for managing the processes used by the organization. The strategic direction of the organization is limited to some extent by the effectiveness of its processes. The process will, over time, provide the information about how well that strategy is being played out. Second, because the strategic view is long-term, and covers many projects using many different tools and techniques, and possibly more than one process, the data from project to project or from year to year is not comparable unless the detailed data is summarized to allow it to be combined with other, possibly different detail data.

Each strategic manager will have his or her own views about which information is needed to manage the organization. These views will influence the specific measures taken and the analyses performed on those measures. This data is used to make decisions about the overall direction of the organization, use of particular technologies, skill requirements, and the assessment of the organizational health. If the organization's goals are stated in measurable terms, the strategic data can be used to determine if and how well those goals are being met.

The measures used at this level tend to be indirect measures of external process attributes, to use Fenton's terms (Fenton 1991). Measures of products, projects, and resources tend to be summarized as means or medians, with some indication of variability. The strategic view tracks trends of these summary statistics. The desired trend may be downwards or upwards, depending on the goals of the measurer and the measurements being taken. These are general goals, and the mean product per unit resource, or vice versa, will be the measure tracked. Variability in these summary measures will also be watched, as increasing variability means that funny things are starting to happen.

One of the biggest difficulties at this level is making sure that the measures taken are used in a meaningful way, in the sense that meaningfulness is defined in measurement theory. For example, if the measures collected do not support the interval or ratio scales, it makes no sense to track their means. In fact, it can lead to some dangerous decisions. If you are merely curious about measurement theory, it is briefly covered in Chapter 5. If you just have to know more right now, skip to Chapter 5, then come back. You may have to read Chapter 4 to understand some of the mathematics in Chapter 5.

Examples of the measures used at the strategic level include (this does not constitute an endorsement of any of these measures on my part):

- Unit cost (labor hours/function point, for example)
- Cycle time (project days/function point)
- Defect rates (delivered defects/function point)

- Maintenance efficiency (function points/equivalent full-time person)
- Asset management
  - Capitalized cost of software inventory
  - Average age (years/function point)—or even a FIFO or LIFO system
  - Replacement schedule
  - Replacement cost (function points * current rate per function point)

The strategic view also performs several forms of variance analysis. The trend of variances (of several factors) may be one of the indirect measures tracked. Variance analysis determines how close the actual values are to plan. A high variance (far off the mark, in either direction) on a particular project may mean several things, from a particularly difficult problem to poor project execution to environmental factors. Variance that is always high usually points to environmental factors, such as a poor planning process or attributes of the environment that are not accounted for in the planning model. The tools and techniques used in standard cost accounting can be applied to software measurement data. This is especially true of variance analysis techniques. The only real difference between software measurement data and cost accounting data is that some of the former measures might be expressed in units other than dollars.

Tactical View

The tactical point of view is concerned with the performance of individual projects. As the name implies, the tactician is responsible for the execution of the organization's processes, making use of the selected tools, methods, techniques, and resources to create the organization's products. The tactical focus is on the project. The measures tend to be task-oriented, but draw from process, product, and resource measures to create project measures. There are no direct project measures, which leads some to believe that a project is not an object of measurement in its own right. This issue will be discussed in the next section.

A project may create several products, each with its own characteristics. The typical software project creates at least two products: software and user documentation. These two products differ in their basic natures, and in the skills, tools, and processes required to produce them. These different natures often require the use of different product measures. Thus, the product measures used at the tactical level may be limited to a particular product or blended through summarization to mask the effects of particular characteristics or technology. At this level, product measurement data is used to compare actual results to target results, such as tracking the growth of the requirements or the defect discovery rate during inspection or testing activities. Product measures may be used to predict values of certain indirect project measures, such as using product size to predict cost and schedule.

Projects consume resources, including talent, money, and time. One of the more important project measures is resource consumption. This is a specific instance of an indirect process measure, since it combines one or more resource measures with other measures, such as the ratio of product size to time used or time used to time allocated.

Estimates of product measures such as size, resource measures such as available staff hours, and process measures such as staff hours per unit size are used to plan the project. Some product measures, and some project measures, may be used to determine the skill requirements for the project. In a highly constrained project, for example, a project manager may choose to use the best people available.

The primary user of tactical measurement data is the project manager. During the course of the project, the actual values of many measures are compared with the estimated or planned values. Any variances are noted and investigated. A variance of the actual from the plan may indicate a problem requiring corrective action or may indicate that the plan needs revision.

Examples of the tactical uses of measurement data include:

- Planning
  - Structuring the project into specific tasks
  - Resources (time and skill level) required for each task
  - Activities and processes required to complete the tasks
  - Cost of materials and consumable resources required for the project
- Controlling
  - Actual effort-to-date by activity or product deliverable
  - Progress-to-date, using earned value or percentage completion measures
  - Expected effort required to complete—this may be based on planned usage rates at actual progress or on actual usage rates at planned progress—these two views provide different information and highlight different issues
  - Target performance using target values of product measures
  - Defect data, such as defect rates, containment effectiveness, correction efficiency, cost of rework, or any of a number of other uses of defect information

Technical View

Strategic and tactical measurement have many similarities. Indeed, the major difference seems to be one of focus. Technical measurement, however, is a different animal altogether. These fundamental differences arise from a variety of sources. Technical measurement tends to be focused upon a single product or process. The primary measures used at this level are used as details and are not summarized. Technical measures are highly dependent on the technology in the product and are extremely sensitive to changes in that technology. Physically, all measurement takes place at the technical level. All measures used at the strategic and tactical levels are built from fundamental technical measures. Strategic and tactical users of measurement data depend on technical users to supply the data.

The primary user of technical measurement data is the software engineer. The focus is on a selected set of internal product or process attributes. The particular attributes of interest may vary over the course of a project, within an activity, or across different measurement purposes. Measurement data supports and influences technical decisions, such as the choice of design approaches, design tradeoffs, and data structure and algorithm selection.

Some examples of technical measurement include:

- Using measures of coupling and cohesion to assess the need to adjust the design
- Using measures of size and complexity to choose between alternative implementations
- Using defect rates and direct product measures to look for cause and effect relationships, for the ultimate purpose of modifying a process
- Using effort and productivity data to assess and evaluate the effects of using a new tool or method

OBJECTS OF MEASUREMENT

One of the first obligations of a measurement effort is to identify those objects which are to be measured. We then measure attributes of those objects. We group these objects into four classes: processes, projects, products, and resources.

Many frameworks, like Fenton's (1991), include only processes, products, and resources. They combine projects into processes. Projects are different enough and important enough, for reasons discussed shortly, to elevate them to the status of a class of measurement object. The measurement framework in this book is built, in part, on this premise.

Each class of objects has two types of attributes (Fenton 1991):

- *Internal*: Those attributes which can be measured purely in terms of the process, project, product, or resource itself
- *External*: Those attributes which can only be measured with respect to how the process, project, product, or resource relates to its environment

Internal attributes are often measured directly—that is, the value of the attribute can be determined just by looking at it. Sometimes, they must be measured using the values of other internal measures, in which case they are called indirect measures. External attributes are almost always measured with indirect measures.

Processes

Fenton (1991, p. 43) defines a process as a set of "software related activities which normally have a time factor." He gives as examples the activities of "constructing a specification document" or "developing a software system from requirements capture through release to a customer." Fenton further claims that time slices "which do not correspond to any coherent software activity" can also be considered as processes. Fenton's definition seems to have been accepted by a large number of people, as his definition is cited frequently in the literature.

This definition seems inadequate: It implies that a process does not exist apart from a project. In fact, processes can be managed independently of any use of the process, similar to the way that classes can be managed independent of any object of those classes. The very notion of process improvement—and a repeatable process—implies a definition of process that is very different from Fenton's.

Second, a project applies a process, or parts of several processes, to a specific problem. Theoretically, if you use the same process on the same problem, using the same resources, your project will result in the same product. Of course, this never works. Part of the unique nature of every project is the set of goals and constraints under which the project is working. Changes to any of these can result in markedly different products, at fundamental levels, even if the process, problem, and resources are held constant.

To remedy this problem, I propose using a different definition of process, borrowed from some other disciplines. The new definition is:

A process is the set of activities, methods, practices, techniques, and tools used by an organization to develop its products.

An instance of a process is a time slice that is bounded by a start and stop date. These instances may coincide with the dates for a particular project, a particular product, a particular activity, or some period of calendar time. Note that a project is an instance of a process, among other things. The reverse isn't always true: An instance of a process does not always coincide with a project.

Further, a process has future and historical components. You can define and discuss a process that has never been used. Process improvement makes changes to the process, an instance of which will only be created the next time it is used. The historical component of a process is the set of versions of the process that were used in the past. All of these instances may be the same, or not. The relative performance of different versions of a process allows you to determine whether a particular process change was beneficial.

Processes are measured by comparing instance measurements to each other over time. The separation of the process from its instances is important because you can measure the trends of a process over time. If you call each instance a separate process, as Fenton and others do, you can't really measure process trends without some very confusing terminology.

Direct internal process attributes include:

- Time, execution or calendar time, such as labor hours or months
- Resources consumed, such as budget dollars, labor hours, or machine cycles
- Iterations, such as number of test cases performed
- Number of incidents of a specific type, such as the number of errors detected, number of errors corrected, or the number of staff members

Indirect internal process measures include:

- Average cost per error
- Defect insertion rate
- Defect detection rate
- Defect correction rate
- Defect containment

External process measures include:

- Productivity—the unit of product produced per unit of input—which is affected by several factors, including the tools and methods employed
- Stability of the process or the lack of variation
- Variation—the extent to which instances of the process differ from each other

Products

Products are the deliverables created during the course of a project. They include plans, requirements listings, functional specifications, design diagrams, design calculations, design notes, source code, test cases, test results, and anything else that is the residue left over from applying a process and resources to a problem. The point is that a product can include just about anything that results from a project. Some of these products are interesting to measure; others are not. Not all products are delivered to the customer. Some products help with internal maintenance activities and some exist only to document decisions made during the project.

External product attributes include understandability, usability, reusability, and maintainability. Internal product attributes include size, complexity, functionality, modularity, reuse, redundancy, defects, coupling, and cohesion. Some of these internal attributes are directly measured; others are measured indirectly. Products are measured directly in a *white box* fashion by examining their internals. Products are measured indirectly in a *black box* fashion by examining their behavior in specific situations.

Resources

Resources are those objects that serve as input to the processes used on a project. Resources include people, tools, materials, methods, time, money, training (or generally, knowledge and skill), and products from other projects. Internal attributes of resources include cost (both to acquire and to use), capability, and constraints on use. External attributes include performance. Performance of people might mean their productivity. Performance of tools and methods might mean their effects on the productivity of the people resources or the quality of the products.

Resource consumption is an important measure which is both a process and resource measure. The resource aspect of consumption is the amount of the resource used or the amount remaining. The consumption rate over time is the process aspect. Both the processes used and the resources themselves influence these measures. Consumption is the quantity of resources used during an activity. For people, this is measured in terms of labor hours, labor months, or labor years. For materials, consumption is measured in the units by which the material is used.

Resource consumption is divided into product output to arrive at the overall productivity of a project, a set of projects, or an entire organization. When measuring productivity in this manner, you must be careful to match the unit of product output to the measure of value received from that output. In manufacturing, each unit made has the potential to produce a certain amount of profit. In software, this output-to-value relationship is often difficult to define.

Projects

A project is the relationship between instances of the following classes of items:

- A problem to be solved
- Internal and external goals and standards
- Processes, methods, and techniques
- Resources: people, tools and equipment, money, time
- Internal and external constraints placed upon the project and/or the use of resources, including those due to the operating environment
- A product: one or more defined deliverables

Charles Gray (1981, p. 1) says that a project "is a complex of non-routine activities that must be completed with a set amount of resources and within a set time interval." Projects and processes are different entities. A project uses an instance of a process. The historical aspect of a process is the combination of the instances taken over a number of projects.

The goals and constraints imposed on a project can have a material effect on the outcome of that project, including the nature of the resulting product, and even on the eventual success or failure of the project itself. Two projects that solve the same problem can result in very different outcomes as the goals and constraints change. To see an example of this, refer to DeMarco's description of Weinberg's Coding Wars in DeMarco (1982).

Projects can be measured in several ways:

- Instance measurements of processes and resources
- Internal and external measures of the problem being solved, such as its size and complexity
- Internal and external measures of the product to assess performance relative to goals, standards, constraints, and the requirements defined in the problem
- Progress measures which combine different views of product measures, such as actual size completed at a point in time versus the size scheduled to be completed at that point in time
- Project performance measures, including cost versus budget, actual flow time versus planned flow time, and product quality

The size and complexity of the problem may be the only true internal project measures. Nearly all other measures used on a project are process, resource, or product measures.

The complete framework is shown in Figure 1.4. The intersections between the views and the objects (the boxes in the figure) contain measures of the object that are meaningful to the view. The process of filling these boxes is covered in Chapter 3.

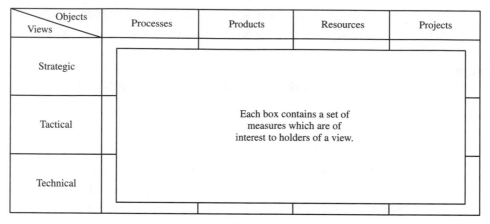

Objects Views	Processes	Products	Resources	Projects
Strategic				
Tactical	Each box contains a set of measures which are of interest to holders of a view.			
Technical				

Figure 1.4 *Measure matrix for the measurement framework.*

THE ROLES OF TECHNICAL MEASUREMENT IN DESIGN

Each point of view in the framework has its own uses for measurement. Each view has different needs for information. While each view may use many of the same measures as the other views, it uses them in different ways to answer different questions. Since this is a book about technical measurement, the focus will be exclusively on the roles technical measures can play during the design process. As you can see, measurement is a powerful and useful design tool.

I have been around software measurement for a long time. I also have experience using measurement data in the design of nonsoftware products. I have noticed some common uses for measurement data during the design process. While some uses look rather unique on the surface, if you look at them in terms of the questions being answered, the commonalties come into focus. I have identified five separate and distinct uses of technical measures (Whitmire 1994), as shown in Table 1.1. Others identify more, or fewer. Fenton (1991), for example, identifies only two uses of measurement: prediction and assessment. But, as the following discussion indicates, estimation and prediction are different, and so are comparison and assessment. You might notice also that Fenton's book, which is about mea-

**Table 1.1 Roles of Technical Measurement
in Design**

1. Estimation
2. Prediction
3. Assessment
4. Comparison
5. Investigation

surement research, is full of examples of the use of technical measures for investigative purposes.

Estimation

Estimation combines measures taken from existing products with historical and environmental data to determine likely resource requirements for future products or future activities. These future products and activities may be related to the same or different projects.

For example, the size of a set of requirements can be combined with historical and environmental data to estimate the time and effort needed to develop the remaining products for the project. This is the form of estimation most familiar to software developers. The data from a similar application, built in a similar environment, can be used to estimate the resources required for the current project. Another use of estimation is to use product size, its defect rate, the volatility of the product components, and the productivity of the organization to estimate the required level of maintenance effort.

The inclusion of historical and environmental data is important. It is impossible to estimate in the absence of knowledge about the history of the organization for which the estimate is being made. Estimates made under these conditions are nothing more than guesses. The effects of the current environment on the performance of the organization are important, since changes to the environment can completely invalidate the use of historical data for estimation.

Prediction

Prediction uses measures from existing products to determine the likely future values of measures of the same or other products. Prediction differs from estimating in that estimation relies heavily on historical and environmental data, and often converts product measures into project or process measures. Prediction can be based on internal or external models of the product or other factors. Prediction and estimation also serve two different purposes. Estimation determines the likely amount of resources required to build a product or perform an activity. Prediction determines likely values of product measures.

One well-known example of prediction is to use certain test results to predict the mean time to failure of the product once it is delivered. Another example of prediction is to use measures of design characteristics to predict those portions of the software most likely to contain errors.

Assessment

Assessment compares measures from a product or process to predetermined values set by law, standards, project-specific goals, targets, constraints, or customer requirements to determine the product's or process's conformance. An example of assessment is measuring characteristics of an organization's process to the standard required to be assessed at a given level in the Software Engineering Institute's

Capability Maturity Model (CMU/SEI 1995). Another example is to compare the level of coupling in a design to the group standard for levels of coupling. A review to determine how effectively a product meets its requirements is another example of the assessment role. The key concept for assessment is that the values to which measures are compared are determined either before the comparison is made or are set by outside parties.

Comparison

The primary purpose of the comparison role is to make design tradeoffs. The measures of two or more products or processes are compared in order to choose one from among them or for ranking them according to some scheme. The biggest difference between comparison and assessment is that the measures used in comparison are all taken from instances of products or processes and not predetermined values.

Comparison is, in my view, the most important, and least used, use of measurement during the design process. There are many, many decisions I must make during the course of design that can be rendered easier, or even automatic, by the appropriate use of the appropriate data.

For example, given two design alternatives, both of which solve the same design problem, which is the better choice? How do you decide whether to use a list or an array in a given situation? In software, we tend to rely on what we know, folklore, and myth, in that order. Rarely do we take the time to measure the effects of one alternative over the other on the overall design. In another case, we may be trying to decide between two design alternatives with different space-time tradeoffs. The choice between them will be driven by the goals and constraints on the project, but measurement data must be used to determine which alternative best meets those goals.

Often, the goal of the design process is to determine the product structure that will optimize several conflicting goals while still performing the intended function. This can become a multiaxis optimization problem. It is not possible to come even close to knowing which potential solution is the best (best optimizes the various goals) by intuition. Even the best designers, those who seem to use intuition, are really using measurement. The next time you see a really good designer, ask her how she makes her design choices. If she describes characteristics for which she looks, she is using a form of measurement.

Investigation

Investigation is the use of measurement data from a product or process to support or refute an hypothesis. This describes the basic scientific experiment. The whole scientific method describes the conditions and protocols governing the collection and interpretation of measurement data to support or refute an hypothesis. Investigation includes any use of measurement designed to answer a question of the form "What happens when . . . ?", "What causes . . . ?", or "Why . . . ?".

DESIGN AND CODE MEASUREMENT

To date, the vast majority of the measurement effort, both in research and in practice, has been the development and application of measures based on source code. There are several significant problems with this. Most obviously, code-based measures are available much too late in the development cycle to be of any use to the designer. I have had many experiences where I developed the code according to a design, then discovered through some code-based measurement that the design needed revision. Not only did I have to revise the design, but this often meant a complete or near-complete rewrite of the code.

Many important characteristics of a design are not visible in the code. While they may be useful to the programmer of a particular module, code-based measures simply do not tell much about the designs. The range of possible module sizes is not completely dependent on the design for the module. Module size is a function of many factors, including language, coding style, and skill. Likewise, the number of operators and operands (Halsted 1977) used in a module are more dependent on the mood and ability of the programmer than on the design. Of course, the amount of coupling between modules is completely dependent on the design, if the design was taken to that level, so this problem is prevalent, but not universal.

As a discipline, we do not really understand many of the relationships between module characteristics and design characteristics. Most of the relationships between design and module, in terms of cause and effect, which are used daily are based on supposition and folklore, and are not yet supported by hard evidence. This doesn't make them invalid; it just makes them matters of myth rather than fact. One of the key relationships about which very little is known is that between design structure and module performance, in terms of executable code size, memory usage, or speed. In some situations, this relationship is very important and is often *the* critical relationship in the project. Other design decisions are based upon characteristics of the design that can be measured only during the design process; these characteristics are often masked by the structure of the code.

Measures used lower in our measurement framework are more sensitive to changes in the technology or environment than those appearing higher; technical measures are the most sensitive to these changes (Whitmire 1994). This is both deliberate and necessary. Measures used in the higher levels of the framework must, by necessity, be insensitive to technology and environment factors. This is the only way you can use the same measure over different projects and not get meaningless garbage as a result, not that anyone would ever do that, of course. Conversely, measures used in the lower levels must be more sensitive to technology and environment factors. This is the only way we can account for these factors in our designs.

At the technical level, even small changes in the technology, environment, or even the nature of the design components themselves, can render the definition of a measure meaningless or obsolete (Whitmire 1994). The concept underlying a measure, such as coupling, may not change; it will always deal with the interactions between design components. But the nature of coupling—its semantics—and the ways coupling can be measured can be altered dramatically. In the case of cohesion, for example, several people (Fenton 1991; Ott et al. 1995) have suggested that one or two new forms of cohesion be defined specifically for object-oriented software in addition to the forms first presented by Myers (1976).

To use measurement during the design process, you must measure the components of the design directly, not indirectly through the resulting code. This is particularly true if you want to make use of measurement to influence the course of the design. To measure design components, you need to first name them, then understand something about them which you can measure. To begin this process, let's explore ways in which object-oriented software differs from software which is not object-oriented.

OBJECT-ORIENTED SOFTWARE IS DIFFERENT

The biggest difference between object-oriented software and software that is structured in some other means, aside from the structure itself, is that the inherent complexity of the software moves from the source code into the design—into the interactions between objects (Church and Sheppard 1995b). In typical non-object-oriented software, the inherent complexity is embodied in the structure of the code itself. Functions tend to be longer and more complex. More of the code is imperative in nature; that is, a larger proportion of the size of the code is devoted to executable instructions. Interactions between modules, while they can be traced, are hidden in the code, often to the point of being nearly invisible.

In typical object-oriented software, the inherent complexity lies in the interactions between objects. Functions (object methods) tend to be shorter than functional software, often much shorter. There also tend to be more methods in object-oriented software than functions in non-object-oriented software. A much larger percentage of the total size of the code is declarative in nature; that is, a larger portion is devoted to describing the structure and contents of the objects than in instructions about how to perform the functions.

This migration of complexity is accompanied by a migration in the concern of the designer. More emphasis is placed on the interfaces between objects in object-oriented software. Indeed, one of the major benefits of the object-oriented approach is that once the interfaces are agreed upon, both in structure and in semantics (the contract for the interface), the implementation of a particular function is not really relevant. As long as a method lives up to its contract, the only people who really care about its internals are the person who wrote it and those who must come along afterwards and maintain it.

Consequently, many practitioners are finding that measures defined around structured code do not lend themselves to use with object-oriented code (Roberts 1992). This is not to say that code-based measures such as source lines of code or McCabe's various complexity measures (McCabe 1976) can't be used on object-oriented software. They can be used, but only on individual methods and functions. In object-oriented software, very little of interest is happening within an individual method or function. The interesting action takes place when these individual methods work together to accomplish some larger task.

THREE DIMENSIONS OF SOFTWARE

This last section deals with a part of the framework that is orthogonal to the discussion so far. It focuses on the nature of one of the products of a design, the software itself. Our purpose is to try to gain an understanding of software's fundamental nature so that we might better identify ways in which we can measure it.

DeMarco (1982) states that three perspectives are required to fully describe any piece of software. He goes on to say that in fact, these three perspectives are the *only* ones required to fully describe a piece of software. Some people take issue with that. Zachmann (1987) has identified as many as eight perspectives. I am convinced that many, if not most, of Zachmann's perspectives can be boiled down into the three proposed by DeMarco. DeMarco bases this premise on the analogy of needing three views to fully describe the shape of a solid. You might notice that while these three views fully specify the physical structure and shape of the object, they do not tell us everything we might want to know about it, such as its mass, its density, or its composition. The same can be said for software. The three perspectives of software may tell us only the size of the software in three dimensions and say nothing about other aspects of the software, such as its complexity, its correctness, or other interesting information.

DeMarco's three perspectives, or dimensions, combine to create a complete view of the size of the software as shown in Figure 1.5 and are informally defined as:

- *Function*: A partitioned view of what the system does
- *Data*: A partitioned view of what the system remembers
- *Behavior*: A partitioned view of the different behavioral states that characterize the system

Some applications are clearly dominated by one of the three dimensions and fall into one of the following categories: data-strong, function-strong, or control-strong (Whitmire 1992a). In other applications the dominant dimension is not so clear; these are considered to be hybrid applications. In object-oriented software, the categories can be applied to individual objects, providing some interesting insights into the nature of a particular piece of software.

It is worth noting here that individual objects have the same characteristics as whole applications (Whitmire 1993). This is an important and very useful concept, since it allows us to treat a single object as we would any whole application, including the measurement tools and techniques which we can apply. While the following discussion is presented in terms of applications, you can substitute "object" for "application" and it will still be meaningful.

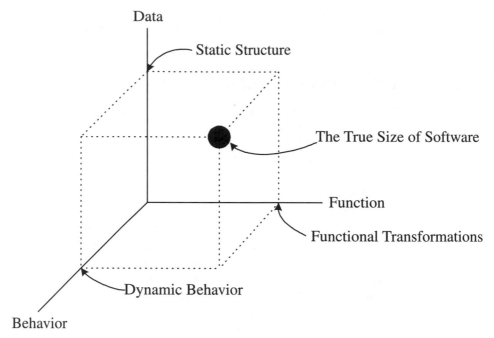

Figure 1.5 *The three dimensions of software.*

Static Structure (Data)

Data is the information that must be remembered by the application (DeMarco 1982). This "memory" may be required for an indefinite period of time, from very short (during the execution of a process) to very long (a permanent database). The data has a structure which is static in nature. It is a snapshot of the internal and external structure of the data at any given point in time. The structure includes both the entities about which things are to be remembered and the relationships between those entities.

The data dimension models the entities or objects from the real world that are represented in the application in terms of their descriptive characteristics and the relationships between them. Here, "models" is the key word, since an application will only remember the information about an entity that is relevant to the work of the application. The relationships may be represented by constraints on the values of certain pieces of information or they may be modeled more completely, depending on the needs of the application and the capabilities of its designers.

Data-strong applications, or applications with a strong data dimension, derive their size from the structure of the retained or static data, and the effect that structure has on the human-machine interface at the boundary of the application (Whitmire 1992a). Data-strong applications tend to model, or maintain information about, real-world entities, both physical and otherwise. The entity in the world and its model in the application are clearly distinguishable from each other. Typically, the model in the application is a limited view of the entity itself.

The use of data modeling techniques provides the structure of the data dimension. In object-oriented software, the data dimension is described by the static class or object models.

Functional Transformations (Function)

A function is a transformation of an incoming stream of data into an outgoing stream of data and is governed by a set of rules (DeMarco 1982; Davis 1990). Davis calls these rules semantic statements; they control when a function can be triggered.

Function-strong applications, or those with a strong function dimension, derive their size from the processing required to transform the input data into the output data. This processing is expressed in the mathematics of the application domain. In fact, the mathematics of the domain is *the* major source of functional size. This information can be used in measurement [in particular, see 3D function points in Whitmire (1995)].

Function-strong applications tend to model the behavior of real-world entities, rather than the entities themselves. They model the phenomena and processes that operate on those entities. The focus is on the way the entity reacts to those processes, and not on information about the entity, as in a data-strong application. Some function-strong applications exist only to perform certain sets of calculations and may not model any specific entity or class of entities.

The function dimension models the processing performed by the application, including both the specific steps in that processing and the rules which control it. Here, we use a limited definition of the word "processing" that includes only that processing which changes or transforms data from one form into another. Typical business applications may include forms of processing which are explicitly excluded from the definition (any type of data processing that does not change the form or nature of the data, such as searching, sorting, grouping, and reporting).

This separation of transformations from other forms of processing was not part of DeMarco's intentions. It came about while attempting to derive the three dimensions from domain models which contained the implication of perfect technology (where nontransformation types of processing are not required). We were interested in identifying that part of the domain model that could be considered function, and mathematical transformations were the only form of processing that could not be removed from a domain model which contained only the essential elements of the model (McMenamin and Palmer 1992), that is, based upon perfect technology.

Process modeling techniques result in a description which includes the function dimension. These results may also include other forms of processing which are not part of the function dimension. In object-oriented software, the function dimension is contained in the object interaction or communication models. One of the two primary purposes of use cases (Jacobsen et al. 1992) is to identify the functional transformations required of the system (the other is to identify the objects of the system—its data dimension).

Dynamic Behavior (Control)

Behavior is the state-dependent response of an application, or an object, to an external or internal event. This response triggers an action which may or may not result in a transition to a new state. Sometimes, the response to a given event varies among different states. That is, an application's response to an event will be different if the event occurs while in one state than it would be if the event occurred in a different state. Consider an automated teller machine (ATM). You can press any button at any time. The ATM may or may not respond to a particular button, or may respond to a particular button differently, depending upon its current state. For instance, an ATM will recognize the number keys only when it is expecting you to enter a number of some kind.

Control-strong applications, or applications with strong control dimensions, derive their size from the size of their state space and the number of events to which they need to respond (Whitmire 1992a). Control-strong applications tend to perform real work, rather than model entities that exist outside the application. Indeed, control-strong applications are often part of real-world entities. They monitor and control processes and react to control or influence the process in a time scale defined by the process, not the computer (Mellichamp 1983; Chonoles and Gilliam 1995). It is not possible to separate control-strong software from its environment. Indeed, it becomes *part of* the environment.

The behavior dimension models the possible states assumed by the application or object and the transitions among and between those states. The behavior dimension is the result of state modeling techniques. In object-oriented software, the behavior dimension is represented by the combined state models of the system objects.

SUMMARY

In this chapter a general framework has been developed which can be used to classify and focus your measurement efforts. This framework is built around three basic views of software measurement and four classes of entities which can be measured. The three views are:

- *Strategic*: Concerned with the long-term performance of an organization
- *Tactical*: Concerned with the short-term performance of an individual process
- *Technical*: Concerned with many details of products and processes that influence the design of products and the processes used to create them

The four objects classes of entities are: processes, products, resources, and projects.

The five basic roles that measurement data can play in technical measurement activities were identified and discussed. The five roles are: estimation, prediction, assessment, comparison, and investigation.

The differences between measuring design artifacts and code artifacts, and why we need to focus on design artifacts, were discussed. We also discussed some of the differences between object-oriented software and software that is not object-oriented, and how those differences can influence the ways in which we can measure the software.

Then the fundamental three-dimensional nature of software was presented. The three dimensions are: static structure (data), functional transformations (function), and dynamic behavior (control). The characteristics from each dimension that can cause inherent size in a piece of software were noted, as was the fact that individual objects also have these same dimensions.

2

AN OBJECT-ORIENTED DESIGN PROCESS

Mostow (1985, quoted in Booch 1994, p. 22) suggests that the purpose of design is to construct a system that:

- Satisfies a given functional specification
- Conforms to limitations of the target medium
- Meets implicit or explicit requirements on performance and resource usage
- Satisfies implicit or explicit design criteria on the form of the artifact
- Satisfies restrictions on the design process itself, such as its length or cost, or the tools available for doing the design.

Put this way, it is a wonder anything is ever designed. These goals are very often in conflict, handing the designer an optimization problem in which no solution is clearly better than any other. In these circumstances, a well-defined design process can offer guidance in how to make design tradeoff decisions. A good process will not specify one particular solution over another, but will guide the designer through a thinking process which ultimately leads to a choice. A process, however well-defined, will never replace the talents of a good designer. A good process together with a good designer can lead to reliably good designs on a consistent basis.

In this chapter, I present a design process that has evolved over several years and many projects to show how an informal process can be a well-defined process and to illustrate how measurement can be used during design to help make design tradeoff decisions. As I discuss measurement throughout the rest of the book, this process will give you some idea of what I am talking about.

The first section, "An Informal, Defined Design Process," is an overview of the design process, briefly touching on all of the "steps." The following section introduces the four domains of design around which the design steps are organized. "Problem Definition" describes the problem definition process in some detail, indicating ways in which measurement might be used. The section "Selecting the Design Approach" discusses the selection of the design approach and why this step is important enough to warrant the position it is given within the total process. The final sections cover the actual design steps in greater detail. The design portion of the process is emphasized here because this is a book about design, and because nearly all of the problems I have encountered during the construction and testing phases of my projects were the result of rushed or neglected design.

AN INFORMAL, DEFINED DESIGN PROCESS

My design process grew out of my own experiences on projects, those of other projects I witnessed, and the experiences of other people with whom I have talked. On nearly every project which was not trivial (I have done several trivial projects over the years—those programs coded and implemented over a lunch hour), I encountered two major issues again and again. This design process was developed primarily to help me address these issues.

First, I am never sure the design is correct. I constantly worry whether I have all of the requirements, whether I have identified *all* of the objects I need. I also worry about whether I have identified *only* the objects I need. I do not have confidence in any innate ability to filter out the correct objects from a set of requirements, nor do I believe that any particular object discovery method will work in every instance.

Second, I really dislike having to redo large portions of my code because I need to change an interface to get at some piece of data. I especially dislike this effort when I could have avoided the rework in the first place by 10 minutes of effort during design to identify the data needed by each function and to map out its retrieval by the function. This is a design activity which usually gets neglected, at large expense, in the rush to get coding.

The design process covers the entire life cycle of a software product, from conception through retirement, and includes the following basic steps:

1. *Project planning*: Define the boundaries of the project, including the scope of work, the project goals, the project constraints, the set of tasks, the identification of project risks, and an initial estimate of the resources required.

2. *Requirements gathering*: Determine the requirements, preferences, expectations, and constraints of the various groups of users and customers.

3. *Selecting the design approach*: Use the goals and requirements of the project to select what the design should emphasize, which will materially affect the basic shape of the design.

4. *Problem domain design*: Identify the objects, roles, and responsibilities within the problem domain.

5. *Application domain design*: Identify and refine those objects from the problem domain which will actually be implemented in the application.

6. *Physical packaging design*: Determine how the source code will be packaged into modules, with an eye towards minimizing the compile and link times during modifications, and minimizing the requirement to recompile working code because some object it depends upon has changed.

7. *Construction*: Write, compile, and unit test the source code.

8. *Implementation*: Integrate the components of the system, let the customers test it, and install it.

9. *Change management*: Track and control changes to requirements, design, and source code, and determine the point at which the application should be retired based on the cost of further changes to the application.

That the process is heavily oriented towards design is deliberate. In this day of rapid application development (RAD), where programmers and users sit down together and visually create a prototype, this much emphasis on design may seem out of place. Perhaps it is. I have found, however, that those design steps not explicitly done before code is cut are done implicitly during the coding process and are never done very well. I firmly believe that anything important in software development is reflected in the design. Design is the second most important activity in software engineering, after requirements gathering. While the requirements tell you *what* is to be done, the design contains all of the information about *how* it will be done. With a good and complete design, code construction can be turned into activity which can be fully automated. In writing, the real work precedes the actual putting of words to paper (or computer screen). In software, the real work precedes the cutting of code.

This process is criteria-based—that is, each step defines a set of goals and gives some idea of the information to be gathered and decisions to be made during that step. These information requirements are presented as a set of questions to be answered or as a small checklist. The process does not define a set of artifacts to be produced, since they are usually defined as part of a selected method. Also, the process does not name, nor assume, any particular method. The choice of method is like the choice of tools: It is up to the individual designer.

The name "step" is perhaps a misnomer, as these are not steps to be executed sequentially. It is permissible, even encouraged, to perform several of the requirements and design steps repeatedly in rapid succession, what George Yuan (1995) calls a "depth-first" approach. In practice, these steps are often done simultaneously in the mind of the designer.

This process is my personal process. I do not advocate that people adopt it as their own. I believe that one purpose of a defined design process is to make up for the designer's inherent weaknesses. You can think of it as making up in definition what I lack in innate skill. Since you and I are different people, we have a different sets of weaknesses. Consequently, our design processes will be different.

THE FOUR DOMAINS OF DESIGN

As described in this book, design is really two different activities: analysis and true design. The material in this section relies heavily on Yuan (1995). Analysis is the activity of discovering, understanding, and describing properties of real-world objects and their behaviors in the problem domain. These properties cannot be changed by the designer. True design is the activity of building the system architecture and each system component. This involves inventing and specifying classes and their properties in the solution domains. It is very difficult to separate the two and I have given up trying.

Yuan describes an application using four domains, shown in Figure 2.1. Each domain is briefly discussed here. I highly suggest you read Yuan's paper—it is one of those rare gems that is both readable and useful. It is also very important. Incidently, each of Yuan's four domains includes all three of DeMarco's dimensions, so this is not a different or conflicting view of software.

Problem Domain

The first domain is the problem domain. It contains abstractions of those objects that are part of and interact with the application. The perspective is from that of the user and system requirements. Not all objects which interact with a system are part of the system. In particular, the problem domain may contain representations of people, organizations, and other applications, none of which are within the scope of the current problem, but which nonetheless must be understood to completely define the application. Problem domain design is a systems engineering effort in which you determine the software application's allocation of work. The "system" may be a business process or a true hardware/software system.

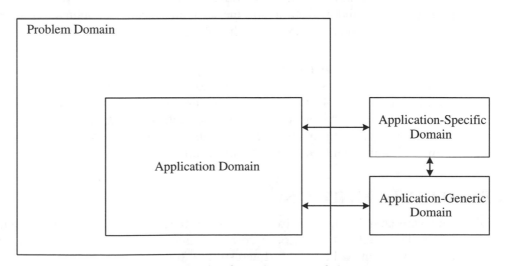

Figure 2.1 *The four domains of design.*

The problem domain can be divided into subdomains as necessary. These subdomains may divide the system along the lines of organizations, business processes, policies, resources, and knowledge. Abstractions in the problem domain (they may or may not be thought of as classes) are related through the three basic relationships of generalization/specialization, association, and aggregation. The problem domain design can be expressed using the same tools, notations, techniques, and measures used for the other domains. This raises the very real potential for using object-oriented design methods to design, document, and analyze business processes. That this is even possible is a matter of some controversy.

Application Domain

The application domain is the first level of the solution domains. It contains those abstractions from the problem domain that will actually be implemented as system objects. Application domain design, along with the domains which follow, is the software engineering portion of building an application. There may be a one-to-one mapping between some abstractions in this domain and some of those in the problem domain. There may be many-to-one mappings between other sets of abstractions. Some of the abstractions in the problem domain may not be mapped into the application domain at all. The perspective is that of the designer and programmer. Like the problem domain, the application domain can be divided into subdomains as required. Abstractions in the application domain are related through relationships of inheritance, uses, and contains, which are implementations of those in the problem domain. A contains or uses relationship can be implemented through by-value, by-reference, or key value containment.

Application-Specific Domain

This domain contains support classes crafted specifically for this application. It may be divided into subdomains, which often run vertically through the application. Possible subdomains include the user interface, communication, event handlers, database interface, exception handling, object management, and caching.

Application-Generic Domain

This domain contains support classes and system objects with generic behavior used by multiple applications. These include container classes, generic data structures, database management systems, user interface classes, messaging mechanisms, and operating system services. This domain also includes purchased and borrowed components such as kits and frameworks.

PROBLEM DEFINITION

This step actually involves two activities: project planning and requirements gathering. The goal is to develop a correct, complete, and unambiguous description of the problem to be solved. Interestingly, this step is almost never completed, yet we still manage to develop the occasional successful piece of software.

The main concerns during this step are:

- Size of the problem in terms of its requirements.
- Complexity of the problem.
- Completeness of the description—do we have all of the requirements?
- Sufficiency of the description—do we have enough of the requirements to proceed?

Measurement can help with the first two concerns. You can measure the size and complexity of a problem. Unfortunately, there is little help for the last two. At this point, you can only say whether the requirements you have are complete and/or sufficient after the fact. Quality of abstraction, represented by the design characteristics sufficiency, completeness, and cohesion can help you assess your requirements by comparing the abstractions in the various design domains to the object they represent in the problem itself. Use cases and scenarios, role playing, and games are other ways designers and users can build confidence that all, or nearly all, of the requirements have been identified.

Project Planning

Project planning involves placing boundaries around the problem—sort of like building a fence within which you try to place the problem. The planning step involves such activities as defining the project scope, setting goals and constraints, assessing the risks, breaking down the project into manageable tasks, estimating resource requirements, and making task assignments to project personnel.

The plan represents part of the problem definition since it puts boundaries around the requirements which will likely be included in the application. Some organizations are very good at planning projects and others wouldn't know a plan if it came through the window tied to a rock. Yet every organization, whether explicitly or implicitly, performs all of these activities with widely varying degrees of success.

Requirements Gathering

I used to call this step requirements extraction, since it felt a lot like pulling teeth. Over time, I've gotten better at getting people to tell me what they want, thanks to people like Donald Gause and Gerald Weinberg (1989). Briefly, this step involves defining the overall system requirements—those features which are required—and the preferences and expectations of the customers. Gause and Weinberg provide some wonderful tools to assist in this process, including several ways to test for ambiguity in requirements statements.

Requirements gathering is missing from nearly every method published. One of the first things I noticed about structured analysis (DeMarco 1978), and any of several object-oriented analysis methods, is that they all assumed that you had in hand a statement of the requirements of the system. Not until Gause and Weinberg did anyone ever actually talk about how to get those requirements. I highly recommend their book.

SELECTING THE DESIGN APPROACH

Another oft-neglected step in the design process is to explicitly select the design approach most suitable to the problem. Many people think that one approach is better than all others and try to use it on every problem. This simply doesn't work. As Shaw (1995) shows, different approaches to the same problem can lead to vastly different designs, and even different architectures with significantly different properties. Sharble and Cohen (1993) demonstrate this phenomenon very clearly when they apply two approaches to the very same set of requirements. Their experiment is discussed a little later.

The goal of this process step is to match as closely as possible the approach to be taken during design with the nature of the problem, balanced against the project goals, targets, and constraints. The nature of the problem is determined by the relative importance or influence of each of the three dimensions defined in Chapter 1: static structure, functional transformations, and dynamic behavior. Measurement can be used effectively to weigh the relative importance of each dimension. My favorite technique is to use 3D function points (Whitmire 1995) as a triple (d, f, b) of data size, transformation size, and behavior size. The relative values of these three sizes give me some idea of where to place the emphasis in my design effort. This method works surprisingly well, but there are probably others that work as well or better.

Currently, there are five separately identified design approaches: data-driven, process-driven, event-driven, interaction-driven, and responsibility-driven. Each emphasizes a different aspect of the problem, each has its own strengths and weaknesses, and each can lead a designer in very different directions. While each approach develops each of the three dimensions, they differ in the way they go about it. The approaches are named for the characteristics of the objects they concentrate on first and the method they use to identify the objects. Thus, each approach defines objects from a different primary point of view. The data-driven and responsibility-driven approaches are currently the most commonly used. Each is used in two or more of the object-oriented methods currently available.

Different problem types may require a specific approach. Problems of the same type but with different goals and constraints may require different approaches. A competent software engineer should be at least familiar enough with each approach to be able to explain why a given approach is being used on a particular problem. An expert software engineer should have some experience with each approach, to the point where he or she has a feel for the best approach for a given problem, set of goals, and constraints. At the very least, the expert software engineer should have enough knowledge to be able to justify the use of a given approach on a given problem, preferably with quantitative information.

To select the approach to use in a particular situation, you want to analyze the requirements, goals, and constraints, looking for patterns of characteristics that maximize the effects of an approach's strengths and minimize the effects of its weaknesses. There are often conflicting goals and constraints, so the selection of the design approach is often an optimization problem. One important point to remember is that all of the approaches ultimately result in a complete model of the structure, function, and behavior dimensions, but each approach emphasizes a different aspect of a problem.

The Object–Oriented Brewery

Sharble and Cohen (1993) conducted one of a very few, if not the only, experiment to determine the relative effectiveness of different approaches to a design. They designed the same system using the data-driven and responsibility-driven approaches. When they were done, they compared the two designs using a set of several measures. In every measure, the data-driven design scored worse than the responsibility-driven design, leading them to conclude that the responsibility-driven approach was superior. One of the authors is an experienced data-driven designer and the other is an experienced responsibility-driven designer, so they believe that each approach was given a fair shot.

There are some things you should consider before you go applying the responsibility-driven approach to every problem (which is just what some methodologists think you should do!). First, this is only one experiment, and should be repeated several times by several different teams before we take the results at face value. Second, the application they developed was a real-time control system, a control-strong application, used to control the brewing processes in a brewery. The same results might not be attained if the experiment were to be conducted on a data-strong or function-strong application. Third, each designer used a particular method to apply his approach. Using different methods that encompass the same approaches could lead to different results. Finally, the experiment compared only the data-driven and responsibility-driven approaches, completely ignoring the others. These concerns do not invalidate the results at all; they only urge caution before generalizing the results to other domains, or to using other methods, or to using other approaches.

The five approaches, their primary strengths, and their primary weaknesses are summarized in Table 2.1 and briefly discussed in the following subsections.

Data–Driven

The data-driven approach focuses on the static data or information model contained in the problem domain. It is one of the two most commonly used approaches, being built into several object-oriented methodologies. It views objects primarily by their component parts and static structural relationships with one another. The main influence for the approach is data or information modeling. The objects in a system developed with this approach tend to map to the entities in the information model.

The data-driven approach has several strengths. It tends to identify the objects about which information must be retained, including both active and passive objects. Active objects are those which perform some part of the function required by the application. Passive objects are only acted upon or provide responses to queries from other objects. Objects which exist only to interface to one or more

Table 2.1 The Five Design Approaches

Approach	Strengths	Weaknesses
Data-Driven	• Identifies passive and active objects • Maps easily to existing relational data models • Easier transition for those with data modeling experience	• Difficult to tell passive objects from active • Leads to unnecessary complexity in system responsibility allocation • Internal structure shows through external interface • Interactions tend to be attribute-based
Process-Driven	• Includes all functions in design • Maps easily from a set of dataflow diagrams • Easier transition for those with process modeling experience	• May not map to domain objects • Leads to designs with high coupling and low cohesion • Objects are function-oriented • Passive objects are often missed • Algorithms tend to be identified too early in design process • Algorithms and objects cannot be easily separated
Event-Driven	• Packages interaction with environment into coherent units • Good for some control-strong applications • Objects tend to map to external devices • Captures communication with environment • Helps build complete model of state application	• Does not help build complete state model of each object • Design coalesces around groups of events and responses • Easy to miss essential objects and collaborations
Interaction-Driven	• Clearly defines external communication for an object	• Provides no help with identifying sets of objects or classes
Responsibility-Driven	• Focuses on required behavior • Packages responsibilities into coherent contracts • Clearly defines expectations for a class • Usually results in fewer classes • May lead to less complex designs in some domains • Easy to map requirements into design • Good for some control-strong applications	• Limits view of object to one point of view • May not identify all essential classes • Concentrates on active objects and may miss passive objects • May lead to unintuitive class structures for data-strong and function-strong applications

database tables are examples of passive objects. The object model created by the data-driven approach maps closely to existing relational database structures. It also maps closely to the data models that exist in many organizations. The transition to the data-driven approach to object-oriented design may be easier for those with experience in data modeling techniques.

The data-driven approach also has several weaknesses. It is difficult to tell passive objects from active objects in a data-driven object model. This difficulty could lead to unnecessary complexity in the allocation of system responsibilities (Sharble and Cohen 1993). The internal structure of an object developed with the data-driven approach tends to show through the public interface of the object. Interaction with the object tends to be attribute-based—messages query and set attribute values rather than request services. Some references on the data-driven approach are: Shlaer and Mellor (1988); Embley, Kurtz, and Woodfield (1992); Rumbaugh et al. (1991); Coad and Yourdon (1991b); and Booch (1994).

Process-Driven

The process-driven approach focuses on the functions performed in the problem domain's process model. It views objects primarily by the functions they perform. The main influence in the approach is process modeling. The objects in an object model developed using the process-driven approach tend to map in a loose fashion to the high-level processes in the problem domain.

The process-driven approach has several strengths. It ensures, or at least helps to ensure, that all of the functions and processes in the specification are included in the design. The object model maps easily from a set of dataflow diagrams and may make for an easier transition for those experienced in structured analysis and decomposition.

The process-driven approach also has several weaknesses. The objects tend to be identified by process and may not map well to the real-world objects, leading to designs with high coupling and low cohesion. I have seen process-driven designs that have no discernible relationship to reality, yet appear to correctly solve the problem ("appear" being the operative word). Objects in a process-driven model tend to be function-oriented, when they may not need to be. Passive objects are often left out of the design completely or not considered in a timely manner. Use of the process-driven approach often (usually) results in the selection and specification of algorithms too early in the design process. Finally, the process-driven approach may lead to cases where the algorithms and the objects which use them cannot be easily separated, hampering reuse of either the algorithms or the objects. One reference for this approach is Embley, Kurtz, and Woodfield (1992).

Event-Driven

The event-driven approach focuses on the events to which the system must respond and the actions taken in response to those events. It views objects primarily by the events to which they respond. The main influence in the approach is event-response modeling. The objects in an object model tend to map to sets of related events.

The event-driven approach, too, has several strengths. It packages the system's interaction with its environment into neat, coherent units. The results are similar to those of the responsibility-driven approach, but the packages are event-response pairs. It is good for modeling real-time applications. The objects in the design tend to map to the external devices with which the system must interact. The event list captures, to a large degree, the communication between the device and the application. The event-driven approach makes it fairly easy to build a complete state model of the application. It may not help in building the complete state model for each object, however.

The event-driven approach also has its share of weaknesses. The design tends to coalesce around groups of events and responses, rather than abstractions in the problem domain. It is very easy to miss essential objects and collaborations, especially those passive objects which may not respond directly to external events. References for this approach include Page-Jones and Weiss (1992) and Shlaer and Mellor (1992).

Interaction–Driven

The interaction-driven approach focuses on object interactions and the constraints those interactions must satisfy. It views objects primarily by their interactions with other objects, both internal and external to the application. The main influence is communication modeling. The objects in the object model tend to map to groups of related messages.

Very little has been written about this approach. It is given a brief mention in Wirfs-Brock, Wilkerson, and Wiener (1990), but nothing has been published about experiences with the approach, its strengths, or its weaknesses. My own brief attempts at using it have resulted in very little knowledge about its good and bad points. I have managed to identify one major strength and one major weakness.

The interaction-driven approach defines clearly the external communications for a class. This goes a long way towards defining the external interface for the class. The approach provides almost no help in identifying the correct set of classes, however. This would seem to limit the interaction-driven approach as a follow-on to help define the external interfaces on a set of classes identified using some other approach.

Responsibility–Driven

The responsibility-driven approach focuses on the various responsibilities of the application, in terms of the actions required to fulfill the requirements. It views objects primarily by the roles and responsibilities they have in the application. The main influence is role playing. The objects in the object model tend to map to groups of related responsibilities, with an *object-in-charge* being defined for each one. Sometimes, objects are invented to serve as object-in-charge.

The responsibility-driven approach has many strengths. It focuses on the required behavior of the application and packages sets of responsibilities into coherent groups called contracts. It defines clearly the external expectations of a class and delays decisions about attributes and functions (the structure of a class) until more is known. This approach usually results in fewer problem domain classes, which often leads to less complex applications. It also provides an easier mapping from requirements to design components.

The responsibility-driven approach is not without weaknesses. It limits the view of an object to that of the current application, leading to potentially sufficient but incomplete classes. It may not identify all of the essential classes in the domain. The approach tends to concentrate on active objects and may miss many of the passive objects in the domain. It may also lead to non-intuitive class structures for data-strong and function-strong applications. References include Wirfs-Brock, Wilkerson, and Wiener (1990) and Booch (1994).

PROBLEM DOMAIN DESIGN

Problem domain design is the activity during which the problem domain model takes shape. Many people insist on calling it analysis. Granted, a large portion of the work in this activity is analysis, but it is truly a design function. Analysis, as an activity, consists of tearing things apart to see how they are put together and how they work. Design, on the other hand, is a synthesis activity, a building up. The purpose of problem domain design is to build a model of the problem domain.

There is another reason for calling problem domain design a design activity. During the process of building the model, the designer must often decide where to put features of the problem domain. These decisions usually involve tradeoffs of some kind and are not always determined by the problem domain itself. The choice of objects is not always clear-cut; it is often a matter of debate or preference. The placement of responsibilities is not always a given, either. A designer relies upon experience and intuition when making these decisions. The main purpose of this book is to make measurement, specifically technical measurement of products, one of the designer's primary tools for making these decisions.

Problem domain design builds the problem and application domains. The goal of this activity is effective or correct operation of the application. The driving force is the requirements. This activity seeks to identify abstractions, structures, functions, and attributes necessary to solve the problem. The process involves allocation and assignment of roles, responsibilities, attributes, and functions among the identified abstractions. It involves the assignment of abstractions to identified subdomains and includes the selection of those abstractions in the problem domain which will become the application domain. Those abstractions which fall outside of the application domain must be provided interfaces through which they can interact with and influence the operation of the application.

This last task, establishing the boundary of the application, is vital to the success of the project and should be approached with care. One advantage to working the problem and application domains together is that placement of the boundary can be fluid, at least for this activity. The boundary can be adjusted as appropriate to optimize the application domain for the goals of the project. This optimization should be based on technical measurement, of course.

The main issues for the designer at this point are:

- *Sufficiency*: Does the model contain enough real-world facts and concepts to implement the application at hand?
- *Completeness*: Does the model contain enough real-world facts and concepts to be generally useful to the entire enterprise, the entire industry, or to the market at large?
- *Cohesion*: Does each abstraction or composite structure faithfully represent one and only one real-world fact or concept, including all of its roles, responsibilities, and expectations?

Together, these issues address what I call the quality of abstraction. Problem domain design consists of eleven basic steps, which are summarized in Table 2.2. Each step addresses some failing in a past design project. As each step is presented, some of the tasks and concerns, as well as ways in which measurement can help address these issues, will be discussed. While there are many ways to make use of measurement data in this step, the measures are by necessity crude and unrefined. Just be patient, more refined measures are available as more information about the design becomes known.

Identify System Responsibilities

System responsibilities refer to the functions the application must perform in the business domain. Identifying them requires naming the business functions (domains) which the application will either support or perform. It includes defining the products which the application will produce, in terms of their content and their form. These responsibilities and products should be defined and described in the language of the business domains. This could mean plain English text, structured English, process descriptions, enumerated lists of items, use cases (Jacobsen et al. 1992), or mathematical formulae.

Completion of this step amounts to developing a set of requirements. You may think of this step as a checklist of sorts to help you identify areas in which your requirements are lacking. In one project or another, I forgot to include one or more areas, for which I later paid dearly. The tasks included in this step need not be done in the sequence presented. They may be done in any order or in parallel if you have the resources.

The set of system responsibilities and products collectively compose the requirements for the application. Group these requirements by common business function, by common type, or by whatever means is helpful. This grouping defines business domain-level "transactions" through the application. Use case modeling is a very useful tool for this exercise.

Identify groups of users, customers, and others who have a stake in the application. Classify them according to their areas of interest, skill level, and potential

Table 2.2 Problem Domain Design Steps

Step	Measurement Concerns
1. Identify system responsibilities	• Population of ○ System responsibilities ○ Products ○ Users ○ External events ○ Threads of execution • Equivalence classes of users • Functionality • Volume
2. Identify problem domain abstractions	• Population of ○ Abstractions ○ Points of view by abstraction ○ Points of view (union of abstractions) • Sufficiency • Completeness • Cohesion
3. Identify structures	• Population of ○ Abstractions added ○ Structures ○ Relationships by type • Cohesion
4. Identify communication patterns	• Population of communication links ○ Into each abstraction ○ Out of each abstraction
5. Identify timing and concurrency constraints	• Population of timing constraints • Population of concurrency constraints • Scope of each concurrency constraint
6. Identify and describe attributes	• Population of attributes by abstraction • Population of attribute domains • Scope of attribute domain (by domain)
7. Identify instance connections	• Population of association
8. Identify abstraction states	• Population of states by abstraction • Population of invariant terms
9. Identify services	• Population of ○ Services by abstraction ○ Preconditions by service ○ Postconditions by service ○ Calculations by service
10. Identify message connections	• Population of message links • Population of message links by abstraction pairs
11. Simplify the model	• Sufficiency • Completeness • Cohesion

volume of application use. This will provide you with a user profile which can be used to develop a portion of your test plan. Note that an individual person may belong to more than one group.

Identify external events to which the system must respond. For each event, identify the application's required response. These event responses may become additional system responsibilities not otherwise included in the requirements. They also provide much of the information required to develop the state models later in the process.

Identify threads of execution through the application. Look for coherent activities that cut across major parts of the application. Think in terms of using the application to perform each of the system responsibilities. When performing one, a user may take several paths through the application based on the circumstances. This defines to a large extent the navigation paths through the user interface, as well as the application itself. For each thread which cannot be mapped completely to a previously identified system responsibility, create a new one and add it to the set.

If you were paying close attention, there are several potential measures which might be useful. The most obvious is the number of system responsibilities. You may also want to track the number of products, the number of groups of requirements, the number of groups of users, the number of users in each group, the number of external events, and the number of threads of execution. All of these counts provide different views of the size of the application. The size of the application measured in this way does not represent functionality, but does provide some indication of the number of requirements for the application. Each of these items can be tracked independently. As system responsibilities are added during the process, the growth of the requirements can be tracked at the item level. You can use measures such as 3D function points (Whitmire 1995) to measure the application size in terms of functionality. You can also use the measure for breadth- and depth-of-scope, developed in Chapter 7, to track the degree of support the application provides to the business process.

These measurements cannot be compared across applications or organizations. They can be used for estimating, but only in a project-oriented organization with a fairly stable environment, including people, tools, techniques, and platforms. The reasons for these restrictions will become apparent in Chapter 4, where the analytical tools which may be applied to measurement data are discussed, and Chapter 5, where measurement theory is discussed.

Identify Problem Domain Abstractions

Choosing the abstractions in the problem domain is one of the most critical steps in object-oriented design. I use *choosing* rather than *finding*, as most people do, because I have found that the designer often has considerable latitude for making tradeoff decisions. Of course, this latitude is constrained to some narrow sets of choices, but choices do exist, nevertheless. I use the term *abstractions* rather than *classes* because it has been my experience that every abstraction in the problem domain turns into at least two classes in the application and sometimes as many as five classes for distributed applications. By using a different term, a lot of confusion is avoided.

For me, the biggest issues faced by this activity are the two biggest issues faced during the entire design effort. They are:

1. Have you identified all of the abstractions you need in the problem domain to build this application?

2. Have you identified only those abstractions needed to build this application?

The first issue deals with sufficiency, while the second deals with efficiency. Both issues deal with completeness. I have created designs which were missing important abstractions from the problem domain and I have created designs which contained a galaxy of problem domain abstractions. Neither of these extremes is a good situation; both lead to substantial and costly rework down the road. This activity is designed to help you be confident that you have identified all of the abstractions required to build the application, that is, to fulfill the system responsibilities, and that you have identified only those abstractions required to discharge those responsibilities.

For each system responsibility, identify the real-world entities, concepts, ideas, policies, organizations, people, events, and applications which contribute in some way to meeting the responsibility. Each of these "things" becomes an abstraction in the problem domain. Recall from the section on the four domains of design that the problem domain may include abstractions which will not become part of the application. Include abstractions that both affect and are affected by the execution of the system responsibility.

Each system responsibility will thus be the source of a set of abstractions. The set of abstractions required for the application is the union of the sets for each system responsibility. Abstractions which appear in more than one set need only be included in the problem domain once. You do need to be aware, though, of the point of view each system responsibility takes for each abstraction. In fact, you need to examine each abstraction in the set from different points of view, which will usually be aligned with organizations, business functions, or business processes. Identify all of the points of view for each abstraction which are relevant to the enterprise. At this point, a simple list of points of view for each abstraction is sufficient. These lists will be used later in the design process to determine the abstraction's properties. Generally, each point of view will see a given abstraction as a different set of properties. This concept is discussed further in Chapter 6.

This activity contributes many new measures to the design effort. Among the more important measures are the number of abstractions and the number of points of view for each abstraction. The set of points of view, taken as the union of the sets of points of view for each abstraction, and its population counts are valuable measures, as well. You may want to determine the average number of points of view for each abstraction, but I'm not sure what you would do with it. Abstractions with many points of view will probably be more important to the enterprise and this application. They are certainly the best candidates to be designed in such a way to be easily reused in the future, for this application and other applications. Even at this early stage in the development process, measurement is giving you a good feel of the size and shape of your application and of the potential for reuse. If some of these abstractions exist in another application, you can examine them to see if they can be used or modified to be used. If not, you can plan to build them with reuse in mind.

Here is one other point. The number of abstractions, and the number of points of view for an abstraction, are not important numbers by themselves. You shouldn't plan to target a set number of abstractions. Nor should you limit the number of points of view to some artificial value, such as 7 plus or minus 2. The numbers as they naturally occur in the problem domain are important to help understand what it is you are facing. At this point, just understanding the problem domain is a pretty big task.

Identify Structures

Abstractions do not exist independently. They work together, sometimes dynamically and sometimes by participating in static structures with other abstractions. This activity is basic data modeling. The purpose is to compose simple abstractions into relevant structures and to decompose complex abstractions into structures of simpler abstractions. Usually, this activity results in the addition of new abstractions to the problem domain. Sometimes, abstractions are removed from problem domain. The resulting model is a more stable and useful model upon which to build the application.

There are two basic kinds of structures (Booch 1994; Coad and Yourdon 1991a; Rumbaugh et al. 1991). Generalization-specializations are structures in which some abstractions adopt and extend the properties of others. Since individual properties have not yet been defined, these structures must be identified based on the knowledge the designer has of the problem domain. The discipline of data modeling is helpful in this effort. The other basic structure is the whole-part structure, where one abstraction contains or is composed of other abstractions, or where one abstraction plays a master role to another's detail role. Whole-part structures most often result in the addition of new abstractions at this point, since they are the easiest to identify with the information at hand. Later on in the process, you will have more information for creating additional generalization-specialization structures.

You want to track the number of abstractions added and removed during this activity. You may also want to track the number of structures in the application. For each structure, the number of participating abstractions will give some idea of its complexity. Be careful, though. At this point you are dealing with units of abstractions. Some of these abstractions will be more complex than others once the properties are all defined. Complexity at this point is not the complexity of the application. It is the complexity of the abstraction structure, which is interesting and useful, but shouldn't be managed in terms of targets or standards, since the model at this point simply reflects the structure of the problem domain.

Identify Communication Patterns

System responsibilities create the need for abstractions to communicate with one another. These communication links create dynamic relationships between objects of each abstraction. All messages passed within the application will flow along these communication links. Together, these links form the network over which information will pass within the application. As such, it is vital to understand the basic nature of this network. These links, more than any other type of object-to-object relationship, define the complexity of the application.

The total communication network for even a small application is exceedingly complex. It is easy to build, if you take it one responsibility at a time. Ivar Jacobsen's use cases (Jacobsen et al. 1992) are a disciplined, defined way to build the communication network one responsibility at a time. Jacobsen provides a convenient way to document these subnetworks, too. The total network for the application is the union of the subnetworks for each responsibility. Links which appear on more than one subnetwork need only be included in the total network once.

Often, attributes and methods are identified during the course of developing the network. As they are identified, record them. This will save work in later activities.

The total number of communication links is the best indication of the application's overall complexity available at this point in the process. Likewise, the number of links going to each abstraction or structure gives you an idea of the complexity of the external interface of the abstraction. The number of links going out from each abstraction gives you an idea of the dependence of the abstraction on the rest of the application and the exposure or risk of changes to the abstraction due to changes to other parts of the application. You may want to study Chapter 8 on complexity and Chapter 9 on coupling.

Identify Timing and Concurrency Constraints

Some problem domains contain inherent timing and concurrency constraints. Such constraints often lead to the discovery of new attributes and methods. All of these, constraints, attributes, and methods, should be added to the model as they are discovered.

The number of timing constraints gives you some idea of the critical nature of the application. A high number—high is undefined at this point—indicates that the execution of methods in the application may be fairly restricted, which will very likely increase the design time substantially. The number of concurrency constraints gives you an idea of the shape of the application in terms of its linearity or parallel operation. Concurrency constraints also increase the design time, but not nearly as much as timing constraints. They may indicate the need for system objects in the application-specific or application-generic domains to control access to constrained resources. Both of these are red flags, and should be heeded, although there is nothing you can do to avoid them—they are part of the problem domain, after all.

Identify and Describe Attributes

For each abstraction in the problem domain, look for descriptive characteristics. Name the properties of each abstraction which need to be exposed in the application. These will form your first cut at the set of attributes for each abstraction. Over the course of the rest of the design, you will doubtless discover additional attributes. When you do, add them to the model as soon as they are discovered and update your attribute-based measurements.

As attributes are discovered, they must be defined in terms of their type, their name, and the domain from which possible values may be drawn. From experience, I can guarantee that it is easier to do this as they are discovered than to wait for some later activity. If you wait, you will either forget why the attribute is important (and delete it at your peril) or not define it until you start to build the application. Many attributes are accompanied by constraints. When this is the case, they must also be identified and defined as they are discovered.

The number of attributes in an abstraction reflects the size of the set of properties of the abstraction of interest in the application. Attributes create work, both for the designer and for the application itself. The number of attributes is one of the contributors to the size of an abstraction.

Identify Instance Connections

Look for groups of abstractions which share a key or identifying attribute. The attribute must be the primary identifier in one abstraction, and either part of the primary identifier or a regular attribute in the other abstractions. These shared attributes form and anchor the association relationships in the model.

Look for one-to-one, one-to-many, and many-to-many relationships. For each such relationship, if the relationship itself contains attributes other than the shared attributes, create an abstraction which includes them. Add the relationship links to the model. This is another activity from data modeling, and helps to uncover existence and other constraints placed on an abstraction by other abstractions. Nearly all many-to-many relationships require the addition of a new associative abstraction to the domain model. Many one-to-many relationships require the use of a container abstraction, which will be added later on—the type of container and where it is located are important implementation decisions.

Like structural relationships, associations contribute to the complexity of the application. The more densely the abstractions are related, by whatever type of relationship, the more complex the application. At this point, a count of associations by type is the best you can do in terms of measurement.

Identify Abstraction States

There are several sources of state information buried in the abstraction model at this point. Status attributes are those that exist only to track the state of an abstraction. They may legitimately be part of the problem domain, but are most often the results of system thinking. If this is the case, remove them from the model, especially if the different states tracked by the attributes can be distinguished by other means.

Sometimes, attribute values are constrained by the values of other attributes. When this happens, these other attributes create a unique state for each possible value from their domain. If multiple attributes work in combination, then each possible combination of values forms a unique state. At other times, the value of an attribute is controlled by other circumstances. When this is the case, each set of circumstances identifies a unique state. Some responsibilities can only be fulfilled under certain circumstances. These circumstances, if not already identified, also form unique states.

Any message received by an abstraction can be considered an external event. When some events occur, one or more of the attributes may change as the abstraction responds. When this is the case, the set of values before the event is a different state from the set of values after the event.

As states are identified, include them in the model. You may notice that some states share the same values for each of the attributes in the abstraction. These are duplicate states and all but one of them may be eliminated from the model. Thus far, you have built only part of the state model for each abstraction. You have identified only the potential states for the abstractions, not the connections, or transitions, between them. Track the number of states for each abstraction. Abstractions with more states are inherently more complex than abstractions with fewer states. You will also note that the number of states for an abstraction that are relevant to the model is usually very small compared to the number of possible states for the abstraction. The number of possible states is a function of the number of attributes and the cardinality of the domain sets for each attribute.

Identify Services

For each system responsibility, each participating abstraction must provide some set of services in order to meet the responsibility. These services form the start of the set of methods for the abstractions. Each system responsibility has one abstraction which is in charge for that responsibility. This is the abstraction responsible for initiating the application's action to fulfill the responsibility. If the responsibility is triggered by an event outside the application boundary, the abstraction which first detects the event is the abstraction in charge. The abstraction in charge for each responsibility may require additional services to trigger the work of the other abstractions. If so, add them to the model.

Each service must be defined. Through experience, this definition has grown to resemble a formal specification. This is one of two instances where I strongly advocate the use of formal specification methods, such as the Z language (Spivey 1992)—the other will be noted during the logical design activity. For each service:

1. Name the service.
2. Describe the service.

3. List the preconditions for the service which exist in the problem domain. Preconditions are conditions which must be met in order for the service to execute.

4. List the postconditions for the service which exist in the problem domain. Postconditions are conditions which the service must guarantee to be true upon completion.

5. List the invariants from the problem domain which affect the execution of this service. Invariants are conditions which are both preconditions and postconditions, plus those conditions which *must never be false* in a stable state; some design methods allow invariants to be violated during transitions between stable states.

6. List the states in which this service may be requested. These are usually covered by the preconditions, but this is not always the case.

7. Identify the attributes required by the service as input parameters. For each parameter, identify its owner and source. The owner and/or source of the parameter must be in scope and visible to this service. Identifying them here leads to a list of scope and visibility requirements which can be very useful during later design activities. Many times I have found I needed an attribute and ended up changing a dozen interfaces to make it available to the service because its source was no longer in scope or was not visible. This problem is particularly annoying, since it generates more rework in the construction activity than nearly any other design error and it is so easy to avoid with this little effort.

8. Identify the attributes to be modified or returned by the service as output parameters or side effects.

9. Identify the services required of other objects. This should be readily apparent from the communication network for the system responsibilities. If new services are required, add them, and their communication links, to the model. Include these messages in the postconditions for the service.

10. If the processing steps for the service are defined by the problem domain, document them. Processing steps in the problem domain may include specific tasks, but usually consist of mathematical calculations. Do not specify specific algorithms at this point. Do not specify processing that is dependent upon or assumes anything about the internal structure of the data (including database table structures). These considerations will be covered later.

The number of services for each abstraction is an important measure. Even more useful, however, is the number of preconditions, postconditions, and invariants for each service. Also useful is the number of processing steps or calculations for each service. Record and track these values by service within each abstraction. The list of owners of the input parameters gives some idea of the exposure of the service, and thus the abstraction, to changes in other components of the application. This is a component of the volatility of the abstraction. Volatility is discussed at length in Chapter 15.

Identify Message Connections

Message connections exist between a pair of abstractions when a service of one abstraction must invoke or make use of a service in another abstraction. These connections were identified in step nine when identifying services. Rather than simply linking abstractions together, message connections link specific pairs of services together. Message connections are one-way, from the calling service to the called service. Attributes returned by the service are listed as output parameters. Message connections which connect the same calling and called service may be combined.

Message connections are the fourth major type of abstraction relationships which exist in a model. Like structural and association relationships, message connections contribute to the complexity of the application. All abstraction relationships are a form of coupling—discussed in Chapter 9—and should be of concern to the designer. Therefore, track the counts of message connections, both in total and between specific pairs of abstractions. Abstractions which have many message connections are highly dependent on one another (depending on the direction of the connections) and may create a highly volatile situation.

Simplify the Model

When you complete the above steps, you will usually have one unholy mess of a model. This is where design takes over from analysis. Calculate the complexity, coupling, sufficiency, completeness, and volatility for each abstraction and the model as a whole. To reduce model complexity, combine abstractions and messages. To reduce abstraction complexity, add generalization-specialization or aggregation structures. You can see that model and abstraction complexity are probably a tradeoff. Your job here is to optimize them. What "optimize" means depends on your project, its goals, targets, and constraints.

When the model is substantially complete, or when you even think it is, revisit every abstraction, structure, state, attribute, and service. You must keep a component if it:

- Is essential to the fulfillment of one or more system responsibility
- Adds to the understanding of the model
- Simplifies the model

LOGICAL DESIGN

Logical design is the activity during which the application takes its final form. Logical design begins with architectural issues and ends with detailed implementation issues. It stops short of packaging the design components into modules for construction. This separation is not arbitrary. The concerns of application design are very different from those of module packaging design. An apt analogy is the difference in electrical engineering between circuit design and packaging design. The concerns of the circuit designer are electrical in nature: current, voltages, charges, and radio frequency (RF) interference. The concerns of the packaging designer are more physical than electrical: size, shape, and heat dissipation characteristics, as well as RF interference. The circuit designer creates a schematic; the packaging designer creates the circuit board layout. So it is with logical and physical software design.

The logical design activity completes the application domain and builds the application-specific and application-generic domains. The goal is efficient operation of the application. This activity seeks to identify useful abstract classes, support classes, task classes, and patterns for implementation. This activity is also responsible for the allocation of the required functionality among the architectural layers or design components. The primary issues for the designer are:

- Cohesion
- Complexity
- Class coupling
- Volatility
- Similarity
- Primitiveness
- Completeness (in terms of the portion of the requirements represented in the design)

Logical design has eight basic steps, summarized in Table 2.3. Like problem domain design, the steps need not be completed in any particular order, although some information in the later steps is provided by earlier steps (these instances are noted as they occur). At each step, measurement data and manipulation techniques can assist the designer in making the necessary tradeoffs.

Develop the Architecture

The first task is to determine the type of architecture appropriate for this application. This involves selecting the degree of distribution and independence of the various architectural components. The architecture of an application can vary from unified, with all components on the same platform and within the same process, to client-server, with some components on the client side and some components on the server side, to distributed peer-to-peer, where components can be anywhere at anytime. The nature of the problem, the geographical distribution of users and data, and the tools selected to build the application all influence its basic architecture. (While it is preferable to select tools *after* the architecture has been defined, they are more often than not selected before this is done.)

The application's architecture will contain basic components found to some degree in any application. These include the application domain, user interface, data management, task and process management, network interface, interprocess communications, and utility functions (Yuan 1995). Some components, such as

Table 2.3 Logical Design Steps

Step	Measurement Concerns
1. Develop the architecture	• Size (all views) • Complexity • Sufficiency • Cohesion • Volatility
2. Map the problem domain abstractions to system objects	• Sufficiency • Completeness • Complexity • Cohesion
3. Refactor domain classes	• Size (all views) • Complexity • Primitiveness • Volatility • Similarity
4. Identify support classes	• Completeness • Complexity • Similarity • Primitiveness • Volatility
5. Define object life cycles	• Sufficiency • Completenss • Coupling
6. Perform make-buy analysis	• Cost to build (population, functionality) • Cost to buy • Time to build • Time to receive • Complexity • Coupling • Volatility
7. Modify problem domain and logical designs	• All characteristics
8. Identify methods for each class	• Size • Complexity • Primitiveness • Volatility • Coupling • Similarity

the application domain, are products of other activities in the design process. Other components need to be identified and created in this step. Each component will assume some of each system responsibility; this allocation is a painstaking, trade-off-ridden process. There are many ways to allocate system responsibilities among architectural components; some are better than others under one set of conditions, while different allocations are better under other conditions.

The designer's task in this step is to allocate the system responsibilities among the components in such a way as to optimize the issues being addressed. These issues are not always complimentary; sometimes they can seem arbitrary. When based on measurement data, even seemingly arbitrary decisions can be explained. I often perform this step several times on a project. I will develop a set of components and test the measurement results against what I think the targets ought to be. I select the set of components which has the "best" set of values and still satisfies my intuition about how well it might work. I've not always examined multiple architectures in this step. Occasionally, I have built some or most of an application, found the architecture to be lacking, and have had to make major architectural changes. In one project, I had to add a missing layer. Late in a project, this can be very expensive, both for the project and for you personally.

Map the Problem Domain Abstractions into System Objects

The major task in this step is to determine the boundary of the application. Some of the abstractions in the problem domain will never be implemented as part of the application. Usually, these represent people or organizations, but the separation is not always so clean-cut. Sometimes, an abstraction must be excluded because you don't have the resources or you don't understand it well enough to build it. A key measure at this point is the number of problem domain abstractions remaining within the application domain. The ratio of included (or excluded) abstractions to the total problem domain is also an interesting number: It is the proportion of the problem which is being implemented (or the portion of the problem not being implemented) and gives a sense of the scope of the application. This idea is discussed in great detail in Chapter 7, where a new measure for the scope of an application is developed.

The application domain classes must be mapped into the classes in the application-specific and application-generic domains. The key measure here is that all of the classes in the application domain are mapped in some way. This mapping need not be one-to-one. It is possible for several classes from the application-specific and/or the application-generic domains to cooperate to perform the responsibility of a single class in the application domain. This is one reason to use the term *abstractions* when discussing the problem domain.

Refactor Domain Classes

It is probable that the domain classes, as they exist after the first pass through this process, are more tightly coupled, less cohesive, more complex, less sufficient, and less complete than they should be. This step is a deliberate effort to take another look at the domain classes and improve as many of their characteristics as possible. Refactoring means moving attributes and methods from one class to another or from two classes into a common third class which then becomes a superclass. This is the first time you look at the design with an eye towards inventing classes for your own purposes—to improve the design—rather than trying to get a complete picture of the problem.

This is the most difficult step, in my opinion, because it holds the most choices and has the least guidance available: You are pretty much on your own. I have often worried over a choice among alternatives during this step with no clue as to how to choose among them, that is, until I started using design measures to make these choices. Measurement is an essential tool for this step since it helps determine those alternatives which have the most desirable characteristics. Measurement data on the same problem will not always lead to the same answer every time, since different projects have different goals and constraints, and these have a material effect on which set of characteristics are "desirable."

Identify Support Classes

For the application-specific domain, the support classes include those that support views, database access, communication services, system interfaces, event dispatching, exception handling, object management, and caching, among others (Yuan 1995). For the application-generic domain, the support classes include those that serve as containers, generic data structures, database management, user interface services, messaging mechanisms, and operating system access (Yuan 1995). The purpose of this step is to identify those support classes needed to implement the application. This is the first step in what most people call detail design. The most important measures from this step are the number of support classes added to the design and the changes in the total design coupling and complexity values.

It is important that this step be performed after the domain classes have been refactored. From personal experience, refactoring the domain classes is much easier before the design becomes "polluted" with support classes. After the support classes are added, the application domain classes become much harder to identify. Also, seemingly minor changes to the domain classes can have a material effect on the set of support classes required.

Define Object Life Cycles

Every object in the system has a life cycle—it is created by some other object, performs its function, then is destroyed. It is critical that the life cycle for every object be identified explicitly and documented, particularly the creation and destruction events. These events consume and release resources, and need to be carefully planned. Failing to do so can result in resource leaks—mostly memory, but other resources can be leaked as well. It is also important to identify the object(s) responsible for these events. This can help you spot holes in the design.

I have encountered a few cases, in my designs and in others, where the object responsible for the destruction of another was no longer available—it had been destroyed earlier—leaving a major resource leak in the design. While this is an important step, the only real measure is the portion of classes, both domain and support classes, for which these events have been identified. You can use the analysis techniques in Chapter 6 to help determine when objects are, or should be, created and destroyed. The set of objects remaining in scope after completion of a system responsibility can tell you a lot about the quality of your design (see, in particular, the discussion of the set *ActiveObjects* on page 250).

Perform Make-Buy Analysis

Some of the support classes will have to be built, some can be purchased, and some can be used from previous projects. If you have been doing this for awhile in the same domain, you may be able to borrow domain classes from previous projects. Several companies are working on domain classes to market to an industry, so you may be able to purchase some of your domain classes. Deciding which classes to build and which to acquire from some other source is a very important decision. First of all, the effort required to build the system from this point is directly determined by the set of classes you choose to build. Using classes from other sources may decrease your construction costs, but they may increase your acquisition and training costs. This is a classic make-buy decision found in every engineering discipline and is usually based on technical and financial measurement data. The objective is to optimize your technical characteristics and your financial costs according to the goals and constraints of your project.

Modify Problem Domain and Logical Designs

At any time during the course of this activity, some characteristics of the design may go out of whack. If you are using design measurement data, this departure from the norm or plan will be easy to spot. If you make a small design change, and then discover that your global complexity increases too much, you may want to rethink the change. This is not so much a discrete step as an awareness of the design characteristics throughout the logical design activity. Measurement data is absolutely essential in the effective performance of this step. A good designer will make use of whatever tools are at his or her disposal, including all sorts of technical product measures. The object theory in Chapter 6 provides a way to mathematically model a design change and the characteristics of the resulting design. With this technique, you can test a design change on paper without actually changing your model. This can be useful, especially when the cost to back a change out of your model is high.

Identify Methods for Each Class

The logical design activity usually adds many new classes to the design. Often, the application-specific and application-generic class may add two to three times (or more) the number of classes found in the application domain. This is a substantial explosion of new classes. The methods for every one of these new classes, or at least for those classes to be built, must be identified and defined using the same process used to define services. For each method:

1. Name the method.
2. Describe the method.
3. List the preconditions for the method.
4. List the postconditions for the method.
5. List the invariants which affect the execution of this method.
6. List the states in which this method may be requested.
7. Identify the attributes required by the method as input parameters. For each parameter, identify its owner and source.
8. Identify the attributes to be modified or returned by the method as output parameters or side effects.
9. Identify the methods required of other objects.
10. Determine the processing steps for the method. This is the proper time to define the processing steps, including algorithms, for the methods and services of every class, including those in the application domain.

Important measures from this step include the number of methods for each class, and the size of each class in terms of a measure such as 3D function points. You can also apply design measures used for non-object software to individual methods, including cyclomatic complexity and source lines of code estimates.

PHYSICAL DESIGN

Physical design is the packaging of the classes and objects in the logical design into modules. Booch (1994) notes that choosing the right objects and classes, then organizing them into modules are independent design decisions. Physical design, as described here, takes a sideways view of the problem. Instead of trying to solve the problem itself, which is the objective of the other design activities, physical design focuses on building and packaging the product. This activity allocates the design components from all four domains into physical modules. The goal is efficient builds. You are seeking to minimize the impacts of changes to one design component on the others in the design, not just from the point of view of having to change their designs, but from the point of view of having to rebuild them, either compiling or linking them.

This activity is usually very informal and is often invisible. The lack of good packaging design becomes apparent only after you have triggered your tenth 15-minute compile and link cycle for the day. I have often repackaged my designs out of frustration, and usually at considerable cost. The packaging of design components can affect their logical design. Like everything else in design, the problem is one of optimization within constraints.

The benefits of sound, deliberate packaging design can be staggering. If your compile and link cycles take five minutes each, and you can cut that to three minutes, you have saved 40 percent of your compile and link time. At 10 or more such cycles per day, that can be close to half an hour not spent waiting for the computer. During the debugging process, I usually run 40 to 50 compile cycles per day (this is a symptom of an incomplete design, but I end up doing it anyway). You can see how any savings at all can equal big gains in overall time savings. (Of course, there is a downside—the only time I can get coffee is while the computer is compiling and linking, so I end up getting much less coffee during the day.)

The issues facing the designer during this activity include:

- Scope control
- Class visibility
- Module coupling
- Module cohesion
- Similarity
- Characteristics of the module dependency graph, including cycle detection, abstraction level, morphology (the shape of the graph), and any other characteristics of a directed graph which might be useful (see Chapter 4 and Fenton 1991)

As important as the physical design is, it is a fairly simple activity which has only four basic steps, summarized in Table 2.4. Unlike the other design activities,

Table 2.4 Physical Design Steps

Step	Measurement Concerns
1. Determine the visibility requirements	• Coupling • Complexity • Similarity • Volatility • Module cohesion
2. Allocate classes to modules	• Coupling • Volatility • Structural cohesion • Size (population, length, volume)
3. Examine physical design for cycles	• Coupling • Size (length) • Graph path analysis
4. Modify problem domain, logical, and physical designs	• All of the above characteristics

where the steps can be done in different orders, or even in parallel, the steps in this activity are best done in the sequence given. The main reason for this is the output of each step serves as input into the following step.

Determine the Visibility Requirements

This step requires examining the design for structural and communication links between classes. Every such link implies a dependency of one class on the other. A specialization is dependent on its generalization. A composite class is dependent on its component classes, so aggregations create dependencies in the opposite direction as generalization-specializations. The dependencies in an association can be tricky to sort out. Usually, the set of attributes upon which the association is built is a natural part of one of the classes, and a foreign part of the other. When this is the case, the class for which the attributes are foreign is the dependent class. In those cases where an association results in an associative class, the associative class is dependent upon all of the other classes which participate in the relationship. Message connections create dependencies from the sender to the receiver.

Inter-class dependencies in the logical design indicate visibility requirements in the physical design. In order for a class to send a message to another class, the sending class must be able to "see" the receiving class. That is, an object of the receiving class must be alive and in the same scope as the sending object. Furthermore, the sending object must know about and understand the receiver's public interface. Inter-class visibility requirements mean that the modules in which those classes reside must also be visible. Module dependencies exist whenever class dependencies exist and are in the same direction.

The important measures for this step are the number and types of class dependencies. While these dependencies are all part of the coupling of the design, the single value for coupling does not help you during this activity.

Allocate Classes to Modules

The purpose of this step is to allocate the classes to modules in such a way that inter-module dependencies are minimized. When you compile and link, you compile and link modules, not classes. For this reason, it is acceptable design practice to place all classes in a single structure, an aggregation, for example, in the same module. Offsetting this, however, is the size of the modules. The goal is to minimize the total compile time. With an incremental compiler, or a good make utility, you can minimize the total compile time by keeping the size of each module as small as practical, given that inter-module dependencies may cause multiple modules to be recompiled, even if their source code was not changed.

Examine Physical Design for Cycles

Once the initial allocation is made, you need to explicitly look for cycles in the module dependency graph. This graph is built by making the modules the vertices and the dependencies between modules the edges. The edges in this graph are directional, since the dependencies are directional. A cycle is a path in a directed graph which leads back to the starting point. In other words, if you can start at a module, follow the dependency paths, and end up back at that starting module, you have a cycle.

Cycles in the dependency graph can wreak havoc on the builds for the application. At best, you will compile modules which don't need to be compiled; at worst you will get your compiler or make utility so wrapped up it can't finish the job. I have seen this happen—actually, I have caused this to happen. Have you ever seen a make utility in an infinite loop?

John Lakos (1992) is the only person I have seen doing research in this area. He has recently published a more comprehensive work on the subject, but it appeared too late to be used as reference for this book.

Modify Physical, Logical, and Problem Domain Designs as Appropriate

As with other design activities, whenever you uncover a situation which requires that you change the physical, logical, or problem domain designs, make the change. The best time to make design changes is when you discover they are required. Putting them off will only make things worse. You will forget why the change needs to be made, and may end up making matters worse, or the cost to make the change will be higher.

In all of these steps, the measures mentioned at the start of this section will help detect the need for design changes, and will help with the decision process. Measurement is an essential element of the designer's toolkit, one which I have found to be more useful than methods and CASE tools.

SUMMARY

This chapter has presented the design process I have developed over several years and several projects. This process is formal in areas where my intuition is weak. Your process will be different, since you have a different set of weaknesses. The design of a software application consists of four domains: problem, application, application-specific, and application-generic. The design process consists of five major activities: problem definition, selecting the design approach, problem domain design, logical design, and physical design. Each activity focuses on a different aspect of the problem and solution. The physical design activity focuses on the packaging of the components defined during the other activities into physical modules from which the physical system will be built. Each activity has different goals and issues. Measurement can help with each activity, by highlighting areas which need attention and by helping the designer choose between alternatives.

In this chapter, I have attempted to show you the importance and usefulness of technical measurement as a design tool. I have found measurement and analysis to be an important addition to my toolkit. Many useful analysis techniques do not exist yet; one is included in Chapter 6, and I am continuing to explore others. Using measurement as a design tool is one of the more important ways we can turn the art of software development into an engineering discipline.

3

SELECTING A SET OF MEASURES

Perhaps the most difficult part of starting to measure is deciding what to measure and how to measure it. To solve this problem, you need to eventually select a set of measures which you will then collect and analyze—both of which are major tasks. Selecting a set of measures means culling through a list of many hundreds of potential measures to find those few to help you run your business, improve your process, or analyze your design.

This chapter has two purposes: to provide a method for selecting a set of measures within the context of an organization or specific project and to make the material in this book more complete by including some of the "how" along with the "why" and the "what."

Over the years, several methods have emerged to help select a set of measures. Some of these are proprietary, in the sense that some consulting firm has attached a name to their method. Others are embedded in seemingly unrelated documents, such as quality standards. One approach, however, has emerged that is simple, direct, effective, and in the public domain.

One word of caution is in order before proceeding. Fenton (1991) notes that the use of approaches such as the one presented here do not help clarify the problems caused by lack of rigor and may actually aggravate them. The rigor is required when selecting the objects and attributes which will be measured. Anyone can collect measurement data. To collect meaningful data requires that you understand what it is you are attempting to measure. If you have read to this point from the beginning, you have some idea of how to proceed. More information about measurement data and how to use it is included in Chapters 4 and 5.

THE GOAL QUESTION METRIC APPROACH

To be effective, measurement must be (Basili, Caldiera, and Rombach 1994a):

1. *Focused on specific goals*: To help distinguish what is important from what is unimportant.

2. *Applied to all life cycle products, processes, resources, and projects*: To ensure consistent coverage and to provide valid data over time.

3. *Based on interpretations of the objects being measured.*

The Goal Question Metric approach was developed in the Software Engineering Laboratory at NASA Goddard Space Flight Center. It was initially used to determine a set of measures for a single project. It has since been expanded to become the goal setting step in an evolutionary quality improvement approach—The Quality Improvement Paradigm—within an overall organizational framework—The Experience Factory—dedicated to building the software competencies of entire organizations, then making them available to projects. The approach has been used successfully by many organizations over several years, including my own projects and some at Hewlett-Packard (Grady 1992).

The Goal Question Metric approach is based on a three-level model of measurement, shown in Figure 3.1 (Basili, Caldiera, and Rombach 1994a):

1. *Conceptual level* (goal): A goal is defined for an object (process, product, resource, or project), for a variety of reasons, with respect to various models or issues (quality, for example), from various points of view, and relative to a particular environment. Goals are discussed in the next section.

2. *Operational level* (question): A set of questions is developed to verify or assess the achievement of a particular goal. Questions are discussed further in the section titled "Questions."

3. *Quantitative level* (metric): A set of data is associated with each question in order to answer it in a quantitative way. The data can be objective or subjective and are discussed in the section on measure selection.

The full process has six basic steps:

1. Develop a set of goals.

2. Develop an operational model.

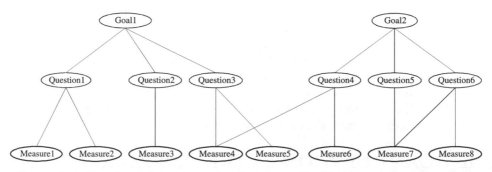

Figure 3.1 *The Goal Question Metric approach, illustrated. Reprinted, by permission of John Wiley & Sons, Inc., from J. Marciniak, ed.,* Encyclopedia of Software Engineering. © *1994 by John Wiley & Sons, Inc.*

3. Determine the measures needed.

4. Develop a mechanism to collect and analyze the data.

5. Collect, validate, and analyze the data in real time and feed back to the projects.

6. Analyze the data in a post mortem fashion.

Each step is discussed in more detail in the sections which follow.

Occasionally, you will find that no measures exist which can satisfactorily address one or more of your questions. When this happens, you can either change your questions, or build a measure. Building a measure is not as difficult as it sounds. The section on measure construction presents a technique for building a measure from the understanding which comes from answering your questions in empirical, everyday terms.

GOAL SETTING

A goal is defined for an object (process, product, resource, or project), for a variety of reasons, with respect to various models or issues, from various points of view, and relative to a particular environment (Basili, Caldiera, and Rombach 1994a). A goal is an expression which includes purpose, perspective, and environment (Fenton 1991):

- *Purpose*: To (characterize, evaluate, predict, motivate) the (process, product, resource, or project) in order to (estimate, predict, compare, assess, or investigate) it.

- *Perspective*: To examine the (cost, effectiveness, correctness, defects, changes, characteristics) from the viewpoint of the (developer, manager, customer).

- *Environment*: The environment consists of process factors, people factors, problem factors, methods, tools, constraints, and project goals.

Alternatively, a goal can be seen as a five-tuple of purpose, issue, object, viewpoint, and environment, as illustrated in Figure 3.2 (Basili, Caldiera, and Rombach 1994a). For example:

$$G = (purpose, issue, object, viewpoint, environment)$$

$$G_1 = (improve, timeliness, change request, project manager, development process)$$

This format makes it possible to store and manipulate goals as objects, bringing to mind all sorts of possibilities for automated support for storing, manipulating, and tracking goal statements. It is fairly easy to take English goal statements and convert them into a five-tuple described here. If you cannot identify all five components, it is very likely the goal statement is incomplete or is not really a goal at all.

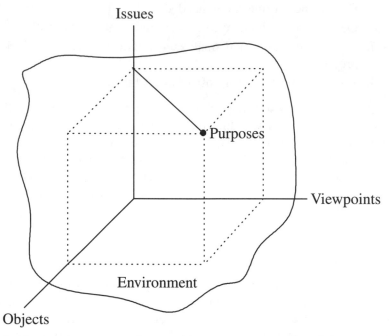

Figure 3.2 *The components of a goal statement. Reprinted, by permission of John Wiley & Sons, Inc., from J. Marciniak, ed.,* Encyclopedia of Software Engineering. © *1994 by John Wiley & Sons, Inc.*

The measurement framework developed in Chapter 1 contains three basic levels: strategic, tactical, and technical. Each of these levels has a different view of the organization and a different set of goals for the organization. Even within a level, there may be constituents or groups of stakeholders who hold several views of the organization or have several sets of goals. The first task of selecting a set of measures is to identify all of these goals; that means identifying all of the constituencies.

A constituency is a group of stakeholders with a common view or a common set of goals. A stakeholder is any person or group with a stake in the process under consideration—the software development process in this case. Each person's stake is a personal interest in the success (or failure) of the process. Since all stakeholders have a personal interest, they have some expectations of the process; these can be formed into goals for the process itself. It is important that you identify all groups of stakeholders or you may miss some very important goals, and disappoint some people with significant influence over the process.

You may group together the goals at each level in the framework. If yours is like most organizations, the goals at the strategic level will influence and be reflected in the goals at the tactical and technical levels. Likewise, the goals at the tactical level will influence and be reflected in the goals at the technical level. At times, the goals at different levels are conflicting. It often falls to the technical level to resolve these conflicts, creating the optimization problems so often faced in real projects.

For example, a possible strategic goal for the organization might be to increase product quality as measured by some selected measure. This goal will filter down to the technical level and influence the process used to build the product, including the use of inspections, more rigorous design, more testing, and so on. At the same time, a tactical goal might be to get the product out the door as soon as possible or to meet the planned schedule at all costs (these are real goals; do they sound familiar?). On the surface, this tactical goal appears to conflict with the strategic goal of increasing quality. It now falls to the technical level to resolve this apparent conflict. In this situation, the designer will use the strategic goal to set product quality goals for the project and use the tactical goal as a constraining factor. This may cause the designer to modify the design and implementation process, including the choice of method, tool set, or techniques. Or, this may cause the designer to ignore one goal in favor of the other, choosing the goal with the highest reward or lowest penalty.

The process of goal setting at the technical level begins with a systematic examination of the environment. This examination involves:

1. Collecting the measurement goals for the strategic and tactical levels.
2. Examining the requirements for the project.
3. Looking at targets provided by the customers.
4. Identifying the applicable standards.
5. Understanding the policies and strategies of the organization.
6. Understanding the processes and products of the organization.
7. Having a model of the organization.

From this information, you develop the goal statements which are then used to develop a model, as described in the next section.

QUESTIONS

From the goals come questions. These questions have two purposes: to define implicitly the model used in the goal and to define how the model will be used to assess achievement of the goal. There are three groups of questions (Basili, Caldiera, and Rombach 1994a):

- *Group 1*: Questions about the object with respect to the overall goal of the specific measurement model
- *Group 2*: Questions about the attributes of the object which are relevant with respect to the issues of the specific measurement model
- *Group 3*: Questions which help evaluate characteristics of the object which are relevant with respect to the specific measurement model

In these groups, the specific measurement model is the one defined in the goals and to be brought to light through the questions. Typically, stakeholders have mental models of the objects they wish to measure which influence the ways they measure those objects, and thus the goals they have for the measurement activity. Each group of questions highlights successive levels of details in the implicit mental model. Group 1 questions deal with the top level—the overall goal of the model, the purpose for the measurement activity. Group 2 questions deal with the individual issues in the environment and relate them to attributes of the objects to be measured. Group 3 questions deal with specific characteristics of the attributes of the objects to be measured. That is, if the attribute in group 2 is size, the group 3 questions seek to name the characteristics of size which are relevant. In one model, the relevant characteristics may be the physical dimensions of an object, while another model may be more interested in the volume of space occupied by the object. An example, borrowed from Basili, Caldiera, and Rombach (1994a), goes something like this:

- Goal:
  - *Purpose*: Improve
  - *Issue*: Timeliness of
  - *Object*: Change request processing
  - *Viewpoint*: Project manager's viewpoint
- Group 1 questions:
  - What is the current change request processing speed?
  - Is the documented change request process actually performed?
- Group 2 questions:
  - What is the deviation of the actual change request process time from the estimated time?
  - Is the performance of the process improving?
- Group 3 questions:
  - Is the current performance satisfactory from the viewpoint of the project manager?
  - Is the performance *visibly* improving?

These questions should give you an increasingly detailed guide to deciding how and what to measure in order to answer them. The idea is to determine quantitative answers to these questions, which leads us to the final step, the selection or construction of specific measures.

MEASURE SELECTION

Measures are selected to provide quantitative answers to each question, which define the model implicit in each goal. This may sound repetitive, but it contains an important axiom: Collect only the measures necessary to assess the achievement of your goals. This is a an effective way to limit the data you collect and it defines a clear purpose for each measure. People tend to be more willing to provide data when they know how it will be used and the data they provide tends to be more accurate. When you collect a set of measures, people will behave to improve whatever is being measured. If you are measuring the wrong things, this natural behavior may cause your processes to move in the wrong direction. On the other hand, when your measures are aligned with your goals, improvement in the measures naturally leads to, or at least towards, achievement of the goals.

Measures may be objective or subjective. Objective measures depend only on the object being measured, not on the viewpoint from which the measurement is being taken. Subjective measures depend on both the object being measured and the viewpoint from which they are being taken. You need to consider several factors when trying to decide whether to use objective or subjective measures (Basili, Caldiera, and Rombach 1994a):

- *The amount and quality of existing data*: Use whatever is available first, provided it helps answer the questions and provided that it has a sound theoretical basis. Measures which fail either one of these tests can end up doing more harm than good.

- *The maturity of the objects being measured*: Maturity, in this sense, is the level of knowledge we have about the object being measured, its attributes, the relationships between the attributes, and the relationships between the attributes and those of other objects. For mature objects, you can apply objective measures. For less mature objects, you may have to resort to subjective measures.

- *The learning process*: Models need refinement and adaptation. Measures must help evaluate both the object and the reliability of the model.

The Goal Question Metric approach helps translate a set of goals into a set of relevant measures aligned with those goals. It helps, but does not guarantee it. It is always possible to get sidetracked at the point of actually selecting the measures. It is very tempting to choose a measure because it is available, it is cheap to collect, or because you have a tool which collects it automatically. It is also very tempting to not choose a measure because it is difficult or costly to collect. Both of these views completely miss the point. The objective is to measure whether and how well you are achieving your goals. Measures which don't support this objective are mere noise at best, and dangerous at worst. Failing to collect measures which do support this objective is tantamount to saying you don't really care whether you meet your goals. If that is really the case, you don't need to measure and you don't need to set goals, either. If you are serious about meeting your goals, you will be serious about collecting the data which proves, or disproves, that you are meeting them. It's really that simple.

MEASURE CONSTRUCTION

Occasionally, and often when working with object-oriented software, you find that you need to measure a characteristic for which a suitable measure just isn't available. The problem is compounded by the fact that many existing measures are simply not suitable for any purpose. At times, you will find yourself trying to make a design decision on an attribute for which no one has even attempted to create a measure. You need to be able to create measures on-the-fly. Any measure you create should have a firm grounding in both your empirical understanding of the attribute in question and measurement theory.

This section presents a process for building theoretically valid measures from an empirical understanding of some characteristic. I used this process to construct the measures in Chapters 7 through 15. It works and it isn't as difficult to use as the prospect might at first sound. The process involves the basic steps:

1. Determine your requirements for measurement.
2. Analyze the model.
3. Select the target structure.
4. Construct a representation.

If you are the least bit imaginative, you will recognize immediately the four basic software development steps: define requirements, analyze the requirements, design a candidate implementation, and build the application. These four basic steps and those of my process are strikingly similar. The process results in an empirical relational structure which is guaranteed—in the sense that it has already been mathematically proven—to map to a real numerical structure with the properties of a particular scale type.

The technical material in this section is presented in Chapters 5 and 6. You may read this section without a thorough understanding of the technical aspects of the material. You can even *use* this process without a thorough understanding of these technical aspects. If you are unfamiliar with the scale types of measurement theory, or the dependence that measurement has upon models, you may want to read the first few sections of Chapter 5, then return and finish this section.

I placed the process description ahead of the technical material because it fit in nicely with the measure selection process and addresses one of the major weaknesses in the Goal Question Metric approach. I expect that you will learn this rather simple process much faster than you will learn the specific requirements for each of the empirical relational structures that comprise the bulk of Chapter 5. If that is the case, you will be referring to Chapter 5 much more often than this section. On the other hand, whenever you enter a new situation in which you have to select, and possibly build, a set of measures, having all of the processes in one place will be convenient.

Without this process, you can use known measures, or the structures I describe in Chapters 7 through 15, to measure the characteristics in those chapters. With this process, you can measure any characteristic you can describe. It's like giving you a free fish, which feeds you for one meal, or teaching you how to fish, which will feed you for the rest of your life.

Determine the Requirements for Measurement

Building an empirical relational structure is much like building an application in at least one other important aspect: If you don't have a goal in mind, any old design will do. So, you must do a little planning before you start building. You need to have a set of requirements so you know what to build and an understanding of any constraints which might limit your options. Requirements are obtained from the type of representation, or scale type, you want. You are constrained by the types of elements and relationships in your model of what you are trying to measure.

The first consideration is: What do you want to be able to do with the measurement data? What kinds of analysis do you wish to perform on the data? In Chapter 1, I described five roles or uses for technical measurement: estimation, prediction, assessment, comparison, and investigation. The role which you intend for the measure you are building has a major influence on the requirements for the empirical relational structure from which it is built.

If you are trying to build a prediction system, for example, you may want to perform some pretty sophisticated statistical analysis on a fairly large set of sample data. The more sophisticated the analysis, the more stringent the scale requirements. The more stringent the scale requirements, the more severe the structural constraints. Most prediction systems will require measures which are at least the interval scale and work better with ratio or absolute scale measures.

If you are constructing your measure for comparison purposes, you may be satisfied with an ordinal scale measure. For assessment and investigation purposes, a nominal scale measure may suffice. Many of the most useful assessment and investigation measures are binary nominal scale measures (yes or no questions). That is, they classify objects into one of two classes. For many purposes, this is good enough.

Like many other forms of engineering, your reasons for doing something have a major effect on the effort required to do it. When building a representation, a measure, the key is to construct a measure that is good enough, and only just good enough, to meet your needs.

Now that you know which scale type you need for your measure, you can use Tables 3.1 through 3.4 to determine the types of structures available. The structures are grouped by scale type and are described in detail in Chapter 5. To my knowl-

Table 3.1 Ordinal Scale Structures

Structure	Section	Page
Separable one-dimensional betweenness	Ordinal Representations	163
Separable one-dimensional separation	Ordinal Representations	165
Proximity metric	Unidimensional Spatial Proximity Representations	208
Factorial proximity with one-factor independence	Multidimensional Spatial Proximity Representations	217

Table 3.2 Interval Scale Structures

Structure	Section	Page
Positive difference (on a set of objects)	Difference Representations	173
Algebraic difference	Difference Representations	174
Cross-modality ordering	Difference Representations	176
Finite, equally spaced difference	Difference Representations	177
Absolute difference	Difference Representations	178
Strongly conditional absolute difference	Difference Representations	179
Nonadditive conditional probability	Probability Representations	187
Conditional decision (on decisions)	Probability Representations	189
Additive conjoint	Conjoint Representations	192
Bisymmetric	Conjoint Representations	197
Equally spaced, additive conjoint	Conjoint Representations	198
n-Component additive conjoint	Conjoint Representations	199
Nonsolvable n-component additive conjoint	Conjoint Representations	200
Multiplicative polynomial conjoint	Conjoint Representations	203
Distributive polynomial conjoint (on components A_1 and A_2)	Conjoint Representations	204
Dual-distributive polynomial conjoint (on component A_3)	Conjoint Representations	205
Intradimensional difference	Multidimensional Spatial Proximity Representations	212
Interdimensional additive	Multidimensional Spatial Proximity Representations	213
Additive-difference	Multidimensional Spatial Proximity Representations	215
Additive-difference metric ($r > 1$)	Multidimensional Spatial Proximity Representations	215
Feature proximity (on each dimension for nonextensive structures)	Feature Proximity Representations	216
Feature proximity (on multidimensional attribute)	Feature Proximity Representations	216
Solvable concatenation	Nonadditive Representations	225

Table 3.3 Ratio Scale Structures

Structure	Section	Page
Closed extensive	Extensive Representations	165
Closed periodic	Extensive Representations	166
Extensive with no essential maximum	Extensive Representations	167
Extensive with at least one essential maximum	Extensive Representations	168
Entropy	Extensive Representations	169
Extensive multiples	Extensive Representations	172
Positive difference (on a set of differences)	Difference Representations	174
Algebraic difference, pairs of	Difference Representations	175
Distributive polynomial conjoint (on components $A_1 \times A_2$ and A_3)	Conjoint Representations	201
Dual-distributive polynomial conjoint (on components A_1 and A_2)	Conjoint Representations	205
Segmentally additive proximity	Unidimensional Spatial Proximity Representations	209
Additive-difference metric ($r = 1$)	Multidimensional Spatial Proximity Representations	215
Feature proximity (on each dimension for extensive structures)	Multidimensional Spatial Proximity Representations	215
PCS	Nonadditive Representations	221
Intensive concatenation	Nonadditive Representations	225

edge, this is the only reference of structures by scale type, either in the software engineering literature or in the literature at large. My search for such a reference led me into measurement theory in the first place.

Table 3.1 contains structures which produce ordinal scale measures. Table 3.2 contains structures which produce interval scale measures. Table 3.3 contains structures which produce ratio scale measures. Table 3.4 contains structures which produce absolute scale measures. Each table gives the structure name, the section in Chapter 5 which contains the empirical requirements for the structure, and the page on which the definition for the structure begins.

You now have a set of potential structures, along with their structural requirements, and are ready to pare down your list of choices.

Analyze the Model

This is an elimination step. Its purpose is to eliminate those potential structures which either do not fit what you are trying to measure or whose structural requi-

Table 3.4 Absolute Scale Structures

Structure	Section	Page
Archimedean qualitative probability	Probability Representations	183
Modified qualitative probability	Probability Representations	185
Countably additive qualitative probability	Probability Representations	186
Qualitative probability with equivalent atoms	Probability Representations	186
Vectorial qualitative probability	Probability Representations	186
Archimedean qualitative conditional probability	Probability Representations	188
Conditional decision (on events)	Probability Representations	189

rements cannot be met by your model. The approach is to take a structure, identify its requirements, and see if you can find the elements, relations, and operations required by the structure in your model. Eliminate any structure for which you cannot meet the requirements.

It is possible that all potential structures for a scale type are eliminated, meaning that your model cannot support measurement on the scale you want. In this case, you have two options: Modify your model so it can meet the requirements for at least one structure (see Chapter 9 on coupling) or modify your measurement requirements to loosen the structural constraints (see the first example in Chapter 7 on size).

The actual comparison of structural requirements and model capabilities can be very technical, varying from an informal discussion to a formal mathematical proof. A formal proof is sometimes required to show that the model has the properties necessary to support the structure. If the model is stable, this proof need be constructed only once; it is possible that someone else has already done it for you. Most often, a less-than-formal discussion of how the model can meet the structural requirements is all that is necessary. This is the tactic used in Chapters 7 through 15.

Once a model has been shown to possess a certain set of properties, further consequences of those properties can be assumed without further proof. In a mature environment, this analysis process may consist of simply finding and confirming the results of earlier work. At worst, it means constructing a formal or informal proof yourself.

Mechanically, the process begins by stating, in the form of a theorem, that the model has a certain property. This theorem is then either confirmed or rejected using mathematical reasoning. Proof that a model does *not* possess a certain property is as important as proof that it does.

As an example, compare the requirements for a closed extensive structure (Chapter 5) to the formal object model (Chapter 6). For this discussion, assume that the results of the first step determine that you require a ratio scale measure. Since all closed extensive structures lead to ratio scale measures, they are on the list of potential structures. Further assume that you are looking for some form of size measure, say population (Chapter 7), that is supported by your model. In other words, you are testing your model to see if it supports a closed extensive structure which represents a population measure.

The section "Extensive Representations" in Chapter 5 contains a set of requirements for a closed extensive structure. These are (all of the various terms, relations, and conditions are defined in Chapters 4, 5, and 6):

1. The structure (model elements and an ordering relation) forms a weak order (it is both transitive and connected).
2. The concatenation operation is weakly associative.
3. The ordering relation is monotonic under concatenation.
4. You can select a unit of population such that you can construct a strictly bounded sequence of your unit; all such sequences have a finite length.
5. From requirements 1 and 3, infer that you can define a reasonable ordering relation—that is, you can define a way to order your measured objects in terms of observed populations of some characteristic.
6. From requirement 2, infer that you can define a reasonable concatenation operation.

The first task is to identify the characteristic of the population which you are trying to measure. In the model, you could use classes in the design, attributes in a class, methods in a class, or objects or messages in a use case.

Next, define your empirical ordering relation. Given that population is essentially set membership, it seems reasonable to define your ordering relation using the cardinalities of the various population sets.

The set union operation is the first thing that comes to mind when considering the concatenation operation. Concatenation is the operation by which some object is tacked onto the end of another object. As developers, we do this all the time with strings of characters. It seems reasonable that set union would be a good concatenation operation for sets.

We've already run into a problem: Extensive measurement requires that the resulting representation be additive under concatenation. The structural requirements imposed by the closed extensive structure exist largely to ensure this additivity. In particular, the condition of monotonicity provides for additivity in the representation. The problem is that set union is not additive in general, and unless we can guarantee that any two sets we choose to concatenate will be disjoint, we cannot use set union to construct a closed extensive structure.

Having eliminated the closed extensive structure from the list of possibilities, we must test each structure which remains on the list until we find one supported by our model. There may only be one such structure, there may be no such structures, or there may be more than one such structure. This last case leads to the third step.

Select the Target Structure

You will often end up with more than one structure which meets all measurement requirements and can be supported by your model. When this happens, you need to resort to more pragmatic concerns, such as ease of measurement and the alignment of the measure with your purposes. If only one structure is left on your list, you can skip this step.

Ease of measurement deals with the effort required to collect the data or calculate the measure. If the measurement can be automated—by getting a population count from a tool, for example—then so much the better. All else being equal, the measure which is easier to collect is your best option (but all else is very rarely equal).

The alignment issue deals with how well the characteristic measured by a potential structure aligns with your measurement goals. For example, if you are concerned about populations of attributes among your classes, a structure which measures populations of methods or populations of attribute domains may not meet your goals.

This issue is an explicit part of the *third* step in the process because it will cause you to rethink your goals in light of a set of potential structures known to satisfy your technical requirements. It is also possible that during the process of defining the relations and operations, you strayed off the track a little. This step then becomes one of realignment and is a good reality check.

The purpose is to select one structure from among those remaining on your list. It may be the case that more than one of these is aligned with your goals, but they can be ordered with respect to the quality of their alignment (which is itself a measurement problem). If this is true, you can select the structure that is most closely aligned with your goals.

If you cannot eliminate all but one structure using this technique, you can rely on ease of measurement, available tool support, or personal preference to make the decision. Ease of measurement is a subjective matter. If you must collect the data by hand, you want a structure where the elements can be easily identified with little risk for gross error. In other words, you want to be able to identify the elements quickly and still be able to get a reasonably accurate measure. On the other hand, if you have a tool which can readily provide measures based on a more complex structure, it may be more practical to use what the tool gives you.

Once you get your list down to one potential structure, you can move on to the fourth step.

Construct the Representation

In this step, you construct your actual measure, a representation from your chosen empirical relational structure into a numeric relational structure. The step requires the completion of four tasks:

1. Map the structure elements to numeric elements.
2. Map the empirical relations and operations to numeric relations and operations.
3. Select a unit.
4. Validate the representation (this is the measurement equivalent of testing).

Much of the work in these tasks may have been done implicitly as you worked through empirical structures.

Mapping the elements of your empirical structure entails selecting the numerical elements you wish to use in your measure. Most often, elements are mapped into the set of real numbers, but real numbers are by no means the only option. Instead, you can choose to map your elements into the set of positive real numbers, the set of integers, the set of natural numbers, or even some other number system such as complex numbers. You might also choose to map your empirical elements into vectors of numbers (of some kind). Using vectors of numbers, while more complex than simple or scalar numbers, may result in more valid measures since we sometimes resort to questionable practices to get a set of numbers down to a single value (Fenton 1991).

Mapping empirical relations and operations requires finding numeric relations and operations which they can support. This means finding numeric relations and operations with a set of properties that can be subsumed by the set of properties our empirical relations and operations possess. In other words, our empirical relations and operations must be at least as restrictive as the numeric relations and operations to which we wish to map.

The requirements imposed by many empirical relational structures are a direct result of mapping empirical relations and operations, particularly operations, into an assumed set of numeric operations. This set of numeric operations is explicitly identified in the representation condition for a given empirical relational structure.

Getting back to the earlier example, an extensive structure must satisfy two conditions. Given two objects a and b, we must be able to find a real-valued function ϕ such that

$$a \succeq b \Leftrightarrow \phi(a) \geqslant \phi(b)$$

and
$$\phi(a \circ b) = \phi(a) + \phi(b)$$

where $\circ$ is our empirical concatenation operation. In this case, the selection of such a structure implies mapping the structural elements into the real numbers, the relation $\succeq$ into the numeric relation $\geqslant$, and the operation $\circ$ into the numeric operation $+$. Thus, the results of the first two tasks are determined by our choice of empirical structure. This is often the case in real life.

Note that, while the requirements for an extensive structure *imply* that we map our elements, relations, and operations as we did, they do not necessarily *require* such a mapping. If we can find a number system with a $\geq$ relation which has all of the properties as for the real numbers, and likewise with a + operation, we can map to that alternative system. The lesson here is to look at the *real* requirements, not just the *stated* requirements. As good software developers, you already know how to do that, right?

Next, we need to select a unit. In a ratio scale measure, the choice of unit is arbitrary: Any unit will do. We can always convert from one unit to another by multiplying by a constant. The English and metric units for distance are a familiar example of such arbitrariness in unit selection. For interval scale measures, both the unit and the zero point are arbitrary. Such is the case for the Fahrenheit and Celsius scales for temperature. For ordinal measures, you only need to preserve ordering, so even your selection of sets of values is arbitrary. For nominal scale measures, you only need to be able to distinguish among groups of measured objects, so you aren't even restricted to number systems. If you are working with an absolute scale, however, such as the count of certain elements, there are no arbitrary choices.

Thus, the less stringent your structural constraints, the more work you have to do for this task. This task is easiest when working with absolute scale measures, since all of your choices are determined by your chosen structure, although you do need to explicitly define what gets counted. For the less stringent scales, many of these decisions will be subjective. That's fine, as long as you can explicitly define your choices and they are consistent with each other.

The final task is to validate the newly constructed representation. Validation has two parts: validating the mapping with respect to the structure and validating the measure experimentally. Validation of the mapping with respect to the structure is built into this process. Any measure that results from applying these four steps will be valid in this sense.

Experimental validation amounts to performing a system test of the measure. The question to be answered is: Does this measure really measure what you think it does? This validation can be done with a complex empirical experiment or a simple test against reality. The effort put into validation is driven by your use for the measure. If you are using the measure for comparison, assessment, or investigation purposes, a simple test is sufficient validation. Such a test consists of applying the measure to at least four different objects, ordering those objects empirically, checking that the empirical ordering of the objects matches the ordering with respect to the measure, and perhaps performing one or more empirical operations and comparing the results with the respective numeric operations. Any failure of this test invalidates your measure and you need to redo the last task or perhaps all four steps.

If your measure is to be used for prediction or estimation purposes, you must perform a controlled empirical experiment, which may consist of comparing measurement results to past actual data, if you have good past actual data. In the absence of good historical data, you would be forced to gather data from the field (field observations) or conduct explicit field experiments. Either of these is a very expensive proposition.

SUMMARY

This chapter describes a proven, reliable method for selecting or constructing a set of measures which are aligned with the organizational or project goals. By aligning the measures with the goals, the organization or project has a quantitative way to determine whether the goals are being met and, if not, by how much they are being missed. This information can be used by management, and by designers in the case of technical measures, to determine when corrective action is necessary and where that action should be targeted.

This three-step method is deceptively simple. First, you need to define the goals with which measures should be aligned. Then, you ask questions which, when answered, help you determine your progress towards these goals. Finally, you determine the measures which help answer the questions. This method is aptly called the Goal Question Metric method.

I have added a fourth step which can be used to construct measures when no suitable measure can be found. This technique contains four steps of its own and moves you from an empirical understanding of a characteristic—being able to describe it, but not measure it—to being able to measure it with a representation of a known scale type. The four basic steps in this process follow roughly the four basic steps of application development: define the requirements, analyze the model, design the application, and build the application. This process was used to construct the measures in Chapters 7 through 15. It works.

Part II

TECHNICAL FOUNDATIONS

Measurement, like software engineering itself, is a technical activity. Both are based, to a large extent, on discrete mathematics—the study of sets, relations, operations, and structures built from these basic blocks. The chapters in Part II contain all of the technical material used throughout the book.

Chapter 4 covers the basics of discrete mathematics. It is organized by structure, beginning with the most basic and progressing to the most complex. Here, increasing complexity means either increasing structure or increasing levels of abstraction. One section covers statistical inference and analysis; another covers the mathematics behind algorithmic complexity.

Chapter 5, as large as it is, contains a concise summary of measurement theory. The early sections in the chapter provide the basic structure of measurement theory. The section on scale types provides new information on how to determine the scale type of any given measure. The major portion of the chapter is devoted to mathematical requirements for various types of empirical relational structures. Measures for which the empirical model meets these conditions are guaranteed, mathematically, to create a numeric model of the given scale type. I used this chapter extensively in writing the materials for Part III. I found it more convenient than my source material, and hope you find it as convenient. In the process of writing Part III, I found and corrected several errors in Chapter 5. Any that remain are entirely my responsibility.

Chapters 4 and 5 may be skipped upon your initial reading. They contain reference material to allow the book to stand on its own. As you use the techniques in this book, you will need to refer to these chapters. Including them makes such reference more convenient. Your only risk in skipping them is that some of the terms and constructs in chapters 6 through 15 may be unfamiliar and confusing.

Chapter 6 presents a formal theory of objects. This theory includes a model based on the algebraic structure of categories. This model can formally describe most of the characteristics which we will find of interest during design (I did have to add one extension in a chapter in Part III).

The theory also includes an algebraic manipulation technique for testing a design, before any code is written. Even though the technique requires a complete description of the design, it does not require the implementation-level details that often get in the way of prototyping a design. I use this technique to avoid having to rewrite my code to correct design errors. As this is a new technique, we'll see over time how well it actually works. I expect it to be indispensable, just as static and dynamic analysis techniques are indispensable to structural and mechanical engineering.

4

MATHEMATICAL STRUCTURES

Civil and structural engineering are built on a foundation of Newtonian physics. Electrical engineering is built upon a foundation of electromagnetism. Chemical engineering is built upon a foundation of chemistry. It has been said, and oft repeated, that software development can never become a "true" engineering discipline because it is not built on a foundation of a hard natural science. Let's face it, computer science is not physics. Nor is it the foundation for software engineering. Computer science is built upon a foundation of mathematics and studies certain aspects of computing and software, such as programming language semantics and compiler construction theory. Some aspects of software engineering, such as algorithm selection and design, data structure selection, and many other design decisions are based upon computer science. Software itself, however, is rooted firmly in discrete mathematics.

Discrete mathematics is the study of noncontinuous (discrete) sets of objects and the operations which manipulate those objects. The entire field of discrete mathematics is sometimes called abstract algebra. Sets, relations, and functions form the basic foundations for all of algebra, and even all of mathematics. I have one algebra text which manages to define the real numbers (a continuous set of numbers) in terms of sets and operations (Foldes 1994). This chapter presents an introduction to the algebraic structures used in this book. Discrete mathematics and abstract algebra are wonderful tools for understanding many things in the world, including software objects and how they interact with each other. In fact, the terms "object" and "class" have the same meaning in software that they have in mathematics. As you will see in Chapter 5, the whole of measurement theory is based upon the notion of sets, relations, and some structures built from these components, such as groups and fields.

The purpose of this chapter is to acquaint you with the language of discrete mathematics. It does not contain enough for you to become competent in any single subject. To do that, you will need to refer to some of the sources upon which this chapter is based. The most concise, in my opinion, is Stephan Foldes's book *Fundamental Structures of Algebra and Discrete Mathematics* (1994). It presents a complete and (fairly) easy to follow buildup of algebraic structures from sets through categories. Except as noted, my primary reference for this chapter is Foldes (1994).

The first section covers the basics of sets, relations, and functions. Since they form the basic foundations for discrete mathematics, this material is a little more comprehensive than the rest. You will find the language of set theory pervades throughout not only this book, but nearly all of software engineering and even nearly all of mathematics. While most of the material in the section relies on Foldes (1994), I first learned most of what I know about set theory from Woodcock and Loomes (1989), which takes a slightly different slant than Foldes. Some of that slant is reflected in this section.

The second section covers the basic algebraic structures from groupoids through topological spaces. These structures are lumped together for a couple of reasons. First, each succeeding structure is built upon the previous structure by adding new structural requirements. Thus, each structure, with some exceptions, is a specialization of the structure which precedes it. Groups, fields, and vector spaces play a significant role in the mathematics of objects. While represented in terms of categories, the mathematics of object manipulation rests upon an algebraic foundation. As condensed as this section is, you should be able to at least understand the terms as they are used later.

The third section presents graphs. Directed and nondirected graphs play an important role in the study of software. Graphs and graph theory are used extensively in the studies of a great many aspects of software, including coupling and complexity.

The next section introduces categories. Mathematically, categories are rather new, having been invented in the early 1940s to help explain some aspects of other structures (Mac Lane 1994). Categories are an abstraction of all of the other algebraic structures included in the chapter. They represent an extension and unification of the various algebraic structures. Categories are new to most people and can be rather arcane. They can also be used to explain a lot of interesting notions. The basic axioms of category theory are very simple and it amazing what you can do with them. This material relies on Mac Lane (1994), Pierce (1991), and Barr and Wells (1995).

The object theory in Chapter 6 is built on a categorical foundation. Categories allow tying together the various views of objects, classes, and designs encountered in the development of object-oriented software. The language of categories can describe nearly all aspects of both the static and dynamic nature of software. This section is important since it provides the basis for much of the remainder of the book.

Various statistical analysis and inference techniques are summarized in the next section. Both parametric and nonparametric techniques are covered. These techniques provide the tools to analyze and understand measurement data after we collect it. While by no means complete, the techniques presented in this section are typical of the statistical techniques I have encountered in my work in measurement. The material relies on a variety of sources, most notably Myers (1990), Krzanowski and Marriott (1994), and Sprent (1993).

The final section provides a brief introduction to algorithmic complexity analysis. More computer science than mathematics, the study of algorithmic complexity has taken on a mathematical language of its own. This language is used to study some of the different aspects of software size (not complexity).

SETS, RELATIONS, AND FUNCTIONS

The notion of a set as a collection of objects is central to many sciences, including software engineering. Sets allow the precise and unambiguous description of a collection of objects, from a variety of viewpoints, using a variety of techniques. Set theory forms the foundation for much of mathematics, including algebra and measurement theory.

Sets

A *set* is a well-defined collection of objects. The objects which belong to the set are called *members* or *elements*. A set is completely defined by its elements. The easiest way to define a set is to list its members, as in $S = \{1, 2, 3\}$. This method is called set specification *by extension*. A set may be described by specifying one or more properties which all of its members must satisfy, as in $S = \{n : \mathbb{Z} \mid 1 \leq n \leq 3\}$ ($\mathbb{Z}$ denotes the set of all integers and will be used throughout this book). This expression is read as "the set of all n which are elements of the set of integers such that n is greater than or equal to one and less than or equal to three." This method is called set specification *in comprehension*. A set may be described by specifying the shape or form of its members, as in $S = \{n : \mathbb{Z} \cdot n^2\}$. This is set specification *in comprehension by form*. These last two may be combined, as in $S = \{n : \mathbb{Z} \mid 1 \leq n \leq 100 \cdot n^2\}$, which gives $S = \{1, 4, 9, 16, 25, 36, 49, 64, 81, 100\}$.

Set membership is one of the very basic notions in set theory. To declare that an object x is a member of a set A, write $x \in A$. To declare that object y is not a member of a set A, write $y \notin A$. One basic axiom of set theory states that every object x is a member of the *singleton* (one-element) set that contains it: $\forall x \cdot x \in \{x\}$, where the notation $\forall x$ means "for all x." This axiom is known as the *axiom of set membership*. A set which has no members is the *empty set* and is written as $\{\,\}$ or $\varnothing$. Two sets A and B are *equal* if all of the members of A are members of B and all of the members of B are members of A. When this is the case, sets A and B have *exactly* the same members, and you write $A = B$. If A and B are not equal, write $A \neq B$. A set B is a *subset* of a set A if all of the members of B are members of A, and you write $B \subseteq A$. A is called a *superset* of B, and you write $A \supseteq B$. The set B is a proper subset of A if B is a subset of A and $B \neq A$, and you write $B \subset A$.

The *union* of two sets A and B is the set whose members belong to A, B, or both, and is written $A \cup B$. The *intersection* of two sets A and B is the set whose members belong to both A and B, and is written $A \cap B$. Two sets A and B are *disjoint* if their intersection is the empty set: $A \cap B = \varnothing$. When $B \subseteq A$, the *set difference* $A \backslash B$ is the set of members of A which are not members of B. The *Boolean sum, symmetric difference*, or *coproduct* of two sets A and B is the set of members of A which are not in B, in union with the set of members of B which are not in A, and is written $A + B = (A \backslash B) \cup (B \backslash A)$.

The members of a set can themselves be sets. The concept of sets being members of sets is so important that some mathematicians believe that *every* set has sets as members and can produce strong arguments in favor of this idea. For some particularly interesting examples, see Foldes (1994). One set of sets is particularly useful, so much so that it is given a special name and its own symbol. This set contains as its members all of the subsets of a given set A, including both $\varnothing$ and A itself. This set is called the *power set* of A and is written $\mathbb{P}(A)$, $\mathbb{P}A$, or 2^A.

The *distributed union* of a set of sets A is the set of all elements which are members of some member set of A and is written $\cup A$. The *distributed intersection* of a set of sets A is the set of all elements which are members of all member sets of A and is written $\cap A$.

Given two objects x and y, the sets $A = \{x, y\}$ and $B = \{y, x\}$ are *pairs*, and are in fact equal. If $x = y$, then the pairs A and B are both singleton, since $\{x, y\} = \{y, x\} = \{y\} = \{x\}$. The pairs A and B are *not* ordered since $A = B$. The *ordered pair* $\langle x, y \rangle$ is a pair of objects in which x is the *first object* and y is the *second object*. Two ordered pairs $\langle x, y \rangle$ and $\langle a, b \rangle$ are *equal* if and only if $x = a$ and $y = b$. If $x \in A$ and $y \in B$, then the set of all ordered pairs $\langle x, y \rangle$ is the *Cartesian product* or *cross product* of A and B, and is written $A \times B$. The notion of Cartesian products can be generalized to more than two sets and creates ordered n-tuples, where n is the number of sets in the Cartesian product: $\langle a_1, a_2, ..., a_n \rangle \in A_1 \times A_2 \times ... \times A_n$. Note that the following sets are not equal:

- $A_1 \times A_2 \times A_3$ is a set of ordered triples.
- $A_1 \times (A_2 \times A_3)$ is a set of ordered pairs, the second object of which is also an ordered pair.
- $(A_1 \times A_2) \times A_3$ is a set of ordered pairs, the first object of which is also an ordered pair.

Relations

Given two sets A and B, we can define a *relation* from A to B as a *mapping* of elements of A to elements of B, forming a set of ordered pairs $\langle a, b \rangle$ where $a \in A$ and $b \in B$. A relation R from A to B is thus a subset of $A \times B$, where for some $a \in A$ and $b \in B$, we write $\langle a, b \rangle \in R$, $a \mapsto b \in R$ or aRb. The relation R from A to B is sometimes written as $R: A \leftrightarrow B$. It is not required that $R: A \leftrightarrow B$ contain every pair of $A \times B$. Thus $R: A \leftrightarrow B \subseteq \mathbb{P}(A \times B)$, which allows R to be empty (the *empty relation*) or contain $A \times B$ (the *full relation*), or anything in between.

A relation between two sets is called a *binary* relation. A relation between different sets, as in $R: A \leftrightarrow B$, where $A \neq B$, is called a *heterogeneous* relation. It is possible to define a relation between members of the same set, as in $R: A \leftrightarrow A$. Such a relation is called a *homogeneous* relation and maps elements of A onto (possibly) other elements of A. A special case of a homogeneous relation is the *identity relation* $I_A: A \leftrightarrow A$ which maps each element of A onto itself.

In a relation $R: A \leftrightarrow B$, the set A is called the *source* and the set B is called the *target*. Those members of the source of a relation R which appear as the first object in any ordered pair in R are collectively called the *domain* of R. More formally,

$$\text{dom } R = \{x : A \mid R : A \leftrightarrow B \wedge (\exists a \in A, \exists b \in B \cdot \langle a, b \rangle \in R \wedge a = x)\}$$

$$(4.1)$$

Those members of the target of a relation R which appear as the second object in any ordered pair in R are collectively called the *codomain*, *range*, or *image* of R. More formally,

$$\text{cod } R = \{y : B \mid R : A \leftrightarrow B \wedge (\exists a \in A, \exists b \in B \cdot \langle a, b \rangle \in R \wedge b = y)\}$$

$$(4.2)$$

The *inverse* of a relation $R: A \leftrightarrow B$ is $R^{-1}: B \leftrightarrow A$ such that $\langle a, b \rangle \in R \Leftrightarrow \langle b, a \rangle \in R^{-1}$ (the notation $\Leftrightarrow$ means "if and only if"). You can *compose* a pair of relations $R: A \leftrightarrow B$ and $S: B \leftrightarrow C$ to get $R \mathbin{\S} S: A \leftrightarrow C$ if the codomain of R equals the domain of S. This is called *relational composition*. Relational composition is *associative*: $R \mathbin{\S} (S \mathbin{\S} T) = (R \mathbin{\S} S) \mathbin{\S} T$. A homogeneous relation R is *reflexive* if it contains the identity relation—it relates every member of A to itself:

$$R \text{ is } reflexive \Leftrightarrow (\forall x : A \cdot \langle x, x \rangle \in R) \qquad (4.3)$$

It is *irreflexive* if it relates no member of A to itself:

$$R \text{ is } irreflexive \Leftrightarrow (\forall x : A \cdot \langle x, x \rangle \notin R) \qquad (4.4)$$

It is *symmetric* if whenever $\langle x, y \rangle \in R$, we also have $\langle y, x \rangle \in R$:

$$R \text{ is } symmetric \Leftrightarrow (\forall x, y : A \cdot \langle x, y \rangle \in R \Rightarrow \langle y, x \rangle \in R) \qquad (4.5)$$

The notation $A \Rightarrow B$ means "if A then B" or "A implies B." It is *antisymmetric* if whenever $\langle x, y \rangle \in R$ and $\langle y, x \rangle \in R$, then x and y are the same object:

$$R \text{ is } antisymmetric \Leftrightarrow (\forall x, y : A \cdot \langle x, y \rangle \in R \wedge \langle y, x \rangle \in R \Rightarrow x = y)$$

$$(4.6)$$

It is *asymmetric* if whenever $\langle x, y \rangle \in R$, we cannot have $\langle y, x \rangle \in R$:

$$R \text{ is } asymmetric \Leftrightarrow (\forall x, y : A \cdot \langle x, y \rangle \in R \Rightarrow \langle y, x \rangle \notin R) \qquad (4.7)$$

It is *transitive* if whenever $\langle x, y \rangle \in R$, and $\langle y, z \rangle \in R$, we have $\langle x, z \rangle \in R$:

$$R \text{ is } transitive \Leftrightarrow (\forall x, y, z : A \cdot \langle x, y \rangle \in R \wedge \langle y, z \rangle \in R \Rightarrow \langle x, z \rangle \in R)$$

$$(4.8)$$

R is a *preorder* on A if it is reflexive and transitive. A preorder which is also antisymmetric is an *order*. An order is *total* (a *total order*) if aRb or bRa hold for all $a, b \in A$. A preorder which is also symmetric is called an *equivalence relation*. If R is an equivalence relation on a set A, then a subset B of A is an *equivalence class*, or *class*, with respect to R if and only if $\exists a \in A$ such that $B = \{b \mid \langle a, b \rangle \in R\}$. The set of equivalence classes for R on A form a *partition* of A—that is, the set A is a disjoint union of its equivalence classes ($\cap A = \varnothing$). The subset relation $A \subseteq B$ is reflexive, symmetric, and transitive. The proper subset relation $A \subset B$ is irreflexive, asymmetric, and transitive.

For a relation $R: A \leftrightarrow A$, the *reflexive closure* of R is the smallest reflexive relation which contains R, and is written R^r. The *symmetric closure* of R is the smallest symmetric relation containing R and is written R^s. The *transitive closure* of R is the smallest transitive relation containing R and is written R^t. The *reflexive transitive closure* of R is the smallest relation containing R which is reflexive and transitive (a preorder) and is written R^*. Thus we have the following facts:

1. R is reflexive $\Leftrightarrow R = R^r$.
2. R is symmetric $\Leftrightarrow R = R^s$.
3. R is transitive $\Leftrightarrow R = R^t$.
4. R is reflexive and transitive $\Leftrightarrow R = R^*$.

The reflexive closure of the empty relation is the identity relation for any set A: $\varnothing^r = \mathrm{id}_A$. The reflexive, symmetric, transitive, and reflexive transitive closures for the identity relation on any set are the identity relation: $\mathrm{id}_A{}^r = \mathrm{id}_A{}^s = \mathrm{id}_A{}^t = \mathrm{id}_A^* = \mathrm{id}_A$. The composition of a reflexive transitive closure of any relation R with R is the transitive closure of R: $R^* \, \S \, R = R^t$. The composition of the transitive closure of any relation R with R is the transitive closure of R: $R^t \, \S \, R = R^t$. The transitive closure of the transitive closure of any relation R is the transitive closure of R: $(R^t)^t = R^t$. The inverse of the transitive closure of any relation R is the transitive closure of the inverse of R: $(R^t)^{-1} = (R^{-1})^t$. The same is true of the reflexive transitive closure: $(R^*)^{-1} = (R^{-1})^*$. If the composition of two relations R and S are commutative ($R \, \S \, S = S \, \S \, R$), then the transitive closure of the composition is the composition of the transitive closures: $R \, \S \, S = S \, \S \, R \Rightarrow (R \, \S \, S)^t = R^t \, \S \, S^t$.

Let $(a_i \mid i \in n + 1) = (a_0,...,a_n)$ be a sequence of $n + 1$ distinct elements ($n \in \mathbb{N}$, $\mathbb{N}$ is the set of natural numbers $\{1, 2,...\}$, $n \geq 1$, and $a_i \neq a_j$ if $i \neq j$). The relation defined by $P = \{(a_i, a_{i+1}) : i \in n\}$ is called a *path* of *length* n from a_0 to a_n. If $n \geq 2$, then $P \cup \{a_n, a_0\}$ is called a *cycle* of length $n + 1$. A binary relation R is called *acyclic* if no relation $P \subseteq R$ is a cycle. Informally, a path is a string of elements strung together by a relation. A cycle is a path that passes through the same element more than once.

Relational Algebra

A relation can be viewed as a matrix or table where each column represents a set in the Cartesian product from which the relation is drawn. The *arity* or *degree* of the relation is the number of columns it contains. Each row in the matrix or table is a tuple from the Cartesian product. This view of a relation as a table forms the mathematical basis for relational databases. While this is very interesting, it is not the subject of this book. A class in software, ignoring for the moment its operations, is also a relation in this sense. It is a table formed by the Cartesian product of one or more domain sets, some of which may be other classes. Each domain set contains the permissible values for each attribute in the class. The rows of the table represent the various states an object of the class can occupy over the course of its life. This concept will be explored in much more detail in Chapter 6. For now, the notion is described only as a motivation for the topic of this subsection: a set of operations which manipulate relations.

Formally, we form an algebra consisting of a set of relations, drawn from various domains, and a set of operations. When we study algebras in the next section, you will see that we have indeed formed an algebra. This particular algebra we call *relational algebra*, for obvious reasons. The main purpose of this discussion is to explain the operations of relational algebra as they will be used to explain the manipulation of classes in a design in Chapter 6.

In the database world, each column in a relation is called an *attribute*. The name of the attribute is usually the name of the domain set from which the values of the attribute are drawn. This convention is adopted for both this section and the discussion of classes in Chapter 6. Rather than come up with names for the attributes, we will simply designate them by a letter A, B,... representing the name of the domain set. We will use the letters R, S,... to represent the relations themselves. We write $R.A$ to denote the attribute from the domain A in the relation R. In the database world, a relation will have one or more distinguished attributes, called *keys*, which help identify a tuple as distinct from all other tuples. We are not concerned with keys, either here or in Chapter 6, and will not discuss them any further.

The operations of relational algebra include set union, set intersection, set difference, and Cartesian product, already discussed. Here, the concentration will be on several new operations: projection, selection, quotient, join, and semijoin. These particular operations will prove very useful. The material for this subsection relies on Ullman (1988).

Projection

With projection, we remove some of the attributes from a relation, and perhaps rearrange some of the remaining attributes. If R is a relation of arity k, the notation $\pi_{i_1, i_2, \dots, i_m}(R)$, where the i_j are distinct integers in the range 1 to k, represents the *projection* of R onto components i_1, i_2,..., i_m which forms the set of m-tuples $\langle a_1, a_2,..., a_m \rangle$ such that for some k-tuple $\langle b_1, b_2,..., b_k \rangle$ in R, $a_j = b_{i_j}$ for $j = 1, 2,..., m$. For example, the projection $\pi_{3,2}(R)$ is determined by taking from each tuple in R the third and second components, in that order, and forming a new 2-tuple, R'. You can use the names of the attribute domain sets instead of numbers, which will eliminate the necessity of keeping the columns of R in any particular order. Thus, if the relation R is $R(A, B, C, D)$, the relation $\pi_{3,2}(R) = \pi_{C,B}(R) = R'(C, B)$.

In Chapter 6, the notation $\pi_i(R)$ will be used to represent the ith domain set of the relation R. In this usage, $\pi_i(R)$ represents the entire domain set for the ith attribute.

Selection

Selection describes a set of tuples from a relation R which satisfies a set of criteria. Each of these tuples contains one value for each attribute in the relation R; all of the columns in R are in each of the selected tuples. Selection can become some-what complex in the way you specify the conditions you want each selected tuple to satisfy.

The general notation $\sigma_F(R)$ represents the *selection* of all tuples in R which satisfy the conditions given by the function F. Define F to be a function involving constants and attribute numbers or names, arithmetic comparison operators, and logical connectives. Constant values which are drawn from numeric domains are unadorned in the function F. Constant values drawn from domains such as strings are enclosed in single quotes, as in 'Smith.' Attribute numbers or names are pre-ceded by '$\$$' as in $\$1$ or $\$A$. All of the arithmetic comparison operators $<$, $=$, $>$, $\leq$, $\neq$, and $\geq$ are allowed, as are all of the logical connectives $\wedge$ (and), $\vee$ (or), and $\neg$ (not). For example, the selection $\sigma_{\$1 > \$3}(R)$ represents the set of tuples from R for which the value of the first attribute is greater than the value of the third attribute.

For our purposes, the specification of a row number as a condition for selection is also allowed. The notation $\sigma_i(R)$ represents the ith tuple in the relation R. This notation will be used to specify a particular state in the state space of a class in Chapter 6.

Quotient

In a sense, the quotient operation is the inverse of the Cartesian product operation, but not completely. The quotient of two relations, taken in Cartesian product with the second of the original two relations provides tuples which are all contained in the first relation, although not all of the tuples in the first relation are necessarily in the Cartesian product. Formally, given two relations R and S of arities r and s, respectively, with $r > s$ and $S \neq \varnothing$, the *quotient* of R and S, denoted $R \div S$, is the set of $(r - s)$-tuples $\langle a_1,..., a_{r-s} \rangle$ such that for all s-tuples $\langle a_{r-s+1},..., a_r \rangle$ in S, the tuple $\langle a_1,..., a_r \rangle$ is in R. The quotient operation can be defined in terms of projection, Cartesian product, and set difference as

$$R \div S = \pi_{1,2,...,r-s}(R) \backslash \pi_{1,2,...,r-s}((\pi_{1,2,...,r-s}(R) \times S) \backslash R) \qquad (4.9)$$

Join

The join operation on two relations can best be described as a restriction placed on their Cartesian products. That is, the join operation first forms the Cartesian product of two relations, then selects those tuples from the results which satisfy a given set of criteria. We will define two types of joins: the θ-join and the natural join. The natural join will be most useful for our purposes.

The θ-*join* of relations R and S on attributes i and j, denoted $R \underset{i\theta j}{\bowtie} S$, where θ is an arithmetic comparison operator, is shorthand for $\sigma_{\$i\theta\$(r+j)}(R \times S)$, where R is of arity r. If θ is $=$, then the operation is called an *equijoin*.

The *natural join*, denoted $R \bowtie S$, selects from the Cartesian product $R \times S$ those tuples where the values of attributes common to both relations match. To compute $R \bowtie S$, first take the Cartesian product $R \times S$. Then, for each attribute A that appears in both R and S, select from $R \times S$ those tuples for which the value of A in R agrees with A in S, or $R.A = S.A$. Finally, for each attribute A, project out the column $S.A$ and rename the column $R.A$ to simply A. Formally, if $A_1, A_2,..., A_k$ are all attributes in both R and S, we have

$$R \bowtie S = \pi_{i_1, i_2, ..., i_m}\ \sigma_{R.A_1=S.A_1 \wedge R.A_2=S.A_2 \wedge ... \wedge R.A_k=S.A_k}(R \times S) \qquad (4.10)$$

where $i_1, i_2,..., i_m$ is the list of attributes in $R \times S$, in order, except for the attributes $S.A_1, S.A_2,..., S.A_k$. The natural join operation is used to combine classes in Chapter 6.

Semijoin

The semijoin relation has the effect of selecting those rows from R which are contained in the natural join of R and some other relation. Formally, the *semijoin* of relations R and S, denoted $R \ltimes S$, is the projection of the natural join of R and S onto the attributes of R. Formally,

$$R \ltimes S = \pi_R(R \bowtie S) \qquad (4.11)$$

where R, as a subscript of π, denotes the attributes of the relation R. Equivalently,

$$R \ltimes S = R \bowtie \pi_{R \cap S}(S) \qquad (4.12)$$

Functions

A *function* is a relation which is deterministic in the sense that a function f from A to B always maps a particular element of A to the same element of B. A *partial function* f from A to B is a function which maps an element of A onto at most one element of B, but every element of A need not be mapped onto an element of B. We denote the set of all partial functions f from A to B by $f: A \twoheadrightarrow B$. A *total function* f from A to B maps *every* element of A onto at most one element of B. We denote the set of all total functions f from A to B by $f: A \rightarrow B$. In most branches of mathematics, the term "function" usually refers only to total functions; this convention will be adopted throughout the book. "Partial function" will be used to refer to a partial function. For any (partial) function f: $A \to B$ ($f: A \nrightarrow B$), if an object $a \in A$ is mapped to an object $b \in B$, we write $f(a) = b$ or $f\ a = b$ or $\langle a, f(a) \rangle \in B$. We prefer $f\ a = b$ to avoid unnecessary parentheses. If $a \in A$ and $b \in B$ are in $f: A \nrightarrow B$ or $f: A \to B$, we say that b is the *value* of f at a.

Given two functions $f: A \to B$ and $g: B \to C$, we can create a *composite function* in the following way. For each $a \in A$ the value of $f\ a$ is in B and the value of $g(f\ a)$ is in C. Taking this as a single step, we have $g\ f: A \to C$, and $(g\ f)(a) = g(f\ a)$. There is a general convention that the function *arrow* $A \to B \to C$ is *right associative*: $A \to B \to C = (A \to B) \to C$, while function application is left associative: $(g\ f)(a) = g(f\ a)$. In general, $g\ f$ means "f first, then g" and may be denoted $g \circ f$.

Certain types of functions have special names. A function $f: A \to B$ is *surjective*, or is a *surjection*, if every $b \in B$ is a value of $f\ a$ for *at least* one $a \in A$. A function $f: A \to B$ is *injective*, or is an *injection*, if every $b \in B$ is a value $f\ a$ for *at most* one $a \in A$. A function $f: A \to B$ is *bijective*, or is a *bijection*, if it is both a surjection and an injection. Figure 4.1 illustrates these types.

If $f: A \to B$ and $g: B \to C$ are injections, then so is the composite $g\ f$: $A \to C$. If $f: A \to B$ and $g: B \to C$ are surjections, then so is the composite $g\ f: A \to C$. If $f: A \to B$ and $g: B \to C$ are bijections, then so is the composite $g\ f: A \to C$. To prove that a function f is an injection, we assume $f\ x = f\ x'$ and show that $x = x'$. If a set A is a subset of a set B, the *inclusion function* $i: A \to B$, defined as $i\ x = x$, is an injection. When $A = B$, the inclusion function $i: A \to B$ is sometimes called the *identity function*. A function $f: A \to B$ has an *inverse* function $g: B \to A$ if, for all $a \in A$ and $b \in B$, $g\ f\ a = a$ and $f\ g\ b = b$.

Since functions are sets of ordered pairs, we can take their union, their intersection, and so on. Given two functions $f: A \to B$ and $g: A \to B$, the union of f and g is always a relation, but is a function only if f and g are disjoint ($f \cap g = \varnothing$), or if f and g map elements in both domains consistently ($f\ a = g\ a$). More formally,

$$\forall f, g : A \to B \cdot f \cup g \in B \Leftrightarrow \forall a : A \mid a \in (\text{dom } f \cap \text{dom } g) \cdot f\ a = g\ a$$
$$(4.13)$$

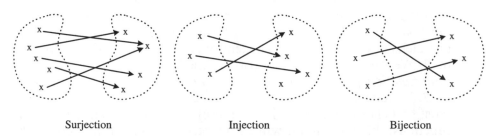

| Surjection | Injection | Bijection |

Figure 4.1 *Three types of functions.*

If f and g produce different results for some common domain element, you can avoid ambiguity by saying you prefer one function, say g, over f. This is written $f \oplus g$ and is called *function overriding* (Woodcock and Loomes 1989). We say that g *overrides* f or f *is overridden by* g. This has the effect of removing those elements of f which belong to dom f from (dom $f \cap$ dom g), leaving (dom $f \cap$ dom g)\dom f. The domain of g is unaffected. Function overriding can be used to model polymorphism in software. Function overriding has some interesting properties:

1. It is idempotent: $f \oplus f = f$.
2. It is associative: $f \oplus (g \oplus h) = (f \oplus g) \oplus h$.
3. It has left unity: $\varnothing \oplus f = f$.
4. It has right unity: $f \oplus \varnothing = f$.

If f and g have disjoint domains, function overriding is commutative: dom $f \cap$ dom $g = \varnothing \Rightarrow f \oplus g = g \oplus f$.

The *cardinality* of a set is the number of elements it contains. The cardinality of a set A, written as $|A|$ or $\#A$, is a bijection from $A \rightarrow \mathbb{N}_n$, where $\mathbb{N}_n = \{1, 2, 3,..., n\}$. We say that the *size* of A is n, and write $|A| = n$. The size of the empty set is zero: $|\varnothing| = 0$. A set A is *finite* if it is empty, or $|A| = n$ for some positive integer n. A set that is not finite is *infinite*. A nonempty set is infinite if and only if there is an injection from $\mathbb{N}$ to A ($\mathbb{N}$ is the set of all natural numbers). If, for an infinite set A, we can construct an injection $f: \mathbb{N} \rightarrow A$ which is also a surjection, we say that A is *countable*. If we cannot construct such a bijection, we say that A is *uncountable* (Biggs 1985).

Paradoxes in Set Theory

Applied without limits, the axioms of set theory can lead to some very interesting paradoxes. Since you can specify any set by describing its members, you can create sets such as "the set of all sets which are not members of themselves," which is a legal description, but every member violates one of the axioms. To avoid paradoxes, mathematicians will restrict the application of set theory to some fixed given universe U. An additional requirement for a set is that it be a member of this universe. Such a set $u \in U$ is called a *small set*. Given a universe U and two sets $u, v \in U$, you can construct various sets:

- $\{u, v\}$: The set with u and v as its elements
- $\langle u, v \rangle$: The ordered pair
- $\omega = \{0, 1, 2,...\}$: The infinite set of all finite ordinals
- $u \times v = \{x, y \mid x \in u, y \in v\}$: The Cartesian product
- $u = \{v \mid v \subseteq u\}$: The power set
- $x = \{y \mid y \in z \text{ for some } z \in x\}$: The union of a set x of sets

Set theory limited to a fixed universe in this way is based on the Zermelo-Fraenkel axioms (Foldes 1994). Some mathematicians assume instead the Gödel-Bernays axioms (Gödel 1940). These axioms consider sets and classes. A *set x* is an *element* of the universe U: $x \in U$, and a *class* c is defined to be any *subset* of the universe U: $c \subseteq U$. All sets are classes; not all classes are sets. Classes which are not sets—subsets of U but not elements of U—are called *proper classes*.

Lattices

Let $\langle A, \preceq \rangle$ be a preordered set ($\preceq$ is a preorder relation on A) and let $B \subseteq A$. An element $b \in B$ is *minimal* if $\nexists b' \in B$ such that $b' < b$. The element b is the *minimum* of B if $b < x$ for all $x \in B \backslash \{b\}$. The element b is *maximal* if $\nexists b' \in B$ such that $b < b'$. The element b is the *maximum* of B if $x < b$ for all $x \in B \backslash \{b\}$. An element $a \in A$ is a *lower bound* of B if $a < b$ for all $b \in B$. The element a is the *greatest lower bound* of B (*glb*) if, in addition, $a' \preceq a$ for every other lower bound a' of B. An element $a \in A$ is an *upper bound* of B if $b \preceq a$ for all $b \in B$. The element a is a *least upper bound* of B (*lub*) if, in addition, $a \preceq a'$ for every other upper bound a' of B.

An order $\langle A, \preceq \rangle$ is a *lower semilattice*, or *meet semilattice*, if every two elements $a, b \in A$ have a glb. We write $a \wedge b$ for glb$\{a, b\}$. An order $\langle A, \preceq \rangle$ is an *upper semilattice*, or *join semilattice*, if every two elements $a, b \in A$ have a lub. We write $a \vee b$ for lub$\{a, b\}$. A *lattice* is both a lower and an upper semilattice. Every nonempty finite set in a lattice has both a glb and a lub. The order $\langle A, \preceq \rangle$ is a *complete lattice* if every subset $B \subseteq A$ has both a glb and a lub, denoted $\wedge B$ and $\vee B$, respectively. An interesting point is that the set of closure systems on any given set S, when ordered by inclusion, forms a complete lattice. Closure systems will be explained in the next section.

GROUP STRUCTURES

This section explores a series of algebraic structures. An *algebra* is a set, called the *carrier set*, together with one or more operations. A generic algebra, called a *universal algebra*, is defined at the end of this section. The "structure" in an algebraic structure usually refers to conditions which are applied on the operations. Sometimes, these conditions apply to the members of the carrier set. The fewer the conditions, the simpler the structure.

Let's begin with the simplest structure and add conditions as we move to more advanced structures, then conclude with a discussion of the universal algebra. When most people encounter algebraic structures, those structures use the integers or real numbers as the carrier set and the common arithmetic operations as the structure operations. Algebras need not be limited to the real numbers and arithmetic operations. The carrier set can be *any* set of objects that meets the constraints of set theory. Indeed, algebras are most useful when applied to sets which are not numbers of any kind. Structures which can be shown to be one of the algebraic structures in this chapter have many known properties which allow you to apply a great deal of previous work in the theory concerned. This ability can be very useful in the study of software structures.

Groups

Four structures are discussed in this section, all of which are built from a carrier set and a single binary operation. An algebraic group is the fourth and most complex of these structures.

A *groupoid* is a set A together with a closed binary operation $*: A \rightarrow A$. It is denoted by the couple $\langle A, * \rangle$. When there are two elements $x, y \in A$, you usually write $x * y$, or simply xy, rather than $*(x, y)$. Saying that $*$ is *closed* simply means that for all $x, y \in A$, $x * y \in A$. Any structure with a set and a closed binary operation forms a groupoid. The set C of subsets of A which are closed under $*$ forms an algebraic closure system. A *subgroupoid* is a set $C \in C$ ($C \subseteq A$) together with the restriction of $*$ to $C \times C$, and is denoted by $\langle C, * \rangle$. A function between two groupoids $\langle A, *_A \rangle$ and $\langle B, *_B \rangle$, $h: A \rightarrow B$, is a *homomorphism* if $h(x *_A y) = h(x) *_B h(y)$ for all $x, y \in A$. In shorthand, $h: \langle A, *_A \rangle \rightarrow \langle B, *_B \rangle$. Under a homomorphism, an element of A is mapped onto an element of B. Furthermore, this mapping is *structure preserving*—that is, the relationships between elements of A is reflected in the relationships between elements of B.

A homomorphism which is bijective is called an *isomorphism*. A homomorphism from a groupoid $\langle A, * \rangle$ onto itself is called an *endomorphism*. An isomorphism from a groupoid onto itself is an *automorphism*. Two groupoids $\langle A, *_A \rangle$ and $\langle B, *_B \rangle$ are said to be *isomorphic* if there exists an isomorphism between them.

A *congruence* relation on a groupoid $\langle A, * \rangle$ is an equivalence relation, denoted $\equiv$, on A such that for all $x, x', y, y' \in A$, $x \equiv x'$ and $y \equiv y' \Rightarrow x * y \equiv x' * y'$.

A *semigroup* is a groupoid for which the binary operation $*$ is associative: for all $x, y, z \in A$, $(x * y) * z = x * (y * z)$. A *sub-semigroup* is a subgroupoid of a semigroup. A *semigroup homomorphism* (*isomorphism*) is a homomorphism (isomorphism) between two semigroups.

An element $e \in A$ is a *neutral element* under $*$ if and only if $e * x = x * e = x$ for all $x \in A$. A *monoid* is a semigroup with a neutral element. A subset B of A which also contains the neutral element e and the operation $*$ restricted to B form a *submonoid*. A *monoid homomorphism* (*isomorphism*) is a homomorphism (isomorphism) between two monoids.

An element x^{-1} is an *inverse* of x under $*$ if both $x, x^{-1} \in A$ and $x * x^{-1} = x^{-1} * x = e$. A *group* $\langle A, * \rangle$ is a monoid such that for all $x \in A$, $x^{-1} \in A$. A group for which the operation $*$ is commutative—that is for all $x, y \in A$, $x * y = y * x$—is called an *abelian group* or *commutative group*. For a group homomorphism $h: A \rightarrow B$, the class of the neutral element in the congruence of A induced by h is called the *kernel* of h and is denoted Ker h.

A *subgroup* is a set $B \subseteq A$ such that B and the operation $*$ restricted to B form a group. Note that B must contain the neutral element e, as well as the inverse element x^{-1} for all $x \in B$. A subgroup $\langle B, * \rangle$ of $\langle A, * \rangle$ for which $B \subset A$ is called a *proper subgroup*.

Rings and Fields

A *ring* is a set A with two binary operations $+$ and $\cdot$, denoted by $\langle A, +, \cdot \rangle$, such that:

1. $\langle A, + \rangle$ is a commutative group, with $+$ called *sum* or *addition*, and with a neutral element denoted by 0_A, or just 0.

2. $\langle A, \cdot \rangle$ is a commutative semigroup, with $\cdot$ called *product* or *multiplication*.

3. The product is *distributive* over the sum: $x \cdot (y + z) = x \cdot y + x \cdot z$ for all $x, y, z \in A$.

In a ring where $\langle A, \cdot \rangle$ is a monoid (not a general requirement), the neutral element for $\cdot$ is denoted by 1_A, or just 1, and is called the *ring identity element*. There is at most one identity element in a ring. In some texts, the multiplication operation need not be commutative. A subring of $\langle A, +, \cdot \rangle$ is any subgroup of $\langle A, + \rangle$ that also a sub-semigroup of $\langle A, \cdot \rangle$. The set of subrings forms an algebraic closure system on A.

A *ring homomorphism* from a ring $\langle A, +, \cdot \rangle$ to a ring B is a group homomorphism $h: \langle A, + \rangle \rightarrow \langle B, + \rangle$ that is also a multiplicative semigroup homomorphism from $\langle A, \cdot \rangle$ to $\langle B, \cdot \rangle$. The composition of two ring homomorphisms $h: \langle A, +, \cdot \rangle \rightarrow \langle B, +, \cdot \rangle$ and $g: \langle B, +, \cdot \rangle \rightarrow \langle C, +, \cdot \rangle$ is a ring homomorphism from $\langle A, +, \cdot \rangle$ to $\langle C, +, \cdot \rangle$. The identity mapping on each ring is a ring homomorphism. The inverse of a bijective ring homomorphism is a ring homomorphism. A bijective ring homomorphism is called a *ring isomorphism*. Two rings $\langle A, +, \cdot \rangle$ and $\langle B, +, \cdot \rangle$ are *isomorphic* if there exists a ring isomorphism between them. An *ideal* is a subgroup I of $\langle A, + \rangle$ such that $a \in I$ and $c \in A \Rightarrow ac \in I$ [$ac = a \cdot c$]. A *proper ideal* is one where $I \subset A$.

A *field* is a ring where the nonzero elements form a group under multiplication. Formally, given a ring $\langle A, +, \cdot \rangle$, the set $A \backslash \{0\}$ and the operation $\cdot$ form a group. A *subfield* of a field $\langle F, +, \cdot \rangle$ is any subring of $\langle F, +, \cdot \rangle$ which also forms a field.

Vector Spaces

Given a commutative group $\langle V, + \rangle$, you can take the set of endomorphisms over V—those homomorphisms $h: V \rightarrow V$—and call it End V. Suppose that you also have a field $\langle F, +, \cdot \rangle$ and a function $p: F \rightarrow$ End V such that both $\langle F, \cdot \rangle \rightarrow \langle$End $V, \circ \rangle$ and $\langle F, + \rangle \rightarrow \langle$End $V, + \rangle$ hold. Here, $\circ$ is the composition of endomorphisms over V, and $\langle$End $V, + \rangle$ is defined by $(\sigma + \tau)(x) = \sigma(x) + \tau(x)$ for all $x \in V$ and $\sigma, \tau \in$ End V. The tuple $\langle V, +, p \rangle$ is called a *vector space* over the field F. The elements of V are called *vectors*, and the elements of F are called *scalars*. For a vector v and a scalar α, write $\alpha \cdot v$ or αv instead of $[p(\alpha)](v)$, and call this a *vector space product*. The $+$ operation on End V is called *vector addition* or *vector sum*. Denote the neutral *null vector* in the group V by $\overline{0}$, which is the addition identity. The additive inverse for any vector v is written $-v$.

Since p is a homomorphism, you have, for all $\alpha, \beta \in F$ and $v \in V$, $(\alpha + \beta)v = \alpha v + \beta v$ (right distributivity), $(\alpha\beta)v = \alpha(\beta v)$ (mixed associativity), $0v = \overline{0}$, $1v = v$, $(-1)v = -v$, $\alpha\overline{0} = \overline{0}$, and $\alpha(-v) = (-\alpha)v = -(\alpha v)$. A *scalar multiple* of a vector v is any vector of the form αv where α is a scalar. When F and p are clear, or can be understood from the context, refer to the "vector space V."

A subset U of V is a subspace if it is a subgroup of $\langle V, + \rangle$ and $\alpha v \in U$ for every scalar α and $v \in U$. Subspaces form an algebraic closure system on V.

Given any set of vectors $M \subseteq V$, and a finite family of scalar multiples $(\alpha_i v_i : i \in I)$ of elements v_i of M, the sum

$$\sum_{i \in I} \alpha_i v_i \qquad (4.14)$$

is a *linear combination* of elements of M. A set of vectors M is *linearly independent* (or *independent*) if no $v \in M$ belongs to the subspace generated by $M \setminus \{v\}$—that is, no element of M is a linear combination of any other elements of M. A set of vectors C is *linearly dependent* (or *dependent*) if it is not independent. A dependent set C is called a *circuit* if it is minimal—if every proper subset of C is independent.

A subset B of V is called a *basis* of the space V if any of the following equivalent conditions are met:

1. B is a maximal independent set.
2. B is a minimal generating set for the entire space V.
3. B is independent and generates V.

Every vector space V has a basis. Each independent set of vectors is contained in some basis. Two bases of a given vector space V are *equipotent*—they have the same cardinality. The cardinality of a basis of a space V is called the *dimension of V* and is denoted dim V. If U is a subspace of V, then dim $U \leq$ dim V. If V has finite dimension and $U \neq V$, the dim $U <$ dim V.

Given two vector spaces V and W over the same field F, a mapping $h: V \to W$ is a *linear mapping* if it is a group homomorphism from $\langle V, + \rangle \to \langle W, + \rangle$ and if for all $\alpha \in F$, $x \in V$, $h(\alpha x) = \alpha h(x)$. The composition of two linear mappings $h: V \to W$ and $g: W \to Z$ is a linear mapping $g\ h: W \to Z$. The identity mapping on each vector space V is a linear mapping. The inverse of a bijective linear mapping is also a linear mapping. A bijective linear mapping $h: V \to W$ is called an *isomorphism* from V to W, and V and W are said to be *isomorphic*. Any two vector spaces over the same field that have the same dimension are isomorphic—an isomorphism between them can *always* be found. Any isomorphism from V to V is called an *automorphism* of V. Under composition, the set of all automorphisms of V is a group, denoted $\langle$Aut $V, \circ \rangle$. All of the linear mappings V to V are called *endomorphisms* and they form a monoid under composition: $\langle$End $V, \circ \rangle$. For a linear map $h: V \to W$, we have dim $V =$ dim(Ker h) + dim(cod h).

Given a basis B of a vector space V over a field F, you can find a finite family of nonzero scalars $(\alpha_u : u \in I, \alpha \in F)$ indexed by a subset I of B such that:

$$v = \sum_{u \in I} \alpha_u u \qquad (4.15)$$

This set $I \subseteq B$ is called the *support* of V in B. For every basis element $u \in B$, you define the *u*th *coordinate function* c_u with respect to B from V to F by:

$$c_u(v) = \begin{cases} \alpha_u & \text{if } u \in I \\ 0 & \text{otherwise} \end{cases} \qquad (4.16)$$

As a notational convention, given any field F and a positive integer n, the notation F^n will denote the vector space $F^{[1,n]}$ ($F_1 \times F_2 \times ... \times F_n$). A typical vector ($v(i)$: $i \in [1, n]$) in F^n shall also be written as an n-tuple $\langle v_1, v_2,..., v_n \rangle$. The *inner product* or *dot product* of any two vectors $v, w \in F^n$ is defined as the element

$$\sum_{i=1}^{n} v(i) \cdot w(i) \qquad (4.17)$$

of the field F, and is denoted by $v \cdot w$. The dot product is both commutative and distributive: for $u, v, w \in F^n$, we have $v \cdot w = w \cdot v$ and $u \cdot (v + w) = (u \cdot v) + (u \cdot w)$. Two vectors are *orthogonal* if their dot product is zero. If two vectors $v, w \in F^n$ are orthogonal, and $u = v + w$, then $v \cdot v + w \cdot w = u \cdot u$. For those of you still awake, this is the Pythagorean theorem stated in terms of vector spaces. To prove it, use as F the real numbers and create a vector space of dimension two on a flat sheet of paper. In this space, orthogonal vectors are represented by perpendicular line segments. If two such line segments share a common endpoint, vector addition is represented by a line segment connecting the unconnected ends of the two original segments, as shown in Figure 4.2.

Given any two natural numbers m and n, an $m \times n$ *matrix* over a field F is a family $a = (a_{ij}: 1 < i < m, 1 < j < n)$ of elements of F indexed by the set of couples of integers (i, j). The field element a_{ij} is the matrix's *entry at position* i, j (or *in row* i, *column* j). For each fixed i, $(a_{ij} : 1 < j < n)$ is called the ith *row vector of* a and is denoted $\bar{a}_i$. $\bar{a}_i$ is a vector in F^n. For each fixed j, $(a_{ij} : 1 < i < m)$ belongs to F^n and is called the jth *column vector*, denoted by $a_{[j]}$.

Topological Spaces

The couple $\langle T, C \rangle$ is a *topological space*, where T is any set and C is a closure system on T such that the empty set is closed, and the union of any two closed sets is closed. The closure system C is often referred to as the *topology* or *topological closure system* on T. The elements of T are called *points*. A point x of T is *close to*, or *is approximated by*, a set $A \subseteq T$ if x belongs to the closure $\bar{A}$ of A

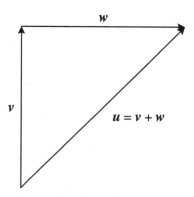

Figure 4.2 *Vector addition. Does this look familiar?*

in the closure system C. We also say that x is a *closure point* or *adherence point* of A. A subset B of T is *open* if its complement $(B' = T\backslash B)$ is closed. On any set T, there is at least the *discrete topology* in which all subsets of T are closed and the *trivial topology* where $\varnothing$ and T are the only closed sets.

If $C \subseteq C'$ for two topologies on the same set T, then C' is *finer than*, or a *refinement of*, C. This defines a *refinement order* on the set τ of all topologies on T. The trivial and discrete topologies on T are the minimum and maximum of τ, respectively.

For any subset S of T, the *inherited topology* on S is $\{S \cap C: C \in C\}$. A homomorphism $h{:}T \to T'$ between topological spaces is said to be *continuous* when for every $x \in T$ and $A \subseteq T$, if A approximates x, then $h[A]$ approximates $h(x)$. Topological homomorphisms preserve approximation. The following conditions are equivalent for any function $h{:}\ T \to T'$ between topological spaces:

1. h is continuous.
2. Whenever $B \subseteq T'$ is closed, the inverse image $h^{-1}[B]$ is closed in T.
3. Whenever $B \subseteq T'$ is open, $h^{-1}[B]$ is open in T.

The composition of continuous functions $h{:}\ T \to R$ and $g{:}\ R \to S$ is a continuous function $g\,h{:}\ T \to S$. The identity function on each topological space is continuous. All constant functions are continuous.

An upper section F of a lattice L that is closed under the meet operation $[(x \wedge y) \in F$ for $x, y \in F]$ is called a *filter in the lattice L*. The set of filters form an algebraic closure system on L. A *proper filter* is a filter on L that is distinct from L. For any $x \in L$, the section $[x, \to)$ is a filter, called the *principal filter* generated by x. An *ultrafilter* is a maximal member of the inclusion-ordered set of proper filters. A principal filter $[x, \to)$ is an ultrafilter if and only if x is an atom.

Consider a filter U on a set $V \times V$. Each member of U is a binary relation on V. We think of these relations as expressing some notion of proximity, though not necessarily in numerical terms. Assume that:

1. For every $x \in V$ and $E \in U$, $(x, x) \in E$.
2. For every $E \in U$ the dual relation $E^* \in U$.
3. For every $E \in U$ there is some $D \in U$ such that for every $x, y, z \in V$, $(x, y) \in D$ and $(y, z) \in D$ together imply that $(x, z) \in E$.

The couple $\langle V, U \rangle$ is called a *uniform space* or *uniformity* on V. The members of U are called *entourages* or *uniform entourages*. The *standard uniformity* on V consists of all reflexive relations. The *trivial uniformity* on V has $U = \{V \times V\}$.

The standard uniformity on $\mathbb{R}$ has some interesting properties. Let d be a function from $V \times V$ to $\mathbb{R}$ for any set V. Assume that for every $x, y, z \in V$:

1. $d(x, y) \geqslant 0$.
2. $d(x, y) = 0 \leftrightarrow x = y$.
3. $d(x, y) = d(y, x)$.
4. $d(x, y) + d(y, z) \geqslant d(x, z)$ (the triangle inequality).

The function d is called the *distance function* on V, and $\langle V, d \rangle$ is called a *metric space*. For any connected graph $\langle V, E \rangle$ (graphs are covered in the section on graphs), the graph-theoretic distance function on $V \times V$ makes the vertex set into a metric space. The function $d = |x - y|$ makes $\mathbb{R}$ into a metric space. Every metric space $\langle V, d \rangle$ gives rise to a uniform space $\langle V, U_d \rangle$, where U_d is the filter on $V \times V$ generated by the set of relations of the form $\{(x, y) \in V \times V: d(x, y) < \varepsilon\}$ for some positive real ε. The metric space defined on a connected graph gives rise to a discrete uniformity. Not all uniformities arise from metric spaces—those that do are called *metric uniformities*.

Uniformities give rise to, or *determine*, topological spaces. Let $\langle T, U \rangle$ be any uniform space. For $E \in U$ and $x \in T$, define $N_e(x) = \{y: (x, y) \in E\}$ and for $A \subseteq T$ define:

$$\bigcup_{x \in A} N_e(x) \tag{4.18}$$

Define the closure $\overline{A}$ of each $A \subseteq T$ by:

$$\overline{A} = \bigcap_{E \in U} N_e(A) \tag{4.19}$$

The set $C = \{\overline{A}: A \subseteq T\}$ of closed sets is a topological closure system on T. Thus, $\langle T, C \rangle$ is a topological space, called the *uniform topology corresponding to* or *determined by* U. If the uniformity U is a metric uniformity, then the corresponding uniform topology is called a *metric topology*. In the topological space T, for every $x \in T$ and entourage E, $N_e(x)$ is a *topological neighborhood* of x. Also, $N_e(A)$ is a topological neighborhood of every $A \subseteq T$.

Assume that $A \subseteq T$ is closed and $x \notin A$, but $x \in T$. Then there is a uniform entourage E such that $N_e(x) \cap A = \varnothing$ (x and A are in *disjoint neighborhoods*). A topological space in which every closed set A and any point $x \notin A$ are contained in disjoint neighborhoods is called *regular*. Also, the point is *separated from* the closed set A, meaning they can be enclosed in disjoint neighborhoods. All uniform topologies are regular. Topological spaces for which pairs of distinct points can be separated are called *Hausdorff spaces*. All metric topologies are Hausdorff spaces (the Hausdorff separation theorem). Regularity does not imply Hausdorff separation.

Universal Algebras

So far, you have seen several algebraic structures, all consisting of a set and one or more operations of various arities or orders. After seeing all of these structures, a pattern should be emerging. This generic pattern is developed in this section.

A *universal algebra*, or *algebra*, is a couple $\langle U, (f_i: i \in I) \rangle$ where U is any set and $(f_i: i \in I)$ is a family of operations $f_i: U^{n(i)} \to U$, $n \in \mathbb{Z}$ for $i \in I$. The notation $U^{n(i)}$ denotes the cross product of U taken $n(i)$ times (U^2 means $U \times U$). The $n(i)$ denote the *arity* or *order* of the operations f_i. The arity of an operation is the number of parameters it requires when written in functional format. For example, $+(x, y)$ is the functional notation for the binary operation of addition, normally written in *infix notation* $x + y$, and for which $n(i) = 2$. The family $(n(i): i \in I)$ is the *type* of the algebra. The set I is usually an ordinal. Often the algebra $\langle U, (f_i: i \in I) \rangle$ is written as $\langle U, f_i: i \in I \rangle$ for convenience. If a set $S \subseteq U$ is closed under all the operations f_i, $i \in I$, then $\langle S, f_i \mid S^n(i) : i \in I \rangle$ is also an algebra of type $(n(i) : i \in I)$, and is called a *subalgebra* of U.

Let $\langle U, f_i : i \in I \rangle$ and $\langle V, f_i : i \in I \rangle$ be two algebras of the same type. A *universal homomorphism*, or *homomorphism*, from the algebra U to the algebra V is a map $h: U \to V$ such that for all $i \in I$ and $(x_0,..., x_{n-1}) \in U^{n(i)}$, $h(f_i(x_0,..., x_{n-1})) = f_i(h(x_0),..., h(x_{n-1}))$. Write $h: \langle U, f_i : i \in I \rangle \to \langle V, f_i : i \in I \rangle$ to denote such a homomorphism. A bijective universal homomorphism is called a *universal isomorphism*, or *isomorphism*, and two algebras mapped by an isomorphism are *isomorphic*. The composition of two universal homomorphisms $h: \langle U, f_i : i \in I \rangle \to \langle V, f_i : i \in I \rangle$ and $g: \langle V, f_i : i \in I \rangle \to \langle W, f_i : i \in I \rangle$ is a homomorphism $g\,h: \langle U, f_i : i \in I \rangle \to \langle W, f_i : i \in I \rangle$. The identity mapping of any universal algebra $\langle U, f_i : i \in I \rangle$ is a homomorphism $i: \langle U, f_i : i \in I \rangle \to \langle U, f_i : i \in I \rangle$. The inverse of a bijective homomorphism is also a homomorphism.

A groupoid is an algebra $\langle U, f_0 \rangle$ for which $I = 1 = \{\emptyset\}$ (a set whose only member is the empty set) and f_0 is binary ($n(0) = 2$). A monoid is an algebra $\langle U, f_0, f_1 \rangle$ of type $(2, 1)$ where f_0 is the binary product ($n(0) = 2$) and f_1 is the nullary constant operation e—where e is the neutral element ($n(1) = 0$). A group with neutral element e is an algebra $\langle U, f_0, f_1, f_2 \rangle$ of type $(2, 0, 1)$ where f_0 and f_1 are as for monoids, and f_2 is the unary operation giving the inverse of each group element. A ring $\langle U, +, \cdot \rangle$ corresponds to an algebra $\langle U, +, 0_U, f_2, \cdot \rangle$ of type $(2, 0, 1, 2)$ where 0_U is the nullary constant corresponding to the ring's zero element and f_2 is the unary additive inverse operation—this algebra can also be written as $\langle U, +, 0, -, \cdot \rangle$. A lattice is an algebra $\langle U, \wedge, \vee \rangle$ of type $(2, 2)$. Universal homomorphisms and isomorphisms for groupoids, monoids, groups, and rings are the same as the structure-specific homomorphisms and isomorphisms described in this section.

For any universal algebra U, the set of subalgebras forms an algebraic closure system on U. A closure system C on a set U is algebraic if and only if C coincides with the subalgebra closure system of some universal algebra U.

A *congruence relation* on a universal algebra U is an equivalence relation $\equiv$ on U such that for every $i \in I$ with $n(i) = n$, if $x_0 \equiv x'_0,..., x_{n-1} \equiv x'_{n-1}$ then $f_i(x_0,..., x_{n-1}) = f_i(x'_0,...,x'_{n-1})$.

Universal algebras will become important in Chapters 6 through 15 where from time to time the class of an object is represented as a universal algebra.

GRAPHS

Graphs are a particularly useful structure for studying software. Many kinds of software structures can be represented as a graph. Most graphical representations of software, including dataflow models, entity-relationship models, state transition models, class models, and even use case models, can be considered as an algebraic graph. This is good news as many characteristics of graphs are well known and can aid in the design of software. Many of these characteristics can translate directly into software measures. Because of graph representations, we can define concepts like the shape of a design, or the depth of an inheritance tree, or the concept of cycles in a class dependency diagram. Dependency relationships are particularly suited for representation as graphs.

Fundamentally, graphs are just another algebraic structure and could have been included in the previous section. Like other algebraic structures, graphs are based on a set and relationships between elements of the set. Because of their importance and usefulness, an entire section is devoted to algebraic graphs.

Let V be any set and E be any set of two-element subsets of V. Then $G = \langle V, E \rangle$ is called a *graph*. The elements of V are called *vertices* and the elements of E are called *edges*. Note that because E consists of two-element sets, the concept of an edge having the same vertex at both ends is not part of this definition. Since we will need such a construct, we will modify the definition a bit later. Any two vertices forming an edge are called *adjacent*. If E consists of all nonsingleton pairs of vertices, then G is called a *complete graph*. If $V = \varnothing$, then $E = \varnothing$, and $G = \langle V, E \rangle$ is called the *empty graph*. The *complement* $\overline{G}$ of a graph $G = \langle V, E \rangle$ is the graph whose vertex set is V and whose edges join pairs of vertices not joined in G: $G = \langle V, E \rangle$, $\overline{G} = \langle V, \{\{x, y\} : x, y \in V \wedge \{x, y\} \notin E\}\rangle$. Graphs can be composed by taking the unions of their vertex and edge sets. Formally, given two graphs $G_1 = \langle V_1, E_1 \rangle$ and $G_2 = \langle V_2, E_2 \rangle$, the composition $G_1 \circ G_2 = \langle V_1 \cup V_2, E_1 \cup E_2 \rangle$.

The binary *adjacency relation* R on V is defined by xRy if $x, y \in V$ and x and y are adjacent, that is if $\{x, y\} \in E$. The adjacency relation is irreflexive and symmetric. In fact, every irreflexive and symmetric binary relation on a set V is the adjacency relation on a graph. A *walk* is a sequence of edges connected by an adjacency relation in which an edge can appear more than once. *Paths* and *cycles* form in graphs and correspond to the relation-theoretic notions discussed in the first section of this chapter. If P is a relation-theoretic path in the adjacency relation of a graph $G = \langle V, E \rangle$ from a vertex a to a vertex b, then the edge set $\{\{x, y\}: (x, y) \in P\}$ is called a *path in the graph G from a to b* or *the path between a and b*. If C is a relation-theoretic cycle in the adjacency relation, then $\{\{x, y\}: (x, y) \in C\}$ is a *cycle in the graph G*. Informally, a path between vertices a and b in a graph is a sequence of edges such that the first edge is (a, x) and the last edge is (y, b), and no edge appears more than once. A cycle is a path from a to a through at least one other vertex. The number of edges in a walk, path, or cycle is its *length*. A graph without a cycle is called *acyclic* or a *forest*. A connected acyclic graph is called a *tree*.

The *vertices on the walk*, *on the path*, or *on the cycle*, are those that belong to the edges of the walk, path, or cycle. If more than one walk or path exists between two vertices a and b, then those with the least possible length are called *geodesics* between a and b. The *distance* between a and b, denoted by $d(a, b)$, is the length of a geodesic, or 0 if $a = b$. A graph is *connected* if between any two distinct vertices there is a path. The distance in a connected graph is always defined and for any $a, b, c \in V$ there is the *triangle inequality*: $d(a, b) + d(b, c) \geqslant d(a, c)$. The *diameter* of a connected graph is the maximal distance or the length of the longest geodesic (Biggs 1990). A vertex $v \in V$ of a graph is a *cut-vertex* if removal of v results in a graph which is *disconnected* (no longer connected). The *vertex interval* between a and c, denoted by $I(a, c)$, is the set $\{b \in V: d(a, b) + d(b, c) = d(a, c)\}$. We say that $K \subseteq V$ is a *convex set* of vertices if $a, c \in K \Rightarrow I(a, c) \subseteq K$. Convex sets constitute an algebraic closure system on V.

Given two graphs $G_1 = \langle V_1, E_1 \rangle$ and $G_2 = \langle V_2, E_2 \rangle$, G_2 is a *subgraph* of G_1 if $V_2 \subseteq V_1$ and $E_2 \subseteq E_1$. If $G_2 \neq G_1$, then G_2 is a *proper subgraph* of G_1. If $V_2 = V_1$, then G_2 is a *spanning subgraph* of G_1. If G_2 is a tree, it is called a *spanning subtree* of G_1. If $E_2 = \{\{x, y\} \in E_1: x, y \in V_2\}$, then G_2 is called a *full* or *induced subgraph* of G_1.

Given two graphs $G_1 = \langle V_1, E_1 \rangle$ and $G_2 = \langle V_2, E_2 \rangle$, a function $\alpha: V_1 \rightarrow V_2$ is a *homomorphism* if for every $e \in E_1$, $\alpha(e) \in E_2$. If α is a bijection, then it is an *isomorphism*, and graphs G_1 and G_2 are *isomorphic*. Two graphs are the *same* or *equal* if they are isomorphic.

The *valency* of a vertex v in a graph $G = \langle V, E \rangle$ is the number of edges in G, elements of E, which contain v, denoted $\delta(v)$. Formally, $\delta(v) = |\{e \in E \mid v \in e\}|$. The sum of the values of the valency, taken over the vertices v in a graph, is equal to twice the number of edges:

$$\sum_{v \in V} \delta(v) = 2|E| \qquad (4.20)$$

For any graph G, the preorder closure of the adjacency relation is an equivalence relation on the set of vertices. The subgraph of G induced by each equivalence class is connected and is called a *connected component*. In a forest, all connected components are trees. In a tree, every path between distinct vertices is unique; a set of vertices is convex only if it induces a subgraph that is also a tree; the vertices on a path from a to b are the members of the interval $I(a, b)$.

An *orientation* of a graph $G = \langle V, E \rangle$ is a binary relation D on V which is irreflexive and antisymmetric such that $E = \{\{x, y\}: xDy\}$. A graph with an orientation is called a *directed graph* because the edges are really ordered pairs based on the relation D. Alternatively, a directed graph D is a set of vertices V and a subset A of $V \times V$, denoted $D = \langle V, A \rangle$. The members of A are often called *arcs*. Note that arcs in a directed graph are ordered pairs of vertices while the edges in a graph are unordered two-element sets of vertices—(x, y) versus $\{x, y\}$. In a directed graph, the *indegree* of a vertex is the number of edges which terminate at the vertex. For a vertex a, the indegree $\overleftarrow{\delta}(a)$ is the cardinality of the set $\{\{x, y\}: xDy \wedge y = a\}$. The *outdegree* of a vertex in a directed graph is the number of edges which originate at the vertex. For a vertex a, the outdegree $\overrightarrow{\delta}(a)$ is the cardinality of the set $\{\{x, y\}: xDy \wedge x = a\}$.

The following discussion on flowgraphs, from Fenton (1991), has somewhat of a software flavor, but can nevertheless be applied to nonsoftware domains. A *flowgraph* is a directed graph with a *start vertex*, the *source*, with indegree = 0, and a *stop vertex*, the *sink*, with outdegree = 0, and for which all other vertices lie on a walk. Vertices with an outdegree of one are *procedure vertices*. Vertices with an outdegree >1 are *predicate vertices*.

Flowgraphs can be *composed* by making the stop vertex of one flowgraph and the start vertex of another flowgraph coincide in the new composition flowgraph. This process can also be called *concatenation* or *sequencing*, a notion which cannot be applied to graphs in general. The inverse of composition is *decomposition* and involves removing an edge between two vertices to make two separate flowgraphs, each with its own start and stop vertices.

If x is a procedure vertex in the flowgraph F, you can create a new flowgraph $F(F'$ on $x)$ by making x the start vertex of F' and replacing the edge leading from x with the flowgraph F'. This is called *nesting* of flowgraphs and can be applied to directed graphs generally only if an edge is replaced by a flowgraph.

Prime flowgraphs are those which cannot be decomposed into other flowgraphs using nesting and sequencing. Every flowgraph has a unique decomposition into a hierarchy of prime flowgraphs. A flowgraph is fully described by its decomposition tree. Note that decomposition is an isomorphism between a flowgraph and its decomposition tree.

The *morphology* or *shape* of a graph can be expressed in a number of ways (Fenton 1991). A directed graph is a *directed tree* if it has only one vertex with indegree = 0, the *root vertex*, and more than one vertex with outdegree = 0, the *leaf vertices*. In any nondirected tree, any vertex lying on more than one edge can be the root vertex, and the leaf vertices are those lying on only one edge. All of these measures apply to directed and nondirected trees. Some apply to all graphs.

The *size* of a graph is the number of vertices, or $|V|$. The *depth* or *height* of a tree is the length of the longest path from the root vertex to a leaf vertex. The depth of a tree is also its diameter. A *level* of a tree is the set of vertices for which the distance to the root vertex is the same. Formally, a level is $\{v \in V: d(root, v) = x$ for some $x \in \mathbb{Z}\}$. The *name* of the level is x. The *width* of a tree is the cardinality of the maximal level—the level with the most vertices. The *girth* of a graph is the length of the smallest cycle contained in the graph. If the graph contains no cycles, then the girth = 0.

Tree impurity is, informally, the extent to which a graph deviates from being a tree (Fenton 1991). Tree impurity, denoted $m(G)$, has the following properties:

1. $m(G) = 0$ if and only if G is a tree.

2. $m(G_1) > m(G_2)$ if G_1 differs from G_2 only by the addition of an edge.

3. For $i = 1, 2$, let E_i denote the number of edges in G_i, and V_i the number of vertices; if $V_1 > V_2$ and $E_1 - V_1 + 1 = E_2 - V_2 + 1$, then $m(G_1) < m(G_2)$—the spanning subtree of G_1 has more edges than the spanning subtree of G_2, but the number of additional edges of the graph over and above the spanning subtree is the same in both cases.

4. For all graphs G, $m(G) \leq m(K_v) = 1$ where v is the number of vertices, $|V|$, and K_v is the complete graph with v vertices.

These properties mean that $m(G)$ lies in the interval $[0, 1]$ $(0 \leqslant m(G) \leqslant 1)$. The tree impurity measure is the number of edges in the graph G more than the spanning subtree of G divided by the maximal number of edges more than the spanning subtree of a complete graph with the same number of vertices as G. Formally,

$$m(G) = \frac{2(e - v + 1)}{(v - 1)(v - 2)} \tag{4.21}$$

where e is the number of edges, $|E|$, and v is the number of vertices, $|V|$.

CATEGORIES

Categories are based on the observation that many properties of mathematical systems can be represented more simply using a graphical language. Category theory was initially developed in the early 1940s as a language for discussing other structures. Categories were discovered in 1942 by Eilenburg and Mac Lane (Mac Lane 1994) as part of a study in another area of mathematics. During the late 1940s and into the 1950s, categories became a structure in their own right. Eilenburg and Mac Lane first studied categories as structures in 1945. Even today, category theorists are discovering new fundamental truths about categories. Many of these new discoveries are not universally accepted.

At first, categories present some strange concepts, and even some rather funny terminology. The important point is that categories are primarily a way to describe and discuss the properties of other mathematical objects from afar—a way to identify and discuss the common properties of different objects whose basic theories often use very different terminology for the same concept. Categories present a unifying approach to the study and manipulation of different structures. It is in this spirit that they are even included in this chapter. They provide the fundamental language and notation for discussing objects and classes in Chapter 6.

At its core, categorical notation consists of diagrams with arrows. Each arrow $f: X \to Y$ represents a function—a set X, a set Y, and a rule mapping $x \mapsto f\,x$ which assigns each element $x \in X$ to an element $f\,x \in Y$. Start with the basics and elaborate from there. We closely follow the outline of the first couple of chapters of Pierce's book (1991) because it provides a logical introduction of concepts for those new to categories.

Categories

A *category* C includes:

1. A collection of *objects*.

2. A collection of *arrows*, also called *morphisms*.

3. Operations assigning to each arrow f an object dom f, called its *domain*, and an object cod f, called its *codomain*—write $f: a \to b$ or $a \xrightarrow{f} b$ to show that dom $f = a$ and cod $f = b$; the collection of all arrows with domain a and codomain b is written $C(a, b)$ or $\hom(a, b)$.

4. A composition operator $\circ$ assigning to each pair of arrows f and g, with cod $f =$ dom g, a *composite* arrow $g \circ f$: dom $f \to$ cod g or $g\, f$: dom $f \to$ cod g, also written $g\, f$, which satisfies the following *associative law*: For any arrows $f: a \to b$, $g: b \to c$, and $h: c \to d$ (a, b, c, and d are not necessarily distinct objects), we have $h \circ (g \circ f) = (h \circ g) \circ f$.

5. For each object a, and *identity arrow* $\mathrm{id}_a: a \to a$ which satisfies the following *identity law*: For any arrow $f: a \to b$, we have $\mathrm{id}_b \circ f = f$ and $f \circ \mathrm{id}_a = f$.

A couple of examples will serve to illustrate these concepts. These particular examples were chosen because they appear over and over in the application of category theory to computer science. You will also see the second example show up frequently in measurement theory. As a notational convention, the names of "standard" or well-known categories such as these examples and those we define ourselves will be shown in boldface type.

As the first example, the category **Set** has as objects all sets and as arrows all total functions between sets. Composition of arrows is the usual set-theoretic function composition. Identity functions are the identity arrows. For each total function $f: a \to b$, we have dom $f = a$ and cod $f = b$ (here, a and b are sets). We know from set theory that functions can be composed, and that functional composition is associative, so the associativity law holds. Also, since the identity functions can be composed with any other function, the identity law holds.

The second example is the category **Poset**, which has as objects all partially ordered sets and as arrows all total functions which are order-preserving. Recall that a partial ordering $\leq_A$ on a set A is a reflexive, transitive, and antisymmetric relation on the elements of A for which:

1. $a \leq_A a$, for all $a \in A$.
2. $a \leq_A b \leq_A c$ implies $a \leq_A c$, for all $a, b, c \in A$.
3. $a \leq_A b$ and $b \leq_A a$ implies $a = b$, for all $a, b \in A$.

An *order-preserving* (or *monotone*) function from $\langle A, \leq_A \rangle$ to $\langle B, \leq_B \rangle$ is a function $f: A \to B$ such that $f\, a$, $f\, b \in B$ and $a \leq_A b$ implies $f\, a \leq_B f\, b$ for all $a, b \in A$. Since an order-preserving function on a partially ordered set is just a function on a set, composition of order-preserving functions holds and so does the associativity law. There is also for each partial order $\langle A, \leq_A \rangle$ an identity function id_A which is order-preserving and satisfies the identity law.

It is sometimes convenient to identify the identity arrow id_a with the object a itself, writing $\mathrm{id}_a: a \to a$, or $1_a = a = \mathrm{id}_a$ as may be convenient. Any object is thus completely interchangeable with its identity arrow, leading to discussions which are "arrows-only." An *arrows-only category* C consists of arrows, certain ordered pairs $\langle g, f \rangle$, called the *composable pairs* of arrows, and an operation assigning to each composable pair $\langle g, f \rangle$ an arrow $g\, f$, called its *composite*. If $\langle g, f \rangle$ is a composable pair, we say that $g\, f$ is defined. An identity arrow u of C is defined to be an arrow $f\,u = f$ whenever $f\,u$ is defined and $u\,g = g$ whenever $u\,g$ is defined. The arrows must then satisfy the following axioms:

1. The composite $(h\,g)\,f$ is defined if and only if the composite $h\,(g\,f)$ is defined. When either is defined, they are equal, and the triple composite is written as $h\,g\,f$.
2. The triple composite $h\,g\,f$ is defined whenever both $h\,g$ and $g\,f$ are defined.
3. For each arrow g of C, there exist identity arrows u and u' of C such that $u'\,g$ and $g\,u$ are defined.

The arrows of any objects-and-arrows category satisfy these arrows-only axioms. Likewise, an arrows-only category satisfies the objects-and-arrows axioms if the identity arrows are taken as objects. Thus, any category can be treated either as objects-and-arrows or arrows-only as may be convenient.

Nine other categories are presented, not so much as examples, but because they will be useful in our further discussions as they have some interesting properties. The category **0** has no objects and no arrows. The category **1** has object and one arrow, the identity arrow for the object. The category **2** has two objects, two identity arrows, and one non-identity arrow from one object to the other. It does not matter which object is the domain of this arrow. The category **2** is represented graphically by:

$$id_a \left(\quad a \xrightarrow{\quad\quad f \quad\quad} b \quad \right) id_b \qquad (4.22)$$

The category $\downarrow\!\downarrow$ is a category with two objects, two identity arrows, and two nonidentity arrows with the same domain and codomain, which are called *parallel arrows*. This category is represented by:

$$id_a \left(\quad a \underset{g}{\overset{f}{\rightrightarrows}} b \quad \right) id_b \qquad (4.23)$$

The category **3** has three objects—call them a, b, and c—three identity arrows, and three other arrows: $f: a \to b$, $g: b \to c$, and $h: a \to c$. Category **3** can be depicted graphically as:

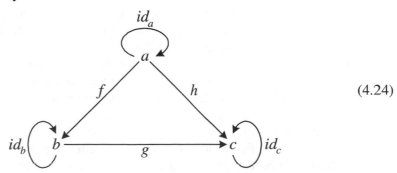

$$(4.24)$$

A *monoid* is a category with one object. Each monoid is determined by the set of all of its arrows, the identity arrow, and the rule for composition of arrows. Since any two arrows have a composite, a monoid can be described as a set M with a binary operation $M \times M \to M$ which is associative and has an identity. These operations can be defined as $\mu\colon M \times M \to M$ and $\eta\colon \mathbf{1} \to M$ such that the diagram

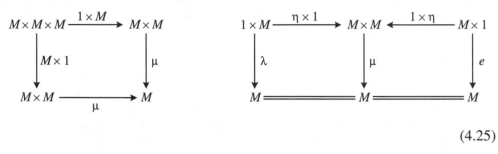

$$(4.25)$$

commutes, where $\lambda\langle 0, x \rangle = x$ and $e\langle x, 0 \rangle = x$. Categories and monoids share a special relationship. For any category C and any object $a \in C$, the set $\hom(a, a)$ of all arrows $a \to a$ forms a monoid.

A *group* is a category with one object in which every arrow has a two-sided inverse under composition. A preorder is a category P in which, given objects p and p', there is at most one arrow $p \to p'$. In any such preorder P, define a binary relation $\leqslant$ on the objects with $p \leqslant p'$ if and only if there is an arrow $p \to p'$ in P. This binary relation is reflexive since there is an identity arrow $p \to p$ for each object p. It is transitive because the arrows can be composed. The category δ has as objects all finite ordinals and as arrows all order-preserving functions $f\colon m \to n$ ($i \leqslant j$ in $m \Rightarrow f\, i \leqslant f\, j$ in n). We call this the *simplical category*. Note that the categories monoid and group just described also describe exactly the algebraic structures monoid and group which were covered in the section on group structures. Note also that the definition of preorder just given describes exactly the axioms for a preorder in set theory: a set with a reflexive transitive binary relation.

Every algebraic structure (system) covered in the section on group structures can be represented as a category. These specific systems are presented because of their usefulness in the measurement of software. Generally, the elements of the system's underlying sets will be the objects and suitable functions which preserve the system's internal structure will be the arrows. Universal algebras can be represented as categories along these same lines. This fact forms the basis for the model of objects presented in Chapter 6.

A category is *discrete* when all of its arrows are identity arrows. Every set X is the set of objects of a discrete category and every discrete category is determined by its objects. Thus, discrete categories are sets and every set can become a category by adding an arrow $x \to x$ for each $x \in X$.

Given any arbitrary category C, you can view the objects as *formulas* and the arrows as *proofs*. An arrow $f\colon a \to b$ is considered a proof of the logical implication $a \Rightarrow b$. The identity arrow $\mathrm{id}_a\colon a \to a$ represents the reflexivity axiom $a \Rightarrow$

a, and composition of arrows represents the transitivity of implication, as given by the inference rule:

$$\frac{f\colon a \to b;\ g\colon b \to c}{g \circ f\colon a \to c} \tag{4.26}$$

The concept of *duality* plays a major role in category theory. In simple terms, duality means to "reverse all arrows." For a category *C*, the objects of the *dual category* C^{op} are the same as those in *C*. The arrows in C^{op} are the opposites of those in *C*. That is, an arrow $f\colon a \to b$ in *C* corresponds to an arrow $f\colon b \to a$ in C^{op}. Most definitions in category theory come in dual pairs: product/coproduct, pullback/pushout, and so on, with a "co-*x*" in category *C* being the same as *x* in C^{op}. Further, any statement about a category can be transformed into a statement about its dual by exchanging the words "domain" and "codomain" and reversing the order of composition. If a statement *S* is true of a category *C*, the statement S^{op} is true of the category C^{op} by definition. This very important property, called the *duality principle*, is used to get two results for the price of one: You only have to prove a result in one category and its dual result is automatically proved in the dual category.

A category *B* is a *subcategory* of *C* if each object of *B* is an object of *C*, for all objects *b* and *b'* in *B*, $B(b, b') \subseteq C(b, b')$, and composites and identity arrows in *B* are the same in *C*.

Diagrams

The graphical representation of a category can be formalized using the notion of a *diagram*. A diagram in a category *C* is a directed graph, that is, a collection of *vertices*, labeled as the objects of *C*, and *directed edges*, labeled as the arrows of *C*. In a diagram in *C*, an arrow $f\colon a \to b$ is represented by a directed edge from *a* to *b* and labeled *f*. Diagrams are often used to state and prove properties of categorical constructions. You can think of it as a graphical proof; this notion will become very handy in discussions about the behavior of software. A statement about a category is represented by a walk through the diagram. Composition of arrows in represented by following a sequence of edges. Two sets of statements are equivalent if their respective walks through the diagram start and end at the same pair of objects (have a common *source* and a common *sink*). Normally, you include in a diagram only those statements you are exploring. Otherwise, the diagram of even a small category can become very messy very quickly.

When you have two or more equivalent sets of statements in a diagram, it is said the diagram *commutes*. Formally, a diagram in a category *C* commutes, or *is commutative*, if, for every pair of vertices *x* and *y* in *C*, all the walks in the diagram from *x* to *y* yield, by the composition of labels, equal arrows from *x* to *y*. The associative law can be represented by the commutative diagram:

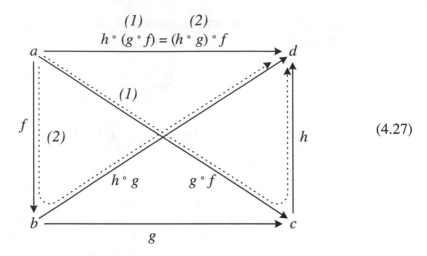

$$(4.27)$$

The unit law can be represented by the commutative diagram:

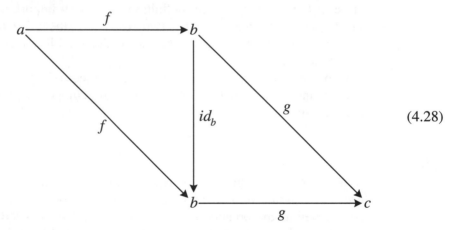

$$(4.28)$$

Commutative diagrams can be "composed" by overlaying their common objects and arrows. Because of arrow composition, the composition of two or more commutative diagrams also commutes. For example, if the diagrams

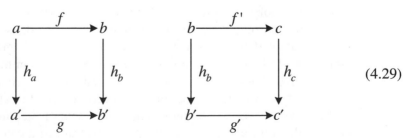

$$(4.29)$$

both commute, then the composite diagram

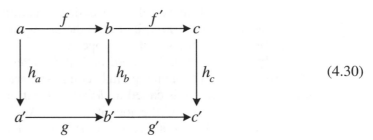

(4.30)

also commutes. If the two inner squares (the original diagrams) commute, then the outer rectangle (the composite diagram) also commutes. This is a general property of commutative diagrams.

Monis, Epis, Isomorphisms, and Idempotents

An arrow $f: b \to c$ in a category C is a *monimorphism*, or a *moni*, or *is monic*, if, for any pair of arrows in C $g: a \to b$ and $h: a \to b$, the equality $f\,g = f\,h$ implies that $g = h$. A moni is *left-cancelable* since it can always be canceled when it appears on the left. In **Set**, the monis are the injective functions, but this does not hold in all categories. The composite of two monis is also monic. If a composite $g\,f$ is monic, so is f.

An arrow $f: a \to b$ in a category C is an *epimorphism*, or an *epi*, or *is epic*, if, for any pair of arrows in C $g: b \to c$ and $h: b \to c$, the equality $g\,f = h\,f$ implies that $g = h$. An epi is *right-cancelable*, since it can always be canceled when it appears on the right. In **Set**, the epis are the surjective functions, but again, this does not hold in all categories. The composite of two epis is also epic. If a composite $g\,f$ is epic, so is g.

An arrow $f: a \to b$ is an *isomorphism* if there is an arrow $f^{-1}: b \to a$, called the *inverse of f*, such that $f^{-1} \circ f = \mathrm{id}_a$ and $f \circ f^{-1} = \mathrm{id}_b$. The objects a and b are said to be *isomorphic*. Two objects that are isomorphic are often said to be *identical up to an isomorphism* or *within an isomorphism*. An object a with a property P is said to be *unique up to an isomorphism* if every object satisfying P is isomorphic to a.

A *left inverse* for an arrow $h: a \to b$ is an arrow $l: b \to a$ with $l \circ h = \mathrm{id}_a$, and is called a *retraction* for h. Any arrow with a left inverse is monic. A *right inverse* for an arrow $h: a \to b$ is an arrow $r: b \to a$ with $h \circ r = \mathrm{id}_b$. A right inverse, which is usually not unique, is also called a *section* of h. If h has a right inverse, it is epic. If $g\,h = 1_a$, then h is a *split moni* and g is a *split epi*. The composite $f = h\,g$ is an *idempotent*. An arrow $f: b \to b$ is called *idempotent* when $f \circ f = f$, or $f^2 = f$. An idempotent is *split* when there exist arrows g and h such that $f = h \circ g$ and $g \circ h = 1$.

Universal Constructions

A *universal construction* is a class of objects and accompanying arrows that share a common property and pick out the terminal objects when the class is considered as a category. Each universal construction is paired with its dual, which is called a *co-universal construction*, in which the arrows are all reversed and pick out the initial objects with the specified property.

An object t is *terminal* or *final* in C if for every object a in C there is exactly one arrow $a \to t$ (which may include composite arrows). An arrow from a terminal object to any object a is called a *global element* or *constant* of a. If t is terminal, the only arrow $t \to t$ is the identity arrow. Any two terminal objects in C are isomorphic. Dually, an object s is *initial* in C if to every object a in C there is exactly one arrow $s \to a$. In the category **Set**, the empty set is an initial object and every singleton set is terminal. A *null object* z in C is an object which is both initial and terminal. If C has a null object, it is unique up to an isomorphism. For any two objects a and b of C, there is a unique arrow $a \to z \to b$ (the composite through z) called the *zero arrow* from a to b. Any composite with a zero arrow is also a zero arrow.

Two of the more common and important universal constructions are that of a product and its dual, the coproduct. A *product* of two objects a and b in a category C is an object $a \times b$, together with two *projection arrows* $\pi_1 \colon a \times b \to a$ and $\pi_2 \colon a \times b \to b$, such that for any object c and pair of arrows $f \colon c \to a$ and $g \colon c \to b$ there is exactly one *mediating arrow* $\langle f, g \rangle \colon c \to a \times b$, making the diagram

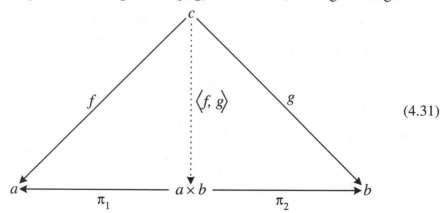

(4.31)

commute—that is, $\pi_1 \circ \langle f, g \rangle = f$ and $\pi_2 \circ \langle f, g \rangle = g$. Dashed arrows are used to indicate arrows which we assert to exist in a commutative diagram when the rest of the diagram is filled in appropriately. If a category C has a product $a \times b$ for every pair of objects a and b, we say that C has *all binary products*, or *has products*. Although we usually refer to the object $a \times b$ as the product, it is important to remember that the arrows π_1 and π_2 are also part of the definition. It is more accurate to define the product as the tuple $\langle a \times b, \pi_1, \pi_2 \rangle$.

The dual notion of the product is the coproduct and corresponds to set-theoretic symmetric difference, while the product corresponds to set-theoretic Cartesian product or cross product. A *coproduct* of two objects a and b is an object $a + b$, together with two *injection arrows* $\iota_1 \colon a \to a + b$ and $\iota_2 \colon b \to a + b$, such that for any object c and any pair of arrows $f \colon a \to c$ and $g \colon b \to c$ there is exactly one arrow $[f, g] \colon a + b \to c$, making the diagram

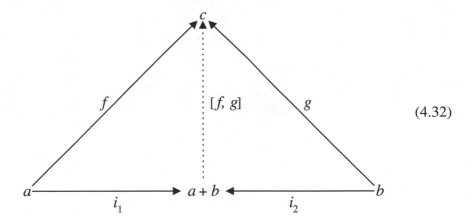

(4.32)

commute.

You can generalize the notions of product and coproduct to families of objects. The product of a family $(a_i)_{i \in I}$ of objects indexed by a set I consists of an object $\Pi_{i \in I} A_i$ and a family of projection arrows $(\pi_i: (\Pi_{i \in I} a_i) \to a_i)_{i \in I}$ such that for each object c and family of arrows $(f_i: c \to a_i)_{i \in I}$ there is a unique arrow $\langle f_i \rangle_{i \in I}: c \to (\Pi_{i \in I} a_i)$ such that the diagram

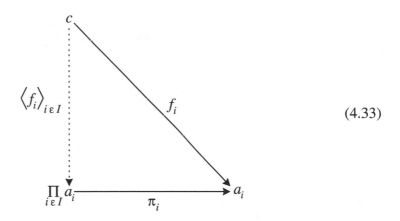

(4.33)

commutes for all $i \in I$.

The coproduct of a family $(a_i)_{i \in I}$ of objects consists of an object $\Sigma_{i \in I} a_i$ and a family of injection arrows $(\iota_i: a_i \to (\Sigma_{i \in I} a_i))_{i \in I}$ such that for each object c and family of arrows $(f_i: a_i \to c)_{i \in I}$ there is a unique arrow $[f_i]_{i \in I}: (\Sigma_{i \in I} a_i) \to c$ such that the diagram

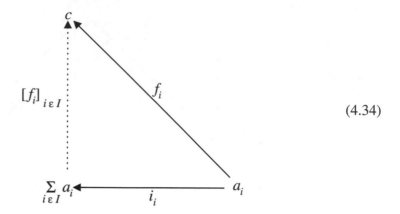

(4.34)

commutes.

A second basic universal construction is the equalizer of two arrows. An arrow $e: x \to a$ is an *equalizer* of a pair of arrows $f: a \to b$ and $g: a \to b$ if $f\,e = g\,e$ and whenever $e': x' \to a$ satisfies $f\,e' = g\,e'$, there is a unique arrow $k: x' \to x$ such that $e \circ k = e'$, making the diagram

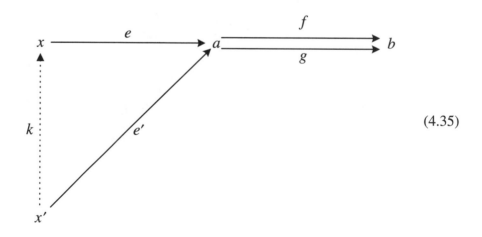

(4.35)

commute.

The dual of an equalizer is called a coequalizer. Given a pair of arrows $f, g: a \to b$, a *coequalizer* of $\langle f, g \rangle$ is an arrow $u: b \to x$ such that $u\,f = u\,g$, and if $k: x \to x'$ has $k\,y = u'$, then $k\,u = u'$ for a unique arrow $u': b \to x'$. Graphically, a coequalizer is:

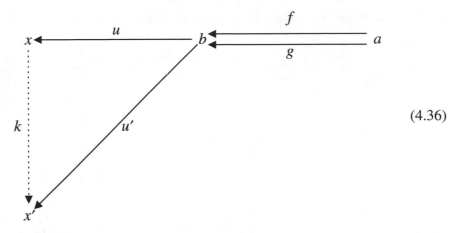

(4.36)

Another important categorical construct is the pullback of two arrows. A *pullback* of two arrows $f: a \to c$ and $g: b \to c$ is an object p and a pair of arrows $g': p \to a$ and $f': p \to b$ such that $f\,g' = g\,f'$

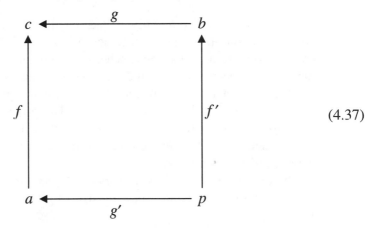

(4.37)

and if $i: x \to a$ and $j: x \to b$ are such that $f\,i = g\,j$

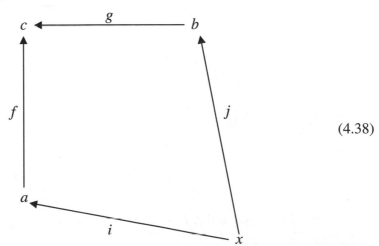

(4.38)

then there is a unique $k: x \rightarrow p$ such that $i = g' k$ and $j = f' k$

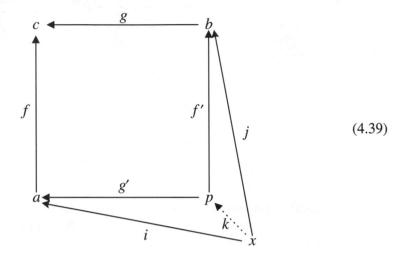

(4.39)

The arrow f' is commonly called a pullback or *inverse image* of f along g, and g' is commonly called a pullback of g along f. The source of this terminology comes from the category **Set**, which is often the case in category theory. If, in **Set**, the arrows $f: a \rightarrow c$ and $g: b \rightarrow c$ exist, with common codomain c, the pullback object p is the subset of the Cartesian product $a \times b$ defined by $p = \{(x, y) \mid x \in a, y \in b, \text{ and } f(x) = g(y)\}$. The projections f' and g' are defined by $f'(a, b) = b$ and $g'(a, b) = a$. It is helpful to think of the pullback as a kind of constrained product, where the constraints are the equations which make the first diagram (4.37) commute.

The dual of a pullback is a *pushout*. A *pushout* of two arrows $f: c \rightarrow a$ and $g: c \rightarrow b$ is an object p and a pair of arrows $g': a \rightarrow p$ and $f': b \rightarrow p$ such that $g' f = f' g$

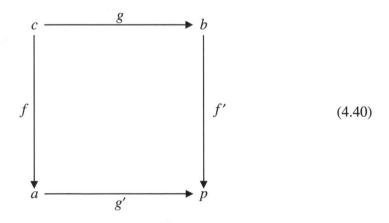

(4.40)

and if $i: a \rightarrow x$ and $j: b \rightarrow x$ are such that $i f = j g$

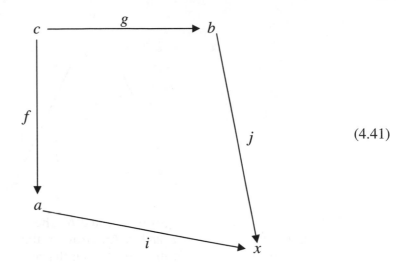

(4.41)

then there is a unique $k: p \longrightarrow x$ such that $i = k\ g'$ and $j = k\ f'$

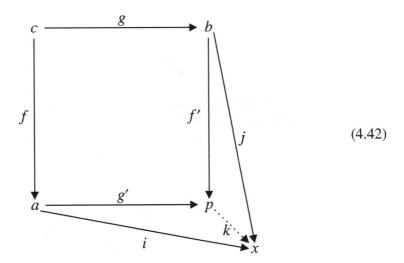

(4.42)

You can generalize the notion of universal and co-universal constructions to generic relationships between objects. Given two objects a and b in a category C, you can describe a class of tuples $\langle x, x_1, x_2 \rangle$ where $x_1: x \longrightarrow a$ and $x_2: x \longrightarrow b$:

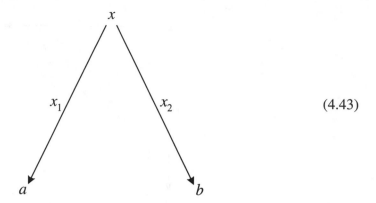

$$(4.43)$$

These tuples are called *wedges* over a and b. These wedges form the objects of a *category of wedges* over a and b. An arrow in this category, m: $\langle w, w_1, w_2 \rangle \rightarrow \langle x, x_1, x_2 \rangle$, is an arrow in C, m: $w \rightarrow x$, such that $w_1 = x_1 m$ and $w_2 = x_2 m$:

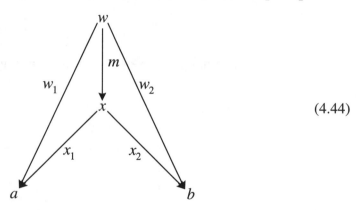

$$(4.44)$$

A terminal object in the category of wedges, say $\langle t, t_1, t_2 \rangle$, is one with a unique arrow to it from each wedge:

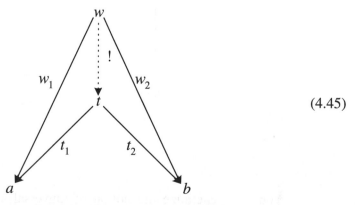

$$(4.45)$$

The objects defined by a universal construction are said to *be universal among* those objects having the given property. The objects are also said to *have the universal property*.

Limits

The universal and co-universal constructions seen so far, including the concept of wedges, are a specific instance of the still more general notions of limits and colimits. Let C be a category and D a diagram in C. A *cone* for D is an object x in C and arrows $f_i \colon x \to d_i$, where each d_i is an object in D, such that for each arrow g in D, the diagram

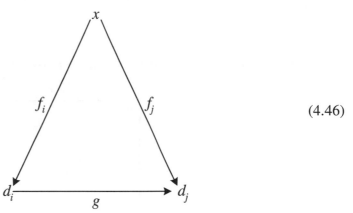

(4.46)

commutes. Denote a cone by $\{f_i \colon x \to d_i\}$.

A *limit* for a diagram D is a cone $\{f_i \colon x \to d_i\}$ with the property that if $\{f_i' \colon x' \to d_i\}$ is another cone for D, then there is a unique arrow $k \colon x' \to x$ such that the diagram

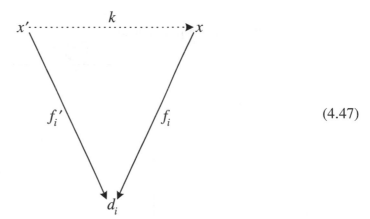

(4.47)

commutes for every d_i in D.

The cones for a diagram D form a category and a limit is a terminal object in this category. Since terminal objects are unique up to isomorphism, so are limits.

An example might help. Let D be the diagram:

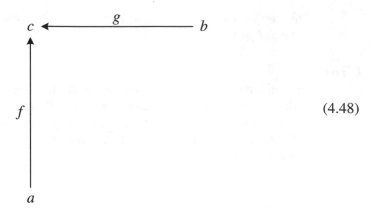

(4.48)

A cone for D is an object x and three arrows f', g', and h such that the diagram

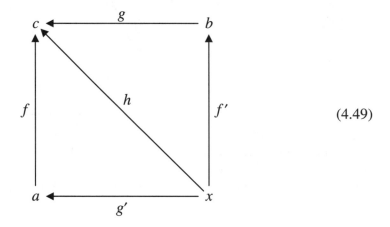

(4.49)

commutes. This is equivalent to

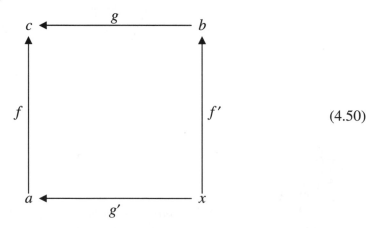

(4.50)

since $f\,g' = g\,f' = h$.

If x, f', and g' form a limit, then they have the universal property among objects and arrows which makes diagram (4.50) commute. That is, given any object x' with arrows f'', g'', and h' making the diagram

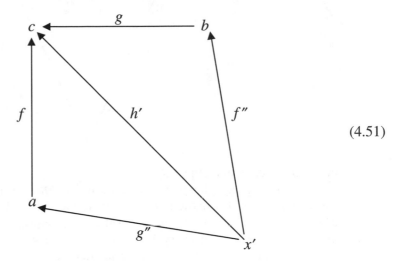

(4.51)

commute, there will be a unique arrow $k : x' \rightarrow x$ such that $f'' = f' k$, $g'' = g' k$, and $h' = h\, k$, as shown by:

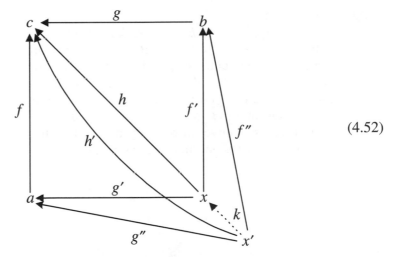

(4.52)

Since $f\, g'' = h' = g\, f''$, you can ignore h', showing that a limit of D is a pullback of f and g.

The dual of a cone is a cocone. The dual of a limit is a colimit. A *cocone* for a diagram D in C is an object x of C and a collection of arrows $f_i: d_i \rightarrow x$ such that $f_j\, g = f_i$ for each g in D. A *colimit* or *inverse limit* for D is a cocone $\{f_i: d_i \rightarrow x\}$ with the co-universal property that for any other cocone $\{f'_i: d_i \rightarrow x'\}$ there is a unique arrow $k: x \rightarrow x'$ such that the diagram

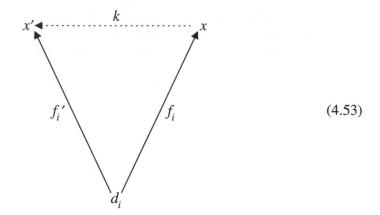

$$(4.53)$$

commutes for every object d_i in D.

Not all diagrams have limits or colimits. One of the more useful pieces of information about a particular category is knowing whether it does, in fact, have a limit. The *limit theorem* states that if D is a diagram in C with sets V of vertices and E of edges, and if every V-indexed and every E-indexed family of objects in C has a product and every pair of arrows in C has an equalizer, then D has a limit.

Exponentiation

In set theory, if A and B are sets, the collection $B^A = \{f: A \rightarrow B\}$ of all functions with domain A and codmain B is itself a set. In some categories C, the set of arrows with domain a and codomain b, denoted $C(a, b)$, is representable as an object b^a of C. This does not hold for all categories. To present this notion in categorical terms, you need to define a function eval: $(B^A \times A) \rightarrow B$ as eval(f, a) $= f(a)$. On input (f, a), with $f: A \rightarrow B$ and $a \in A$, we get $f(a) \in B$. Note that eval posseses a universal property among all functions $g: (C \times A) \rightarrow B$: for each g, there is exactly one function curry$(g): C \rightarrow B^A$ such that the diagram

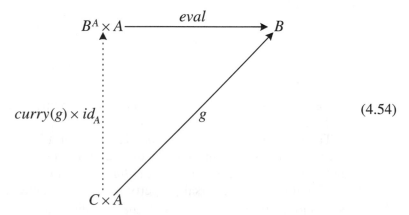

$$(4.54)$$

commutes. The arrow curry(g) $\times$ id$_A$ denotes a product mapping. On input (c, a), it yields (curry(g)(c), a).

Any given $c \in C$ determines a function in B^A by fixing the first argument of g to be c and leaving the second argument free. Define g_c to be the curried version of g for a given $c \in C$: $g_c(a) = g(c, a)$. Thus curry(g) is the function that takes each c to the appropriate curried version of g: curry(g)$(c) = g_c$. Now, for any $(c, a) \in C \times A$, you have:

$$(\text{eval} \circ (\text{curry}(g) \times id_A))(c, a) = \text{eval}(\text{curry}(g)(c), a)$$

$$= \text{eval}(g_c, a)$$

$$= g_c(a)$$

$$= g(c, a). \tag{4.55}$$

Not only does curry make diagram (4.54) commute, it is the only function which does so.

Formally, given a category C with all binary products with objects a and b, an object b^a is an exponential object if there is an arrow eval$_{ab}$: $(b^a \times a) \rightarrow b$ such that for any object c and arrow g: $(c \times a) \rightarrow b$ there is a unique arrow curry(g): $c \rightarrow b^a$, making

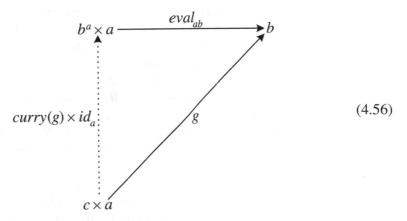

$$\tag{4.56}$$

commute. That is, eval$_{ab}$(curry(g) $\times$ id$_a$) = g.

If a category C has an exponential b^a for every pair of objects a and b, then C is said to *have exponentiation*. Categories with exponentials and products for all pairs of objects are special enough to have a name: A *Cartesian closed category* (CCC) is a category with a terminal object, binary products, and exponentiation.

Functors

A *functor* is a morphism between categories. For categories B and C, a functor T: $C \rightarrow B$ with domain C and codomain B consists of two related functions:

1. The *object function* T assigns each object $c \in C$ to an object $T c \in B$.
2. The *arrow function* T assigns each arrow $f: c \rightarrow c'$ in C to an arrow $T f: T c \rightarrow T c'$ in B such that $T(\mathrm{id}_c) = \mathrm{id}_{Tc}$ and $T(g \circ f) = T g \circ T f$ whenever $f \circ g$ is defined in C.

Like categories, functors can be described in an arrows-only fashion. A functor is a function $T: C \rightarrow B$ from the arrows f in C to the arrows $T f$ in B, such that each identity in C is mapped to an identity in B and each composable pair $\langle f, g \rangle$ in C is mapped to a composable pair $\langle T g, T f \rangle$ in B with $T g \circ T f = T(g \circ f)$.

A functor which "forgets" some or all of the structure of an algebraic system is called a *forgetful* or *underlying* functor. Forgetful functors make possible the mappings of a structured system, such as a group, to a much simpler, underlying system, such as a set. The arrows in the more structured system are mapped to their underlying cousins.

Functors may be composed. Given two functors $C \xrightarrow{T} B \xrightarrow{S} A$ between categories A, B, and C, the composite functions $c \mapsto S(T c)$ and $f \mapsto S(T f)$ on objects c and arrows f of C define a functor $S \circ T: C \rightarrow A$, called the *composite* of S with T. For each category B there is an identity functor $I_B: B \rightarrow B$ which acts as an identity for functor composition.

An *isomorphism* $T: C \rightarrow B$ is a functor T from C to B which is a bijection on both arrows and objects. Equivalently, a functor $T: C \rightarrow B$ is an isomorphism if and only if there is a functor $S: B \rightarrow C$ for which both the composites $S \circ T$ and $T \circ S$ are identity functors. S is the *two-sided inverse* of T, $S = T^{-1}$.

A functor $T: C \rightarrow B$ is *full* when to every pair c, c' of objects of C and to every arrow $g: T c \rightarrow T c'$ of B, there is an arrow $f: c \rightarrow c'$ of C with $g = T f$. The composite of two full functors is full. A functor $T: C \rightarrow B$ is *faithful*, or is *an embedding*, when to every pair c, c' of objects and to every pair $f_1, f_2: c \rightarrow c'$ of parallel arrows in C, the equality $T f_1 = T f_2: T c \rightarrow T c'$ implies that $f_1 = f_2$. Composites of faithful functors are faithful. Faithfulness is not a complementary or dual property to forgetfulness.

All of the functors described so far are *covariant* functors. A *contravariant* functor is one which maps objects to objects as before, but maps arrows to arrows in the opposite direction. Thus, a contravariant functor $\overline{T}: C \rightarrow B$ maps each object c of C to an object $\overline{T} c$ of B, and each arrow $f: c \rightarrow c'$ of C to an arrow $\overline{T} f: \overline{T} c' \rightarrow \overline{T} c$ of B. A contravariant functor from C to B is the same as a covariant functor from C^{op} to B.

Natural Transformations

Given two functors S, $T: C \rightarrow B$, a *natural transformation* $\tau: S \xrightarrow{\cdot} T$ is a function which assigns to each object c of C and arrow $\tau_c = \tau c: S c \rightarrow T c$ of B in such a way that every arrow $f: c \rightarrow c'$ in C yields a commutative diagram:

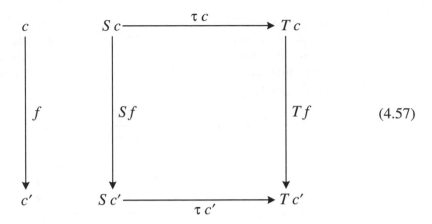

$$(4.57)$$

When this holds, τ_c: $S\,c \rightarrow T\,c$ *is natural in* C. If you think of the functor S as giving a picture in B of all of the objects and arrows of C, then a natural transformation τ is a set of arrows *mapping* or *translating* the picture S into the picture T. Alternatively, τ may be thought of as *superimposing* the picture S onto the picture T, or *morphing* S into T. You can represent this morphing with the commutative diagram:

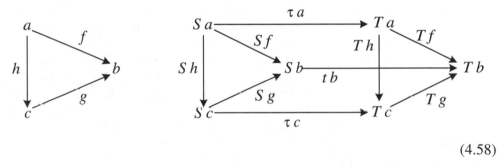

$$(4.58)$$

$\tau\,a$, $\tau\,b$, and $\tau\,c$ are the *components* of τ. A natural transformation is often called a *morphism* of functors.

An arrow e: $a \rightarrow b$ is *invertible* in C if there is an arrow e': $b \rightarrow a$ in C with $e' \circ e = \mathrm{id}_a$ and $e \circ e' = \mathrm{id}_b$. If such an e' exists, it is unique and is written as $e' = e^{-1}$. Two objects a and b are *isomorphic* in a category C if there is an invertible arrow (an isomorphism) e: $a \rightarrow b$. When this holds, write $a \cong b$. The relation isomorphism is reflexive, symmetric, and transitive (it is an equivalence relation).

A natural transformation τ with every component $\tau\,c$ invertible in B is called a *natural equivalence*, or better, a *natural isomorphism*. In symbols, τ: $S \cong T$. The inverses $(\tau\,c)^{-1}$ in B are the components of a natural transformation τ^{-1}: $T \overset{\cdot}{\rightarrow} S$. An *equivalence* between categories C and D is defined as a pair of functors S: $C \rightarrow D$, T: $D \rightarrow C$ together with a natural isomorphism $I_C \cong T \circ S$, $I_D \cong S \circ T$. This allows you to compare categories which are "alike" but of very different "sizes" (the size of a category is given by the number of objects it contains).

Given categories C and B, you can consider all functors $R, S, T,...: C \to B$. If $\sigma: R \xrightarrow{\cdot} S$ and $\tau: S \xrightarrow{\cdot} T$ are two natural transformations, their components for each $c \in C$ define composite arrows $(\tau \cdot \sigma)\, c = \tau\, c \circ \sigma\, c$ which are the components of a transformation $\tau \cdot \sigma: R \xrightarrow{\cdot} T$. The composite $\tau \cdot \sigma$ is a natural transformation since the diagram

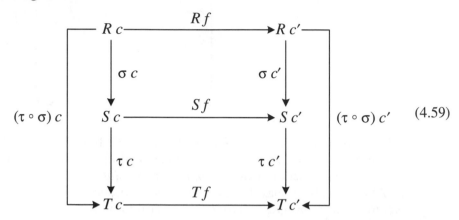

$$(\tau \circ \sigma)\, c \qquad\qquad\qquad\qquad\qquad\qquad (\tau \circ \sigma)\, c' \qquad (4.59)$$

commutes. The composition of natural transformations is associative. Further, each functor T has an identity, the natural transformation $\iota_T: T \to T$ with components $\iota_{TC} = 1_{TC}$. Hence, given categories B and C, you can construct a functor category $B^C = \mathrm{Funct}(C, B)$ with objects the functors $T: C \to B$ and arrows the natural transformations between pairs of functors. The set of arrows, the *hom-set*, for this category is variously written as $\mathrm{Nat}(S, T) = B^C(S, T) = \{\tau \mid \tau: S \xrightarrow{\cdot} T \text{ natural}\}$.

Functor categories are used often. For any category B, the functor category B^1 is isomorphic to B, $B^1 = \mathrm{Funct}(\mathbf{1}, B) = \{T \mid T: \mathbf{1} \to B\}$. The functor category B^2 is called the category of arrows of B, $B^2 = \{T \mid T: \mathbf{2} \to B\}$. The objects of B^2 are arrows $f: a \to b$ of B and its arrows $f \to f'$ are those pairs $\langle h, k \rangle$ of arrows in B for which the square

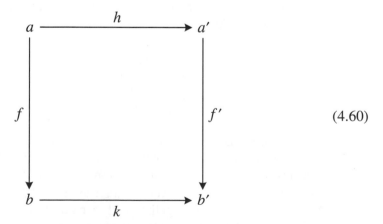

$$(4.60)$$

commutes.

So far, the composition of natural transformations between functors which are between the same two categories has been defined, as in the diagram:

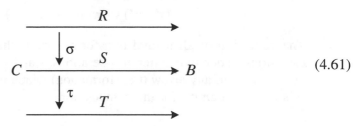

$$(4.61)$$

Such composition is often called *vertical*, for obvious reasons. There is another form of composition called *horizontal*. Given the functors and natural transformations in the diagram

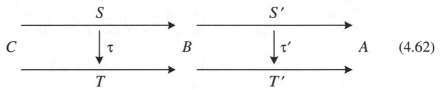

$$(4.62)$$

you may form first the composite functors $S' \circ S$ and $T' \circ T$: $C \to A$, then construct a square

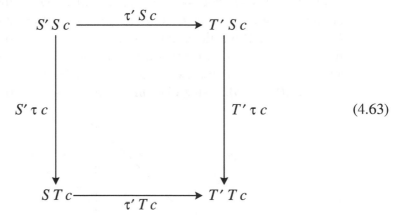

$$(4.63)$$

which commutes because τ and τ' are both natural. Now, define $(\tau' \circ \tau) c$ to be the *diagonal* for this square: $(\tau' \circ \tau) c = T' \tau c \circ \tau' S c = \tau' S c \circ S' \tau c$. $\tau' \circ \tau$: $S' S \xrightarrow{\cdot} T' T$ is natural. The composition $\langle \tau, \tau' \rangle \to \tau' \circ \tau$ is also associative and has identities. More generally, given three categories and four transformations

$$(4.64)$$

the vertical and horizontal transformations are related by the identity (the *interchange law*):

$$(\tau' \cdot \sigma') \circ (\tau \cdot \sigma) = (\tau' \circ \tau) \cdot (\sigma' \circ \sigma) \tag{4.65}$$

The collection of all natural transformations is the set of arrows of two different categories under two different operations, $\cdot$ and $\circ$, which satisfy the interchange law. Moreover, any arrow (transformation) which is an identity for the composition $\circ$ is also an identity for the composition $\cdot$.

Product Categories

Given two categories B and C, we construct a new category $B \times C$, called the *product* of B and C. An object of $B \times C$ is a pair $\langle b, c \rangle$ of objects $b \in B$ and $c \in C$. An arrow $\langle b, c \rangle \rightarrow \langle b', c' \rangle$ of $B \times C$ is a pair $\langle f, g \rangle$ of arrows $f: b \rightarrow b'$ in B and $g: c \rightarrow c'$ in C. The composite of two arrows in $B \times C$

$$\langle b, c \rangle \xrightarrow{\langle f, g \rangle} \langle b', c' \rangle \xrightarrow{\langle f', g' \rangle} \langle b'', c'' \rangle \tag{4.66}$$

is defined in terms of the composites in B and C by $\langle f', g' \rangle \circ \langle f, g \rangle = \langle f' \circ f, g' \circ g \rangle$.

Functors $B \xleftarrow{P} B \times C \xrightarrow{Q} C$ are called *projections* of the product and are defined on arrows by $P \langle f, g \rangle = f$ and $Q \langle f, g \rangle = g$, and on objects by $P \langle b, c \rangle = b$ and $Q \langle b, c \rangle = c$. Projections have the property that given any category D and two functors $B \xleftarrow{R} D \xrightarrow{T} C$, there is a unique functor $F: D \rightarrow B \times C$ with $P \circ F = R$ and $Q \circ F = T$. These two conditions require that $F\,h$, for any arrow h in D, must be $\langle R\,h, T\,h \rangle$. Using diagrams, F is constructed by:

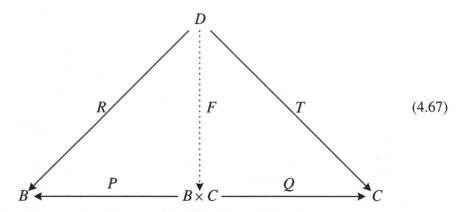

$$(4.67)$$

This property of the product category states that the projections P and Q are "universal" among pairs of functors between B and C. Product categories will prove very useful in your dealings with objects in software.

Two functors $U: B \rightarrow B'$ and $V: C \rightarrow C'$ have a product $U \times V: B \times C \rightarrow B' \times C'$ which may be defined on objects as $(U \times V)\langle b, c \rangle = \langle U\,b, U\,c \rangle$ and on arrows as $(U \times V)\langle f, g \rangle = \langle U\,f, V\,g \rangle$. This functor product $U \times V$ may be described as the unique functor which makes the diagram

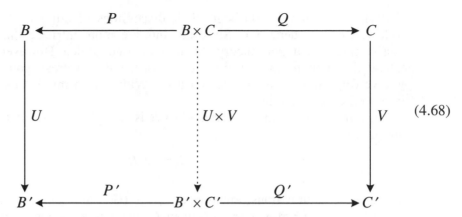

$$(4.68)$$

commute. The product operator $\times$ is a pair of functions:

1. To each pair B, C of categories a new category $B \times C$.

2. To each pair U, V of functors a new functor $U \times V$.

When $U' \circ U$ and $V' \circ V$ are defined, then $(U' \times V') \circ (U \times V) = (U' \circ U) \times (V' \circ V)$. Thus, the operator $\times$ is also a functor.

The definition of $F: D \rightarrow B \times C$ defines functor *to* a product category. A functor $S: B \times C \rightarrow D$ is a functor *from* a product category and is also called a *bifunctor on B and C*. Bifunctors are functors of two variables, one in B and one in C. Bifunctors occur frequently and are another useful category pattern. Given a bifunctor $S: B \times C \rightarrow D$, fixing one argument gives an ordinary functor on the remaining argument.

The bifunctor is thus determined by two arrays of one-variable functors in the following way. Let B, C, and D be categories. For all objects $c \in C$ and $b \in B$, let $L_c: B \rightarrow D$ and $M_b: C \rightarrow D$ be functors such that $M_b(c) = L_c(b)$ for all b and c. Then there exists a bifunctor $S: B \times C \rightarrow D$ with $S(-, c) = L_c$ for all c and $S(b, -)$ for all b if and only if for every pair of arrows $f: b \rightarrow b'$ and $g: c \rightarrow c'$ you have $M_{b'} g \circ L_c f = L_{c'} f \circ M_b g$. These equal arrows in D are then the values of $S(f, g)$ of the arrow function of S.

You may also form products of three or more categories, or combine the construction of opposite categories and process categories.

Given two functors S, S': $B \times C \rightarrow D$, define α to be a function which assigns to each pair of objects $b \in B$, $c \in C$ an arrow $\alpha(b, c)$: $S(b, c) \rightarrow S'(b, c)$ in D. Call α *natural in b* if for each $c \in C$ the components $\alpha(b, c)$ for all b define $\alpha(-, c)$: $S(-, c) \xrightarrow{\cdot} S'(-, c)$ as a natural transformation of functors $B \rightarrow D$. Call α *natural in c* if for each $b \in B$ the components for all c define $\alpha(b, -)$: $S(b, -) \xrightarrow{\cdot} S'(b, -)$ as a natural transformation of functors $C \rightarrow D$. A function α: $S \xrightarrow{\cdot} S'$ is a natural transformation of bifunctors if and only if $\alpha(b, c)$ is natural in b for each $c \in C$ and natural in c for each $b \in B$.

Adjoints

The notion of adjoint was developed by Kan in 1958 (Mac Lane 1994; Pierce 1991). Many mathematical constructs are examples of adjoints. Both Mac Lane

(1994) and Pierce (1991) begin their discussions of adjoints with an example, followed by the definition. Since adjoints are more intricate than anything else you've seen in category theory, this may be a good idea. However, this chapter is intended not to teach you about categories, but to refresh your memory when you've forgotten some specific construct. With that in mind, let's launch directly into the heart of adjoints.

An *adjunction* from categories C to B is a triple $\langle F, G, \varphi \rangle: C \rightharpoonup B$ where F and G are functors

$$C \underset{G}{\overset{F}{\rightleftarrows}} B \tag{4.69}$$

and φ is a natural transformation $\varphi: I_C \overset{.}{\rightarrow} (G \circ F)$ such that for each object $c \in C$ and each arrow $f: c \to G\,b$ in C, there is a unique arrow $f^{\#}: F\,c \to b$ in B making the diagram

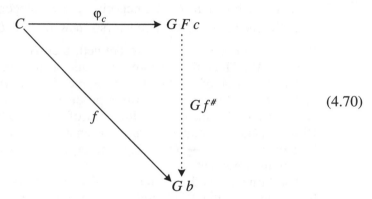

$$\tag{4.70}$$

commute. We call the pair $\langle F, G \rangle$ an *adjoint pair* of functors. F is the *left adjoint* of G, and G is the *right adjoint* of F. The natural transformation φ is the *unit* of the adjunction.

Each adjunction is associated with another natural transformation $\varepsilon: (F \circ G) \overset{.}{\rightarrow} I_B$, called the *counit* of the adjunction. The counit has the property that for each arrow $g: F\,c \to b$ in B there is a unique arrow $g^*: c \to G\,b$ in C making the diagram

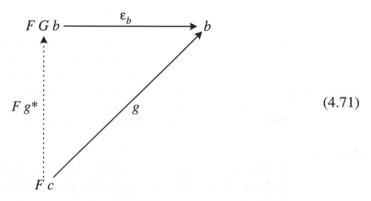

$$\tag{4.71}$$

commute. The existence of a unit transformation implies the existence of a counit transformation and vice versa. Thus, you can decide whether to look for a unit or counit as a matter of choice when you are trying to establish the existence of an adjunction. The unit and counit are not dual constructs, as duality was defined earlier in this section.

A given functor F may or may not have a right or left adjoint. The forgetful functor on several algebraic structures has a left adjoint, the *free algebra* functor, which takes a set A to the free algebra generated by the elements of A and a function $f: A \rightarrow A'$ to the homomorphic extension of f. The right adjoint, when it exists, usually defines a subset with some kind of closure property. Adjoints have many useful properties. Left adjoints preserve colimits and right adjoints preserve limits.

Normally, categorists think of adjoints in terms of an isomorphism between hom-sets $B(F\ c,\ b) \cong C(c,\ G\ b)$ that is natural in both c and b. That is, it is a two-variable natural transformation between hom-functors $B(f\ -,\ -)$ and $C(-,\ G\ -)$ that preserves structure as both c and b vary, and is also a bijection for all c and b. This bijection can be presented as:

$$\frac{c \rightarrow Gb}{Fc \rightarrow b} \tag{4.72}$$

Put yet another way, adjointness occurs when there is an exact correspondence between arrows $F\ c \rightarrow b$ in B and $c \rightarrow G\ b$ in C, making the diagram

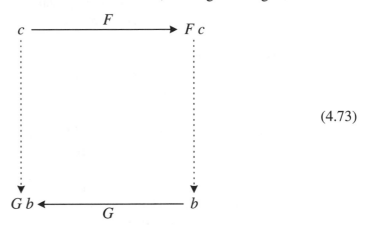

$$\tag{4.73}$$

commute.

For a short bit, let's explore some of the more esoteric properties of adjoints, universal arrows, and limits. There appears to be a strong connection among these concepts; exploiting these connections makes it easier to show that when two of the three exist, the third is present also.

Every adjunction yields a universal arrow. The hom-set $B(F\ c,\ b)$ contains the identity $1: F\ c \rightarrow F\ c$. Call the φ-image of this arrow η_c. By Yoneda's Proposition (Mac Lane 1994), this η_c is a universal arrow $\eta_c: c \rightarrow G\ F\ c$, $\eta_c = \varphi(1_{Fx})$, from $c \in C$ to G. The adjunction gives a universal arrow of this type for every object $c \in C$. Moreover, the function $c \mapsto \eta_c$ is a natural transformation $I_c \rightarrow G\ F$ because every diagram

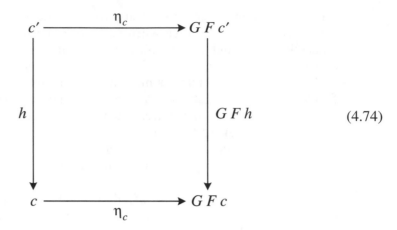

$$(4.74)$$

commutes. Yoneda's Proposition and Yoneda's lemma are very important contributions to category theory. You should consult Mac Lane (1994) to study these further.

Mac Lane (1994) gives a theorem that provides five different ways to construct an adjunction $\langle F, G, \varphi \rangle$: $C \rightharpoonup B$. Rather than reproduce the theorem, here is a list of the five methods:

1. With functors F, G, and a natural transformation η: $1c \xrightarrow{\cdot} G\,F$, where each η_c: $c \rightarrow G\,F\,c$ is universal from G to c, φ is defined by $\varphi\, f = G\,f \circ \eta_c$: $c \rightarrow b$.

2. With the functor G: $B \rightarrow C$, for each $c \in C$ an object $F_0\, c \in B$, and a universal arrow η_c: $c \rightarrow G\,F_0\, c$ from c to G, the functor F has F_0 as the object function and is defined on arrows h: $c \rightarrow c'$ by $G\,F\,h \circ \eta_c = \eta_{c'} \circ h$.

3. With functors F, G, and a natural transformation ε: $F\,G \xrightarrow{\cdot} I_B$ such that each ε_b: $F\,G\,b \rightarrow b$ is a universal arrow from F to b, φ^{-1} is defined by $\varphi^{-1}\, g = \varepsilon_b \circ F\,g$: $F\,c \rightarrow a$.

4. With the functor F: $C \rightarrow B$, for each $b \in B$ an object $G_0\, b \in C$, and a universal arrow ε_b: $F\,G_0\, b \rightarrow b$, the functor G has G_0 as the object function and is defined on arrows h: $b \rightarrow b'$ by $\varepsilon_b \circ F\,G\,h$.

5. With functors F, G and natural transformations η: $I_C \xrightarrow{\cdot} G\,F$ and ε: $F\,G \xrightarrow{\cdot} I_B$ such that both composites

$$G \xrightarrow{\eta G} G\,F\,G \xrightarrow{G\varepsilon} G \qquad \text{and} \qquad F \xrightarrow{F\eta} F\,G\,F \xrightarrow{\varepsilon F} F \qquad (4.75)$$

are identity transformations, φ is defined by $\varphi\, f = G\,f \circ \eta_c$: $c \rightarrow b$ and φ^{-1} is defined by $\varphi^{-1}\, g = \varepsilon_b \circ F\,g$: $F\,c \rightarrow a$.

Because of method five, the adjunction $\langle F, G, \varphi \rangle$ is often denoted by $\langle F, G, \eta, \varepsilon \rangle$: $C \rightharpoonup B$. Method five also describes an adjunction by two simple identities

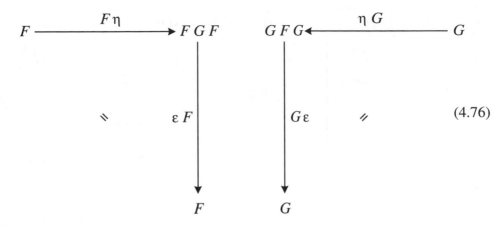

$$(4.76)$$

on the unit and counit of the adjunction. These *triangular identities* do not explicitly include objects of the categories C and B, and are thus easy to manipulate. This is convenient for discussing properties of adjunctions. A corollary in Mac Lane (1994) is that any two left-adjoints of a functor are naturally isomorphic. If you've found one, you've found them all.

Comma Categories

If b is an object of the category C, the category of *objects under b* $(b \downarrow C)$ has as objects all pairs $\langle f, c \rangle$ where $c \in C$ and $f: b \to c$ is an arrow in C, and as arrows $h: \langle f, c \rangle \to \langle f', c' \rangle$ those arrows $h: c \to c'$ of C for which $h \circ f = f'$. Thus, an object in $(b \downarrow C)$ is an arrow in C, and an arrow in $(b \downarrow C)$ is a commutative triangle with top vertex b:

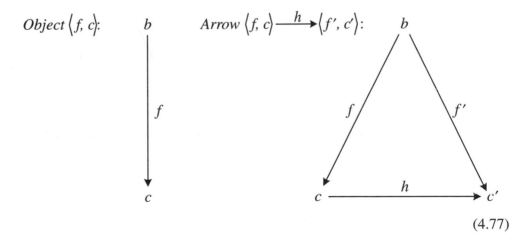

$$(4.77)$$

The composition of arrows in $(b \downarrow C)$ is given by the composition in C of the base arrows of these triangles.

Given $b \in C$, the category $(C \downarrow b)$ of *objects over b* has:

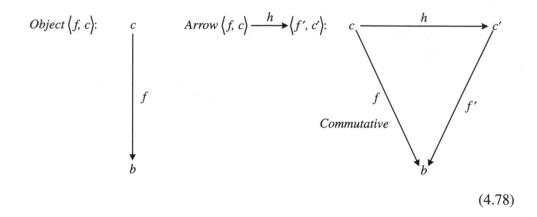

(4.78)

If $b \in C$ and $S: D \to C$ is a functor, the category $(b \downarrow S)$ of *objects S-under b* has as objects all pairs $\langle f, d \rangle$ with $d \in D$ and $f: b \to S\, d$, and as arrows $h:$ $\langle f, d \rangle \to \langle f', d' \rangle$ all those arrows $h: d \to d'$ in D for which $f' = S\, h \circ f$. In pictures, you have:

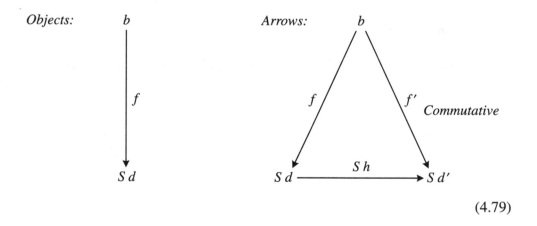

(4.79)

Composition is given by composition of the arrows h in D. Note that equality of arrows $h = h'$ in $(b \downarrow S)$ means $h = h'$ in D.

If $b \in C$ and $S: D \to C$ is a functor, the category $(S \downarrow b)$ of *objects S-over b* has:

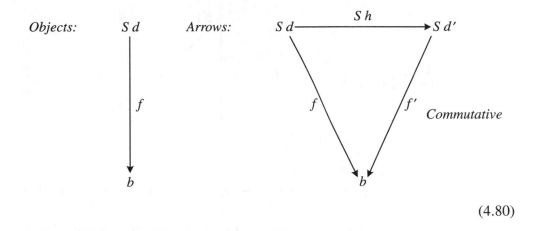

$$(4.80)$$

The general construction is, given categories and functors $E \xrightarrow{T} C \xleftarrow{S} D$, the *comma category* $(T \downarrow S)$ has:

1. *As objects*: all triples $\langle e, d, f \rangle$ with $d \in D$, $e \in E$ and $f: T e \to S d$.
2. *As arrows*: $\langle e, d, f \rangle \to \langle e', d', f' \rangle$ all pairs $\langle k, h \rangle$ of arrows $k: e \to e'$ and $h: d \to d'$ such that $f' \circ T k = S h \circ f$.

In pictures, with the square commutative, you have:

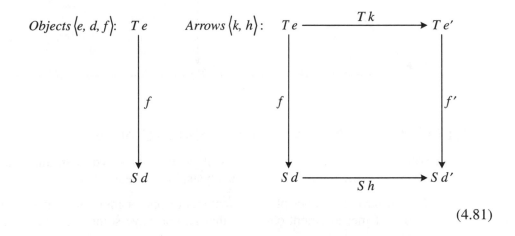

$$(4.81)$$

The composite $\langle k', h' \rangle \circ \langle k, h \rangle$ is $\langle k' \circ k, h' \circ h \rangle$ when composition is defined. The construction of the comma category can be visualized by the commutative diagram of categories and functors

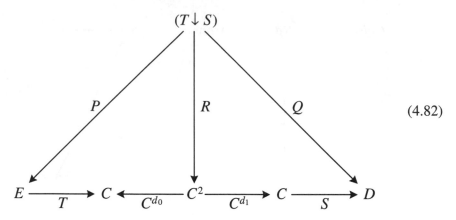

$$(4.82)$$

where d_0 and d_1 are the two functors $\mathbf{1} \to \mathbf{2}$, the functor category C^2 is a category of arrows of C, and the functors C^{d_0} and C^{d_1} are the functors which send each arrow f to its domain d_0 and codomain d_1. The functors P and Q are the projections of the comma category. The functors P, Q, and R are defined on objects by the diagram:

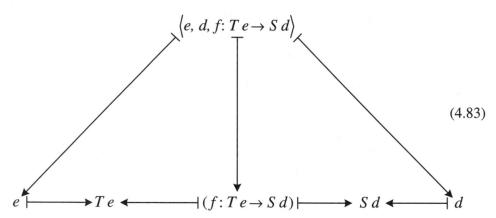

$$(4.83)$$

STATISTICAL ANALYSIS AND INFERENCE

A collection of measurement data is of no use unless you can analyze it to determine what the data mean. By "analysis," it is meant that:

1. You have a number of measurements of one or more attributes from a number of measurement objects—that is, you have some measurement data.

2. You expect the measurement objects to be comparable—you are not comparing apples and oranges.

3. You want to determine the characteristics of the attribute values for objects of the same types—summary statistics—and the relationships between attribute values for objects of the same or different types.

Many statistical techniques depend upon data that is based upon the interval or ratio scales, and which is randomly distributed. Many software measures fail on one or both counts. Nominal and ordinal measures cannot be analyzed with classical statistical methods. For these measures, the robust techniques must be used. Some of the robust techniques cannot be applied to nominal measures. The various measurement scales: nominal, ordinal, interval, ratio, and absolute, are discussed at length in the section on scales in Chapter 5.

To further complicate matters, a measure or model validated on one project or set of data may not be valid on another model or set of data because of differences in the environment. Nominal measures help here to classify environments so you can be reasonably sure that a model is appropriate for your set of circumstances. When you use nominal, and sometimes other scale, measures this way, you are really creating equivalence classes which partition the data by gathering projects into groups so that all projects within a group have similar properties.

This section describes the two classes of summary and relationship statistics: parametric and nonparametric, sometimes called the robust statistics. In general, *parametric* statistical methods can be used for interval and ratio scale measures. *Nonparametric* statistical methods are used for nominal and ordinal scale measures. It is valid to use nonparametric methods on measures of all scales, but they lack certain powers of differentiation relative to the parametric methods. For this reason, it is common practice to use the parametric methods whenever their application is valid.

The selection of the material to include in this section is based on Fenton (1991). Many of the test definitions are also based on Fenton (1991). Most of the definitions of and information about the nonparametric tests are based on Sprent (1993). The discussions about multiple variable analysis, including principal component analysis, is based on Krzanowski and Marriott (1994).

Summary Statistics

A set of data can be characterized in terms of its center point and its spread. The *center point* describes the point around which the data is somewhat symmetrical. This symmetry is defined differently for the different types of statistical methods. For the parametric methods, the values below the center point account for about one-half of the sum of all of the values. For the nonparametric methods, the values below the center point account for about one-half of the data points by count. The *spread* gives you an idea of the closeness of the data points around the center point, or the variability in the data. The smaller the spread, the more tightly packed the data are around the center point.

Sets of measurement data on the interval or ratio scales can be summarized using the mean, standard deviation, and variance values. The *mean* is

$$\bar{x} = \frac{1}{n} \sum_{i=1}^{n} x_i \tag{4.84}$$

where n is the number of observations $(1 \leqslant i \leqslant n)$, x_i is the value of the ith observation, and $\bar{x}$ is the mean of the sample observations. The *standard deviation* is:

$$S_D = \sqrt{\frac{1}{n} \sum_{i=1}^{n} (x_i - \bar{x})} \qquad (4.85)$$

The *variance* is:

$$= S_D{}^2 \qquad (4.86)$$

The mean defines the center point of the data set and the variance describes the spread of the data.

Robust or nonparametric summary statistics use the median and quartiles to define the center point and spread of the data. The median and quartiles can be applied to data from the ordinal, interval, and ratio scales. The summary statistics for nominal scale data are the *frequency*, the number of observations at each value, and the *mode*, the frequency with the highest number of observations. This is the last you will see of statistical methods for the nominal scale.

The *median m* is the value for which half of the values of the data set are larger and half are smaller. The *upper fourth u* is the median of those values larger than m. Those values above u are the *upper quartile*. The *lower fourth l* is the median of those values smaller than m. The values below l are the *lower quartile*. The *box length* is $d = u - l$. The *upper tail* is $u + 1.5d$, and the *lower tail* is $u - 1.5d$. Both tails are truncated to the nearest actual data point. Values outside of the tails are called *outliers*.

Normally, the median, upper, and lower tails are shown on a graphical display of the data set. Outliers are always shown explicitly. A sample of a graphical display is shown in Figure 4.3.

Relationships between Attributes

There are many ways to test for a relationship between attributes. The simplest test for such a relationship is to print a scatter plot of pairs of values and stare at

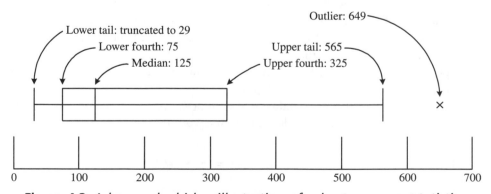

Figure 4.3 *A box-and-whisker illustration of robust summary statistics.*

it for a good long while. Each point on the plot represents a pair of values: one for each attribute for a measurement point. If, after a time, a pattern begins to appear, there may be a real relationship lurking in the data.

There are several statistical tests you can use, depending on the number of attributes and the quality of your data. Quality here refers to the scale from which your data comes. Like summary statistics, these relationship tests come in two flavors: parametric and nonparametric.

Parametric tests are more powerful in that they provide more accurate results. Parametric tests also have greater restrictions. Many tests assume a normal or random distribution. When measuring software, you usually won't find a random distribution. What looks random is more likely the result of a complex but poorly understood relationship between more than two variables. Parametric tests can be used only on data from the interval and ratio scales.

There are several ways to overcome these restrictions. You can attempt to determine the true distribution of your data and use tests appropriate for that distribution. This is often a difficult task. You can attempt to transform your data into a scale which conforms more closely to the normal distribution. Several types of transformations are discussed in this section. Or, you can use nonparametric methods and robust statistics.

In this section, five statistical methods for determining and analyzing relationships between attributes will be presented along with the mechanics for using each method. The presentation includes any assumptions and limitations which apply to the method or its use. Emphasis is placed on one of the methods, principal component analysis, in terms of the amount of coverage, for several reasons:

1. It is a method for creating indirect measures from collections of direct and other indirect measures.

2. It uses a given set of data to select and weight the principal components, which amounts to built-in correlation.

3. It can be used with a wide variety of measures, and includes a means of rescaling measures to a common scale.

4. It can be used with either parametric or nonparametric data.

5. It is fairly flexible in its applications.

Correlations

The most used, and most misused, statistical test is correlation. Correlation measures the extent to which the value and direction of change in one attribute is tied to that of another attribute. Correlations can also be run between more than two attributes. *Pearson's product moment correlation coefficient r* is:

$$r = \sum_{i=1}^{n} \frac{(x_i - \bar{x})(y_i - \bar{y})}{\sqrt{n \cdot \text{var}(x) \cdot \text{var}(y)}} \tag{4.87}$$

Pearson's correlation requires data from the ratio scale and assumes a normal distribution (Sprent 1993).

Two attributes are highly correlated in a positive relationship—an increase in the value of one attribute is accompanied by (not "leads to" or "causes") an increase in the value of the other—if the correlation coefficient is close to 1.0. Two attributes are highly correlated in a negative relationship—an increase in the value of one attribute is accompanied by a decrease in the value of the other—if the correlation coefficient is close to -1.0. Two attributes are not correlated if the correlation coefficient is close to 0.0.

There are four possible explanations for an observed relationship:

1. The value of the first attribute is a direct or indirect result of the value of the second (cause and effect).

2. The value of the second attribute is a direct or indirect result of the value of the first (again, a cause and effect).

3. Both values are the direct or indirect results of a third, unknown attribute.

4. The two values are the direct or indirect results of different, perhaps unrelated, unknown attributes.

The point is that knowing a relationship exists does not allow you to infer anything about the *nature* of that relationship.

Robust correlation can be used when the data do not justify parametric correlation. *Spearman's rank correlation coefficient* uses the ranks of the observed values. Each value is numbered 1, 2, . . . , n in order from the smallest through the largest. When two values are the same, only one of the observations is used. The number thus assigned to an observation becomes its rank. The correlation coefficient is calculated the same as Pearson's correlation coefficient, substituting ranks for values. A simplified form of Spearman's rank correlation coefficient is

$$r_s = 1 - \frac{6 \sum_{i=1}^{n} (r_i - s_i)^2}{n(n^2 - 1)} \tag{4.88}$$

where r_i is the rank assigned to x_i and s_i is the rank assigned to y_i.

Kendall's rank correlation coefficient is based on a relationship between pairs of data points. It can be used to provide partial correlation coefficients which can help determine if a relationship between two attributes is due to a third attribute. Kendall's coefficient is easiest to calculate if the x data are arranged in ascending rank order. Paired rankings are obtained by allocating ranks to the y data, forming a pair (x-rank$_i$, y-rank$_i$), (r_i, s_i). Kendall's coefficient is based on the notion that if there is an association between the x and y data, arranging the x data in ascending rank order should show an increasing trend in the y data if there is a positive relationship and a decreasing trend if there is a negative relationship. After arranging the paired differences as described, assign $s_j - s_i$ for $i = 1, 2,..., n - 1$ and $j > i$ as $+1$ if $s_j - s_i > 0$ and -1 if $s_j - s_i < 0$. A positive difference is called a *concordance* and a negative difference is called a *discordance*. Ties are ignored; one of the tied values is dropped from the sample. If there is a significant number of ties, relative to the number of data points in the sample, then the results of any correlation test must be considered inconclusive. Kendall's correlation coefficient τ is

$$\tau = \frac{n_c - n_d}{\frac{1}{2} n(n-1)} \qquad (4.89)$$

where n_c is the number of concordances and n_d is the number of discordances.

According to Sprent, the two tests, Spearman's and Kendall's, generally provide very similar results, although Spearman's rank correlation coefficient may be more sensitive to some outliers.

Regression

The purpose of *regression analysis* is to fit a line or curve to a set of plotted data points while minimizing the distance of any actual data point from the line. Regression analysis assumes that a relationship between the two or more attributes being fitted has been established, and that the intent now is to determine what that relationship might be. Regression analysis can try to fit many types of curves to the data: linear, polynomial, or exponential.

The most basic form of regression analysis is called *linear regression* or *least squares analysis*. Least squares analysis attempts to fit a straight line to a scatter plot of pairs of values. These pairs represent observed values of two attributes. The basic model is

$$y_i = \alpha + \beta x_i + \varepsilon_i \qquad (4.90)$$

where y_i is the ith observation of the y attribute, x_i is the ith observation of the x attribute, α is the estimated point at which the line intercepts the y-axis (the *intercept*), β is the estimated angle of the line relative to the x-axis (the *slope*), and ε_i is an unobservable random variable, sometimes called an *error term*. The objective is to minimize

$$\sum_{i=1}^{n} (y_i - \hat{y}_i)^2 \qquad (4.91)$$

where $\hat{y}_i$ is the estimated value of the ith observation of the y-attribute using the fitted line, and y_i is the actual value of the ith observation of the y-attribute (Myers 1990).

Least-squares regression analysis is subject to several assumptions (Sprent 1993):

1. The observations are independent of each other.
2. The data are homogeneous.
3. The data are normally distributed.
4. The ε_i are independently normally distributed with mean 0 and variance σ^2 (the square of the standard deviation).

In software, it is often the case that one or more, or all, of these assumptions are violated (Fenton 1991).

Robust regression often yields results similar to least squares regression when the assumptions for least squares regression hold. When the assumptions do not hold, robust regression may be the only alternative, assuming a straight line is the best fit for the data. This can usually be determined by looking at the scatter plot. One robust regression technique is Thiel's method, first proposed in 1950 (Sprent 1993). Thiel's method makes no assumptions about the distribution of the data. The method estimates the slope of the regression line by the median of the slopes of all lines adjoining pairs of points with different x values. For two points (x_i, y_i) and (x_j, y_j), the slope is:

$$b_{ij} = \frac{y_j - y_i}{x_j - x_i} \tag{4.92}$$

The median of all of b_{ij} is the estimated slope $b*$ which serves as an estimate for β. An estimate for α, $a*$, is suggested by the median of all $a_i = y_i - b*x_i$. You could also use $\hat{a} = \text{med}(y_i) - b* \text{med}(x_i)$ in which case you find that your regression line passes through the median, where the least squares line passes through the mean. If n is even, estimate b as $b = \text{med}(b_{i,i+1/2n})$ for $i = 1, 2,...,$ $1/2n$. If n is odd, estimate b as $b = \text{med}(b_{i,i+1/2(n+1)})$ for $i = 1, 2,..., 1/2(n - 1)$. In the abbreviated method, estimate α as for the full method.

Multivariate Regression

When more than two attributes are being compared, *multivariate regression* is used. The multivariate linear regression model attempts to fit a line to the data in each of p dimensions, where p is the number of variables (Krzanowski and Marriott 1994). The model has the form

$$Y = \beta X + \varepsilon \tag{4.93}$$

where Y is an $n \times p$ matrix, n is the number of observations, X is an $n \times (q + 1)$ matrix (y is a function of $(x_1, x_2,..., x_q)$ and the α constant is given by $x_0 = 1$), β is a $(q + 1) \times p$ matrix, and ε is an $n \times p$ matrix. The residuals of each p-variable observation, the rows of ε, are independent, but the residuals of the individual y values are an unknown covariance matrix E. The assumptions of this model include $E(\varepsilon) = 0$ (an $n \times p$ matrix), and $\text{cov}(\text{vec } \varepsilon) = E \times I$ where E is $p \times p$ and I is $n \times n$.

Transformations

When a relationship between two attributes appears to be nonlinear, one method used to make it more linear is to apply a *transformation* (Fenton 1991). A transformation is a mathematical function applied to a measurement. Tukey's ladder contains a set of possible transformations (the "top" is at the left):

$$x^3 \quad x^2 \quad x \quad x^{1/2} \quad \log x \quad -x^{-1} \quad -x^{-2} \quad -x^{-3} \tag{4.94}$$

The ladder is used to transform the independent variable (the x variable). If the relationship between the dependent (the y variable) and independent variable is positive and convex, transform the independent variable by moving down the ladder. If the relationship is positive and concave, transform the independent variable by moving up the ladder. Transforming the dependent variable changes its scale and is not recommended. An example of a transformation is a logarithmic plot, where each division on the scale is a factor of 10.

Principal Component Analysis

It is often the case that a single measure, or even a small number of measures, do not adequately characterize a piece of software. Many measurement tools provide several measures, from a dozen to nearly a hundred. Trying to build a model based on a couple of dozen measures amounts to building a model with a couple of dozen dimensions. Each measure contributes a line of axis to the model. To further complicate matters, many of the lines of axis might be parallel, or nearly so. This problem is called collinearity; failing to account for it renders the data misleading, at best, and can lead to incorrect conclusions, at worst.

Principal component analysis was developed to combat this collinearity problem. The general form of a principal component is

$$x_{ij} = \sum_{\alpha=1}^{q} a_{i\alpha} b_{j\alpha} + e_{ij} \tag{4.95}$$

where $i = 1, 2,..., n$, $j = 1, 2,..., p$, and $q < p$ represents the number of retained principal components, leaving the error term e_{ij}. The terms a and b may be seen as the "scores" of the subjects on the components, and the "loadings" or "weights" of the variables on the components, and represent the scoring of the rows and columns in the data matrix X. Here, n is the number of observations and p is the number of variables (Krzanowski and Marriott 1994).

Often, the data matrix is replaced with a three-way matrix, with element x_{ijk}. This structure represents n observations of p variables over q groups, or at q points in time ($i = 1,..., n$, $j = 1,..., p$, $k - 1,..., q$). Each component then takes the form

$$x_{ijk} = \sum_{\alpha=1}^{m} a_{i\alpha} b_{j\alpha} c_{k\alpha} + e_{ijk} \tag{4.96}$$

which generates m triplets, and for a given m, provides a unique solution (Krzanowski and Marriott 1994).

The main idea behind principal components is to represent the main structural elements of a set of data in terms of a smaller number of variables. Another goal is for the selected set or variables to contribute lines of access which are as perpendicular to each other as possible. The method selects components so that they are as orthogonal (perpendicular) as possible and, taken together, explain as much of the variability of the data as possible.

If the original variables are not measured on the same scale, they need to be rescaled. Usually, all of the variables are scaled by dividing them by their standard deviations.

The variance-covariance matrix is replaced by the correlation matrix. This will cause the first component to be dominated by the variables that are strongly correlated, whether positively or negatively. The trace of the correlation matrix, and the sum of the eigenvalues, is the number of variables.

In biology, the first principal component tends to be dominated by measures of the size of an organism, since these tend to be strongly collinear (Krzanowski and Marriott 1994). In fact, the first principal component is often ignored when discussing similarities and differences between organisms. In software, the first principal component is also often dominated by size measures.

Some care is necessary when the principal components calculated from a set of data are taken to be estimates of the principal components of the population. The ith principal component a_i, and its eigenvalue λ_i, are consistent estimates of the ith population principal component only if the variance and covariance estimates are consistent, and the ith population eigenvalue is unique. Sometimes, rotation of components can help in cases where eigenvalues are very similar (see Khoshgoftaar and Lanning (1995) for an example of this rotation process).

Since the principal components are selected from the set of data, it is natural to ask whether two populations—such as two pieces of software—have the same principal components. If the variance and covariance matrices of the population are the same, they have the same principal components. In other cases, the population covariances may have the same eigen vectors, but different eigenvalues, meaning they have parallel axes, but different magnitudes.

Comparing principal components from different data sets is subject to certain limitations. A model that has parallel axes, but unequal covariance matrices, is difficult to justify except on the assumption that unobservable side effects are operating on all of the groups, but with different strengths. In software, this is probably a valid assumption, since there are many factors that we choose not to observe. Essentially, this implies a factor model, and may be better analyzed using confirmatory factor analysis (Krzanowski and Marriott 1994). Also, any significance tests based on the assumption of multivariate normality is likely to be very sensitive to that assumption. This means that tests which assume the normal distribution of values for the variables are likely to be invalid if that assumption does not hold.

Aside from the limitations discussed so far, there are two main problems to be solved while using principal component analysis (Krzanowski and Marriott 1994):

1. How to determine which variables are informative and which are noise, along with a related issue: how many components are needed.

2. How to determine if a variable is redundant and can be discarded.

While several criteria for variable selection have been suggested, six are given here and appear in Krzanowski and Marriott (1994).

Option 1: Use the proportion of the variance explained by each variable as a guide. If the first two or three components account for 90 percent or more of the variation, the rest may be irrelevant. This is a subjective decision and can be misleading—a single component dominated by size can account for most of the variation, while most of the interesting information is in the other components.

Option 2: Components with variances below a certain level may be rejected. If components are calculated on the basis of the correlation matrix, components with variances less than one are often discarded. If one variable is independent of the rest, it will appear as a component with a variance of slightly less than one, but still be informative. So, the dividing line between those components retained and those discarded is subjective.

Option 3: If the accuracy of the observed measurement is known, stop extracting components when the remaining unexplained variance approaches the error in the measurements. This probably doesn't work when measuring software, since the error of measurement is almost never known.

Option 4: Bartlett (1950) derived a sphericity test of the hypothesis that after removing k principal components, the data can be regarded as being derived from $p - k$ uncorrelated variables of equal variance (Krzanowski and Marriott 1994). The test is a modified likelihood ratio test, is based on the normal distribution, and is asymptotically valid. It takes the form

$$\left(n - \frac{2p + 11}{6}\right)(p - k) \log \left(\frac{a_0}{g_0}\right) \approx X^2_{(p-k+2)(p-k-1)/2} \qquad (4.97)$$

where a_0 and g_0 are the arithmetic and geometric means, respectively, of the $p - k$ eigenvalues $\lambda_{k+1},..., \lambda_p$. The test was proposed in the context of factor analysis and can be regarded as a test for the existence of any other common factors. If the data are normally distributed, and the sample is sufficiently large (neither of which generally hold in software), a nonsignificant result is an indication that there is no point in extracting any more principal components. This does not mean, of course, that the remaining components contain no useful information.

Option 5: A "scree plot" is made of the eigenvalues λ_i against i. The eigenvalues are in descending order and often the plot will fall towards zero with a gradually decreasing slope. Sometimes, the plot will drop sharply for the first few values, then much more slowly. This "elbow" suggests that the components corresponding to the eigenvalues from that point on are part of the random error of the model. This division point is also subjective (Krzanowski and Marriott 1994).

Option 6: Each element x_{ij} of the data matrix X is left out in turn and is estimated from the rest of the data (the reduced rank singular value decomposition). The accuracy of the approximation is then based on the sum of the squares of the differences between the actual and estimated values. This is the PRESS statistic, where

$$\text{PRESS}(m) = \frac{1}{np} \sum_{i=1}^{n} \sum_{j=1}^{p} (\hat{x}_{ij}^{(m)} - x_{ij})^2 \qquad (4.98)$$

and where $\hat{x}_{ij}^{(m)}$ is the estimate of x_{ij} based on the first m principal components. The number of components retained is given by

$$W_m = \frac{\text{PRESS}(m - 1) - \text{PRESS}(m)}{\text{PRESS}(m)} \frac{p(n + 1)}{n + p - 2n} \qquad (4.99)$$

where W_m is the increase in predictive information supplied by the mth component, divided by the average predictive information provided by the other $m - 1$ components. If W_m is small, the inclusion of the mth component has little effect on the accuracy of the estimate. If $W_m < 1$, the mth component appears to carry less information than the average of the other $m - 1$ components, and may be discarded with little adverse effect. Krzanowski suggests a cutoff of $W_m = 0.9$ to allow for bias and error. The main problem with this method is that it is extremely intensive computationally, especially the calculations of the $\hat{x}_{ij}^{(m)}$s (Krzanowski and Marriott 1994).

ALGORITHMIC COMPLEXITY

Algorithmic complexity is a measure of the complexity of a problem in terms of the computational resources (time and space) required to execute an algorithm (Fenton 1991). We would like a way to express the idea that an algorithm that requires time proportional to its input to execute is more efficient than an algorithm that requires time proportional to the square of its input.

The mathematical formalism to order the efficiencies of algorithms is called the *big O notation*. The O stands for *order* and is the dominating term of a function $f(n)$, ignoring constant multiples. Thus, $O(n)$ is basically the same as $O(2n)$ or $O(10n)$. The big O notation captures the asymptotic behavior of functions. When n is large, only the big O term really matters. In the function $f(n) = 2n^3 + n + 3n^2$, the only important term for large values of n is $2n^3$. Dropping the multiplier 2 leaves $O(f(n)) = n^3$, written as $O(n^3)$. It is important to note that $O(p)$ is a set: It is the set of functions which asymptotically dominate p. There is a well-defined partial order over the order functions, given by set inclusion:

$$O(1) \subset O(\log n) \subset O(n) \subset O(n \log n) \subset O(n^2) \subset O(c^n) \subset O(n!)$$
$$O(n^i) \subset O(n^j) \qquad \text{for all } i < j \qquad\qquad (4.100)$$
$$O(n^i) \subset O(c^n) \qquad \text{for all integers } i$$

Some of the big O sets are common enough to be named. If $f(n)$ is:

- $O(1)$, $f(n)$ has *constant* complexity.
- $O(\log n)$, $f(n)$ has *logarithmic* complexity.
- $O(n)$, $f(n)$ has *linear* complexity.
- $O(n^2)$, $f(n)$ has *quadratic* complexity.
- $O(c^n)$, $f(n)$ has *exponential* complexity.

This is a true measure of efficiency. The numerical relation system is the set N consisting of all the $O(p)$s. The numerical relation to which you map the empirical relation "more efficient" is set inclusion. The intuitive notion of feasibility can be mapped to the numerical relation polynomially bounded. Any big O set which is included in $O(n^i)$ for some i is *polynomially bounded* (at least $O(c^n)$). Polynomially bounded algorithms can be implemented for large n—they are *feasible*. This is not the case for algorithms which are not polynomially bounded—they are said to be *infeasible*.

SUMMARY

I have presented a lot of mathematics in this chapter. Much of this math will be used in the exploration of measurement theory and the measurement of software. Some of this math will be encountered in the real world as you try to solve the problems you face with software.

You have studied sets, relations, and functions in some detail and have touched on various algebraic structures from groupoids through topological spaces. More emphasis was given to graphs and categories because these particular structures seem to help explain much of the static and dynamic nature of software. Some time was spent exploring statistical analysis and inference techniques, since these are required to make sense out of the data you collect as you measure. Finally, you have looked at a way to measure the efficiency of an algorithm as a function of the size of its input.

I do not expect you to read this material more than once. I found I needed to learn it in order to understand other concepts. I expect you to refer to it on occasion and have included it so that you have most of what you need to measure software in one book.

5

MEASUREMENT THEORY

Measurement characterizes an attribute of an object in terms of a number or symbol. More precisely, a measure maps an empirical relationship between two objects into a numerical relationship between two numbers or symbols. Measurement as a process has three fundamental requirements: a model of the empirical relationship in the form of an empirical relational structure, a model of the numeric relationship in the form of a numerical relational structure, and a structure-preserving mapping between the two. This mapping must faithfully reflect the properties of the attribute in the numerical system. This process is known as fundamental measurement and leads to fundamental measures of the attribute. A measure is fundamental if it directly characterizes an empirical property and does not require the prior measurement of some other property (Krantz et al. 1971).

Measurement plays an essential role in all science and engineering. It seems strange that more attention isn't paid to measurement theory in the physical sciences. Physics and chemistry do not concern themselves with measurement as theory, only as practice. Papers in journals on the science of measurement seem to deal more with the mechanics of measurement rather than the principles of measurement.

Softer sciences, such as psychology, economics, and software, must approach measurement much more carefully. In many cases you are not sure whether certain attributes can even be measured. If they can, you are not certain as to how to measure them or what you can do with the measurements when you have them. The analysis of measurement data and the construction of new measurement systems have thus been a source of major work among behavioral and computer scientists. Some of this work is very good, while some of it, well, isn't.

Fundamental measurement can present difficult theoretical and empirical obstacles. You cannot always find an easy way to fundamentally measure some interesting attribute. Sometimes, you cannot find *any* way to measure it. To avoid these issues, you are often tempted to instead measure some other, more easily measured, attribute you believe to be related to the original. Those of us in software are particularly guilty of this sin as this has become the accepted practice. Many measures are "validated" by assessing their relationship to existing measures. This may be a good way to proceed, provided that you understand the basic attributes themselves. "But to treat such indirect measures as objective definitions of unanalyzed concepts is a form of misplaced operationalism" (Krantz et al. 1971, p. 32). Some software measurement experts, such as Fenton and Zuse, have been preaching this gospel all along, and it may do some good to hear it from other disciplines.

Careful analysis of an attribute is not possible until a way is devised to say that one object possesses more of the attribute than another. Once you can order objects in some way, you can then look for additional structure, such as finding two or more factors that affect the ordering. Then, search for qualitative or empirical laws satisfied by the ordering and additional structure. While the classification of objects does not require ordering, it is a method of measurement. Such classification is chiefly useful for assisting in the search for additional structure—all equivalence classes are based on nominal measurement.

Unlike fundamental physical measurement, which tends to be unidimensional, many theories of measurement which appear to apply to social science or computer software are inherently multidimensional. These theories deal simultaneously with several measures and the laws which connect them. These theories suggest new qualitative laws which must be tested. Even if these laws are wrong, you can learn much if the violations are systematic—you learn more from your mistakes than from your successes.

The work on fundamental measurement representation is a fairly recent development in the behavioral sciences. It contrasts with an older field called psychometrics and scaling theory. Most psychometric work is based on numerical rather than empirical relations. The goal is to represent numerical data by numerical relations that are more compact and more revealing than the original data. These alternative numerical relations are mostly geometric in nature. Most of the scaling procedures assume the validity of the proposed model, producing a best-fit numerical representation—whether the model is appropriate or not. This work underlies the various forms of statistical inference covered in the section entitled "Statistical Analysis and Inference" in Chapter 4.

In this chapter you will study the qualitative conditions required for a particular representation to hold and look for the appropriate qualitative models to support particular numerical representations. This chapter relies on the three-volume set *Foundations of Measurement* (Krantz et al. 1971; 1989; 1990) which contains the most concise, organized, and complete presentation on measurement theory I could find.

I digress for a moment to discuss what should be a major issue in software engineering. After studying Fenton (1991), I felt as if I had only part of the story. I was looking for the mathematical requirements for the interval and ratio scales, but they were not specifically mentioned in his book. The book contains a well-annotated bibliography. Two of the sources in that bibliography with the most favorable notes were Krantz et al. (1971) and Roberts (1979). After studying Roberts (1979), I discovered that much of *his* material was from Krantz et al. (1971). When I secured my copy of Krantz et al., I discovered it was the first volume of a set. I had seen the second volume cited in some other works, so I investigated further and discovered the third volume quite by accident. As I began to study them, I was in for a shock.

Fenton and Zuse are the two most quoted authors in the software engineering literature on the subject of measurement theory. Both of these authors have written extensively on the subject (Fenton 1991; Kitchenham, Pfleeger, and Fenton 1995; Zuse 1991; Zuse, 1994; as well as several other titles). Both of these authors draw heavily from the *Foundations* set. Most other authors in software engineering refer to Fenton and Zuse as the authorities on measurement theory.

Fenton (1991) repeatedly discusses "the Representation Condition (sic)" as if there were only one such condition. Zuse (1991, 1994) claims, indirectly, that extensive measurement is the only way to achieve the ratio scale (these highly technical terms are explained in this chapter). Both of these views are simply wrong. Measurement theory, especially work done in the last decade, provides several representations which lead to the ratio or interval scale. In fact, except for the ordinal representations discussed in the section on "Ordinal Representations" in this chapter, *all* of the representations in this chapter lead to interval or higher scales. My shock was the realization that the entire basis for measurement theory in software engineering was built on an incomplete foundation, and that none of the really useful portions of that foundation were present. In short, *no discussion on measurement theory in the context of software engineering is based on complete information.*

I had originally planned to include a much briefer summary of the theory in this book. Like every other author in software engineering, I was prepared to base my summary on the work of Fenton and Zuse. After this discovery, I changed my plans. Many of the structures presented in the later sections, particularly conjoint and the various proximity structures, are very useful in understanding and measuring software. Many of the claims of measurement "purists" can be refuted with arguments based on these structures. Many additional insights into software measurement can be gained by understanding these structures. As you study them, you will begin to see the patterns of the mathematical structures reflected in your software.

To the best of my knowledge, this chapter is the only *complete* summary of measurement theory in the software engineering literature. This is both good news and bad news. It is bad news because we have neglected to question the basic assumptions and claims of those who tell us what we don't know. This is a major weakness in the field and one of the reasons we continuously seek silver bullets. It is good news because it is here, in print, for everyone's use. I don't claim to be an expert on measurement theory. I have, however, come to accept Krantz, Luce, Suppes, and Tversky as experts in measurement theory because theirs is the only major work on the subject. Their sources come from economics, metaphysics, psychology, and sociology, where the real work is being done. I hope to add software engineering to that list.

This chapter is organized by the type of representation, basically following the order of presentation in the *Foundations* set. The first section "Axioms and Procedures" describes the types of axioms needed in order to build representations from empirical structures. It also gives the three known basic procedures for actually building these representations. "Models, Attributes, and Measures" discusses the central nature of models in measurement and is based on Basili et al. (1994b). The third section provides an overview of the representational theory of measurement, which is what the approach to measurement taken in the rest of the chapter is called. The section presents, in general terms, each of the five components of this approach.

The fourth section entitled "Scales" discusses the notion of scale types which describe the forms of the numerical representations constructed in later sections. This section summarizes the five basic scale types, the basic forms of their representations, and the allowable transformations on a representation of each type. It also contains material which is less than 10 years old on finding scale types for representations of a more general nature. The majority of the material in the section covers this very new ground (for mathematics). I include it because there are some structures in software which do not meet all of the conditions for any structure in the following nine sections. Armed with this new material, you can invent not only new measures, but also new empirical structures and their representations, then determine their scale types. Given the state-of-the art in software measurement, this section contains material essential for the advancement of that art.

The conditions required of each kind of structure are given in the next nine sections starting with "Ordinal Representations." These sections include representations which, on appearances, may not be directly usable in the measurement of software. However, I have been required to find and use these structures either as part of an application or in some other endeavor. I'm sure you will find occasion to use them, too.

Each of the structures is given a name which can be used as a shorthand reference. The structures are presented in terms of the conditions or axioms they must satisfy in order to construct the given representation. One common example of such an axiom is that the ordering relation be at least a weak order—it must be both transitive and connected.

The structural sections are followed by a discussion of indirect measures. All of the representations in this chapter are fundamental measures and are thus direct measures. Indirect measures are those which use one or more fundamental measures of one or more attributes to measure, indirectly, another supposedly related attribute. Conjoint measurement, from an earlier section, presents an interesting problem. Conjoint measurement at first glance appears to be indirect measurement. It is not. The theories of conjoint measurement measure the attribute and its components *simultaneously*. Indirect measurement requires first the measurement of two or more attributes, then their combination using a mathematical model of some kind. This is a fine distinction and one not worth dwelling on.

The next section "Prediction Systems" provides additional requirements for using measurement as part of a prediction system. It is followed by a discussion of two ways to validate a new measure, theoretically and empirically, and several validation criteria. Some issues related to measure validation are also presented.

The final section focuses on a current debate on the applicability of measurement theory to software engineering. This debate includes some very recent work by Briand, El Emam, and Morasca (1995). I present both sides, as fairly and concisely as possible, then declare that both sides completely miss the point. I explain why I feel this way, but you need to read the rest of this chapter before you understand my position.

AXIOMS AND PROCEDURES

Measurement as a process has two fundamental components. First are the conditions which a representation in numbers or symbols imposes on an empirical structure. These conditions are characterized as axioms which are then used to frame the representation and uniqueness theorems. It is these theorems which, when proven, allow you to measure. Second are the basic procedures for assigning numbers to empirical objects. Once you know, through the representation and uniqueness theorems, that measurement is possible, you apply one of three basic procedures for actually constructing your measure.

Types of Axioms

The axioms imposed on various empirical structures fall into three basic classes: necessary, nonnecessary, and Archimedean. *Necessary* axioms are those conditions which are mathematically necessary as a consequence of the representation being constructed. *Nonnecessary* or *structural* axioms are used to limit the set of structures which satisfy the axiom set. The set of necessary conditions lead to a set of structures which might require a more complex proof for the representation and uniqueness theorems, so limit the allowable structures to a more manageable set. There are three types of structural axioms:

1. Those which demand the system be nontrivial—that a certain set be nonempty.

2. Those which require the set be finite or countable.

3. Those which assert that solutions actually exist for certain classes of equations—these are often called *solvability* axioms.

The *Archimedean* axiom, which is necessary, is based on the Archimedean property of real numbers: For any positive number x, no matter how small, and for any number y, no matter how large, there exists an integer n such that $nx \geqslant y$. Put another way, the set of integers for which $y > nx$ is finite. This axiom is imposed as a condition on the empirical structure because you are trying to map that structure to the real numbers (usually) and the property must be reflected in the empirical structure. Empirical structures for which the Archimedean axiom does not hold cannot be represented in the real numbers; some other representation is required. The Archimedean axiom is usually stated in the form: Every strictly bounded standard sequence is finite. Both "standard sequence" and "strictly bounded" are defined within the context of a particular representation.

Procedures of Measurement

This chapter presents several sets of structures which lead to fundamental measurement. While there are many such structures, it is interesting to note that there are only three basic procedures for assigning numbers to objects or events: ordinal measurement, counting of units, and solving inequalities.

Ordinal Measurement

In *ordinal measurement*, you are simply trying to find a numerical representation which faithfully reflects the relative order of a set of objects in terms of some attribute. To perform ordinal measurement, first find or determine an ordering relation for the objects themselves. This is a mental means for sorting the objects in some order (usually ascending) in terms of the attribute you are trying to measure. To do this, you need a reliable way to say that one object has more of an attribute than another. The process is like a typical bubble sort where each object is compared to every other object in the set and an exchange takes place when the first object has more of the attribute than the second. Once the objects are ordered in this way, assign a number to each object so that the natural sort order of the numbers matches exactly the sort order of the objects.

Obviously, a particular object can be assigned a great many distinct numbers. The only requirement for ordinal measurement is that the number sequence matches exactly the object sequence. This introduces the notion of allowable transformations. A transformation is a mapping of one number sequence or representation onto another. For ordinal measures, any transformation which preserves the order of the numbers relative to the order of the objects is allowable. Any strictly increasing function from one set of numbers to another set satisfies these requirements and thus forms the set of allowable transformations for ordinal measures.

Counting of Units

The *counting of units* procedure depends upon an empirical concatenation operation and the construction of a standard sequence of objects. As an example, take three rods; call them a, b, and c. The ordering relation consists of laying two rods, say a and b, side-by-side so they coincide on one end and observing how the other ends compare. In this case, you are measuring the attribute length. If the end of rod a extends beyond the end of rod b, you say that a is *longer* than b and write $a > b$. You also say that rod b is *shorter* than rod a and write $b < a$.

The *concatenation operation* consists of laying two rods end-to-end so they form a line, which is denoted by $a \circ b$. Construct a *standard sequence* by selecting one of the rods to be your unit of measure. Then create, or imagine, some number of "perfect copies" of your selected rod and measure the other rods by concatenating copies of the unit rod until you have approximated the length of the rod you are measuring. If three copies of rod c are shorter than rod b, and four copies of rod c are longer than rod b, you say that the length of rod b is between $3c$ and $4c$. If you give the length of rod c a name, say one *foot*, you can now say that rod b is between 3 and 4 feet in length.

This procedure is also called *extensive measurement* and is the basis for nearly all measurement in the physical sciences. Note that the choice of unit was arbitrary. You could just as easily have chosen rod a as the unit and defined its length as 1 yard, for example. Note also that the length of rod b was expressed as a multiple of the length of the unit rod.

Given a unit e, if a rod is as long as n copies of e, it is ne units long. This can also be expressed as $\phi(b)/\phi(e)$ where $\phi(e) = 1$ (Krantz et al. 1971). Since you can express the length of any other rod, say e', in terms of a number of copies of rod e, say α copies, you can use rod e' as your unit and convert all measurements in multiples of e to multiples of e' by multiplying them by α. This is a general transformation of all extensive measures: given a function ϕ expressed in terms of e, you can create a function ϕ' expressed in terms of e' by multiplying by some constant α which represents the length of e' in terms of e, or $\phi' = \alpha\phi$. To most of us, this is familiar as a conversion factor between units. The fact that you can use such a factor is a direct result of the fact that you are performing extensive measurement. Were you not using the counting of units procedure, you could not find a simple constant conversion factor. The conditions required by extensive measurement are strong and are given in a later section.

Solving Inequalities

There are times when it is impractical to construct a standard sequence. At times, it may not even be possible to construct a standard sequence. When this is the case, you can use the final procedure, the *solving of inequalities*. For example, suppose you have four rods, a, b, c, and d, which are found to satisfy:

$$a \circ d > b \circ c > a \circ c > d > c > b > a \qquad (5.1)$$

You can map each rod to a number, as $a \to x_1$, $b \to x_2$, $c \to x_3$, and $d \to x_4$, and map the concatenation operation $\circ$ to the addition operation $+$ on numbers. From the above you know the following must be true:

$$x_1 + x_4 - x_2 - x_3 > 0$$

$$x_2 + x_3 - x_1 - x_3 > 0$$

$$x_1 + x_3 - x_4 > 0$$

$$x_4 - x_3 > 0 \qquad (5.2)$$

$$x_3 - x_2 > 0$$

$$x_2 - x_1 > 0$$

Any simultaneous solution to this set of inequalities is a valid representation of the lengths of rods a, b, c, and d.

It is possible that no simultaneous solution, and thus no representation, exists. The solving of inequalities procedure involves two very important assumptions:

1. The numbers assigned to each rod are additive—if $a \circ c \sim b$, then $x_1 + x_3 = x_2$.

2. Ratios of the numerical assignments are unique, regardless of the unit chosen.

Measurement by solving inequalities has many applications. Also, many empirical operations other than addition can be used, as you will see.

MODELS, ATTRIBUTES, AND MEASURES

A measure is used to characterize some property of a class of objects quantitatively (Basili et al. 1994b). To do so, you must have a model of the property to be measured. A given property can have more than one model, which can lead to more than one way to measure it (Basili et al. 1994b). One of the first tasks in measuring a property of an object is to identify or develop a model of that property. A model is an abstract representation of an object (Fenton 1991). By necessity or design, a model includes only those details about the object which are of interest to your current purpose and leaves the other details out. Thus, all models are in some sense incomplete representations of their real-world counterparts.

There are two types of models (Fenton 1991; Basili et al. 1994b):

1. Attribute models in which an external attribute of an object (process, product, resource, or project) is represented by one or more internal attributes. For example, defining complexity in terms of the number and types of components in an object is an attribute model for complexity. As Basili et al. (1994b, p. 649) put it, "Models of this type are generally used to characterize qualitative aspects in a quantitative way."

2. Relationship models establish a relationship, generally a mathematical function, among one attribute and a list of others. For example, a model of effort might be defined as a function of product size and certain other internal and external process, project, and resource attributes. Again from Basili et al. (1994b, p. 649): "Models of this type are used either to represent the relationship among qualitative aspects or to describe a relationship among qualitative aspects in terms of their quantitative characterizations." Here, the quantitative characterizations of the qualitative aspects refer to attribute models of those aspects.

To repeat, measures are intended to characterize attributes or properties of objects. Measures are based upon models of these attributes or properties. Multiple models of an attribute or property can exist. In order to measure something, then, you must identify the entities or objects to be measured, identify the attributes or properties we are measuring, then identify or develop a model appropriate to your current environment for each attribute and property. When selecting measures, it is important to understand the model upon which they are based. If you select measures that are not built on your model, you will not be measuring what you think you are measuring. Likewise, all of the measures in a set should be based on the same model if they are to be combined in any way. Mixing measures from different models is like mixing oil and water: It isn't easy, it doesn't last, it doesn't help anyone, and lots of birds get killed.

Since models are by necessity merely abstract representations of their real-world counterparts, a model needs to be tailored to a specific environment. Tailoring means to map the elements of the abstract model to the concrete elements in your environment. Often, this mapping is clear and direct. Sometimes, it is somewhat obscure and requires significant thought and imagination. It is beyond the scope of this book to offer techniques for tailoring abstract models. My purpose here is to simply point out that such tailoring needs to occur and can be difficult in some cases.

The point of this section is to highlight the absolute dependence of measurement on abstract models. For many objects in software engineering, models exist and can be used as a basis for measurement. For many other objects, including some of the most important objects, coherent models do not yet exist. To measure these objects, you must either use a partial model that exists, wait for better models, or create one that is good enough for your purposes. In some ways, this amounts to building your own ruler. Unfortunately, given the state of measurement in software engineering, and especially object-oriented software engineering, building your own ruler is a prerequisite to measuring nearly anything.

THE REPRESENTATIONAL THEORY OF MEASUREMENT

The representational approach to measurement seeks to represent empirical observations in a numerical structure. You try to build numerical *representations* which faithfully reflect what you observe in your empirical structure. The approach has three main components (and two types of theorems which we'll get to later):

1. An empirical relational structure.
2. A numerical relational structure.
3. A mapping from the empirical structure into the numerical structure.

Recall from Chapter 4 that a relational structure is a set of objects and a set of relations and operations among those objects. An empirical relational structure is thus a set of empirical objects, such as software objects or modules, and a set of empirical relations between them, such as message connections or relationships, and operations, such as combination or concatenation. For any attribute of interest, at least one of the relations must be an ordering of the objects in terms of that attribute. This ordering is the most basic condition for measurement: If you cannot say that one object has more of an attribute than another, you cannot measure them in terms of that attribute, except to classify them nominally.

Formally, you denote an empirical relational structure as $\langle A, R_0,..., R_n \rangle$ where A is the set of objects and $R_0,..., R_n$ are the relations and operations. Typically, the first relation, R_0, is the ordering relation and is denoted by $\succeq$. Often, the second relation, R_1, represents the concatenation operation, when one is defined, and is denoted by $\circ$. The empirical relational structure thus becomes, $\langle A, \succeq, \circ, R_2,..., R_n \rangle$. These relations and operations are selected to explain or capture your intuitive understanding about, or observed relationships between, objects in terms of the attribute you are trying to measure.

The numerical relational structure consists of a set of numbers, symbols, or structures, such as vectors, and a set of numerical relations and operations. Typically, the set of real numbers, denoted $\mathbb{R}$, is the selected set of numbers. Occasionally, it is convenient to use some other set of numbers, such as the positive reals, denoted $\mathbb{R}+$, the integers, denoted $\mathbb{Z}$, or the positive integers, denoted $\mathbb{Z}+$ (or $\mathbb{N}$), a set of symbols, or even vectors of numbers or symbols. The numerical operations and relations are selected so they faithfully represent the relations and operations in the empirical structure. The mappings between structures are called *homomorphisms* and take each empirical object to a number, each empirical relation to a numerical relation, and each empirical operation to a numerical operation, all in such a way that the relationships and operations between empirical objects are preserved in the numerical structure. Such mappings are called *structure-preserving*.

Both the empirical and numerical relational structures can be represented as categories. The objects of the empirical category are the empirical objects. The arrows of the empirical category are the relations and operations between objects. The objects of the numerical category are the numbers, symbols, or vectors of your numerical relational structure. The arrows of the numerical category are the relations and operations between numbers. The mapping between them is thus a structure-preserving functor.

Measurement, in categorical terms, is a matter of finding a functor between an empirical category and a suitable numerical category which preserves the structure embedded in the empirical category. The functor must satisfy all of the conditions of the representation condition for the type of structure represented by the empirical category. Using categorical concepts does not make these functors easier to find, but it does give a way to represent your structures graphically and allows you to construct graphical proofs that your chosen structures do indeed meet the conditions required of them. To my knowledge, measurement has not been expressed in terms of categories, but such an expression fits well with the object model in Chapter 6, which is based on categories.

The mappings between structures are constrained by two types of theorems: a representation theorem and a uniqueness theorem. The *representation theorem*, also called the *representation condition*, sets forth the conditions or axioms which must be satisfied by the empirical structure in order for the mapping to take place and be meaningful. Each structure has its own representation theorem. The theorem states that an empirical relational structure which meets the specified conditions can be used to construct a representation into the real numbers (usually) of the form given in the theorem. The conditions are usually imposed by the structure of the numerical system to which you are trying to map your empirical structure. The *uniqueness theorem*, or *uniqueness condition*, defines the mathematical transformations that map one homomorphism to another. Put another way, the uniqueness theorem defines the relationships between different mappings or representations.

You can think of a representation as an embedding of an empirical structure into a numerical structure. The representation theorem shows how to construct this embedding and the uniqueness theorem describes the different embeddings that are possible.

SCALES

In the representational approach, the triple formed by the empirical structure E, the numerical structure N, and the mapping ϕ between them is called a *scale* (Fenton 1991). Denote a scale by $\langle E, N, \phi \rangle$. The representation theorem constrains the mapping itself, which controls the relationship between the structures. The uniqueness theorem controls the relationship between mappings. Relationships between mappings are described in terms of transformations. Representations are nothing more than functional mappings or functors between categories; transformations are mappings between functions or functors (and must qualify as natural transformations). The uniqueness theorem constrains the possible transformations between mappings so that the scale type is preserved. The set of transformations permitted by the uniqueness theorem determines the scale's type.

The Conventional View of Scales

In 1946, Stevens (1946; 1951) identified five different scale types based on the group of transformations determined by the automorphisms on the empirical structure. Recall from Chapter 4 that an *automorphism* is a one-to-one homomorphism, an isomorphism, from a set onto itself. Stevens classified his scale types based on the number of points which remain invariant under the automorphisms of the empirical structure. Later work has revealed that Stevens's scale types are too limited in scope, an issue which will be taken up later.

For now, the scale types given by Stevens will be listed for several reasons. First, Stevens gave a name to each scale type which is convenient for discussing them. While limited, Stevens's classification is essentially correct as far as it goes—I will add to it later, not replace it. Stevens's scale types also provide a useful framework for the rest of this section. The scale types are ordered from less unique to more unique. Each type is defined in terms of its defining relations—those that remain invariant under the set of permissible transformations. Next, the uniqueness of each scale type is discussed in terms of the number of points which can be mapped onto themselves under two transformations without the transformations being identical (the same transformation). Finally, the statistics appropriate for each scale type are discussed. This information relies on Siegel and Castellan (1988).

Nominal Scale

Objects are assigned to numbers or symbols as a form of classification. Nothing can be said about the ordering of the classes. It can only be said that two objects in the same class—with the same nominal value—are equivalent in terms of the attribute by which the objects are classified. The defining relation is equivalence. The allowable transformations include all one-to-one mappings of the form $x \rightarrow f(x)$. The mathematical group formed by these transformations is called the *homeomorphism group*—which consists of all one-to-one mappings or *isomorphisms*.

The only requirement for using a nominal scale is that the objects which are equivalent in terms of the property being measured are assigned to the same number or symbol value. Formally, given two objects a and b, $a \sim b \Leftrightarrow \phi(a) = \phi(b)$. No points are unique under transformations. As long as all objects with the same value under one mapping have the same new value under the new mapping, the transformation is valid.

Appropriate statistics include the frequency, mode, and the contingency coefficients. Appropriate statistical tests include nonparametric tests which do not depend on ordering or ranking.

Strictly speaking, use of the nominal scale is not measurement; it is classification. The mathematical operation is the creation of equivalence classes which partition the set of objects into a set of scale values. Valid transformations are those which preserve this partitioning.

Ordinal Scale

Objects are assigned numbers or symbols so they may be ranked and ordered. Given two objects which are adjacent in the ordering, you can say that one object has at least as much of the attribute as the object next to it. The relation is generally denoted by $a \succeq b$ where a is the first object mentioned in the comparison just given. The defining relation is greater than, in addition to the equivalence relation from the nominal scale. The allowable transformations include all strictly increasing functions of the form $x \rightarrow f(x)$ so that order is preserved under the transformation. The group of functions formed by these transformations is also a homeomorphism group, but is restricted to those isomorphisms which are strictly increasing.

To use an ordinal scale, an empirical structure must have an empirical ordering relation which is a weak order. A weak order is one which is transitive and connected, and the objects of the structure must be countable. Formally:

1. $a \succeq b \Leftrightarrow \phi(a) \geqslant \phi(b)$.

2. $a \succeq b \vee b \succeq a$ (connected).

3. $a \succeq b \wedge b \succeq c \Rightarrow a \succeq c$ (transitive).

No points are unique under transformations, as the only requirement is that the order of the points is preserved by the transformation.

Appropriate statistics include the median, quartiles, the upper fourth, the lower fourth, box length, and the upper and lower tails, in addition to those appropriate for the nominal scale. Appropriate statistical tests include all nonparametric tests, including Kendall's rank correlation coefficient τ, the Spearman rank correlation coefficient r_s, and Kendall's ω.

Interval Scale

Objects are assigned numbers in such a way that, in addition to order, the ratio of intervals between objects is preserved under transformations. Given four objects a, b, c, and d, you can say that an object, say a, has at least as much of an attribute as another object, say b. Assuming the same for objects c and d, you can also say that the difference between a and b, called the *interval ab*, is some multiple of the difference between c and d. Formally:

1. $a \succeq b \Leftrightarrow \phi(a) \geq \phi(b)$.

2. If $c \succeq d \wedge a \succeq b \Leftrightarrow \phi'(a) \geq \phi'(b)$, then

$$\frac{\phi(a) - \phi(b)}{\phi(c) - \phi(d)} = \frac{\phi'(a) - \phi'(b)}{\phi'(c) - \phi'(d)}. \tag{5.3}$$

The defining relation is the ratio of any two intervals, in addition to greater than of the ordinal scale and equivalence of the nominal scale.

The allowable transformations can take one of two forms, depending on the domain of the numerical structure. If the domain is all real numbers, the allowable transformations take the form $x \rightarrow rx + s$, where $r > 0$. These transformations form the *positive affine group*. If the domain of the numerical structure is restricted to the positive real numbers, which is often the case in software measurement, the allowable transformations take the form $x \rightarrow tx^r$, where $r > 0$. These transformations form the *power group*, which is prevalent in the transformations of physical dimensions. An interval scale of the power group is called a *log-interval scale*. A transformation is called a *translation* if $r = 1$ or the transformation is the identity which maps every point onto itself. A transformation is called a *dilation* if $r \neq 1$.

The requirements for an interval scale representation vary for different structures. Detailed conditions are given in later sections starting with "Extensive Representations" on page 164.

For interval and log-interval scales, two points are unique under the permissible transformations. For both types of scales, the zero point and the unit of measure are arbitrary choices.

Appropriate statistics include the arithmetic mean, standard deviation, and variance, in addition to those appropriate for the ordinal scale. Appropriate statistical tests include all parametric and nonparametric tests, including the Pearson product-moment correlation coefficient and the multiple product-moment correlation coefficient, subject to assumptions about the distribution of the data.

Ratio Scale

Objects are assigned numbers in such a way that, in addition to order and ratios of intervals, the ratio of scale values is preserved under transformations. The ratio scales have the additional property that the smallest scale value is zero, and that an object can have a null characteristic of an attribute. Given two objects a and *b* with *a* ⪰ *b*, not only can you say that *a* has at least as much of an attribute as *b*, but also you can define a standard sequence of units and say that object *a* has some multiple of units of the attribute more than *b*. This implies further that the scale values assigned to an object are additive over the concatenation operation on the empirical structure. Formally, given objects *a*, *b*, *c*, and *d*:

1. $a \succeq b \Leftrightarrow \phi(a) \geqslant \phi(b)$.

2. $a \sim nb \Leftrightarrow \phi(a) = n\phi(b)$.

3. $a \circ b \sim c \circ d \Leftrightarrow \phi(a) + \phi(b) = \phi(c) + \phi(d)$.

The defining relation is the ratio of two scale values, or

$$\frac{\phi(a)}{\phi(b)} = \frac{\phi'(a)}{\phi'(b)} \tag{5.4}$$

in addition to the defining relations for the interval, ordinal, and nominal scales. It is possible to build ratio scales from structures for which concatenation is not additive or is not defined. Later sections contain several examples of such structures.

The allowable transformations can take one of two forms, depending on the domain of the numerical structure. If the domain is the real numbers, the transformations may be of the form $x \rightarrow x + s$, which is called the *translation group*, or of the form $x \rightarrow rx$, where $r > 0$, which is called the *similarity group*. A scale whose transformations are in the translation group is called a *difference scale*. Note that a difference scale is a form of the ratio scale. If the domain is restricted to the positive real numbers, all transformations take the form $x \rightarrow rx$, where $r > 0$ (the similarity group).

The requirements for a ratio scale representation are quite strong and vary for different kinds of structures. Detailed conditions are given later in the chapter.

For ratio scales, one point is unique under the permissible transformations and only the unit of measure is an arbitrary choice as the zero point is determined by the representation.

Appropriate statistics for ratio scale values include the geometric mean and coefficient of variation, in addition to all those appropriate for the interval scale. Appropriate statistical tests include all parametric and nonparametric tests, subject to assumptions about the distribution of the data.

Absolute Scale

The absolute scale represents counts of objects, cardinality of sets, and probabilities. Both the unit of measure and the zero point are determined by the representation. The only automorphism is the identity, so the only permissible transformation is the identity. All statistics and statistical tests appropriate for the ratio scale are appropriate for the absolute scale.

A More General View of Scales

The material in this section was developed during the late 1980s and was first published in book form in Krantz et al. (1990). This material is newer than object-oriented software development, which gives you some idea of the real age of measurement theory. While work in this field has been ongoing since the late 1800s, many important new advances have come about only in the last decade. As far as I know—and I looked—what appears in this section is the only reference for this material in the software engineering literature. While highly technical and somewhat advanced—it makes use of mathematics covered in Chapter 4—you can use it to determine the scale types of any representation for structures not discussed elsewhere in this chapter. In other words, if you have an empirical structure which does not fit one covered in the sections on pages 160–226, you can still determine a representation and its scale type from this material.

If you look at the transformations between the various representations of a given scale type, note they have some number of parameters or degrees of freedom. You can view this number, N, in two ways:

1. A transformation exists for which some set of N arbitrary distinct points are mapped to some other set of N distinct points in such a way that ordering among the values is preserved.

2. Given that two transformations agree at N distinct points, they are identical—that is, they agree at every point.

The first notion is called *homogeneity* and describes the sizes of two arbitrarily selected sets of points which can always be mapped into each other by a member of the transformation group. The second notion is called *uniqueness* and describes the smallest number of distinct points which are fixed (go to themselves under a transformation) and forces the transformation to be the identity map. Usually, these two numbers agree, but this is not always the case.

In the conventional view of scales, the degree of homogeneity and the degree of uniqueness, denoted by the pair (H, U), are always the same. The nominal and ordinal scales are homogeneous for all points, and unique at no points, which is denoted by (∞, ∞). The interval and log-interval scales are denoted by the pair $(2, 2)$. The ratio and difference scales are denoted by the pair $(1, 1)$.

Now let's formally define the notions of homogeneity and uniqueness. These definitions make use of the following general concepts. Some of these concepts are repeated from the discussions on sets and algebras in Chapter 4, but are included here for convenience. Build a structure from a nonempty set A, a nonempty set J, and for each $j \in J$, a relation S_j of finite order (a finite number of parameters) on A. For our purposes, the set A can contain either the empirical objects or the numbers or symbols to which the objects will be mapped. The set J usually contains integers, but this is not required. The *order* of a relation S_j is given by an integer $n(j)$, which represents the number of parameters for the relation. The relation S_j is included in $A^{n(j)}$ which is the set of all relations S_j for which the order is n.

Then, $A = \langle A, S_j \rangle_{j \in J}$ is called a *relational structure*. When J is finite or countable, you can write $\langle A, S_0, S_1,... \rangle$. If one relation is a weak or total order, you usually replace S_0 with $\succeq$, and write $\langle A, \succeq, S_j \rangle_{j \in J}$ and call the structure *weakly* or *totally ordered*. If A is a subset of $\mathbb{R}$ and S_0 is $\geq$, you usually replace A with R

and S_j with R_j, and write $\boldsymbol{R} = \langle R, \geqslant, R_j \rangle_{j \in J}$, and call it an *ordered numerical structure*.

If A and A' are relational structures with the same index set J, and if, for each $j \in J$, the order(S_j) = order(S'_j); then A and A' are said to be *isomorphic* if and only if there is a one-to-one mapping φ from A *onto* A' such that for all $j \in J$ and all $a_1, a_2,...,a_{n(j)} \in A$:

$$(a_1, a_2,..., a_{n(j)}) \in S_j \Leftrightarrow [\varphi(a_1), \varphi(a_2),..., \varphi(a_{n(j)})] \in S'_j \qquad (5.5)$$

The mapping φ is called an *isomorphism*. If φ is not one-to-one, it is called a *homomorphism*. If A is a totally ordered structure, and $\boldsymbol{R}$ is a totally ordered numerical structure, and A and $\boldsymbol{R}$ are isomorphic, then $\boldsymbol{R}$ is said to be a *numerical representation* of A. This is the essence of measurement: *the construction of an isomorphism from some empirical structure*, that which we are trying to measure, *onto a suitable numerical structure*. Sounds simple enough, but like a great many things, it is easier said than done.

Suppose $A = \langle A, \succeq, S_j \rangle_{j \in J}$ is a totally ordered relational structure, G its group of homomorphisms, and M and N are nonnegative integers. G is said to be *M-point homogeneous* if and only if for each $a_i, b_i \in A$, $i = 1,..., M$, such that $a_1 > a_2 > \cdots > a_M$ and $b_1 > b_2 > \cdots > b_M$, there exists an automorphism $\alpha \in G$ such that $\alpha(a_i) = b_i$, $i = 1, 2,..., M$. G is said to be *N-point unique* if and only if for every $\alpha, \beta \in G$ and $a_i \in A$, $i = 1, 2,..., N$, such that $a_1 > a_2 > \cdots > a_N$, if $\alpha(a_i) = \beta(a_i)$, $i = 1, 2,..., N$, then $\alpha(a) = \beta(a)$ for all $a \in A$. If G is M-point homogeneous, then A is also M-point homogeneous. A is *homogeneous* if it is M-point homogeneous for some $M \geqslant 1$. If G is N-point unique, then A is also N-point unique. A is unique if it is N-point unique for some $N < \infty$. A is said to be of *scale type* (M, N) if and only if its largest degree of homogeneity is M and its smallest degree of uniqueness is N. If the structure is homogeneous for all M, set $M = \infty$. If the structure is unique for any finite N, set $N = \infty$. These definitions are from Narens (1981a; 1981b).

Homogeneity is a strong concept which greatly restricts the possible structures. Thus, the conditions under which homogeneity hold are extremely important. There is one very simple test: No single element can be distinguished from any other element solely in terms of the properties of the structure. Under automorphisms, any element may be mapped to any other element and the structural relations must be preserved.

Currently, there are only four general results about how structures, the degree of homogeneity, and the degree of uniqueness interact. The first result describes the how homogeneity and uniqueness in the presence of structural properties are either assumed or easily proven in certain cases. Given a totally ordered relational structure A, the following hold:

1. If for some integer $M > 1$, the cardinality of $A > M$, and A is M-point homogeneous, then A is $(M - 1)$-point homogeneous.

2. If A is N-point unique, then A is $(N + 1)$-point unique.

3. If A is of scale type (M, N) and the cardinality of $A > M$, then $M \leqslant N$.

The second result describes the powerful relationship between homogeneity and structure. Given a totally ordered relational structure A that is M-point homogeneous, if for each $j \in J$, order$(S_j) \leq M \leq |A|$, then A and $\langle A, \succeq \rangle$ have the same homomorphism group. If in addition, $\langle A, \succeq \rangle$ is isomorphic to $\langle \mathbb{R}, \geq \rangle$ then either for some $j \in J$, $M < $ order(S_j) or A is of scale type (∞, ∞). For example, a concatenation structure $\langle A, \succeq, \circ \rangle$ that has a representation into the real numbers and that is not of scale type (∞, ∞), must have $M \leq 2$, since order$(\circ) = 3$. Usually, the (∞, ∞) case can be ruled out, leaving us with $M \leq 2$ (and either an interval or a ratio scale).

The third and fourth results describe special ties between structure and uniqueness. To deal with uniqueness, some additional concepts are needed. Consider a totally ordered relational structure A. Suppose F is a function on A of order n. F is A-invariant if and only if for each automorphism α of A, and $a_1, a_2,..., a_n \in A$,

$$\alpha F(a_1, a_2,..., a_n) = F[\alpha(a_1), \alpha(a_2),..., \alpha(a_n)] \qquad (5.6)$$

If B is a subset of A, and F is a collection of generalized operations (functions and partial functions), then C is the *algebraic closure* of B under F if and only if A is the smallest set that includes B and, for each F in F, if $c_i \in C$, then $F(c_1,..., c_n) \in C$. Such a closure always exists. If, for some integer N, the algebraic closure under F of each subset with N distinct points is order dense in A, then A is N-point unique.

An automorphism α of a totally ordered relational structure is said to be a *dilation* if and only if it has a fixed point $\alpha(a) = a$, and it is said to be a *translation* if and only if it is either the identity or not a dilation. The set of dilations is denoted D. The set of translations it denoted T. The union of D and T includes all of the automorphisms, or $G = D \cup T$. The identity I is the sole element of the intersection of D and T, or $D \cap T = \{I\}$. The identity is both a dilation and a translation.

If A is a totally ordered relational structure and T is its set of translations, then the following hold:

1. T is a group under functional composition.
2. T is 1-point unique ($N = 1$).
3. Each dilation, aside from the identity, and each translation have a point in common.

If A is N-point unique, its automorphisms commute (for $\alpha, \beta \in G$, $\alpha \beta = \beta \alpha$), and no point is singular in the sense that it is a fixed point for every automorphism, then A is 1-point unique.

If you limit your focus to the real relational structures, properties that determine the scale type can be defined formally. To be applied to general measurement, these properties are determined by analyzing the representation onto or into the real numbers for a given empirical structure.

To define these properties, some concepts from group theory are needed. Suppose $\succeq'$ is an ordering on a group F, and H is a subgroup of F. H is said to be *convex* in F if and only if for each $\alpha \in F$ there exists $\beta \in H$ such that both $\beta \succeq' \alpha$ and $\beta \succeq' \alpha^{-1}$, then $\alpha \in H$. H is said to be *normal* if and only if for $\alpha \in F$, $\alpha H \alpha^{-1} = H$. If A is an ordered relational structure and G is its group of automorphisms, the *asymptotic order* $\succeq'$ on G is defined by:

$$\alpha(b) \succeq' \beta(b) \Leftrightarrow \text{for some } b \in A \qquad \alpha(a) \succeq' \beta(a) \text{ for all } a > b \qquad (5.7)$$

If $R = \langle \mathbb{R}, \geqslant, R_j \rangle_{j \in J}$ is a numerical relational structure that is homogeneous and unique, then the following are true:

1. R is either 1- or 2-point unique ($N = 1, 2$).
2. The asymptotic order on G is a total order and there is a subgroup H of G with the following properties:
   - H is the minimal nontrivial convex subgroup of G.
   - H together with the asymptotic order is an Archimedean ordered group.
   - $H = T$ (the translations of G).
   - H is normal.
   - H is of scale type (1, 1)—*ratio*.
3. If D is nontrivial, then D is homogeneous.
4. R is of scale type (1, 1)—*ratio*—if and only if it is isomorphic to a real structure whose automorphisms are in the difference group.
5. R is of scale type (2, 2)—*interval*—if and only if it is isomorphic to a real structure whose automorphisms are in the affine group.
6. R is of scale type (1, 2)—*interval*—if and only if it is isomporphic to a real structure whose automorphisms are a proper subgroup of the affine group that properly includes the difference group.

No real structure is of type (M, M) for $M > 2$ ($2 < M < \infty$) (Narens 1981b). No real structure is of type $(M, M + 1)$ for $M > 1$ ($1 < M < \infty$) (Alper 1985).

These results apply only to the real numbers. For structures based on proper subsets of $\mathbb{R}^+$, we do not know what classes of transformation groups correspond to scale types (1, 1), (1, 2), and (2, 2), so we generally choose between representations for which the automorphism group is a subgroup of the affine or power groups. These are not the only options, but are matters of convention (Krantz et al. 1990).

For scale types $(0, N)$, where $N < \infty$, the absolute scales, Alper (1987) showed that any $(0, N)$ case can occur. Since so little is known about these structures (Krantz et al. 1990), they will not be discussed any further.

Before proceeding, some additional definitions are needed. A real relational structure $R = \langle R, \geqslant, R_j \rangle_{j \in J}$ is a *real unit structure* if and only if $R \subseteq \mathbb{R}+$ and there is some $T \subseteq \mathbb{R}^+$ such that:

1. T is a group under multiplication.
2. T maps R into R—for each $r \in R$, $t \in T$, $tr \in R$.
3. T restricted to R is the set of translations in R.

Suppose $C = \langle A \times P, \succeq \rangle$ is a conjoint structure (see the section on Conjoint Representations), $a_i, b_i \in A$, $i = 1,..., n$, and S is a relation of order n on A. The ordered n-tuples $(a_1,..., a_n)$ and $(b_1,..., b_n)$ are *similar* if and only of there exist p, $q \in P$ such that for each $i = 1,..., n$, $(a_i, p) \sim (b_i, q)$. S is *distributive in* **C** if and only if for each $a_i, b_i \in A$, $i = 1,..., n$, if $(a_1,..., a_n) \in S$ and $(b_1,..., b_n)$ is similar to it, then $(b_1,..., b_n) \in S$. A structure is distributive in **C** if and only if each of its defining relations are distributive in **C**.

If the translations for a structure **A** form a homogeneous, Archimedean (commutative), ordered group, you can always find a log-interval scale representation of the form taken by the power group $(x \to tx^r, r > 0, t > 0)$ if **A** is order dense. Further, you can find a real unit structure to which **A** is isomorphic. Further still, if the real unit structure is 1-point unique, you can represent **A** with a ratio scale. In addition, you can find an Archimedean, solvable conjoint structure **C** with a relational structure **A**' on the first component that is isomorphic to **A** provided **A**' is distributive in **C**. This conjoint structure satisfies the Thomsen condition (solvability and the Thomsen condition are defined in the sections "Conjoint Representations" and "Nonadditive Representations").

This is an extremely important result. If you have an axiom system for a relational structure, the first step is to look at its translations. If they form a homogeneous, Archimedean, ordered group, you can represent the structure numerically as a homogeneous, real unit structure *with at least a log-interval scale*. If the real unit structure is also 1-point unique, *you have a ratio scale representation.* The significance of these results, due to Luce (1987), is that representation on a log-interval or even a ratio scale is *not dependent on extensive measurement, or even upon having an empirical concatenation operation.* The key is for a structure lying on one component of an Archimedean, solvable conjoint structure to have translations that form a homogeneous, Archimedean, ordered group.

If the conjoint structure **C** is, in addition to being Archimedean, unrestrictedly A-solvable, and restrictedly P-solvable, then **A** is 1-point homogeneous: Its scale type is either $(1, 1)$ or $(1, 2)$. If **A** is also Dedekind complete, then given a mapping $\varphi: A \to \mathbb{R}^+$, **A** has a homogeneous representation, and there exists a mapping $\psi: P \to \mathbb{R}^+$ such that $\varphi\psi$ is a representation of **C**: **C** has a multiplicative representation. Further, if **C** is unrestrictedly P-solvable, and there is a Dedekind complete relational structure on P that, under some $\psi: P \to \mathbb{R}^+$, has a homogeneous unit representation, then for some real constant ρ, $\varphi\psi^\rho$ is a representation of **C**. These results highlight two things:

1. We need not postulate that **C** has a product representation, since we can derive this from the uniqueness of the translations of **A** and the assumption that **A** is distributive in **C**.

2. The multiplicative representation is not restricted to extensive or even concatenation structures—it holds for any structure that is isomorphic to a real unit structure.

The notions of A-solvability, P-solvability, and Dedekind completeness are defined for generic structures in the section on "Nonadditive Representations."

If $A = \langle A, \succeq, \circ \rangle$ is a homogeneous concatenation structure ($M \geq 1$), $\succeq$ is a total order, and $\circ$ is partial operation, then:

1. The partial operation ○ is closed on *A*.

2. Either ○ is idempotent ($\forall a \in A$, $a \circ a \sim a$), weakly positive ($\forall a \in A$, $a \circ a > a$), or weakly negative ($\forall a \in A$, $a \circ a > a$).

3. If ○ is idempotent, the structure is intern and dense; if ○ is weakly positive or weakly negative, it is unbounded.

4. If *A* is weakly positive or negative, then $M = 1$; if it is idempotent, then $M \leq 2$.

5. If *A* is unique ($N < \infty$), then it is of scale type (1, 1), (1, 2), or (2, 2); in the last two cases, it is necessarily idempotent.

Thus, if *A* is unique and either weakly positive or weakly negative, it has a ratio scale representation. If *A* is unique and idempotent, it has at least an interval scale representation (Luce and Narens, 1983; 1985).

If *A* is a positive concatenation structure (PCS—defined in the section "Non-additive Representations"), it is sufficient to show that it is Dedekind complete and that its group of automorphisms *G* is order-dense to conclude that *A* is homogeneous (Cohen and Narens 1979). If *A* is a closed PCS whose automorphism group is dense, then *A* is embeddable in a PCS that has a unit representation, and every automorphism of *A* extends to one of the PCS in which *A* is embedded (Narens 1985).

If *A* is an idempotent concatenation structure that is also closed, solvable, and Dedekind complete, it is homogeneous if and only if there exists some translation $\tau \in T$, $\tau \neq \iota$, such that for some integer *n*, $\theta(\tau, \iota, n)$, $\theta(\tau^{-1}, \iota, n) \in T$, where $\theta(a, b, n)$ is defined by:

$$\theta(a, b, n) = \begin{cases} a \circ b & \text{if } n = 1 \\ \theta(a, b, n - 1) \circ b & \text{if } n > 1 \end{cases} \tag{5.8}$$

To use this result, due to Luce (1986), you must find some nontrivial translation τ of *A* and verify that for each integer *n*, $\theta(\tau, \iota, n)$ is a translation. If this condition is satisfied for some τ, then it holds for all τ. It does not matter which translation is examined first. The fact that you are not given a translation to examine first is somewhat unsatisfactory, but is the best you can do at this point (Krantz et al. 1990).

You have seen how to define homogeneity and uniqueness on one factor of a conjoint structure but it is less clear what should be done with the other factor. Two-factor conjoint structures will be analyzed in the sections "Conjoint Representations" and "Nonadditive Representations," but the discussion of *n*-factor conjoint structures is limited to the special cases of conjoint representations. Only two-factor conjoint structures are considered here.

To work with such structures, we need to define homogeneity and uniqueness on the group of factorizable automorphisms (defined in the section "Nonadditive Representations"). Given a conjoint structure $C = \langle A \times P, \succeq \rangle$ and its group of automorphisms *F*, *F* is *component M-point homogeneous* if and only if for strictly increasing sequences of *M* elements $\{a_i\}$, $\{b_i\}$, $\{p_i\}$, and $\{q_i\}$ ($a_1 < a_2 < a_3 <$

$\cdots < a_m$, etc.) there are factorizable automorphisms $\langle \theta, \eta \rangle$ and $\langle \theta', \eta' \rangle$ such that $\theta(a_i) = b_i$, $\eta(p_m) = q_m$, $\theta'(a_m) = b_m$, and $\eta'(p_i) = q_i$, $i = 1,..., m$. F is *component N-point unique* if and only if for all sequences $\{a_i\}$ and $\{p_i\}$ such that $\{a_i p_i\}$ is strictly increasing, and for all $\langle \theta, \eta \rangle$, $\langle \theta', \eta' \rangle$ in F such that $\theta(a_i) = \theta'(a_i)$ and $\eta(p_i) = \eta'(p_i)$:

1. If $\{a_i\}$ is strictly increasing, then $\theta = \theta'$.

2. If $\{p_i\}$ is strictly increasing, then $\eta = \eta'$.

If C is component M-point homogeneous, then C is M-point homogeneous. If C is N-point unique, then C is component N-point unique. If C is restrictedly solvable and Archimedean, then its group of automorphisms is either component 1- or 2-point unique (Krantz et al. 1990).

A *singular point* for a general relational structure is one which remains fixed under all automorphisms of the structure. To define a singular point in a conjoint structure, you must first be able to find a singular point on each component separately. If $C = \langle A \times P, \succeq \rangle$, then if a_0 is a singular point on the A factor, and p_0 is a singular point on the P factor, then $a_0 p_0$ is a singular point on the conjoint structure.

Determining whether a factor has a singular point requires factoring the automorphisms for the conjoint structure and testing the groups formed by each factor's automorphisms. If C is unrestrictedly solvable and Archimedean, and $a_0 p_0 \in A \times P$ is a singular point, then the group of factorizable automorphisms F is component 2-point unique—an interval scale of type $(1, 2)$ or $(2, 2)$.

The set $A^+ = \{a \mid a \in A \wedge a > a_0\}$ and I_{A^+} is the PCS on A^+ induced by C via $a_0 p_0$. F_{A^+} is the restriction of the A-factors in F to A^+. Likewise, $A^- = \{a \mid a \in A \wedge a_0 > a\}$ and I_{A^-} is the PCS on A^- with the inequalities reversed. F_{A^-} is the restriction of the A-factors in F to A^-. Similar definitions can be applied to P for I_{P^+}, I_{P^-}, F_{P^+}, and F_{P^-}. If $F_{A^+ \times P^+}$ is component 1-point homogeneous on $A^+ \times P^+$, then:

1. F_{A^+} is the automorphism group on I_{A^+} and is of scale type $(1, 1)$—a ratio scale.

2. F_{A^-} is the automorphism group on I_{A^-} and is of scale type $(1, 1)$.

3. F_{P^+} is the automorphism group on I_{P^+} and is of scale type $(1, 1)$.

4. F_{P^-} is the automorphism group on I_{P^-} and is of scale type $(1, 1)$.

For conjoint structures with no singular point, look to the following. If $C = \langle \mathbb{R} \times \mathbb{R}, \geqslant \rangle$ is a real conjoint structure that is unrestrictedly solvable, and its group of factorizable automorphisms satisfies 2-point uniqueness and component 2-point homogeneity, and both F_i satisfy 2-point uniqueness, then C satisfies the Thomsen condition (see the section "Conjoint Representations"; and Krantz et al. 1990).

ORDINAL REPRESENTATIONS

Ordinal measurement is based upon an ordering relation $\succeq$ on a set. The structural requirements for ordinal measurement are fairly simple, in mathematical terms.

Transferring these simple mathematical requirements to an empirical structure is often very difficult, and sometimes impossible.

The basic requirements for ordinal measurement are laid down in Cantor's theorem, which was proven in 1895 (Krantz et al. 1971): If a set A is countable, and $\langle A, \succeq \rangle$ is a simple order, then there exists a real-valued function ϕ on A such that for all $a, b \in A$:

$$a \succeq b \Leftrightarrow \phi(a) \geq \phi(b) \tag{5.9}$$

Cantor's theorem is the representation condition for ordinal measurement. The uniqueness of the function ϕ has not yet been established.

A *simple order* is a structure formed by a set A and a binary relation $\succeq$, denoted $\langle A, \succeq \rangle$, that satisfies the following:

1. Connectedness: $a \succeq b \vee b \succeq a$.
2. Transitivity: $a \succeq b \wedge b \succeq c \Rightarrow a \succeq c$.
3. Antisymmetry: $a \succeq b \wedge b \succeq a \Rightarrow a \sim b$ (a and b are equivalent).

A structure $\langle A, \succeq \rangle$ which is only connected and transitive is called a *weak order*. Weak orders arise often in empirical structures. If the set A is finite, the presence of a weak order is a sufficient condition for a representation ϕ to exist (Krantz et al. 1971). Most empirical structures consist of finite sets, especially in software, although some are countable. Only a very few abstract entities are uncountable.

Having provided the general requirements for ordinal measurement, let's explore two more ordinal structures which highlight some of the ways a simple order can be constructed. Both of these examples come from geometry (Krantz et al. 1989). The first is from affine geometry and the second is from projective geometry. Both define ordering in terms of the notion of betweeness on a line, but each does so in a very different way.

Betweenness Structures

The affine geometry defines betweenness as a ternary relation B on a set A by $B(a, b, c) \Leftrightarrow a \mid b \mid c$. This notation indicates that b is between a and c in the sense that the interval ac is at least as much as both the intervals ab and bc, or $ac \succeq ab, bc$. It is possible for b to be either a or c. Here, the interval is the distance between two points along the line which connects them. Points a, b, and c are *collinear*: They lie on the same line.

Given a nonempty set A and a ternary relation B, $U = \langle A, B \rangle$ is a *one-dimensional betweenness structure* (Krantz et al. 1989) if and only if the following all hold for every $a, b, c, d \in A$:

1. $a \mid b \mid a \Rightarrow a = b$.
2. $a \mid b \mid c \Rightarrow c \mid b \mid a$.
3. $a \mid b \mid c \wedge b \mid d \mid c \Rightarrow a \mid b \mid d$.
4. $a \mid b \mid c \wedge b \mid c \mid d \wedge b \neq d \Rightarrow a \mid b \mid d$.
5. $a \mid b \mid c \vee b \mid c \mid a \vee c \mid a \mid b$.

U is *separable* if and only if there is a finite or countable order-dense subset of A: That is, there is a finite or countable $C \subseteq A$ such that for all $a, c \in A$ with $a \neq c$, there exists $b \in C$ such that $a \mid b \mid c$. Or, the structure U is separable if there is at least one point between any two distinct points. This requirement can cause problems in many of the discrete structures encountered in software.

For the affine geometry, the **representation condition** is: If $U = \langle A, B \rangle$ is a separable one-dimensional betweenness structure, then there is a real-valued function φ such that for all $a, b, c \in A$,

$$a \mid b \mid c \Leftrightarrow [\varphi(a) \leq \varphi(b) \leq \varphi(c) \vee \varphi(c) \leq \varphi(b) \leq \varphi(a)] \qquad (5.10)$$

(Krantz et al. 1989). The **uniqueness condition** is: If φ' is another function which satisfies these conditions, then there exists a strictly monotone function $h: \mathbb{R} \rightarrow \mathbb{R}$ such that for all $a \in A$, $\varphi'(a) = h[\varphi(a)]$ (φ is an **ordinal scale**) (Krantz et al. 1989). As a convention, I will define any new structures needed for the representation or uniqueness conditions first, then give the representation condition, followed by the uniqueness condition. These two conditions will be labeled in **boldface** type to make them easy to spot. In general, there will be only one such pair for each structure, and only one structure will be described in a subsection.

Separation Structures

The projective geometry requires the quaternary relation of separation. The axioms of separation for projective order on the line also characterize order on the circle. Intuitively, when we have $ab\ S\ cd$, then the points a and b separate the points c and d, and conversely, as shown in Figure 5.1. When the points are on a line and projected onto another line through a point not on either line, separation order is preserved, as shown in Figure 5.2. Note that under projection, while separation order is preserved, betweenness order may not necessarily be preserved.

The axioms for separation form a strict order, corresponding to numerical less than. Betweenness forms an inclusive order, corresponding to numerical less than or equal to. Given a nonempty set A and a quaternary relation S on A, the structure $U = \langle A, S \rangle$ is a *one-dimensional separation structure* (Krantz et al. 1989) if and only if the following all hold for every $a, b, c, d, e \in A$:

1. $\neg(ab\ S\ ac \vee ab\ S\ cc)$.
2. $ab\ S\ cd \Rightarrow cd\ S\ ab$.

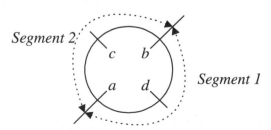

Figure 5.1 *A geometric betweenness structure (Krantz et al. 1989).*

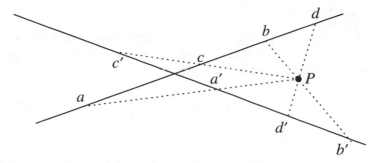

Figure 5.2 *A geometric separation structure (Krantz et al. 1989).*

3. *ab S cd* ⇒ *ab S dc.*
4. *ab S cd* ⇒ ¬(*ac S bd*).
5. *ab S cd* ∧ *ae S db* ⇒ *ab S ce.*
6. If *a*, *b*, *c*, and *d* are distinct, then *ab S cd* ∨ *bc S ad* ∨ *ca S bd.*

U is *separable* if and only if there is a finite or countable order-dense subset of *A*: There is a finite or countable subset $C \subseteq A$ such that for all *a*, *b* ∈ *A* with *a* ≠ *b*, there exist *c*, *d* ∈ *C* with *ab S cd*. Or, there is always a pair of points that separate any two distinct points. As with betweenness, not all discrete structures are separable.

For the projective geometry, the representation condition is based on the notion of cross ratios. Let a_i, *i* = 1, 2, 3, 4, be four distinct points on a line, and let the coordinate of a_i be x_i. The *cross ratio* of these four points in terms of their coordinates is

$$\frac{x_1 - x_2}{x_1 - x_4} \cdot \frac{x_3 - x_4}{x_3 - x_2} \tag{5.11}$$

where you have $a_1a_3 \, S \, a_2a_4$ and $x_1 < x_2 < x_3 < x_4$. The set of real numbers must include ∞, so define the numerical structure to be based on $\mathbb{R}^* = \mathbb{R} \cup \{\infty\}$. For the algebra, assume:

1. $x + \infty = \infty + x = x - \infty = \infty - x = \infty.$
2. If $x \neq 0$, then $x\infty = x/0$ and $x/\infty = 0$.
3. If $x_4 = \infty$, then the cross ratio is:

$$\frac{x_1 - x_2}{x_3 - x_2} \tag{5.12}$$

More generally, if *a*, *b*, *c*, and *d* are real numbers such that $ad - bc \neq 0$ and $x = \infty$, then:

$$\varphi(x) = \frac{ax + b}{cx + d} = \frac{a}{c} \tag{5.13}$$

4. As for order, $x < \infty$.

For the projective geometry, the **representation condition** is: If $U = \langle A, S \rangle$ is a separable one-dimensional separation structure, then there exists a function φ: $A \to \mathbb{R}^*$ such that for all $a, b, c, d \in A$,

$$ab \, S \, cd \Leftrightarrow \frac{\varphi(a) - \varphi(c)}{\varphi(a) - \varphi(d)} \cdot \frac{\varphi(b) - \varphi(d)}{\varphi(b) - \varphi(c)} < 0 \qquad (5.14)$$

(Krantz et al. 1989).

For the uniqueness condition, it is necessary to define the concept of a projective monotone function. A function h: $\mathbb{R} \subseteq \mathbb{R}^* \to \mathbb{R}' \subseteq \mathbb{R}^*$ is *projectively monotone* if and only if h is strictly monotone or there exists a partition $(\underline{\mathbb{R}}, \overline{\mathbb{R}})$ of $\mathbb{R}$ such that every element of $\underline{\mathbb{R}}$ is less than every element of $\overline{\mathbb{R}}$ and either h is strictly increasing on $\underline{\mathbb{R}}$ and on $\overline{\mathbb{R}}$, and for every x in $\underline{\mathbb{R}}$ and every x' in $\overline{\mathbb{R}}$, $h(x') < h(x)$, or h is strictly decreasing on $\underline{\mathbb{R}}$ and on $\overline{\mathbb{R}}$, and for every x in $\underline{\mathbb{R}}$ and every x' in $\overline{\mathbb{R}}$, $h(x) < h(x')$.

The **uniqueness condition** is: If $U = \langle A, S \rangle$ is a separable one-dimensional separation structure, and φ and φ' are two representing functions (satisfying the representation condition), and $\mathbb{R}$ is the range of φ and $\mathbb{R}'$ is the range of φ', then there exists a projective monotone function h: $\mathbb{R} \to \mathbb{R}'$ such that for all $a \in A$, $\varphi'(a) = h[\varphi(a)]$ (φ is an **ordinal scale**) (Krantz et al. 1989).

EXTENSIVE REPRESENTATIONS

This section focuses on several structures which can be measured extensively. Extensive measurement is so ingrained into our way of thinking that most of us use it every day without realizing it. The measurement of length is the most obvious and familiar use of extensive measurement. The measurement of linear distance, the measurement of mass, and the measurement of volume are also common examples of extensive measurement. Many measurement experts within software engineering (and many other fields) feel that extensive measurement is the only "true" form of measurement. Some, particularly Zuse (1990) and to some extent Fenton (1991), believe that extensive measurement is the only kind that leads to ratio scale representations. You will see, in other sections, that this is simply not the case. Here, though, you will see why they think that way.

Extensive measurement can occur whenever the ordering relation $\succeq$ and the concatenation operation $\circ$ are both defined. Extensive measurement makes use of the counting of units procedure, and depends on the ability to concatenate the units end-to-end, thereby constructing a standard sequence, to approximate the object being measured. Extensive structures, those empirical structures to which extensive measurement can be applied, must satisfy two basic conditions (Krantz et al. 1971):

1. The representation $a \to \phi(a)$ must be order-preserving: $a \succeq b \Leftrightarrow \phi(a) \geq \phi(b)$.

2. The representation $a \to \phi(a)$ must be additive under concatenation: $\phi(a \circ b) = \phi(a) + \phi(b)$.

In any particular case, a theory of extensive measurement is a set of assumptions, or axioms, formulated in terms of the conditions required by a structure so that the relation ϕ and the concatenation $\circ$ do satisfy these conditions. Extensive measurement leads to ratio scale representations. That is, the assignment of numbers to the attribute is dependent only upon the choice of the unit used to construct the standard sequence. In extensive measurement, a standard sequence can always be constructed.

Not all structures can form extensive structures. In some cases, a natural interpretation of the concatenation operation leads to nonadditive representations. For example, in dealing with sets, the general set union operation is nonadditive, but does represent a natural interpretation of the concatenation operation. Note, however, that the union of two disjoint sets, $A \cup B$ where $A \cap B = \emptyset$, is additive and has been used in extensive measurement (Krantz et al. 1971). The nonadditive situation can be partially dealt with by using transformation functions to convert the results of measurement into an additive function (see Krantz et al. 1971; and the last subsection on construction techniques). In other cases, no natural empirical interpretation of the concatenation operation can be found.

Now let's explore, in order of increasing complexity, the different types of empirical structures known to lead to extensive measurement. The following conventions will be used during the exploration.

Start with a nonempty set A which contains the objects $a, b, c, ...$ you wish to measure. Add a binary relation $\succeq$ on A which is interpreted as meaning $a \succeq b$ holds if and only if the object a has at least as much of some defined property or attribute as object b. Write $a \sim b$ if and only if both $a \succeq b$ and $b \succeq a$ hold; write $a > b$ if and only if $a \succeq b$, but not $b \sim a$. Add a binary operation $\circ: A \times A \to A$ which is assumed to be closed for the moment (this restriction is loosened later). Interpret $a \circ b$ to be an object in A which is obtained by concatenating or composing objects a and b in some defined way. Denote the structure by $\langle A, \succeq, \circ \rangle$.

Closed Extensive Structures

A triple $\langle A, \succeq, \circ \rangle$ is a *closed extensive structure* (Krantz et al. 1971) if and only if the following hold for all $a, b, c, d \in A$:

1. *Weak order*: $\langle A, \succeq \rangle$ is a weak order, that is, $\succeq$ is:
  - *Transitive*: $a \succeq b \wedge b \succeq c \Rightarrow a \succeq c$
  - *Connected*: $a \succeq b \vee b \succeq a$
2. *Weak associativity*: $a \circ (b \circ c) \sim (a \circ b) \circ c$.
3. *Montonicity*: $a \succeq b \Leftrightarrow a \circ c \succeq b \circ c \Leftrightarrow c \circ a \succeq c \circ b$.
4. *Archimedean*: If $a > b$, then for any $c, d \in A$, there exists a positive integer n such that $na \circ c > nb \circ d$, where na is defined inductively as $1a = a$, $(n + 1)a = na \circ a$.

If, in addition, a closed extensive structure satisfies $a \circ b \succeq a$ (*positivity*), it is called a *positive closed extensive structure* (Krantz et al. 1971).

The **representation condition** is: $\langle A, \succeq, \circ \rangle$ is a closed extensive structure if and only if there exists a real-valued function ϕ on A ($\phi: A \to \mathbb{R}$) such that for all $a, b \in A$:

1. $a \succeq b \Leftrightarrow \phi(a) \geq \phi(b)$ (ϕ is order preserving).   (5.15a)

2. $\phi(a \circ b) = \phi(a) + \phi(b)$ (ϕ is additive under concatenation).   (5.15b)

(Krantz et al. 1971.) The **uniqueness condition** is: Another real-valued function ϕ' satisfies conditions (5.15a) and (5.15b) if and only if there exists $\alpha > 0$ such that $\phi' = \alpha\phi$, or, for all $a \in A$, $\phi'(a) = \alpha\phi(a)$ (ϕ is a **ratio scale**). The structure is *positive* if and only if for all $a \in A$, $\phi(a) > 0$.

The form of these conditions, "if and only if," may look strange to you. You can think of the phrasing as "if you have a structure that satisfies thus and so, then there exists a real-valued function . . ." and you would be correct, but only partially. Strictly speaking, the "if a, then b" construct means that if a is true, you can assume b, but if b is known to be true, you can infer nothing about a. The "a if and only if b" phrasing indicates that if either a or b is known to be true, you can assume the other. For our representations, this means that not only can you find such a function when conditions 1 through 4 are met, but that when you encounter such a function which satisfies the representation condition, then any empirical structure to which it can be mapped meets conditions 1 through 4 previously given. The "if and only if" phrasing will be used consistently throughout this chapter.

To use these conditions to construct an extensive representation, it is sufficient to show that your empirical relational structure meets conditions 1 through 4 (and positivity, if that is important). The uniqueness condition asserts that you may select any arbitrary object $a \in A$ to be the unit object in your standard sequence. You can find an $\alpha > 0$ such that you can express any standard sequence in terms of any other standard sequence based on some other object $b \in A$.

Some closed extensive structures exhibit a periodic nature, where given a period p, $a \circ p \sim a$. Familiar examples of such periodic structures are clock time and angle. Periodic structures require modifications to the monotonicity and Archimedean axioms. In a periodic structure, monotonicity fails if you don't account for the fact that a concatenation operation may cause a, b, neither a nor b, or both a and b to complete a period. So, $\langle A, \succeq, \circ \rangle$ is a *closed periodic extensive structure* (Krantz et al. 1971) if and only if the following hold for all $a, b, c \in A$:

1. *Weak order*: $\langle A, \succeq \rangle$ is a weak order.

2. *Weak associativity and weak commutativity*: $\langle A, \circ, \sim \rangle$ satisfies $(a \circ b) \circ c \sim a \circ (b \circ c)$ and $a \circ b \sim b \circ a$.

3. *Monotonicity*: $a \succeq b$ if and only if either:

$$a \circ c \succeq b \circ c \succeq c,$$

$$c > a \circ c \succeq b \circ c, \text{ or}$$

$$b \circ c \succeq c \succeq a \circ c$$

4. Archimedean: If $a > b$, then there exists a positive integer n such that $a > na$ and $nb \succeq b$, where $1a = a$ and $(n + 1)a = na \circ a$.

The structure $\langle A, \succeq, \circ \rangle$ has an *identity* $e \in A$ if for all $a \in A$, $a \circ e \sim e \circ a \sim a$.

The **representation condition** for closed periodic extensive structures is: $\langle A, \succeq, \circ \rangle$ is a closed periodic extensive structure if and only if there exists a unique function $\phi: A \rightarrow [0, \alpha]$ such that for all $a, b \in A$:

1. $a \succeq b \Leftrightarrow \phi(a) \geqslant \phi(b)$.   (5.16a)

2. $\phi(a \circ b) = \phi(a) + \phi(b) \pmod{\alpha}$.   (5.16b)

3. $\phi(e) = 0$.   (5.16c)

(Krantz et al. 1971.) The **uniqueness condition** is: Another real-valued function ϕ' satisfies conditions (5.16a), (5.16b), and (5.16c) if and only if there exists $\alpha > 0$ such that $\phi' = \alpha\phi$, or, for all $a \in A$, $\phi'(a) = \alpha\phi(a)$ (ϕ is a **ratio scale**) (Krantz et al. 1971).

Nonclosed Extensive Structures with No Essential Maxima

An extensive structure is *nonclosed* if the results of concatenating objects $a, b \in A$ is not an object in A ($a \circ b \notin A$). This can result from several conditions, the most common of which is that the set A is finite and simply doesn't contain the element which results from the operation. This is nearly always the case in software measurement—there are very few examples of infinite sets in software, one of which is the set of states for a container which can contain generic objects.

The axioms given in this subsection apply to an extensive structure with no essential maximum. A structure has an *essential maximum* if there is an object $z \in A$ such that for all $a \in A$, $z \succeq a$ and $a \circ z \sim z$ (that is, the concatenation operation is defined for z, but always results in z). The speed of light in relativistic velocity is such an essential maximum.

For this set of axioms, a set of ordered pairs B are defined to be a subset of $A \times A$. The set B contains all $\langle a, b \rangle$, $a, b \in A$, for which $a \circ b \in A$. The quadruple $\langle A, \succeq, B, \circ \rangle$ is an *extensive structure with no essential maximum* (Krantz et al. 1971) the following hold for all $a, b, c \in A$:

1. $\langle A, \succeq \rangle$ is a weak order.

2. If $\langle a, b \rangle \in B$ and $\langle a \circ b, c \rangle \in B$, then $\langle b, c \rangle \in B$, $\langle a, b \circ c \rangle \in B$, and $(a \circ c) \circ b \succeq a \circ (b \circ c)$.

3. If $\langle a, c \rangle \in B$ and $a \succeq b$, then $\langle c, b \rangle \in B$ and $a \circ c \succeq c \circ b$.

4. If $a > b$, then there exists $d \in A$ such that $\langle b, d \rangle \in B$ and $a > b \circ d$.

5. If $\langle a, b \rangle \in B$, then $a \circ b > a$.

6. Every strictly bounded standard sequence is finite, where $a_1,\ldots, a_n,\ldots$ is a *standard sequence* if for $n = 2,\ldots, a_n = a_{n-1} \circ a$, and it is *strictly bounded* if for some $b \in A$ and for all a_n in the sequence, $b > a_n$.

Axiom 6 is the Archimedean axiom. Both a standard sequence and the notion of strict boundedness in the statement of the axiom will be defined for each structure since these definitions depend on the nature of the structure.

The **representation condition** is: If $\langle A, \succeq, B, \circ \rangle$ is an extensive structure with no essential maximum, then there exists a function $\phi: A \to \mathbb{R}^+$ such that for all $a, b \in A$:

1. $a \succeq b \Leftrightarrow \phi(a) \geqslant \phi(b)$. $\hfill$ (5.17a)
2. If $\langle a, b \rangle \in B$, then $\phi(a \circ b) = \phi(a) + \phi(b)$. $\hfill$ (5.17b)

(Krantz et al. 1971.) The **uniqueness condition** is: If another function ϕ' satisfies conditions (5.17a) and (5.17b), then there exists a real number $\alpha > 0$ such that for all nonmaximal $a \in A$, $\phi'(a) = \alpha\phi(a)$ (ϕ is a **ratio scale**) (Krantz et al. 1971).

Nonclosed Extensive Structures with Essential Maxima

In the previous subsection, an *essential maximum element z* of a set A was defined as one for which $z \succeq a$ for all $a \in A$; and $z \circ a \sim z$ for all $a \in A$. In software, essential maxima occur in situations where saturation points exist. One example is a measure based on a proportion of a total, such as the percentage of use cases mapped into a design. If all of the use cases are mapped, the essential maximum of 100 percent is reached. Adding a new use case, which is also mapped, leaves the measure at 100 percent.

Define the structure by modifying axioms 5 and 6 of the definition of an extensive structure with no essential maximum. A structure $\langle A, \succeq, B, \circ \rangle$ is an *extensive structure with at least one essential maximum* (Krantz et al. 1971) if the following hold for all $a, b, c \in A$:

1. $\langle A, \succeq \rangle$ is a weak order.
2. If $\langle a, b \rangle \in B$ and $\langle a \circ b, c \rangle \in B$, then $\langle b, c \rangle \in B$, $\langle a, b \circ c \rangle \in B$, and $(a \circ c) \circ b \succeq a \circ (b \circ c)$.
3. If $\langle a, c \rangle \in B$ and $a \succeq b$, then $\langle c, b \rangle \in B$ and $a \circ c \succeq c \circ b$.
4. If $a > b$, then there exists $d \in A$ such that $\langle b, d \rangle \in B$ and $a > b \circ d$.
5. If $\langle a, b \rangle \in B$ and a is not an essential maximum, then $a \circ b > a$.
6. If a standard sequence is strictly bounded by an element which is not an essential maximum, the sequence is finite.

Suppose that $\langle A, \succeq, B, \circ \rangle$ is an extensive structure with at least one essential maximum z. The structure $\langle A', \succeq', B', \circ' \rangle$ is defined as follows:

1. A' is the subset of all nonmaximal elements of A ($z \notin A'$).
2. $\succeq'$ is the restriction of $\succeq$ to A'.
3. $B' = \{ \langle a, b \rangle \mid a, b \in A' \wedge \langle a, b \rangle \in B \wedge a \circ b \in A' \}$.
4. $\circ'$ is the restriction of $\circ$ to B'.

If A' and B' are nonempty, then $\langle A', \succeq', B', \circ' \rangle$ is an extensive structure with no essential maximum as defined in the previous subsection.

The **representation condition** is: If $\langle A, \succeq, B, \circ \rangle$ is an extensive structure with at least one essential maximum z, and $\langle A', \succeq', B', \circ' \rangle$ is an extensive structure with no essential maximum such that $A' = A \setminus \{z\}$, and there exist $x, y \in A'$ such that $\langle x, y \rangle \in B$ and $x \circ y \sim z$, then there exists $\phi: A \to \mathbb{R}^+$ such that for all $a, b \in A$:

1. $a \succeq b \Leftrightarrow \phi(a) \geqslant \phi(b)$.   (5.18a)
2. If $\langle a, b \rangle \in B'$, then $\phi(a \circ b) = \phi(a) + \phi(b)$.   (5.18b)
3. $\phi(z) = \inf\{\phi(x) + \phi(y) \mid \langle x, y \rangle \in B \wedge x \circ y \sim z\}$.   (5.18c)

(Krantz et al. 1971.) The **uniqueness condition** is: If another function ϕ' satisfies conditions (5.18a), (5.18b), and (5.18c), then there exists a real number $\alpha > 0$ such that for all nonmaximal $a \in A$, $\phi'(a) = \alpha\phi(a)$ (ϕ is a **ratio scale**) (Krantz et al. 1971).

Conditionally Connected Extensive Structures

In some structures, the connectedness of $\langle A, \succeq \rangle$ is not valid for all pairs $a, b \in A$. There may be cases where neither $a \succeq b$ nor $b \succeq a$ hold. An example is where the set A is the set of all possible states which can be assumed by an object (software or otherwise). If the relation $a \succeq b$ is interpreted to mean that an object in state b can transition to state a, then there may be some pairs of states for which this relation does not hold. In these cases (for these pairs), $\langle A, \succeq \rangle$ is not connected.

Extensive measurement on such a structure can still be performed by modifying the axioms which the structure must satisfy. Given the structure $\langle A, \succeq, \circ \rangle$, define A_0 as:

$$A_0 = \{x \mid x \in A \wedge \forall a \in A \; x \succeq a \Rightarrow a \succeq x\} \qquad (5.19)$$

Thus, A_0 contains all of the pairs $a, b \in A$ for which connectedness holds. We further assume that A_0 is closed under concatenation, and that for all elements $b \in A$ for which $a \succeq b$ holds, at least one b is in A_0 (axioms 7 and 8 in the following list).

The structure $\langle A, \succeq, \circ \rangle$ is an *entropy structure* (Krantz et al. 1971) if you define A_0 as in (5.19) and the following axioms are satisfied for all $a, b, c, d, x, y \in A$:

1. *Quasi ordering*: The relation $\succeq$ is reflexive and transitive.
2. *Conditional connectedness*: If $a \succeq b$ and $a \succeq c$, then either $b \succeq c$ or $c \succeq b$.
3. *Weak associativity* [$(a \circ b) \circ c \sim a \circ (b \circ c)$] and *weak commutativity* [$a \circ b \sim b \circ a$].
4. *Monotonicity*: $a \succeq b \Leftrightarrow a \circ c \succeq b \circ c$.

5. If for some $n \in \mathbb{N}$, $na \succeq nb$, then $a \succeq b$ ($1a = a$, $(n + 1)a = na \circ a$).

6. *Archimedean*: If $a > b$ and either $c \succeq d$ or $d \succeq c$, then there exists $n \in \mathbb{N}$ such that $na \circ c \succeq nb \circ d$.

7. If $x, y \in A_0$, then $x \circ y \in A_0$.

8. For each $a \in A$, there exists $z \in A_0$ such that $a \succeq z$.

To facilitate construction of the mapping $\phi: A \rightarrow \mathbb{R}^+$, define a component of content as follows: A function $\chi: A \rightarrow \mathbb{R}$ is a *component of content* for the entropy structure $\langle A, \succeq, \circ \rangle$ if and only if, for all $a, b \in A$, $a \succeq b \Rightarrow \chi(a) \geqslant \chi(b)$; and $(a \circ b) = \chi(a) + \chi(b)$. A component of content is nontrivial if $\chi \neq 0$.

The **representation condition** is: If $\langle A, \succeq, \circ \rangle$ is an entropy structure, then there exists a family C of components of content and a function $\phi: A \rightarrow \mathbb{R}^+$ such that, for all $a, b \in A$:

1. $a \succeq b \Leftrightarrow \phi(a) \geqslant \phi(b) \lor \forall \chi \in C \; \chi(a) = \chi(b)$.   (5.20a)

2. $\phi(a \circ b) = \phi(a) + \phi(b)$.   (5.20b)

3. $\phi(a) = 0 \Leftrightarrow a \in A_0$.   (5.20c)

(Krantz et al. 1971.) The **uniqueness condition** is: Another function ϕ' satisfies (5.20a), (5.20b), and (5.20c) if and only if there exists a real number $\alpha > 0$, such that $\phi'(a) = \alpha\phi(a)$ (ϕ is a **ratio scale**) (Krantz et al. 1971).

Condition (5.20a) of the representation condition states that $a \succeq b$ only if a and b are comparable in A. To be comparable, there must be a family of additive measures which do not change between a and b: $\chi(a) = \chi(b)$ for all $\chi \in C$. Put another way, if a and b are not comparable (if neither $a \succeq b$ nor $b \succeq a$), then there is a nontrivial component of content for which $\chi(a) \neq \chi(b)$. In empirical terms, when moving from b to a (as in $a \succeq b$), only those qualities measured by ϕ are allowed to change. Objects a and b must have some qualities in common which do not change. For software objects, as in the earlier example, this would mean that two states, a and b, must have at least one attribute value in common in order to move from state b to state a, and that only the attributes included in ϕ are allowed to change values.

Alternative Numerical Representations

Not all representations of extensive structures need to be additive. If $\langle A, \succeq, \circ \rangle$ is an extensive structure with no essential maximum, we know that we can find an additive function ϕ which maps it to $\langle \mathbb{R}^+, \geqslant, + \rangle$.

Suppose there exists some different binary operation $\oplus$ on $\mathbb{R}$ such that $\psi: \langle A, \succeq, \circ \rangle \rightarrow \langle \mathbb{R}, \geqslant, \oplus \rangle$ and is "additive" in $\oplus$ over $\circ$. The images of $\langle A, \succeq, \circ \rangle$ under ψ must also satisfy the axioms of an extensive structure with no essential maximum. This means that the image of ψ can be mapped additively into $\langle \mathbb{R}^+, \geqslant, + \rangle$ by some function f:

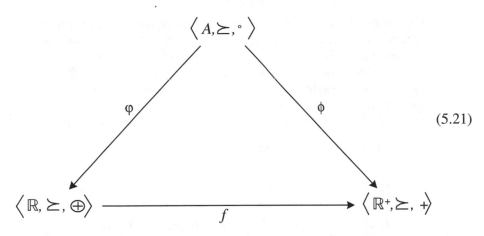

(5.21)

This allows you to choose between ϕ and ψ since $\phi = f(\psi)$. Since both ψ and ϕ are additive:

$$\psi(a) + \psi(b) = \psi(a \circ b)$$
$$= f^{-1}[\phi(a \circ b)]$$
$$= f^{-1}[\phi(a) + \phi(b)]$$
$$= f^{-1}[f(\psi(a)) + f(\psi(b))] \qquad (5.22)$$

More generally, you have

$$x \oplus y = f^{-1}[f(x) + f(y)] \qquad (5.23)$$

or

$$g(x + y) = F[g(x), g(y)] \qquad (5.24)$$

(Aczél 1966). This allows you to use nonadditive representations where they are convenient, since you can always convert back to an underlying additive representation so long as you can define the operation $\oplus$.

Construction Techniques

You have seen the conditions required of an empirical structure in order to know you can measure it extensively. That is, given an empirical relational structure which satisfies one of the sets of axioms in this section, you know you can find a function ϕ such that $\phi\colon \langle A, \succeq, \circ \rangle \to \langle \mathbb{R}^+, \geqslant, + \rangle$, or a function $\psi\colon \langle A, \succeq, \circ \rangle \to \langle \mathbb{R}, \geqslant, \oplus \rangle$. But there is little in these sets of axioms which helps determine any particular ϕ or ψ.

The aim of this subsection is to provide a means of constructing a function ϕ given an empirical relational structure $\langle A, \succeq, \circ \rangle$. We do this by restricting ourselves to concatenation operations of the form na, and excluding all those of the form $a \circ b$ where $\neg(a \sim b)$. You want to be able to handle cases where na is not necessarily in A. Further, you cannot merely specialize the previous results because whenever $a \circ a \in A$ and $a \succeq b$, then $a \circ b \in A$, which you don't want. So, a new axiom system is needed which consists solely of elements na.

Let A be a nonempty set; $\succeq$ a binary relation on A; B a nonempty subset of $\mathbb{N} \times A$; and f a function from B into A, which is written as $f(n, a) = na$. The quadruple $\langle A, \succeq, B, f \rangle$ is a *structure of extensive multiples* (Krantz et al. 1971) if and only if the following hold for all $a, b \in A$ and $m, n, p, q \in \mathbb{N}$:

1. $\langle A, \succeq \rangle$ is a weak order.

2. $\langle 1, a \rangle \in B$ and $1a \sim a$.

3. If $\langle n, a \rangle \in B$, then $n \geqslant m$ if and only if $\langle m, a \rangle \in B$ and $na \succeq ma$.

4. If $\langle m, a \rangle, \langle p, a \rangle, \langle n + q, b \rangle \in B$, $nb \succeq ma$, and $qb \succeq pa$, then $\langle m + p, a \rangle \in B$ and $(n + q)a \succeq (m + p)a$ (note that by axiom 2, $\langle n + q, b \rangle \in B \Rightarrow \langle n, b \rangle \in B \wedge \langle q, b \rangle \in B$).

5. If $b > a$, then there exist $c \in A$ and $n \in \mathbb{N}$ such that $\langle n + 1, c \rangle \in B$ and $b \succeq (n + 1)c \succeq nc \succeq a$.

6. Any strictly bounded standard sequence is finite, where $a_1, a_2, \ldots$ is a standard sequence if, for $n = 2, \ldots,$ $a_n = na$.

Given an extensive structure with no essential maximum $\langle A, \succeq, B, \circ \rangle$, we can construct a structure of extensive multiples $\langle A, \succeq, B', f \rangle$ by defining B' and na recursively as $\langle 1, a \rangle \in B'$ and $1a \sim a$ for all $a \in A$, if $\langle n - 1, a \rangle \in B'$ and $\langle (n - 1)a, a \rangle \in B$, then $\langle n, a \rangle \in B'$ and $na = (n - 1)a \circ a$, and for $\langle n, a \rangle \in B'$, $f(n, a) = na$.

The **representation condition** is: If $\langle A, \succeq, B, f \rangle$ is a structure of extensive multiples, then there exists a positive, real-valued function ϕ on A such that for all $a, b \in A$ and $n \in \mathbb{N}$:

1. $a \succeq b \Leftrightarrow \phi(a) \geqslant \phi(b)$.   (5.25a)
2. $\langle n, a \rangle \in B \Rightarrow \phi(na) = n\phi(a)$.   (5.25b)

(Krantz et al. 1971.) The **uniqueness condition** is: If another function ϕ' satisfies (5.25a) and (5.25b), then there exists a real number $\alpha > 0$ such that $\phi'(a) = \alpha\phi(a)$ (ϕ is a **ratio scale**) for all nonmaximal $a \in A$ (Krantz et al. 1971).

These conditions say that you need only to identify the subsystem of multiples in order to construct an extensive measure. Also, because of the way standard sequences work, you need only to actually construct objects of the form $2^i e$, where $i = 0, 1, 2, \ldots$ and e is your chosen unit.

DIFFERENCE REPRESENTATIONS

The basic idea behind difference measurement is the creation of standard sequences of intervals between elements, with indifference of ordering interpreted as equal spacing. Difference measurement can be used in those cases where pairs of intervals between elements $\langle ab, cd \rangle$ can be compared but no preexisting extensive measurement is available. We distinguish between the intervals ab and ba. Also, unless certain properties are met by the ordering of intervals, the use of a calibrated, extensive scale will not yield constant results.

The view of difference measurement I provide in this section is concerned with intervals ordered along a straight line, or unidimensional interval measurement. Interval ordering which requires a more complex, multidimensional structure is discussed in later sections that cover geometric representations.

Hölder (1901) showed that intervals on a line can be reduced to extensive measurement. In extensive measurement, standard sequences of the form a, $a \circ a$, $a \circ a \circ a$,... or na were created, where n is a natural number. In difference measurement, a standard sequence has the form a_1, a_2, a_3,... where $a_2 a_1 \sim a_3 a_2 \sim$ ··· . Equivalent intervals are grouped into a set of equivalence classes. Pairs of equivalence classes can be concatenated by selecting end-to-end intervals within the two classes and taking the equivalence class of the overall interval as the result of the concatenation. Given this idea, the axioms required for difference measurement are just those required to show that concatenation of equivalence classes is well defined and that the hypotheses of Hölder's theorem are satisfied.

This section takes the approach of defining difference measurement in terms of extensive measurement. It is also possible to define extensive measurement in terms of difference measurement. Now let's explore several difference structures, each of which has some different characteristics and lends itself to solving slightly different problems.

Positive Difference Structures

Let's begin with a nonempty set A, which is interpreted to be the set of endpoints of all intervals along some single dimension, such as a straight line in a plane or on a curved surface. Take a subset A^* of $A \times A$ to be the set of all positive intervals. Define a positive interval in terms of the empirical structure you are attempting to measure and state that if $ab \in A^*$, then $ba \notin A^*$. Finally, add a binary relation $\succeq$ on A^*.

Positive difference structures lead to some interesting results. If A^* is merely a partial order, then you obtain a ratio scale measure ψ on A^*. If A^* is a total order, you obtain, in addition, the difference representation $\psi(ab) = \phi(a) - \phi(b)$, where ϕ is an interval scale measure on A. The term "positive" implies that A^* is a strict partial order—that is, it is irreflexive, which means that $aa \notin A^*$. Since A^* is transitive (because it is a weak order) and irreflexive, it is also asymmetric—if $ab \in A^*$, then $ba \notin A^*$ as has already been stated.

A triple $\langle A, A^*, \succeq \rangle$ is a *positive difference structure* (Krantz et al. 1971) if and only if the following hold for all $a, b, c, a', b', c' \in A$, and all sequences $a_1, a_2,..., a_i,... \in A$:

1. $\langle A^*, \succeq \rangle$ is a weak order.
2. $ab, bc \in A^* \Rightarrow ac \in A^*$.

3. $ab, bc \in A^* \Rightarrow ac > ab, bc$.

4. $ab, bc, a'b', b'c' \in A^* \wedge ab \succeq a'b' \wedge bc \succeq b'c' \Rightarrow ac \succeq a'c'$.

5. If $ab, cd \in A^*$ and $ab > cd$, then there exists $d', d'' \in A$ such that ad', $d'b, ad''$, and $d''b \in A^*$ and $ad' \sim cd \sim d''b$ (this is a nonnecessary solvability condition which asserts that a given positive interval cd can be copied within any larger positive interval ab using either a or b as an endpoint of the copy).

6. If $a_1, a_2, ..., a_i, ...$ is a strictly bounded sequence—$a_i + {}_1a_i \in A^*$ and $a_{i+1}a_i \sim a_2a_1$ for all a_i, a_{i+1} in the sequence, and for some $d'd'' \in A^*$, $d'd'' \succeq a_ia_1$ for all a_i in the sequence—then it is finite (this is the Archimedean axiom).

The **representation condition** is: If $\langle A, A^*, \succeq \rangle$ is a positive difference structure, then there exists $\psi: A^* \to \mathbb{R}^+$ such that for all $a, b, c \in A$:

1. $(ab, cd \in A^* \Rightarrow ab \succeq cd) \Leftrightarrow \psi(ab) \geqslant \psi(cd)$.   (5.26a)

2. $ab, bc \in A^* \Rightarrow \psi(ac) = \psi(ab) + \psi(bc)$.   (5.26b)

3. If, for all $a, b \in A, a \neq b$, either ab or $ba \in A^*$, then there exists $\phi: A \to \mathbb{R}$ such that for $ab \in A^*$, $\psi(ab) = \phi(a) - \phi(b)$.   (5.26c)

(Krantz et al. 1971.) The **uniqueness condition** is: If ψ' also has the same properties as ψ, then there exists a real number $\alpha > 0$ such that $\psi' = \alpha\psi$ (ψ is a **ratio scale**); if ϕ' has the same properties as ϕ, then there exists a constant β such that $\phi' = \phi + \beta$ (ϕ is an **interval scale** since the domain is over all of the real numbers) (Krantz et al. 1971; 1990).

To use these conditions to construct the mappings ψ and ϕ, it is sufficient to show that an empirical relational structure satisfies axioms 1 through 6 for ψ, and additionally that A^* is a total order for ϕ. The uniqueness condition asserts that you can use any interval $ab \in A^*$ as the basis for a standard sequence of intervals. You can find $\alpha > 0$ such that you can express any standard sequence of intervals in terms of any other standard sequence of intervals based on some other interval $cd \in A^*$. If A^* is a total order, you can construct a mapping ϕ on A which is an interval scale, allowing you to define $\psi(ab)$ in terms of $\phi(a) - \phi(b)$, or vice versa. Further, you can choose any arbitrary starting point β and preserve your structure.

Algebraic Difference Structures

An algebraic difference structure is one in which both positive and negative intervals appear. The basis for this structure is to define a subset of positive intervals $A^* = \{ab \mid ab > aa\}$ which is a positive difference structure. The subset of negative intervals is defined using the usual sign reversal axiom: $ab \succeq cd \Rightarrow dc \succeq ba$.

Given a nonempty set A and a binary relation $\succeq$ on $A \times A$ (a quaternary relation on A), the couple $\langle A \times A, \succeq \rangle$ is an *algebraic difference structure* (Krantz et al. 1971) if and only if the following hold for all $a, b, c, d, a', b', c' \in A$ and for all sequences $a_1, a_2, ..., a_i, ... \in A$:

1. $\langle A \times A, \succeq \rangle$ is a weak order.

2. $ab \succeq cd \Rightarrow dc \succeq ba$.

3. $ab \succeq a'b' \wedge bc \succeq b'c' \Rightarrow ac \succeq a'c'$.

4. If $ab \succeq cd \succeq aa$, then there exist d', $d'' \in A$ such that $ad' \sim cd \sim d''b$.

5. If $a_1, a_2, \ldots, a_i, \ldots$ is a strictly bounded standard sequence—$a_{i+1}a \sim a_2 a_1$ for every $a_i a_{i+1}$ in the sequence, with $\neg(a_2 a_1 \sim a_1 a_1)$, and there exist d', $d'' \in A$ such that $d'd'' > a_i a_1 > d''d'$ for all a_i in the sequence—then it is finite (this is the Archimedean axiom).

The **representation condition** is: If $\langle A \times A, \succeq \rangle$ is an algebraic difference structure, then there exists a real-valued function ϕ on A such that, for all $a, b, c, d \in A$:

$$ab \succeq cd \Leftrightarrow \phi(a) - \phi(b) \geqslant \phi(c) - \phi(d) \qquad (5.27)$$

(Krantz et al. 1971.) The **uniqueness condition** is: If ϕ' has the same properties as ϕ, then there are real constants α, β, with $\alpha > 0$, such that $\phi' = \alpha\phi + \beta$ (ϕ is an **interval scale**) (Krantz et al. 1971).

If you have a ϕ which provides an interval scale, then $\psi = e^\phi$ gives a ratio representation:

$$ab \succeq cd \Leftrightarrow \psi(a)/\psi(b) \geqslant \psi(c)/\psi(d) \qquad (5.28)$$

Note that a ratio representation is *not* the same as a ratio *scale* representation. Conversely, any positive-valued ψ which has this property yields a difference representation ϕ by taking logarithms.

More generally, let L be an interval in $\mathbb{R}$ and f be any strictly increasing function from $\mathbb{R}$ into L. Define ψ and $\odot$ by $\psi(a) = f[\phi(a)]$, $a \in A$, and $x \odot y = f[f^{-1}(x) - f^{-1}(y)]$, $x, y \in L$. Thus, $\psi(a) \odot \psi(b) - f[\phi(a) - \phi(b)]$. This makes ψ a homomorphism that carries $\succeq$ into the numerical relation defined by ordering of the $\odot$ values. This allows for a wide choice of alternative equivalent numerical representations, the most convenient of which is the ratio representation with $L = \mathbb{R}^+$ and $f = exp$. The ψ representation is invariant under transformations of the form $T_{\alpha,\beta} = f(\alpha f^{-1} + \beta)$, where α, β are real and $\alpha > 0$, which means that all ψ representations are interval scales.

It has been shown that positive difference structures lead to ratio scale measures, and that algebraic difference structures lead to interval scale measures. Now, let's see how to take two distinct algebraic difference structures based on the same underlying cross product and arrive at a ratio scale measure of the underlying set. This is an important result, since it allows you to construct a ratio scale measure out of two different interval scale measures on the same set of intervals.

Let $\langle A \times A, \succeq_1 \rangle$ and $\langle A \times A, \succeq_2 \rangle$ both be algebraic difference structures. Let ϕ_1 be a difference representation for $\succeq_1$, and ϕ_2 be a ratio representation for $\succeq_2$. Then, $\alpha_1(\phi_1 + \beta)$ is also a difference representation for $\succeq_2$. The objective is to find a ϕ such that:

$$\alpha_1(\phi_1 + \beta) = \phi = \alpha_2 \phi_2^\gamma \qquad (5.29)$$

Since β, γ, and α_1/α_2 will be uniquely determined by any solution, if one exists, then ϕ is a ratio scale representation on A. The **representation condition** is: Let $\succeq_1$ and $\succeq_2$ be disjoint quaternary relations on a set A such that $\langle A \times A, \succeq_1 \rangle$ and $\langle A \times A, \succeq_2 \rangle$ are algebraic difference structures. Suppose that for all a, b, c, d, a', b', $c' \in A$, $ab \succeq_1 aa \Leftrightarrow ab \succeq_2 aa$. If $aa' \succeq_1 bb'$ and $cc' \succeq_2 bb'$, then if $a'b' \succeq_1 b'c'$, then $ab \succeq_1 bc$. Then, there exists $\phi: A \to \mathbb{R}$ such that for all a, b, c, $d \in A$:

1. $ab \succeq_1 cd \Leftrightarrow \phi(a) - \phi(b) \geq \phi(c) - \phi(d)$ (5.30a)

2. $ab \succeq_2 cd \Leftrightarrow \phi(a)/\phi(b) \geq \phi(c)/\phi(d)$.   (5.30b)

(Krantz et al. 1971.) The **uniqueness condition** is: If ϕ' is any other function with these properties, then there exists a real $\alpha > 0$ such that $\phi' = \alpha\phi$ (ϕ is a **ratio scale**) (Krantz et al. 1971).

It is possible to obtain interval scale measures for difference structures using just strict inequalities. To do this, you need to modify your construction axioms. The solvability axioms (axiom 5 for positive difference structures and axiom 4 for algebraic difference structures) help you construct standard sequences of intervals, allowing the expression of any interval ab as a number of exact copies of an interval cd. If you use strict inequalities, you can no longer create exact standard sequences, but only approximate sequences.

For any $cd > cc$, let $G(cd)$ denote the family of sequences such that if $\{a_i\} \in G(cd)$, then for all a_n, a_{n+1} in $\{a_i\}$, $a_{n+1}a_n \succeq cd$. Let $L(cd)$ be the family of sequences where $cd > a_{n+1}a_n$. An exact standard sequence, if one exists, is in $G(cd)$. Now modify the solvability axioms as follows:

Axiom 4′: If $ab \succeq cd > c'd' \succeq aa$, then there exist x, $y \in A$ such that both $cd > ay > c'd'$ and $cd > xb > c'd'$ hold.

Axiom 5′: If $cd > cc$, the sequence a_1, a_2,..., a_i is in $G(cd)$, and $ab > a_ia_1$ for all a_i in the sequence, then the sequence is finite.

Axiom 4′ asserts that A is dense in the sense that between any two nonequivalent points, there exists a third point which is not equivalent to either of them. When inequalities are easier to observe than equalities, axiom 4′ may be easier to verify than axiom 4. Axiom 4′ may also be easier to refute than axiom 4. Thus, a difference structure based on strict inequalities may be more convenient than a standard algebraic difference structure.

Cross-Modality Ordering

An algebraic difference structure is built upon an ordering relation $\succeq$ on a cross product of a set. It is simple to extend this concept to the case where $\succeq$ is defined on the set of all pairs from any of $A_1 \times A_1$,..., $A_n \times A_n$, or $\bigcup_{i=1}^{n} A_i \times A_i$. Cross-modality matching establishes an equivalence relation $\sim$ on $\bigcup_{i=1}^{n} A_i \times A_i$. The relation $\sim$ may be extended to $\succeq$ in a number of ways.

Given nonempty sets A_1,..., A_n and a binary relation $\succeq$ on $\bigcup_{i=1}^{n} A_i \times A_i$, $\langle A_1$,...,

A_n, $\succeq\rangle$ is a *cross-modality ordering structure* if and only if the following hold for all i, j with $1 \leq i, j \leq n$ and all a_i, b_i, $c_i \in A_i$, a'_j, b'_j, $c'_j \in A_j$:

1. $\langle \bigcup_{i=1}^{n} A_i \times A_i, \succeq \rangle$ is a weak order.

2. $a_i b_i \succeq a'_j b'_j \Rightarrow b'_j a'_j \succeq b_i a_i$.

3. $a_i b_i \succeq a'_j b'_j \wedge b_i c_i \succeq b'_j c'_j \Rightarrow a_i c_i \succeq a'_j c'_j$.

4. Both of the following hold:

- There exists d_1, $e_1 \in A_1$ such that $a_i b_i \sim d_1 e_1$.
- $\langle A_1 \times A_1, \succeq \rangle$ satisfies axiom 4 for an algebraic difference structure

($\langle A_1 \times A_1, \succeq \rangle$ is the restriction of $\langle \bigcup_{i=1}^{n} A_i \times A_i, \succeq \rangle$ to A_1).

5. $\langle A_1 \times A_1, \succeq \rangle$ satisfies the Archimedean axiom (axiom 5) for an algebraic difference structure.

Axioms 4 and 5 here require that $\langle A_1 \times A_1, \succeq \rangle$ be an algebraic difference structure.

The **representation condition** is: If $\langle A_1, ..., A_n, \succeq \rangle$ is a cross-modality ordering structure, then there exists functions ϕ_i from A_i to $\mathbb{R}^+$, $i = 1, ..., n$, such that for all i, j, $1 \leq i, j \leq n$, and all a_i, $b_i \in A_i$, a'_j, $b'_j \in A_j$:

$$a_i b_i \succeq a'_j b'_j \Leftrightarrow \phi_i(a_i)/\phi_i(b_i) \geq \phi_j(a'_j)/\phi_j(b'_j) \qquad (5.31)$$

(Krantz et al. 1971.) The **uniqueness condition** is: If ϕ'_i are any other functions with these properties, then there exist positive numbers $\alpha_1, ..., \alpha_n$ and γ such that $\phi'_i = \alpha_i \phi_i^\gamma$, $i = 1, ..., n$ (the ϕ_i are **interval scales** of the power group, since their domains are limited to the positive real numbers) (Krantz et al. 1971). The representation condition provides that a cross-modality ordering structure may be mapped to a set of ratio representations (of an interval scale). The uniqueness condition allows the permissible transformations $\phi'_i = \alpha_i \phi_i^\gamma$, $i = 1, ..., n$, where γ is independent of i. Thus, if the scale is fixed in one continuum, say A_1, then the other scales are **ratio scales** (Krantz et al. 1971).

Finite, Equally Spaced Difference Structures

A finite, equally spaced structure of any type, such as extensive or difference, corresponds to a single finite standard sequence of the more general structure. Thus, a finite, equally spaced difference structure is really nothing more than a single finite standard sequence of a difference structure.

To formulate the idea of equal spacing, define the concept of immediate successor. Let $\langle A \times A, \succeq \rangle$ satisfy axioms 1 through 3 of any difference structure and let A^* be defined by $ab \in A^* \Leftrightarrow ab > aa$ (the subset of positive intervals). Define a relation J on A: for all a, $b \in A$, aJb if and only if $ab \in A^*$ and there exists no $c \in A$ such that both ac, $cb \in A^*$. The notation aJb says that a is the immediate successor to b and there is no intervening object $c \in A$.

Given a finite nonempty set A and a binary relation $\succeq$ on $A \times A$, the pair $\langle A \times A, \succeq \rangle$ is a *finite, equally spaced difference structure* (Krantz et al. 1971) if and only if the following hold for all a, b, c, d, a', b', $c' \in A$:

1. $\langle A \times A, \succeq \rangle$ is a weak order.

2. $ab \succeq cd \Rightarrow dc \succeq ba$.

3. $ab \succeq ab' \wedge bc \succeq b'c' \wedge ac \succeq ac'$.

4. $aJb \wedge cJd \Rightarrow ab \sim cd$—this asserts that any two intervals between an element and its immediate successor are equivalent.

The **representation condition** is: If $\langle A \times A, \succeq \rangle$ is a finite, equally spaced difference structure, then there exists $\phi: A \rightarrow \mathbb{R}$ such that, for all $a, b, c, d, \in A$:

$$ab \succeq cd \Leftrightarrow \phi(a) - \phi(b) \geq \phi(c) - \phi(d) \tag{5.32}$$

(Krantz et al. 1971.) The **uniqueness condition** is: If a function ϕ' has the same properties, then there exist real α, β, with $\alpha > 0$, such that $\phi' = \alpha\phi + \beta$ (ϕ is an **interval scale**) (Krantz et al. 1971). There exist functions ϕ satisfying these conditions which are integer-valued.

Absolute Difference Structures

In an absolute difference structure, we wish to represent unordered differences along a single dimension:

$$ab \succeq cd \Leftrightarrow |\phi(a) - \phi(b)| \geq |\phi(c) - \phi(d)| \tag{5.33}$$

Instead of the sign reversal axiom that $ab \succeq cd \Rightarrow dc \succeq ba$, there is $ab \sim ba > aa \sim bb$ for $a \neq b$. Suppose $\langle A \times A, \succeq \rangle$ is a weak order and $ab \sim ba > aa \sim bb$ for $a \neq b$. Then, b is *between* a and c, denoted $a \mid b \mid c$, if and only if $ac \succeq ab, bc$. This notion of betweenness will be used to simplify axioms 3 and 4 below.

Given a set A with at least two elements, a binary relation $\succeq$ on $A \times A$, the pair $\langle A \times A, \succeq \rangle$ is an *absolute difference structure* (Krantz et al. 1971) if and only if the following hold for all $a, b, c, d, a', b', c' \in A$, and all sequences $a_1, a_2,...,$ $a_i,... \in A$:

1. $\langle A \times A, \succeq \rangle$ is a weak order.

2. If $a \neq b$, then $ab \sim ba > aa \sim bb$.

3. Both of the following hold:
   - If $b \neq c$, $a \mid b \mid c$, and $b \mid c \mid d$, then both $a \mid b \mid d$ and $a \mid c \mid d$.
   - If $a \mid b \mid c$ and $a \mid c \mid d$, then $a \mid b \mid d$.

4. If $a \mid b \mid c$, $a' \mid b' \mid c'$, and $ab \sim a'b'$, then $bc \succeq b'c' \Leftrightarrow ac \succeq a'c'$.

5. If $ab \succeq cd$, then there exists d' with $a \mid d' \mid b$ and $ad' \sim cd$.

6. $a_{i+1} \mid a_i \mid a_1$ for all i, successive intervals are equal and nonnull, and $a_i a_1$ is strictly bounded.

The **representation condition** is: If $\langle A \times A, \succeq \rangle$ is a finite, equally spaced difference structure, then there exists $\phi: A \rightarrow \mathbb{R}$ such that, for all $a, b, c, d \in A$:

$$ab \succeq cd \Leftrightarrow |\phi(a) - \phi(b)| \geq |\phi(c) - \phi(d)| \tag{5.34}$$

(Krantz et al. 1971.) The **uniqueness condition** is: If a function ϕ' has the same properties, then there exist real α, β, with $\alpha > 0$, such that $\phi' = \alpha\phi + \beta$ (ϕ is an **interval scale**) (Krantz et al. 1971).

Suppose $\langle A \times A, \succeq \rangle$ is an absolute difference structure. Choose distinct elements x, $y \in A$ (A must have at least two elements). Define A^* to be the set of all $ab \in A \times A$ such that at least one of the following hold:

1. $a \mid x \mid y$, $b \mid x \mid y$, and $ax > bx$.
2. $\neg(a \mid x \mid y)$, $\neg(b \mid x \mid y)$, and $bx > ax$.
3. $a \mid x \mid y$ and $\neg(b \mid x \mid y)$.

Let $\succeq^*$ be the restriction of $\succeq$ to A^*. Then, $\langle A, A^*, \succeq^* \rangle$ is a positive difference structure, with $ab \in A^*$ or $ba \in A^*$ for $a \neq b$.

Strongly Conditional Difference Structures

In some cases, pairs of objects can be compared, or ordered, only when one of the objects is common to both pairs. Such situations arise in the social sciences, especially when different subjects are trying to match responses with a stimulus (see Krantz et al. 1971 for an example). In this subsection, the primitives are a set A and a binary relation $\succeq$ on $A \times A$ which is connected only for pairs whose second component is in common. Thus, ac is comparable to bd only if $c = d$. This property is called *strongly conditional connectedness* (Krantz et al. 1971). The representation you are aiming for is:

$$ac \succeq bc \Leftrightarrow |\phi(a) - \phi(c)| \geq |\phi(b) - \phi(c)| \qquad (5.35)$$

A strongly conditionally connected ordering of pairs can contain information about the ordering of pairs which have no common element. To see this, let's introduce the concepts of midpoint, betweenness (slightly modified from before), and extreme points.

Let $\sim$ be a symmetric binary relation on $A \times A$. For a, b, $c \in A$, c is a *midpoint* of a and b if and only if $(a = b = c) \vee (a \neq b \wedge ac \sim bc)$. For any two elements in A, a unique midpoint exists. Use the operation notation $a \circ b$ to denote the midpoint of a and b. The similarity between the notation for midpoint and the notation for concatenation is deliberate. Here, the midpoint operation is a form of concatenation. Because of the symmetry of $\sim$, you have $a \circ b = b \circ a$.

Therefore, b is *between* a and c, denoted $a \mid b \mid c$, if and only if both $ac \succeq bc$ and $ca \succeq ba$. This definition of betweeness is slightly different than the previous definition. It is more suited for strongly conditionally connected relations. As before, $a \mid b \mid c$ is still equivalent to $c \mid b \mid a$, but it is no longer true that for any a, b, c, one of them is always between the other two based only on this definition.

If $X \subset A$, then $a \in A$ is an *extreme point* of X if and only if, for all x, $y \in X$, either $x \mid y \mid a$ or $y \mid x \mid a$.

Now take these definitions and extend the relation $\succeq$ to pairs which do not have an element in common. For a, b, c, $d \in A$, define $ab \succeq^* cd$ if and only if one of the following holds:

1. $a \mid c \mid d \mid b$ or $a \mid d \mid c \mid b$ (*cd* is wholly contained in *ab*).

2. $a \mid b \mid c \mid d$ or $a \mid c \mid b \mid d$, and $(a, b \circ c) \succeq (d, b \circ c)$.

3. Condition 2 holds after exchanging *a* and *b*, or *c* and *d*, or both.

Conditions 2 and 3 describe the possible ways in which *ab* and *cd* may be either disjoint or interlocking. If either is the case, $ab \succeq^* cd$ if and only if $(a, b \circ c) \succeq (d, b \circ c)$. These conditions are illustrated in Figure 5.3.

It is possible to determine whether $ab \succeq^* cd$ without finding the midpoint $b \circ c$. Suppose you have $a \mid b \mid c \mid d$, and some *e* such that $b \mid e \mid c$, with $ce \succeq be$ and $ae \succeq de$. From this, infer that *e* is on the *b* side of the midpoint of $b \circ c$. Since $ae \succeq de$, you must have $(a, b \circ c) \succeq (d, b \circ c)$ and so $ab \succeq^* cd$. You need the inequality $ce \succeq be$ only for cases where the data sample does not have a midpoint, but does contain a point *e*.

Given a set *A* with at least two elements, a binary relation $\succeq$ on $A \times A$, and the operations $\sim$, $\circ$, and $\mid$ previously defined, the pair $\langle A \times A, \succeq \rangle$ is a *strongly conditional absolute difference structure* (Krantz et al. 1971) if and only if the following hold for all *a*, *a'*, *b*, *b'*, *c*, *d* $\in$ *A* and all sequences $a_1, a_2,..., a_i,...$ of elements of *A*:

1. Either $ac \succeq bc$ or $bc \succeq ac$, and if $ac \succeq bd$, then $c = d$.

2. If $aa \succeq ba$, then $a = b$.

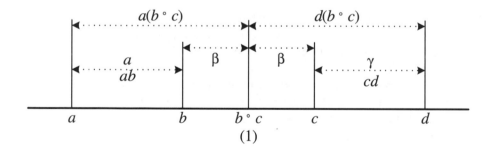

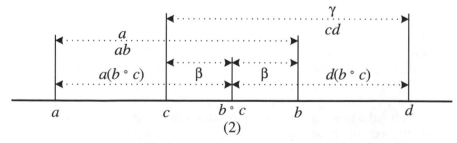

Figure 5.3 *Nonassociative concatenation (Kranzt et al. 1971).*

3. Transitivity:
   (a) $ad \succeq bd \wedge bd \succeq cd \Rightarrow ad \succeq cd$,
   (b) $ac \succeq bc \wedge cb \succeq ab \Rightarrow ca \succeq ba$, and
   (c) $ad \succeq bd \wedge db \succeq cb \wedge bc \succeq ac \Rightarrow da \succeq ca$;
   furthermore, $>$ holds in each conclusion if $\sim$ does not hold in the respective antecedents.

4. Both of the following hold:
   (a) $b \neq c \wedge a \mid b \mid c \wedge b \mid c \mid d \Rightarrow a \mid b \mid c \mid d$
   (b) $a \mid b \mid c \wedge a \mid c \mid d \Rightarrow a \mid b \mid c \mid d$

5. A midpoint $a \circ b$ exists.

6. Bisymmetry: $(a \circ b) \circ (c \circ d) = (a \circ d) \circ (b \circ c)$.

7. Weak monotonicity: If a is an extreme point of $\{a, a', b, b'\}$, $ac \succeq bc$, and $a'c \succeq b'c$, then $(a \circ a', c) \succeq (b \circ b', c)$. Furthermore, $>$ holds in the conclusion unless $\sim$ holds in both antecedents.

8. Solvability: If $a \mid b \mid c$, then there exists $e \in A$ such that $b \circ e = a \circ c$.

9. Archimedean: If $a_1, a_2, ..., a_i, ...$ is a strictly bounded standard sequence— $a_2 = a_1$; for any a_{i+1}, a_i, a_{i-1} in the sequence, $a_{i+1} \circ a_{i-1} = a_i$; and there exist $e, f \in A$ such that for every a_i in the sequence, $e \mid a_i \mid f$—then it is finite.

Axiom 1 asserts strong conditional connectedness. Axiom 2 asserts positiveness. Axiom 3(a) asserts transitivity when there is a common second element. Axiom 3(b) asserts a limited form of transitivity. Axiom 3(c) asserts transitivity in the face of two reversals such that the first and last terms have a common element. Axiom 4 asserts betweenness. Axiom 5 asserts the existence of midpoints. If a true midpoint does not exist, you can use any point in between and solve inequalities. Axiom 6 is bisymmetry and asserts the internal consistency of midpoints. Axiom 7 asserts a very weak monotonicity which says that if c is an extreme point of $\{a, a', b, b'\}$ (c is either to the left or right of all of these points) and if $ac \succeq bc$ and $a'c \succeq b'c$, then $(a \circ a', c) \succeq (b \circ b', c)$. Intuitively, this axiom says that if c is closer to b than it is a, and closer to b' than it is a', then it is closer to the midpoint $b \circ b'$ than it is the midpoint $a \circ a'$.

The **representation condition** is: If $\langle A \times A, \succeq \rangle$ is a strongly conditionally connected absolute difference structure, then there exists a function $\phi: A \rightarrow \mathbb{R}$ such that, for all $a, b, c, \in A$:

$$ac \succeq bc \Leftrightarrow |\phi(a) - \phi(c)| \geq |\phi(b) - \phi(c)| \qquad (5.36)$$

(Krantz et al. 1971.) The **uniqueness condition** is: If a function ϕ' has the same properties, then there exist real α, β, with $\alpha > 0$, such that $\phi' = \alpha\phi + \beta$ (ϕ is an **interval scale**) (Krantz et al. 1971).

PROBABILITY REPRESENTATIONS

In probability measurement, a number between 0 and 1 is attached to an entity called an *event*. An event is a subset of a set called the *sample space*. The sample space represents all possible observations which might be made in a particular situation. Given a nonempty set X, the sample space, and a nonempty family of subsets of X called E, then E is an *algebra of sets* on X if and only if for every A, $B \in E$: $-A \in E$; and $A \cup B \in E$. Furthermore, if whenever $A_i \in E$, $i = 1$, 2,..., it follows that $\cup_{i=1}^{\infty} A_i \in E$, then E is closed under countable unions and is called a α-*algebra* on X. The elements of E are the events. In this definition, $E \subseteq \mathbb{P} X$, A, $B \subseteq X$, and $-A$ denotes the complement of A, defined as $-A = X \backslash A$. E is also closed under intersections and differences. In other words, for any A, $B \in E$, $A \cap B \in E$ and $A \backslash B \in E$.

The objective in probability measurement is to construct a function from E onto [0, 1], creating what is called a *probability space*. The function is usually denoted $P(x)$ and is interpreted as being the probability that event x will occur. Probability measurement can be used in any situation where the mapping is onto [0, 1], including the measurement of proportions and percentages.

The following definition of numeric probability was first stated explicitly by Kohmogorov (1933) and axioms 1 through 3 are called the *Kohmogorov axioms*. Given a nonempty set X, an algebra of sets on X E, and a function P from E into the real numbers, the triple $\langle X, E, P \rangle$ is a *finitely additive probability space* (Krantz et al. 1971) if and only if the following hold for all A, $B \in E$:

1. $P(A) \geqslant 0$.
2. $P(X) = 1$.
3. If $A \cap B = \varnothing$, then $P(A \cup B) = P(A) + P(B)$.

It is a *countably additive probability space* (defined but not named in Krantz et al. 1971) if, in addition:

4. E is an α-algebra of sets on X.
5. If $A_i \in E$, and $A_i \cap A_j = \varnothing$, $i \neq j$, i, $j = 1$, 2,..., then $P(\cup_{i=1}^{\infty} A_i) = \Sigma_{i=1}^{\infty} P(A_i)$.

The objective is to determine the conditions under which an ordering $\succeq$ on E has an order-preserving function P which satisfies this definition—that is, which leads to a finite or countably additive probability space $\langle X, E, P \rangle$. This ordering is to be interpreted empirically as "at least as probable as." The question then becomes one of acceptable empirical methods to determine $\succeq$. The basic debate in probability theory is how to objectively order the probability of events. One method, called "personal probability" (Savage 1954), is introduced here because of its notation.

If a and b are outcomes, and A is an event, we denote an act or decision as $a_A \cup b_{-A}$ to indicate that the decision or act has outcome a if event A occurs, and outcome b if event A does not occur. Events and outcomes can be combined in this notation to describe virtually any act. The notation itself is used heavily in the representation of conditional expected utility.

If outcome a is preferred to outcome b, and the act $a_A \cup b_{-A}$ is preferred to the act $a_B \cup b_{-B}$, we may conclude that event A is more probable than event B, in the judgment of the decision maker being observed. Such a representation can be used in the simulation of software designs, or in the ranking of preferred designs or requirements, if we choose to represent sets of designs or requirements rather than events. The ability to apply probability representations to cases where preference rather than probability is being measured is the reason preference representations are included in this chapter.

Unconditional Probability Representations

In this subsection, a representation for unconditional qualitative probability will be developed. Given a nonempty set X, an algebra of sets E, and an equivalence relation $\sim$ on E, a sequence $A_1,..., A_i,...$, where $A_i \in E$, is a *standard sequence relative to* $A \in E$ if and only if for $i = 1, 2,...$, there exists $B_i, C_i \in E$ such that:

1. $A_1 = B_1 \wedge B_1 \sim A.$
2. $B_i \cap C_i = \emptyset.$
3. $B_i \sim A_i.$
4. $C_i \sim A.$
5. $A_{i+1} = B_i \cup C_i.$

If event A_i is assumed to correspond to i disjoint copies of A, then it follows that A_{i+1} corresponds to $i + 1$ disjoint copies of A. A_{i+1} equals the disjoint union of B_i, which is equivalent to A_i, and C_i, which is equivalent to A. This sequence will become part of the Archimedean axiom for the representation condition.

Given a nonempty set X, an algebra of sets on X E, and a binary relation $\succeq$ on E, the triple $\langle X, E, \succeq \rangle$ is a *structure of qualitative probability* (Krantz et al. 1971) if and only if for every $A, B, C \in E$:

1. $\langle E, \succeq \rangle$ is a weak order.
2. $X > \emptyset$ and $A \succeq \emptyset.$
3. If $A \cap B = A \cap C = \emptyset$, then $B \succeq C \Leftrightarrow A \cup B \succeq A \cup C.$

The structure is *Archimedean* if and only if in addition:

4. For every $A > \emptyset$, any standard sequence relative to A is finite.

Axioms 1 through 4 are all necessary to represent qualitative probability, but are not sufficient. To arrive at a set of conditions which are both necessary and sufficient, we must add:

5. Given a structure of qualitative probability $\langle X, E, \succeq \rangle$, if $A, B, C, D \in E$ are such that $A \cap B = \emptyset$, $A > C$, and $B \succeq D$, then there exist $C', D', \mathbf{E} \in E$ such that:
   - $\mathbf{E} \sim A \cup B$
   - $C' \cap D' = \emptyset$
   - $\mathbf{E} \supset C' \cup D'$
   - $C' \sim C \wedge D' \sim D$

Axiom 5 states that if A and B are disjoint, if A is more probable than C, and if B is at least as probable as D, then somewhere in the structure there is an event

E that is equally probable as $A \cup B$, and that **E** includes disjoint subsets C' and D' which are equivalent to C and D, respectively. This axiom is violated by any finite structure whose equivalence classes fail to form a single standard sequence.

The **representation condition** is: If $\langle X, E, \succeq \rangle$ is an Archimedean structure of qualitative probability which also satisfies axiom 5, then there exists a unique order-preserving function P from E into the unit interval $[0, 1]$ such that $\langle X, E, P \rangle$ is a finitely additive probability space, or:

1. $P(A) \geqslant 0 \; (A \in E)$.   (5.37a)
2. $P(X) = 1$.   (5.37b)
3. $A, B \in E \wedge A \cap B = \varnothing \Rightarrow P(A \cup B) = P(A) + P(B)$.   (5.37c)

(Krantz et al. 1971.) The **uniqueness condition** is: Since P is unique, P is an **absolute scale** (Krantz et al. 1971).

The crucial property, if $A \cap B = \varnothing$, then $P(A \cup B) = P(A) + P(B)$, is formally similar to the additive property of extensive measurement if $\cup$ is treated like the concatenation operation $\circ$. To make this explicit, the condition $A \cap B = \varnothing$ needs to be restated as a restriction on the concatenation operation, such as $\langle A, B \rangle \in \boldsymbol{B}$ where $\boldsymbol{B} \subset E \times E$. Thus, an ordering of an algebra of sets can be interpreted as a type of extensive measurement if the sets are collections of objects rather than events. Such an interpretation will be used in the measurement of objects and classes.

If the ordering $\succeq$ on E is based on choices among acts, or preferences among alternatives, then the axioms of qualitative probability can be restated as assumptions about observable choices. Let E be an algebra on X and $\boldsymbol{C}$ a set of outcomes, consequences, or alternatives. Let $a_A \cup b_B \cup c_C$ be the act that has outcome a if event A occurs, b if event B occurs, or c if event C occurs. Denote the preference relation by $\succeq^*$. Note that it is a weak order on both the outcome set $\boldsymbol{C}$ and the set of acts $\boldsymbol{A}$. More formally, it is a subset of $(\boldsymbol{C} \times \boldsymbol{C}) \cup (\boldsymbol{A} \times \boldsymbol{A})$. Permutations among acts do not matter: $a_A \cup b_B \cup c_C = a_A \cup c_C \cup b_B$. Three-outcome sets with two identical outcomes become two-outcome sets: $a_A \cup b_B \cup b_C = a_A \cup b_{B \cup C} = a_A \cup b_{-A}$. Define a relation $\succeq$ on E as $A \succeq B$ if and only if for all $a, b \in \boldsymbol{C}$, if $a \succeq^* b$, then $a_A \cup b_{-A} \succeq^* a_B \cup b_{-B}$.

To summarize, a structure $\langle X, E, \succeq \rangle$ is a structure of qualitative probability if and only if:

1. All outcomes $a, b, c, d \in \boldsymbol{C}$.
2. $A, B, C \in E$ and partition X.
3. All acts are in $\boldsymbol{A}$.
4. $\succeq^*$ is a weak order on a subset of $(\boldsymbol{C} \times \boldsymbol{C}) \cup (\boldsymbol{A} \times \boldsymbol{A})$.
5. If $a >^* b$, $c \succeq^* d$, and $a_A \cup b_{-A} \succeq^* a_B \cup b_{-B}$, then $c_A \cup d_{-A} \succeq^* c_B \cup d_{-B}$.
6. If $a >^* b$, then $a_X \cup b_\varnothing >^* a_\varnothing \cup b_X$ and $a_A \cup b_{-A} \succeq^* a_\varnothing \cup b_X$.
7. If $a_A \cup b_B \cup c_C \succeq^* a_{A'} \cup b_B \cup b_{C'}$, then $a_A \cup a_B \cup c_C \succeq^* a_{A'} \cup a_B \cup b_{C'}$.
8. There exist $a, b \in \boldsymbol{C}$ with $a >^* b$.

Axiom 5 states that $\succeq$ is connected and transitive, so it is a weak order. Axiom 6 states that $X > \varnothing$ and $A \succeq \varnothing$ and, since outcome a is strictly preferable to b, the certainty of a is preferable to the certainty of b, and the possibility of a given event A is at least as preferable as the certainty of b. Axiom 7 states that if two acts have a common outcome b when event B occurs, the contingency of b_B is irrelevant between them and b can be replaced without affecting the choice. This is an example of the *extended sure-thing principle* and leads to expected utility representations.

Modifications to Unconditional Probability

This subsection considers three modifications to the unconditional probability structures. The first is for situations in which $P(A)$ and $P(B)$ may exist, but $P(A \cap B)$ need not, such as might arise in quantum mechanics. $P(A \cap B)$ is interpreted as the probability of both events A and B occurring together. The second modification allows you to apply probability measurement to structures requiring countably additive representations rather than just finitely additive representations. The third modification allows you to create a representation for a single standard sequence which covers all nonnull equivalence classes in E.

The first modification requires that we redefine the notion of an algebra of sets. Given a nonempty set X and a family of subsets of X E, then E is a *QM-algebra of sets* on X if and only if, for every $A, B \in E$: $-A \in E$; and $A \cap B = \varnothing \Rightarrow A \cup B \in E$. Furthermore, if E is closed under countable unions of mutually disjoint sets, then E is called a *QMα-algebra*. Then, we modify axiom 3 of the definition of a qualitative probability structure to state:

> **3'.** Suppose that $A \cap B = C \cap D = \varnothing$. If $A \succeq C$ and $B \succeq D$, then $A \cup B \succeq C \cup D$. Moreover, if either hypothesis is $>$, then the conclusion is $>$.

This new structure is called a *modified structure of qualitative probability* (defined in Krantz et al., 1971, as a *QM-structure of qualitative probability*).

The **representation condition** is: If E is a QM-algebra of sets on X and if $\langle X, E, \succeq \rangle$ is a structure of qualitative probability which satisfies axiom 3' rather than 3, then there exists a unique function P from E into the unit interval $[0, 1]$ such that $\langle X, E, P \rangle$ is a finitely additive probability space and P preserves the ordering of $\succeq$ on E (Krantz et al. 1971). The **uniqueness condition** is: Since P is unique, P is an **absolute scale** (Krantz et al. 1971).

To make the second modification, which allows you to create a countably additive representation, you need the additional concept of monotone continuity. If $\langle X, E, \succeq \rangle$ is a structure of qualitative probability and E is an α-algebra, $\succeq$ is *monotonically continuous* if and only if for any sequence $A_1, A_2,...$ in E and any B in E, if $A_i \subset A_{i+1}$ and $B \succeq A_i$ for all i, then $B \succeq \cup_{i=1}^{\infty} A_i$. Then, a finitely additive probability representation of a structure of qualitative probability, on an α-algebra, is *countably additive* if and only if it is monotonically continuous.

You can use this concept of monotone continuity to modify the structural axiom (axiom 5). This modification uses the concept of a probability atom. Numerically,

A is an *atom* if $P(A) > 0$ and if $A \supset B$ (A contains or includes B), then either $P(B) = P(A)$ or $P(B) = 0$. Formally, given a weak order $\succeq$ of an algebra of sets E, an event $A \in E$ is an atom if and only if $A > \varnothing$ and for any $B \in E$, if $A \supset B$, then $A \sim B$ or $B \sim \varnothing$.

Two additional concepts are needed: fineness and tightness. A structure is *fine* if, for every $A > \varnothing$, there exists a partition $\{C_1,..., C_n\}$ of X such that $A \succeq C_i$ for every $i = 1,..., n$. For $A, B \in E$, define $A \sim^* B$ if for all $C, D > \varnothing$ such that $A \cap C = B \cap D = \varnothing$, then $A \cup C \succeq B \cup D$ and $B \cup D > A$. The structure is *tight* if whenever $A \sim^* B$, then $A \sim B$.

Putting this all together, we have defined a *countably additive structure of qualitative probability* (defined but not named in Krantz et al. 1971). The **representation condition** is: If $\langle X, E, \succeq \rangle$ is a structure of qualitative probability, E is an α-algebra, $\succeq$ is monotonically continuous on E, and there are no atoms, then the structure is both fine and tight, there is a unique order-preserving function P, and it is countably finite (Krantz et al. 1971). The **uniqueness condition** is: Since P is unique, P is an **absolute scale** (Krantz et al. 1971).

The third modification allows the construction of a single finite standard sequence of probabilities. This requires replacing the structural axiom (axiom 5) with some sort of equal-spacing axiom. The simplest characterization of such a structure is one with a finite number of equivalent atoms. If $A \succeq B$, then there exists $C \in E$ such that $A \sim (B \cup C)$ (axiom 6). There is an event which, when combined with B, makes the combination equally as probable as event A. We call this a *structure of qualitative probability with equivalent atoms* (defined but not named in Krantz et al. 1971). The **representation condition** is: If $\langle X, E, \succeq \rangle$ is a structure of qualitative probability such that X is finite and axiom 6 holds, then there exists a unique order-preserving function P on E such that $\langle X, E, P \rangle$ is a finitely additive probability space. Moreover, all atoms in E are equivalent (Krantz et al. 1971). The **uniqueness condition** is: Since P is unique, P is an **absolute scale** (Krantz et al. 1971).

In cases where axiom 5 does not hold, you can still construct an order-preserving probability measure for a finite algebra of sets. Define a vectorial characteristic function v for E as the one-to-one mapping of E into $\mathbb{R}^n$ defined by $v(A) = \overline{A} = (\overline{A}_i,..., \overline{A}_n)$, where for any $i = 1,..., n$:

$$\overline{A}_i = \begin{cases} 1 & \text{if } x_i \in A \\ 0 & \text{if } x_i \notin A \end{cases} \tag{5.38}$$

Each A in E is represented by a unique vector of zeroes and ones in $\mathbb{R}^n$. Let $\overline{E} = \{\overline{A} \mid A \in E\}$ and E^+ be its additive closure with respect to componentwise vector addition. Define $\sim_I$ as: for any $x, y \in E^+$, let $x \sim_I y$ if and only if there exist $a_1,..., a_n, b_1,..., b_n \in \overline{E}$ such that $x = \overline{a}_1 + \cdots + \overline{a}_n$, $y = \overline{b}_1 + \cdots + \overline{b}_n$, and for $j = 1,..., n$, $a_j \sim b_j$. Define $>_I$ as: $x >_I y$ if and only if there exist $c_1,..., c_n, d_1,..., d_n \in \overline{E}$ such that $x = \overline{c}_1 + \cdots + \overline{c}_n$, $y = \overline{d}_1 + \cdots + \overline{d}_n$, $c_j \succeq d_j$ for $j = 1,..., n$, and for some j, $\neg(d_j \succeq c_j)$. This is called a *vectorial structure of qualitative probability* (defined but not named in Krantz et al. 1971). The **representation**

condition is: Let X be a finite nonempty set, E an algebra of sets on X, and $\succeq$ a reflexive binary relation on E satisfying $X > \emptyset$ and $A \succeq \emptyset$ for all $A \in E$, then there exists P satisfying:

1. $A > B \Rightarrow P(A) > P(B)$. $\hspace{5cm}$ (5.39a)
2. $A \sim B \Rightarrow P(A) = P(B)$. $\hspace{4.5cm}$ (5.39b)
3. $P(A) \geqslant 0$. $\hspace{6.8cm}$ (5.39c)
4. $P(X) = 1$. $\hspace{6.8cm}$ (5.39d)
5. $A \cap B = \emptyset \Rightarrow P(A \cup B) = P(A) + P(B)$ if and only if
   $>_I$ is irreflexive. $\hspace{6cm}$ (5.39e)

(Krantz et al. 1971.) The **uniqueness condition** is: Since P is unique, P is an **absolute scale** (Krantz et al. 1971).

Conditional Probability

Conditional probability is the probability that an event A will occur given that an event B has already occurred. The outcome must be in both A and B; that is, it must be an element of $A \cap B$. Numerically, $P(A \mid B) = P(A \cap B)/P(B)$ provided that $P(B) > 0$. Ordinary unconditional probability is a special case of conditional probability where $B = X$. The goal is to form a structure under which a qualitative relation on the form $A \mid B \succeq C \mid D$ (read: A given B is at least as probable as C given D) can be represented by a probability measure:

$$A \mid B \succeq C \mid D \Leftrightarrow P(A \cap B)/P(B) \geqslant P(C \cap D)/P(D) \hspace{2cm} (5.40)$$

Given a nonempty set X, an algebra of sets on X E, a subset N of E which contains all null events, and a binary relation $\succeq$ on $E \times (E - N)$ [$E - N = E \backslash N$], the quadruple $\langle X, E, N, \succeq \rangle$ is a *structure of qualitative conditional probability* if and only if for every $A, B, C, A', B', C' \in E$ (or $E - N$, whenever the symbol appears to the right of $/$) the following hold:

1. $\langle E \times (E - N), \succeq \rangle$ is a weak order.
2. $X \in E - N$ and $A \in N$ if and only if $A \mid X \sim \emptyset \mid X$.
3. $X \mid X \sim A \mid A$ and $X \mid X \succeq A \mid B$.
4. $A \mid B \sim A \cap B \mid B$.
5. Suppose that $A \cap B = A' \cap B' = \emptyset$. If $A \mid C \succeq A' \mid C'$ and $B \mid C \succeq B' \mid C'$, then $A \cup B \mid C \succeq A' \cup B' \mid C'$; if either hypothesis is $>$, then the conclusion is $>$.
6. Suppose that $A \supset B \supset C$ and $A' \supset B' \supset C'$. If $B \mid A \succeq C' \mid B'$ and $C \mid B \succeq B' \mid A'$, then $C \mid A \succeq C' \mid A'$; if either hypothesis is $>$, then the conclusion is $>$.

The structure is *Archimedean* if, in addition,

7. Every standard sequence is finite, where $\{A_i\}$ is a standard sequence if and only if for all i, $A_i \in E - N$, $A_{i+1} \supset A_i$, and $X \mid X > A_i \mid A_{i+1} \sim A_1 \mid A_2$.

Add the following axiom to make this axiom system both necessary and sufficient:

8. If $A \mid B \succeq C \mid D$, then there exists $C' \in E$ such that $C \cap D \supset C'$ and $A \mid B \sim C' \mid D$.

This axiom says that E is sufficiently rich so that whenever $A \mid B \succeq C \mid D$, we can add just enough to C to make $C' \mid D$ equivalent to $A \mid B$.

The **representation condition** is: If $\langle X, E, N, \succeq \rangle$ is an Archimedean structure of qualitative conditional probability for which axiom 8 holds, then there exists a real-valued function P on E such that for all $A, C \in E$ and all $B, D \in E - N$:

1. $\langle X, E, P \rangle$ is a finitely additive probability space. $\hspace{2cm}$ (5.41a)
2. $A \in N$ if and only if $P(A) = 0$. $\hspace{3.8cm}$ (5.41b)
3. $A \mid B \succeq C \mid D \Leftrightarrow P(A \cap B)/P(B) \geq P(C \cap D)/P(D)$. $\hspace{0.5cm}$ (5.41c)

(Krantz et al. 1971.) The **uniqueness condition** is: Since P is unique, P is an **absolute scale** (Krantz et al. 1971).

You can find cases where an ordering of conditional probability satisfies the multiplicative property of axiom 6, but not the additive property of axiom 5. To create a nonadditive representation of conditional probability, replace axioms 5, 6, and 8 with the following:

5'. If $A \in N$ and $A \supset B$, then $B \in N$.

6'. Suppose that $A \supset B \supset C$ and $A' \supset B' \supset C'$. If $B \mid A \succeq B' \mid A'$ and $C \mid B \succeq C' \mid B'$, then $C \mid A \succeq C' \mid A'$. Moreover, if either hypothesis is $\succ$, then the conclusion is $\succ$.

8'. If $A \mid B \succeq C \mid D$, then there exists a $C' \in E$ such that $C \cap D \supset C'$ and $A \mid B \sim C' \mid D$; if, in addition, $C \in E - N$, then there exists a $D' \in E$ such that $D \supset D' \supset C \cap D$ and $A \mid B \sim C \mid D'$.

The last part of axiom 8' adds the condition that just enough can be removed from $D - C$ to obtain a subset D' such that $A \mid B \sim C \mid D'$. The **representation condition** is: Let $\langle X, E, N, \succeq \rangle$ satisfy the conditions of a structure of conditional probability, except that axioms 5, 6, and 8 are replaced with 5', 6', and 8', respectively; then there exists a function Q from $E - N$ to $(0, 1]$ such that:

1. $Q(X) = 1$. $\hspace{8cm}$ (5.42a)
2. $A \cap B, C \cap D \in E - N \Rightarrow A \mid B \succeq C \mid D \Leftrightarrow$
   $Q(A \cap B)/Q(B) \geq Q(C \cap D)/Q(D)$. $\hspace{2.5cm}$ (5.42b)

(Krantz et al. 1971.) The **uniqueness condition** is: If Q' is any other function with the same properties, then $Q' = Q^\alpha$, for $\alpha > 0$ (Q is an **interval scale**). These conditions restrict $\succeq$ to $(E - N) \times (E - N)$; we do not have Q defined on elements of N (Krantz et al. 1971).

Conditional Expected Utility

The theory of expected utility deals with making decisions when their consequences are certain. The model used to measure expected utility can also be used for selecting among alternatives. Like probability, conditional expected utility is built upon an algebra of subsets E of a given nonempty set X. The elements of E represent chance events to which probabilities will ultimately be assigned. A second primitive is a subfamily N of null events. These are events to which the probability of zero will be assigned. The third primitive is a nonempty set C which contains the set of possible consequences.

Construct a set of functions, called *conditional decisions*, or just *decisions*, from $E - N$ (E without the null events) into C. These decisions are "conditional" in the sense that we assume that a fixed, nonnull event has occurred. When a decision is considered, the event becomes the universe of possibilities, and each conditional decision specifies the consequences associated with each of the possible events in the restricted universe.

Formally, for $A \in E - N$, any function f_A from A into C is a *conditional decision on A*. To every $x \in A$, the decision assigns a *consequence*, denoted $f_A(x)$, from C. f_A is not defined for x in $X - A$. The notation f_A makes the conditioning event, which is the domain of the decision, explicit: in this case, it is A. The set of functions $f_A: A \in E - N \rightarrow C$ is called the *set of conditional decisions*, denoted D. A binary preference relation $\succeq$ is defined on the elements of D, such that for $a, b \in D$, $a > b$ means that a is preferable to b, and $a \sim b$ means indifference between a and b.

You can combine events and their decision sets as follows: if A and B are disjoint events, $A \cap B = \varnothing$, and if f_A and g_B are two conditional decisions, then $f_A \cup g_B$ is the decision conditional on $A \cup B$ defined by:

$$(f_A \cup g_B)(x) = \begin{cases} f_A(x) & \text{if } x \in A \\ g_B(x) & \text{if } x \in B \end{cases} \tag{5.43}$$

The set of decisions D must be closed in two senses:

1. If $f_A, g_B \in D$, and $A \cap B = \varnothing$, then $f_A \cup g_B \in D$.
2. If A and B are nonnull events, $B \subset A$, and $f_A \in D$, then the restriction of f_A to B is also in D.

The objective is to arrive at a representation of the structure $\langle X, E, N, C, D, \succeq \rangle$. We wish to establish that a finitely additive probability measure P exists on E and that a real-valued function u exists on D such that for all $f_A, g_B \in D$:

1. $R \in N \Leftrightarrow P(R) = 0$. (5.44a)
2. $f_A \succeq g_B \Leftrightarrow u(f_A) \geq u(g_B)$. (5.44b)
3. $A \cap B = \varnothing \Rightarrow u(f_A \cup g_B) = u(f_A)P(A \mid A \cup B) + u(g_B)P(B \mid A \cup B)$.
(5.44c)

Suppose that E is an algebra of subsets on a set X, N is a subset of E, C is a set, D is a set of functions whose domains are elements of $E - N$ and whose images are subsets of C, and $\succeq$ is a binary relation on D. Then, $\langle X, E, N, C, D, \succeq \rangle$ is a *conditional decision structure* (Krantz et al. 1971) if and only if the following hold for all $A, B \in E - N$, $R, S \in E$, and all $f_A, f_A{}^i, f_{A \cup B}, g_B, g_B{}^i, h_A{}^i, k_B{}^i \in D$, where $i \in \mathbb{N}$:

1. *Closure*:
   If $A \cap B = \emptyset$, then $f_A \cup g_B \in D$.
   If $B \subset A$, then the restriction of f_A to B is in D.

2. *Weak order*: $\langle D, \succeq \rangle$ is a weak order.

3. *Union indifference*: If $A \cap B = \emptyset$ and $f_A \sim g_B$, then $f_A \cup g_B \sim f_A$.

4. *Independence*: If $A \cap B = \emptyset$, then $f_A^1 \succeq f_A^2$ if and only if $f_A^1 \cup g_B \succeq f_A^2 \cup g_B$.

5. *Compatibility*: If $A \cap B = \emptyset$, $f_A^i \sim g_B^i$, $i = 1, 2, 3, 4$, $f_A^1 \cup k_B^1 \sim f_A^2 \cup k_B^2$, and $h_A^1 \cup g_B^1 \sim h_A^2 \cup g_B^2$, then $f_A^3 \cup k_B^1 \succeq f_A^4 \cup k_B^2$ if and only if $h_A^1 \cup g_B^3 \succeq h_A^2 \cup g_B^4$.

6. *Archimedean*: If $A \cap B = \emptyset$, M is a sequence of consecutive integers, $\neg(g_B^0 \sim g_B^1)$, and $f_A^i \cup g_B^1 \sim f_A^{i+1} \cup g_B^0$ for all i, $i + 1 \in M$, then either M is finite, or $\{f_A^i \mid i \in M\}$ is unbounded.

7. *Nullity*:
   If $R \in N$ and $S \subset R$, then $S \in N$.
   $R \in N$ if and only if for all $f_{A \cup B} \in D$ with $A \cap R = \emptyset$, $f_{A \cup B} \sim f_A$, where f_A is the restriction of $f_{A \cup B}$ to A.

8. *Nontriviality*:
   $E - N$ has at least three pairwise disjoint elements.
   $D/\sim$ has at least two distinct equivalence classes.

9. *Restricted solvability*:
   If A and g_B are given, then there exists $h_A \in D$ for which $h_A \sim g_B$.
   If $A \cap B = \emptyset$ and $h_A^1 \cup g_B \succeq f_{A \cup B} \succeq h_A^2 \cup g_B$, then there exists $h_A \in D$ such that $h_A \cup g_B \sim f_{A \cup B}$.

You can reformulate axioms 5 and 6 if you define the notion of a standard sequence. Take $E - N$ and let M be a sequence of consecutive integers (finite or infinite, positive or negative, or both). A set of decisions $\{f_A^i \mid f_A^i \in D, i \in M\}$ is a standard sequence if for some B in $E - N$, $A \cap B = \emptyset$, and g_B^0, $g_B^1 \in D$ with $\neg(g_B^0 \sim g_B^1)$, then for all i, $i + 1 \in M$, $f_A^i \cup g_B^1 \sim f_A^{i+1} \cup g_B^0$. Axiom 5 then becomes: If $\{f_A^i \mid i \in M\}$ and $\{h_B^i \mid i \in M\}$ are any two standard sequences such that, for some j, $j + 1 \in M$, $f_A^j \sim h_B^j$ and $f_A^{j+1} \sim h_B^{j+1}$, then for all $i \in M$, $f_A^i \sim h_B^i$. Axiom 6 becomes: Any strictly bounded standard sequence is finite.

The **representation condition** is: If $\langle X, E, N, C, D, \succeq \rangle$ is a conditional decision structure, then there exist real-valued functions u on D and P on E such that $\langle X, E, P \rangle$ is a finitely additive probability space, and for all $A, B \in E - N$, $R \in E$, $f_A, g_B \in D$:

1. $R \in N \Leftrightarrow P(R) = 0$.   (5.45a)

2. $f_A \succeq g_B \Leftrightarrow u(f_A) \geq u(g_B)$.   (5.45b)

3. $A \cap B = \emptyset \Rightarrow u(f_A \cup g_B) = u(f_A)P(A \mid A \cup B)$
   $\quad + u(g_B)P(B \mid A \cup B)$.   (5.45c)

(Krantz et al. 1971.) The **uniqueness condition** is: Since P is unique, P is an **absolute scale**; if u' is another function on D with the same properties, then there exist real numbers α, β, $\alpha > 0$, such that $u' = \alpha u + \beta$ (u is an **interval scale**) (Krantz et al. 1971).

CONJOINT REPRESENTATIONS

Many of the attributes we wish to measure, especially in software, are not of a structure which can lead to direct extensive measurement. Usually, this is due to a lack of an extensive concatenation operation. Often, such attributes are composites of two or more components, each of which affects the attribute in question.

You can construct composite measurement scales which preserve the observed order of the entity being measured. Each scale constructed for the composite attribute is a function of the scales of its components. The theories that lead to these representations allow the simultaneous measurement of the attributes and their components. Such measurement is called *conjoint measurement*.

Many conjoint constructions are possible. The most basic conjoint structures are those which have two components and lead to additive representations. The basic two-component additive conjoint structure can be modified in a variety of ways. Another interesting structure is the bisymmetric conjoint structure which provides a concatenation-like operation which may be idempotent, nonassociative, and noncommutative, conditions which are encountered frequently in software.

The notion of additive conjoint measures can be generalized to cases which have more than two components. Surprisingly, the more general case is simpler than the two-component case. To close the discussion, some nonadditive conjoint structures, all of which are varieties of polynomial representations, will be explored.

Because we are interested in finding interval and ratio scale measures, we are limited to using the counting of units or the solving of inequalities procedures. With conjoint structures, this involves constructing sequences in two or more dimensions simultaneously or solving a set of simultaneous inequalities in two or more variables.

In practice, we have evolved two basic experimental designs: constructive and factorial. In the constructive design, the object is to construct a standard sequence. In a two-dimensional additive situation, select a point of origin $a_0 p_0$ and some unit $a_1 p_0$. Then search for a p_1 which solves the equation $a_1 p_0 \sim a_0 p_1$. Next, look for a p_2 which satisfies $a_1 p_1 \sim a_0 p_2$, and for an a_2 which satisfies $a_2 p_0 \sim a_1 p_1$, and also $a_2 p_0 \sim a_0 p_2$, for which the solutions must coincide. If the model thus built is valid, the scale values are obtained by counting the number of equally spaced levels for each factor. In some contexts, constructive designs are difficult to use. One reason is that as the sequence grows, the effects of random error and biases are magnified at each level.

The other basic type of experiment is the factorial design, where the levels of the factors, and the factors themselves, are selected in advance. These preselected factors are then compared against actual data, testing for a specific representation. In factorial designs, the necessary axioms can be tested. The nonnecessary axioms cannot be tested.

However, even if the necessary axioms are met, and even if the solvability assumptions are accepted based on other information, it does not follow that the data possess a representation of the kind being investigated. The existence of a particular representation for a particular set of data depends on the solution to a set of simultaneous linear or polynomial inequalities. "One must demonstrate that the system obtained by translating the observed order relations into equations and inequalities, according to the appropriate measurement model, has a simultaneous solution" (Krantz et al. 1971, p. 426).

Additive Representations of Two Components

A basic tenet of conjoint measurement is that the attributes and underlying components exhibit two distinct forms of independence. The first form of independence requires that each component be independently realizable: You must be able to select the value of one component without regard to the value of the other. Formally, given two components $a \in A_1$ and $p \in A_2$, ap must be a realizable entity, or $ap \in A_1 \times A_2$ [ap is the same as $\langle a, p \rangle$]. Realizability may fail for either or both of two reasons. You may be limited to a $B \subset A_1 \times A_2$ due to practical reasons. In software, possible combinations of values from A_1 and A_2 may be restricted by an invariant condition imposed by the application domain. Or, the two components may be related by an empirical law. Theories of conjoint measurement apply only when the values of components can be selected independently and the ordering relation is over the whole of $A_1 \times A_2$.

The second form of independence requires that the two components contribute their effects to the attribute independently. The general form of the representation you are trying to construct is a set of real-valued functions ϕ_i on A_i, $i = 1, 2$, and a function $F: \mathbb{R} \times \mathbb{R} \rightarrow \mathbb{R}$, one-to-one for each component, such that for all $a, b \in A_1$ and $p, q \in A_2$:

$$ap \succeq bq \Leftrightarrow F[\phi_1(a), \phi_2(p)] \geq F[\phi_1(b), \phi_2(q)] \qquad (5.46)$$

When such a representation exists, the structure $\langle A_1, A_2, \succeq \rangle$ is said to be *decomposable*.

A special case is where the components contribute their effects noninteractively, which is called additive independence. Additive independence is used heavily in inferential statistics. Additive independence uses a function $F(x, y) = x + y$, so that equation (5.46) reduces to:

$$ap \succeq bq \Leftrightarrow \phi_1(a) + \phi_2(p) \geq \phi_1(b) + \phi_2(q) \qquad (5.47)$$

This is the general form of principal component analysis, a statistical technique to reduce the dimensions (number of independent variables) in an analysis problem. One issue that must be considered when using a technique such as principal component analysis is whether the derived empirical structure satisfies the axioms of additive conjoint measurement.

Let's formally define independence. A relation $\succeq$ on $A_1 \times A_2$ is *independent* if and only if, for all $a, b \in A_1$, $ap \succeq bp$ for some $p \in A_2$ implies that $aq \succeq bq$ for every $q \in A_2$, and, for $p, q \in A_2$, $ap \succeq aq$ for some $a \in A_1$ implies that $bp \succeq bq$ for every $b \in A_1$. For an independent relation $\succeq$ on $A_1 \times A_2$, define $\succeq_1$ on A_1: For $a, b \in A_1$, $a \succeq_1 b$ if and only if for some $p \in A_2$, $ap \succeq bp$. Define $\succeq_2$ on A_2: For $p, q \in A_2$, $p \succeq_2 q$ if and only if for some $a \in A_1$, $ap \succeq aq$.

Several additional properties are needed to construct the conjoint structure. A relation $\succeq$ on $A_1 \times A_2$ satisfies *double cancellation* provided that, for every $a, b, f \in A_1$ and $p, q, x \in A_2$,

$$ax \succeq fq \wedge fp \succeq bx \Rightarrow ap \succeq bq \qquad (5.48)$$

When $\succeq$ is replaced with $\sim$, we have the *Thomsen condition*. The Thomsen condition is important enough to restate explicitly: For every $a, b, f \in A_1$ and $p, q, x \in A_2$,

$$ax \sim fq \wedge fp \sim bx \Rightarrow ap \succeq bq \qquad (5.49)$$

A relation $\succeq$ on $A_1 \times A_2$ satisfies *triple cancellation* provided that, for every $a, b, f, g \in A_1$ and $p, q, x, y \in A_2$,

$$ax \succeq by \wedge fy \succeq gx \wedge gp \succeq fq \Rightarrow ap \succeq bq \qquad (5.50)$$

This property, with $\succeq$ replaced by $\sim$, is called the *Reidmeister condition* in the theory of webs.

Suppose $\succeq$ is an independent weak order on $A_1 \times A_2$. For any set N of consecutive integers (positive or negative, finite or infinite), a set $\{a_i \mid a_i \in A_1, i \in N\}$ is a *standard sequence on component one* if and only if there exist $p, q \in A_2$ such that $\neg(p \sim q)$ and for all i, $i + 1 \in N$, $a_i p \sim a_{i+1} q$. A standard sequence $\{a_i \mid i \in N\}$ is *strictly bounded* if and only if there exist $b, c \in A_1$ such that for all $i \in N$, $c >_1 a_i >_1 b$. Similarly, a set $\{p_i \mid p_i \in A_2, i \in N\}$ is a *standard sequence on component two* if and only if there exist $a, b \in A_1$ such that $\neg(a \sim b)$ and $ap_i \sim bp_{i+1}$. A standard sequence $\{p_i \mid i \in N\}$ is *strictly bounded* if and only if there exist $x, y \in A_2$ such that $x >_2 p_i >_2 y$. In words, these conditions define that a standard sequence on A_1 such that the interval from a_i to a_{i+1} is equivalent to the interval from p to q, and that moving one notch in one direction in one component and one notch in the opposite direction on the other component maintains equivalence. Likewise for A_2. These standard sequences form the basis for the Archimedean axiom.

A relation $\succeq$ on $A_1 \times A_2$ satisfies *unrestricted solvability* provided that, given three of $a, b \in A_1$ and $p, q \in A_2$, the fourth exists so that $ap \sim bq$. It satisfies *restricted solvability* provided that:

1. Whenever there exists $a, b', b'' \in A_1$ and $p, q \in A_2$ for which $b'q \succeq ap \succeq b''q$, then there exists $b \in A_1$ such that $ap \sim bq$.
2. Whenever there exists $p, q', q'' \in A_2$ for which $bq' \succeq ap \succeq bq''$, then there exists $q \in A_2$ such that $ap \sim bq$.

Given a relation $\succeq$ on $A_1 \times A_2$, component A_1 is *essential* if and only if there exist $a, b \in A_1$ and $p \in A_2$ such that $\neg(ap \sim bp)$. Component A_2 is essential if and only if there exist $a \in A_1$ and $p, q \in A_2$ such that $\neg(ap \sim aq)$.

Now, let's present the full set of conditions. Given two nonempty sets A_1 and A_2 and a binary relation $\succeq$ on $A_1 \times A_2$, the triple $\langle A_1, A_2, \succeq \rangle$ is an *additive conjoint structure* (Krantz et al. 1971) if and only if the following hold:

1. $\langle A_1 \times A_2, \succeq \rangle$ is a weak order.
2. $\succeq$ is independent.
3. $\succeq$ satisfies the Thomsen condition.
4. $\succeq$ satisfies restricted solvability.
5. Every strictly bounded standard sequence is finite.
6. Each component is essential.

The structure is *symmetric* if and only if, in addition:

7. For $a, b \in A_1$, there exist $p, q \in A_2$ such that $ap \sim bq$, and for $p', q' \in A_2$, there exist $a', b' \in A_1$ such that $a'p' \sim b'q'$.

If you replace the Thomsen condition with double cancellation in axiom 3, and replace restricted solvability with unrestricted solvability in axiom 4, and at least one component is essential, you still have a symmetric, additive conjoint structure.

The **representation condition** is: If $\langle A_1, A_2, \succeq \rangle$ is an additive conjoint structure, then there exist functions $\phi_i : A_i \to \mathbb{R}$, $i = 1, 2$, such that for all $a, b \in A_1$ and $p, q \in A_2$:

$$ap \succeq bq \Leftrightarrow \phi_1(a) + \phi_2(p) \geqslant \phi_1(b) + \phi_2(q) \qquad (5.51)$$

(Krantz et al. 1971.) The **uniqueness condition** is: If ϕ_i', $i = 1, 2$, are two other functions with the same property, then there exist constants $\alpha > 0$, β_1, and β_2 such that $\phi_1' = \alpha\phi_1 + \beta_1$ and $\phi_2' = \alpha\phi_2 + \beta_2$ (ϕ_1 and ϕ_2 are **interval scales**) (Krantz et al. 1971). Note that the change in unit, α, is the same for both components.

Alternative Constructions

In this rather long subsection, several modifications to the basic theory for additive conjoint structures are discussed. These modifications may make it possible to use conjoint measurement in cases where it could not be used otherwise.

It is possible to drop the Archimedean axiom, at least for additive conjoint structures, by defining a standard sequence $\{a_i \mid a_i \in A_1, i \in I\}$ and $\{p_i \mid p_i \in A_2, i \in I\}$, $I = \{0, 1, 2,...\}$, giving real-valued functions ϕ_1 on $\{a \mid a \in A_1 \wedge a_i \succeq_1 a \succeq_1 a_j$ for some $i, j \in I\}$ and ϕ_2 on $\{p \mid p \in A_2 \wedge p_i \succeq_2 p \succeq_2 p_j$ for some $i, j \in I\}$ such that:

1. $\phi_1(a_i) = i$ and $\phi_2(p_i) = i$.
2. $a \succeq_1 b \Rightarrow \phi_1(a) \geqslant \phi_1(b)$ and $p \succeq_2 q \Rightarrow \phi_2(p) \geqslant \phi_2(q)$.

Dropping the Archimedean axiom allows for strictly bounded standard sequences which are infinite.

Given an additive conjoint structure, you can define a representation $\psi = \psi_1 \oplus \psi_2$, where $\oplus$ is some numerical operation other than addition. As with extensive measurement, there exist strictly increasing functions f, f_1, and f_2 such that $\phi = f\psi$, $\phi_1 = f_1\psi_1$, and $\phi_2 = f_2\psi_2$, and $x \oplus y = f^{-1}[f_1(x) + f_2(y)]$. Conversely, any such system of functions provides a representation into the real numbers that is additive in $\oplus$.

The typical transformations that preserve such a representation are $T_{\alpha,\beta_i}^{f_i} = f_i^{-1}(\alpha f_i + \beta_i)$, $i = 0, 1, 2$, where $f_0 = f$, $\beta_0 = \beta_1 + \beta_2$, and $\alpha > 0$. This is the same two-parameter group in which $T_{1,0}$ is the identity and $T_{1/\alpha,-\beta/\alpha}$ is the inverse to $T_{\alpha,\beta}$. The most common such transformation is where $f_0 = f_1 = f_2 = \log$ and $x \oplus y = \exp(\log x + \log y) = xy$, or $T_{\alpha,\beta}(\psi) = \exp(\alpha \log y + \beta) = \gamma\psi^\alpha$, where $\gamma = \exp \beta$.

You can find a set of functions f, f_1, and f_2 such that $f[F(x, y)] = f_1(x) + f_2(y)$ [$x = \psi_1$, $y = \psi_2$] provided that the equation holds for open intervals of real numbers and we impose suitable smoothness conditions on the functions (Scheffé 1959). Formally, suppose that X, Y, and Z are open intervals of real numbers and that $F: X \times Y \to Z$ is such that Fxy exists everywhere on $X \times Y$ and that $FxFy \neq 0$. There exist $f: Z \to \mathbb{R}$, $f_1: X \to \mathbb{R}$, and $f_2: Y \to \mathbb{R}$ such that f'' (second derivative of f) exists, f' (first derivative of f) is nonzero, and $f[F(x, y)] = f_1(x) + f_2(y)$ if and only if there is an integrable function $G: Z \to R$ such that $Fxy/FxFy = G(F)$. Moreover,

$$f(F) = c_1 \int \exp\left[-\int G(F)\, dF \right] dF + c_2, \qquad (5.52a)$$

$$f_1(x) = \int F_2(z, y)f'[F(z, y)]\, dz + c_3, \qquad (5.52b)$$

and

$$f_2(y) = f[F(x, y)] - f_1(x). \qquad (5.53)$$

Some interpretations are more natural to think of as differences rather than sums, leading to a representation of the form:

$$ap \succeq bq \Leftrightarrow \phi_1(a) - \phi_2(p) \geq \phi_1(b) - \phi_2(q) \qquad (5.54)$$

Since

$$\phi_1(a) - \phi_2(p) \geq \phi_1(b) - \phi_2(q) \Leftrightarrow \phi_1(a) + \phi_2(q) \geq \phi_1(b) + \phi_2(p)$$

$$(5.55)$$

you define dual relations $\succeq$ and $\succeq'$ on $A_1 \times A_2$ as follows: For $a, b \in A_1$ and p, $q \in A_2$, $ap \succeq bq \Leftrightarrow aq \succeq' bp$. If two relations are dual, then transitivity and double cancellation are dual properties, and independence, restricted and unrestricted solvability, and the Archimedean property, are self-dual properties. This means that a difference representation can always be made into an additive representation, and vice versa, provided the structure $\langle A_1, A_2, \succeq \rangle$ satisfies the requisite axioms.

As noted earlier, the theory of additive conjoint measurement had been developed only for $B = A_1 \times A_2$. There are times when you want to apply such measurement to $B \subset A_1 \times A_2$. This situation most often arises in experiments on data sets. Even though the theory doesn't address these situations directly, you can patch together a representation.

Given some subset B that resembles a convex or closed region of the plane, you can almost cover it with a set of overlapping rectangles, each of which is an additive conjoint structure. That is, you can find an additive representation for each of the rectangles. If the areas of overlap are sufficiently large to form additional additive conjoint structures, you can choose representations for each overlapping rectangle so they coincide in the overlapping region, due to the uniqueness condition. You can extend this process throughout the entire subset B, provided that certain consistency requirements are met. Since these requirements have not been formally developed, the best you can hope for is an approximate representation built according to these procedures. The concept is illustrated in Figure 5.4.

You can view the orderings $\succeq_1$ on A_1, $\succeq_2$ on A_2, and $\succeq$ on $A_1 \times A_2$ as three orderings $\succeq_1$, $\succeq_2$, and $\succeq_3$ on A if A_1 and A_2 are equivalence classes. Take $\succeq_1$ to be the first coordinate, $\succeq_2$ as the second coordinate, and $\succeq$ as the ordering induced by $\succeq_3$ on $(A/\sim_1) \times (A/\sim_2)$. With these orderings, your choice of which of the variables is dependent is a matter of convention. Given the representation $\phi = \phi_1 + \phi_2$, you could just as easily write $\phi_1 = \phi + (-\phi_2)$ or $\phi_2 = \phi + (-\phi_1)$. Some objects have a natural product structure which leads us to choose a particular variable as dependent. Other objects present no natural choice, so you rely on convention or convenience.

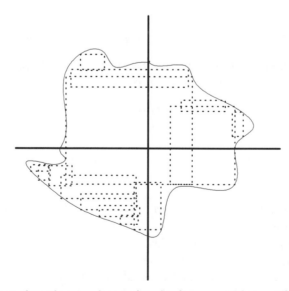

Figure 5.4 *Approximating an irregular enclosure with two-factor rectangles (Krantz et al. 1971).*

To make conjoint measurement on the orderings $\succeq_1$, $\succeq_2$, and $\succeq_3$, you need one new axiom: If $a \succeq_1 b$, then $a \succeq_2 b$ if and only if $a \succeq_3 b$, and if $a \succeq_2 b$, then $a \succeq_1 b$ if and only if $a \succeq_3 b$, and if $a \succeq_3 b$, then $a \succeq_1 b$ if and only if $a \succeq_2 b$. Basically, this axiom states that if a and b are equivalent in two orderings, then they are equivalent in the third as well.

Additive conjoint measurement involves the measurement of three variables ϕ, ϕ_1, and ϕ_2 which are linearly related and have essentially the same status. Either component of the Cartesian product could be defined as a Cartesian product with the other two variables as components. In many representation situations, several factorial decompositions (sets of components) may be considered. The selection of the appropriate structure is a nontrivial and often very difficult problem. Each of the candidate structures must be examined empirically to see if it satisfies the conditions for additive conjoint measurement. There are no general methods for discovering whether a particular structure can be decomposed so as to satisfy additivity. It could very well be the case that none of the candidate structures satisfy the conditions. In this case, either a new structure needs to be found or another representation must be sought. With conjoint measurement, it is very apparent that we are operating on the leading edge of measurement theory.

Bisymmetric Structures

Bisymmetric structures arose out of the study of the behavior of means of pairs of numbers. Such a structure contains a binary operation $\circ: A \times A \rightarrow A$, which looks like concatenation (the operation, not just the symbol), but may be idempotent ($a \circ a \sim a$), and need not be associative or commutative. The operation of combining two classes in software (set union) is an example of such an operation.

Suppose that A is a nonempty set, that $\succeq$ is a binary relation on A, and that $\circ$ is a binary operation from $A \times A$ into A. The triple $\langle A, \succeq, \circ \rangle$ is a *bisymmetric structure* (Krantz et al. 1971) if and only if the following hold for all a, b, b', b'', $c, d \in A$:

1. $\langle A, \succeq \rangle$ is a weak order.
2. *Monotonicity*: $a \succeq b \Leftrightarrow a \circ c \succeq b \circ c \Leftrightarrow c \circ a \succeq c \circ b$.
3. *Bisymmetry*: $(a \circ b) \circ (c \circ d) \sim (a \circ c) \circ (b \circ d)$.
4. *Restricted solvability*: If $b' \circ c \succeq a \succeq b'' \circ c$ (or $c \circ b' \succeq a \succeq c \circ b''$) then there exists $b \in A$ such that $b \circ c \sim a$ (or $c \circ b \sim a$).
5. *Archimedean*: Every strictly bounded standard sequence is finite, where $\{a_i \mid a_i \in A, i \in \mathbb{N}\}$ is a standard sequence if and only if there exist p, $q \in A$ such that $p > q$ and, for all $i, i + 1 \in \mathbb{N}$, $a_i \circ p \sim a_{i+1} \circ q$, or for all $i, i + 1 \in N$, $p \circ a_i \sim q \circ a_{i+1}$.

The notion of bisymmetry can best be explained graphically, as shown in Figure 5.5.

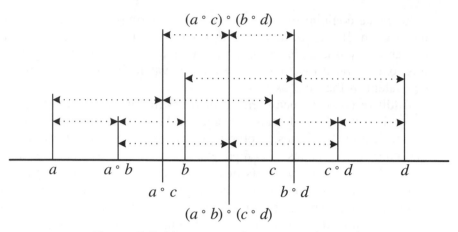

Figure 5.5 *Bisymmetry (Krantz et al. 1979).*

The **representation condition** is: If $\langle A, \succeq, \circ \rangle$ is a bisymmetric structure, then there exist real numbers $\mu > 0$, $\nu > 0$, and λ and a real-valued function ϕ on A such that, for $a, b, \in A$:

1. $a \succeq b \Leftrightarrow \phi(a) \geq \phi(b)$.   (5.56a)

2. $\phi(a \circ b) = \mu\phi(a) + \nu\phi(b) + \lambda$.   (5.56b)

(Krantz et al. 1971.) The **uniqueness condition** is: If μ', ν', λ', and ϕ' is another representation satisfying (5.56a) and (5.56b), then there exist constants $\alpha > 0$ and β such that $\phi' = \alpha\phi + \beta$ (ϕ is an **interval scale**), with $\lambda' = \alpha\lambda + \beta(1 - \mu - \nu)$, $\mu' = \mu$, and $\nu' = \nu$ (Krantz et al. 1971).

This representation has some interesting properties. If $\circ$ is idempotent—for all $a \in A$, $a \circ a \sim a$—then $\lambda = 0$ and $\mu + \nu = 1$. If $\circ$ is commutative, and if there exist $a > b$, then $\mu = \nu$. If $\circ$ is both idempotent and commutative, then $\mu = \nu = 1/2$, and $\lambda = 0$. If $\circ$ is associative as well as commutative, and there exist $a > b$, then $\mu = \nu = 1$.

Equally Spaced Additive Structures

Occasionally, you run across a bisymmetric structure with built-in standard sequences. If the structure happens to be finite, which is typical of the kinds of software structures we wish to measure, so much the better. A finite, equally spaced bisymmetric structure is a very special case. Not only can you drop the solvability and Archimedean conditions, which is usual with finite equally spaced structures, but you also drop bisymmetry.

Suppose that A is a finite set, $\succeq$ is a binary relation on A, B is a nonempty subset of $A \times A$, and $\circ$ is a function from B into A. The structure $\langle A, B, \succeq, \circ \rangle$ is an *equally spaced, additive conjoint structure* (defined but not named in Krantz et al. 1971) if and only if the following hold for all $a, b, c, d \in A$:

1. $\langle A, \succeq \rangle$ is a weak order.

2. If $ac, bc \in B$, then $a \succeq b \Leftrightarrow a \circ c \succeq b \circ c$.

3. If $ab \in B$, then $ba \in B$ and $a \circ b \sim b \circ a$.

4. $aa \in B$ and $a \circ a \sim a$.

5. If $bc \in B$, aJb, and cJd, then $ad \in B$ and $a \circ d \sim b \circ c$, where J is defined as aJb if and only if for all $c \in A$, exactly one of the following hold: $c \succeq a$ or $b \succeq c$.

The **representation condition** is: If $\langle A, B, \succeq, \circ \rangle$ is an equally spaced, additive conjoint structure, then there exists a real-valued function ϕ on A such that for every $a, b \in A$:

1. $a \succeq b \Leftrightarrow \phi(a) \geqslant \phi(b)$. $\qquad\qquad\qquad\qquad\qquad\qquad\qquad$ (5.57a)

2. $ab \in B \Rightarrow \phi(a \circ b) = [\phi(a) + \phi(b)]/2$. $\qquad\qquad\qquad\qquad$ (5.57b)

(Krantz et al. 1971.) The **uniqueness condition** is: If ϕ' is another real-valued function which has these properties, then there exist real numbers $\alpha > 0$ and β such that $\phi' = \alpha\phi + \beta$ (ϕ is an **interval scale**) (Krantz et al. 1971).

Additive Representations of *n* Components

There are many times when three or more components affect the attribute of interest. This situation requires that we generalize our definitions and theorems. First, there is the notion of independence. A relation $\succeq$ on $\times_{i=1}^{n} A_i$ is *independent* if and only if, for every $M \subset \mathbb{N}$, the ordering $\succeq_m$ induced by $\succeq$ on $\times_{i \in M} A_i$ for fixed choices $a_i \in A_i$, $i \in \mathbb{N} - M$ is unaffected by those choices.

Next, generalize restricted solvability. A relation $\succ$ on $\times_{i=1}^{n} A_i$ satisfies *restricted solvability* if and only if, for each $i \in \mathbb{N}$, whenever $b_1,..., b_i',..., b_n \succeq a_1,..., a_i,..., a_n \succeq b_1,..., b_i'',..., b_n$, there exists $b_i \in A_i$ such that $b_1,..., b_i,..., b_n \sim a_1,..., a_i,..., a_n$.

The Archimedean axiom and the essentialness of components were both defined in terms of single components and so do not need to be redefined.

Suppose that A_i, $i \in \mathbb{N}$, $n \geq 3$, are nonempty sets and that $\succeq$ is a binary relation on $\times_{i=1}^{n} A_i$. The structure $\langle A_1,..., A_n, \succeq \rangle$ is an *n-component additive conjoint structure* (Krantz et al. 1971) if and only if the following hold:

1. $\langle \times_{i=1}^{n} A_i, \succeq \rangle$ is a weak order.

2. $\succeq$ is independent over n components.

3. $\succeq$ satisfies restricted solvability for n components.

4. Every strictly bounded standard sequence is finite.

5. At least three components are essential.

The **representation condition** is: If $\langle A_1,..., A_n, \succeq \rangle$ is an n-component additive conjoint structure, then there exist real valued functions ϕ_i on A_i, $i \in \mathbb{N}$, such that:

$$a_1,..., a_n \succeq b_1,..., b_n \geqslant \sum_{i=1}^{n} \phi_i(a) \geqslant \sum_{i=1}^{n} \phi_i(b) \qquad (5.58)$$

(Krantz et al. 1971.) The **uniqueness condition** is: If $\{\phi_i'\}$ is another family of functions with these properties, then there exist real numbers $\alpha > 0$ and β_i, $i \in \mathbb{N}$, such that $\phi_i' = \alpha\phi_i + \beta_i$ (the ϕ_i are **interval scales**) (Krantz et al. 1971). For $n \geqslant 3$, you need to test for solvability, the Archimedean property, weak ordering, and independence. You don't need to worry about any form of cancellation.

In situations where solvability cannot be tested, the following technique can be used to construct an additive representation. Let $A = A_1 \times \cdots \times A_n$ be a finite set with A_i and A_j pairwise disjoint for $i \neq j$, and let $\succeq$ denote a reflexive binary relation on A. Suppose the sets $A_1,..., A_n$ contain $k_1,..., k_n$ elements, respectively, and let $k = \Sigma_{i=1}^n k_i$. Thus, $Y = \cup_{i=1}^n A_i$ contains k elements: $y_1,..., y_k$ (since the A_i and A_j are disjoint sets, the cardinality of the union operation is additive). An isomorphism v of A into $\mathbb{R}^k$ ($\mathbb{R}_1 \times \cdots \times \mathbb{R}_k$) is defined by $v(a) = \boldsymbol{a} = (\boldsymbol{a}_1,..., \boldsymbol{a}_k)$ where for any $l = 1, 2,..., k$,

$$\boldsymbol{a} = \begin{cases} 1 & \text{if } y_l \text{ is a component of } a \\ 0 & \text{otherwise} \end{cases} \tag{5.59}$$

Each a in A corresponds to a vector $\boldsymbol{a}$ in $\mathbb{R}^k$. Let $\boldsymbol{A} = \{\boldsymbol{a} \mid a \in A\}$ and let A^+ be the closure of $\boldsymbol{A}$ with respect to componentwise vector addition (A^+ is the smallest semigroup of vectors in $\mathbb{R}^k$ which contains $\boldsymbol{A}$; the elements of A^+ all have non-negative integer components). Formally, $A^+ = \{x \in \mathbb{R}^k \mid x = \boldsymbol{a}_1 + \cdots + \boldsymbol{a}_m, \boldsymbol{a}_j \in \boldsymbol{A}, j = 1,..., m, m = 1, 2,...\}$.

Define $\sim_I$: For any $x, y \in A^+$, let $x \sim_I y$ if and only if there exist $\boldsymbol{a}_1,..., \boldsymbol{a}_m$, $\boldsymbol{b}_1,..., \boldsymbol{b}_m \in \boldsymbol{A}$ such that $x = \boldsymbol{a}_1 + \cdots + \boldsymbol{a}_m$, $y = \boldsymbol{b}_1 + \cdots + \boldsymbol{b}_m$, and for $j = 1,..., m$, $a_j \sim b_j$. Define $>_I$: $x >_I y$ if and only if there exist $\boldsymbol{c}_1,..., \boldsymbol{c}_m, \boldsymbol{d}_1,..., \boldsymbol{d}_m \in \boldsymbol{A}$ such that $x = \boldsymbol{c}_1 + \cdots + \boldsymbol{c}_m$, $y = \boldsymbol{d}_1 + \cdots + \boldsymbol{d}_m$, $c_j \succeq d_j$, $j = 1,..., m$, and for some j, $\neg(d_j \succeq c_j)$. The relation $\succeq_I$ is $\sim_I \cup >_I$. The irreflexivity of $>_I$ is a necessary and sufficient condition for the existence of an additive representation. We call $\langle A, \succeq \rangle$ a *nonsolvable n-component additive conjoint structure* (defined but not named in Krantz et al. 1971). The **representation condition** is: The relation $>_I$ is irreflexive if and only if there exists a real-valued function ϕ on Y and ψ on A such that for all $a, b \in A$:

1. $\psi(a) = \psi(a_1,..., a_n) = \Sigma_{i=1}^n \phi(a_i)$. $\qquad\qquad\qquad\qquad$ (5.60a)

2. $a \sim b \Rightarrow \psi(a) = \psi(b)$. $\qquad\qquad\qquad\qquad\qquad\qquad$ (5.60b)

3. $a > b \Rightarrow \psi(a) > \psi(b)$. $\qquad\qquad\qquad\qquad\qquad\qquad$ (5.60c)

(Krantz et al. 1971.) The **uniqueness condition** is: If A has an order-preserving additive representation, then there exist vectors $z_1,..., z_m$ in $\mathbb{R}^k$, and an integer j, with $0 \leqslant j \leqslant m$, such that z satisfies, for all $a, b \in A$, $a \sim b \Rightarrow z \cdot \boldsymbol{a} = z \cdot \boldsymbol{b} \wedge a > b \Rightarrow z \cdot \boldsymbol{a} > z \cdot \boldsymbol{b}$ if and only if $z = \Sigma_{i=1}^n \alpha_i z_i + c$ where c is any vector whose components are all equal, $\alpha_i \geqslant 0$ for $i \leqslant j$, and $\alpha_i > 0$ for $i > j$ (ϕ and ψ form an **interval scale** only in the special case where $m = 1$; otherwise, they form something *between* an **ordinal scale** and an **interval scale**) (Krantz et al. 1971).

Polynomial Conjoint Structures

In many cases, the ordering of objects requires the use of two or more components, but they do not combine in an additive way. There are three basic polynomial representations: multiplicative, distributive, and dual-distributive. Their forms and the differences between them will be explained later. In order to work with polynomial representations, a few concepts need to be defined first.

Like additive conjoint structures, our goal is to find representations for a binary relation $\succeq$ on $A = \times_{i=1}^{n} A_i$, as a structure $\langle \times_{i=1}^{n} A_i, \succeq \rangle$, such that for all $a, b \in A$,

$$a \succeq b \Leftrightarrow F[\phi_1(a_1),..., \phi_n(a_n)] \geq F[\phi_1(b_1),..., \phi_n(b_n)] \tag{5.61}$$

where F is some form of polynomial. A function F of n real variables is a *polynomial* if it is a linear combination of products of the variables raised to nonnegative powers, or

$$F(x_1,..., x_n) = \sum_{k=1}^{m} \alpha_k x_1^{\beta_{1k}} x_2^{\beta_{2k}} \cdots x_n^{\beta_{nk}} \tag{5.62}$$

where $\alpha_k \in \mathbb{R}$ and $\beta_{ik} \in \mathbb{N} \cup \{0\}$. Normally, the multipliers of the form $x_i^0 = 1$ are omitted for clarity.

It is much easier to specify sufficient conditions for a representation to exist for a special class of polynomials: the *simple* polynomials. Members of this class can be split into either a sum or a product of two polynomials that have no common variables, and such that both of these smaller polynomials can be split further, until only single variables are left. For example, $x_1 + x_2$ splits into the sum of x_1 and x_2. $x_3 x_4$ splits into the product of x_3 and x_4. $(x_1 + x_2)x_3 x_4$ splits into the product of $(x_1 + x_2)$ and $x_3 x_4$. Formally, let $X = \{x_1,..., x_n\}$. The set $S(X)$ of simple polynomials in $x_1,..., x_n$ is the smallest set of polynomials such that:

1. $x_i \in S(X)$, $i = 1,..., n$.
2. If Y_1 and Y_2 are nonempty subsets of X with $Y_1 \cap Y_2 = \varnothing$, $F_1 \in S(Y_1)$ and $F_2 \in S(Y_2)$, then $F_1 + F_2$ and $F_1 F_2$ are in $S(X)$.

There are just four classes of simple polynomials in three variables:

1. *Additive*: $x_1 + x_2 + x_3$.
2. *Distributive*: Such as $(x_1 + x_2)x_3$.
3. *Dual-distributive*: Such as $x_1 x_2 + x_3$.
4. *Multiplicative*: $x_1 x_2 x_3$.

There are 10 classes of simple polynomials in four variables: four formed by adding a fourth variable to each of the previous classes, four formed by multiplying each of the previous classes by a fourth variable, plus $(x_1 + x_2)(x_3 + x_4)$ and $x_1 x_2 + x_3 x_4$.

A factor A_i, $i = 1,..., n$ in $\times_{i=1}^{n} A_i$, is *independent* of another factor A_j, $i \neq j$, $j = 1,..., n$, if and only if the induced relation $\succeq_i$ on A_i is independent of the choice of any value in A_j, for all $j \neq i$. If more than two factors are involved, that is, if $n > 2$, the other factors are held constant while testing A_i against A_j.

For any simple polynomial, if A_i is not independent of $\times_{i \neq j} A_j$, then only three different relations can be induced over A_i. The induced weak order $\succeq_i$ over A_i will remain unchanged when multiplied by a positive value in some other factor A_j, $i \neq j$, denoted S^+. The induced weak order $\succeq_i$ over A_i will be reversed when multiplied by a negative value, denoted S^-. The induced weak order $\succeq_i$ over A_i will degenerate when multiplied by a zero value, denoted S^0. In each of these three cases, we say that A_i is *sign dependent* on A_j. Assume that at least one S^+, S^-, or S^0 is nonempty, that is, the value of an A_j factor exists. When two or three of S^+, S^-, or S^0 are nonempty, it is called proper sign dependence. Note that S^+, S^-, and S^0 on a factor A_j partition the set A_j.

So far, we have discussed the independence or sign dependence of a factor A_i on another factor A_j, $j \neq i$. The independence of the joint effect of two or more factors from fixed or selected values of the other factors can also be discussed, as well as the notion of joint sign dependence; that is, where two or more factors are jointly sign dependent upon a third factor, or two or more other factors. The notions of single factor independence and sign dependence are not necessarily related to joint independence or joint sign dependence—one does not always lead to the other. You need to test for each type of independence separately.

For the distributive model, $(x_1 + x_2)x_3$, the Thomsen condition must hold for the induced order on $A_1 \times A_2$ for any fixed a_3. Likewise, taking $A_1 \times A_2$ as a single factor combined with A_3, a multiplicative version of the Thomsen condition must hold for $(A_1 \times A_2) \times A_3$. For the dual-distributive model, $x_1 x_2 + x_3$, the induced order on $A_1 \times A_2$ must satisfy multiplicative versions of the two-factor additive conjoint measurement conditions. The additive (version of the) Thomsen condition is repeated: A relation $\succeq$ on $A_1 \times A_2$ satisfies the Thomsen condition provided that, for every $a_1, b_1, c_1 \in A_1$ and $a_2, b_2, c_2 \in A_2$,

$$a_1 c_2 \sim c_1 b_2 \wedge c_1 a_2 \sim b_1 c_2 \Rightarrow a_1 a_2 \sim b_1 b_2 \qquad (5.63)$$

The *multiplicative* (version of the) *Thomsen condition* is: For every $a_1, b_1, c_1 \in A_1$ and $a_2, b_2, c_2 \in A_2$

$$a_1 c_2 \sim c_1 b_2 \wedge c_1 a_2 \sim b_1 c_2 \wedge (c_1 \notin A_1{}^0 \vee c_2 \notin A_2{}^0) \Rightarrow a_1 a_2 \sim b_1 b_2$$

$$(5.64)$$

The provision that either $c_1 \notin A_1{}^0$ or $c_2 \notin A_2{}^0$ means that any value c_1 or c_2 is nonzero to prevent division by zero. This form of the Thomsen condition was introduced by Roskies (1965).

If each A_i is independent of $\times_{j \neq i} A_j$, you need a special cancellation condition to distinguish the distributive and dual-distributive cases. Suppose that $\succeq$ is a binary relation on $A = A_1 \times A_2 \times A_3$. We say that *distributive cancellation* holds if and only if, for all $a, b, b', c \in A$,

$$a_1 b_2 a_3 \succeq b_1' c_2 c_3 \wedge b_1 a_2 a_3 \succeq c_1 b_2' c_3 \wedge b_1' b_2' a_3 \succeq b_1 b_2 a_3 \Rightarrow a \succeq c \qquad (5.65)$$

Suppose that $\succeq$ is a weak order on A, and that A_1 and A_2 are sign dependent on each other. We say that *dual-distributive cancellation* holds if and only if, for all $a, b, c, d, e \in A$, with $e_2 \notin A_2^0$,

$$a_1c_2c_3 \sim c_1d_2b_3 \wedge$$

$$d_1a_2a_3 \sim b_1e_2d_3 \wedge$$

$$d_1c_2d_3 \sim e_1d_2a_3 \wedge$$

$$c_1e_2e_3 \sim e_1b_2e_3 \wedge$$

$$a_1e_2e_3 \sim d_1b_2e_3 \Rightarrow a_1a_2b_3 \sim b_1b_2c_3 \qquad (5.66)$$

One last notion, unrestricted solvability, is needed before the representation and uniqueness conditions for the three polynomial models can be presented. Suppose that $\succeq$ is a weak order on $A = A_1 \times A_2 \times A_3$ and that each factor is sign dependent on the other two. We say that *unrestricted solvability* holds if and only if, for all $a, b \in A$ for which $\langle b_i, b_j \rangle \in (A_i^0 \times A_j^0)$, $i, j = 1, 2, 3$, $i \neq j$, there exists $c \in A$ such that

$$a \sim b_1b_2c_3 \sim b_1c_2b_3 \sim c_1b_2b_3 \qquad (5.67)$$

where $a = a_1a_2a_3$.

Multiplicative Polynomial Conjoint Structures

First, the representation and uniqueness conditions for the multiplicative model will be presented, then the tests to determine if the multiplicative model applies to the empirical structure will be covered. Recall that the model in three real variables is $x_1x_2x_3$. A structure $\langle A_1 \times A_2 \times A_3, \succeq \rangle$ is a *multiplicative polynomial conjoint structure* (defined but not named in Krantz et al. 1971) if and only if the following hold:

1. $\langle A, \succeq \rangle$ is a weak order.
2. Each pair of factors is jointly sign dependent on the third.
3. Every strictly bounded standard sequence in each factor (using the other pair of factors as the second component) is finite.
4. Unrestricted solvability holds.

The **representation condition** is: If $\langle A_1 \times A_2 \times A_3, \succeq \rangle$ is a multiplicative polynomial conjoint structure, then there exist real valued functions ϕ_i on A_i, $i = 1$, 2, 3, such that, for all $a, b \in A$:

$$a \succeq b \Leftrightarrow \phi_1(a_1)\phi_2(a_2)\phi_3(a_3) \geq \phi_1(b_1)\phi_2(b_2)\phi_3(b_3) \qquad (5.68)$$

(Krantz et al. 1971.) The **uniqueness condition** is: If ϕ_i', $i = 1$, 2, 3, are real-valued functions with the same properties, then

$$\phi_i'(a_i) = \begin{cases} \alpha_i[\phi_i(a_i)]^\beta & \text{if } \phi_i(a_i) \geq 0 \\ -\alpha_i[-\phi_i(a_i)]^\beta & \text{if } \phi_i(a_i) < 0 \end{cases} \qquad (5.69)$$

where the α_i and β are real numbers, $\beta > 0$, and α_1, α_2, $\alpha_3 > 0$ (the ϕ_i are **log-interval scales** on each component) (Krantz et al. 1971).

To use the multiplicative model on a particular empirical structure, the following tests must be performed in the order given (the tests are given in increasing order of strength and difficulty for testing):

1. $\langle A = A_1 \times A_2 \times A_3, \succeq \rangle$ forms a weak order.
2. Each factor is properly sign dependent on each of the other two factors.
3. Each pair of factors is sign dependent on the third factor.
4. The Archimedean property holds.
5. Unrestricted solvability holds.

Distributive Polynomial Conjoint Structures

The distributive model in three variables is $(x_1 + x_2)x_3$. A structure $\langle A_1 \times A_2 \times A_3, \succeq \rangle$ is a *distributive conjoint structure* (defined but not named in Krantz et al. 1971) if and only if the following hold:

1. $\langle A, \succeq \rangle$ is a weak order.
2. $A_1 \times A_2$ and A_3 are sign dependent on each other.
3. $\langle A_1 \times A_2, A_3, \sim \rangle$ satisfies the multiplicative Thomsen condition.
4. Distributive cancellation holds.
5. For any induced ordering on $A_1 \times A_2$, every strictly bounded standard sequence in one component is finite.
6. Unrestricted solvability holds.
7. $(A_1 \times A_2)^0$ and A_3^0 are nonempty—there are zero-valued members of $A_1 \times A_2$ and A_3.

The **representation condition** is: If $\langle A_1 \times A_2 \times A_3, \succeq \rangle$ is a distributive conjoint structure, then there exist real-valued functions ϕ_i on A_i, $i = 1, 2, 3$, such that, for all $a, b \in A$,

$$a \succeq b \Leftrightarrow [\phi_1(a_1) + \phi_2(a_2)]\phi_3(a_3) \geq [\phi_1(b_1) + \phi_2(b_2)]\phi_3(b_3) \qquad (5.70)$$

(Krantz et al. 1971.) The **uniqueness condition** is: If ϕ_i' are real-valued functions with the same properties, then $\phi_1' = \alpha\phi_1 + \beta$, $\phi_2' = \alpha\phi_2 - \beta$, and $\phi_3' = \gamma\phi_3$, where α, β, γ are real numbers with α, $\gamma > 0$ (ϕ_1 and ϕ_2 are **interval scales** on components A_1 and A_2, $\phi_1 + \phi_2$ is a **ratio scale** on component $A_1 \times A_2$, and ϕ_3 is a **ratio scale** on component A_3) (Krantz et al. 1971).

To use the distributive model on a particular empirical structure, the following tests must be performed in the order given:

1. $\langle A, \succeq \rangle$ forms a weak order.
2. Each factor is either independent of or sign dependent on each of the other two factors.
3. One pair of factors is jointly sign dependent on the third and all other pairs are independent of the third.

4. Distributive cancellation holds.

5. The Archimedean property holds.

6. Unrestricted solvability holds.

7. The multiplicative Thomsen condition holds for $\langle A_1 \times A_2, A_3, \succeq \rangle$.

8. Some of the values in the pair of factors which is jointly dependent on the third are zero valued, and some of the values in the third factor are zero valued.

Dual-Distributive Polynomial Conjoint Structures

The dual-distributive model in three variables is $x_1x_2 + x_3$. A structure $\langle A_1 \times A_2 \times A_3, \succeq \rangle$ is a *dual-distributive conjoint structure* (defined but not named in Krantz et al. 1971) if and only if the following hold:

1. $\langle A, \succeq \rangle$ is a weak order.

2. $A_1 \times A_2$ and A_3 are mutually independent and A_1 and A_2 are mutually sign dependent.

3. $\langle A_1 \times A_2, A_3, \sim \rangle$ satisfies the additive Thomsen condition.

4. Dual-distributive cancellation holds.

5. Regarding $\langle A_1 \times A_2, A_3, \succeq \rangle$ as a two-component structure, each component has the property that every strictly bounded standard sequence is finite.

6. Unrestricted solvability holds.

7. A_1^0 and A_2^0 are nonempty.

The **representation condition** is: If $\langle A_1 \times A_2 \times A_3, \succeq \rangle$ is a dual-distributive conjoint structure, then there exist real valued functions ϕ_i on A_i, $i = 1, 2, 3$, such that, for all $a, b \in A$,

$$a \succeq b \Leftrightarrow \phi_1(a_1)\phi_2(a_2) + \phi_3(a_3) \geq \phi_1(b_1)\phi_2(b_2) + \phi_3(b_3) \qquad (5.71)$$

(Krantz et al. 1971.) The **uniqueness condition** is: If ϕ_i' are real-valued functions with the same properties, then $\phi_1' = \alpha_1\phi_1$, $\phi_2' = \alpha_2\phi_2$, and $\phi_3' = \alpha_1\alpha_2\phi_3 + \beta$, where α_1, α_2, and β are real numbers with α_1, $\alpha_2 > 0$ (ϕ_1 and ϕ_2 are **ratio scales** on components A_1 and A_2, and ϕ_3 is an **interval scale** on component A_3) (Krantz et al. 1971).

To use the dual-distributive model on a particular empirical structure, the following tests must be performed in the order given:

1. $\langle A, \succeq \rangle$ forms a weak order.

2. Each factor is either independent of or sign dependent on the other two factors.

3. One pair of factors is jointly sign dependent on the third and all other pairs are independent of the third.

4. Distributive cancellation does not hold.

5. Dual-distributive cancellation does hold.

6. The Archimedean property holds.

7. Unrestricted solvability holds.
8. The additive Thomsen condition holds using $(A_1 \times A_2)$ as the first component and A_3 as the second.
9. A_1^0 and A_2^0 are nonempty.

Polynomial Structures with No Solvability

For the polynomial structures seen thus far, unrestricted solvability is the structural assumption. We would like to be able to measure data for which either we cannot test for solvability or it does not hold. Factorial data and a proposed measurement model create a set of polynomial inequalities. Generally, for each element $a_1,...,$ a_n in $A_1 \times \cdots \times A_n$, define a polynomial p with unknowns for $a_1,..., a_n$. If the proposed model is decomposable (is a simple polynomial), there will be one unknown for each a_i in A_i and the set $Y = \cup_{i=1}^n A_i$ is the set of all unknowns. If the model is not decomposable, Y may contain several unknowns for some a_i in A_i.

The relation $\succeq_I$ between polynomials is defined by: If p corresponds to $a_1,...,$ a_n and q corresponds to $b_1,..., b_n$, then $p \succeq_I q \Leftrightarrow a_1 \cdots a_n \succeq b_1 \cdots b_n$. Let $R[Y]$ denote the set of all polynomials in the unknowns of Y with real numbers as coefficients. For p, q in $R[Y]$, write $p = q$ whenever the equation $p = q$ is an algebraic identity (as in $x_1 x_2 - x_1 x_2 = x_3 - x_3$). $R[Y]$ is a ring with respect to the usual addition and multiplication of polynomials. A set of polynomial inequalities in the unknowns of $Y = \cup_{i=1}^n A_i$ has a solution if and only if the corresponding relation $\succeq_I$ on $R[Y]$ can be extended to a weak order $\succeq_{II}$ such that $\langle R[Y], \succeq_{II} \rangle$ is an Archimedean weakly ordered ring ($\succeq_{II}$ induces an Archimedean ordered ring structure on $R[Y]/\sim_{II}$).

Now, determine the necessary and sufficient conditions to allow such an extension to be constructed and tested. Let $\succeq_I$ be a relation on $R[Y]$. A pair of relations $\langle \sim_{II}, \succeq_{II} \rangle$ is called a *regular extension* of $\succeq_I$ if and only if the following hold for all $p, q \in R[Y]$:

1. $p \sim_{II} q$ whenever one of the following holds:
   Extension: $p \sim_I q$.
   Polynomial identity: $p = q$.
   Closure: There exist p', p'', q', q'' with $p' \sim_{II} q'$ and $p'' \sim_{II} q''$ such that either $p = p' + p''$, $q = q' + q''$, or $p = p'p''$, $q = q'q''$.
2. $p >_{II} q$ whenever one of the following holds:
   Extension: $p >_I q$.
   Additive closure: There exist p', p'', q', q'' with $p' >_{II} q'$ and $p'' >_{II} q''$ such that $p = p' + p''$ and $q = q' + q''$.
   Multiplicative closure: There exist p', q', r with either $r >_{II} 0$, or $q' >_{II} p'$ and $0 >_{II} r$, such that $p = p'r$ and $q = q'r$.

Any binary relation on $R[Y]$ has at least one regular extension (the *universal extension*) and a unique minimal regular extension. If there exists an extension of $\succeq_I$ such that $\langle R[Y], \succeq_I \rangle$ is a weakly ordered ring, and if $\langle \sim^*, >^* \rangle$ is the minimal regular extension of $\succeq_I$, then $>^*$ is irreflexive. Irreflexivity of the minimal regular extension implies all of the cancellation and independence conditions.

These results are summarized as follows: A set of polynomial inequalities in the unknowns of Y has a solution if and only if the corresponding relation $\succeq_I$ on $R[Y]$ has a regular extension $\langle \sim_{II}, >_{II} \rangle$ such that $\succeq_{II}$ is Archimedean and connected, and $>_{II}$ is not universal. The cancellations in the general case form an infinite chain and they cannot all be tested. No practical general methods exist to determine the solvability of a set of simultaneous polynomials: You must proceed by trial and error.

Concluding Remarks Regarding Polynomial Representations

In general, components or component groups which are mutually sign dependent are multiplied and lead to log-interval or ratio scales. Components or component groups which are mutually independent are added and lead to interval scales.

There are many cases where a simple polynomial cannot be found—the tests for additive, multiplicative, distributive, and dual-distributive models all fail. In these cases, the Cartesian products of the components contain common factors, and the tests and properties described here do not help find the correct polynomial model. This does not mean that polynomial conjoint measurement cannot take place. Rather, it means that no representation and uniqueness conditions have been explicitly stated. These cases push the state-of-the-art for measurement beyond what we currently know: You are on your own (although you can use the material in the section on scales if you are adventurous). The tests provided in this section to determine the appropriate model are heuristics, since the conditions required to define the finite, irreflexive binary relations which correspond to sign dependence have not been discovered.

To generalize these results to four or more variables, the following three classes of cancellation conditions are required:

1. Thomsen conditions to permit the construction of binary operations corresponding to each addition or multiplication which enters the polynomial.
2. Cancellation conditions which guarantee that two different concatenations, both corresponding to addition or both corresponding to multiplication, do in fact coincide.
3. A cancellation condition which guarantees the distributive law holds for multiplication over addition.

Note that all empirical structures which can be measured using polynomial conjoint measurement must form an algebraic ring, except for additive conjoint structures, which need only form an algebraic group.

UNIDIMENSIONAL SPATIAL PROXIMITY REPRESENTATIONS

In this section, the notion of a proximity structure will be developed. More time will be spent on the preliminaries—developing conditions for preliminary but required structures—than was done for previous structures for two reasons. First, the proximity structures developed in this section can be used to represent additive distance along a straight line in a plane or on a curved surface. They thus constitute a visualization of extensive measurement but with a slightly different set of conditions for the empirical structure. Second, the proximity structures provide the building blocks for multidimensional representations discussed in the next section. Some new terminology from the field of geometry is also introduced.

A set A and a binary relation $\succeq$ on $A \times A$ form a *proximity structure* (Krantz et al. 1989) if and only if the following axioms hold for all $a, b \in A$:

1. $\langle A \times A, \succeq \rangle$ is a weak order.
2. $(a, b) > (a, a)$ whenever $a \neq b$.
3. *Minimality:* $(a, a) \sim (b, b)$.
4. *Symmetry:* $(a, b) \sim (b, a)$.

The notation (a, b) denotes the distance from a to b along a straight line which is fully contained within the geometric surface, be it a plane or a curved surface of some kind. The structure is *factorial* if and only if $A = \times_{i=1}^{n} A_i$.

In some cases, axiom 2 may fail, especially when a and b are distinct but otherwise indistinguishable to the observer. This situation will arise frequently in software, where two instances of the same class can have identical values for all of the attributes of the class, yet be two different objects. In these cases, the proximity analysis should be applied to the appropriate equivalence classes. For software, this means that we should limit our proximity analysis to classes, rather than objects. We can get around this limitation by including the object identifier as an explicit attribute, rather than as an implicit attribute.

We can define an ordinal representation on a proximity structure if and only if $(A \times A)/\sim$ has a finite or countable order dense subset. A subset B of A is *order dense* in A if and only if for all $a, c \in A$ such that $a > c$, there exists $b \in B$ such that $a \succeq b \succeq c$. Further, $\langle A, \succeq \rangle$ must be a simple order, which is a slightly stronger condition than a weak order. The **ordinal scale** measure is a real-valued function $\delta: A \times A \rightarrow \mathbb{R}$, which is called a *metric*, and which meets all of the following conditions, for all $a, b, c, d \in A$:

1. $\delta(a, b) > 0$ unless $a = b$, and $\delta(a, a) = 0$.   (5.72a)
2. $\delta(a, b) = \delta(b, a)$.   (5.72b)
3. $\delta(a, b) + \delta(b, c) \geq \delta(a, c)$ (this is the *triangle inequality*).   (5.72c)
4. $(a, b) \succeq (c, d) \Leftrightarrow \delta(a, b) \geq \delta(c, d)$.   (5.72d)

(Krantz et al. 1989.) The usual format for presenting the representation and uniqueness conditions is not used here because this is not our desired representation. It can be useful, but we try not to settle for ordinal measures if we can do better.

In mathematics, and especially geometry, the term "metric" is reserved to describe a function from $A \times A \rightarrow \mathbb{R}$ which meets conditions (5.72a) through (5.72d). The use of the term "metric" for any other type of measure is imprecise at best and misleading at worst. That is why, throughout this book, I use the term "measure" to describe the results of any mapping, and use "metric" only to describe true geometric distance measures.

By imposing stronger conditions on the proximity structure $\langle A, \succeq \rangle$, you can construct a better representation. A structure $\langle A, \succeq \rangle$ is *segmentally additive proximity structure* (Krantz et al. 1989) if and only if the following hold for all $a, c, e, f \in A$:

1. If $(a, c) \succeq (e, f)$, then there exists $b \in A$ such that $(a, b) \sim (e, f)$ and for all $a', b', c' \in A$, both of the following hold:
   - $(a, b) \succeq (a', b') \wedge (a', c') \succeq (a, c) \Rightarrow (b', c') \succeq (b, c)$
   - $(c, b) \succeq (c', b') \wedge (c', a') \succeq (c, a) \Rightarrow (b', a') \succeq (b, a)$
2. If $e \neq f$, then there exist $b_0,..., b_n \in A$ such that $b_0 = a$, $b_n = c$, and $(e, f) \succeq (b_{i-1}, b_i)$, $i = 1,..., n$.

A segmentally additive structure is *complete* if and only if the following hold for all $a, c, e, f \in A$:

3. If $e \neq f$, then there exist $b, d \in A$, with $b \neq d$, such that $(e, f) > (b, d)$.
4. Let $a_1,..., a_n,...$ be a sequence of elements of A such that for all $e, f \in A$, if $e \neq f$, then $(e, f) \succeq (a_i, a_j)$ for all but finitely many pairs $\langle i, j \rangle$. Then there exists $b \in A$ such that for all $e, f \in A$, if $e \neq f$, then $(e, f) \succeq (a_i, b)$ for all but finitely many i.

Axiom 1 is the segmental solvability condition which specifies that for any distinct $a, c \in A$ ($a \neq c$) and for any nonnegative $\alpha \leq \delta(a, c)$, there is a point b on a segment from a to c whose distance from a is exactly α. Axiom 2 is the Archimedean condition which leads to equivalent distances. Axiom 3 is a nondiscreteness condition which specifies that there is no smallest positive distance. Axiom 4 expresses the completeness property of metric spaces: Every Cauchy sequence has a limit. General metric spaces and Cauchy sequences are defined in the geometric literature, are briefly mentioned in Chapter 4, but are not defined specifically in this chapter.

For future convenience, let's define the ternary relation $\langle a, b, c \rangle$ for all $a, b, c \in A$ to hold if and only if for all $a', b', c' \in A$,

1. $(a, b) \succeq (a', b') \wedge (a', c') \succeq (a, c) \Rightarrow (b', c') \succeq (b, c)$.
2. $(c, b) \succeq (c', b') \wedge (c', a') \succeq (c, a) \Rightarrow (b', a') \succeq (b, a)$.

This is axiom 1 for the segmentally additive proximity structure.

The **representation condition** is: If $\langle A, \succeq \rangle$ is a segmentally additive proximity structure, though not necessarily complete, then there exists a real-valued function $\delta: A \times A \to \mathbb{R}$ such that, for any $a, b, c, d \in A$, $\langle A, \delta \rangle$ is a metric space, and

$$(a, b) \succeq (c, d) \Leftrightarrow \delta(a, b) \geq \delta(c, d) \tag{5.73a}$$

and

$$\langle a\ b\ c \rangle \Leftrightarrow \delta(a, b) + \delta(b, c) = \delta(a, c) \tag{5.73b}$$

(Krantz et al. 1989.) The **uniqueness condition** is: If δ' is another metric on A satisfying these conditions, then there exists $\alpha > 0$ such that $\delta' = \alpha\delta$ (δ is a **ratio scale**) (Krantz et al. 1989). If $\langle A, \succeq \rangle$ is a complete segmentally additive proximity structure, then $\langle A, \delta \rangle$ is a complete metric space with additive segments, and also forms a **ratio scale** (Krantz et al. 1989).

MULTIDIMENSIONAL SPATIAL PROXIMITY REPRESENTATIONS

Many measurement problems take the form of trying to order a set of objects using a set of attributes that forms an n-dimensional metric space. The values of each attribute can be plotted in n-dimensional space to create an ordering based on the proximity of the points of each object. This measurement technique makes use of multidimensional proximity representations. Such representations can be used to measure the similarity of values of attribute sets and to measure the similarity of the attribute sets themselves. The latter problem is called feature proximity measurement and is covered in the next section since it requires a slightly different set of conditions.

The most common form of metric is a family called the *power metric, Minkowski r-metric,* or the L^P metric. In the power metric model, there is a real-valued function on A^n ($A_1 \times A_2 \times \cdots \times A_n$) and a constant $r \geq 1$ such that the distance between $a = a_1 \cdots a_n$ and $b = b_1 \cdots b_n$ is given by

$$\delta(a,b) = \left[\sum_{i=1}^{n} |\varphi_i(a_i) - \varphi_i(b_i)|^r \right]^{1/r} \tag{5.74}$$

In Euclidean geometry, setting $r = 2$ and $n = 2$ gives the familiar distance formula between two points lying in a plane. Note that the a_i, b_i, $i = 1,\ldots, n$, can be nominal scale values.

The power metric model includes the following four assumptions:

1. *Decomposability*: The distance between objects is a function of componentwise contributions.

2. *Intradimensional subtractivity*: Each componentwise contribution is the absolute value of an appropriate scale difference.

3. *Interdimensional additivity*: The distance is a function of the sum of componentwise contributions.

4. *Homogeneity*: Affine (straight) lines are additive segments.

If the empirical structure violates any of these assumptions, it cannot be measured with a power metric. However, each assumption comes with its own structure which can be used to measure proximity.

Decomposable Structures

A factorial proximity structure (see the previous section) $\langle A = \times_{i=1}^{n} A_i, \succeq \rangle$ satisfies *one-factor independence* if and only if the following holds for all $a, a', b, b', c, c', d, d' \in A$: If the two elements in each of the pairs (a, a'), (b, b'), (c, c'), and (d, d') have identical components on all but one factor, and the two elements in each of the pairs (a, c), (a', c'), (b, d), and (b', d') have identical components on the remaining factor, then $(a, b) \succeq (a', b') \Leftrightarrow (c, d) \succeq (c', d')$. One-factor independence is closely related to the notion of independence in the theory of conjoint measurement. Basically, one-factor independence asserts that if a set of pairs of elements differ with respect to the ith factor only, then for each $i = 1,..., n$, the induced ordering of $A_i \times A_i$ is independent of the (fixed) components of the remaining $A_j \times A_j$, $j \neq i$.

A measure can be built from what is available so far. Call this structure $\langle A, \succeq \rangle$ a *factorial proximity structure with one-factor independence* (defined but not named in Krantz et al. 1989). The **representation condition** is: If a structure $\langle A, \succeq \rangle$, for which $(A \times A)/\sim$ has a finite or countable order-dense subset and satisfies one-factor independence, then there exists a real-valued function f of n arguments, and real-valued functions ψ_i, defined on $A_i \times A_i$, $i = 1,..., n$, such that, for all $a, b, c, d \in A$:

$$\delta(a_1 \cdots a_n, b_1 \cdots b_n) = F[\psi_1(a_1, b_1),..., \psi_n(a_n, b_n)] \qquad (5.75a)$$

and

$$(a_1 \cdots a_n, b_1 \cdots b_n) \succeq (c_1 \cdots c_n, d_1 \cdots d_n)$$
$$\Leftrightarrow F[\psi_1(a_1, b_1),.., \psi_n(a_n, b_n)]$$
$$\geq F[\psi_1(c_1, d_1),..., \psi_n(c_n, d_n)] \qquad (5.75b)$$

(Krantz et al. 1989.) The **uniqueness condition** is: F is increasing in each of its arguments and $\psi_i(a_i, b_i) = \psi_i(b_i, a_i) > \psi_i(a_i, a_i) = \psi_i(b_i, b_i)$ for $a_i \neq b_i$, $i = 1,...,$ n (F and each ψ_i are **ordinal scales**) (Krantz et al. 1989).

Any factorial proximity structure which satisfies these conditions can be recast as a decomposable conjoint structure by regrouping each pair of n-tuples (a, b) $= (a_1 \cdots a_n, b_1 \cdots b_n)$ as an n-tuple of pairs $ab = (a_1, b_1) \cdots (a_n, b_n)$. This recast conjoint structure is the induced conjoint structure $\langle A^*, \succeq \rangle$ for the proximity structure $\langle A, \succeq \rangle$.

Intradimensional Subtractive Structures

Intradimensional subtractivity is a property of each factor, or dimension, independently of the others. It is an extension of the absolute difference structure described in the section "Difference Representations." Thus, the metric δ, if one can be formed, takes the form

$$\delta(a, b) = F[|\psi_1(a_1) - \psi_1(b_1)|,..., |\psi_n(a_n) - \psi_n(b_n)|] \qquad (5.76)$$

where F is an increasing function in each of its n arguments and $|\psi_i(a_i) - \psi_i(b_i)|$ is the coordinatewise difference between a and b along the ith dimension. In other words, each dimension $\langle A_i \times A_i, \succeq_i \rangle$ must be able to support an absolute difference structure, where $\succeq_i$ is the induced ordering defined by one-factor independence.

Suppose that $\langle A, \succeq \rangle$ is a factorial proximity structure that satisfies one-factor independence. Let $\succeq_i$ denote the induced order on $A_i \times A_i$. We say that b *is between* a and c, denoted by $a \mid b \mid c$, if and only if $(a_i, c_i) \succeq_i (a_i, b_i), (b_i, c_i)$ for each i. We say that $\langle A, \succeq \rangle$ satisfies the *betweenness axioms* if and only if the following hold for all $a, b, c, d, a', b', c' \in A$:

    1. If a, b, c, d differ in at most one factor, and $b \neq c$, then
- $a \mid b \mid c \wedge b \mid c \mid d \Rightarrow a \mid b \mid d \wedge a \mid c \mid d$
- $a \mid b \mid c \wedge a \mid c \mid d \Rightarrow a \mid b \mid d \wedge b \mid c \mid d$

    2. If a, b, c, a', b', c' differ in at most one factor, $a \mid b \mid c$, $a' \mid b' \mid c'$, and $(b, c) \sim (b', c')$, then $(a, b) \succeq (a', b') \Leftrightarrow (a, c) \succeq (a', c')$.

A factorial proximity structure $\langle A, \succeq \rangle$ satisfies restricted solvability if and only if, for all e, f, d, a, $c \in A$, if $(d, a) \succeq (e, f) \succeq (d, c)$, then there exists $b \in A$ such that $a \mid b \mid c$ and $(d, b) \sim (e, f)$. A factorial proximity structure $\langle A, \succeq \rangle$ satisfies the Archimedean axiom if and only if, for all a, b, c, $d \in A$, with $a \neq b$, any sequence $e_k \in A$, $k = 0, 1, \ldots$, such that $e_0 = c$, $(e_k, e_{k+1}) > (a, b)$ and $(c, d) > (c, e_{k+1}) > (c, e_k)$ for all k is finite.

    Putting this all together, $\langle A, \succeq \rangle$ is an *intradimensional difference structure* (defined but not named in Krantz et al. 1989) if and only if the following hold:

    1. $\langle A, \succeq \rangle$ is a factorial proximity structure.

    2. One-factor independence.

    3. The betweenness axioms.

    4. Restricted solvability.

    5. The Archimedean axiom.

The **representation condition** is: If $\langle A, \succeq \rangle$ is an intradimensional difference structure, then there exist real-valued functions ψ_i defined on A_i, $i = 1, \ldots, n$, and a real-valued function F that increases in each of its n arguments such that

$$\delta(a, b) = F[|\psi_1(a_1) - \psi_1(b_1)|, \ldots, |\psi_n(a_n) - \psi_n(b_n)|] \qquad (5.77a)$$

and

$$(a, b) \succeq (c, d) \Leftrightarrow \delta(a, b) \geq \delta(c, d) \qquad (5.77b)$$

(Krantz et al. 1989.) The **uniqueness condition** is: If ψ_i' are functions with the same properties as ψ_i, then there exist real numbers α_i, β_i, $\alpha_i > 0$ for all i, such that $\psi_i' = \alpha_i \psi_i + \beta_i$, and if F' is another function with all of the properties of F, then there exist real numbers α, β, $\alpha > 0$, such that $F' = \alpha F + \beta$ (each ψ_i and F are **interval scales**, as is the resulting metric δ) (Krantz et al. 1989).

Interdimensional Additive Structures

Interdimensional additivity assumes that the perceived distance between objects is expressible as an additive combination of n functions of the components on n factors of the form

$$\delta(a,b) = G\left[\sum_{i=1}^{n} \varphi_i(a_i, b_i)\right] \qquad (5.78)$$

where the φ_i are the decomposable representations of each factor and G is an increasing function in one argument. Thus, interdimensional additivity is an extension of additive conjoint measurement.

A factorial proximity structure $\langle A, \succeq \rangle$ satisfies independence if for all a, a', b, b', c, c', d, $d' \in A$, if the two elements of each of the pairs (a, a'), (b, b'), (c, c'), and (d, d') have identical components on one factor, and the two elements of each of the pairs (a, c), (a', c'), (b, d), and (b', d') have identical components on all the remaining factors, then $(a, b) \succeq (a', b') \Leftrightarrow (c, d) \succeq (c', d')$. Thus, if $a_i \sim a_i'$ and $b_i \sim b_i'$, then for $(a, b) \succeq (a', b')$ to hold, the ordering of a and b must be independent of the ith factor. You should be able to change the common value of a and a', and b and b', and still have $(a, b) \succeq (a', b')$ hold.

A factorial proximity structure $\langle A, \succeq \rangle$ with $A = A_1 \times A_2$ satisfies the Thomsen condition if and only if, for all a_i, b_i, c_i, d_i, e_i, $f_i \in A_i$, $i = 1, 2$,

$$(a_1 e_2, b_1 f_2) \sim (e_1 c_2, f_1 d_2) \wedge (e_1 a_2, f_1 b_2) \sim (c_1 e_2, d_1 f_2)$$
$$\Rightarrow (a_1 a_2, b_1 b_2) \sim (c_1 c_2, d_1 d_2) \qquad (5.79)$$

A factor A_i, $i = 1, ..., n$, is essential if and only if there exist $a, b \in A$ that coincide on all but the ith factor and that satisfy $(a, b) > (a, a)$. Thus, whenever $(a, b) \sim (a, a)$, the factor A_i is inessential. When independence holds, inessential factors can be eliminated, and n can be reduced to only the essential factors. This is the key idea behind principal component analysis.

Taking what we have so far, $\langle A, \succeq \rangle$, where $A = A_1 \times \cdots \times A_n$ is an *interdimensional additive proximity structure* (defined but not named in Krantz et al. 1989) if and only if the following hold:

1. $\langle A, \succeq \rangle$ is a factorial proximity structure.
2. $\langle A, \succeq \rangle$ satisfies independence.
3. $\langle A, \succeq \rangle$ satisfies restricted solvability.
4. In the induced conjoint structure, each pair of factors satisfies the Archimedean axiom.
5. If $n = 2$, $\langle A, \succeq \rangle$ must satisfy the Thomsen condition, if $n \geq 3$, the Thomsen condition is not required.

The **representation condition** is: If $\langle A, \succeq \rangle$ is an interdimensional additive proximity structure, then there exist real-valued functions ψ_i defined on $A_i \times A_i$, $i = 1, ..., n$, such that, for all $a, b, c, d \in A$:

$$(a_1 \cdots a_n, b_1 \cdots b_n) \succeq (c_1 \cdots c_n, d_1 \cdots d_n)$$
$$\Leftrightarrow \sum_{i=1}^{n} \psi_i(a_i, b_i) \geq \sum_{i=1}^{n} \psi_i(c_i, d_i) \qquad (5.80)$$

(Krantz et al. 1989.) The **uniqueness condition** is: If ψ_i', $i = 1, ..., n$, is another set of functions satisfying this relation, then there exists real numbers $\alpha > 0$, β_i such that $\psi_i' = \alpha \psi_i + \beta_i$, $i = 1, ..., n$ (each ψ_i is an **interval scale**) (Krantz et al. 1989). If $n = 2$, these representation and uniqueness conditions hold, provided that the Thomsen condition is also satisfied.

Additive–Difference Structures

Additive-difference structures combine intradimensional difference structures with interdimensional additive structures. Models based on this combination take the form

$$\delta(a,b) = G \left\{ \sum_{i=1}^{n} F_i[|\varphi_i(a_i) - \varphi_i(b_i)|] \right\} \tag{5.81}$$

where G and F_i, $i = 1,..., n$ are all increasing functions in one argument.

A factorial proximity structure $\langle A, \succeq \rangle$ is an *additive-difference structure* (Krantz et al. 1989) if and only if the following hold:

1. The betweenness axioms.
2. Independence.
3. The Thomsen condition, if $n = 2$.
4. Restricted solvability.
5. The Archimedean axiom.

The **representation condition** is: If $\langle A, \succeq \rangle$ is an additive-difference factorial proximity structure, then there exist real-valued functions $\varphi_1,..., \varphi_n$ defined on $A_1,..., A_n$, respectively, and increasing functions $F_1,..., F_n$ each defined on $\mathbb{R}$, such that for all $a, b, c, d \in A$,

$$(a_1 \cdots a_n, b_1 \cdots b_n) \succeq (c_1 \cdots c_n, d_1 \cdots d_n)$$

$$\Leftrightarrow \sum_{i=1}^{n} F_i[|\varphi_i(a_i) - \varphi_i(b_i)|]$$

$$\geq \sum_{i=1}^{n} F_i[|\varphi_i(c_i) - \varphi_i(d_i)|] \tag{5.82}$$

(Krantz et al. 1989.) The **uniqueness condition** is: If φ_i', $i = 1,..., n$, are another set of functions with these properties, then there exist real numbers $\alpha_i > 0$, β_i such that $\varphi_i' = \alpha_i \varphi_i + \beta_i$, and if F_i' is another set of increasing real-valued functions in one argument, then there exists real number $\alpha > 0$, β_i, such that $F_i' = \alpha F_i + \beta_i$ (each φ_i and F_i are **interval scales**) (Krantz et al. 1989).

This model expresses proximity between objects in terms of two sets of scales. The transformations of one set $\{\varphi_i\}$ apply to the components of the object along each dimension. The transformations of the other set $\{F_i\}$ apply to the absolute values of componentwise differences and describe their relative contribution to the overall proximity of the object to other objects.

Additive–Difference Metric Structures

An additive-difference structure provides a measurement between objects that differ along several dimensions. The resulting measure may not be a metric, however, because the triangle inequality $\delta(a, b) + \delta(b, c) \geq \delta(a, c)$ may not hold. Also, the additive-difference structure need not have additive segments. In order to be a metric, the functions F_i must satisfy certain conditions:

1. They must be continuous and convex, so that $F_i(x) = F(t_i x)$, $t_i > 0$, for all x in F_i, $1 \leq i \leq n$. The function log $F(e^x)$ is convex.

2. The functions F_i must all be identical except for a change in the unit of their domains (this follows from 1).

3. The metric is of the form:

$$\delta(a,b) = F^{-1} \left\{ \sum_{i=1}^{n} F[|\varphi_i(a_i) - \varphi_i(b_i)|] \right\} \qquad (5.83)$$

4. The metric δ must have additive segments.

The power metric, with $F(x) = kx^r$, $r \geq 1$, $k \geq 1$, is the only family of functions which meets all of these conditions.

A structure $\langle A, \succeq \rangle$ is an *additive-difference metric structure* (defined but not named in Krantz et al. 1989) if and only if it is a complete, segmentally additive, factorial proximity structure which is also an additive-difference structure. The **representation condition** is: If a structure $\langle A, \succeq \rangle$ is an additive-difference metric structure, then there exist a unique $r \geq 1$ and real-valued functions φ_i defined on A_i, $i = 1,..., n$, that are **interval scales**, such that, for all a, b, c, $d \in A$,

$$(a, b) \succeq (c, d) \Leftrightarrow \delta(a, b) \geq \delta(c, d) \qquad (5.84a)$$

where

$$\delta(a,b) = \left[\sum_{i=1}^{n} |\varphi_i(a_i) - \varphi_i(b_i)|^r \right]^{1/r} \quad [F(x) = kx^r] \qquad (5.84b)$$

(Krantz et al. 1989.) The **uniqueness condition** is: δ is a **log-interval scale**; if $r = 1$, then δ is a **ratio scale** (Krantz et al. 1989).

FEATURE PROXIMITY REPRESENTATIONS

Dimensional metric models are based on the representation of objects as points in a multidimensional coordinate space and the use of metric distance to represent proximity between objects. While useful, these representations are based on assumptions which are not always valid. In many cases, subtractivity, additivity, and the triangle inequality fail on a systemic basis.

In this section, we seek a model of proximity that interprets objects as sets of features and represents proximity of two objects in terms of their common and distinctive features. The common features are represented by the set intersection of their respective feature sets. The distinctive features are represented by the set difference of their respective feature sets, one object relative to the other. The goal is to obtain a model of the form

$$\delta(a, b) = \alpha\varphi(a - b) + \beta\varphi(b - a) - \theta\varphi(a \cap b) \qquad (5.85)$$

where δ represents the dissimilarity between the two objects. This model is known as the *contrast model* and was introduced by Tversky (1977). Alternatively, we could look for model of similarity by reversing all of the signs, as in:

$$\delta(a, b) = \theta\varphi(a \cap b) - \alpha\varphi(a - b) - \beta\varphi(b - a) \qquad (5.86)$$

This representation will be seen again in Chapter 14, when dealing with similarity.

If you set $\alpha = \beta = 0$, the model reduces to the *common features model*, in which proximity depends only on $\varphi(a \cap b)$. An alternative is to set $\theta = 0$ and $\alpha = \beta = 1$ so that $\delta(a, b) = \varphi(a - b) + \varphi(b - a)$. If φ is additive, you obtain the symmetric difference model which defines a metric distance between sets. The contrast model can also handle asymmetric proximities when α and β are unequal.

In the following discussion, let S denote a nonempty set and A be a family of subsets of S. Interpret A as the set of objects and S as the set of all possible relevant features of A (the universe of features). Thus, each object $a \in A$ is a subset of S. For each pair $(a, b) \in A \times A$ you can form the subsets $a - b$, $b - a$, and $a \cap b$. Do not assume that $A = \mathbb{P}S$, nor that every subset can appear as a set of common or distinctive features. Instead, $A \subset \mathbb{P}S$ and the possible sets of common and distinctive features are defined by A.

The family S_D of difference subsets is $\{a - b \mid a, b \in A\}$. The family S_C of common subsets is $\{a \cap b \mid a, b \in A\}$. Assume that the sets S_D and S_C are ordered with respect to their contribution to dissimilarity. Because proximities may be asymmetric, assume two weak orders on S_D. To this framework, add as primitives an ordering of pairs of objects (*dissimilarity*) and three orderings of feature sets (*salience*). From this model, you conclude that $a - b$ exceeds $c - d$ whenever $b - a = d - c$, $a \cap b = c \cap d$, and $(a, b) \succeq (c, d)$. Likewise, you conclude that $a \cap b$ exceeds $c \cap d$ whenever $a - b = c - d$, $b - a = d - c$, and $(c, d) \succeq (a, b)$.

Given a pair (a, b), $\succeq_1$ represents the contribution of $a - b$, $\succeq_2$ represents the contribution of $b - a$, and $\succeq_3$ represents the contribution of $a \cap b$, which is also the ordering of S_C. All three weak orders are assumed to be monotone with respect to set inclusion. The dissimilarity ordering $\succeq$ is a weak order of $A \times A$, $\succeq_1$ and $\succeq_2$ are weak orders of S_D, and $\succeq_3$ is a weak order of S_C. The pair (a, b) *dominates* (a', b') if $a - b \succeq_1 a' - b'$, $b - a \succeq_2 b' - a'$, and $a' \cap b' \succeq_3 a \cap b$. When (a, b) dominates (a', b'), $(a, b) \succeq (a', b')$. Suppose that b is between a and c in the sense that $a \cap c \subseteq b \subseteq a \cup c$, which is denoted $a \mid b \mid c$. By monotonicity of $\succeq_3$ for set inclusion together with dominance, we conclude that $(a, c) \succeq (a, b)$ and $(a, c) \succeq (b, c)$. One final assumption is that each $\succeq_i$ is nondegenerate—it contains at least two equivalence classes.

The structure $\langle S, A, \succeq, \succeq_1, \succeq_2, \succeq_3 \rangle$ is called a *proximity feature-structure* (Krantz et al. 1989) if it has all of these characteristics. To map a proximity feature-structure into an additive conjoint measurement model, take the sets of equivalence classes induced by the weak orders $\succeq_i$ to be the additive factors or dimensions. Thus, let $X_1 = S_D/\sim_1$, $X_2 = S_D/\sim_2$ and $X_3 = S_C/\sim_3$, and map $A \times A$ into a subset Y of $X_1 \times X_2 \times X_3$ by $(a, b) \rightarrow ([a - b], [b - a], [a \cap b])$ where $[\ ]$ designates the equivalence class determined by the set inside the brackets. Call $[a - b]$, $[b - a]$, and $[a \cap b]$ the first, second, and third components of (a, b). Using dominance, you can define a relation $\succeq$ on Y that is homomorphic to $\succeq$ on $A \times A$:

$$([a - b], [b - a], [a \cap b]) \succeq ([a' - b'], [b' - a'], [a' \cap b'])$$
$$\Leftrightarrow (a, b) \succeq (a', b') \tag{5.87}$$

If $A \times A$ has a countable order-dense subset, you can map $\langle Y, \succeq \rangle$ and each $\langle X_i, \succeq_i \rangle$ homomorphically into $\langle \mathbb{R}, \geqslant \rangle$, getting an order-preserving function δ on $A \times A$ of the form

$$\delta(a, b) = F[\varphi_1(a - b), \varphi_2(b - a), \varphi_3(a \cap b)] \tag{5.88}$$

with F strictly increasing on its first two components and strictly decreasing on its third component. Put another way, an ordinally scalable proximity feature-structure is decomposable.

A proximity feature-structure is *partially factorial* if for any $a, b, c, d, e, f, g \in A$ such that $a - b \succeq_1 c - d$, $b - a \succeq_2 f - e$, $a \cap b \succeq_3 g \cap h$, there exist a', $b' \in A$ such that $a' - b' \sim_1 c - d$, $b' - a' \sim_2 f - e$, and $a' \cap b' \sim_3 g \cap h$. This structure is weaker than the usual factorial structure in two ways: It requires equivalence and not equality—two structures can be identical yet still be distinct and the feature set is restricted in that it is bounded by the components of some pair of objects in A. For any $a, b \in A$, define $Y_1 = \{x_1 \mid [a - b] \succeq_1 x_1\}$, $Y_2 = \{x_2 \mid [b - a] \succeq_2 x_2\}$, and $Y_3 = \{x_3 \mid [a \cap b] \succeq_3 x_3\}$. Then $Y(a, b) = Y_1 \times Y_2 \times Y_3$ is the Cartesian product bounded by (a, b).

Let $\langle S, A, \succeq, \succeq_1, \succeq_2, \succeq_3 \rangle$ be a proximity feature-structure. The pairs (c, d) and (e, f) are factorially comparable if their components lie in a common Cartesian product bounded by (a, b), or: $a - b \succeq_1 c - d$, $e - f$; $b - a \succeq_2 d - c$, $f - e$; and $a \cap b \succeq_3 c \cap d$, $e \cap f$. The structure is *factorially connected* if for any two pairs $(c, d) \succeq (e, f)$ there exist $(a_0, b_0) \cdots (a_n, b_n)$ with $(a_0, b_0) = (c, d)$ and $(a_n, b_n) = (e, f)$ such that $(a_{i-1}, b_{i-1}) \succeq (a_i, b_i)$, $i = 1, ..., n$, and all adjacent pairs in the sequence are factorially comparable.

We say that (a, b) and (c, d) *agree* on the first component if $a - b \sim_1 c - d$. They agree on the second component if $b - a \sim_2 d - c$, and they agree on the third component if $a \cap b \sim_3 c \cap d$. A proximity feature-structure is independent if and only if: If the pairs (a, b) and (c, d) agree on two components, the pairs (a', b') and (c', d') agree on the same components, the pairs (a, b) and (a', b') agree on the remaining component, and (c, d) and (c', d') also agree on the remaining component, then $(a, b) \succeq (a', b') \Leftrightarrow (c, d) \succeq (c', d')$.

A proximity feature-structure satisfies restricted solvability if and only if $(a, b) \succeq (c, d) \succeq (e, f)$ implies that there exist (p, q) in $A \times A$ such that $(p, q) \sim (c, d)$, and (p, q) agrees with (a, b) and (c, d) on all components for which (a, b) agrees with (c, d). A proximity feature-structure is Archimedean if and only if for all $a, b, c, d \in A$, $a \neq b$, any sequence $e_k \in A$, $k = 0, 1, ...$, such that $e_0 = c$, $(e_k, e_{k+1}) > (a, b)$ and $(c, d) > (c, e_{k+1}) > (c, e_k)$ for all k is finite.

A proximity feature-structure is *uniform* if and only if $S_D = S_C(\{a - b \mid a, b \in A\} = \{a \cap b \mid a, b \in A\})$ and $\succeq_1, \succeq_2,$ and $\succeq_3$ are identical. Uniformity says that the salience ordering of feature sets is the same for all three components.

Uniformity also implies that all φ_i are monotonically related. At first glance, uniformity looks a little strange. One case in which uniformity can occur is where every feature is a member of at least two objects and no feature is a member of all objects.

Consider an independent proximity feature-structure. For distinct $i, j \in \{1, 2, 3\}$, let $\succeq_{ij}$ be the ordering induced on a subset of $X_i \times X_j$ by holding the remaining component fixed. The structure is *invariant* if and only if it is uniform and for any distinct i, j and any distinct k, l in $\{1, 2, 3\}$:

$$(xy \sim_{ij} x'y' \wedge x'y \sim_{ij} x''y') \Rightarrow (xz \sim_{kl} x'z' \wedge x'z \sim_{kl} x''z') \qquad (5.89)$$

In effect, if x, x', x'' is a standard sequence in component i relative to component j, then it should also form a standard sequence in component k relative to component l.

A proximity feature-structure is *extensive* if and only if each of the following is true whenever $x \subseteq S$ is disjoint from $a \cup b \cup c \cup d$ and $a \cup x, b \cup x, c \cup x$, and $d \cup x \in A$:

$$(a, b) \succeq (c, d) \Leftrightarrow (a \cup x, b) \succeq (c \cup x, d)$$

$$\Leftrightarrow (a, b \cup x) \succeq (c, d \cup x)$$

$$\Leftrightarrow (a \cup x, b \cup x) \succeq (c \cup x, d \cup x) \qquad (5.90)$$

To summarize, the **representation condition** is: If $\langle S, A, \succeq, \succeq_1, \succeq_2, \succeq_3 \rangle$ is a proximity feature-structure that is partially factorial, factorially connected, and satisfies independence, restricted solvability, and the Archimedean axiom, then there exist nonnegative functions φ_i on X_i, $i = 1, 2, 3$, such that

$$(a, b) \succeq (c, d) \Leftrightarrow$$
$$\varphi_1(a - b) + \varphi_2(b - a) - \varphi_3(a \cap b)$$
$$\geqslant \varphi_1(c - d) + \varphi_2(d - c)$$
$$- \varphi_3(c \cap d) \qquad (5.91)$$

(Krantz et al. 1989.) Since

$$\delta(a, b) = \varphi_1(a - b) + \varphi_2(b - a) - \varphi_3(a \cap b) \qquad (5.92a)$$

and

$$\delta(c, d) = \varphi_1(c - d) + \varphi_2(d - c) - \varphi_3(c \cap d) \qquad (5.92b)$$

you can restate the representation condition as

$$(a, b) \succeq (c, d) \Leftrightarrow \delta(a, b) \geqslant \delta(c, d) \qquad (5.92c)$$

For the conditions given in the representation condition, there is no fixed relationship between the φ_i. If the structure is uniform, then $\varphi_i = H_i(\varphi)$ for some function φ on $X_1 = X_2 = X_3$, and for some increasing functions H_i, $i = 1, 2, 3$

(the φ_i are monotonically related to each other). If the structure is invariant, then $\varphi_i = \gamma_i \varphi$, $\gamma_i \geq 0$, $i = 1, 2, 3$ (the φ_i are linearly related to each other). If the structure is extensive, then each φ_i is finitely additive, and includes feature additivity, that is:

$$\varphi_i(x \cup y) = \varphi_i(x) + \varphi_i(y) - \varphi_i(x \cap y) \qquad (5.93)$$

The **uniqueness condition** has three parts:

1. For structures which are not extensive, there exist real numbers $\alpha > 0$, β_i, $i = 1, 2, 3$ such that $\varphi_i' = \alpha \varphi_i + \beta_i$ (each φ_i is an **interval scale**) (Krantz et al. 1989).
2. For structures which are extensive, there exist real numbers $\alpha_i > 0$, $i = 1, 2, 3$, such that $\varphi_i' = \alpha_i \varphi_i$ (each φ_i is a **ratio scale**) (Krantz et al. 1989).
3. Since we have essentially a three-component additive conjoint structure, there exist real numbers $\alpha > 0$, β such that $\delta' = \alpha \delta + \beta$ in all cases (δ is an **interval scale**) (Krantz et al. 1971).

NONADDITIVE REPRESENTATIONS

Extensive structures, which led to additive representations have already been presented. In all of these structures, the empirical concatenation operation was assumed or required to be associative. That is, given a structure $\langle A, \succeq, \circ \rangle$, for all a, b, $c \in A$, $a \circ (b \circ c) \sim (a \circ b) \circ c$. In the section "Conjoint Representations," we also studied additive conjoint structures in which an attribute was composable from two or more independent components, each of which formed separate additive structures. Independence of each component from the others was a key assumption. When we combined independence with associativity, we were able to create structures in which we could add the representations of each component.

Many conjoint structures have components which are not independent: They interact in some way. These structures fall into two classes: those in which the interaction can be eliminated by a monotonic transformation of the resulting conjoint scale and those in which the concatenation operation is essentially nonassociative. The vector product operation is an example of an operation which is neither associative nor commutative. Weighted averages are another example. In this section, we are concerned only with those cases in which the concatenation operation is nonassociative, which can be viewed as a generalization of extensive and/or additive conjoint structures. Let's begin by developing some necessary concepts.

Concatenation Structures

To study nonassociative operations, it is necessary to introduce the notion of a concatenation structure, of which there are several types. Suppose that A is a nonempty set, $\succeq$ is a binary relation on A, and $\circ$ is a partial binary relation on A

with a nonempty domain B. The structure $A = \langle A, \succeq, \circ \rangle$ is a *concatenation struc-ture* if and only if the following hold:

1. *Weak order*: $\langle A, \succeq \rangle$ is a weak order.
2. *Local definability*: If $a \circ b$ is defined ($a, b \in B$), $a \succeq c$, and $b \succeq d$, then $c \circ d$ is defined.
3. *Monotonicity*:
    - If $a \circ c$ and $b \circ c$ are defined, then $a \succeq b$ if and only if $a \circ c \succeq b \circ c$.
    - If $c \circ a$ and $c \circ b$ are defined, then $a \succeq b$ if and only if $c \circ a \succeq c \circ b$.

A concatenation structure can be specialized in a number of ways. These def-initions are given in Krantz et al. (1990). It is:

- *Closed* if and only if $a \circ b$ is defined for all $a, b \in A$.
- *Positive* if and only if whenever $a \circ b$ is defined, $a \circ b > a, b$.
- *Negative* if and only if whenever $a \circ b$ is defined, $a, b > a \circ b$.
- *Idempotent* if and only if $a \sim a \circ a$ whenever $a \circ a$ is defined.
- *Intern* if and only if whenever $a > b$ and $a \circ b$ or $b \circ a$ is defined, $a > a \circ b > b$ and $a > b \circ a > b$.
- *Intensive* if and only if it is both intern and idempotent.
- *Associative* if and only if whenever one of $(a \circ b) \circ c$ or $a \circ (b \circ c)$ is defined, the other is also defined and they are equivalent.
- *Bisymmetric* if and only if it is closed and $(a \circ b) \circ (c \circ d) \sim (a \circ c) \circ (b \circ d)$.
- *Autodistributive* if and only if it is closed and both $(a \circ b) \circ c \sim (a \circ c) \circ (b \circ c)$ and $c \circ (a \circ b) \sim (c \circ a) \circ (c \circ b)$. These are sometimes called *right* and *left autodistributivity*, respectively.

A concatenation structure is:

- *Halvable* if and only if it is positive and, for each $a \in A$, there exists $b \in A$ such that $b \circ b$ is defined and $a \sim b \circ b$.
- *Restrictedly solvable* if and only if, whenever $a > b$, there exists $c \in A$ such that either $b \circ c$ is defined and $a \succeq b \circ c > b$ or $a \circ c$ is defined and $a > a \circ c \succeq b$.
- *Solvable* if and only if given a and b, there exist c and d such that $a \circ c \sim b \sim d \circ a$.
- *Dedekind complete* if and only if $\langle A, \succeq \rangle$ is Dedekind complete: Every non-empty subset of A that has an upper bound has a least upper bound in A.
- *Continuous* if the operation $\circ$ is continuous as a function of two variables, using the order topology on its range and the relative product order topology on its domain. A more concrete definition of continuity specialized to the positive concatenation structure will be given later.

In the section "Axioms and Procedures" the necessity of an Archimedean ax-iom for representing any empirical structure in the real numbers was discussed.

In general, an Archimedean axiom specifies the conditions under which the basic process of counting of equal units using standard sequences produces an appropriate scale value for any object to be measured. In positive concatenation structures, a standard sequence is constructed by selecting an element a and inductively constructing the sequence as a, $a \circ a$, $(a \circ a) \circ a$,... . In idempotent structures, each of these is equivalent to a. In nonassociative concatenation structures, there are many ways to construct a sequence of concatenated elements, all of which differ only in the placement and quantity of the parentheses, and all of which produce a potentially different scale value.

There are three types of sequences: standard, difference, and regular. A more general form of the Archimedean axiom is: Every bounded sequence of a given type is finite, where the type of the sequence must be specified. For nonidempotent structures, all three types of sequences can be defined. A *standard sequence* is any set $\{a(n) \mid n \in J\}$ where $J = \{1, 2,..., n\}$ and is finite, or $J = \{1, 2,...\}$ and is infinite. The notation $a(n)$ denotes a concatenated with itself n times, and $a(0) = a$. A *difference sequence* is any set $\{a_j \mid j \in J\}$, with J either finite or infinite, if there exist b, $c \in A$, with $\neg(b \sim c)$, such that $\forall j, j + 1 \in J, a_{j+1} \circ b \sim a_j \circ c$. A *regular sequence* is any set $\{a_j \mid j \in J\}$, with J either finite or infinite, if there exist b, $c \in A$, with $c > b$, such that $\forall j, j + 1 \in J, a_{j+1} \circ b > a_j \circ c$ and $b \circ a_{j+1} > c \circ a_j$ (Krantz et al. 1989)

A concatenation structure is a *PCS* (Krantz et al. 1989) if and only if it is positive, restrictedly solvable, and Archimedean in standard sequences. Here, PCS stands for *positive concatenation structure*, but means much more than that, given the conditions in the definition. A PCS which is associative is extensive. A PCS in which $A \subseteq \mathbb{R}^+$ and $\succeq$ is the usual ordering $\geqslant$ of $\mathbb{R}^+$ restricted to A is a numerical PCS and is usually denoted $\boldsymbol{R} = \langle R, \geqslant, \otimes \rangle$.

Given two PCSs, $\boldsymbol{A} = \langle A, \succeq, \circ \rangle$ and $\boldsymbol{A}' = \langle A', \succeq', \circ' \rangle$, a function $\varphi: A \to A'$ is a homomorphism of A into A' if and only if the following hold:

1. $a \succeq b \Leftrightarrow \varphi(a) \succeq' \varphi(b)$.
2. If $a \circ b$ is defined, then $\varphi(a) \circ' \varphi(b)$ is defined and $\varphi(a \circ b) = \varphi(a) \circ' \varphi(b)$.

A homomorphism is a *measurement representation* if and only if the structure A' is a numerical PCS.

The set of homomorphisms of a PCS into a fixed (preselected) PCS satisfies 1-point uniqueness. If φ and ψ are two homomorphisms that agree at one point, then they agree at every point, except possibly at one maximal point. Further, these homomorphisms can be ordered. If $\varphi(a) \succeq' \psi(b)$ at one nonmaximal point b, then $\varphi(a) \succeq' \psi(a)$ for every nonmaximal point $a \in A$.

If $\boldsymbol{A} = \langle A, \succeq, \circ \rangle$ is a PCS, then there exists a numerical PCS $\boldsymbol{R}$ such that there is a homomorphism φ of A into R. Further, if φ is a homomorphism of A into R, then φ' is another such representation if and only if there is a strictly increasing function h from $\varphi(A)$ onto $\varphi'(A)$ such that, for all $a \in A$, $\varphi'(a) = h[\psi(a)]$ and such that the numerical operations $\otimes$ and $\otimes'$ are related as follows: $x \otimes' y$ is defined if and only if $h(x) \otimes h(y)$ is defined, and when they are defined, $x \otimes' y$

$= h^{-1}[h(x) \otimes h(y)]$. In other words, *every* empirical PCS has at least an ordinal representation in the numerical PCS $\boldsymbol{R} = \langle R, \geqslant, \otimes \rangle$.

The definition of a set of permissible transformations required to develop a uniqueness condition is more difficult than for extensive structures because there is no definite numerical operation in hand. If φ and ψ are both homomorphisms from a PCS $\boldsymbol{A}$ *onto the same* numerical PCS $\boldsymbol{R}$, and if h is the increasing function that takes φ into ψ, then $\varphi^{-1}h\varphi = \varphi^{-1}\psi$ is an isomorphism of $\boldsymbol{A}$ onto itself. Such an isomorphism is called an automorphism. The permissible transformations for the representation of a concatenation structure are defined by the characteristics of the set of automorphisms for the structure. Further, the set of automorphisms for a particular structure form a group under functional composition.

For a PCS, the automorphism group forms an Archimedean ordered group. The ordering for the group, $\succeq'$, is natural to the group, since for any two automorphisms α and β and for all $a \in A$, $\alpha \succeq' \beta \Leftrightarrow \alpha(a) \succeq \beta(a)$. This automorphism group is also isomorphic to a subgroup of the similarity group $x \to rx$, $x > 0$, $r > 0$. One such subgroup is the ratio scale case, which corresponds to the entire set of positive real numbers. Two other possibilities are $r = 1$, which leads to an absolute scale, and the discrete group of the form $x \to k^n x$ where $k > 0$ and is fixed, and n ranges over the positive and negative integers. The discrete group is the familiar form taken by conversion factors in the physical sciences, and also forms a ratio scale.

Conjoint Structures

Now let's generalize additive conjoint structures to form nonadditive conjoint structures. Heavy use will be made of the information on concatenation structures just given. A key fact developed here is that both intensive and conjoint structures induce an operation that can be decomposed into a PCS.

First, define a general conjoint structure. Suppose A and P are nonempty sets, and $\succeq$ is a binary relation on $A \times P$. Then, $\boldsymbol{C} = \langle A \times P, \succeq \rangle$ is a *conjoint structure* if and only if the following hold for each $a, b \in A$ and $p, q \in P$:

1. *Weak ordering*: $\succeq$ is a nontrivial weak ordering.
2. *Independence*:
   - $ap \succeq bp \Leftrightarrow aq \succeq bq$
   - $ap \succeq aq \Leftrightarrow bp \succeq bq$
3. $\succeq_A$ and $\succeq_P$ are total orders, where $\succeq_A$ is the induced weak order on A, and $\succeq_P$ is the induced weak order on P.

$\boldsymbol{C}$ is said to satisfy the Thomsen condition if and only if for all $a, b, c \in A$ and $p, q, r \in P$,

$$ar \sim cq \wedge cp \sim br \Rightarrow ap \sim bq \qquad (5.94)$$

For $a_0 \in A$ and $p_0 \in P$, $\boldsymbol{C}$ is solvable relative to $a_0 p_0$ if and only if:

1. For each $a \in A$, there exists $\pi(a) \in P$ such that $ap_0 \sim a_0 \pi(a)$.

2. For each $ap \in A \times P$, there exists $\xi(a, p) \in A$ such that $\xi(a, p)p_0 \sim ap$.

C is *unrestrictedly A-solvable* if and only if for each $a \in A$ and $p, q \in P$, there exists $b \in A$ such that $ap \sim bq$. C is *unrestrictedly P-solvable* if and only if for each $p \in P$ and $a, b \in A$, there exists $q \in P$ such that $ap \sim bq$. C *solvable* if it is both A-solvable and P-solvable.

Let J be an infinite or finite interval of integers. Then a sequence $\{a_j \mid a_j \in A, j \in J\}$ is a *standard sequence on A* if and only if there exist $p, q \in P$ such that $\neg(p \sim_P q)$, and for all $j, j + 1 \in J$, $a_{j+1}p \sim a_jq$. The sequence $\{a_j \mid a_j \in A, j \in J\}$ is bounded if and only if for some $c, d \in A$, $c \succeq a_j \succeq d$ for all $j \in J$. C is said to be Archimedean if every bounded standard sequence is finite.

Given a conjoint structure $\langle A \times P, \succeq \rangle$ that is solvable relative to $a_0p_0 \in A \times P$, the Holman induced operation on A relative to a_0p_0, denoted $\circ_A$, is defined by $a \circ_A b = \xi[a, \pi(b)]$ where π and ξ are as previously defined. Let A be a nonempty set, $\succeq$ a binary relation on A, $\circ$ a binary operation on A, and $a_0 \in A$. Then the structure $A = \langle A, \succeq, \circ, a_0 \rangle$ is a *total concatenation structure* (Krantz et al. 1990) if and only if the following hold:

1. $\succeq$ is a total order.
2. $\circ$ is monotonic.
3. The restriction of A to $A^+ = \{a \mid a \in A \wedge a > a_0\}$ is a PCS.
4. The restriction of A to $A^- = \{a \mid a \in A \wedge a < a_0\}$ but with the reverse order $\preceq$ is a PCS [$\langle A^-, \preceq, \circ \rangle$ is a PCS].
5. For all $a \in A$, $a \circ a_0 = a_0 \circ a = a$ (a_0 is the identity for $\circ$).
6. For all $a \in A^+$ and $b \in A^-$, there exist $p, q \in A$ such that $p \circ b$ and $q \circ a$ are defined and $p \circ b > a$ and $b > q \circ a$.

A total concatenation structure is isomorphic to a total concatenation structure on the reals and has at least an ordinal representation. A total concatenation structure is 2-point unique, with a_0 always being one of the common points.

If C is a conjoint structure that is solvable relative to a_0p_0 and $\circ_A$ is the Holman induced operation, then $\circ_A$ is closed and monotonic, and is positive over A^+ and negative over A^-. If, in addition, C is Archimedean, then both $I_{A^+} = \langle A^+, \succeq_{A^+}, \circ_{S+} \rangle$ and $I_{A^-} = \langle A^-, \succeq_{A^-}, \circ_{A^-} \rangle$ are Archimedean in standard sequences. If C is both solvable and Archimedean, then I_A is a closed, solvable, total concatenation structure (I_A is C without a_0 in A).

If A is Archimedean in differences, then C is Archimedean. If A is solvable and Archimedean in standard sequences, then C is solvable and Archimedean. If C is a conjoint structure that is solvable at a point, then C satisfies the Thomsen condition, and $\circ_A$ is associative and commutative. If in addition, C is a solvable conjoint structure, then the induced operations are invariant in the sense that for every $a, b, c, d \in A$ and every pair of induced operations $\circ_A$ and $\circ'_A$,

$$a \circ_A b \succeq c \circ_A d \Leftrightarrow a \circ'_A b \succeq c \circ'_A d \tag{5.95}$$

Thus, Archimedean, solvable conjoint structures give rise to concatenation structures with PCS substructures on the positive and negative parts. Since any PCS has a real interpretation, so do Archimedean, solvable conjoint structures.

Suppose $C = \langle A \times P, \succeq \rangle$ is a conjoint structure, and α is an order automorphism of C. Then α is *factorizable* if and only if there exist functions θ and η, where θ is an isomorphism of A onto A, and η is an isomorphism of P onto P, such that $\alpha = \langle \theta, \eta \rangle$ and $\alpha(ap) = \theta(a)\eta(p)$. Factorizable automorphisms are the results of independent factors in a conjoint structure. The assumptions of factorizable automorphisms, interval scale representability, and a representation into $\mathbb{R}^+$ forces the Thomsen condition.

Let $C = \langle A \times P, \succeq \rangle$ be solvable at points $a_0 p_0$ and $a_0' p_0'$ and suppose that $\alpha = \langle \theta, \eta \rangle$ maps $a_0 p_0$ to $a_0' p_0'$. Let π and π' denote the mappings of A to P relative to these points $[ap_0 \sim a_0 \pi(a)$ and $a'p_0' \sim a_0' \pi'(a')]$. α is an automorphism of C if and only if $\eta\pi = \pi'\theta$ and either or both of θ and η are isomorphisms of the induced Holman structures. If the conjoint structure has sufficient factorizable automorphisms, then the induced operations are all basically the same.

Let $A = \langle A, \succeq, \circ \rangle$ be a concatenation structure. Then, for each $a \in A$, define *left multiplication* a^L by $a^L(b) = a \circ b$, for all $b \in A$ for which $a \circ b$ is defined. Define *right multiplication* a^R by $a^R(b) = b \circ a$ for all $b \in A$ for which $b \circ a$ is defined. In a conjoint structure, any pair of multiplications in the Holman structures on each factor generates a factorizable transformation. In general, this transformation is not an automorphism. When there is solvability at a point and such pairs of multiplications do yield an automorphism, then the Thomsen condition is satisfied.

If $A = \langle A, \succeq, \circ \rangle$ is a closed concatenation structure, then the conjoint structure induced by A is $C = \langle A \times A, \succeq' \rangle$ where for all $a, b, c, d \in A$, $ab \succeq' cd \Leftrightarrow a \circ b \succeq c \circ d$. If, in addition, A is solvable, C is unrestrictedly solvable. If for each $a \in A$ there exist $b, c \in A$ such that $a = b \circ c$, then the converse holds as well. C is Archimedean if and only if A is Archimedean in differences. If A is idempotent and α is a mapping of A onto A, then α is an automorphism of A if and only if $\langle \alpha, \alpha \rangle$ is a factorizable automorphism of C.

If $A = \langle A, \succeq, \circ \rangle$ is a concatenation structure and α is an automorphism of A, then α is a dilation at a if and only if $\alpha(a) = a$, and it is a translation if and only if either it is the identity or is not a dilation for any $a \in A$.

Suppose A is a closed, idempotent, solvable concatenation structure, I_a is the total concatenation structure induced on A via the Holman induced operations on A relative to $a_0 p_0$ and the conjoint structure induced by A, and α is an automorphism of A. Then, α is a dilation at a if and only if α is an automorphism of I_a, and α is a translation if and only if α is an isomorphism of I_a onto $I_{\alpha(a)}$, where $\alpha(a) \neq a$. Further, if A is also Archimedean in differences, then the set of dilations at a form commutative subgroup.

Basically, an idempotent concatenation structure can be decomposed into a family of induced total concatenation structures that are all isomorphic under the translations of the idempotent structure. Further, the dilations of the idempotent concatenation structure are the automorphisms of the induced total concatenation structures. In short, you can take any suitably solvable concatenation structure and induce a total concatenation structure by first inducing a conjoint structure, and be sure you have a set of automorphisms to help determine the uniqueness of your representation.

Recall that a concatenation structure is halvable if it is positive and for each $a \in A$ there exists $b \in A$ such that $b \circ b$ is defined and $a \sim b \circ b$. Another way to look at it is that, in such a structure, a is "double" b. Put still another way, a and b are related by a doubling function, which we now define. Let A be a nonempty set, $\succeq$ a binary relation on A, and * a partial, intensive operation on A. Suppose that $B \subseteq A$ and δ is a function from B into A. Then δ is a *doubling function* (Krantz et al. 1990) of $A = \langle A, \succeq, * \rangle$ if and only if for all $a, b \in A$, the following hold:

1. δ is strictly monotonic increasing.
2. If $a \in B$ and $a \succeq b$, then $b \in B$.
3. If $a > b$, then there exists $c \in A$ such that $b * c$ is defined and in B, and $a > \delta(b * c)$.
4. If $a * b$ is defined and in B, then $\delta(a * b) > a, b$.
5. If $a_n \in A$, $n = 1, 2,...$, are such that if $a_{n-1} \in B$, then $a_n \sim \delta(a_{n-1}) * a_1$, and for any b, either there is an integer n such that $a_n \notin B$ or $a_n \succeq b$; such a sequence is called a *standard sequence of* δ.

If A is an intensive concatenation structure with a doubling function, then either the doubling function is unique, or there is just one other doubling function and their domains differ by just one point b, the functions agree on their common domain, and the double of b is maximal in A.

Suppose A is a nonempty set, $\succeq$ is a binary relation on A, and $\circ$ and * are two closed operations on A such that for each $a, a', b, b' \in A$, $a \circ b \sim a' \circ b'$ if and only if $a * b \sim a' * b'$. Define the function θ by $\theta(a \circ b) = a * b$. Then, $\langle A, >, \circ \rangle$ is a PCS with *half element function* $\theta[a \sim \theta(a) \circ a]$ if and only if $\langle A, >, * \rangle$ is an intensive concatenation structure with doubling function θ^{-1} defined on all of A (Krantz et al. 1990).

If A is an intensive concatenation structure with a doubling function, B is the related PCS, and A has no maximal element, then the automorphism groups of A and B are identical. If an intensive structure does not have a doubling function, it is not related to a PCS, and its automorphisms have two degrees of freedom.

Representations of Solvable Conjoint and Concatenation Structures

A conjoint structure that is unrestrictedly solvable and Archimedean induces a total concatenation structure which is made up of two PCSs, each of which has a real representation. Thus, the conjoint structure, which is called a *solvable concatenation structure* (defined but not named in Krantz et al. 1990), also has a real representation. Formally, the **representation condition** is: If $C = \langle A \times P, \succeq \rangle$ is a conjoint structure that is Archimedean and solvable, then there exist a numerical operation $\oplus$ and functions φ from A and ψ from P into $\mathbb{R}$ such that

$$\varphi(a_0) = 0 \qquad \psi(p_0) = 0 \tag{5.96a}$$

$$x \oplus 0 = x \qquad 0 \oplus y = y \tag{5.96b}$$

$$ap \succeq bq \Leftrightarrow \varphi(a) \oplus \psi(p) \geq \varphi(b) \oplus \psi(q) \tag{5.96c}$$

$$\psi = \varphi\pi^{-1}[ap_0 \sim a_0\pi(a)] \tag{5.96d}$$

(Krantz et al. 1990.) Suppose that under these conditions, $\varphi \oplus \psi$ and $\varphi' \oplus \psi'$ are two representations of $C = \langle A \times P, \succeq, a_0p_0 \rangle$ with $\varphi(A) = \varphi'(A)$ and $\psi(P) = \psi'(P)$. The **uniqueness condition** is: If for some $a \in A$, $\varphi(a) = \varphi'(a)$, then $\varphi \equiv \varphi'$ and $\psi \equiv \psi'$. Note that the representation is 2-point unique because the point (a_0, p_0) is mapped to $(0, 0)$ and there are really two degrees of freedom (φ and ψ form **ratio scales** on A and P, respectively, and combine to form an **interval scale** on C) (Krantz et al. 1990).

A concatenation structure that is closed, solvable, and Archimedean in difference sequences is isomorphic to a real concatenation structure and is either 1- or 2-point unique. In other words, a closed, solvable, Archimedean (in differences) concatenation structure has a representation which is either a ratio or an interval scale.

If $A = \langle A, \succeq, * \rangle$ is an intensive concatenation structure with doubling function δ, $\oplus$ a partial binary numerical operation on $\mathbb{R}^+$ with half-element function h, and φ a mapping from A into $\mathbb{R}^+$, then φ is a $\oplus$-*representation* (Krantz et al. 1990) of A if and only if for all $a, b \in A$:

1. $a \succeq b \Leftrightarrow \varphi(a) \geq \varphi(b)$.
2. If $a * b$ is defined, $\varphi(a * b) = h[\varphi(a) \oplus \varphi(b)]$.
3. If a is in the domain of δ, $\varphi(a) = h\varphi\delta(a)$.

The **representation condition** is: If A is an intensive concatenation structure with doubling function δ, then there exist $\varphi: A \to \mathbb{R}^+$ and a binary operation $\oplus$ on $\mathbb{R}^+$ such that φ is a $\oplus$-representation of A, and

$$a \succeq b \Leftrightarrow \varphi(a) \geq \varphi(b) \tag{5.97a}$$

$$\varphi(a * b) = h[\varphi(a) \oplus \varphi(b)] \tag{5.97b}$$

$$\varphi(a) = h\varphi\delta(a) \tag{5.97c}$$

(Krantz et al. 1990.) The **uniqueness condition** is: If two such $\oplus$-representations φ and φ' agree at one point, then they are identical (φ and φ' are 1-point unique and are thus **ratio scales**) (Krantz et al. 1990).

INDIRECT MEASURES

Even if you can measure an attribute directly, you can often get a more accurate measure by doing so indirectly. For example, the direct measurement of the attribute speed of an object is at best an ordinal scale (Kyburg 1984). It can be said that an object a is going faster than an object b (relative speed). This statement will be meaningful, true in this case, for any rescaling. But not very much can be said about the speed of either object individually. When you measure speed indirectly, say in terms of time and distance, you get a ratio scale and a more accurate measure of speed.

Attributes that are measured indirectly are defined to be external attributes of the object with which they are associated. External attributes must be defined in terms of internal attributes in such a way that consensus is achieved on the definition (Fenton 1991). You need to get people to accept the model and its relationships.

A scale M is an indirect scale if it is defined in terms of some functions M_1, $M_2,..., M_n$, for $n > 0$, such that M and M_i satisfy the condition $E(M_1, M_2,..., M_n, M)$. For speed, $E(m, v, d)$ is $d = m/v$. The analysis of the scale type for an indirect scale M is similar to that of a direct scale. The scale type of an indirect scale M will generally be the weakest of the scale types of the M_i (Fenton 1991). You may recognize that indirect scales form conjoint structures, with each of the M_i forming a component. When analyzing an indirect scale, make use of the information on conjoint and concatenation structures presented in earlier sections.

PREDICTION SYSTEMS

In order for a measure, or set of measures, to be used for prediction, they must be part of a prediction system. A *prediction system* contains (Littlewood 1988):

1. A mathematical model that represents the measures and their relationships to each other.

2. A statistical inference procedure for determining the unknown values of the model parameters.

3. A prediction procedure which combines 1 and 2 to allow you to make statements about future values.

Each of the three components is equally important, since two predictions made using the same model, but different parameter values, will yield different results.

The model is usually expressed in the form of an equation for an indirect measure. For example, the COCOMO model (Boehm 1981) for effort is *effort* = $a(size)^b$ where *effort* is measured in person-months, *size* is measured in thousands of delivered source instructions, and the values of a and b depend upon the type of development. For in-house development, called *organic*, $a = 2.4$ and $b = 1.05$. For semidetached development (geographically or organizationally distributed teams), $a = 3.0$ and $b = 1.12$. For embedded real-time software, $a = 3.6$ and $b = 1.20$. The model assumes that the type of development is known and can be readily determined.

If the size is known, the model can be solved for effort, although this is not really prediction—if the size is known with certainty, so is the effort, since the product has already been created! If the size is unknown when the model is used, there must be a way to determine the size from the available data. If specifications are available, we would like to base the size estimate on them. Thus, a way is needed to predict size, in thousands of delivered source instructions, from the specifications.

This leads to the second component: a way to infer the values of model parameters that are unknown at the time of model application. The procedure must be tailored to the specific environment, as must the model itself. This means that each organization, based on it own experience, must develop the means to predict these model parameter values. This is where historical data plays a major role in prediction. Good, high-quality historical data provides the information to build both the model and the inference procedure.

The third component provides a way of interpreting the results. One aspect of this interpretation is to determine if the results of the prediction are reasonable and/or significant. There are several statistical methods for testing the predictive quality of a model (now complete with estimated parameter values that were previously unknown).

Two aspects of this investigation are the model's *quality of fit* and its *predictive quality* (Szabo and Koshgoftaar 1995). Quality of fit is evaluated using the R^2 statistic, where R^2 is the ratio of the sum of squares of the prediction error to the total sum of the squares, or

$$\frac{\sum_{i=1}^{n} (\hat{y}_i - \bar{y})^2}{\sum_{i=1}^{n} (y_i - \bar{y})^2} \tag{5.98}$$

where y_i is the actual value of the dependent variable at observation i ($i = 1,...,$ n), $\hat{y}_i$ is the predicted value of the dependent variable at observation i, and $\bar{y}$ is the mean value of the y_is. The closer R^2 is to 1.0, the higher the quality of fit. The correlation of actual values (y_i) to the predicted values ($\hat{y}_i$) of the dependent variable is $\sqrt{R^2}$. This and other potential statistical tests for quality of fit are discussed in the section "Statistical Analysis and Inference" in Chapter 4.

Predictive quality can be assessed using the *PRESS* statistic (for Prediction Sum of Squares). *PRESS* is defined by

$$PRESS = \sum_{i=1}^{n} (y_i - \hat{y}_i)^2 \tag{5.99}$$

where n is the number of observations, y_i is the value of the dependent variable at observation i, and $\hat{y}_i$ is the predicted value of the variable from a regression model fitted with all *except* the ith observation. This version of the *PRESS* statistic differs from that in Chapter 4 because this version applies to only one component, while the version in Chapter 4 can be applied to models with more than one dependent variable. This version is from Szabo and Koshgoftaar (1995).

With this test, n different regression models are each fitted with $n - 1$ observations and are used to predict the ith observation, where i here assumes each of the values $i = 1,..., n$, in turn. Lower values of *PRESS* indicate better predictive quality. See Myers (1990) for more discussion.

There is a way to compare the predictive quality of two models to determine if one is (statistically) significantly better than the other (Szabo and Koshgoftaar 1995). The process uses a t-test on the paired *PRESS* residuals, $\hat{e}_i = (y_i - \hat{y}_i)$, squared, or $\hat{e}_i^2$, to determine if the two models are significantly different. Formally, the hypotheses are H_0: $\mu_D = 0$ (the null hypothesis) and H_a: $\mu_D > 0$ where μ_D is the mean of the population. Let n be the number of observations where $i = 1,..., n$, S_d the sample standard deviation, and $\hat{e}_{ij}$ the ith *PRESS* residual for model j. The test is

$$T = \frac{\overline{D}}{S_d/\sqrt{n}} \tag{5.100}$$

where

$$\overline{D} = \frac{1}{n} \sum_{i=1}^{n} (\hat{e}_{i,model1}^2 - \hat{e}_{i,model2}^2) \tag{5.101}$$

T has a t-distribution with $n - 1$ degrees of freedom. For a given level of significance α, the critical region is identified using a table of critical values for the t-distribution, with $T > t_\alpha$. If T is inside the critical region, reject the null hypothesis and conclude that model 2 is significantly better, from a statistical viewpoint, than model 1. If T is outside of the critical region, then accept the null hypothesis and conclude that the two models are not statistically different.

I should mention that these tests can only be used for measures from the interval, ratio, or absolute scales. This does not mean that a prediction system cannot be based on a model with nominal or ordinal scale measures. It does mean that the techniques of single and multiple linear regression, and tests of quality of fit and predictive quality, cannot be used on such models. For these models, the robust regression methods can be used, but are rather complicated (Sprent 1989; and the section "Statistical Analysis and Inference" in Chapter 4).

VALIDATION

Validation in software measurement has three facets: validating the measures themselves either empirically or theoretically, measuring the reliability of the measures, and validating any prediction systems you might base on the measures. Validation of a software measure is the process of ensuring that the measure does indeed satisfy the representation condition for the attribute being measured (Fenton 1991; Kitchenham, Pfleeger, and Fenton 1995). This is much easier said than done. One of the chief difficulties with the empirical validation of software measures is the filtering out of the effects of other factors on the value of the measure.

This is especially true in software, where we really don't understand all of the interactions between components. This lack of understanding makes it difficult to evaluate many software measures from a theoretical standpoint as well.

Schneidewind (1994) gives six criteria that a validation process must check (after the conditions of the representation condition are satisfied): association, consistency, discriminating power, tracking, predictability (for prediction systems), and repeatability. All of these terms are defined in Schneidewind (1994). Association is the extent to which a variation in the value of an attribute is explained by the variation in the measure. This amounts to determining a confidence level in the mapping from the attribute value to the measure value. Consistency is the extent to which the value of an attribute and the value of the measure share rankings when the results of multiple measurements are sorted in order. Ideally, if the attribute values $a_1, a_2,..., a_n$ are sorted in ascending order by value, the same sort applied to the measure values $m_1, m_2,..., m_n$ should put the values in the same order, so that pairings of the sorted values have the same index number.

Discriminative power is the extent to which a value of a measure can be used to partition a set of attribute measures in a way that $m_i > m_c \Leftrightarrow a_i > a_c \wedge m_i \le m_c \Leftrightarrow a_i \le a_c$. Tracking is the extent to which changes in the value of the measure follow changes in the value of the attribute. Predictability is the extent to which the value of a measure at some point in time can be used to determine the value of the attribute at some later point in time. This applies more to validation of prediction systems than it does to validation of individual measures, since the other elements of a prediction system materially affect the results of the prediction. Repeatability is the extent to which repeated attempts to measure an attribute of some constant value results in measures with the same value. Schneidewind (1994) provides several statistical tests, both parametric and nonparametric, for each criterion.

Measure reliability has three components (Reynolds and Zannoni 1994): observer variability, entity variability, and environment variability. Observer variability is the likelihood that the value of a measure will be the same from measurement to measurement given the same situation. Random measurement error plays a role in this component. Entity variability considers changes that may happen to the entity during the course of measurement, whether caused by the act of measurement or some other factor. Environment variability considers uncontrollable aspects of the environment that introduce noise into the measurement process.

The purpose of assessing a measure's reliability is to determine the variability in the measure value caused by each of the three components. The statistical tests for this assessment are included in those given by Schneidewind (1994). The process of assessing a measure's reliability involves collecting lots of data over a long period of time. This usually involves the use of carefully designed experiments.

Validation of a prediction system, in a given environment, is the process of establishing the accuracy of the predictions by empirical means—by comparing the model's predicted values with known actual values for the given environment

(Fenton 1991). The predictive quality of the system has three components (Reynolds and Zannoni 1994): predictive validity, content validity, and construct validity. Predictive validity is the extent to which the predicted values at some point in time show a strong association with the actual values at some later point in time (this is Scheidewind's test of predictability). Content validity is the extent to which the central tendency, the variation, and the scale of the predicted values are consistent in some respect with the actual values. Construct validity is the extent to which the variables or components that contribute to the predicted values do indeed have some relationship with the actual values.

Most users of software measures are really users of prediction systems. Often, parts of the system are missing. Also often, the components of the predicted value either do not have any established relationship to the actual value or some of the factors that do affect the value are missing.

This latter problem is the case with many size measures. Size is often used to predict the effort required to build a software application. This effort is translated into both the estimated cost and the estimated schedule for the project. We know, both from study and experience, that many factors other than size affect the time and effort required to produce a piece of software. These other factors include the type of problem being solved, the skill and experience of the team members, the availability and use of tools, and the goals of the project. Some prediction systems, such as COCOMO (Boehm 1981), attempt to take some of these factors into account. Unfortunately, we don't really understand the relationship between many of these factors and effort. Even worse, the relationships between some factors and effort appear to be interrelated with other factors (not independent), and some relationships appear to be variable.

These problems make validation of software measures, and particularly prediction systems, very difficult. In most disciplines, measure validation happens in carefully controlled experiments. In software, controlled experiments are nearly impossible, in some areas of measurement, because the subject being measured, the developers, actually changes between experiments—they learn while they are doing.

However, to use a measure during the design process, for most of the purposes given in Chapter 1, it is sufficient to validate the measure as described at the start of this section—to show that it meets the representation condition and satisfies five of Scheidewind's six criteria (all except predictability).

MEASUREMENT THEORY AND SOFTWARE ENGINEERING

In the software engineering community, there is currently debate about the application of measurement theory to software measurement. There are two sides to this debate, which is not unusual. What is unusual is that both sides miss the point completely.

One side, whose primary proponents are Fenton (1991) and Zuse (1991), argues that the scale type of a measure should determine the types of statistical tests we can use to analyze the values of the measure. They take the view that certain tests are inappropriate for use on measures of certain scale types. Much of their information is included in the section on "Scales." From another angle, this view says that, given a measure, we should first determine its scale type, then use only those tests appropriate for that scale. This view talks in terms of prescribing (allowing) and proscribing (prohibiting) certain tests for each type of scale. Unfortunately, this view is being called the measurement-theoretic approach to software measurement. I will explain later why I think this is unfortunate.

As a specific example, Zuse (1991) maintains that, among other things, complexity measures must be additive. This requirement allows the use of extensive measurement to be used for measuring complexity, because extensive measurement leads to the ratio scale. Understand: The goal here is that complexity be a ratio scale measure and extensive measurement is but one way to achieve this goal. Zuse provides no other grounds for requiring extensive measurement and thus additivity. This view is becoming increasingly accepted as valid in the software engineering literature (Bieman and Ott 1994; Chidamber and Kemerer 1994; Fenton 1994).

The other view, whose main proponents are Briand, El Emam, and Morasca (1995), argues that the measurement-theoretic approach is too rigorous for our current knowledge of software. This view has some support in nonsoftware disciplines, especially in the behavioral sciences. Their main argument is that limiting the kinds of tests which can be used on measurement data of certain scale types can cause us to miss many conclusions, which may only be approximate, that we might otherwise find by using "invalid" tests. Briand and colleagues argue that the measurement goals should determine the scale, and thus the types of analysis techniques, under which the data should be used, not the other way around. As support, they assert that sometimes it is very difficult to determine the scale type of a particular measure. They use Cyclomatic Complexity as an example (McCabe 1976). As an aside, the key to determining the scale type of a measure is to identify the empirical structure upon which it is based and examine the homogeneity and uniqueness of the structure's group of automorphisms. For Cyclomatic Complexity, the key question is: "Just what is being measured?"

In addition to the rigorous requirements for using certain statistical tests, Briand, El Emam, and Morasca (1995) raise strong objection to the requirement that a measure of software complexity be additive. They argue convincingly that additivity for complexity is counterintuitive. While the discussion in their paper centers mainly around Weyuker's properties (Weyuker 1988), their main point is that a measure of an attribute should follow our intuition for that attribute. As an example, they make the statement that additivity for a size measure is a natural requirement.

Briand, El Emam, and Morasca argue for pragmatism to be the guide in software measurement. The tests used on a measure should be appropriate for the types of questions for which answers are sought, without regard for the scale type of the measure. Fenton (1991, 1994) and Zuse (1991, 1994) argue that a measure's scale type should determine the types of tests used. I said earlier that both views missed the point; now I will explain why.

The unstated assumption in both views is that the current crop of software measures is worth studying. The measurement-theoretic approach would require that, given a measure, you first determine its scale type, then use the tests appropriate for that scale. The other view would have you use the tests appropriate for the questions you are posing, ignoring the scale type of the measure. I have to ask, though, if the scale type of a measure cannot be determined, can we even call it a measure?

Both of these views start with a given measure and go from there. I propose a different approach. I suggest we start with the questions to which we want answers, which is the second step in the Goal Question Metric approach described in Chapter 3. These questions will require the use of certain kinds of information from a measurement data set, such as central tendency, variation, and relationships between various factors. Our accuracy requirements may cause us to want to use parametric tests over nonparametric tests. Since parametric tests require the use of interval or ratio scale measures, we then go looking for structures from which to construct them. If existing measures for the attribute of interest do not qualify, we have the information, presented in this chapter, to invent measures that do qualify. This is the essence of the measure construction technique I provide in Chapter 3.

The key is not to look for specific measures, but to look for required scale types. Then, we can use the information in this chapter to select a basic structure which is likely to provide the right kind of measure. In that sense, the empirical structures in this chapter form a set of structural patterns. These patterns determine the requirements for our empirical structures, which we then try to construct.

Our inability to construct a structure of a particular type is not a problem with the theory, but reflects the limits of our understanding about software. The proper response in this case is not to abandon or weaken our reliance on measurement theory, but to increase our understanding of what we are trying to study. This should be the goal of software engineering research.

For example, if a ratio scale is a reasonable requirement for a complexity measure, is extensive measurement the best way to get there? Is the requirement of additivity a reasonable one to impose on a complexity measure? Just what is complexity anyway? There is by no means common agreement on any of these answers. Unlike size (or maybe not—size has never been formally defined in the literature), we have not developed an intuitive or empirical understanding of complexity on which we can all agree. Until this is done, measurement is nearly impossible. In fact, there is no common intuitive understanding of what constitutes size in software. I explore software size in Chapter 7 and complexity in Chapter 8, in order to develop my own intuition about these concepts. From there, I work to build specific measures for these attributes.

A truly "measurement-theoretic" approach to software engineering, then, is to start with the structural requirements for different kinds of measurement and seek to find or build empirical structures in software which meet these requirements. Valid measures will fall out of these efforts. We do not start with measures, then see what we can do with them, nor do we take a set of measures and do whatever we want with them. Given the allowable transformations on each scale type, getting to a particular measure is not nearly as important as what we learn about software as a result of this effort.

SUMMARY

A lot of ground has been covered in this chapter—from the basic ideas behind physical measurement to the limits of what is known about other forms of measurement. You now have the tools to begin building measures from the theory out, something that has not yet been done in software engineering. We have, in this chapter, the requirements our empirical models must satisfy in order for measurement of a given kind to take place. We also know the limitations of any measures we do use.

We have learned some important practical matters, as well as some important theoretical aspects of measurement. We have the tools at our disposal to venture into uncharted measurement waters, inventing measures on-the-fly, while knowing full well what we are trying to do, and whether we are succeeding.

As you use the information in this chapter, through repeated references, you will become familiar with it. This familiarity will allow you to recognize patterns in your software, patterns which match the various kinds of empirical structures presented in this chapter. As you gain experience with these patterns, you will recognize ways to measure software that you did not previously recognize. When you do, please tell others, so they, too, can benefit from your discovery.

6

A THEORY OF OBJECTS

From Chapter 5, we learned we cannot measure an object without a model of that object which supports the construction of measurement representations. The model must faithfully represent and be able to explain our empirical understanding about the nature and structure of individual objects, and ways in which they interrelate. A single model should support the measurement of many characteristics, both static and dynamic. Such a model must be formal—based on mathematics—in order to serve as a reliable foundation for measurement.

In this chapter, a formal model of objects based on category theory (Mac Lane 1994; Pierce 1991; Barr and Wells 1995) is introduced. This model allows the measurement of both static and dynamic properties of a design. I also introduce a set of analysis techniques which allow the dynamic manipulation of a design, including the simulation of its behavior in reponse to an external event. The chapter describes fully the model and the accompanying analysis techniques. It does not, however, describe the empirical structures, based on the model, which help measure size, complexity, coupling, cohesion, sufficiency, completeness, primitiveness, similarity, and volatility, which are described in the chapters of Part III.

Categories are a mathematical structure which generalizes and unifies the many algebraic structures of discrete mathematics. They are a major tool in the exploration and study of programming languages. Using categories, you can move between algebraic structures along pathways which preserve structure as you move from simple to complex, and which strip away structure as you move from complex to simple. These pathways are well-defined and, in fact, are mathematical functions. Categories provide several universal constructs which explain many things in object-oriented software.

The model describes the structure of a class in terms of its attributes and methods. It describes the state space for a class as a cross product of attribute domains, and consequently describes the state of an individual object as a selection from this state space. It describes the operations of a class as transitions between states and it allows the definition of message passing and method binding mechanisms. The model also allows the modeling of both static and dynamic relationships between classes and between objects.

The model consists of five categories: **Class**, **DesignState**, **Design**, **Message**, and **Method**. The measurement of static properties of a design use the categories **Class** and **DesignState**. The objects in the category **Class** are the attribute domains and the individual states in the state space. The arrows are projection functions representing individual attributes, functions between states representing the operations or methods of the class, and selection functions from the state space to individual states. The objects in the category **DesignState** are the software classes in the design. The arrows are the relationships between classes: generalization, association, aggregation, and message links. These two categories allow the direct measurement of such empirical concepts as size, complexity, coupling, primitiveness, and similarity, and the indirect measurement of cohesion, sufficiency, completeness, and volatility.

The third category, **Design** is used for algebraic simulation of the design's behavior, dynamic design analysis, and the algebraic manipulation of the design structure itself. Objects in this category are design states. The arrows of the category are operations which alter the design. When combined, all three categories allow you to measure a design's static characteristics or to determine a design's response to an external event *either before or after applying a sequence of design changes*. With this model, not only can you measure the complexity of a design, but you can measure the complexity of a design after applying a set of modifications, without actually modifying the design models themselves.

The categories **Message** and **Method** are used to define the universal mechanisms of message passing and message binding. The objects in both categories are atoms of content for messages, interpreted as parameters of methods. The arrows are all selection functions.

The mathematics of these techniques are surprisingly simple. Models of the empirical design characteristics are based on basic theories from sets and functions, graphs, lattices, and other algebraic structures, including category theory itself. The operations which allow altering the structure of the design are based on relational algebra. Predicate calculus is the basis for analyzing a particular design's behavior under stimulus. Together, the model and techniques form a theory of objects which allows the static measurement of design properties as well as the testing of the design while still on paper.

As motivation for the model, and to provide a set of requirements for our theory, let's first discuss three types of analysis we might want to apply to a design. The model itself is developed in the next four sections. The analytical techniques which complete the theory are provided in the section entitled "Analytical Techniques." "Potential for Tool Support" explores the potential for tools which support this theory and can significantly assist with the design process.

ANALYZING DESIGNS

In software engineering, the terms analysis and design carry many meanings. They are used primarily to describe sets of activities, each with different purposes. Analysis is exploratory in nature. Analysis activities work to discover the requirements of an application, or to discover the essential models of an application or business domain. It is used to discover properties of things which already exist and involves the tearing apart of a thing—working from the whole to the various parts.

Design is creational in nature. Design activities work to build models of an application, or to create the essential models of an application or business domain. Design is used to build a thing which does not yet exist and involves the synthesis of a thing—the putting together of various parts to make a whole.

The design of an application, taken as a noun, can be viewed as a thing in its own right. A design exists; it has properties and contains parts. We can apply the activities of analysis to a design to discover its properties and identify its parts. Theoretically, we can analyze any design. Practically, any analysis technique not based on a theory, or at least on a formal model, of a design cannot tell us much about the design.

So, why would we want to analyze a design? Doesn't testing the code tell us whether the software is correct? What can we learn from the design itself?

In nearly every engineering discipline, the design is accompanied by a set of calculations. In structural, civil, and mechanical engineering, the calculations determine whether a structure built according to the design can withstand its intended load. They also determine the limits of a design: its maximum load, maximum shock, tolerance for vibration and wear, temperature ranges, moisture limits, and the design life of the structure. In electrical engineering, the calculations determine the electrical properties of the design: the size of the power supply, the maximum current flow, the maximum and minimum voltage levels, and the magnetic fields generated by the design. These calculations are an integral part of the design; no design is complete without them. They help determine whether the design satisfies its specifications; that is, whether a product built according to the design will perform as intended. The motivation for including them is that the cost of doing the calculations is far less than the cost of not doing them, which may mean building a product to an inadequate design.

Software engineering is no different. In a typical project, I invest many hours into building code before it is at a point where I can test the design. This effort is usually on the order of staff weeks and can run into staff years on large projects. If the design proves to be inadequate, all of this effort is waste. The rework required to fix design defects has been the root cause of every schedule slippage I have ever experienced in 17 years of professional programming. The rework can be saved by investing a few additional hours in the design effort and by testing the design before the code is built.

In a team environment, it is often necessary to discuss design issues as a team. Among the reasons for such discussion is the selection of a design from among a set of alternatives. In these settings, it is not possible to build each of the alternatives in order to test them. Teams need to be able to analyze the design in terms of static properties and dynamic behavior during the design process.

The techniques in this chapter are intended for use by individuals during the design process. They can be used equally well at the blackboard or whiteboard during a team design session.

Since software is not based on physical science, we can't calculate physical limits for a software design. Software designs do have many properties: size, complexity, coupling, cohesion, sufficiency, completeness, primitiveness, similarity, volatility, response to an external event, timing constraints, and resource constraints. Some of these are static properties of the design as an object. Others are static or dynamic properties of the designed product as it executes. Both sets of properties can be extracted from a well-defined design using the analysis techniques in this chapter.

Static Analysis

Designs, being objects, have a set of properties. Discovering these properties can take two forms (Wand 1989):

1. Discovering a property from among the set and naming it—resulting in the set of properties which define the kind to which a design belongs.
2. Discovering the current value of a property—resulting in a set of values which determine the state of the design.

The first form of discovery is an analysis problem and aims to identify and define a set of properties which describes the object. The second form of discovery is a measurement problem and is the motivation for this entire book.

The set of properties of an object serve to completely describe the object. If complete, the set of properties allows you to distinguish any object from any other object if its kind and to distinguish any kind of object from any other kind. This discovery process is rooted in the science of ontology, which is a branch of the philosophy of physics (Bunge 1977). Using this process, we seek to characterize a set of objects so that we may understand them, discuss them, and even measure them.

For object-oriented designs, a set of properties has evolved over the years. These properties are the results of discussions about design criteria, the objective being to distinguish "good" designs from "bad" designs. Part III of this book contains a set of nine properties. Several of these properties will appear on almost everyone's list of important concerns. Some will appear on fewer lists. Two of the properties appear only on my list so far. I discuss each property in detail in Chapters 7 through 15. This set of properties is the result of my discovery process. Further consideration of each property, including why it is part of the set, will be delayed until these chapters.

For now, let's turn to the second form of discovery: Assigning a value for a property to an object. This is the essence of measurement and makes this form of discovery the more important of the two for our purposes.

Measurement carries with it the assumption that the property being measured is important to us—that we derive benefit from measuring the property. Measurement further assumes that we can assign numbers or symbols to objects in such a way as to draw meaningful conclusions from the results of the assignment. This last assumption is the source of the structural constraints imposed by measurement theory.

Let's assume for the moment that the set of properties given in Chapters 7 through 15 is sufficient for our goals: Creating better object-oriented designs. Next, we determine how to build a representation of each property into the real number, the integers, or some set of numeric symbols. The numeric structure we choose, and the constraints that structure places on our empirical model, is determined by the type of measure we wish to construct. That, in turn, is determined by the ways we wish to use the results of measurement.

The purpose of static analysis, as defined here, is to assist with decision-making during the design process. We want to analyze designs for any of the five technical measurement purposes described in Chapter 1. Measurement of the properties in Part III will help us decide whether one design is better than another and which design best meets our project goals.

Some design decisions involve the whole design or major parts of it. These decisions are called global decisions. Global decisions include selection of the overall architecture, choosing between design patterns, and the selection of the design or development approach to take. Other design decisions are more local in nature, involving individual and small groups of design elements. Local decisions include whether to split a class into two or more parts, whether to combine two classes into one, and whether to use a separate class to represent some algorithm or process.

Dynamic Analysis

Dynamic analysis applies to the behavior of a design as it executes. Normally, dynamic analysis is performed on a design by testing the code constructed according to the design. It is clear that testing a design in this manner is a very inefficient way to determine whether a design is correct. Instead, we would like to determine the design's behavior before construction of code. This would allow us to "test" a design before any time and effort is invested into building code that may be wrong no matter how closely it matches the design.

The analogy I will employ is physical stress analysis from structural or mechanical engineering, although circuit analysis from electrical engineering may prove to be a better analogy. In a mechanical structure, the design is stressed by applying a force, usually a load or vibration, to a point in the structure. The analysis consists of calculating the behavior of the design in terms of the way it responds to the force. This analysis can be performed on individual parts or on assemblies of parts. The purpose is to discover the behavior of the parts and assemblies under load or stress. This information is used to determine the limits of the design.

In this analogy, the objects themselves represent the parts in a mechanical structure. The relationships between objects represent the joints or contact points between parts. The design as a whole represents the physical structure as a whole. The design must include both the static and dynamic properties of each object. An external event represents the physical load. The analysis involves calculating the response of the design to this external event.

In a structure, calculate and follow the lines of force through each component and the interfaces between components. In an object-oriented design, the lines of force are replaced with paths of messages and state transitions which propagate through the design much as electrical signals propagate through a circuit. To perform the analysis, take a design, assume a steady state, apply an event, and track the message and state changes until a new steady state is reached. Define a steady state to be one in which no object of the design changes state without external stimulus. Objects are allowed to send messages while in a steady state; some applications require continuous messages between objects to detect external events.

In structural and mechanical engineering, we can perform stress analysis on a design using mathematical techniques. These techniques are based upon the laws of physics. In a software design, we would like to be able to stress a design using mathematical techniques based upon discrete mathematics and abstract algebra since they form the theoretical basis for software. Dynamic analysis of a design is such a technique.

An analysis technique, whether applied to a physical or software structure, requires these features:

1. A means of mathematically describing both the static and dynamic properties of the design.
2. A means of mathematically describing an initial state, including the initial state of each component.
3. A means of mathematically describing the load to be applied to the structure.
4. A set of manual or automated mathematical tools and techniques to trace the lines of force and determine each component's, and thus the design's, response to those forces.
5. A means to mathematically describe the results of the analysis—in particular a means to identify any failure points which are discovered.

Because software and physical designs can become very complex, stress analysis on the whole design is often impractical (impossible to do within a reasonable period of time). For this reason, stress analysis often is performed at the component level, then at the assembly level, treating an entire assembly as a single component.

We can apply this method to a software design, if the design meets certain criteria:

1. We can mathematically describe the structure of each component.
2. We can mathematically describe the relationships between the components.
3. We can mathematically describe the preconditions and postconditions of each operation for each component.

4. We can mathematically describe an event.

5. We can mathematically trace the response to an event through the design's state space.

The mathematical tools which meet all of these criteria exist and are part of software engineering practice. This is rather surprising given the state of software engineering practice. The use of these tools has been hindered by a number of things:

- They impose strict requirements for a rigorous design definition.
- They currently lack a common underlying model.
- There is a general lack of recognition of the value of and need for analytical techniques.

This chapter will address all of these issues. The technical tools and techniques are provided directly.

When most software engineers encounter the term "formal methods," they immediately think of proving a program or code segment correct using strict mathematical reasoning. This is true of both the proponents and opponents of formal methods. Indeed, formal specification methods were developed with this purpose in mind (Woodcock and Loomes 1989; Gries 1981).

I propose two different uses, both of which seem more practical to me than formal proofs of correctness, yet which actually require more information than a formal proof. The first is as a means to test a design in terms of its response to an event, while the design is still in the form of a model. The second use is to explore potential design changes, in terms of their effects on the static and dynamic properties of the design, before the changes are actually made. Either of these uses would be valuable to an individual engineer working on the design. They are essential when discussing the design and potential design changes in a group setting, such as a design session or a design review or inspection. The static and dynamic analyses of a design should both be included in the material which is reviewed and inspected. Keep these uses in mind as we develop the model and analysis techniques which form the theory.

Simulating Execution

Dynamic analysis concentrates on the results of a single event. Simulation is concerned with the results of several sequential or simultaneous events. Simulation makes use of and builds upon dynamic analysis. Manual dynamic analysis is often feasible. Simulation almost requires automated support. With simulation, it is possible to build working prototypes. It is possible to prototype functions and behavior via mathematical descriptions.

A simulation session or scenario has the following components:

1. A complete description of a design.

2. A description of an initial state.

3. A set of events that occur in a sequence or simultaneously, possibly in the form of a script.

4. Access to the dynamic analysis facilities.

5. A means to visualize or represent the application in its initial state, in action, and in its final state.

The design description, initial state description, and event set are provided by the designer. The simulator provides access to the dynamic analysis facilities and the means to visualize the application in its initial and final states, and in action. The descriptions provided by the designer and the description of the final state produced by the simulator provide a permanent record of the session.

It is possible to encode the design description in a replication of the simulator. This results in an executable version of the design. We have, in effect, a directly executable design which could be used for prototyping or limited production. It is not clear whether the simulator could be built with the performance and robustness required for general production use.

THE CATEGORY *CLASS*

The world is composed of things, which we choose to call objects (Bunge 1977). There are two kinds of objects: *concrete*—called *entities* or *substantial individuals*—and *concepts*. The science of ontology treats concrete objects differently than conceptual objects. In software, all objects are conceptual in that they only *represent* or are *abstractions* or *models* of concrete and conceptual objects in the real world. Thus, representations of concrete objects and representations of conceptual objects will be treated in the same way.

Objects, Properties, and Behavior

Objects possess properties (Bunge 1977). Some properties are observable as attributes, others as behaviors. The properties of an object in software are its attributes and its behaviors. One of the properties of any object, software or otherwise, is its identity. Each object has a unique identity which distinguishes it apart from all other objects. If we perceive that two objects are identical, it means we haven't sufficiently identified the important properties. In this case, we haven't discovered the unique identity. The identity of an object is the property that allows us to observe two cars which are alike in every respect, yet still remain two distinct cars.

The attributes of an object are independent of the their values at any given point in time. An object's *state* is the set of (usually static) attributes plus the current (usually dynamic) values of each attribute (Booch 1994).

An object's *behavior* is how the object acts and reacts, in terms of state changes and message passing. Booch (1994) defines a message as an operation one object performs on another. Stepney, Barden, and Cooper (1992) disagree. To them, an object can perform operations only upon itself and responds to requests to perform those operations. An object is not obligated to perform any service it is not designed to perform. Indeed, an object can fail to respond to any message which it does not understand. I will define what we mean by "understand" a little later. The view of an operation held by Stepney and colleagues matches our ontological view better than Booch's view of an operation. Thus, a *message* is defined as a request one object makes of another to perform a service.

Let's take an evolutionary view of an object. Objects evolve through a set of states of existence in response to, and in cooperation with, other objects through well-defined interfaces. An object's response to a message from another object, or to an external event, is controlled by a strict set of rules, or *laws*, of behavior.

An object thus has two parts: external and internal. The external part of an object constitutes the visible properties of the object. These are the messages which the object understands. Each message includes the conditions which the object requires before responding to a message, called *preconditions*, and those conditions which the object will guarantee after responding to a message, called *postconditions*. Together, these conditions constitute the laws of behavior for the object. The internal part consists of the attributes and methods of the object.

We want to separate the external behavior of an object—the messages to which is responds—from the internal mechanisms for the behavior—the methods. Messages are linked to methods through a mechanism called *binding*, which will be formally defined later.

The external view of an object is an algebraic description of its operations and their results under certain conditions. This description of the external view is called the *functional schema* of the objects (Bunge 1977). The internal view of the object is model-based and must be proven to satisfy the conditions described in the external view.

The properties of an object can be filtered through a set of functions which yield subsets of those properties. Each point of view perceives a subset of the properties of the object. Different points of view may perceive different objects when they are actually beholding the same object. The properties perceived by a given point of view are only those relevant to that point of view. This notion is prevalent in software and forms the basis for the distinction between sufficiency and completeness.

The complete functional schema of an object X is defined as $X_m = \langle M, F \rangle$, where M is the set of all possible points of view, and $F = \langle f_i \mid f_i$ is a function on M and $i = 1, 2,... \rangle$ (F is an ordered tuple) where each f_i represents a property of the object expressed as a function. Each f_i is a function from a point of view in M to a domain of values v_i, denoted as $f_i: M \rightarrow v_i$. Each f_i thus represents an attribute or an operation. Each f_i which represents an attribute is called the *state function for attribute i* and returns the current value for the attribute.

Each point of view can have its own set of state functions and operations. For any given point of view, an object can appear to be in one and only one state at a time. When observed from multiple points of view, an object can appear to be in more than one state at the same time. This is only appearance, because the actual state of the object is the union of all of the apparent states in each point of view.

Classes of Objects

The fundamental unit in object-oriented software is the object. An object was defined as a set of properties—attributes and methods—and a set of functions which return the current values of each attribute relative to a specified point of view. The attributes and state functions are interchangeable, so you can use one or the other to represent both. Ignoring the attribute values, you can describe groups of objects by their sets of attributes and methods. In fact, you can use the set of attributes and methods to partition the set of objects into a (smaller) set of equivalence classes, which are called, simply, *classes*.

Partitioning a set of objects into equivalence classes is a standard set-theoretic operation. It is also *exactly* the operation used to group software objects into software classes. Booch (1994, p. 83) notes that the "structure and behavior of similar objects are defined by their common class." He defines a class as "a set of objects which share a common structure [attributes] and a common behavior [methods]." The relationship between a class and the objects within it can be stated from two points of view:

1. *Class*: The set of properties (attributes and methods) shared by a set of objects within an equivalence class.

2. *Object*: An instance of a class.

The concept of a class can be viewed in a variety of ways, all of which are equivalent:

- A class is a model-based theory of an object.
- The class defines a generic set of attributes and operations which apply to all objects which belong to the class.
- A class is a template for an object (Alencar and Gognen 1992) which is used to construct specific objects.
- A class is a functional schema for an object (Wand 1989).

The notions of classes and partitioning a set of objects will be formally defined after developing some additional concepts.

The Attributes of a Class

Now let's formalize the notions of an attribute, membership in a class, and the state space of a class. This discussion is in terms of classes rather than objects because these concepts apply to all objects in a class in the same way. When we discuss values of attributes and, by extension, states of objects a little later, we will be discussing particular objects, since only objects can have a current state.

First, define the various concepts in terms of an algebraic structure which best matches the empirical structure of the concept. Then, bring all of the concepts together into a single category.

Formally, an *attribute* is the name of a set of potential values, which is called an *attribute domain*, or simply, *domain*. The domain of an attribute defines its type. At times, it will be convenient to treat a domain as a class with a single attribute—feel free to do so. It doesn't matter semantically whether you use attribute domain terminology or class terminology, so there will be no indication when terms are switched. The class under discussion will be made clear by the context. However, a distinction will be made between attribute domains which exist in the problem domain and classes created by the designer.

The class may impose direct limitations on the possible values of an attribute. These limitations are called, collectively, the *class invariant*. In effect, they limit the potential values of an attribute to a subset of its domain. The class invariant may restrict the value of an attribute in combination with the values of other attributes. Limits imposed by the class invariant take one of four forms:

1. Strict limits on the set of potential values, such as $a = 1, 2$, or $a \in \{1, 5, 10, 15\}$.
2. Minimum and/or maximum values, such as $1 \leq a \leq 3$, $a \geq 3$, or $a \leq 100$.
3. Specific values, ranges, minimums, or maximums which depend on the current value of other attributes in the object.
4. Specific values, ranges, minimums, or maximums which depend on the current state of other objects.

The class invariant is a set of conditions, taken in conjunction, which must be satisfied by every object of the class in any steady state defined for the class. As in ontology, define a state as *unsteady* if any condition of the class invariant is violated. Objects enter unsteady states only in response to requests for service from other objects or from a source external to the application. The definition of a class must define the transition from every unsteady state to a steady state. These transitions are part of the defined behavior of the class.

Together, the attribute's domain (type) and the class invariant define the attribute's effective universe. For example, an attribute of type integer is limited to the set $\mathbb{Z}$ of integers. An attribute of type unsigned integer is limited to the set $\mathbb{N} \cup \{0\}$ of natural numbers plus zero. Both of these examples are also limited by the maximum values of each type imposed by the platform on which the software is running.

A *class* is an algebra $\langle A, f_i : i \in I \rangle$ consisting of a set A of attributes and a family $(f_i : i \in I)$ of operations (the class methods). Note that each element of the set A is a set of values, not just a particular value.

The *state space* for a class is a subset of the cross product of the attribute domain sets, or $SS \subseteq A^n$, $A^n = a_1 \times a_2 \times \cdots \times a_n$, $a_i \in A$. The state space consists of n-tuples where n is the cardinality of the set A. Certain n-tuples may not be allowed by the class invariant, and are thus excluded from the state space, hence our defining it as a subset of A^n. The size of the state space is a function of the number of attributes and the number of potential values each attribute can take. The cardinality of A^n places an upper bound on the size of the state space. However large, this size is finite, due either to limitations in the class invariant or in the platform architecture—we cannot yet represent infinity in a computer.

Structurally, the state space can be represented in a number of ways:

1. As a table with n columns, one for each attribute, with each row representing a potential state.
2. As a matrix with n columns, with each row representing a potential state.
3. As a vector space of n dimensions, with each vector representing a potential state.

Since all these views are mathematically equivalent, select the one you find the most convenient, based on your need for structure or analytical tools.

The domain of an attribute is independent of the class to which the attribute belongs. Since the domain is a set of values, any other attribute, in any class, whose domain contains the same set of values has the same domain due to the definition of set equality. This equality, and not just equivalence, is also independent of the name of the attribute. From this, we say that two attributes, regardless of their names in their respective classes, are the *same attribute* if and only if they share domains. Thus, you can define the *scope* of an attribute as the set of classes to which the domain belongs. Formally, the scope of an attribute a is:

$$S_a = \{c : \text{class} \mid b \in c \wedge a = b\} \tag{6.1}$$

Thus far, no category theory has been used to model any concepts. I do so now because you will be using this representation to build further pieces of the model. Define category **Class** with attribute domains as objects and set-theoretic functions as arrows. To the set of objects, add a new object which is the set-theoretic cross product of the attribute domains. In category theory, the cross product of two objects is an object, the cross product, and two arrows, the projection arrows from the cross product object to each of the other objects. So far, the category appears in the diagram

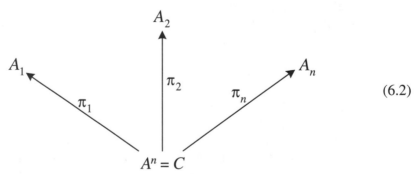

$$\tag{6.2}$$

shown without the identity arrows, where A_1, A_2,..., A_n represent the n attribute domains, and $A^n = C$ represents the state space of class C. The convention of labeling the state space object of a class with the name of the class will be adapted.

The Current Value of an Attribute

Classes have a state space and objects have state. The state of an object contains one and only one value for each of the attributes in the object's class. A given attribute has the same value in every point of view in which it appears. Because of the way the state space was defined, you know the attribute's value is a member of its domain set. You can select a state from within the state space using a selection function σ_j which gives you the jth state. The value of the ith attribute is provided by a projection function π_{ij} from this jth state into an attribute domain. You can think of π_{ij} as providing the value of the ith column of the jth row in a table or matrix. You can map the current value directly from the state space using a selection/projection function σ_{ij} which is defined as $\pi_{ij} \circ \sigma_j$. In categorical terms, the function σ_{ij} causes the lower triangle of the diagram

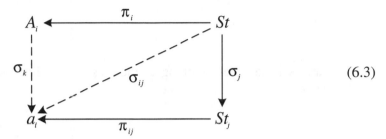

$$(6.3)$$

to commute.

The upper triangle represents an alternative view we won't use much. The arrow π_i is the projection function for the ith attribute and maps the state space of the class to the domain of the attribute. The arrow σ_k is a selection function mapping the attribute value to its domain set ($\sigma_k: A \rightarrow \{a\}$) and is required only to make the triangle commute. Note that k and j are not related since the attribute domain set is unordered and the state is an ordered n-tuple. As a notational convention to avoid clutter. The σ_k arrows will normally be left out of the diagrams.

The state for an object is determined by combining the attribute value diagrams for all of the attributes in a class. The diagram for a 2-attribute class, without the σ_k arrows, would be:

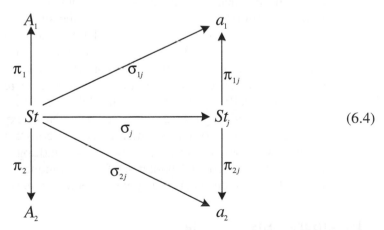

$$(6.4)$$

Other attributes can be added to the diagram in a similar manner. This diagram leads to two simplified diagrams which are equivalent to (6.4). The first is based on the state space,

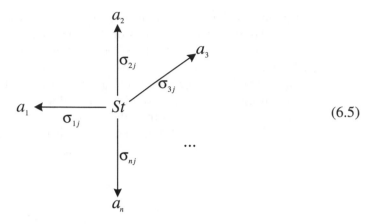

$$(6.5)$$

and is used when working at the class level. The second is based upon a given state,

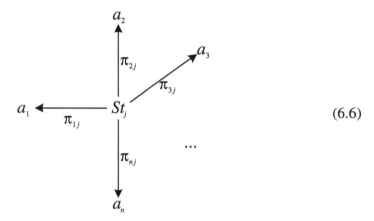

$$(6.6)$$

and is used when working at the object level. In diagram (6.6), the label for the object St_j can be changed to the name of the state taken from the problem domain.

At times, you are interested in isolating a set of states based on the values of a subset of attributes. When you do this, you create a state object which actually represents a set of tuples from the state space, all of which meet a set of selection criteria. You can use the selection operator from relational algebra, σ_θ (Ullman 1988), to specify these criteria in the label of the arrow. As defined, the notation σ_j selects the jth tuple from the state space. Now, expand this definition to include σ_θ where θ is a set of terms which consist of constants, attribute names, arithmetic comparison operators ($<$, $=$, $>$, $\leq$, $\neq$, $\geq$), and logical connectives ($\wedge$, $\vee$, $\neg$). The operator is defined in Chapter 4. This technique allows you to work with only those states which meet your given selection criteria.

The Operations of a Class

In ontology, an event causes an object to transition from one state to another, or possibly to the same state, as determined by its behavior. An event is formally modeled as an ordered pair $E = \langle St_1, St_2 \rangle$ where St_1 is the start state and St_2 is the end state (St_1 and St_2 may be the same state) (Wand 1989). The state St_2 is determined by the behavior of the object and the state St_1 according to the object model for the class of the object. Model the behavior of an object as a set of operations defined for the class. These class operations apply to all objects in the class.

Figure 6.1 shows a diagram for part of a class structure. Only the state space and a selected set of states are shown as objects. The op_i arrows in the figure represent the operations for the class. In this class, the operation or event op_1 causes an object in state St_1 to transition to state St_2. The operation op_1 has *no effect* upon the object if it is in any other state, since there is no arrow labeled op_1 which originates in any other state. The object $\varnothing$ in Figure 6.1 is the *null state*. The Create arrow represents the creation of the object, and the Destroy arrow represents its destruction.

Now let's define the operations Create and Destroy. These two operations are defined implicitly for every class. The Create operation assigns an identifier to a new object, places the object in scope, and leaves the object in the initial state defined for the class. The Create operation is thus a composite of three functions:

1. *AssignId*: Assigns a new identifier.
2. *InScope*: Adds the new identifier to a set, called *ActiveObjects*, which contains the identifiers for all of the currently active (in-scope) objects.
3. *Initialize*: Assigns to each attribute the value defined in the initial state for the class.

Each of these operations is formally defined after defining the form of an object's identifier and discussing the set *ActiveObjects*.

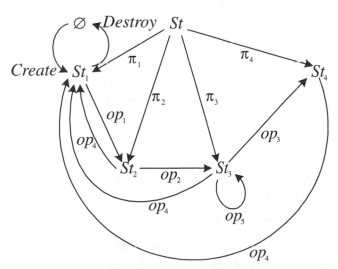

Figure 6.1 *A generic Class diagram.*

An object identifier has the form *class:n* where *class* is the name of the object's class and *n* is an ordinal number denoting the number of objects of the class which have been created. The number *n* is also an upper bound on the number of objects of the class which are currently in existence. It is an upper bound and not necessarily the actual number since some of the created objects may have been destroyed. Define a function id_x which maps the object *x* to its identifier.

The set *ActiveObjects* contains as elements the identifiers for all of the objects currently in scope. Thus, an object *x* is in scope if and only if its identifier is a member of *ActiveObjects* or:

$$x \text{ is in scope} \Leftrightarrow id_x \in \textit{ActiveObjects} \qquad (6.7)$$

Recall that an object is a member of one and only one class. Using this, you can partition the set *ActiveObjects* into sets which contain all of the active objects belonging to the same class. Formally, define a function Class( ) which takes an identifier and returns the class name portion, as in:

$$\text{Class}(\textit{List}{:}1) = \textit{List} \qquad (6.8)$$

Also define a function Instance( ) which takes an identifier and returns the ordinal portion, as in:

$$\text{Instance}(\textit{List}{:}1) = 1 \qquad (6.9)$$

Both Class( ) and Instance( ) are defined to accept either an object identifier, Id_x, or the object itself, *x*. The need for this little bit of polymorphism will become clear. Define the equivalence relation *E* which partitions *ActiveObjects* to be the relation:

$$E = \{a, b \in \textit{ActiveObjects} \mid aEb \Leftrightarrow \text{Class}(a) = \text{Class}(b)\} \qquad (6.10)$$

Since the partition for each class can be ordered by the ordinal portion of the identifier, define the ordering relation $>$ to be:

$$a > b \Leftrightarrow \text{Class}(a) = \text{Class}(b) \wedge \text{Instance}(a) > \text{Instance}(b) \qquad (6.11)$$

If, for two objects *a* and *b*, Class(*a*) $\neq$ Class(*b*), *a* and *b* are *not comparable*. Each class partition has a least upper bound, which is the instance with the greatest ordinal and also the most recently created object of the class. For a class *A*:

$$\text{lub}(A) = b \Rightarrow \forall\, a \cdot \text{Class}(a) = \text{Class}(b)$$

$$A \wedge \text{Instance}(a) \leqslant \text{Instance}(b) \qquad (6.12)$$

Note that Class(*a*) = Class(*b*) and Instance(*a*) = Instance(*b*) if and only if *a* and *b* are the same object:

$$\text{Class}(a) = \text{Class}(b) \wedge \text{Instance}(a) = \text{Instance}(b) \Leftrightarrow a = b \qquad (6.13)$$

You can determine the next identifier by taking the successor to the least upper bound of the class partition. For a new object *x*, you have

$$\text{Instance}(x) = \text{succ}(\text{Instance}(\text{lub}(\text{Class}(x)))) \tag{6.14}$$

where succ is the standard ordinal successor function.

You now have the tools needed to define the function AssignId

$$\text{AssignId}(x) = \text{Class}(x); \text{``:''}; \text{succ}(\text{Instance}(\text{lub}(\text{Class}(x)))) \tag{6.15}$$

which creates both components of the new object's identifier.

The function InScope simply adds the singleton set containing the identifier returned by AssignId to the set *ActiveObjects* through the set union operator:

$$\text{InScope}(x) = \text{ActiveObjects} \cup \{\text{AssignId}(x)\} \tag{6.16}$$

The function Initialize assigns to each attribute the value defined in the initial state for the class. Formally, let a_i be an attribute of class A such that all $a_i \in A$, $i = 1,..., n$, where n is the number of attributes in the class. Further, let initial(a_i) denote the value of a_i in the initial state for A. You then have:

$$\text{Initialize}(x) = \text{initial}(a_1); \text{initial}(a_2);...; \text{initial}(a_n) \tag{6.17}$$

You can now define Create(x) as

$$\text{Create}(x) = \text{InScope}(x); \text{Initialize}(x) \tag{6.18}$$

which in the standard functional composition notation is:

$$\text{Create}(x) = \text{Initialize}(x) \circ \text{InScope}(x) \tag{6.19}$$

The function Destroy(x) is much simpler: It merely removes the object's identifier from the set *ActiveObjects* via set difference:

$$\text{Destroy}(x) = \textit{ActiveObjects} \backslash \{Id_x\} \tag{6.20}$$

Putting All the Pieces Together

Now, let's combine parts of the previous diagrams to form a single representation of a class, a category called **Class**. The category **Class** consists of three types of objects and three types of arrows. The three types of objects are:

1. The state space for the class, labeled with the name of the class.
2. The domain sets for the attributes in the class, labeled with the name of the domain, not the name of the attribute, since a given domain may belong to more than one class as attributes with the same or different names, or more than once to the same class, as attributes with different names.
3. The steady states for objects of the class, labeled with the name for the state used in the application domain.

The three types of arrows are:

1. A projection arrow for each attribute, drawn from the state space to the attribute domain, labeled with the name of the attribute.

2. A selection arrow for each state, drawn from the state space to the state, labeled as σ_x where x is the name of the state.

3. An operation arrow for each event $E = \langle S_1, S_2 \rangle$ drawn from S_1 to S_2, labeled with the name of the method to which the operation corresponds.

There is a one-to-one mapping from the state transitions in the state model to the operation arrows in the category. It is permissible to draw one arrow for an operation for each pair of states for which it represents a valid event, whether or not it has a side effect. Thus, an arrow labeled op_1 may appear more than once in a diagram if the operation is valid in more than one state.

At times, it is informative to add a fourth type of object and arrow. The object represents specific values for specific attributes: constants or ranges of constants. The arrow is the projection function π_{ij} which maps a state to an attribute value. For convenience and to avoid clutter, leave out the σ_k arrows from the attribute domain to the attribute value. Include these new objects and arrows only when they present important information, such as when an attribute is limited to a single value in a given state. These new objects and arrows represent application domain constraints on the value of the attribute in a given state.

You can also identify an initial state for any object of a class by appending an * to the end of the state object label. The initial state for an object is the steady state an object has immediately after it is created. The initial state is exactly described by the postconditions of the Create operation for the class.

The category representation of a simple class *List* which represents a doubly-linked list is given as an example. For this example, assume that the list entries themselves are represented by a different class. The class *List* has, as attributes:

- *head*: A reference to the first entry object in the list.
- *tail*: A reference to the last entry object in the list.
- *current*: A reference to the most recently accessed entry object.
- *count*: A count of the number of entries currently in the list.

The domain for *count* is the set of positive integers and zero, and may have a specified maximum value. The domain for *head*, *tail*, and *current* is the set of valid references as defined for the platform on which this class is implemented. For many platforms, this is the set of positive integers and zero which can be represented in 32 bits or less.

The class *List* has, as methods:

- *AddEntry*: Attaches a given object to the list preceding the *head* entry, adjusting the attributes *tail*, *current*, and *count* as appropriate.
- *DropEntry*: Removes a given object from the list, adjusting the attributes *head*, *tail*, *current*, and *count*, as appropriate.

- *GetCurrent*: Returns the entry object referenced by the attribute *current*.
- *GetNext*: Returns the entry object which follows the entry referenced by the attribute *current* and adjusts *current* to indicate the retrieved object.
- *GetPrevious*: Returns the entry object which precedes the entry referenced by the attribute *current* and adjusts *current* to indicate the retrieved object.
- *GetHead*: Returns the entry object referenced by the attribute *head* and sets *current* to reference the same entry as *head*.
- *GetTail*: Returns the entry object referenced by the attribute *tail* and sets *current* to reference the same entry as *tail*.

The class *List* has four states:

- *Empty*: The list contains no entries: *head*, *tail*, and *current* are null references, and *count* = 0.
- *One*: The list contains one entry: *head*, *tail*, and *current* reference the same entry, and *count* = 1.
- *Two*: The list contains two or more entries, but less than the maximum number of entries as determined by the domain of *count* and the maximum specified in the class invariant: *head* and *tail* refer to different entries, *current* may refer to any entry in the list, and *count* equals an integer representing the number of entries in the list.
- *Full*: The list contains the maximum number of entries as determined by the domain of *count* and the class invariant: If this maximum value of *count* is greater than one, *head* and *tail* refer to different entries, and *current* can refer to any entry in the list. If the maximum value of *count* is one, *head*, *tail*, and *current* refer to the same entry (the states *One* and *Full* are the same). In either case, *count* contains an integer representing the maximum value allowed by its domain as constrained by the class invariant.

The initial state for the class *List* is *Empty*. The diagram for the class *List* is shown in Figure 6.2. As you can see, a diagram for even a simple class can get pretty ugly in a hurry. The main reason is that both static and dynamic elements are shown. Most object-oriented methods create separate models for different elements of the design for this very reason. The intent here is to build a unified mathematical model of a class and its objects, including how they are structured and how they behave, not to develop a new diagram notation for designing classes and applications. The model is supported by all of the currently available object modeling notations.

In category theory, each arrow f in a category is unique since it has a unique pair $\langle \text{dom } f, \text{cod } f \rangle$. In a state model for a class, it is possible to have an arrow labeled f with several pairs $\langle \text{dom } f, \text{cod } f \rangle$, which violates the uniqueness of arrows. To avoid this problem, label each operation arrow in a class category as

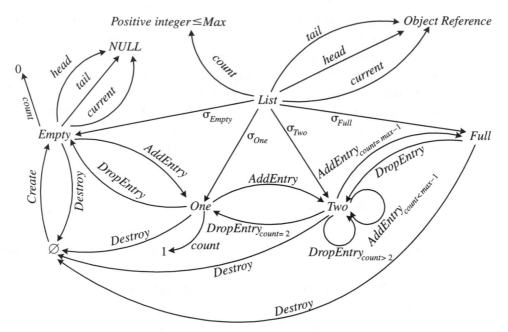

Figure 6.2 *A diagram for the class* List.

$op\langle$dom op, cod $op\rangle$ where op is the name of the operation, the label of the source object replaces dom op, and the label of the sink object replaces cod op. Thus, in the example, the full label for the arrow DropEntry: *One* → *Empty* is Drop-Entry$\langle$*One, Empty*$\rangle$.

In the category **Class**, the Create message is represented as an arrow from the null state $\varnothing$ to the initial state defined for the class. The Destroy message is represented as an arrow from any state in which destruction of the object is allowed to the null state $\varnothing$. In the example, the Create message is the arrow Create: $\varnothing$ → *Empty*, and the Destroy message is all of the arrows Destroy: x → $\varnothing$ where x is any state at which a Destroy arrow originates.

The formal description of the state model is derived in two ways: from the diagram to the operation specification or from the operation specification to the diagram. Going from diagram to specification, the defining attribute values in the states at which an operation arrow begins are the preconditions for the operation. If an operation appears as an arrow between more than one pair of states, the preconditions for the operation are the distributed intersection of the definitions of all of the states at which the arrow starts. Likewise, the postconditions are defined by the distributed intersection of the definitions for the states at which the operation arrow terminates.

Given a specification of an operation, you can derive its role in the diagram. The states from which an operation arrow can originate form a set whose distributed intersection is a superset of the operation's preconditions. Likewise, the states at which an operation arrow may terminate form a set whose distributed intersection is a superset of the operation's postconditions. Whether you start with a diagram or the formal specification depends on your preferences as a designer and the information available to you.

OPERATIONS ON OBJECTS

An object's set of operations is its methods. These are operations *of* an object (or class). Each type of object (class) has its own defined set of operations. The operations of an object are completely determined by the class to which it belongs.

In contrast, the operations you can perform *on* an object are universal to all objects. There are three such operations: message passing, message binding, and state transition. The mechanisms which enable and perform these operations are defined and provided by the software development environment. They are usually defined in the language specification, but may be provided by third-party software such as an object request broker.

Message passing is the only mechanism an object can use to interact with another object. Objects request services of each other by means of passing messages. The contents of any particular message, and the expected response, are controlled by a contract between the sending and receiving objects. These contracts are controlled by the designer and are part of the interface between the two objects. Contracts may be explicitly defined or left as an implicit part of the interface. An object receiving a message may change its state as a result of the message. It may also originate messages to other objects to help perform the requested service.

The receipt of a message triggers the second of the operations: *message binding*. The purpose of message binding is to match the name and contents of a message (the *message signature*) to the name and parameter list of a method (the *method signature*). This matching process is subject to a strict set of rules which are usually defined by the programming language used. Generally, the methods of all superclasses are included in this process, since a subclass behaves as if the methods of its superclasses are defined within the subclass itself. This binding may occur at compile or translation time (*static binding*), or at run time (*dynamic binding*).

At a logical level, the binding operation can be described in terms of preconditions. A message is matched to a method when it satisfies all of the preconditions for the method, including the structural requirements. This view of binding is derived from the method used in the formal specification language Object-Z (Rose 1992). The preconditions for a method of a given name are formed from the conjunction of the preconditions for the service—those specified in the contract—and the successful one-to-one mapping of the contents of the message to the parameters of the method. Since a method signature must be unique within the object's class, this process is deterministic.

Thus, you can know, by looking at the contents of a message, which method will be invoked, if indeed any are invoked. If a match is found for a given message, the matching method is executed. If no match can be found, the behavior of the system is undefined in our model, but is nearly always defined in the software development environment.

The execution of a method may trigger the third and final operation on an object: *state transition*. An object may lie only in a lawful state. A lawful state is one which satisfies all of the class invariants (Wand 1989). When a response to an event causes an object to occupy an unlawful state, the object will cause its own transition to a lawful state which is uniquely determined by the unlawful state. Lawful states are called steady and unlawful states are unsteady. These state-to-state relationships are part of the laws of behavior for the object. In this sense, state transitions are unary operations which are triggered, indirectly, by the object's response to a message. Thus, sending a message to an object is a sequence of two, three, or four universal operations: message passing, message binding, and zero, one, or two state transitions.

The message passing mechanism requires a way to indicate that a method sends a message to another object as a side effect. It is convenient to indicate such an occurrence in the method's postconditions. Use the notation $\lambda x.y\langle a_i \rangle_{i \in I}$ to denote that message y is sent to object x (x is the object identifier, not the class name) with parameters $\langle a_i \rangle_{i \in I}$. I is an ordinal and i denotes the parameter's position in an ordered I-tuple. You can also denote the message as the tuple $\langle y, \langle a_i \rangle_{i \in I}, x \rangle$. This latter notation will be useful as the categorical models are defined.

The binding mechanism requires two categories: one of a message and one of a method. Once a message is sent, the binding mechanism must perform two tasks, in order. First, it must determine if the object to which the message was sent is in scope. Second, if the object is in scope, the binding mechanism must determine whether the receiving object can understand the message—that is, whether it has a method with a signature which matches the message's signature.

A message can be represented as a category with the message parameters as objects and selection functions as arrows. A message is a sequence consisting of the name of the requested service, a parameter for each atom of the message contents, and the identifier of the object to receive the message. The category contains as an additional category object, the message itself. The general form of a message is the ordered tuple $\langle a_1, a_2, ..., a_n \rangle$ where a_1 is the name of the requested service, $a_2, ..., a_n - 1$ are the message contents, and a_n is the identifier for the receiving object. This is the notation previously introduced with $a_1 = y$ and $a_n = x$; its purpose will become clear in a moment. The diagram for the category **Message** is:

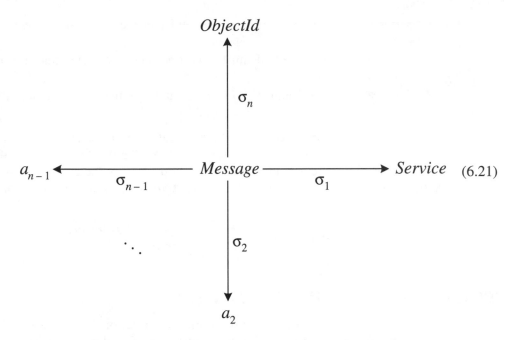

$$(6.21)$$

A method can also be represented as a category with the method name and parameters as objects and selection functions as arrows. Like message atoms, the parameters of a method can be data items of any type. The general form of a method is an ordered m-tuple $\langle p_1, p_2,..., p_m \rangle$ where p_1 is the name of the method and $p_2,..., p_m$ are the method parameters. The diagram for the category **Method** is:

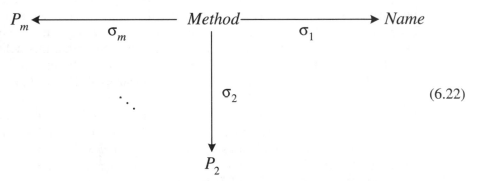

$$(6.22)$$

The similarity between the message and method diagrams is deliberate. The message binding mechanism is a functor bind: **Message** $\rightarrow$ **Method** which maps message atoms and selection arrows $1,..., n - 1$ to parameters and selection arrows $1,..., m$. The atom a_n and its arrow σ_n, which represent the identifier of the receiving object, are stripped out of the message by the message passing mechanism which determines whether the object is in scope. Three obvious preconditions for the binding operation are:

1. *Service* = *Name*: That is, atom a_1 and parameter p_1 must have the same value.

2. $m = n - 1$: The method must have one less parameter than the message has atoms.

3. For $2 \leq i \leq n - 1$ and $2 \leq j \leq m$, a_i and p_j must be the same type for all $i = j$.

When an object is created, its identifier is added to the set *ActiveObjects*. When the object is deleted, its identifier is removed from *ActiveObjects*. Thus, the function to determine whether an object is in scope is a predicate which states that the object's identifier is indeed a member of *ActiveObjects*. You can formalize this as a Boolean function:

$$\text{scope}(x) = \begin{cases} true & \text{iff } x \in ActiveObjects \\ false & \text{otherwise} \end{cases} \qquad (6.23)$$

THE CATEGORY *DESIGNSTATE*

Class relationships define possible or permissible relationships between objects of the classes. An object relationship is an instance of a class relationship. Objects cannot be related in ways that are not included in the set of class relationships. Booch and Rumbaugh define in the Unified Modeling Language (Booch and Rumbaugh 1995) two types of object relationships: generalization and association. To these, I add aggregation and message links.

You now have all the structures needed to model all of the components of a design in a fixed configuration. This fixed configuration is called a *design state* because changes to the configuration cause the design to change state. The current state of a design is modeled as a category, called **DesignState**, with class categories as objects and class relationships as arrows. Note that this definition defines the class relationships as functors, and they are indeed functors.

The diagram for a simple design might appear as in Figure 6.3. This design is a portion of a real-time airlift application. The diagram contains examples of all four types of relationships. The arrows labeled (1) and (2) represent the generalizations. The class *ShipmentItem* is a generalization of both *CargoItem* and *Passenger*. The association relationships, *Has*, *Flies*, *Maps-To*, and *Tracks*, all indicate semantic relationships between objects of the classes involved. The aggregations, *Includes*, *Moves*, *Carries*, and *Indicates*, show whole-part relationships between objects of the classes involved. The message links, Create (two of them), and GetPosition, show examples of communication pathways between objects of the classes involved. Many potential message links are not shown in this example.

The category **DesignState** represents a unification of two or more design models, depending on which design method is used. It is not likely that you would want to use such a cluttered diagram for designing an application. Its purpose, rather, is to serve as the basis for tools and techniques to analyze, measure, and simulate the structure and behavior of the design.

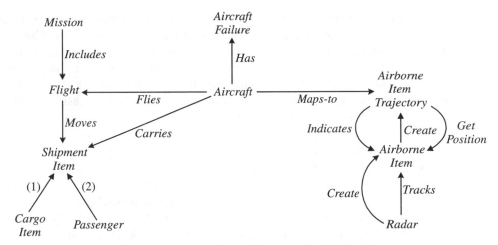

Figure 6.3 *A portion of a sample application.*

To complete the definition of the category **DesignState**, you need to define the identity and composable pairs of arrows. For each object (of the category **Class**), there is a mapping *self*: $a \rightarrow a$ which serves as the identity arrow, which is denoted by an arrow labeled with the name of the class, as in:

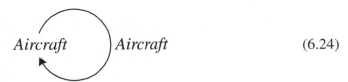

(6.24)

The only composable pairs of arrows in this category are sequences of generalization relationships. When a class is a subclass, and also has one or more subclasses, it is legitimate to draw composition arrows from the lowest-level subclass directly to the highest-level superclass. Composition arrows do not make sense for any other type of relationship.

A sequence of association arrows has no meaning in a class model. It is possible, even likely, that at any given time, a given object of the class which is the codomain of one arrow and the domain of another participates in only one of the two associations. The only way you can have an arrow from class A to class C is if there is an association between objects of A and C, in which case you would have already such an arrow, but it would *not* be a composite arrow.

It is true that an aggregation is a form of nesting of objects. It is also true that nesting of objects is not limited in the number of levels to which the nesting can be carried out. Nevertheless, it is not legitimate to compose aggregation arrows since a containing object has no knowledge of the contents of any object it contains. In other words, you can define a pair of aggregation arrows $g_1: A \rightarrow B$ and $g_2: B \rightarrow C$, but you cannot define a composite arrow $g_2 g_1: A \rightarrow C$ because A has no knowledge of C. This is as it should be. The only way to have such an arrow $g_3 \colon A \to C$ is for an object of A to contain an object of C, in which case you already have an arrow $g \colon A \to C$, but it is *not* the composite of g_2 with g_1.

The same applies to message links. There might well be an arrow $m_1 \colon A \to B$ and an arrow $m_2 \colon B \to C$. The only way to have an arrow $m \colon A \to C$ is for some method of A to send a message to an object of C, in which case you already have an arrow $m \colon A \to C$, but it is not $m_2 m_1$.

To show that **DesignState** is indeed a category, you must show that the arrows, in this case relationships between classes, are true morphisms. Further, you must show that these morphisms are in fact functors between instances of the category **Class**. It may be hard to imagine static class relationships as morphisms, but they are. This is shown informally, rather than through formal proof.

Generalization, association, and aggregation can be formally defined as set-theoretic relations. These definitions use variables A, B, . . . to represent classes. Remember, a class is a set of properties, so it is not inconsistent to refer to a class with a set name. Use f, g, . . . to represent operations, use a, b, . . . to represent objects, and use x, y, . . . to represent attributes of a class or object. To show that object a is a member of class A, write $a \in A$. To show that attribute x is an attribute of class A, write $x \in A$. To show that operation f is a method of class A, write $f \in A$. To refer to the value of attribute x in object a, write $a.x$. To request the service f from object a, write $\lambda a.f(\ )$.

Generalization

A *generalization* is the relationship between a superclass and its subclasses. A class may participate in at most one relationship as a superclass; it may have many subclasses, but it relates to each one in the same way. A class may participate in many generalizations as a subclass. The direction of the relationship is from the specialization (subclass) to the generalization (superclass) and reflects the direction of the object-to-object dependency and class-to-class visibility requirements. For our purposes, a strict supertype/subtype relationship is implied by a generalization relationship. This restriction allows an instance of a subtype to be substituted for an instance of the supertype. This is principle is sometimes called the *Liskov substitution principle* (Liskov 1987, although she attributes the principle to an unpublished thesis by Leavens). This restriction also has implications for resolving name conflicts and redefining operations. A subtype assumes, or *inherits*, the properties of its supertype(s) without them being defined in the subtype (Zuse and Fetcke 1995).

Another form of generalization, called *derivation* (Cusack and Rafsanjani 1992), builds a class from a superclass for the sole purpose of reusing the superclass. This form of generalization is ignored for two reasons:

1. It generally violates the Liskov substitution principle.
2. It can be implemented more effectively and more efficiently through the use of delegation via association or aggregation relationships.

Let A and B be separate classes. In ontological terms, A is a generalization of B if all of the properties of an object of A are in an object of B:

1. $A \subseteq B$.
2. $A \cap B = A$.

This is not to say that class B subsumes class A, as they remain separate classes. In our designs, the properties of A are not strictly members of B, just represented as such by using the generalization relationship. The combination of properties occurs at the moment of instantiation. That is, an object of class B will appear to have all of the properties of class B plus those of class A while the class structure keeps A and B separate.

We can represent a generalization relationship between classes A and B, where A is the generalization of B, categorically with the diagram

$$A \longleftarrow_{\sigma_A} B \tag{6.25}$$

where σ_A is the selection function which pulls the attributes and operations of A out of B. The direction of the arrow is designed to indicate the dependency of class B on class A, and thus the requirement that the definition of A be visible to B.

Association

An *association* is a relationship between classes that implies a set of connections between objects of the classes (Booch and Rumbaugh 1995). An association has a name and two or more roles, one for each class which participates in the relationship. A class may have multiple roles in an association; each is distinct. The roles are used to navigate the association. That is, they can be used to establish the direction of the association. This direction may be the same as, or opposite to, the direction of the object dependency and class visibility requirements. Associations may be subject to three kinds of restrictions (Booch and Rumbaugh 1995):

1. *Multiplicity* (cardinality): Controls how many instances of a class can participate with one instance of another class.
2. *Ordering*: Specifies whether the set of instances of one class attached to one instance of another class is ordered or unordered.
3. *Mutability*: Indicates whether an association can be reassigned to another instance of a class once it has been created, as opposed to destroying an association and building a new one.

Let A and B be separate classes, and X a nonempty subset of the attributes of A. An object $a \in A$ is associated with one or more objects $b \in B$ if there is a set Y of attributes of B such that Y is a permutation of X in terms of domains: An attribute of Y has the same domain as a attribute of X but may have a different name. That is, there is a mapping $f: X \rightarrow Y$ which is bijective and preserves domains but not necessarily names. Since attributes are arrows from a class state space to a domain set, the mapping $f: X \rightarrow Y$ is really a bijection between sets of arrows. Thus, the arrows in X in the category representation of A will have the same codomains as the arrows in Y in the category representation of B, but may have different labels. For a pair of objects $a \in A$ and $b \in B$, the attributes must also have the same values.

These conditions are formally expressed as:

$$\forall x \in X, y \in Y \cdot \exists a \in A, b \in B \mid X \subseteq A \wedge Y \subseteq B \wedge \text{cod } x = \text{cod } y \wedge a.x = b.y$$

$$(6.26)$$

The sets X and Y are called the *anchor sets* for the relationship. Since these two sets are equivalent in terms of domains, which is close enough for our purposes, we can refer to either one as *the* anchor set.

Association relationships can be considered as natural joins between relational tables. Let the classes A and B be two such tables. The objects of class A are the rows in its table representation. Likewise for the objects of class B. Classes A and B are associated by a set of attributes X and the association is written $A_X \bowtie B_X$. If more than two classes participate in an association, such as A, B, and C, where B is an associative class, we write $A_X \bowtie B_{X,Y} \bowtie C_Y$. We depend on the rules of the natural join to associate a row in table A with only those rows in table B for which the values of each attribute in X are the same, and likewise for B, C, and Y.

We can represent an association between classes A and B categorically by adding an arrow f representing the association such that the diagram

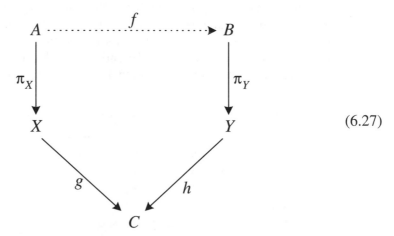

$$(6.27)$$

commutes. In this diagram, the (category) objects X and Y are the anchor sets as previously defined. The arrows π_X and π_Y project the respective anchor sets from the classes A and B. The (category) object C is a set of attribute domains and indicate that the anchor sets X and Y share the same set of attribute domains. C is a subset of the intersection of the codomains of the attribute arrows of A and B.

Formally, start with the diagram

$$A \xrightarrow{\pi_X} X \xrightarrow{g} C \qquad (6.28)$$

where X is the anchor set of attributes, π_X is the set of projection functions from the class A, g is the set of arrows from X to the domain sets

$$g = \{\mathrm{hom}(x, c) \mid x \in X \wedge c \in C\} \qquad (6.29)$$

and C is the set of domain objects for the attributes in X, or the set of codomains for the arrows in g.

Likewise, you can use the diagram

$$B \xrightarrow{\pi_Y} Y \xrightarrow{h} C \qquad (6.30)$$

where Y is the anchor set of attributes, π_Y is the set of projection functions from the class B, h is the set of arrows from Y to the domain sets

$$h = \{\mathrm{hom}(y, d) \mid y \in Y \wedge d \in D\} \qquad (6.31)$$

and D is the set of domain objects for the attributes in Y, or the set of codomains for the arrows in h.

One of the conditions of the association relationship is that the attributes in each anchor set be drawn from the same set of domains. Thus, $C = D$ and we can define g and h as

$$g = \{\mathrm{hom}(x, c) \mid x \in X \wedge c \in C\} \qquad (6.32a)$$

and

$$h = \{\mathrm{hom}(y, c) \mid y \in Y \wedge c \in C\} \qquad (6.32b)$$

The arrow f is drawn from A to B or B to A as appropriate to reflect the dependency and visibility requirements of the relationship.

Aggregation

An aggregation is a special case of association with the connotation of "whole-part" (Booch and Rumbaugh 1995). In an aggregation, one object serves as an attribute of another. It indicates that the association is transitive and antisymmetric. It also indicates, in some cases, that the lifetime of the parts are dependent upon the lifetime of the whole. A multiplicity of one indicates a *physical* aggregation in which a part is physically contained in a single whole and cannot be part of more than one whole. A multiplicity of many indicates a *catalog* aggregation in which a part in a catalog may be used in many assemblies. These definitions are from Booch and Rumbaugh (1995).

I digress to say a word about the lifetimes of the parts and the whole. It is true that in most real-world cases, the lifetime of a part *as a component of the whole* is dependent upon the lifetime of the whole. When the whole ceases to exist, the role of the part as a component also ceases to exist. Parts often survive their composite (the whole) allowing a specific part to become a component in another composite, all the while adhering to the requirement that a part be a component in only one composite *at a time*. When an assembly of parts is disassembled, the assembly ceases to exist, but the parts themselves may very well survive. Anyone who has taken parts from one machine and used them on another has created an example of just this situation.

It is sometimes the case that the part itself ceases to exist. For example, when a customer order record is deleted from a database, the line item records for the order are deleted as well.

Whether the parts survive as independent objects or are destroyed along with the whole should be a deliberate design decision and a prominent part of the design. Either way, it is not an inherent part of the aggregation relationship.

The direction of an aggregation is from the whole to the part. This follows the direction of both the object dependency and class visibility requirements.

Let A and B be separate classes. Class A is an *aggregate* or *composite* and class B is a *component* if A has as an attribute an object of class B: $B \in A$. Classes A and B remain distinct. Objects of class B may be created and destroyed at the request of the objects of class A which contain them, or the B objects may be "owned" by other objects. Aggregation and association differ in that in association, two objects *share* a set of attributes, while in aggregation one object *is* an attribute of the other.

Categorically, the aggregation of class B into class A is represented by the diagram:

$$A \xrightarrow{\quad\quad\quad\quad\quad\quad} B \qquad\qquad (6.33)$$
$$\pi_B$$

The arrow π_B represents the projection of the attribute, an object b of B, to its domain set, the class B. This indicates that any object of class B can be the "value" of the attribute b in an object of class A, subject to the constraints of the class invariant for A. The direction of the arrow also indicates the dependency and visibility requirements of the relationship.

Message Link

A method of one object invokes an operation of another object of the same or different class by sending it a message. The relationship is *Sender*. Method $\rightarrow$ *Receiver*.Message. A *message link* between two classes indicates that at some time, an object of one class can send a message to an object of the other. Message links define the lines of interobject communication. They determine the set of potential messages between objects. Message links are analogous to the phone lines between two points: The presence of a line means it is possible to initiate a call between them; it says nothing about whether such a call is ever made.

In software, the message links are usually identified by the existence of actual messages between objects of the two classes. This is *usually* the case, but not *always* the case. The direction of a message link is from the message sender to the message receiver. This follows both the object dependencies and the class visibility requirements.

Method selection and binding take place within the context of the receiver. Two conditions may prevent the receipt of a message:

1. The receiving object is not in scope.
2. The receiving object does not understand the message—that is, it contains no method to which the message can be bound.

A receiving object is under no obligation to respond to messages which it does not understand. An object which receives a message it does understand is obligated to satisfy the postconditions defined in its external interface subject to the constraints of the preconditions and invariants.

Categorically, a message link is represented by the diagram

$$A \xrightarrow{\quad Msg \quad} B \qquad (6.34)$$

which indicates that an object of class A can send a message to an object of class B. The arrow is labeled with the name of the message. The arrow can start and end at the same class. When this occurs, the arrow *cannot* be interpreted as the identity arrow. The arrow direction reflects the relationship dependency and visibility requirements.

THE CATEGORY *DESIGN*

By modeling the state of a design as a single category, rather than separate models, you create objects for a category in which the arrows are operations which modify the design. This new category, called **Design**, provides the means to:

1. Model the effects of design changes on the state of the design.
2. Trace the history of the design through its previous states.
3. Assess the impact of a potential design change before the change is actually made.

Since this category can become quite large (it is the only category in our model which can actually approach an infinite size), let's adopt the practice of including only those states in which the design has been in the past, and the operations which connect them, plus any of the potential states which would result from changes being considered. You may, if you choose, include states which resulted from changes considered but rejected. No matter how large this category becomes, you, as the designer, will never be working with more than a handful of states and operations at any one time: the current state, a number of changes you may be considering, and the states which would result from those changes.

Operations on Classes

As you work with a design, you modify the set of classes, the set of relationships between classes, or the structure of one or more classes. In doing so, you make use of a surprisingly small number of atomic operations. Each operation causes the state of the design to change. Define these operations as functors which map one design state to another.

Two types of operations are defined: those which alter the internal structure of a class or the set of classes and those which alter the set of relationships between classes. Each type of operation is subject to different sets of constraints and has a different effect on the design.

There are four basic operations which modify the set of classes or alter the structure of a class:

1. Add a new class to the set.
2. Combine two classes into a single class.
3. Extract a subset of attributes and/or methods from a class to form two new, disjoint classes.
4. Delete a class from the design.

One common change to a design is to add or remove properties to or from an existing class. I model these two operations as compositions of two of the four basic operations. Adding properties is the composition of adding a new class composed of the desired new properties and combining this new class with the target class. Removing properties is the composition of extracting the properties from the target class and deleting the new extracted class.

I chose to model these operations as compositions for several reasons. When you add a property to a class, you face two situations: The property is not already part of the design or some other class already contains the property. Only in the first case is it necessary to complete both of the composite operations as defined. If the property is already part of the design, you need only perform the class combination operation. This will be made clearer when these operations are formalized. Likewise, when you remove a property from a class, you do not always want to remove the property from the design. When this is the case, there is no need to perform the class deletion portion of the composite operation. All of the component operations are required as separate atomic operations. Adding new composite operations would lead to nonatomic operations, which you do not want. In addition, since you don't always perform both parts of these composite operations, you would have to add four such operations, none of which would be atomic.

Many of these operations make use of a class which consists of a single property. These singleton classes form the basic building blocks of more complex classes which are more useful. You will see that a given singleton class can be used in more than one nonsingleton class. Using a singleton class more than once also yields an inventory of where and how that property is used. It points out and highlights the scope of the property contained within the singleton class.

There are five basic operations you can use to alter the set of class relationships:

1. Add a generalization.
2. Add an association.
3. Add an aggregation.
4. Add a message link.
5. Drop a relationship.

There are four separate add operations because each is subject to a different set of preconditions. The preconditions for each add operation deal with the structural requirements for each class involved in the new relationship. These requirements will be defined as each relationship type is discussed. The drop operation is subject to no preconditions and can be applied to any type of relationship.

In order to use a class as a subclass, it must behave as if it possesses all of the properties of the superclass. If the superclass were not available, it must make sense for its properties to be physically located in the intended subclasses. This is not so much a structural limitation as it is a design guideline. There is no way to enforce this guideline mathematically. Once the relationship is established, the design will behave as if this condition is true, regardless of whether this is legitimate behavior.

In an association, a set of attributes in each class serves to anchor the relationship. Usually, the identifier or key value of one class appears as an attribute in the other. Sometimes, however, the anchoring attributes are not keys in either class. Regardless of their status as keys, the attributes which make up the anchor set must meet the conditions of an anchor set as defined earlier. The attributes of the classes which will participate in the new association must be such that the anchor sets can be formed before the association is added to the design.

To form an aggregation, the component class must be a legitimate attribute of the composite class.

One precondition for establishing a message link is that a method of the originating class requires the services of the receiving class. You need to know, as a designer, that messages represented by the link are required. In addition, the message described by the link must correspond to a method signature in the receiving class.

To satisfy the preconditions for any of these operations, you may use one of the class operations to alter the classes, then add the new relationship. Most often, however, the preconditions will already be met since class structures are built from information gained during analysis activities. I have found value in the preconditions as a check to see if I have all of the attributes and methods in a class before I complete the design activity. These preconditions also make it possible to build more intelligent tools—tools that can begin to understand the design in a context other than a simple collection of connected objects. The connections will begin to have some meaning to the tool.

Now, let's define formally the operations on classes. All of these operations are arrows between objects in the category **Design** and functors between **DesignState** categories. As functors, each operation has two components: one which operates on classes and one which operates on arrows between classes. Since you also model classes as categories, the component which operates on classes must also be a functor between **Class** categories with two of its own components. One component maps attribute domains in one class category to attribute domains in the other and states in one category to states in the other. The other component maps the arrows between states and between states and attribute domains to their counterparts in the new category. Some of these mappings may cause objects and/or arrows to be dropped, while others may cause objects and/or arrows to be added.

Add a Class

This operation adds a new class category to the design, which requires adding a new object to the category **DesignState**. Denote this operation as $D_2 = D_1 +_C C$. As a functor, the operation adds a new state space, a new set of states, and potentially a new set of attribute domains, along with the appropriate arrows to fully define the new class as a category. The basic model for this operation is set union.

For objects, the operator takes the union of the set of objects in the current design state (classes, or state spaces, attribute domains, and states) with the set of objects to be added (a class, or state space, attribute domains, and states) yielding the objects in a new design state. For arrows, the operator takes the union of the set of arrows in the current design state with the set of arrows to be added, yielding the arrows in the new design state. Note that neither of these operations is necessarily additive, just as set union is not always additive.

Let's work an example. The current design consists of, among other things, two classes A and B, linked by an aggregation relationship, as shown in the diagram:

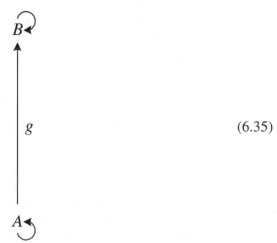

$$g \qquad\qquad (6.35)$$

You wish to add to the design the class C. Eventually, you want to relate C to the other classes in some way, which will require adding some relationships (discussed later). For now, you just want to understand the semantics of adding a class. The new design state is given by the diagram:

(6.36)

And you are done: you have added a new object, the class C, and one new arrow, id_c.

While complete, this definition is not very interesting, nor is it very helpful. To understand what you've really done, it is necessary to look "under the covers." To do this, "explode" each of the class objects into its full category representation. For our purposes, all of the activity involves the state space and attribute domains, so leave the state objects and operation arrows out for the moment. You will discover that this operation is not nearly as simple as it appears.

Start from the beginning, with the class A and its attribute domains, which is represented by the diagram:

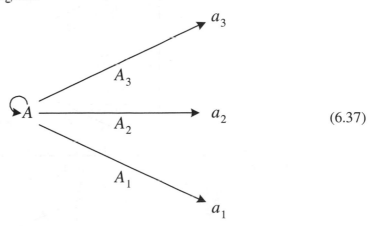

(6.37)

The diagram for class B, also ignoring its states and operations for the moment, is:

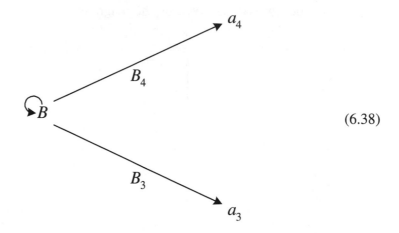

(6.38)

Combining these two diagrams, and adding the aggregation from A to B, you get

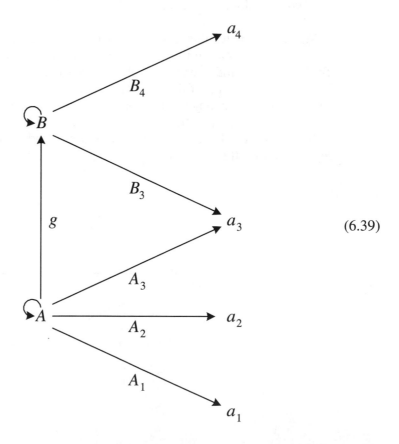

(6.39)

which is a representation of (a portion of) our design with each class "exploded" to expose (part of) its internal structure. The important fact that classes A and B share attribute domain a_3 is represented by showing one object a_3 with arrows from each of the state spaces A and B to a_3. Each arrow is labeled with the name of the attribute, so in our design, the domain a_3 is referred to by the name A_3 in class A and B_3 in class B.

You now want to add class C, which is given by the diagram:

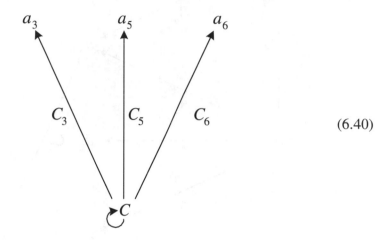

$$(6.40)$$

For objects, you have the operation:

$$\{A, B, a_1, a_2, a_3, a_4\} \cup \{C, a_3, a_5, a_6\}$$
$$= \{A, B, C, a_1, a_2, a_3, a_4, a_5, a_6\} \tag{6.41a}$$

For arrows, the operation is:

$$\{id_A, id_B, A_1, A_2, A_3, B_3, B_4\} \cup \{id_C, C_3, C_5, C_6\}$$
$$= \{id_A, id_B, id_C, A_1, A_2, A_3, B_3, B_4, C_3, C_5, C_6\} \tag{6.41b}$$

Combining these, you have $DS_1 +_C C = DS_2$ as shown by the diagram

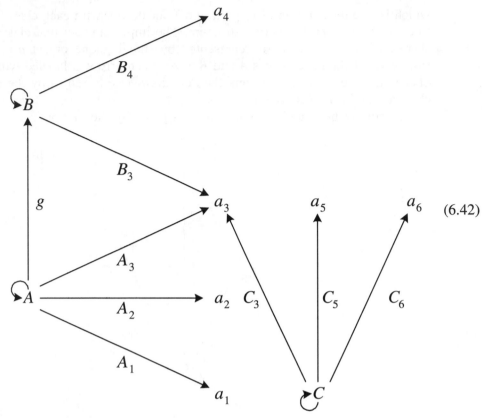

(6.42)

where
$$DS_2 = \langle \text{Obj}(DS_1) \cup [\text{Obj}(C) \backslash \text{Obj}(DS_1)], \text{Arr}(DS_1) \cup [\text{Arr}(C) \backslash \text{Arr}(DS_1)] \rangle \quad (6.43)$$
You can summarize this in pictures by:

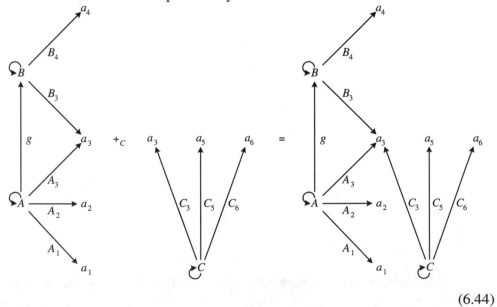

(6.44)

Drop a Class

This operation deletes a class category as an object from the category **DesignState**. Denote this operation by $DS_2 = DS_1 -_C C$. As a functor between two design states, this operation removes a state space, a set of states, a set of operation arrows, a set of attribute arrows, and potentially a set of attribute domains. The basic model for the operation is set subtraction, with a twist.

Viewing classes as unexploded categories, dropping a class is simple set subtraction. To delete the class C from the design state

$$(6.45)$$

simply remove the entire category C from the design state:

$$\{A, B, C\} -_C \{C\} = \{A, B, C\} \backslash \{C\} = \{A, B\} \qquad (6.46)$$

Going under the covers again, it gets more complicated. Any attribute domains not used by any other class can be deleted along with the rest of the objects in the category for the deleted class. But, any attribute domains which are also used by at least one other class cannot be deleted. You can delete only the attribute arrows from the deleted class's state space to these attribute domains. Thus, when viewing classes in exploded form, you are no longer dealing with straight set subtraction.

As an example, delete the class C added in the previous example. Start with the design state:

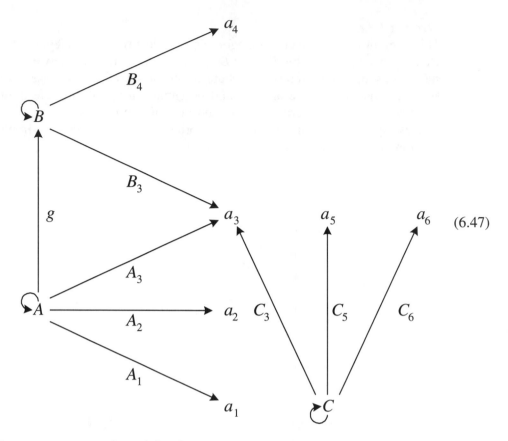

$$(6.47)$$

You can represent class A by the set

$$A = \{A, a_1, a_2, a_3\} \qquad (6.48)$$

class B by the set

$$B = \{B, a_3, a_4\} \qquad (6.49)$$

and class C by the set:

$$C = \{C, a_3, a_5, a_6\} \qquad (6.50)$$

Our current design state DS_1 can be represented by the equation:

$$DS_1 = A \cup B \cup C = \{A, a_1, a_2, a_3\} \cup \{B, a_3, a_4\}$$
$$\cup \{C, a_3, a_5, a_6\} \qquad (6.51)$$

Deleting the class C is the operation

$$(A \cup B \cup C)\backslash C = A \cup B = \{A, a_1, a_2, a_3\} \cup \{B, a_3, a_4\} \qquad (6.52)$$

which gives the desired result and is represented by the diagram:

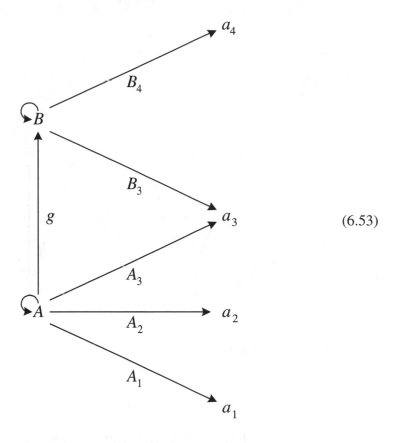

$$(6.53)$$

Note, however, that

$$(A \cup B \cup C)\backslash C \neq \{A, B, C, a_1, a_2, a_3, a_4, a_5, a_6\}\backslash\{C, a_3, a_5, a_6\} \quad (6.54)$$

would result in the set

$$\{A, B, a_1, a_2, a_4\} \quad (6.55)$$

with a_3 missing. Thus, when deleting a class with the object component of the functor, you need to work with the classes in exploded form, but representing the design as a union of class sets. You can't evaluate the union operations since you might lose elements (attribute domains) still needed.

For the arrow component of the functor, the operation is simple set subtraction, since:

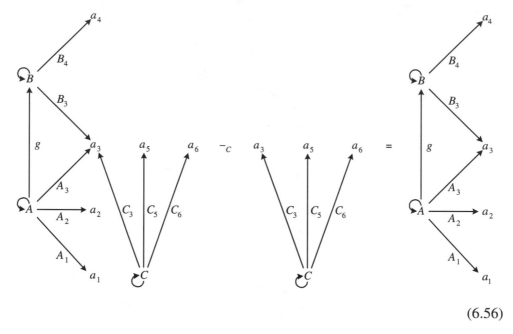

$$(6.56)$$

In set-theoretic terms,

$$\{id_A, id_B, id_C, A_1, A_2, A_3, B_3, B_4, C_3, C_5, C_6\}\backslash\{id_C, C_3, C_5, C_6\}$$

$$= \{id_A, id_B, A_1, A_2, A_3, B_3, B_4\} \qquad (6.57)$$

which is the desired result. This works because while attribute domains are sometimes shared among classes, attribute arrows are never shared. This is also true of state objects and class operation arrows.

The two remaining operations on classes, combining two classes into one, and extracting a subset of attributes and operations out of a class to form two classes, can be defined only by using the exploded view of classes.

Combine Two Classes into One

The purpose of this operation is to take two distinct classes and merge their respective sets of properties, attributes, and methods into a single, new class which is usually, but not always, labeled with the name of one of the merged classes. First the effects of this operation will be noted, then it will be formally defined.

When two classes are combined, the states for both classes are combined as if a natural join is performed on tables formed by the two state spaces. The rows in the new state space are created by combining rows in the two merged state spaces in which common attributes have the same values. The class invariants are joined by logical conjunction. It is possible for the two invariants to contain conflicting conditions such that the combination either resolves to true (all states are possible) or false (no states are possible). Neither of these conditions is desirable, and the conflict must be resolved by the designer. The combined invariant is applied after the two unconstrained state spaces are joined. Operations from both merged classes are then drawn between every pair of states for which the source state satisfies the preconditions and the sink state satisfies the postconditions of the operation.

Class relationship arrows are moved to the new combined class. This can result is an arrow having either its domain or codomain changed. It can also result in two relationship arrows becoming equal, as with attribute arrows, in which case one of the equal arrows is discarded. It doesn't matter which arrow is dropped.

By way of example, combine two classes, A and C, into a new class, called C. Formally, this operation, denoted by $C_{DS_2} = C_{DS_1} \bowtie A_{DS_1}$, is a functor with four component functions. An attribute arrow function, the natural join from relational algebra, denoted $C \bowtie A$, maps the arrows in DS_1 with dom $= A$ to arrows in DS_2 with dom $= C$, relabeling as appropriate and dropping duplicate arrows (those which are equal, after relabeling, to existing arrows). Note that the new state space is a subset of the cross product of combined set of attributes. It is equal to the cross product if none of the attribute domains are shared.

A state function deletes the existing state objects for both classes, combines the class invariants using conjunction, and creates a new set of states which satisfy the combined invariant. This is defined as a surjection from the states of both classes in DS_1 to the states for the new combined class in DS_2 such that each state in DS_2 satisfies the conjunctive class invariant.

An operation arrow function maps the arrows from the states of both classes in DS_1 to the states of the new class in DS_2. This surjective mapping takes the domain of each arrow for each class in DS_1 to all of the state objects for the new class in DS_2 which satisfy the operation's preconditions. This may be a many-to-many mapping. The codomains of each arrow for each class in DS_1 are mapped to all of the state objects for the new class in DS_2 which satisfy the operation's postconditions. This, too, may be a many-to-many mapping. New arrows may be created in DS_2 and will be labeled with the name of the operation. Duplicate arrows, those with the same domain, codomain, and label as some other arrow, are discarded.

A class relationship arrow function maps the arrows for which one of the combined classes is either the domain or codomain to the new class. This surjection preserves relationships between classes.

Note that after combining classes in this way, extracting out one of the old classes is not necessarily an inverse operation. It may not be possible to reconstruct the two original classes from the information contained in DS_2. This will be the case if the intersections of the sets of properties for the two original classes is nonempty.

In categorical terms, this operation is a merging of two categories, preserving relationship functors to or from these categories to other categories. To represent this operation graphically, combine classes A and C in the diagram

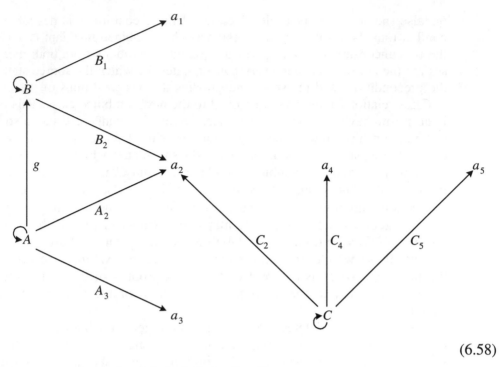

(6.58)

into a new class, also labeled C, in the diagram

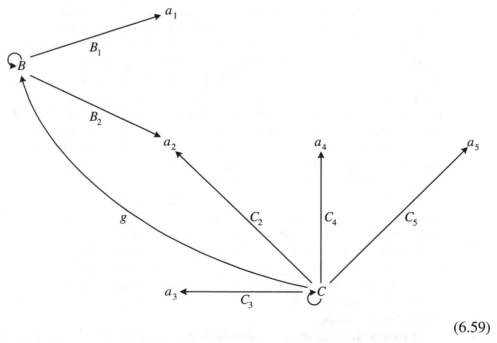

(6.59)

After the operation, object A, representing the state space for class A, has been removed. Arrows A_2 and C_2 have been combined into one arrow, called C_2. You can do this because you first move arrow A_2 from A to C by changing its domain. Since A_2 and C_2 are now equal arrows—they have the same domain and codomain, and will soon have the same label—one of them can be deleted; we chose to delete A_2.

Extract Properties from a Class

In this operation, add a new class to the design, but take all of the attributes and operations from an existing class. In principle, this operation is simpler than adding a new class, because you don't have to add any new attribute domains or attribute arrows. However, it can get rather complicated when dealing with states. You must also add a new state space object.

For attributes, map the arrows for the attributes to be moved to their counterparts in the new design state by changing their (arrow) domains. The state space for the old class is mapped to the new class in the new design state using the projection function of relational algebra, in effect projecting the extracted attributes to the new class. This results in two new sets of states being created out of the cross products of each of the two new sets of attribute domains. Class invariant terms in the source class which are extracted to the new class become the class invariant for the new class. Any term connected to an attribute which gets moved as well as an attribute which does not get moved (such as through an arithmetic comparison operator) is simply dropped (new associations are not created automatically). The state sets for both new classes are created out of their respective state spaces by applying the new class invariants.

Operations extracted to the new class are mapped to the states in the new class by moving their domains and codomains. Domains are mapped to states which satisfy the preconditions of the operation. Codomains are mapped to states which satisfy the postconditions of the operation. Operations which are not moved may have preconditions which are no longer satisfied by their domain states, as some of the attributes in the precondition may have been extracted. Such terms in the precondition are simply dropped—there is not much else to do with them, and they are no longer appropriate components in the precondition. The same is true for codomains and postconditions of operations which are not moved.

Class relationship arrows are copied, except for associations which, follow the attributes which make up their anchor set. If an anchor set is split between the two classes by the extraction, the association is split as well. This means that the anchor set in the class on the other end of the relationship is split into two separate anchor sets, and that class now participates in two relationships, rather than one.

Message links which originate in the source class follow the operations which originate them; side effects are preserved. Message links which terminate in the source class follow the operations which they invoke.

As an example, moving attributes B_2 and B_3, and operations β_1 and β_4 from class B to class C is shown in the diagram:

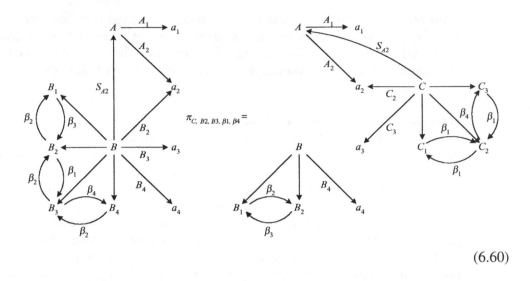

$$(6.60)$$

The operation *might* look like this, depending on the preconditions and postconditions for each operation, and the values represented by each state.

Add a Generalization Relationship

Adding a generalization relationship is a simple operation: There are no preconditions. The significance of this new arrow does not manifest itself until a message is received by the specialization class which invokes an operation of the generalization. The effect of this operation is that the properties of the generalization class are subsequently treated as a subset of the specialization class.

In set-theoretic terms, the operation adds the arrows $g(B, A)$, $g: B \rightarrow A$, to the set $\text{hom}(B, A)$, which will normally be empty before the operation. Denote this operation by $\text{hom}(B, A) \cup \{g(B, A)\}$. In categorical terms, adding a generalization simply adds an arrow between classes in the category **DesignState**. Given two classes A and B in the design state

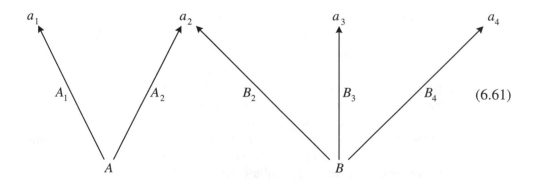

$$(6.61)$$

adding a generalization from B (the subclass) to A (the superclass) gives

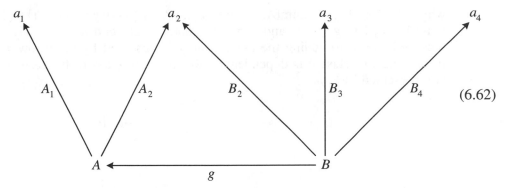

$$(6.62)$$

where g is the new relationship. Note that the semantics of a generalization relationship make the arrow B_2 appear redundant. This may or may not be the case. The two arrows A_2 and B_2 are equal arrows in the sense that they have the same domain and codomain, due to the nature of the generalization relationship, but they may in fact represent different attributes. It is up to the designer to decide whether an arrow can be dropped in this situation.

Operation arrows are only equal if they have the same domain and codomain, the same label, and the same set of preconditions and post conditions. It is unlikely that adding a generalization will create duplicate operation arrows, but it is possible. We do not want to drop seemingly duplicate operation arrows (those where the domain, codomains, and labels match) unless they are truly duplicate, including their side effects (which are specified in the postconditions). It is possible to redefine an inherited operation in a subclass and send a message to the superclass invoking the inherited operation to perform what amounts to default behavior. Therefore, we leave it to the designer to resolve the issue of which operation arrows, if any, are duplicate and can be dropped.

Add an Association Relationship

Adding an association is subject to some fairly strict preconditions. Recall that an association was defined in terms of anchor sets which represent a subset of attribute arrows whose codomains intersect. Pictorially, this situation is depicted by

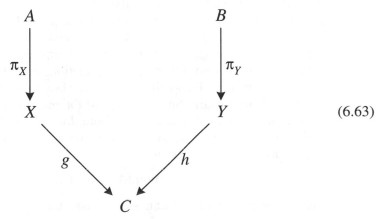

$$(6.63)$$

where $C \subseteq \text{cod}(\{g \in \text{hom}(A, \_), h \in \text{hom}(B, \_) \mid \text{cod } g = \text{cod } h\})$, $X = \{g \in \text{hom}(A, \_) \mid \text{cod } g \in C\}$, and $Y = \{h \in \text{hom}(B, \_) \mid \text{cod } h \in C\}$. This situation must exist prior to adding the association f represented by the arrow $f: A \rightarrow B$, if the object of class A is dependent on the object of class B, the results of which is represented by

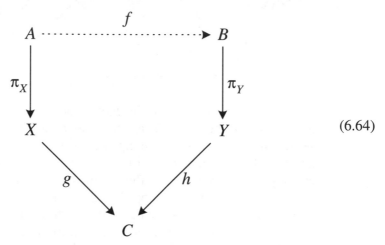

$$(6.64)$$

If the dependency is reversed, so that the object of class B is dependent on the object of class A, then add the arrow $f: B \rightarrow A$. In set-theoretic terms, add the arrow f to $\text{hom}(A, B)$ [or $\text{hom}(B, A)$] via set union, denoted by

$$\text{hom}(A, B) \cup \{f: A \rightarrow B\} \qquad (6.65a)$$

or

$$\text{hom}(B, A) \cup \{f: B \rightarrow A\} \qquad (6.65b)$$

The semantics of a new association are dependent upon the needs of the application. Unlike adding a generalization, adding an association is purely a structural or syntactic matter.

Add an Aggregation Relationship

An aggregation was defined as a relationship in which an object of one class was is an attribute of another class. The first class is the component and the second is the composite or aggregate. In terms of semantics, an aggregation relationship between classes is no different than a relationship between a class and an attribute domain. In fact, as far as the composite class is concerned, the component class *is* an attribute domain. So, let's expand the operation to allow adding aggregation arrows between a class and an attribute domain, as well as between two classes.

In set-theoretic terms, add a new arrow $\pi_B: A \rightarrow B$ to the set $\text{hom}(A, B)$, which is probably empty, via set union:

$$\text{hom}(A, B) \cup \{\pi_B: A \rightarrow B\} \qquad (6.66)$$

The (category) object B can be a class state space (a true aggregation) or an attribute domain. In categorical terms, you are simply adding an arrow between two existing objects, as in:

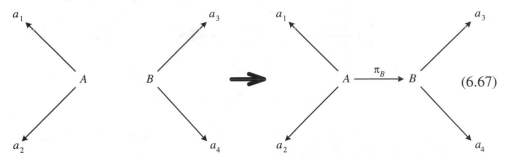

$$(6.67)$$

Add a Message Link

Adding a message link to a design has virtually no effect on the structure of the design. In set-theoretic terms, adding a message link adds a relation to a hom set via set union:

$$\mathrm{hom}(A, B) \cup \{msg: A \to B\}. \tag{6.68}$$

In categorical terms, the operation adds an arrow with dom A and cod B and labeled with the name of the message, as in:

$$(6.69)$$

Drop a Relationship

Dropping a relationship of any kind removes an arrow from the category **DesignState** and has no other effect. The structure of a class, the set of classes, and the set of attribute domain sets are not affected by the operation. There is one glaring exception to this: Dropping an aggregation relationship is the same as dropping an attribute arrow in that an attribute is removed from the state space for the class. This can have a significant effect on the states of the class, as well as the class invariant. It may even affect the preconditions and postconditions of one or more class operations. In that sense, dropping an aggregation is like extracting an attribute from the class and that, in fact, is how you model it.

Dropping a relationship can also have semantic effects when the behavior of the design is simulated. For example, dropping a generalization relationship may mean that some of the attributes and methods assumed to be a part of the class are no longer present. An object of the specialization class may no longer recognize certain messages it once understood.

In set-theoretic terms, the operation removes a relation from a hom set via the set difference operation:

$$\mathrm{hom}(A, B) \backslash \{f: A \to B\} \tag{6.70}$$

In categorical terms, you have:

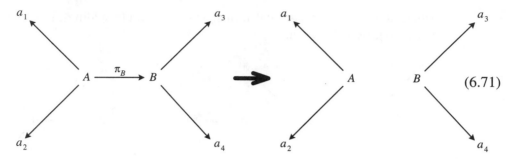

$$(6.71)$$

This completes the development of our formal model of objects and classes, and the designs built from them.

ANALYTICAL TECHNIQUES

For static measurement, measuring things such as size, complexity, and so forth, we need look no further than our formal model. For dynamic measurement, though, we need a way to manipulate that model. By way of review, we need to be able to "execute" our design, with or without contemplated changes, to see how the design will respond to an external event. This amounts to "seeding" a design in a known steady state with an external event and propagating messages between objects of classes in the design until a new steady state is reached.

We define a steady state as one in which the design is essentially at rest: No objects change states without external influence. You might intuitively expect there to be no message traffic in a design at rest, but some applications require continuous message traffic to detect external events. For example, an application may need a polling mechanism which continuously sends messages to monitor the status of a set of sensors.

In this section, a set of mathematical tools is developed to assist in this dynamic analysis. These tools are not new. Rather than invent a new calculus, I borrow from existing calculi and adapt them to our needs. Both calculi are based on models which can be translated into our formal model, which is why the adaptation works. Many of the components of these tools are inherent parts of our model.

I use a form of predicate calculus, adapted from Object-Z (Rose 1992), to describe states and determine the results of executing a method and an adaptation of OPUS (Mens, Mons, and Steyaent 1994b) to describe message passing, message binding, and for describing external events. We have already formally defined the operations needed to evaluate the values of an attribute in a given state and those needed to describe changes to the design. This section completes the theory by defining a way to describe the initial state of a design, a way to describe an event, a way to propagate a set of messages through a design, and a set of inference rules to help simplify complex sequences of message, operations, and states.

Describing States and Operations

Object-Z (Rose 1992) extends the formal specification language Z (pronounced "zed") (Spivey 1992) to describe classes in object-oriented software. Most of the extensions are in notation rather than substance. Many of these extensions modify the scope or applicability of the standard Z operators. The Object-Z notation for the specification of a class is given by:

```
┌─ Class Name [generic parameters] ─────────────────────────
│  visibility list
│  inherited classes
│  type definitions
│  constant definitions
│  state schema
│  initial state schema
│  operation schemas
│  history invariant
└────────────────────────────────────────────────────────────
```

A full description of each of these sections is given in Rose (1992).

Rather than describe all of the extensions here, let's concentrate on those features which are most useful to our purposes: the constant definitions, the state schema, the initial state schema, and the operation schemas. All of these features are basic descriptions of state.

The constant definitions section describes the constants for the class and may name ranges or allowable values of these constants. The value of a constant is set at object creation and is never changed during the life of that object. It is possible for a different object of the class to have a different value for these constants. A constant description for our *List* class might look like:

```
│  max : ℕ
├───────────────
│  max ⩽ 100.
```

The upper line names the type or domain of the constant *max*, in this case the natural numbers. The lower line defines any restrictions placed on the values drawn from the domain.

The state schema describes the state variables of the class and perhaps gives a state predicate. The constants and state variables together comprise the attributes of the class. The domain and restrictions for the constants are taken in conjunction with the state predicate to form the class invariant. The attributes and class invariant are included in the initial state schema and all of the operation schemas implicitly. This means that all attributes are available to these schemas without further definition and all of the conditions in the class invariant are taken in conjunction with any predicates specified in a schema. The state schema for our *List* class might look like:

```
┌──────────────────────────────────────────────────────
│ count: ℕ
│ head, tail, current: Object Reference
├──────────────────────────────────────────────────────
│ count ≤ max
```

Again, the upper line names the domains of the state variables. The lower line places a restriction on the value of any state variable named in the predicate. Here, the state variable *count* is drawn from the natural numbers and is limited to not exceed the value of *max*.

The initial state schema describes the state an object of the class will have immediately after creation. It is possible in Object-Z to describe more than one initial state, although it is not clear how you determine which state to apply to any given object. An initial state for the *List* class, in which we allow only one possible initial state, might look like:

```
┌─ INIT ───────────────────────────────────────────────
│ count = 0
│ head, tail, current = NULL
```

The operation schemas describe the state of an object both before and after the execution of a method, and thus define the preconditions and postconditions of the method. An operation schema includes a Δ-list which names the state variables of the class which may be modified by the operation (the value of constants cannot be changed by a class operation). Operation parameters are defined following the Δ-list. The preconditions and postconditions are a list of predicates taken in conjunction with each other and the class invariant. The postconditions define the final values of state variables, which are indicated by the variable name in primed form, as in *count'*. The operation schema for the AddEntry operation for our *List* class might look like:

```
┌─ AddEntry ───────────────────────────────────────────
│ Δ(count, head, tail, current)
│ entry?: List Entry Reference
├──────────────────────────────────────────────────────
│ count < max
│ entry? ≠ NULL
│ count' = count + 1
│ λentry?.SetNext(head)
│ λentry?.SetPrevious(NULL)
│ head' = entry?
│ count = 0 ⇒ (current' = entry?; tail' = entry?)
```

In this operation, *entry?* represents the new entry to be added to the list (in Z, an input variable is represented by *name?* and an output variable is represented by *name!*). The preconditions for this operation are that the value of *count* is initially less than the value of *max* and the input variable *entry*? is nonnull. As a result of the operation, the value of *count* is incremented by one, SetNext and SetPrevious messages are sent to the entry object, and the value of *head* is set to reference the new entry. If the value of *count* is initially zero, the final values of *current* and *tail* are also set to reference the new entry. This is a complete specification of the AddEntry operation, yet it reveals no details about the data structure used to implement the list in software, nor does it describe the implementation of the operation itself.

One aspect of describing state not yet covered is the description of the initial state for the design, as opposed to the initial state for an object. The state of a design, in preparation for dynamic analysis, includes the descriptions of the initial states for each object, plus a list of those objects in scope at the time the analysis begins. This list can range from empty to a nearly infinite variety, and number, of objects. The mechanism for specifying this list is deceptively simple: You simply name the members of the set *ActiveObjects*.

Propagating Messages

OPUS (Mens, Mens, and Steyaert 1994a; 1994b) is an object calculus developed to support the design of object-oriented programming languages. Part of this calculus is a well-developed scheme for representing the passing of messages and the binding of those messages to methods in a class. We will borrow the ideas of this scheme, though not the notation, to develop our mechanisms for method selection and binding. Part of this mechanism includes checking the set *ActiveObjects* using the function scope( ) to determine if the object to which the message is addressed is in scope.

The form of a message as $\lambda x.y(a_i)_{i \in I}$, where x is the object identifier of the receiving object, y is the name of the message, and $(a_i)_{i \in I}$ is an ordered *I*-tuple which represents the message contents. For binding to occur, the class of x must contain a method m for which the name matches y and the list of parameters $(p_j)_{j \in J}$ matches the message contents of (a_i) on an item-for-item basis. Formally:

$$\lambda x.y(a_i)_{i \in I} \cdot \exists m(p_j)_{j \in J} \in \ Class(x) \ |$$
$$y = m \wedge (\forall i \in I, j \in J \cdot i = j \Rightarrow \mathrm{dom}(a_i) = \mathrm{dom}(p_j) \wedge I = J) \quad (6.72)$$

Also, a different form was defined for both a message and a method. In this alternate form, the message y is an ordered tuple $\langle y, (a_i)_{i \in I}, x \rangle$ and the method m is an ordered tuple $\langle m, (p_j)_{j \in J} \rangle$. The binding mechanism was defined as a functor which mapped all but the last item in the message tuple to the each corresponding item in the method tuple, where the methods used in the mapping are drawn from the class of x.

In OPUS, the method selection mechanism is a simple lookup which compares a message to each method in turn moving from right to left in the object specification. The syntax for OPUS provides a set of reduction rules which govern the lookup and matching process. The reduction rules in OPUS are required since OPUS allows both "ordinary" methods and "constant" methods. A constant method is one which simply returns a constant value. OPUS uses constant methods to represent attributes in an object. They correspond to the state functions in our class model.

In our case, we don't need the reduction rules, since we match tuples directly. More specifically, we require the name of the first item in each tuple to match, and the domains of the remaining items to match when compared on an item-for-item basis. Because of uniqueness requirements, we are not allowed to have two methods with the same signature in any class. This gives us the advantage that our lookup will either find one and only one method which maps to a given message or it will find no such method. Given this simple lookup mechanism, we can perform the lookup by matching categories (mapping objects in Message to objects in Method, and likewise for arrows), by matching tuples, or by using equation (6.72). If we find a match, we can always be assured that we have found *the* method for which we were searching.

We describe an external event as a message to some object in our design. We can represent this message categorically as an arrow from an object which is not part of the design (such as a user) to the object we wish to receive the message. Algebraically, we can just describe the message, as in $\lambda List$:1.AddEntry(*entry*), which denotes sending the AddEntry message, containing the atom *entry*, to the first instance of our *List* class. Binding takes place if scope($List$:1) returns true and if the class *List* contains an AddEntry operation which requires a single parameter of the same type as *entry*.

If binding fails, go no further. However, if binding succeeds, check to see if the preconditions for the AddEntry operation in the class *List* are satisfied. If they are not, go no further. If they are satisfied, assume the postconditions for the operation without further proof. If these postconditions include messages to other objects, repeat this process for each message.

The messages propagating through the design will form a many-branched tree. Evaluate every path on this tree using the analysis techniques. The path through this tree represents a basic tree search problem. You can employ any of three search patterns to this problem: breadth-first, depth-first, and in-order. In this case, due to the possibility of a branch being cut short by binding failure, it seems best to apply the breadth-first pattern. This would mean evaluating all of the messages generated by an object before following the links created by those messages.

Inference Rules

A deductive apparatus allows the manipulation of strings of symbols based on their syntactic shape, without having to assign them any meaning (Woodcock and Loomes 1989). A deductive apparatus has two components: axioms which are primitive statements of a formal language and inference rules which allow us to deduce statements in a formal language as an immediate consequence of other statements. The formal model provides the axioms; we need to develop the inference rules. An inference rule has two parts: the set S_1 of statements you need to apply the rule and a set S_2 of one or more statements that result from applying the rule. An inference rule is denoted by:

$$\frac{S_1}{S_2} \tag{6.73}$$

You can think of an inference rule as a form of allowable substitution: Given the set of statements S_1, you can substitute the statements in S_2 without changing the meaning of the expression. Inference rules are most often used for simplifying a set of statements, such as substituting a single statement for a complex set of statements.

Our model provides for a number of inference rules, in addition to those provided implicitly by propositional and predicate calculus and relational algebra. These rules allow the substitution of classes for objects, objects for classes, methods for messages, messages for methods, and states for sequences of one or more methods.

Object Elimination
Given an object x of class A, denoted $A{:}x$, you can substitute the class A:

$$\frac{A{:}x}{A} \tag{6.74}$$

Object Introduction
Given a class A, you can substitute any object x of the class:

$$\frac{A}{A{:}x} \tag{6.75}$$

Message Elimination
Given a message and a content tuple $\lambda x.y(a_i)$, you can substitute the method $m(p_i)$ of the class A of which x is a member, provided that the message can be bound to the method:

$$\frac{\lambda x.y(a_i)}{m(p_i),\, y = m \wedge m \in Class(x)} \tag{6.76}$$

Message Introduction
Given a method $m(p_i)$ of a class A, you can substitute a message to any object x of the class:

$$\frac{m(p_i),\, m \in A}{\lambda x.y(a_i),\, y = m \wedge x \in A} \tag{6.77}$$

Subtype Substitution
Given an object x of a class A which is a generalization of a class B, you can substitute an object y of class B (this is the Liskov substitution principle, R_g denotes the set of generalization relationships):

$$\frac{x \in A,\ (A,\ B) \in R_g}{y,\ y \in B} \tag{6.78}$$

Method/State Substitution

Given a state S_1 of an object x of a class A, and a method m of the class A, and that the state S_1 satisfies the preconditions of m, you can substitute the resulting state S_2 of m applied to an object in state S_1:

$$\frac{S_1,\ m,\ m:\ S_1 \rightarrow S_2}{S_2,\ \text{with side effects of } m} \tag{6.79}$$

The method/state substitution rule can be applied to a state S_1 and a sequence of methods m_1; m_2;...; m_n applied in the order given:

$$\frac{S_1,\ m_1;\ m_2;...;\ m_n,\ \cup m_i:\ S_1 \rightarrow S_2}{S_2,\ \text{with side effects of each } m_i} \tag{6.80}$$

This allows the substitution of a terminal state for a starting state and a sequence of methods, making the use of predefined method sequences easier to model. The method/state substitution rule can also be applied to design changes and design states:

$$\frac{DS_1,\ o_1;\ o_2;...;\ o_n,\ \cup o_i:\ DS_1 \rightarrow DS_2}{DS_2} \tag{6.81}$$

POTENTIAL FOR TOOL SUPPORT

The formal model and analytical techniques can be implemented in a software tool. Such a tool would be able to take a design from the repository of a design tool, for example, and take static measurements from the design or run simulations against the design. This section briefly describes the potential structure and behavior of such a tool in conceptual terms. To my knowledge, no such tool exists, and what I describe is only one possibility.

Many tools on the market store descriptions of a design. Some of these descriptions are sufficiently complete to allow the generation of code. The "understanding" these tools have of a design is purely structural. Generating code is merely an exercise in translating the description from one form to another. We would like to have a tool that understood our design well enough to tell us how it would behave under a given set of circumstances. Further, we should be able to describe some sequences of design changes, then see how the modified design will behave. This amounts to "executing" a design—before we have written any code.

Such a tool has four major components: a translation mechanism, an inference engine, a means to accept descriptions of design changes, initial states, and seed events, and a means to represent the design both during and after the simulation. A conceptual model of the tool is shown in Figure 6.4.

The translation mechanism converts the design from the native format of a given design tool into the formal model representation described in this chapter. A trans-

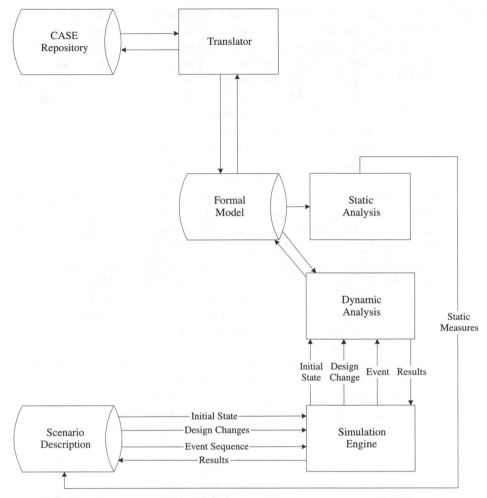

Figure 6.4 *A conceptual model for a theory-based simulator.*

lation mechanism would have to be created for each design tool as it would be a tool-specific back-end. The translation mechanism could be either read-only, reading the design from the design tool and converting it into the formal model, or it could be two-way, also applying changes described in the simulation scenario to the representation of the design in the design tool.

The mechanism to accept design changes, initial states, and event descriptions is part of the user interface of the tool. A sequence of design changes, initial states, and an event or sequence of events constitutes a scenario. The scenario is "executed" by the inference engine.

The inference engine first applies any design changes to the base design, in the order given. The objects of the design are placed in either the initial states described in the scenario or in the initial state defined by the class in the design. Then, the event sequence is triggered. The inference engine works by propagating messages and state changes through the design until a steady state is reached, much like an electronic circuit propagates signals in response to an external voltage source. As a new steady state is reached, the next event in the sequence is triggered. This continues until the event sequence is exhausted.

While the system is active, between the event firing and the reaching of new steady state, the state and activity of the system can be represented visually. Imagine a black screen, like looking into outer space from a spaceship portal. As objects come into scope, they appear in three-dimensional space. Static relationships between classes are be displayed as bonds between objects. The structure would look much like a three-dimensional model of a molecule. Messages are indicated by "rays" or arcs between objects. A message arc displays the values of the message contents, indicates whether binding occurred, and if it did, the results of the requested operation. You can freeze the activity at any point and examine the contents of a message. Remember, no code exists at this point; you are executing the design directly.

After the new steady state is achieved, the inference engine logs the resulting object states along with the initial descriptions of the design, any design changes, the initial states, and the event sequence. Thus, you now have a permanent record of the behavior of a given design in a given set of circumstances. The other portion of the user interface allows you to examine past scenarios and display their final results graphically.

The process as just described can be done by hand: The tools and techniques are given in this chapter. But can you imagine the utility of being able to "watch" your design execute? You can't even do that with code today. As I said, such a tool, to my knowledge, does not exist. When one comes along, I will be first in line to try it out.

SUMMARY

A formal model of objects was developed to use as a basis for static measurement of a software design. The model, based on categories, includes attributes and operations of objects, objects, classes of objects, states of objects and state spaces of classes, operations on classes (design changes), states of the design, and the design as an object.

Along with this model, a set of analytical techniques was developed which allow us to model a design, apply changes to the design, analyze the design's behavior, and even execute the design algebraically, or as part of a new kind of software development tool. These techniques give you a new understanding of your designs, and provide a new way to think and talk about them. With the tool, you can watch the design as it executes, seeing objects come into and go out of scope, seeing the static structures form between objects, and seeing the messages fire, like signals in an electronic circuit. I described one possible architecture for the tool.

After some reflection and discussion, it occurs to me that these techniques could change the way we design software. Design is no longer some abstract activity, full of arcane little diagrams. Design becomes something we can relate to, something we can interact with, something we can understand and discuss, and with the tool, something we can see working (or not working). Perhaps most importantly, design becomes something we can play with. All of this is possible without the expense of first constructing the code. Furthermore, these techniques are not limited to the design of just software.

Part III

DESIGN CHARACTERISTICS

We do not measure designs, we measure characteristics of designs. Designers deem some characteristics more important than others. Different designers use different sets of characteristics. The same designer might use different sets of characteristics on different projects, or at different times within the same project.

The point is that we cannot define, up front, a fixed set of characteristics and provide a set of measures for them. Given this dilemma, and since I am writing this book, I chose the nine characteristics that over the course of my projects have given me the most trouble. No one characteristic, including size, has been an issue on every project. Each project has its own characteristics.

The characteristics of size, complexity, coupling, sufficiency, completeness, cohesion, primitiveness, similarity, and volatility are each covered in separate chapters. The basic format for each chapter is the same. We begin by defining a characteristic from a qualitative, or empirical, perspective. If other authors have written on the subject, I include their discussions and definitions, as well. We then settle on a definition, actually a description, of the characteristic. These definitions usually imply one or more formal properties for a measure of the characteristics. We lay these out explicitly. Most often, the end results meet these properties. In a couple of cases, we have to modify our original set of properties.

Once we have an empirical understanding of a characteristic, we define it in terms of our formal model, which leads to a set of potential empirical relational structures. We examine each of these structures from the perspective of the type of measure it provides and its mathematical requirements. We then apply all of this information, and the measure construction technique from Chapter 3, to construct a measure of our characteristic. Each measure is validated by showing how the elements in the measure satisfy the requirements of the selected structure. Since many of these measures are based on the same structure, some of this discussion is repeated. Each chapter stands on its own.

Of the twelve measures discussed, nine are brand new, as are two of the nine characteristics. These twelve examples should give you ample experience in applying the measure construction technique. You may decide you want to use the measures provided. You have the measures; you have the tools to build your own. The choice is yours.

7

SIZE

On the surface, software size seems an intuitive concept. Upon closer scrutiny, it turns out that size is a rather slippery concept—so slippery, that it has never been defined in the context of software. One of the problems is that our intuitive notion of size varies with the objects we behold and the points of view from which we behold them.

What is the size of an application, for example? Is it the amount of source code, in lines or pages? Is it the number of classes in the design? Is it the average or peak number of concurrent users? Is it the number of records in the database? It is all of these, and then some. The point is that "size" refers to different things at different times and for different types of objects.

In this chapter, the notion of software size is explored in an attempt to discover some basic properties. In "Motivation and Origins," we discuss some of the reasons we measure size, why some measure of size is important. Several forms or aspects of size are discussed in the next section and a small set of views that differ in their empirical properties is settled on. Then, in "Formal Properties" we formally define the properties for each type or view of size followed by a discussion of some possible empirical relational structures, from Chapter 5, which can be used as the basis for building a representation of each view of size. Finally, in the section entitled "Potential Measures," a representation for each view of size is constructed. One of these views of size is new to software and may prove very interesting.

MOTIVATION AND ORIGINS

Size is an internal product attribute that contributes to a great many product, process, and project measures. Size contributes to many of our prediction systems, including those used to estimate effort and schedule for a project. Size also allows us to normalize other product measures, such as defects, which tend to grow along with the size of an application. This normalization allows for more meaningful comparisons between products, processes, or organizations.

For example, the number of defects in an application is related to the size of the application in a strongly positive way. To say that one program has 100 defects and another only one doesn't give much information. Knowing that the first program has 10,000 lines of code and the second has only 10 tells a great deal more. By dividing the number of defects by the number of lines of code, you get a measure of the defect rate, or defect density. This defect density is in the same units for every program for which you have the necessary counts. With this data, you can compare the programs and even order them in terms of their defect densities.

Size is an important component in the rate of development commonly but erroneously measured as productivity. The rate at which you can develop software is different from your productivity because productivity includes non-software activities and products while the development rate is the rate at which you can build software. Given a development rate based on solid historical data, the size of a potential product (in some unit of measure), and a description of the development and production environments, you can develop an accurate estimate for the product. Historically, problems with estimating rest with our inability to accurately estimate the size values and account for the environment.

Size at the component or class level can be used to accurately track progress on a project and generate more accurate management estimates at completion (MEACs). As components are completed, they are checked off and their size is subtracted from the work remaining and added to the work completed. The ratio of work completed to the sum of work completed and work remaining is the percentage complete on the project to date. Subtracting this value from one gives the percentage of work to go. This result can be used to re-estimate the remaining work, which leads to an accurate and up-to-date MEAC.

Size at the component or class level can also be used to measure the level of reuse on a given project. The sum of the sizes for the reused components divided by the sum of the sizes for both reused and built components is the level of reuse.

One apparent result of the use of object technology is the managing of software inventories at the component level, rather than the application level. In this sense, management means acquisition, deployment, maintenance, retirement, and accounting for software assets. Object-oriented software is released at the component level, which may be a single class or a structure of classes. As components are added to inventory, their size is added to the total size of the inventory being managed. When a component is released as a new version, or is replaced with a different component, the size of the old component is deducted from inventory, and the size of the new component is added. If you use dollars as the unit of size (as in dollars spent acquiring or building a component), this process is exactly like managing an inventory of products using actual cost rather than last-in–first-out or first-in–first-out costing schemes.

The size of a product has several origins; the most important is the problem domain. The basic problem being addressed by the software project has a minimum size, which you can measure. Other factors in the problem domain also contribute to the size of the problem. Typically, constraints on processing time, concurrency, safety, integrity, or high volume add to the problem size. They also tend to add to a problem's complexity, but that's a different topic.

Together, the basic size of a problem and the additions caused by problem domain constraints determine the total size of the problem to be solved. This is the *minimum* size for any software solution. The design process, which translates this description of the problem into a description of a software solution, can only add size. In other words, the size of a software solution is always at least as large as the size of the problem.

Now, I've been discussing the size of a problem versus the size of a software solution as if they were independent of each other. Many software engineers do not believe this to be the case. Well, they *are* independent and you can measure them independently. In design, you must measure size in terms of design models. In Chapter 2, there was a discussion of a problem domain model, an application domain model, an application-specific domain model, and an application-generic domain model. The problem domain model is the description of the problem. The application domain model is the description of the problem limited to what you intend to include in the solution. The application, application-specific, and application-generic domains, taken together, describe the software solution. You can measure the sizes of each of these models.

So, a major source of size, in addition to that inherent in the problem, is the designer. There are many reasons to be interested in software size, and that size has many sources.

EMPIRICAL VIEWS

Just as size has many sources, it has many aspects or views. We cannot really discuss a generic concept of size without asking: "In terms of what?" For example, the size of a ship is measured in a number of ways. Most familiar is its length. You can easily compare the lengths of two ships and determine which is longer, but not necessarily which is bigger.

Another measure of a ship's size is its displacement, which is stated in terms of the mass of water the ship displaces. This is not a direct measure of the weight of the ship; it is an indirect measure. Then, there is the ship's draft, which is the distance from the waterline to the lowest point on the ship. The draft represents the minimum depth of water before the ship hits bottom. Another measure of a ship's size is its beam, which is the width of the ship at its widest point. The beam is used to determine the smallest channel the ship may enter or the smallest berth the ship may occupy.

All of these are valid, accepted measures of a ship's size. Yet you cannot use them to order a set of ships in any absolute way. While these measures are all strongly related—longer ships tend to have greater displacement, and possibly greater beams—these relationships are not fixed. Given a set of ships, it is possible that ordering the set on the basis of each measure singly will produce different orderings. It is true of software as well.

Various authors have identified no less than seven distinct views of software size. Some views were identified by several authors and were given different names. I have grouped these views under a common name based on meaning. The views are:

1. *Population*: static counts of various element types (Briand, Morasca, and Basili 1996), including numbers of classes, numbers of methods, and even lines of source code (which is not a design measure).

2. *Length*: The number of elements in a chain of connected elements (Briand, Morasca, and Basili 1996), such as the length of a path in a graph.

3. *Depth*: The length of a path from a root of a tree structure to a leaf node (Yourdon and Constantine 1979). This differs from length in the minor technicality that all paths start at the same element.

4. *Width*: The count of the number of elements at a given level in a tree structure (Yourdon and Constantine 1979). This is the number of elements at the same depth from the tree root.

5. *Functionality*: The amount of function delivered by the product, from a given point of view (Fenton 1991).

6. *Complexity of the underlying problem*: The computational complexity of the theoretically most efficient solution to a problem (Fenton 1991).

7. *Volume*: Dynamic, time-dependent counts of various element types (populations), such as the number of objects in scope, the number of concurrent users (average or peak), the number of transactions per time period, and the number of records in a database.

These seven views can be grouped into four, which I call:

Population
Length
Functionality
Volume

The remainder of this section discusses the mapping of the seven views into the four. The remainder of this chapter will build formal models for each of these four views, leading to one potential measure for each view.

Population is what most people think of when they consider size. Except for function points and similar measures, all commonly used size measures are measures of population. Yet even function points are based on population measures. Any question that begins with "How many . . . ?" leads to a population measure.

Volume differs from population only in the fact that volume measures are dynamic while population measures are static. Volume measures are population measures *at an instant in time*. In contrast, population measures hold over relatively long *intervals of time*.

Another difference is that volume and population measures usually measure very different properties. The properties addressed by volume measures are not properties of the design, although they most certainly influence the design. Further, volume measures cannot be measured directly at design time; they can only be estimated. Volume measures most closely resemble the dynamic load forces in structural engineering.

The complexity of the underlying problem domain, as measured using the Big *O* notation (see Chapter 4) represents the order of time required for an algorithm to process an input set of size n. It is not a measure of size, in static terms, since the order value is fixed for any n measured as a function of n. An $O(n^2)$ problem requires time proportional to the square of the size of the input no matter what the size. Algorithmic complexity is an important dynamic measure which can have significant influence on the design. If the best known solution to a problem is $O(n^3)$, the solution may be feasible for small n, where n is less than some threshold. If n grows beyond this threshold, the solution may no longer be feasible. When deciding to build an application, you should identify the feasibility threshold and determine the likelihood that the size of the input will exceed this value.

Length, depth, and width refer to sequences of elements connected by a common property of some kind. For length, the property is the segments or edges along a path or walk in a graph representation of the software. The only difference between length and depth is that for depth measures, all of the paths or walks must start at the same point. Both length and depth are related to the graph-theoretic notions of a geodesic (the shortest path between a pair of nodes) and distance (the length of a geodesic; see Chapter 4).

Width is a little different. The common property is the length of the path or walk from some start node, or a common depth value. Width is also related to the notions of a geodesic and distance, since width was defined as the number of elements a given distance from a selected root node. We will try to expand this notion of width to other situations while remaining faithful to the idea of distance being constant for all elements considered.

The width of a tree is simply the count of nodes at a given distance from the root. This value is called the *level* of the node. In a graph, ignoring geodesics, a node can lie on more than one level, even if the node selected as the root node does not change. If you apply geodesics and distance, a node can lie on only one level, given a root node. Further, in a graph, the choice of root node is completely arbitrary and you may select any node to be the root. In a directed graph, the choice of root node is constrained, but need not be fixed by the structure.

Functionality started out as an attempt to measure the value received by the user of an application (Albrecht 1984). This notion includes the implicit assumption that the functionality of the delivered software matches the functionality required by the user. Now, we all know that this is often not the case and function measures have been criticized in that regard. However, our inability to deliver true value to the user is not a measurement issue.

Functionality measures can provide a measure of the size of the scope of a project; to answer the question: "Just how big is this thing, anyway?" An interesting use of a functionality measure is to track the variance between the functionality required (measure applied to the problem domain) and the functionality delivered (measure applied to the product delivered).

You can measure the value of an application in terms of functionality used adjusted for the benefits actually gained by the using organization. For example, if an organization uses an application to help provide a service to its customers, and the cost of providing that service goes down, or the revenue gained from that service goes up, the organization has received positive value from the application. If, on the other hand, the cost of providing the service goes up, or the revenue goes down, the organization has received negative value from the application. Of course, there are many ways to measure value and each organization must develop a way that best meets its own needs.

You can take more than one view of functionality, even as it is discussed in terms of these uses. One view is expressed in terms of breadth and depth of scope. Scope is the *area* covered by an application. Given an application domain, an application that is broad in scope includes much of the domain within its boundaries. This may be expressed in terms of the number or proportion of the functions or processes in the domain which are supported at some level by the application. Depth of scope can be considered the level of support provided to a single function or process in the domain.

Thus, an application which fully automates a single process might be viewed as narrow but deep. An application which provides minimal support to many of the domain processes might be viewed as wide but shallow. You can also have narrow and shallow, and broad and deep, applications.

Another view of functionality is the amount of work performed by an application. The amount of work can be expressed in a number of ways, some of which are actually views of volume. You can discuss the work performed by an application in the same terms used to discuss the work performed by a person, group, or organization.

One view of the amount of work, which is actually a view of volume, is the number of pieces of paper, materials, or information processed in an interval of time. You should recognize this as basic productivity. It is not what we are after, however.

Another way to view the amount of work is to look at what the employee must know and what he or she must do with that knowledge in order to perform the work. This is the view of functionality underlying the various function point measures (Albrecht 1984; Jones 1988; Whitmire 1995). These two views of work will be developed further as we build empirical relational structures and then representations for functionality.

Each of these views of size can be characterized from any of the three dimensions—data, function, and control—discussed in Chapter 1. This is done by concentrating on elements within a single dimension as we build our empirical structures for measurement.

To characterize population, assign each element you wish to count to one of the three dimensions. In this sense, a dimension becomes an equivalence class of elements, such as all elements in the data dimension. It is possible that any given element may contribute to more than one dimension, in which case the element is not an atomic element: It is made up of component parts, each of which belongs to one and only one dimension.

Length is a bit trickier, but can lead to some useful insights. In the data dimension, the depth of an inheritance hierarchy provides valuable information about a design. The length of a chain of aggregations can be useful, too, and describes, for example, the level of a part in an indentured bill of materials.

In the behavior or function dimension, the length of a use case gives a view of the cross section of the application involved. You can also characterize a use case (Jacobsen et al. 1992) by its width, which counts the objects at a certain length from the initial object. Here, the segments on the path are the message links between objects. The combination of the length and width of a use case, as a couple (l, w), describes its shape.

Functionality has aspects of all three dimensions. This is the central idea behind functional measures such as DeMarco's Bang (DeMarco 1982) and 3D function points (Whitmire 1995). The structure, size, shape, and content of the static data model, the number and characteristics of the domain-level functions, and the number and types of external events all contribute to the functionality delivered by a software application.

Volume can be characterized in all three dimensions as well. Three important measures of stress on an application are the number of records in the database (data), the number of transactions processed per time period (function), and the sampling rate for external devices or the rate at which external events occur (control).

The measures mentioned in this section serve as examples only. I use them because they are commonly known. They may or may not be worthwhile to you as a designer.

FORMAL PROPERTIES

Aside from the requirements imposed by measurement theory, a measure for an attribute must satisfy certain empirical properties. The properties ensure that any candidate measure of an attribute, in this case size, satisfies our intuition about how a size measure should behave. These properties should help lead us to candidate empirical relational structures, weeding out those which would lead to inappropriate or counterintuitive measures. Using these properties and the technique in Chapter 3, you can construct a theoretically valid and intuitively appealing measure for any attribute you can describe. Let's develop a small set of such properties for each of the views of size identified in the previous section.

Population

Population is fundamentally related to the notion of set membership. A given element is either a member of a given population or not. The population is completely defined by its members, just as a set is defined by its elements. Thus, the formal properties for population and population measures are exactly those used to characterize sets.

In set theory, the size of a set is the number of elements it contains, called its cardinality. Cardinality is simply a count, and so are our potential measures of population. Briand, Morasca, and Basili (1996) listed five properties for a concept they call size, but which we call population. Denote the population of a set A by $\text{pop}(A)$.

Property P1
Population is nonnegative

$$\text{pop}(A) \geq 0 \tag{7.1}$$

where A is some set of elements which is considered as a coherent population (Briand, Morasca, and Basili 1996).

Property P2
Population can be null (Briand, Morasca, and Basili 1996):

$$A = \varnothing \Rightarrow \text{pop}(A) = 0 \tag{7.2}$$

Property P3
The population of combined populations is determined by the standard set union operation:

P3a: Population is additive for disjoint populations (Briand, Morasca, and Basili 1996):

$$A_1 \cap A_2 = \varnothing \Rightarrow \text{pop}(A_1 \cup A_2) = \text{pop}(A_1) + \text{pop}(A_2) \tag{7.3}$$

P3b: Population follows the *sieve principle* in general (Biggs 1985)

$$\text{pop}(A_1 \cup A_2 \cup \cdots \cup A_n) = \alpha_1 - \alpha_2 + \alpha_3 - \cdots + (-1)^{n-1}\alpha_n \tag{7.4}$$

where α_i is the sum of the populations of the intersections taken i at a time. For $n = 3$,

$$\text{pop}(A_1 \cup A_2 \cup A_3) = \alpha_1 - \alpha_2 + \alpha_3 \tag{7.5}$$

where

$$\alpha_1 = \text{pop}(A_1) + \text{pop}(A_2) + \text{pop}(A_3) \tag{7.6a}$$

$$\alpha_2 = \text{pop}(A_1 \cap A_2) + \text{pop}(A_2 \cap A_3) + \text{pop}(A_1 \cap A_3) \tag{7.6b}$$

and

$$\alpha_3 = \text{pop}(A_1 \cap A_2 \cap A_3) \tag{7.6c}$$

Property P4
Population in monotonic increasing; adding elements cannot decrease the population (Briand, Morasca, and Basili 1996):

$$A_1 \subseteq A_2 \Rightarrow \text{pop}(A_1) \leqslant \text{pop}(A_2) \qquad (7.7)$$

Property P5

Population is not synergistic; the population of two merged populations cannot exceed the sum of the two (Briand, Morasca, and Basili 1996):

$$A = A_1 \cup A_2 \Rightarrow \text{pop}(A) \leqslant \text{pop}(A_1) + \text{pop}(A_2) \qquad (7.8)$$

Measurement theory imposes at least one additional property, common to all empirical relational structures given in Chapter 5: Population must form a weak order. Use the notation $A_1 \succ A_2$ to denote the fact that population of A_1 exceeds that of A_2. The notation $A_1 \succeq A_2$ denotes that the population of A_1 is at least as big as that of A_2. Formally, we have Property P6.

Property P6

Population forms a weak order:

$$A_1 \succeq A_2 \vee A_2 \succeq A_1 \qquad (7.9a)$$

and

$$A_1 \succeq A_2 \Leftrightarrow \text{pop}(A_1) \geqslant \text{pop}(A_2) \qquad (7.9b)$$

Many empirical relational structures impose additional, often severe constraints. For example, an extensive representation implies that, in addition to forming a weak order, a representation is also weakly associative, monotonic under concatenation, and Archimedean. This last, the Archimedean property, is required of any representation which targets the real numbers or any subset of the real numbers.

Length

In the previous section, length was defined as the number of elements in a chain of connected elements. We were not particular about just what it is that connects these elements. In some cases, the connections are physical in that they are represented directly in the underlying model. This is the case for elements in a graph which lie on a common path. In other cases, the connections are conceptual in that they are not represented directly in the underlying model. The level of a tree is such a case, since it represents the set of elements which lie at the same distance from the root. The elements of a set need not have any other connection.

Briand, Morasca, and Basili (1996) define a set of properties for length which applies to both physical and conceptual connections. We denote the length of a sequence of elements C by len(C).

Property L1

Length is nonnegative (Briand, Morasca, and Basili 1996)

$$\text{len}(C) \geqslant 0 \qquad (7.10)$$

where C is a chain of connected elements.

Property L2
Length can be null (Briand, Morasca, and Basili, 1996):

$$C = \varnothing \Rightarrow \text{len}(C) = 0 \tag{7.11}$$

Property L3
Length is monotonic nonincreasing for connected elements; adding a new connection between components already in a chain cannot increase the length of the chain (Briand, Morasca, and Basili 1996)

$$c_1 \in C \wedge c_2 \in C \wedge C' = C \cup \{c_1 R c_2\} \Rightarrow \text{len}(C) \geqslant \text{len}(C') \tag{7.12}$$

where R is some relation indicating that c_1 and c_2 are connected in some way.

Property L4
Length is monotonic nondecreasing for elements in different chains; connecting elements in different chains does not decrease the combined length of the two chains (Briand, Morasca, and Basili 1996)

$$c_1 \in c_1 \wedge c_1 \notin C_2 \wedge c_2 \notin C_1 \wedge c_2 \in C_2 \wedge C = C_1 \cup C_2 \wedge C'$$
$$= C \cup \{c_1 R c_2\} \Rightarrow \text{len}(C) \leqslant \text{len}(C') \tag{7.13}$$

where R is again some relation indicating that c_1 and c_2 are connected in some way.

Property L5
The length of a set of disjoint (nonoverlapping) chains is the maximum of the lengths of the member chains (Briand, Morasca, and Basili 1996):

$$C = C_1 \cup C_2 \cup \cdots \cup C_n \wedge C_1 \cap C_2 \cap \cdots C_n = \varnothing$$
$$\Rightarrow \text{len}(C) = \max\{\text{len}(C_1), \text{len}(C_2),..., \text{len}(C)_n)\} \tag{7.14}$$

Like population, length is subject to the additional property, imposed by measurement theory, that it form a weak order. If the target of the representation is the real numbers, or a subset of the real numbers, then the Archimedean property is also imposed. Any particular empirical relational structure will impose additional properties, all of which must be satisfied by the model of length we are using to build our measure.

Functionality

There are no formal definitions of functionality from which we can build a model. Fenton (1991) describes functionality as being based on an intuitive notion of the function a product delivers. The Institute for Electrical and Electronic Engineers (IEEE) (1990) defines a *functional requirement* as "a requirement that specifies a function that a system or system component must be able to perform." Combining these ideas, we get to a definition of functionality as "the sum of the functions required of a system by its collective functional requirements."

However, Fenton's and the IEEE's definitions have a significant conflict. Fenton describes functionality in terms of the function that a system *actually* delivers.

The IEEE implies a definition of functionality in terms of the function the system is *required* to deliver. We know that these two concepts are not always the same. In fact, the difference between them can play a significant role in the success or failure of a project. We can even measure this difference. This problem leads to a slightly different definition of functionality:

> *Functionality is the set of functions derived from the same source; this source may be the set of functions requested, the set of functions delivered, or some other source.*

Note that functionality is not the same as value or utility. Value and utility are related to the amount of benefit the user receives from the system, and may have little, if anything, to do with the functionality either requested or delivered. Of course, the hope is that the functionality delivered closely aligns with the functionality actually needed (but not necessarily requested). Value and utility are also affected by nonfunctional issues such as usability and the cost to acquire, learn, and use the system.

Since functionality is defined as a set of functions, the properties for functionality are the same as those for population. The difference between functionality and population is that population focuses on the elements of a system and functionality focuses on the relationships between elements and on groups of elements. We denote the functionality of a set of functions A by fun(A).

Property F1
Functionality is nonnegative:

$$\text{fun}(A) \geq 0 \tag{7.15}$$

Property F2
Functionality can be null:

$$A = \varnothing \Rightarrow \text{fun}(A) = 0 \tag{7.16}$$

Property F3
Functionality behaves under combination or merging as set union:

F3a: Functionality is additive for disjoint sets of functions:

$$A_1 \cap A_2 = \varnothing \Rightarrow \text{fun}(A_1 \cup A_2) = \text{fun}(A_1) + \text{fun}(A_2) \tag{7.17}$$

F3b: Functionality follows the sieve principle in general

$$\text{fun}(A_1 \cup A_2 \cup \cdots \cup A_n) = \alpha_1 - \alpha_2 + \alpha_3 - \cdots + (-1)^{n-1} \alpha_n \tag{7.18}$$

where α_i is the sum of the populations of the intersections taken i at a time.

Property F4
Functionality is monotonic increasing; adding a new function to a system cannot decrease its functionality:

$$A_1 \subseteq A_2 \Rightarrow \text{fun}(A_1) \leq \text{fun}(A_2) \tag{7.19}$$

Property F5
Functionality is not synergistic; the population of two merged sets cannot exceed the sum of the two:

$$A = A_1 \cup A_2 \Rightarrow \text{fun}(A) \leq \text{fun}(A_1) + \text{fun}(A_2) \tag{7.20}$$

Property F6
Functionality forms a weak order:

$$A_1 \succeq A_2 \vee A_2 \succeq A_1 \tag{7.21a}$$

and

$$A_1 \succeq A_2 \Rightarrow \text{fun}(A_1) \geq \text{fun}(A_2) \tag{7.21b}$$

Additional properties, including the Archimedean property, may be imposed by particular empirical relational structures, depending on the representation you a trying to construct.

Volume

Like population, volume is fundamentally an issue of set membership, with one important difference. With population, an element is either a member of a population or not. An external event and an operation is required to make an element not in a population a member of that population, or an element in a population no longer a member.

Volume, however, includes a time factor. Elements can be added to or removed from a set simply because time has passed. Set membership is determined at a specific point in time. The definition or description of that point in time is essential to fully describe set membership. The volume measured at an instant in time is called *instantaneous volume*. Volume can also include summaries of multiple points in time. Important examples include *peak* and *nominal* or *average volume* over an interval of time. An interval spans one or more contiguous points in time.

This leads to a set of properties similar to those for population, but with a time factor which may be a point in time or a time interval. For each property, a point in time will be denoted by t_i, where i is an integer, usually 1. An interval in time will be denoted by $t_2 - t_1$ where t_2 is assumed to be later than t_1. Denote the volume of a set A at time t by $\text{vol}(A, t)$ and denote the peak volume of a set A over the interval $t_2 - t_1$ by $\text{vol}_p(A, t_2 - t_1)$. Similarly, denote the nominal volume of a set A over the interval $t_2 - t_1$ by $\text{vol}_n(A, t_2 - t_1)$. Normally, the nominal volume is the arithmetic average volume over the interval, but you could use the median volume or some other measure that meets your needs.

Property V1
Volume is nonnegative:

$$\text{vol}(A, t_i) \geq 0 \tag{7.22a}$$

$$\text{vol}_p(A, t_2 - t_1) \geq 0 \tag{7.22b}$$

and

$$\text{vol}_n(A, t_2 - t_1) \geq 0 \qquad (7.22c)$$

Property V2

Volume can be null:

$$A_t = \varnothing \Rightarrow \text{vol}(A, t_i) = 0 \qquad (7.23a)$$

$$\max(A_t, t_2 - t_1) = \varnothing \Rightarrow \text{vol}_p(A, t_2 - t_1) = 0 \qquad (7.23b)$$

and

$$\text{nom}(A_t, t_2 - t_1) = \varnothing \Rightarrow \text{vol}_n(A, t_2 - t_1) = 0 \qquad (7.23c)$$

Property V3

The combination of instantaneous volumes is additive for disjoint volumes and in general follows the sieve principle; additivity does not apply to volumes over intervals of time

$$A_1 \cap A_2 = \varnothing \Rightarrow \text{vol}(A_1 \cup A_2, t_i) = \text{vol}(A_1, t_i) + \text{vol}(A_2, t_i) \qquad (7.24a)$$

$$\text{vol}(A_1 \cup A_2 \cup \cdots \cup A_n, t_i) = \alpha_1 - \alpha_2 + \alpha_3 - \cdots + (-1)^{n-1}\alpha_n \qquad (7.24b)$$

where α_i is the sum of the intersections taken i at a time. Note that in all cases, the volumes must be measured at the same point in time, t_i.

Property V4

Volume is monotonic increasing when the time factor is held constant:

$$A_1 \subseteq A_2 \Rightarrow \text{vol}(A_1, t_i) \leq \text{vol}(A_2, t_i) \qquad (7.25a)$$

$$A_1 \subseteq A_2 \Rightarrow \text{vol}_p(A_1, t_2 - t_1) \leq \text{vol}(A_2, t_2 - t_1) \qquad (7.25b)$$

and

$$A_1 \subseteq A_2 \Rightarrow \text{vol}_n(A_1, t_2 - t_1) \leq \text{vol}(A_2, t_2 - t_1) \qquad (7.25c)$$

Because of the time factor, the measured volume over an interval in time can change simply by changing the time interval. If the volume factor is held constant, and the time interval is shortened, the volume has risen, whether peak or nominal volumes are used. This is reflected in the fact that 10,000 transactions per hour is a higher volume that 10,000 transactions per week. Likewise, if the volume factor is held constant and the time interval is lengthened, the measured volume has decreased. This leads to the fifth property of a volume measure, which is a different view of property V4.

Property V5

Volume rises monotonically in inverse relation to the variation in the time factor, if the volume is held constant:

$$t_2 - t_1 \leq t_3 - t_4 \Rightarrow \text{vol}_p(A_1, t_2 - t_1) \geq \text{vol}(A_1, t_3 - t_4) \qquad (7.26a)$$

and

$$t_2 - t_1 \geq t_3 - t_4 \Rightarrow \text{vol}_n(A_1, t_2 - t_1) \leq \text{vol}(A_1, t_3 - t_4) \qquad (7.26b)$$

Property V6

Volume is not synergistic; the volume of two merged instantaneous volumes cannot exceed the sum of the two, provided the time factor is held constant:

$$A = A_1 \cup A_2 \Rightarrow \text{vol}(A, t_i) \leq \text{vol}(A_1, t_i) + \text{vol}(A_2, t_i) \qquad (7.27)$$

Like property V3, this applies only to instantaneous volumes.

Property V7

Volume forms a weak order. For instantaneous volumes, this ordering can be only on the volume factor, since it is the only factor you can vary. For interval volumes, you can vary either the volume factor or the time factor. Note that the ordering induced by varying the volume factor is the opposite of the ordering induced by varying the time factor.

Like the other views of size, volume measures may be subject to additional constraints imposed by the empirical relational structure you are trying to build. Note that since volume has at least two factors, by definition, you will be constrained to using either a two-factor conjoint structure or a two-dimensional proximity structure (see Chapter 5).

EMPIRICAL RELATIONAL STRUCTURES

Four very different views of size have been explored and each view presents many opportunities for measurement. Measures from each view have their uses; many of these uses are rather important. In this section, we refer to our model from Chapter 6 and build an empirical relational structure for each view. Hopefully, we can build a structure that not only makes intuitive sense, but meets our empirical properties from the previous section. In this section and the next, parts of the measurement construction technique in Chapter 3 will be applied.

For each view of size, we try to discover characteristics of the model which help to explain the phenomena we are trying to measure. For a given view of size, this means trying to discover those characteristics in the model which help to explain our intuitive understanding of size from that point of view. For population, this might mean discovering those elements of the model which, when they increase in number, cause or explain an increase in the apparent size of the design. This is done for each view in turn.

Population

Given that the selection of an empirical relational structure is driven by our goals, we should start the search by naming some goals for measuring population. The most common use of a population measure is as an input to a prediction system for effort, staffing, or schedule—in other words, for estimation. In this case, we would like the units of population to reflect the units of work we need to estimate. It may be that we want a measure of functionality rather than a measure of population.

Many population measures are built from components that are themselves population measures. Weighted methods per class (Chidamber and Kemerer 1994) are often combined with the number of classes (Lorenz and Kidd 1994; and nearly everyone else) to create a compound measure used for estimation. I make this slight digression to point out that the empirical relational structure need not be constructed from a single element of the model. So, use your imagination.

Some authors, such as Chidamber and Kemerer, and Graham (1996), measure the size of a class as the weighted sum of the populations of attributes and methods. For this and similar uses, you need an interval or ratio scale measure. You might also consider a conjoint structure, such as a two-factor structure of attribute and method populations. Such a structure, in fact, serves as the basis for most weighted sum measures (which implies that all weighted sum measures are at best interval scales).

Another use for population measures is investigating cause and effect relationships. For example, you might be trying to discover if there is such a relationship between the population of, say, attributes and the population of defects. Here, the scale requirements, and thus the type of structure, are driven by the types of statistical analysis and inference techniques you wish to use. Most of the more powerful parametric techniques will work with either an interval or ratio scale measure, so stretching for a ratio scale measure may not be worth the effort (and it can often be quite a stretch).

Since population is based on set membership, it is always possible to build a structure which leads to an interval scale due to the properties of the algebra of sets. If you need an additive concatenation operation, you will need to ensure that any populations you combine are disjoint. It is not possible to make additive the populations of two concatenated sets which are not disjoint to begin with. You need to be careful: It is not easy to determine just when you need an additive concatenation operation from when you can do without. Do not attempt to define such an operation just because someone says you need it.

If you are creative, you may find the opportunity to build a probability or conditional utility structure. These structures are concerned with set membership and result in absolute scales on the interval [0, 1]. With only a slight effort, you should be able to recognize the basic pattern shared by percentage-based measures.

Another use of a population measure is to assess the similarity of two or more design elements. Some forms of similarity measurement require the use of a feature proximity structure. Such similarity is covered in Chapter 14.

Length

The concept of length, including depth and width, has many uses in object-oriented software design. One example that comes to mind is comparing the relative length and width measures for several use cases. In object-oriented analysis, a use case is a network of messages that cuts a swath through the object model. A use case can consist of a single chain of messages, one following the other sequentially, or it can contain multiple parallel chains of messages. These multiple chains may or may not converge at the end; it doesn't matter.

If you use your imagination, many forms of comparison begin to look like applications of length, or width, or depth. Anytime there are elements connected by either physical or conceptual links, you should consider length measurement.

The model of length is built on the notion of paths through a graph structure of some kind. You are not limited to trees or even directed graphs. At its core, length is based on the notion of line segments, either in number or in number and length, where the length is represented as a value or weight attached to a segment.

It may not be obvious, but I recognize a geometrical structure based on some notion of distance. In particular, unidimensional and multidimensional spatial proximity structures may prove useful. Of course, if you need an additive concatenation operation, try to build an extensive structure.

Length is also modeled in terms of conceptual connections between design elements. You can use spatial proximity structures here, too. Also, consider the various forms of difference structures. While not based on the idea of geometric proximity, difference structures are excellent for representing intervals and comparing lengths.

Functionality

Perhaps the most common use for a measure of functionality is as a component of an indirect measure of some external attribute, such as construction rate or defect density. Another use of functionality is to compare two applications in terms of their scope or amount of work covered. All of these uses require that a functionality measure be at least an interval scale. While you can order applications in terms of their coverage using an ordinal scale rating, there are often problems with this ordering when applications are compared on two or more dimensions, such as breadth and depth of scope.

The need for interval scale measures limits the search to those structures discussed in Chapter 5, which is not really very limiting. To further narrow the search, you need to focus on the empirical elements that you wish to map to numbers or symbols. This discussion is longer than those for other views because our empirical understanding of functionality is less mature and more exploration is required.

Earlier, two distinct views of functionality were discussed: breadth and depth of scope, and the amount of work performed. From this point on, each view must be discussed separately as we seek to identify the elements of the model which contribute to and explain our empirical understanding.

At first glance, breadth and depth of scope seem very similar to width and height. Given two rectangles of shape (x_1, y_1) and (x_2, y_2), where each element represents a distance along a dimension, it is said that they are the same height if $x_1 = x_2$, the same width if $y_1 = y_2$, the same shape if $x_1/x_2 = y_1/y_2$, and the same size if $x_1 y_1 = x_2 y_2$ (in terms of area covered). We might like our measure of scope to behave in the same way. That is, given two applications of scope (b_1, d_1) and (b_2, d_2), ignoring for the moment that we have absolutely no idea what these numbers mean or how they are constructed, we want to say that the applications are the same breadth if $b_1 = b_2$, the same depth if $d_1 = d_2$, the same shape if $b_1/b_2 = d_1/d_2$, and the same size if $b_1 d_1 = b_2 d_2$. Of course, it is not required that the relationship between b_1 and d_1, and b_2 and d_2, be multiplicative. We could use addition; many existing measures of functionality do just that (function points, for example).

Given this desired behavior, we narrow our structure search to either a two-factor conjoint structure or a multidimensional spatial proximity structure of two dimensions. If we look into a conjoint structure, we still need to find empirical relational structures for breadth and depth separately. Given that our empirical understanding of depth is expressed as a proportion, it might make sense to look into a probability structure of some kind. We then have to work out how we are to combine breadth and depth in order to get the desired behavior.

Breadth of scope can be expressed as the number or proportion of functions in the domain which are supported by the application. The number of functions yields an absolute scale measure on the interval $[0, \infty)$. The proportion of functions yields an absolute scale measure on the interval $[0, 1]$. Both the functions in the domain and those in the application can be represented by means of use cases (Jacobsen et al. 1992).

Consider the directed graph built from the message links through the class structure. This graph, call it R_m, is constructed by ignoring all but the message link arrows in the category **DesignState**. Each use case is a walk through this graph. One potential empirical element for a function is therefore a walk through the graph R_m. If the model included all of the functions in the domain, and not just those you plan to include in your application, you could use this same empirical model to determine the proportion of functions covered: It would be the ratio of walks crossing or contained within the boundary of the application to the total number of walks in the model. Note, though, that even if you use a use case as an empirical element in breadth of scope, you haven't settled on the *number* of use cases as the *representation* of breadth of scope. For a number of reasons, mostly technical, it may be necessary to modify the actual representation in order to construct a measure.

Depth of scope is the level of support provided by the application to any particular function. Here, you face two challenges: to empirically define depth in terms of a single function and to empirically combine depth across functions to determine the depth for the application as a whole.

Empirically, you can define depth of scope by the proportion of a task model enclosed within the application. To do this, you must model precisely both the task as a whole and the portion of the task supported by the application. Since you are working with proportions, and thus percentages, you are led to investigate the various probability structures.

Note that three separate empirical structures are being constructed: one for breadth, one for depth, and one to combine the two. Since breadth and depth are orthogonal, construct each structure independently of the other, and combine them later. This allows the construction of a proximity structure. It is not a necessary requirement for conjoint structures, which construct all representations simultaneously.

Now, let's move to the other view of functionality, expressed in terms of the amount of knowledge and the manipulations of that knowledge required to perform a function. This view can be described as a measure of the information content of a function and the "information dexterity" required to use the information to perform the function.

You can model information empirically as types of data. You are interested in the number of *types* of data, and not the number of *items* of data, since the latter is a measure of volume, not functionality. To determine the information content of a task, build a data model which contains two components:

1. The flows of information into and out of the task's boundary.
2. The structure of the data maintained—added, updated, and deleted—by the task and the information maintained external to the task, but referred to during execution of the task.

Just in case you happen to be dozing, this is the empirical model behind such measures as function points.

You can model information manipulations as the types of operations performed on the data during the course of executing the task. Again, you are interested in the number of *types* of operations, or the number of different operations, and not the number of operation *executions*, again because the latter is a measure of volume. This is the empirical model underlying the function dimension in 3D function points.

As an aside, 3D function points also consider the number of different types of external events to which the system must respond. The idea is that the greater the variety of these events, the more difficult the task. But, in our example, these events are not considered, so they will not be worked into our empirical model. This will leave us with only two of the three dimensions of software. The third dimension can be added later if needed.

The amount of information and the operations required to manipulate it appear to be independent. Thus, you can consider a two-factor conjoint structure or a two-dimensional spatial proximity structure. The proximity structure yields a vector with two components, each of which must have the same unit (in the sense of dimensional analysis). You can leave the proximity vector as a vector, or combine its components into a single value with the same unit as both components. The conjoint structure yields a single value with a different unit than either of its components, each of which may have different units. Which of these two types of structures chosen depends upon whether you can construct models of each component that meet the structural requirements.

You need two different empirical elements for your structure: one to represent types of information and one to represent types of operations. The types of information needed by a job or function come in three basic forms:

1. Static information accumulated over time and controlled, modified, and maintained by the function or application (personal knowledge).
2. Static information accumulated over time, but controlled, modified, and maintained by external sources (reference knowledge).
3. Information which flows into and out of the function during the course of the work (transactional information needed or generated by the function).

Some of you will recognize that all three of these types are represented by the element types in function points (Albrecht 1984). A crucial difference between these information types and those in function points is that the elements in function points are *one specific representation* of information needed to perform a function, while all that's been done here is to identify some empirical elements of information. You have yet to define a unit or mapping to a numerical system, which will necessarily include counting rules for each element mapped. Still, the similarities indicate that function points at least started out in the right direction. Also, the main theoretical criticism of function points (such as Kitchenham, Pfleeger, and Fenton, 1995) is in regards to the construction of the representation, not to the selection of empirical elements.

Selecting empirical elements for operations is a little more difficult. You must almost develop a process model for the function and then use those identified steps as the elements. The primary difficulty is to decide at which level of abstraction you should stop modeling. For example, suppose you are describing a clerical task of filing documents. At one level, the process task is to insert the documents into the file according to the ordering scheme. This description may be good enough or it may not be. To improve it, drop down one level of abstraction and actually describe the mechanisms and decisions in the ordering scheme. You can continue dropping down levels until you have a series of instructions like: "Walk up to the file cabinet; stand facing the cabinet; reach for the drawer handle. . . " Normally, this level is too detailed and a happy medium is somewhere between two extremes.

For now, we weasel out of this situation by saying that the selection of the appropriate level of detail is a representation issue, to be solved later. In fact, it *is* a representation issue. One of the problems that needs to be solved when constructing a representation is to define the units of an empirical element which actually get counted. This is also one of the great failings of many of the existing measures: They don't clearly define just what gets counted and how the chosen unit relates to the empirical elements. For now, it is sufficient to simply select an "atomic operation," to be defined later, as the empirical element for the operational part of the model.

You now have the components for either a spatial proximity structure or a conjoint structure. The information content could, in turn, be either a spatial proximity structure or a conjoint structure. Function points are an example of an additive conjoint structure. How you progress from this point is determined by whether you can meet the structural requirements for either of these types of structures.

Volume

Three different types of volume measures were identified, all based on population counts:

1. Population count at a time t.
2. Nominal (average or median) population during the time interval $t_2 - t_1$.
3. Peak population count during the time interval $t_2 - t_1$.

You can use an empirical structure which leads to an ordinal measure for all of these types, if you are satisfied with using the median value for the nominal volume. You probably will prefer an interval or ratio scale measure so you can measure nominal volume using averages.

So, start with a set of empirical relational structures which can be used to construct representations of population on the interval or ratio scale. From this point on, follow the process for population structures given in this section. The time factor is introduced to construct a representation in the next section.

POTENTIAL MEASURES

As seen in the last section, a given empirical understanding of a characteristic can lead to the selection of more than one potential empirical relational structure. Likewise, the selection of a given empirical relational structure can lead to more than one possible representation. In this section, one potential representation for one empirical relational structure is developed for each view of size. These representations, which will not be named, are examples only. They serve to illustrate the process for creating a representation.

Steps three and four of the measure construction technique, discussed in Chapter 3, will be applied. In these steps, we select a final empirical relational structure and then build a representation by mapping our empirical elements, relations, and operations to numeric elements, relations, and operations—which together form a numerical relational structure. Our major decisions are the selection of empirical and numeric elements, the empirical and numeric relations, and the empirical and numeric operations.

Population

Let us assume, for the moment, that we require an extensive representation for the population of classes in a design. The whys and hows of this decision are not part of our concern in this section. Chapter 5 identifies several potential extensive structures, including closed, positive, periodic, nonclosed with an essential maximum, nonclosed with no essential maximum, and conditionally connected extensive structures.

From a cursory study of this chapter, we conclude that we can probably get by with a closed extensive structure. This conclusion is based on the fact that we are dealing with set of objects of some kind. No matter what we do to these sets, we will always end up with a set of objects, so our structure, whatever else it may be, is closed. Formally, given a set of objects A and an operation $\circ: A \times A \to X$, we can show that the structure $\langle A, \circ \rangle$ is closed since X is always a subset of A. That is, every member of X is always a member of A (if A is defined correctly).

To build a closed extensive structure, we need a set of elements A, a binary relation $\succeq$, and an operation $\circ: A \times A \to A$ such that the structure $\langle A, \succeq, \circ \rangle$ meets the following requirements:

1. $\langle A, \succeq \rangle$ forms a weak order.

2. $\circ$ is weekly associative: $a \circ (b \circ c) \sim (a \circ b) \circ c$.

3. $\succeq$ is monotonic: $a \succeq b \Leftrightarrow a \circ c \succeq b \circ c \Leftrightarrow c \circ a \succeq c \circ b$.

4. The structure is Archimedean: if $a \succ b$, then for any $c, d \in A$, there exists an integer n such that $na \circ c \succ nb \circ d$, where na is defined recursively as $1a = a$, $(n + 1)a = na \circ a$.

In addition, the representation must satisfy the properties for a population measure given previously. All of these properties are implied by the requirements for a closed extensive structure. This means that any measure built from a closed extensive structure—based upon empirical elements, relations, and operations that model population—automatically satisfies all of the properties for population.

The first decision is the selection of empirical elements and the numeric elements to which they will map. Since we are building a representation of the population of classes in a design, an obvious choice for our empirical elements is the set of class category objects in the category **DesignState** (see Chapter 6). An equally obvious choice for a set of numeric elements is the set of cardinal numbers, which is a proper subset of the reals. Our mapping function $\phi: A \rightarrow R$ is $\phi(A) = |A|$ which is the cardinality of the set A.

Extensive structures require a binary relation $\succeq$, from which we can define $\succ$, $\sim$, $\prec$, or $\preceq$. They also require a binary operation $\circ$ (binary from $A \times A \rightarrow A$) which serves as a concatenation operation. Things begin to get a little tricky here. Our requirements dictate that $\succeq$ is transitive, connected, and monotonic under concatenation.

The requirements for transitivity and connectedness are embedded in the condition that $\succeq$ form a weak order. Both of these requirements can be met by mapping $\succeq$ to $\geq$ so that $A \succeq B \Leftrightarrow |A| \geq |B|$. Thus, $A \succeq B$ if (and only if) the set A has at least as many members as the set B. For our purposes, a design state A is bigger than a design state B if A contains more classes. If both design states contain the same number of classes, write $A \sim B$.

Next, we need to define our concatenation operation $\circ$. Since we are dealing with sets of classes in design states, a reasonable choice for concatenation is the AddClass operation defined in Chapter 6. The AddClass operation is a functor with two components: one which operates on the objects of the category **Class** (state spaces, states, and attribute domains) and the other which operates on the arrows of the category **Class** (state selection, class operation, and attribute projection). The basic model for both components is set union. We must now test each component to see if our operation is associative and, together with our relation $\succeq$, monotonic.

Associativity is easy since we already know that set union is associative. Monotonicity is more difficult. Our approach is to attempt to find a situation in which the statement

$$a \succeq b \Leftrightarrow a \circ c \succeq b \circ c \Leftrightarrow c \circ a \succeq c \circ b \qquad (7.28)$$

is false. We use this approach because we need find only one situation which causes the condition to fail. The alternative is a positive proof, which is much more difficult. We need to find a situation in which either

$$a \circ c \succeq b \circ c \qquad (7.29a)$$

or

$$c \circ a \succeq c \circ b \qquad (7.29b)$$

fails. Consider the situation where $c \subseteq a$ ($a \cap c = c$ and $a \cup c = a$) and $c \cap b$ $\varnothing$. Plugging this into (7.28), and substituting $\cup$ for $\circ$ results in:

$$a \succeq b \Leftrightarrow a \cup c \succeq b \cup c \Leftrightarrow c \cup a \succeq c \cup b \qquad (7.30)$$

Substituting a for $a \cup c$ and $c \cup a$ results in:

$$a \succeq b \Leftrightarrow a \succeq b \cup c \Leftrightarrow a \succeq c \cup b. \qquad (7.31)$$

Now, suppose that $|b| + |c| > |a|$, which is entirely possible (set $|a| = 5$, $|b| = 4$, and $|c| = 2$, for example). We know that $|b \cup c| = |b| + |c|$ since $b \cap c = \varnothing$. This would give us

$$|a| < |b \cup c| \qquad (7.32)$$

which causes statement (7.31) to be false; we fail to satisfy monotonicity.

In our model, this situation will arise whenever we combine two design states that have some classes in common. Because of this situation, we cannot, in general, build an extensive structure for the population of classes in a design state. Such a structure can be built only if we can assure ourselves that any pair of design states we wish to combine share no common classes. If we can't be sure of this, we must find some other representation. If we are in a situation where we can weed out common classes before performing the combination, which can sometimes be done, we can use an extensive representation.

We can still use the representation we developed, but we must realize that it is not a ratio scale measure. At least it is not an extensive measure. It may well be the case that we can make our structure meet the requirements for some other structure which leads to the ratio scale. We can be fairly certain, however, that our measure as it stands is an interval scale measure, but we haven't yet tested this assertion. In the interest of space, I leave this test as an exercise for the reader.

Length

For this exercise, assume that we are building a representation for the length of a use case. A use case model takes the form of a directed graph in which the nodes are software objects and the edges are message links. Use cases form a graph rather than a tree in general because it is possible for an object to send a message to an object which is "upstream" from itself; we can have cycles.

The graph will take the basic form of a tree, with a single entry point and one or more termination points, but it is not of necessity strictly a tree. The entry point is the object which receives the initial message from outside the application.

This message represents the application's initial response to an external event. The termination points are objects in the use case which do not send any further messages. If cycles exist, these termination points may be difficult or even impossible to identify.

The length of a use case is defined as the length of the longest geodesic from the entry point to any termination point or the longest geodesic in the graph. A geodesic in a graph is the shortest path between a pair of nodes. The length of the geodesic from node a to node b is defined as the *distance* between a and b, and is written $\delta(a, b)$. The length of the longest geodesic is the graph's *diameter* (Biggs 1990). Geodesics, distance, and diameters are covered in Chapter 4.

Because we are dealing with distances, it is tempting to see if we can construct a unidimensional spatial proximity structure. To do so, we need to be able to construct a segmentally additive proximity structure. One of the requirements for this structure is that for every pair of distinct objects $a, c \in A$, where A is the set of objects in the graph, and for any nonnegative $\alpha \leq \delta(a, c)$, there is a node b on a segment from a to c whose distance from a is exactly α. This is a solvability condition.

If, in our model, we assign every message link the value of one, the distance between adjacent nodes is one and the distance between any two nodes is the number of links between them. We are thus mapping our empirical understanding of length into the set of natural numbers.

The question then is whether this situation does, or can be made to, satisfy the solvability condition. The most likely case for failure is the segment between two adjacent objects. Given two adjacent objects a and c, their distance $\delta(a, c) = 1$. The only way to have an $\alpha \leq \delta(a, c)$ is for α to be either 0 or 1. If $\alpha = 0$, $b = a$, and $\delta(a, b) = 0$, which does indeed satisfy our condition. If $\alpha = 1$, $b = c$, and $\delta(a, b) = 1$, which also satisfies our condition.

We next need to show that our model satisfies the requirements for a proximity structure and the remaining requirement for a segmentally additive structure. If this can be done, our model automatically satisfies the properties for a length measure given earlier.

The requirements for a proximity structure are easy to satisfy with our model. The first requirement is that the structure $\langle A \times A, \succeq \rangle$ is a weak order. That is, the relation $\succeq$ is an ordering of intervals between objects. An interval between two objects a and b is defined as the length of the geodesic between them. Thus, the value of $\delta(a, b)$ is the number of message links along the shortest path from a to b, since each message link was assigned the value of one.

For our model to form a weak order, we need to show that it is both transitive and connected. For transitivity, we require that:

$$(a, b) \succeq (c, d) \land (c, d) \land (e, f) \Rightarrow (a, b) \land (e, f) \qquad (7.33)$$

This is easy to show, since the interval (a, b) is measured in terms of the number of segments between a and b. Thus, $(a, b) \succeq (c, d)$ indicates that there are at least as many segments between a and b as between c and d. Likewise, $(c, d) \succeq (e, f)$ indicates that there are at least as many segments between c and d as between e

and f. Since it is already known that this property holds for $\succeq$ when applied to ordinal numbers, we know that it applies to distance in a directed or undirected graph.

Connectedness requires that:

$$(a, b) \succeq (c, d) \vee (c, d) \succeq (a, b) \tag{7.34}$$

This, too, is easy to show for distances between nodes. Since we mapped the interval (a, b) to the natural number $\delta(a, b)$, and the relation $\succeq$ to $\geq$, we can depend on the connectedness of the $\geq$ relation and natural numbers to show connectedness in our empirical relational system. Both transitivity and connectedness are general properties of distance in a graph.

We next need to show that our empirical relational structure satisfies the second requirement of a proximity structure, namely that $(a, b) > (a, a)$ whenever $a \neq b$. In our case, this is easy. $\delta(a, a)$ is always zero, since we are constrained to using the shortest path between a node and itself. Furthermore, $\delta(a, b)$ is always at least one whenever $a \neq b$, so we always meet this requirement.

The third requirement for a proximity structure is called minimality and requires that $(a, a) \sim (b, b)$, or $\delta(a, a) = \delta(b, b)$. As seen earlier, the distance between a node and itself is always zero, so the minimality requirement is always satisfied.

To meet the fourth requirement, symmetry, we need to ignore the direction of the arrows. Symmetry requires that $(a, b) \sim (b, a)$, or $\delta(a, b) = \delta(b, a)$. When the direction of the arrows is ignored, we can trace backwards, which allows us to meet this requirement.

The last test is the Archimedean condition for a segmentally additive proximity structure and is the most difficult. The Archimedean axiom requires that if $e, f \in A$ (e and f are objects in our use case), and $e \neq f$ (they are distinct), then there exist objects $b_0, b_1, ..., b_n \in A$ such that $b_0 = a$, $b_n = c$, and $(e, f) \succeq (b_{i-1}, b_i)$ for all $i = 1, ..., n$. In English, this axiom requires that we can always find a sequence of objects, starting with a and ending with c, such that for some other pair of objects e and f, the distance between them, $\delta(e, f)$ is as least as much as the distance between each pair of objects between a and c, inclusive.

The easiest way to test our structure against this condition is to pick the most degenerate case we can think of and see if we fail to satisfy it. Suppose that a and c are adjacent. We thus have $\delta(a, c) = 1$, $b_0 = a$, $b_1 = b_n = c$. Since e and f cannot be the same objects, the closest they can be is adjacent, with $\delta(e, f) = 1$. Now the test: The only pair we can test against is (b_1, b_n). Since $b_1 = b_n = c$, $\delta(b_1, b_n) = 0$. Therefore $\delta(e, f) = 1 \geq \delta(b_1, b_n) = 0$, so we meet the Archimedean condition. We can extend this sequence by induction to connect any two nodes.

We have successfully built a representation of the length of a use case by modeling the use case as a directed graph, with objects as nodes and message links as arrows, and by assigning a weight of one to every link. Our representation is in the form of a segmentally additive proximity structure, which leads to the ratio scale (δ is a ratio scale measure). Note that we have built a ratio scale measure without the use of extensive measurement.

Functionality

Two different views of functionality were discussed. One related to the coverage an application provides a business process in terms of breadth and depth of scope. The other views functionality as the amount of work performed, whether by an application or organization of one or more people.

The empirical model for breadth of scope in the first view is based on the number or proportion of tasks within the business process that are supported by the application. The model for depth is based on the proportion of a specific task that is supported by the application. We did not work out a way to combine these two models into a single model of size for the entire application.

The empirical model built into the second view focused on the types of information required, referenced, maintained, and generated by the process being measured. It also included a model of the types of operations performed on that information. This particular model left out the notion of external events to which the process must respond.

In this section, a representation will be built for one of these views. I am tempted to build one for the second view, since I could end up with function points or 3D function points. However great the temptation, building a representation of coverage based on breadth and depth of scope is the more difficult of the two, and potentially the more useful, although both views have a great many uses.

Since the aim is for a representation of the breadth and depth of coverage an application provides to a business process, it makes sense to try for one in terms of percentages. We are trying to build a pair of probability structures: one for breadth and one for depth. Further, we can either leave these as an ordered pair (b, d), or combine them into an additive conjoint structure of two components. We will get an additive conjoint structure, rather than a multiplicative one, because breadth and depth are orthogonal to each other. This fact will be useful when we compare applications of equal coverage as defined by their shape: the sum of breadth and depth, or $b + d$.

A probability structure maps the likelihood of an event occurring into the interval [0, 1]. Since a percentage representation is being built and not a probability representation, some terminology needs translating. Chapter 5 covers several probability structures. Our intuitive understanding of percentages closely resembles a structure of qualitative probability which models unconditional probability. A structure of qualitative probability has five requirements.

First, the structure takes the form of a triple $\langle X, E, \succeq \rangle$ where X is a nonempty set of possible outcomes, E is an algebra of sets on X, and $\succeq$ is a binary ordering relation on E. In the representation of breadth, the set of potential outcomes can be interpreted as the set of functions, subprocesses, or use cases in the business process. For depth, the set of potential outcomes for a given function, subprocess, or use case is full coverage by the application. In other words, assign the value 1 to an application which fully implements a function, subprocess, or use case, and the value 0 to an application which provides no support to a function, subprocess, or use case.

In order to proceed further, we need to partition the business process into sets of discrete "events." Functions, subprocesses, or use cases can be used as the partitioning mechanism. Use cases are a convenient way to model both functions and subprocesses. Here, a subprocess may consist of one or more functions or atomic tasks. The business process is the union of all of the use cases it contains.

In a probability structure, the algebra of sets E is a nonempty family of subsets of X such that for every set $A, B \in E$, $-A \in E$ and $A \cup B \cup E$, where $-A = X \setminus A$. For breadth, if we consider the sets A and B to be two potential sets of coverage, E then becomes a set which contains all of the possible coverages of a business process by an application. For depth, E becomes a set which contains all of the possible levels of coverage of a use case by an application. In general, $E \subseteq \mathbb{P}X$, but in our case, $E = \mathbb{P}X$.

The definition of the ordering relation $\succeq_B$ for breadth is based on the proportion of use cases covered by the application. Thus, if $A \succeq_B B$, application A provides some level of support to at least as many of the use cases in the business process than application B. The definition of the ordering relation $\succeq_D$ for depth is based on the level of support an application provides to a given use case. Thus, if $B \succeq_D A$ for a particular use case, application B provides at least as much support to the use case than application A. Both $\succeq_B$ and $\succeq_D$ are weak orders, since they are both transitive and connected. This follows from our empirical understanding of coverages. The first requirement for constructing a structure of qualitative probability has been satisfied.

The second requirement states that X is nonempty and that a particular event A can be empty. For breadth, this means that our business process must contain at least one use case and that an application need not provide any support to any of the use cases in the business process. For depth, this means that a use case must have some potential for support by an application, but a given application need not provide any support. Both of these situations are obviously covered by our model.

The third requirement states that, given three events A, B, and C, if $A \cap B = B \cap C = \varnothing$, then $B \succeq C \Leftrightarrow A \cup B \succeq A \cup C$. Interpreting this in our scenario is straightforward. For both breadth and depth, interpret A, B, and C to be the coverages provided by three applications, which are conveniently called A, B, and C. For breadth, when we say that $A \cap B = \varnothing$, we mean that A and B support different use cases, with no use cases in common, at any level of depth other than no support at all. For depth, interpret $A \cap B = \varnothing$ to mean that while both applications provide support to the same use case, they do not support any portion of the use case in common—there is no overlapping functionality between them.

For breadth, interpret $A \cup B$ to be the set of use cases in a business process supported by application A, or B, or both. Given this interpretation, the third requirement states that if $B \succeq C$ (B supports at least as many use cases as C), then the combined support by applications A and B is at least as much as the combined support for applications A and C. This seems to be intuitively obvious, so we consider the requirement met for breadth.

For depth, interpret $A \cup B$ to be the support provided to a use case by either application A, or B, or both. Thus, the third requirement states that if application B provides at least as much support to a given use case as application C, then the combined support provided by applications A and B is at least as much as the combined support provided by A and C. This, too, seems intuitively obvious and we consider this requirement met for depth.

The fourth condition—the Archimedean condition—requires some extra work. First, we need to define what a standard sequence relative to A would be like in our structure. Krantz and associates (1971) define such a sequence inductively. A sequence of one set consists of a set A_1, which is also B_1, and which is equivalent to A (it has the same number of elements as A). To build A_2, find a set C_1, which is disjoint from B_1 and is equivalent to A, and take $A_2 = B_1 \cup C_1$. To build A_3, find a set B_2 which is equivalent to A_2, and may in fact be A_2, and a set C_2 which is equivalent to A and disjoint from B_2, and set $A_3 = B_2 \cup C_2$. We continue doing this until we run out of sets to add to our sequence. The requirement is that any such sequence is finite.

For our purposes, it is rather easy to show that we meet the Archimedean condition, since we start out with a finite set. For breadth, create a sequence out of applications that cover the same percentage of use cases, but share no use cases in common. Since every business process has a finite set of use cases, we can create only sequences of finite length, which are often very short as well. For depth, create a sequence out of applications that provide the same level of support to a use case, but which have no overlapping coverage. Like breadth, we cannot create sequences of infinite length. So, we meet the fourth requirement for a qualitative probability structure.

The fifth requirement states that, given four events A, B, C, and D, if A and B are disjoint ($A \cap B = \varnothing$), A is more probable than C ($A \succ C$), and B is at least as probable as D ($B \succeq D$), then somewhere in E is an event F that is equally as probable as $A \cup B$. Furthermore, F contains events C' and D' which are disjoint, with C' equally as probable as C, and D' equally as probable as D.

We interpret the fifth requirement to mean that if, given four applications A, B, C, and D such that A and B do not overlap in breadth or depth, depending on what we are considering, that A provides more coverage than C, and that B provides at least as much coverage as D, then there is an application F which provides the same coverage as A and B combined. Furthermore, there are applications C' and D' which are disjoint, with C' providing the same coverage as C, and D' providing the same coverage as D. To satisfy this requirement, we need only show that we can construct applications which meet these conditions; they do not need to actually exist.

Since, for breadth, X is the set of use cases in a business process, the size of E will usually be pretty small. Define A and B so that $A \cap B = \varnothing$, $C \subset A$, and $D = B$. Then $F = A \cup B$. All we need to do is find a $C' \subset A$ for which $C \cap C' = \varnothing$, and define $D' = D = B$. If $|A| \geq 2$, then we know we can meet this condition. A similar argument can be made for depth, using levels of coverage for a single use case, rather than use cases as wholes.

We have successfully built two structures of qualitative probability: one for breadth of scope and one for depth of scope. The representation of breadth of scope assigns a value from [0, 1] to an application based on the proportion of use cases within a business process to which the application provides some level of support. The representation of depth of scope assigns a value from [0, 1] to an application based on the proportion of a use case included within the application boundary.

There are still several issues left to work in order to create a combined measure. First, we need to decide what is meant when we say that a portion of a use case is inside the application boundary. Do we measure this in terms of objects, information content, functions supported, or what?

Second, the breadth representation applies a single value to the entire application. The depth representation applies a value to each use case included in the application. To get an application-level measure of depth, we need to combine the depth for each use case into a single value. Since probability structures produce values on the absolute scale, we can use any summarization technique to combine the separate values.

An obvious choice for summarization is to use the average depth, in which the representation (.8, .5) tells us that the application covers 80 percent of the use cases in the business process to an average depth of 50 percent. But this can hide a significant amount of information. What if the application supports 8 out of 10 use cases, for a breadth of 80 percent, but covers one of the 8 fully (100 percent) and the other 7 to a much lower extent, so that the average is 50 percent? To solve this problem, we will represent our depth of scope as a triple minimum/average/maximum depth, so that our example might be written as (.8, .05/.5/1.0).

To solve the first problem, count the attributes and methods for each object in the use case, and calculate depth of coverage as

$$d = \frac{\sum_{i=1}^{n} (a_i + m_i)}{\sum_{j=1}^{p} (a_j + m_j)} \tag{7.35}$$

where each i is an object within both the use case and the application, and each j is an object within the use case. This is represented pictorially in Figure 7.1. The a and m represent attributes and methods respectively.

We choose to count both attributes and methods because we model both our use case and application in terms of classes. The application may include or exclude either attributes or methods of the classes in the use case. Thus, to get a truer picture of the application's coverage of a use case, we must consider both types of coverage.

If we are satisfied with a two-part measure, which gives breadth and depth separately, we are done. But, how can we compare two applications in terms of coverage? Suppose application A covers a business process at (.8, .1/.5/.9) and

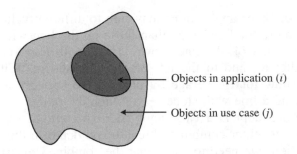

Figure 7.1 *Application support to a function (use case).*

application *B* covers the process at (.7, .4/.7/.9). Which application, *A* or *B*, provides the most total coverage? The short answer is: We can't tell. We need a way to combine the two values.

There are two obvious ways of combining our representations of breadth and depth: We can add them or we can multiply them. To add them, we must be able to construct an additive conjoint structure. To multiply them, we must be able to construct a multiplicative conjoint structure. If the two components are independent, we are constrained to adding them. If the two components are sign-dependent on each other, we must multiply them. Explanations for all of this are found in the section "Conjoint Representations" in Chapter 5.

Since breadth and depth are independent, we have to add them. Figure 7.2 shows a plot of breadth versus average depth. The diagonal line indicates applications with equal functionality. This line is based on the sum of breadth and average depth, and represents those applications whose breadth and average depth

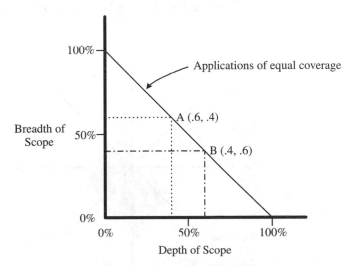

Figure 7.2 *Graphing applications of equal coverage.*

sum to 1.0. Other applications may sum to different values. An application which provides more total coverage than those on the line will lie on a line parallel to, and to the right of, the line shown. Those with less total coverage will lie on a line parallel to, and to the left of, the line shown. With this diagram, we can visually show total coverage by plotting the breadth and average depth values, and drawing a line with slope -1 through the point.

Figure 7.2 depicts a two-factor additive conjoint representation. An obvious question is whether combining breadth and depth in this way is valid. To answer that question, we need to show that the combined measure meets the conditions for such a structure as given in Chapter 5. A quick glance through the section "Conjoint Representations" in that chapter reveals a formidable set of requirements that will take a lot of work to examine. Is there an alternative way to combine breadth and depth so as to compare two or more applications? It turns out there is, and it is very simple and visual in nature.

Total coverage can be depicted by drawing a kiviat diagram with an axis for each use case in the business process. Figure 7.3 shows an example of such a chart. By definition, the maximum potential coverage is all use cases at a level of 100 percent. The plot of such coverage is a regular n-sided polygon, where n is the number of use cases. This also results in all axes showing the same scale.

Next, plot the coverage by an application for each use case by placing a point on the axis for the use case at the level of coverage provided by the application. For a use case that is covered to 50 percent, plot a point half way from the origin to the edge of the regular polygon along the axis representing the use case in question. For zero coverage, plot the point at the origin; for full coverage, plot the point at the edge of the polygon. After plotting the coverage for each use case, we connect the points to create a (usually irregular) polygon for the application.

The same can be done for one or more additional applications. The application that provides the most coverage will create the polygon with the largest area, or the largest portion of the area for the regular polygon. If the area of the regular

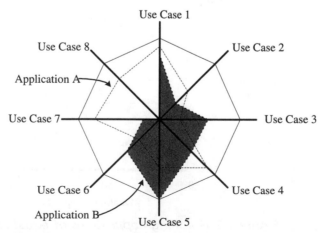

Figure 7.3 *Comparing the coverage of two applications.*

polygon is 100 percent coverage of the business process, the percentage of that area covered by an application's polygon is the percentage of the business process covered by the application.

Volume

Volume is a measure of population modified by a time factor. This factor can be an instant in time or an interval of time. If volume is measured over a time interval, you can measure peak volume, average or nominal volume, or both.

Measurement of nominal volume implies certain requirements of scale, depending on what nominal means. If you use the median of a set of values as the nominal value, you can use a measure from the ordinal or higher scales. If you use the mean of a set of values, you must use a measure from the interval, ratio, or absolute scales.

For measurement of peak volume, you can use a measure from any scale, although a nominal scale measure won't provide any information beyond which volume level occurs most frequently.

In many design situations, an important volume-related question is how much memory a data structure or set of objects will occupy. This is particularly true in situations where the available memory is one of the design constraints. Memory usage is a very real problem, even in personal computer or workstation-based information systems (believe it or not).

For years, the 640 kilobyte limit in the MS-DOS operating system has been considered a severe constraint. In one project, I had to fit 20,000 copies of a particular data structure into memory at the same time. This proved to be quite a design challenge, since these 20,000 copies had to coexist with the operating system, some unknown number of device drivers, other data structures, and the program code. All told, those 20,000 data structures had to occupy less than 300,000 bytes of memory. This project led me to the conclusion that volume is still a relevant design measure.

In this section, a measure for the amount of memory used by the active objects in a design will be developed. I've used this measure many times since I "discovered" it on that project. Since we are looking to make sure we can operate within a fixed limit of memory, let's construct a measure for peak volume. We want the units to be in bytes, so we need to develop two measures: one to measure the peak volume of objects active in memory at any time and a way to size these objects in bytes. The universe of this activity is the objects in the set *ActiveObjects* as defined in Chapter 6.

The strategy is to develop a measure of the size of each object in bytes, then combine the sizes of each object in a class. We have to perform this step because the potential use of class attributes means we can't just add up the byte sizes for each active object. We can then use the same operation to combine the sizes of each class into a single size value. If we can assure ourselves that no attribute values are shared across classes (a characteristic of "good" object-oriented designs), we can simply add the size for each class.

The first task is to select an empirical relational structure for the size of an object in bytes. The simplest structure is the sum of the sizes, in bytes, for each attribute. Since a ratio scale measure is not needed, we can build a less restrictive structure. We can view an attribute as a set of bytes in memory. Most attributes in an object are disjoint sets of bytes, but some attributes share physical memory. The union construct in C++ is one way for multiple attributes to share physical memory. Many purists feel that using such constructs is bad design, and in general it is, but since it happens on occasion, our measure needs to account for it. We can solve this problem by taking the cardinality of the union of the attributes as the size of the object. The elements of an attribute, for this exercise, are bytes of physical memory, so the cardinality of the set of bytes is the size of the attribute in bytes. The nature of set union automatically accounts for common elements, so we have a valid size of the object, in bytes.

When we combine sizes of objects for a given class, we need to account for class attributes. Class attributes are such that all instances of a class share the same instance of the attribute. If one object modifies the value of a class attribute, the value is immediately changed for all other objects of the class. The similarities between this situation and shared physical memory locations should be obvious. To exploit this similarity, we again use set union to create a set which contains the actual instances of all of the attributes for all of the objects of the class currently in scope. The cardinality of this set is the number of attribute instances. We can generalize the formula for this cardinality as

$$n * \text{number of attributes} - (n - 1) * \text{number of class attributes} \quad (7.36)$$

where n is the number of objects of the class currently in scope. To measure this in bytes, we use

$$CS_A = n \sum_{i=1}^{m} |\cup a_i| - (n - 1) \sum_{j=1}^{p} |\cup ca_j| \quad (7.37)$$

where a_i is the set of bytes occupied by attribute i, ca_j is the set of bytes occupied by class attribute j, m is the number of attributes in class A, and p is the number of class attributes in class A. CS_A is the size, in bytes, occupied by all of the objects in the class A that are currently members of the set *ActiveObjects*.

We are now ready to combine the class sizes, the various CS_k, into a total design size, in bytes. For simplicity, assume that no two classes share the same instance of an attribute. When global variables do exist, the same method previously used can be used to calculate the actual size. If our assumption holds true, the total size occupied by a design, in bytes, is

$$DS = \sum_{k=1}^{c} CS_k \quad (7.38)$$

where CS_k is defined by (7.37), and c is the number of classes in the design, which is also the number of partitions in the set *ActiveObjects*.

The measure DS, we have just developed, is the size occupied by a design at some time t. Recall we were interested in measuring the peak size occupied by a design. To find this value, we need to take the maximum value of DS over an interval of time, which could be one execution of the design. Conceptually, this is simple. In practice, it may be very difficult.

As a design is executed, the number of objects of a given class which are in scope changes. So does the mix of classes for which objects are active. We can find situations where a large number of small objects can occupy less total memory that a small number of large objects. One way to find the peak volume is to execute the design, either in code or algebraically, and calculate *DS* every time the membership of *ActiveObjects* changes. Without automated design analysis tools, this can be tedious, but it can be done by hand; that's what I did on that project I mentioned earlier.

SUMMARY

A lot of ground was covered in this chapter. After exploring the nature of software size, four views of size, each with different measurement needs and uses were settled on. Then, formal properties were defined for each view, based on an intuitive understanding of each view's characteristics. Four measures were developed from the ground up, one for each view of size. Beginning with an empirical understanding of a view, a set of goals for measurement was developed which led to a set of potential empirical relational structures. We then examined our model to see if it could support the use of any of the potential structures and selected one structure for each view and constructed a representation—a measure.

For three of the views, we succeeded in constructing a valid measure. For one view, population, we found we could not construct a valid measure using the structure we had originally selected. We thus compromised for a measure on a lesser scale.

This chapter illustrates the technique used to construct new measures using measurement theory and a formal model of objects and designs, described in Chapter 3. With practice, you will become adept at its use; you will be able to construct a measure for any attribute you can clearly define and model.

8

COMPLEXITY

Complexity is perhaps the most studied yet least understood characteristic of software. Fenton (1991) ascribes this to a lack of a unified empirical understanding of complexity as a phenomenon. The many attempts to define complexity fall into two basic groups: those who define it in terms of the effort or resources an external system (person, machine, software application) expends to interact with a software component, and those who define it in terms of a component's structure. This lack of a common empirical understanding has led to a great number of mostly useless measures. In this matter, I share Fenton's view (see Fenton 1991; and Zuse 1994) that no single concept, or measure, can serve such diverse and conflicting aims.

It is useful to begin the exploration of complexity by defining it. Curtis (1980a, p. 102) defines it as ". . . a characteristic of the software interface which influences the resources another system will expend or commit while interacting with the software." Basili (1980) offers a slightly different version: ". . . a measure of the resources expended by a system while interacting with a piece of software to perform to a given task." In both of these definitions, the "other system" can be a person, an external system, or another application. Others define complexity strictly in terms of the effort required by people to understand or use a piece of software. Myers (1976) says: "The complexity of an object is some measure of the mental effort required to understand that object." Henderson-Sellers (1996, p. 166) defines complexity in terms of cognitive effort: "The cognitive complexity of software refers to those characteristics of software that affect the level of resources used by a person performing a given task on it." The IEEE (1990) defines complexity as: "The degree to which a system or component has a design or implementation which is difficult to understand and verify."

The IEEE definition, and to some extent that of Henderson-Sellers, gives some hint that complexity is a characteristic of the product itself. Other definitions of complexity focus on this aspect. Myers (1976 quoted in Zuse 1994, p. 132) offers this: "The complexity of an object is a function of the relationship among the components of the object." Several dictionaries focus on this aspect of complexity as well. *Webster's* (1971) defines complex (an adjective) as: ". . . consisting of composite parts, intricate . . . hard to separate, analyze, or solve." My particular *Webster's* dictionary goes on to explain that the word "complex" applies to situations which are the "unavoidable results of a necessary combining or folding and does not imply fault or failure." That is, complexity is ". . . an essential characteristic of software, not an accidental one" (Brooks 1975). The *Macquarie Dictionary* defines complexity as: "The state or quality of being complex; composed of interconnected parts; characterized by an involved combination of parts . . . an obsessing notion."

The definitions in the previous two paragraphs illustrate the variety of views of complexity. Given this variety, it seems that complexity has several independent aspects. If this is true, as Fenton believes, then no single complexity measure will cover it all. These issues are explored in this chapter. Further, each of these views will be defined, seeking to discover the specific characteristics of the product that contribute to each. Then, some formal properties for complexity (not complexity measures) will be defined that explain and formalize our intuition. The focus will be on the complexity of software due to its internal structure, the discovery of a suitable empirical relational structure, and construction of a representation by which you can measure internal structural complexity.

MOTIVATION AND ORIGINS

Complexity plays an important role in our ability to understand and solve a problem, and to understand, use, and modify a piece of software. Many researchers have linked complexity with the likelihood that a module will contain errors (Curtis 1980a; McCabe 1976; Fountain, Hastings, and Schoonveldt 1994; Fenton 1991; Myers 1976). Others have associated complexity with the effort to test, modify, and maintain software (Lorenz and Kidd 1994; Henderson-Sellers 1996). Certain types of complexity increase the resources required to execute and operate the application (Henderson-Sellers 1996). Complexity is most definitely a factor in the effort required to develop software (Curtis 1980a; DeMarco 1982; Ott et al. 1995). Complexity has been shown to have a negative effect on reliability (Curtis 1980a). Complexity in its various forms is believed to be an indicator of usability, understandability, maintainability, adaptability, reliability, and other factors (Zuse 1994; Henderson-Sellers 1996), but the empirical evidence supporting these relationships is scarce and suspect.

Complexity originates in the problem domain (Booch 1994; Whitmire 1992) in the form of functional requirements, implicit external and internal requirements and constraints, and a lack of ways to capture and communicate these requirements. From personal experience, I can attest that this last source is a *big* problem. Complexity also comes from the development environment. In particular, increased complexity is often the result of the difficulty we have in managing that environment (Booch 1994). For example, a change control process that cannot control and manage requirements changes can add significantly to the complexity of a product.

Software is extremely flexible and this contributes to complexity (Booch 1994). We can do nearly anything in software, at least that's what we believe. One common practice in systems engineering is to allocate problems with known solutions to hardware and everything else to software. We are seeing product lines today whose defining features are contained wholly within their software. Electronic pagers and cellular phones are a prime example of this type of differentiation.

We also have great difficulty characterizing the behavior of discrete systems (Booch 1994). Many software systems appear to have an infinite number of states (while this number is indeed very, very large, it is not infinite). Further, small changes to a system can cause the entire state of the system to change. We cannot map the input into a system to the output using continuous functions. To further complicate things, these mappings don't always lead to deterministic solutions.

A last major source of complexity is the designer himself or herself (Booch 1994; Card and Glass 1990). The problem provides a minimum level of complexity. For any given problem, there are several solutions, each with a varying degree of complexity.

EMPIRICAL VIEWS

Complexity has many origins that lead naturally to multiple views of complexity. Various authors have defined several such views, including one that has not yet been discussed. This section deals with five views of complexity: computational, representational, functional, system, and procedural. Each view is defined and discussed, since they all play a role in the total complexity of a piece of software.

Curtis (1980a) and Henderson-Sellers (1996) discuss a concept they call computational complexity. Computational complexity considers the hardware—processor cycles, memory, and disk space—required to execute the software. These hardware characteristics are often hard constraints, to be met or meet with failure. Computational complexity is covered by the study of algorithmic efficiency (see Chapter 4) as a branch of computer science. It is influential in the design process because is provides information for a number of key design decisions:

1. Whether a feasible solution exists for a problem. Certain problems, such as the traveling salesman problem, are considered to be NP-complete, meaning that there is no known algorithm that will provide an optimal solution. Any given solution can be checked, but the solution itself must be derived through heuristics and approximations.

2. Given that a feasible solution exists, the complexity of the theoretically most efficient solution is defined by Fenton (1991) to be the complexity of the underlying problem itself.

3. Given that a feasible solution exists for some small input size, whether that same solution is feasible as the input size grows.

For any problem, we can trade time complexity for space complexity. This is the classic space-time tradeoff we have all encountered. Time complexity is the processor time required to complete the execution of a program. This factor is often referred to as speed. Solutions with lower time complexity run faster, all else being equal. Space complexity refers to the volume of memory consumed during the course of executing the program. The general belief is that in order to increase the speed at which a program runs—to reduce the time complexity—we must increase the amount of memory we use—increase the space complexity. While this is generally true, it is not always the case.

Neither space or time complexity are truly notions of complexity, as it has been discussed. In truth, they are both forms of volume. Nevertheless, computer science has long considered these to be forms of complexity, so forms of complexity they remain. A well-developed representation for time complexity, covered in the section on "Algorithmic Complexity" in Chapter 4, forms an ordinal scale measure. If we require interval or ratio scale measures of time complexity, or space complexity for that matter, we need to look into representations of volume, not complexity.

Henderson-Sellers (1996) discusses a form of complexity he calls representational complexity. This relates to ". . . the mode of expression in visual form." The basic idea is that for some types of information, a graphical presentation is less complex than a tabular presentation. Patterns and trends in data are much easier to spot if they are presented in graphical form. In other cases, tabular information is easier to grasp than graphical information. Very little work has been done in this area, at least in the software engineering literature. Henderson-Sellers devotes only a very short paragraph to the subject. Representational complexity is a major topic in the literature on human factors and user interface design.

Curtis (1980a) and Henderson-Sellers (1996) also discuss a concept they call psychological complexity. Under this rather broad umbrella, they lump all of the views of software complexity that are of any real use to us as designers. Henderson-Sellers breaks this overall view into three groups: programmer characteristics, problem characteristics, and structural complexity.

Programmer characteristics include experience and knowledge, both of the problem and solution domains. Problem characteristics reflect the difficulties inherent in the problem itself. Problem complexity is sometimes called "difficulty."

Structural complexity is described, ironically, in terms of how it is measured. Measures of structural complexity include characteristics of modules (procedural complexity): style, size, data structure, logic structure, and internal cohesion. Another form of module cohesion is semantic cohesion, and looks not to the physical structure, but to the behavior of the module as seen from the outside. Another aspect of structural complexity is the intermodule metrics, or coupling. Thus, cohesion and coupling are given as forms or evidence of complexity (see also Zuse 1991, 1994).

Card and Glass (1990) take a slightly different approach to complexity. Still dealing with psychological complexity, they give three subtypes: functional, system, and procedural. Functional complexity results from the magnitude and nature of the requirements. It results from the problem and is not in the control of the designer. Card and Glass base this view on Boehm's CPLX attribute (Boehm 1981) and include: control and concurrency issues, computational and mathematical issues, data management issues, and device dependence.

System complexity is under the control of the system designer. It includes such issues as relationships between modules, input and output variables, and the average fan-out from a module. Procedural complexity is under the control of the module designer and includes logic structure, data structure, and similar issues. Procedural complexity is bounded on the bottom by the functional complexity in the problem domain. These interrelated views of complexity are summarized in Figure 8.1.

We view complexity from a structural viewpoint and wish to be able to examine a class or design and determine its complexity apart from any external systems. This removes the requirement to include characteristics of those systems in our empirical structure since we do not always know the characteristics of an external system which must interact with our software. Structural complexity is viewed in terms of how the components of a class or design are interrelated. We are interested in the fact that relationships exist; we are not concerned, at the moment, with what those relationships mean. For a class, consider its elements to be atomic elements: It does not matter to the class under consideration that one component is more complex than another. For a design, consider classes to be atomic elements. The complexity of a design lies in how the classes relate to each other, not in the complexity of each class.

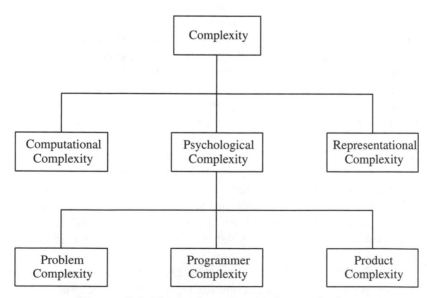

Figure 8.1 *The various types of complexity.*

This is a unique view of complexity in software engineering and is bound to be controversial. However, it lets us view structures of elements as we treat them: atomic elements, be they attributes and methods, or classes. This view also limits complexity to the layer in which we are working. The complexity in more detailed layers can be hidden behind a simple interface, safely beyond our concern. This view allows us to create simple designs out of complex classes, or complex designs out of simple classes (the two differ in how the responsibilities and knowledge of the application are distributed among the classes), or anything in between. It is an intuitive notion that the complexity of a design is independent of the complexity of its individual components, yet this notion has never been reflected in the literature on complexity. This, after all, is one of the points of object-oriented software, is it not?

FORMAL PROPERTIES

There are no less than five sets of formal properties for complexity in the software engineering literature. Weyuker's (1988) were the first and remain the most discussed. Zuse (1991, 1994) lays down a set of formal properties that lead to additive ratio scale measures of complexity (extensive measures). Tian and Zelkowitz (1992) propose a set of properties based upon the expression of a program as an abstract syntax tree. Lakshmanan, Jayaprakash, and Sinha (1991) define a set of properties based on a control-flow model of complexity. Briand, Morasca, and Basili (1996) define a set of properties based on a directed graph model of complexity. Their paper also defines properties for size, length, coupling, and cohesion based on the same model.

The models by Tian and Zelkowitz, Lakshmanan and colleagues, and Briand and colleagues appear not to apply to objects. They were developed in a world of structured modules and all except that of Briand and colleagues are based on a model which consists of a single program. That is, their models seek to explain the complexity found within a single program, what we call procedural complexity. The model of Briand and associates is based on a directed graph representation of a system as a set of elements linked by relations. In their model, a module is a subset of elements and relations between members of this subset.

One of the characteristics of object-oriented software is that the complexity moves from individual functions, the code, into the spaces between objects, the design. Models of complexity based on code segments and sequences of code statements do not help us much.

Like Zuse, Briand and colleagues require that complexity measures be additive when combining disjoint objects. Why should this be so? What intuitive notion leads us to this conclusion? This idea is based on the idea that when combined, the complexities of the components are still visible and must always contribute to the complexity of the whole. This property, in particular, fails to some extent in almost any other system; chemistry is one example that comes to mind. Take water, for example. Water is the combination of hydrogen and oxygen atoms which creates a structure that behaves, for all intents and purposes, as a new element. It is very expensive, in terms of the energy required, to break a water molecule into its components. Any system dealing with water molecules deals only with water molecules, blissfully unaware of even the existence of the hydrogen and oxygen components (under normal physical conditions, that is).

On the other hand, the model of Briand and colleagues is based primarily on the relationships between elements. Complexity as modeled here is influenced by the way in which elements interact with each other. I will take advantage of their model's attributes as I develop another set of formal properties for complexity.

Zuse's main point is that any complexity measure should be built from an extensive structure. This has always struck me as being counterintuitive. First, it does not allow for synergy: The complexity of a composite can exceed the combined complexity of its parts. Nor does it allow for reverse synergy: The complexity of a composite can be less than the combined complexity of its parts. I've seen both cases in real life, both in and out of software. Further, it doesn't seem to make sense to combine complexities when two objects are combined. Complexity ought not to work as size does. It seems more intuitive to throw out the complexities of the combined objects and calculate the complexity of the new object as if the combined parts never existed.

With these points in mind, I now present yet another set of formal properties for complexity. Many of these properties are shared with one or more other sets, especially that of Briand and colleagues. Denote the complexity of a class by $cx_c(C)$, where C is an instance of the category **Class**, and the complexity of a design by $cx_d(D)$, where D is an instance of the category **DesignState**.

Property X1: Complexity is nonnegative (Briand, Morasca, and Basili 1996):

$$cx_c(C) \geq 0 \qquad (8.1a)$$

and

$$cx_d(D) \geq 0 \qquad (8.1b)$$

Property X2: Property can be null (Briand, Morasca, and Basili 1996):

$$C = \emptyset \Rightarrow cx_c(C) = 0 \qquad (8.2a)$$

and

$$D = \emptyset \Rightarrow cx_d(D) = 0 \qquad (8.2b)$$

Property X3: The complexity of a group of elements is symmetrical without regard to the direction of any arrows (modified from Briand, Morasca, and Basili 1996):

$$C_1 = aRb \wedge C_2 = bR^{-1}a \Rightarrow cx_c(C_1) = cx_c(C_2) \qquad (8.3a)$$

and

$$D_1 = aRb \wedge D_2 = bR^{-1}a \Rightarrow cx_d(D1) = cx_d(D_2) \qquad (8.3b)$$

The following properties are a major departure from the properties of any of the sets discussed thus far.

Property X4: There is no fixed relationship between the complexity of a composite and the combined complexities of its components. In fact, the complexities of a set of components do not contribute to the complexity of the composite.

Property X5: Complexity is monotonic nondecreasing; adding a class or relationship to a design, or adding an attribute or method to a class, cannot decrease its complexity:

$$(a \notin C_1 \wedge C_2 = C_1 \cup a) \vee (aRb \notin C_1 \wedge C_2 = C_1 \cup aRb) \Rightarrow cx_c(C_1) \leqslant cx_c(C_2)$$

(8.4*a*)

and

$$(a \notin D_1 \wedge D_2 = D_1 \cup a) \vee (aRb \notin D_1 \wedge D_2 = D_1 \cup aRb) \Rightarrow cx_d(D_1) \leqslant cx_d(D_2)$$

(8.4*b*)

Property X6: Two objects, be they classes or designs, which have similar structures have the same complexity:

$$structure(A) \sim structure(B) \Rightarrow cx_c(A) = cx_c(B) \qquad (8.5a)$$

and

$$structure(A) \sim structure\ (B) \Rightarrow cx_d(A) = cx_d(B) \qquad (8.5b)$$

where structure(x) is a formal description the structure of an object, in terms of its elements and their relationships. Note that property does *not* require that the structures be the *same*—that is, they have the same elements and relationships—only that they be *similar*—that is, they have the same number of elements, with equivalent relationships between them. In formal terms, the category representations of each structure must be isomorphic.

Property X7: Complexity is independent of size. You do not want the population of elements to influence the complexity; you want the complexity to stand on its own. You want to be able to identify more complex structures relative to less complex structures. Intuitively, you can have small, complex structures, and large, simple structures, or any mix of size and complexity. In short, you want any measure of complexity to be orthogonal to size.

Property X8: Complexity forms a weak order; you can order classes, or designs, in terms of their relative complexity.

EMPIRICAL RELATIONAL STRUCTURES

At the end of the section on Empirical views, it was decided to look at complexity from a slightly different point of view than is usually taken. Our empirical model will view complexity in layers. The effect of complexity will be limited to a single layer. Any elements of a layer will be considered as atomic elements, which cannot be broken down. Thus, in the category **DesignState**, the elements will be classes and all classes will be considered equal. In the category **Class**, the elements will be attribute domains and states. Since attribute domains and states are different types of elements, we will need to explore a conjoint structure of some kind for classes.

We will order design states, and classes, in terms of the degree to which their elements are interrelated and consider any type of relationship between elements as contributing to complexity. Of course, different types of relationships contribute in different amounts, at least this is suspected to be the case, so we will have to test for this in our empirical studies. Our model should be able to accommodate different levels of contribution, or weights.

Having defined our empirical view of complexity, we look to the formal model in Chapter 6 to see if it contains elements which can describe this view. It is immediately clear that the arrows in the categories **DesignState** and **Class** meet our needs. Both **DesignState** and **Class** have several types of arrows, some of which are independent of other types and some dependent. This suggests either an additive or mulitplicative conjoint structure, or some combination of both (which is a distributive or dual-distributive conjoint structure depending on how factors are combined).

In the category **DesignState**, we will use the relationship arrows for our units of complexity. Presume, until empirical data proves otherwise, that each type of relationship contributes a different portion to the overall design complexity. Since the various types of relationships are independent of each other, we will look to create an additive conjoint representation for a design's complexity.

In the category **Class**, use attribute projection, class operation, and state selection arrows for the units of complexity. As with designs, presume, until it is proven otherwise, that each type of arrow contributes a different portion to the overall class complexity. The number of state selection arrows is dependent, in part, on the number of attribute projection arrows. The size of the state space is determined by the cardinality of the cross product of the attribute domains, less those states excluded by the class invariant. Without any such constraints, the number of possible states is the product of the cardinalities for each attribute domain. We need to account for this in our model.

Likewise, the number of operation arrows is dependent on two things: the number of operations defined for the class and the number of possible states. An arrow for a given operation originates at every state which satisfies the operation's precondition. Thus, a given operation can be represented by multiple arrows. The maximum number of operation arrows is the product of the number of operations and the number of states. This situation will occur only when every possible state satisfies the preconditions for every defined operation. This may or may not be a rare condition, but it nevertheless provides an upper bound on the number of arrows. We need to account for this in our model.

Both of these situations appear to call for some form of multiplicative, distributive, or dual-distributive conjoint structure. However, there is another angle that is worth considering. In both cases, an upper bound on the number of state selection and operation arrows has been identified. If we define this upper bound to be one in both cases, we have the makings of a probability structure. Thus, we could create a mapping into the interval [0, 1] which would indicate how close we are to having the worst case scenario. We would define a value closer to one as more complex than a value closer to zero. We might, then, look at a structure which combines a count of the number of attribute projection arrows, and the percentage of state selection and operation arrows we actually have to their respective worst cases.

We still need to modify our models, for both designs and classes, to neutralize the effect of the population of elements. In both cases, this can be done simply by taking the ratio of certain types of arrows to the number of elements. For designs, this would mean dividing the whole conjoint structure by the number of classes in the design. This would give us a representation of complexity similar to the density of solids. We could do the same for classes, if we can combine the counts and percentages in an appropriate way.

We have now defined our empirical view of complexity in terms of the formal model. All that's left is to define a specific representation. As usual, this is the most difficult portion of the task.

POTENTIAL MEASURES

There are two empirical models for complexity: one for designs and one for classes. In this section, let's construct a representation for classes. The model for class complexity contains all of the elements for the model of design complexity, and then some. What we learn about measuring class complexity can be directly applied to measuring design complexity.

Our representation will have to address all of the issues and concerns raised in the previous section. In particular, we have to decide what gets counted and how the various counts are combined into a single measure. We also have to figure out how to account for the effects of population on the counts.

The category class contains three types of objects and arrows, but our interest is in how the objects interrelate with one another; so, the focus will be exclusively on the arrows. As discussed in the previous section, the number of state selection and operation arrows are partially dependent on the number of attribute projection arrows. In fact, the number of attributes in a class give an upper bound on the number of states for the class, and thus the number of state selection arrows. The number of attributes and the number of operations defined for a class together provide an upper bound on the number of operation arrows. These are important relationships.

Our representation will have three components, one for each type of arrow, combined in some form of conjoint or proximity structure. Then, we will normalize this entire structure by accounting for the population of attributes in the class. We ignore the number of states in this case because that number is driven, in part, by the number of attributes.

Two of the components, operation arrows and state selection arrows, will be based on probability structures. Define the set X_s (see Chapter 5) for state selection arrows as the set formed by the cross product of the attribute domain sets. The maximum cardinality for this set is the product of the cardinalities for the attribute domain sets. We map this value, whatever it is, to the value one. The set E_s is defined as $\mathbb{P}X_s$. E_s defines the family of possible sets of actual state selection arrows, of which the set in our class is one element. We count the state selection arrows actually in the category and divide it by the cardinality of the set X_s. This gives a mapping into the interval [0, 1], providing us a probability representation for state selection arrows.

Likewise, define the set X_o for operation arrows as the set formed by the cross product of the set of possible states and the set of unique operations defined for the class. The maximum cardinality of the set X_o is the product of the cardinalities of the set X_s and the set of operations. We map this value to one. The set E_o is defined as $\mathbb{P}X_o$ and represents the family of possible sets of operation arrows, of which the set of operation arrows in our class is one element. We count the number of operation arrows actually in the category and divide it by cardinality of the set X_o. Now we have a probability representation for the operation arrows.

Normally, at this point, we have do some legwork to show that our representations actually meet the requirements for probability structures, given in Chapter 5. Fortunately, this is not too difficult for probability structures based on percentages. The one built in Chapter 7 can be used as a basis for these structures. So, we simply say here that we know percentages can be used to build probability structures: been there, done that.

We simply count attribute arrows. This leaves us with three components, one of which is a population count, the other two of which are percentages. We cannot combine these into any kind of coherent representation unless we do some further work.

We also have yet to account for the population of attribute domains and states, the objects in our category, and this may be our opportunity to make that adjustment. The number of attribute arrows is a direct result of the population of attribute domains which contribute to the class. In many cases, the population of arrows is equal to the population of attribute domains. In some cases, a single attribute domain contributes more than one attribute—there is more than one arrow which terminates at the attribute domain. The ratio of attribute domains to attribute arrows has an upper bound of one. Dividing the population of attribute domains by the population of attribute arrows gives us a representation into the interval [0, 1]. This ratio gives a representation of the density of attribute domains relative to the population of attribute arrows. If we use this ratio as a component of complexity, we are saying that for two classes with the same number of attributes (arrows), the class which draws those attributes from the fewest domains is less complex than the other. We are thus ordering our classes based on the number of distinct attribute domains from which they draw their attributes, relative to the number of attributes.

Formally, the set X_a is defined as the set of attribute domains such that it is isomorphic to the set of attribute arrows in the class. The set E_a is $\mathbb{P}X_a$ and contains a family of sets of attribute domains, one of which is the set of attribute domains actually contained in the category for our class. Thus, we have a probability structure representing the density of attribute domain sets relative to the attribute arrows.

We have managed to represent all three components in the same type of structure. The remaining question is twofold: Should we combine these three components into a single value, and if so, how? Since all three components are represented by absolute scale measures on the interval [0, 1], we are not limited to one of the conjoint structures in Chapter 5. We could build a three-dimensional spatial proximity structure. Representing these three ratios as distances in three-dimensional space makes for some intriguing visual possibilities. In addition, we can leave the representation in the form of a vector, rather than a single value, revealing information that a single value might conceal.

Intuitively, we are sure we can represent our three ratios in a three-dimensional additive-difference metric structure, as was used for distance in three dimensions. A quick read through Chapter 5, however, yields a formidable set of requirements. It also yields no less than five different structures, which range from the ordinal to the ratio scales. These five structures are created, with one exception, by adding requirements to simpler structures. With this in mind, we will apply the conditions in Chapter 5 to our empirical model of class complexity until we come to one we cannot satisfy. At that point, if it is reached, we will say that the requirements for the next most complex structure are met, and we will have our measure.

The first set of requirements is imposed by the need for a factorial proximity structure. This structure is defined in the section "Unidimensional Spatial Proximity Representations" in Chapter 5. Given a set A and a binary relation $\succeq$ on $A \times A$, the structure $\langle A \times A, \succeq \rangle$ must satisfy the following five conditions for all a, $b \in A$ to be a factorial proximity structure:

1. $\langle A \times A, \succeq \rangle$ is a weak order.
2. $(a, b) \succ (a, a)$ whenever $a \neq b$.
3. $(a, a) \sim (b, b)$ (minimality).
4. $(a, b) \sim (b, a)$ (symmetry).
5. $A = \times_{n=1}^{n} A_i$.

Starting with the fifth condition, the set A is defined as the cross product of A_s, A_o, and A_a, $A = A_s \times A_o \times A_a$, where A_s is the set of ratios of the cardinalities of the elements of E_s to the cardinality of X_s, A_o is the set of ratios of the cardinalities of the elements of E_o to the cardinality of X_o, and A_a is the set of ratios of the cardinalities of the elements of E_a to the cardinality of X_a. Note that all of these sets are real numbers in the interval [0, 1]. Thus, the three-dimensional space is a cube with sides of length one—there are no units since we are dealing with ratios. This satisfies the fifth condition.

To build a weak order on $\langle A \times A, \succeq \rangle$, we have to order our classes in all three dimensions. This can be done by comparing one dimension at a time while holding the others constant. We can't do much more until we can show that we actually have a multidimensional spatial proximity structure of some kind, which will be done later. Suppose we define three relations $\succeq_s$, $\succeq_o$, and $\succeq_a$, which are the induced orderings on each dimension separately. We can easily define the three relations $\sim_s$, $\sim_o$, $\sim_a$ in terms of these. Given two points in the three-dimensional space, a and b, we can say that:

$$a_s \succeq_s b_s \wedge a_o \sim_o b_o \wedge a_a \sim_a b_a \Rightarrow a \succeq b \tag{8.6a}$$

and

$$a_o \succeq_o b_o \wedge a_s \sim_s b_s \wedge a_a \sim_a b_a \Rightarrow a \succeq b \tag{8.6b}$$

and

$$a_a \succeq_a b_a \wedge a_s \sim_s b_s \wedge a_o \sim_o b_o \Rightarrow a \succeq b \tag{8.6c}$$

Using these results, we can show that our ordering $\succeq$ is both transitive and connected.

The second, third, and fourth conditions all require that the ability to use absolute differences of ratios. We know we can do this, since we draw them from an absolute scale. The second condition states that the interval from a to b is larger than the interval from a to itself. Since $|a - b| > |a - a|$ for all $a \neq b$, a, $b \in A$, we satisfy this condition. The third condition requires that the interval from a point to itself is the same no matter which point is taken. We meet this condition since $|a - a| = |b - b|$ ($= 0$) for all a, $b \in A$. The fourth condition requires that the interval between two points is the same, no matter which direction it is measured from. Since $|a - b| = |b - a|$ for all a, $b \in A$, we meet this condition as well. We have a factorial proximity structure.

To be decomposable, a factorial proximity structure must be one-factor independent. This means that for all a, b, c, d, a', b', c', and $d' \in A$, if the two elements in each of the pairs (a, a'), (b, b'), (c, c') and (d, d') differ in at most one factor, and the two elements in each of the pairs (a, c), (a', c'), (b, d), and (b', d') have identical components on that factor, then $(a, b) \succeq (a', b') \Leftrightarrow (c, d) \succeq (c', d')$. To see if our structure meets this condition, we look at the state selection dimension, our 's' dimension, first. Any results we get for this dimension can be applied to the other two without further work.

We select our points a, b, c, d, a', b', c', and d' so that each of the pairs (a, a'), (b, b'), (c, c') and (d, d') differ in only the s dimension; they are identical in the o and a dimensions. Further, each of the pairs (a, c), (a', c'), (b, d), and (b', d') must be identical in the s dimension; we do not care whether they vary in either of the other two. Then, try to show that $(a, b) \succeq (a', b') \Leftrightarrow (c, d) \succeq (c', d')$, or more precisely, that the interval between a and b is at least as large as the interval between a' and b' if and only if the same is true for (c, d) and (c', d'). The strategy will be to assume that $(a, b) \succeq (a', b')$ is true and show that

$(c, d) \succeq (c', d')$ must be true as well. Then, reverse the process and show that if we assume the second, the first must also be true.

Suppose $(a, b) \succeq (a', b')$. We know that $a_o \sim_o a'_o$, $a_a \sim_a a'_a$, $b_o \sim_o b'_o$, and $b_a \sim_a b'_a$. This means that $(a_s, b_s) \succeq_s (a'_s, b'_s)$. Since $a_s \sim_s c_s$, $a'_s \sim_s c'_s$, $b_s \sim_s d_s$, and $b'_s \sim_s d'_s$, we can thus infer that $(c_s, d_s) \succeq_s (c'_s, d'_s)$. Since $c_o \sim_o c'_o$, $c_a \sim_a c'_a$, $d_o \sim_o d'_o$, and $d_a \sim_a d'_a$, it must be the case that $(c, d) \succeq (c', d')$, giving us half our desired result. The other half is easy to show by swapping c with a, c' with a', d with b, and d' with b' and $\succeq$ with $\preceq$ in all cases. By extension, we can apply the same logic to the o and a dimensions. We have a factorial proximity structure with one-factor independence, which provides us with at least an ordinal scale representation.

The next step is to show that we have an intradimensional difference structure, which is the first structure that can provide an interval scale representation. To do this, we must show that our empirical model satisfies what are called the betweenness axioms, restricted solvability, and the Archimedean axiom.

Given our factorial proximity structure $\langle A, \succeq \rangle$ that satisfies one-factor independence, let $\succeq_i$ denote ordering in each of the three dimensions. We say that b is between a and c, denoted by $a \mid b \mid c$, if and only if $(a_i, c_i) \succeq_i (a_i, b_i)$ and (b_i, c_i) for each $i \in \{s, o, a\}$. For $\langle A, \succeq \rangle$ to satisfy the betweenness axioms, the following must hold for all $a, b, c, d, a', b', c' \in A$:

1. If a, b, c, d differ in at most one factor, and $b \neq c$, then:
    (a) $a \mid b \mid c \wedge b \mid c \mid d \Rightarrow a \mid b \mid d \wedge a \mid c \mid d$
    (b) $a \mid b \mid c \wedge a \mid c \mid d \Rightarrow a \mid b \mid d \wedge b \mid c \mid d$
2. If a, b, c, a', b', c' differ in at most one factor, $a \mid b \mid c$, $a' \mid b' \mid c'$, and $(b, c) \sim (b', c')$, then $(a, b) \succeq (a', b') \Leftrightarrow (a, c) \succeq (a', c')$.

A factorial proximity structure $\langle A, \succeq \rangle$ satisfies restricted solvability if and only if, for all $e, f, d, a, c \in A$, if $(d, a) \succeq (e, f) \succeq (d, c)$, then there exists $b \in A$ such that $a \mid b \mid c$ and $(d, b) \sim (e, f)$. A factorial proximity structure $\langle A, \succeq \rangle$ satisfies the Archimedean axiom if and only if, for all $a, b, c, d \in A$, with $a \neq b$, any sequence $e_k \in A$, $k = 0, 1, \ldots$, such that $e_0 = c$, $(e_k, e_{k+1}) \succ (a, b)$ and $(c, d) \succ (c, e_{k+1}) \succ (c, e_k)$ for all k is finite.

Let's tackle the betweenness axioms first. Since both of these conditions contain the phrase ". . . differ in at most one factor . . . ," we will examine them for the s dimension, holding the o and a dimensions constant, and assume that our objects are all equivalent in the o and a dimensions. This means that, given three classes a, b, and c, we can say that $a \mid b \mid c$ if $a_s \mid b_s \mid c_s$ since they are equivalent in the other dimensions. According to this definition of betweenness, $a_s \mid b_s \mid c_s$ if $(a_s, c_s) \succeq_s (a_s, b_s)$ and (b_s, c_s). In other words, b_s is between a_s and c_s if the interval from a_s to c_s is at least as great as the interval from a_s to b_s and the interval from b_s to c_s. Note that b_s could be either a_s or c_s and the conditions will still be met. Since $a_o \sim_o b_o \sim_o c_o$ and $a_a \sim_a b_a \sim_a c_a$, the definition holds for those dimensions, and we can thus apply betweenness to a, b, and c.

The first betweenness axiom assumes we can find four classes, a, b, c, and d, which differ in at most one factor, and for which $b \neq c$, which means that b and

c are not the same class. The first part of the axiom requires that if $a \mid b \mid c$ and $b \mid c \mid d$, then $a \mid b \mid d$ and $a \mid c \mid d$; that is, if b is between a and c, and c is between b and d, then b and c must both be between a and d. If you place four marbles along a line, this condition is obvious, in the sense that it is easy to see how it is met. This is illustrated in Figure 8.2. The second part of the axiom requires that if $a \mid b \mid c$ and $a \mid c \mid d$, then $a \mid b \mid d$, and $b \mid c \mid d$; that is, if b is between a and c, and c is between a and d, then b must be between a and d, and c must be between b and d. Again, if you place four marbles along a line, as in Figure 8.2, this condition is obvious.

We are working with percentages which vary along the interval [0, 1]. We say that $x \succeq y$ if $x \geq y$ in terms of its value. With this in mind, it is easy to show that the s dimension satisfies the first of the betweenness axioms, and likewise for the o and a dimensions, because we can replace our marbles in Figure 8.2 with percentage values and see that the conditions all hold.

The second of the betweenness axioms assumes six classes, a, b, c, a', b', and c', that differ in only one factor. We will again use the s dimension, assuming the six classes to be equivalent in the o and a dimensions. The axiom requires that if $a \mid b \mid c$, $a' \mid b' \mid c'$, and $(b, c) \sim (b', c')$, then $(a, b) \succeq (a', b') \Leftrightarrow (a, c) \succeq (a', c')$; that is, if b is between a and c, and b' is between a' and c', and the intervals between b and c and b' and c' are the same, then the interval between a and b is at least as great as the interval between a' and b' only when the intervals between a and c, and a' and c' share the same relationship.

We already know how to represent betweenness with our percentages and that we can represent intervals between percentages by taking the absolute value of their difference. Thus, for $(b_s, c_s) \sim_s (b'_s, c'_s)$, it must be the case that $|b_s - c_s| = |b'_s - c'_s|$. In other words, b_s and c_s, and b'_s and c'_s must be the same distance apart, but not necessarily in the same direction; the first two assumptions handle this for us. With this information, we know we can take the interval between b_s and c_s and map it onto the interval between b'_s and c'_s, and get a perfect match.

For b to be between a and c, $|a_s - c_s| \geq |b_s - c_s|$. Likewise for a'_s, b'_s, and c'_s. So, if all of these conditions are met, we need to show that $|a_s - b_s| \geq |a'_s - b'_s|$ only when $|a_s - c_s| \geq |a'_s - c'_s|$. To do this, imagine a pair of two-part line segments, shown in Figure 8.3, for which the second segments match exactly in terms of length. We are trying to show that the first part of the first line segment can be longer than the first part of the second line segment only when the first segment as a whole is longer than the second segment as a whole. Looking at the figure, the intent of the requirement is obvious. Since percentages form an absolute scale, we can use distance analogies to show that our representation indeed meets the requirements.

Restricted solvability requires that if we have classes a, c, d, e, and f, such that the intervals between d and a, e and f, and d and c are given in decreasing

Figure 8.2 *The first betweenness axiom, illustrated.*

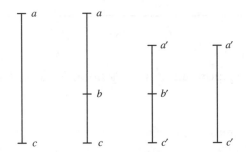

Figure 8.3 *The second betweenness axiom, illustrated.*

order, we must be able to find a class b between a and c and such that the interval between d and b matches the interval between e and f. This situation is illustrated in Figure 8.4. Note these conditions place c between d and a.

Basically, restricted solvability requires that given any two classes, you can always find a third class which is between them. This does not mean that you must actually *have* a class that lies between them, but only that it is possible to *construct* such a class. Betweenness allows the middle class to be one of the end classes, so this is not a difficult requirement. Since percentages are real numbers on the interval [0, 1], and since you can always find a real number between any other two real numbers, we meet this requirement. Since betweenness allows the middle class to coincide with either of the endpoints, you can meet this requirement using a mapping into the integers or even the natural numbers.

The Archimedean axiom is a complicated way of saying that any nonoverlapping sequence of intervals from one class to another, each of which is equivalent to the interval between another pair of classes, is finite. This situation is shown in Figure 8.5. This axiom can be difficult to satisfy. You can weasel out of it, however, by noting that percentages are real numbers on the interval [0, 1]. The Archimedean property of real numbers says that for any real number y, there is a real number x and an a finite integer n such that $nx > y$. This is another way of saying that any sequence of intervals between x and y that is n units long is finite. Since this property holds for the real numbers, it holds for our representation. The number of intervals in the sequence can be very, very large, but even very, very large is finite.

You now have an intrademensional subtractive structure and thus a representation that is at least an interval scale.

In general, two additional requirements must be satisfied in order to achieve an additive-difference structure, which combines an intradimesional subtractive struc-

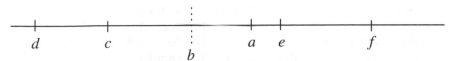

Figure 8.4 *An illustration of restricted solvability.*

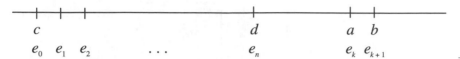

Figure 8.5 *A strictly bounded standard sequence.*

ture with an interdimensional additive structure: the Thomsen condition and independence. Since we are working with three dimensions, the Thomsen condition is not required. Independence requires swapping the requirements for one-factor independence and still being able to show the same results. The addition of the interdimensional additive structure allows our model to account for different contributions of each component.

A factorial proximity structure $\langle A, \succeq \rangle$ satisfies independence if for all a, a', b, b', c, c', d, $d' \in A$, if the two elements of each of the pairs (a, a'), (b, b'), (c, c'), and (d, d') have identical components on one factor, and the two elements of each of the pairs (a, c), (a', c'), (b, d), and (b', d') have identical components on all the remaining factors, then $(a, b) \succeq (a', b') \Leftrightarrow (c, d)(c', d')$. Thus, if $a_i \sim a'_i$ and $b_i \sim b'_i$, then for $(a, b) \succeq (a', b')$ to hold, the ordering of a and b must be independent of the ith factor. We should be able to change the common value of a and a', and b and b', and still have $(a, b) \succeq (a', b')$ hold.

In our model, this means that if we have four classes a, b, a', and b', and we assume $a_s \sim_s a'_s$ and $b_s \sim_s b'_s$, then the ordering of a and b must be based on the o and a dimensions in order for $(a, b) \succeq (a', b')$. Further, we should be able to substitute any other value for a_s and b_s and have achieve the same ordering. Intuitively, our empirical model based on percentages meets this requirement. While all three dimensions depend on the population of attribute arrows, the three ratios are independent of each other. To show this, we select our points a, b, c, d, a', b', c', and d' so that each of the pairs (a, a'), (b, b'), (c, c') and (d, d') are identical in the s dimension; we do not care whether they vary in either of the other two. Further, the each of the pairs (a, c), (a', c'), (b, d), and (b', d') must differ in only the s dimension; they must be identical in the o and a dimensions. We then try to show that $(a, b) \succeq (a', b') \Leftrightarrow (c, d) \succeq (c', d')$. As with the last time we did this, our strategy will be to assume that $(a, b) \succeq (a', b')$ is true and show that $(c, d) \succeq (c', d')$ must be true as well. We can then reverse the process and show that if we assume the second, the first must also be true.

Suppose $(a, b) \succeq (a', b')$. We know that $a_s \sim_s a'_s$, $b_s \sim_s b'_s$, $c_s \sim_s c'_s$, and $d_s \sim_s d'_s$. This means that $(a_s, b_s) \sim_s (a'_s, b'_s)$ and $(c_s, d_s) \sim_s (c'_s, d'_s)$. Since $a_o \sim_o c_o$, $a_a \sim_a c_a$, $a'_o \sim_o c'_o$, $a'_a \sim_a c'_a$, $b_o \sim_o d_o$, $b_a \sim_a d_a$, $b'_o \sim_o d'_o$, and $b'_a \sim_a d'_a$, we can thus infer that $(c, d) \succeq (c', d')$, giving us half our desired result. The other half is easy to show by swapping c with a, c' with a', d with b, and d' with b' and $\succeq$ with $\preceq$ in all cases. By extension, we can apply the same logic to the o and a dimensions. We have an additive-difference structure, which provides a representation on the interval scale, but which also allows for differing contributions by the elements of each dimension to the overall value.

The final step is to see if we can achieve an additive-difference *metric* structure, which gives us a log-interval scale of the form

$$\delta(a, b) = F^{-1} \left\{ \sum_{i=1}^{n} F[|\varphi_i(a_i) - \varphi_i(b_i)|] \right\} \qquad (8.7)$$

where each $F(x)$ takes the form $F(x) = kx^r$, $r \geq 1$, $k \geq 1$. Substituting for $F(x)$, we get

$$\delta(a, b) = \left[\sum_{i=1}^{n} |\varphi_i(a_i) - \varphi_i(b_i)|^r \right]^{1/r} \qquad (8.8)$$

which is the basic form of the power metric. If $r = 1$, the metric δ is a ratio scale, otherwise it is a log-interval scale. For all intents and purposes, a log-interval scale can be used whenever a ratio scale is required.

The only additional requirements for our additive-difference structure to be a metric is that it be complete and segmentally additive. A proximity structure is complete and segmentally additive if and only if the following hold for all a, c, e, $f \in A$ (Krantz et al. 1989):

1. If $(a, c) \succeq (e, f)$, then there exists $b \in A$ such that $(a, b) \sim (e, f)$ and for all a', b', $c' \in A$, both of the following hold:
   - $(a, b) \succeq (a', b') \wedge (a', c') \succeq (a, c) \Rightarrow (b', c') \succeq (b, c)$
   - $(c, b) \succeq (c', b') \wedge (c', a') \succeq (c, a) \Rightarrow (b', a') \succeq (b, a)$
2. If $e \neq f$, then there exist $b_0,..., b_n \in A$ such that $b_0 = a$, $b_n = c$, and $(e, f) \succeq (b_{i-1}, b_i)$, $i = 1,..., n$.
3. If $e \neq f$, then there exist b, $d \in A$, with $b \neq d$, such that $(e, f) \succ (b, d)$.
4. Let $a_1,..., a_n,...$ be a sequence of elements of A such that for all e, $f \in A$, if $e \neq f$, then $(e, f) \succeq (a_i, a_j)$ for all but finitely many pairs $\langle i, j \rangle$. Then there exists $b \in A$ such that for all e, $f \in A$, if $e \neq f$, then $(e, f) \succeq (a_i, b)$ for all but finitely many i.

As we are dealing with percentages, intuition leads us to believe that we should easily construct a segmentally additive metric structure. As usual, the mathematics appears more complex than it is when you tackle one requirement at a time. The first condition is called the segmental solvability axiom. Its purpose is to ensure that spacing within our structure is independent of direction and the location of the starting point. For percentages, this means that we measure distances in terms of absolute values of the differences, and that it does not matter which point is chosen as our starting point. An interval of length (e, f) will always have a length (e, f), no matter what point we choose as e, nor which direction we go from there.

The main clause of the first condition states that given two intervals, the first of which is at least as great as the second, we can always find a point within the first interval, and the length of this new interval is equivalent to the length of the second.

The first part of the first condition is illustrated by the line segments in Figure 8.6a. Looking at points on a line, the condition given by part a is obvious. If we terminate the line segment at 0 and 1, as shown in the figure, we can readily see that the condition holds for percentages and ratios, as long as we are comparing different values of the same ratio; it does not necessarily work if we compare different ratios.

The second part of the first condition is illustrated by the line segments in Figure 8.6b. Since the first condition requires that both parts must hold, we need to find a situation where this works. If we make $a \sim a'$, $b \sim b'$, and $c \sim c'$, as shown in Figure 8.6c, both parts hold and we are still dealing with the relation $\succeq$.

Condition 2, as complex as it looks, is really rather intuitive. All it requires is that we can construct a sequence of intervals, all of which are the same length and positive (their endpoints are distinct), that begin at one point and end at another, these two points forming a larger segment. This condition allows us to mark centimeters on a meterstick. To show this condition holds for percentages, pick two distinct values. Since percentages are real numbers, we know we can always find a number between them. In fact, we can find arbitrarily many points between them. Thus, we can always construct a sequence of equally spaced intervals which together coincide exactly with the larger interval in question.

The third condition says that if we have an interval with distinct endpoints, we can always find another pair of distinct points, the interval between which is smaller than the first. In other words, there is no smallest positive distance. With percentages, this means that given an absolute difference between two values, we can always find another pair of values with a smaller absolute difference. This is obvious.

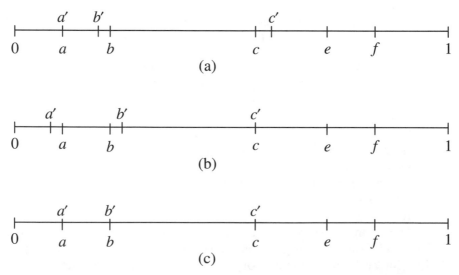

Figure 8.6 *A test for segmented additivity and completeness.*

The fourth condition states, simply, that any sequence of intervals between two fixed points has a finite number of segments. This means that every distance between any pair of points in the space can be measured using a finite sequence of intervals of the same length; every distance between fixed points is finite. This is obvious, when we use real numbers.

We have succeeded in creating an additive-difference metric space, giving us a ratio scale measure of class complexity. This means we can represent our three ratios as points in three dimensions within a space of fixed size and allows us to compare different classes by comparing the volumes of the solids created by the three-dimensional plots of their respective ratios. Imagine a three-dimensional model of a design in which the complexity of each class is represented by the size, in each dimension, of its irregular shape. Such a representation would make it very easy to spot the complex classes, wouldn't it?

This particular representation cannot be applied to designs, although we can calculate the median or average complexities of the classes in the design, along with the quartiles or standard deviations for the class complexities. We can then judge an individual class by the quartile in which it lies or by its complexity in relation to the norm. We have thus constructed a measure of class complexity which we know to be theoretically valid, a ratio scale measure, and for which we can envision some practical use.

SUMMARY

Complexity is a fuzzy notion in software engineering. Many authors have suggested a wide variety of definitions, leading some to the conclusion that we cannot construct a single measure of complexity that serves all of these conflicting needs. Five distinct views of complexity were identified and several others that are expressed in terms of these five were discussed. A view of complexity that stratifies complexity into different layers was settled on. Complexity in one layer is hidden from all others. Then, several formal properties were defined that express our empirical understanding of how complexity behaves in this view.

We looked to our formal model and found several ways to express our view of complexity in terms of that model, leading to several possible empirical relational structures. We created a structure to represent the complexity of a design and a structure to represent the complexity of a class. Then, we developed the class complexity structure into a representation.

We saw once again that the process for creating a representation is a lot of work, but is not difficult if taken one step at a time. In many ways, it is like software engineering itself. The secret is to understand the intuitive descriptions underlying the formal conditions, then select empirical models that we know can meet them. This is not always possible; we may have to try more than one model, or settle for a representation on a lesser scale than we originally wanted.

During this process, we gained an appreciation for the differences of opinion that exist in regards to software complexity. In order to create a representation, we had to select a very simple view of complexity; one which is nonetheless useful in our design efforts. By isolating the complexity of different levels of abstraction into different layers, we can work within a layer without concern about the complexity we hide behind an interface. This view supports one of the tenets of object-oriented software development, in that the complexity of individual elements in a given layer is encapsulated in a lower layer, beyond our concern. Thus, we can view and use classes as components in a design without regard to their internal structure or complexity.

9

COUPLING

Coupling describes the nature and extent of the connections between elements of a system. In mathematics, a *system* is a collection of zero or more interacting or related elements (Berard 1993). The components of a system may be connected in logical ways, physical ways, or both. A system may be a component in a larger system, in which case the smaller system is a *subsystem*. "In general, interactions and interrelationships inside subsystems are stronger than the interactions and interrelationships between and among subsystems" (Simon and Ando, 1961).

Any form of logical or physical connection between elements of a system is defined as a form of coupling. The IEEE defines coupling as "a measure of the interdependence among modules in a computer program" (IEEE 1990). Sommerville (1989) says that coupling is related to cohesion—it is an indication of the strength of interconnectedness between program units. Berard (1993) separates coupling and cohesion by defining coupling in terms of the physical connections between elements, and cohesion in terms of the logical connections between elements.

For objects, Wirfs-Brock, Wilkerson, and Wiener (1990) define coupling between classes as a measure of how much they depend on each other. Several other authors also define coupling as a measure of dependence of one component in a design on another (see, for example, Blair et al. 1991; and Coad and Yourdon 1991). We follow Berard's lead and define coupling as a measure of strength of the physical connections between components of a design. This definition will apply at any level in a design, whether we measure the coupling between class categories, between classes, or between elements of a class.

I digress for a bit, and talk about the connection between coupling and cohesion. Most researchers who measure cohesion define their measures in terms of physical connections between components of a module or class. The data slice method of Bieman and Ott (1994) is one example. As Berard (1993) points out, looking at cohesion in this way confuses cohesion with coupling. I agree; a very different approach to cohesion will be taken in Chapter 12.

MOTIVATION AND ORIGINS

The prime motivation for measuring coupling is for predicting and controlling the scope of changes to a system. Dependencies follow lines of coupling. As the scope of these dependencies increase, so does the portion of the system that must be examined in order to estimate a change. So, too, the likelihood that a necessary change will be overlooked increases, resulting in a particularly nasty form of defect. It is not always the case that a change in one element requires a change in another to which it is tightly coupled. It is the case that the chances of a change being required in the second element are greater, and it must be analyzed.

Ideally, we should be able to change a class, recompile it, rebuild its dynamic library, and begin using the modified class without so much as relinking the remainder of the application. Of course this rarely happens in real life. Often, the best we can do is to merely recompile the rest of the application. Most often, a change in one class causes changes to ripple through the design like shock waves in an earthquake, with much the same effect.

Tightly coupled components cannot be reused separately. This is simply a fact of life. If we try to use a component that is highly dependent on another component, we invariably find that we must use this second component as well. This is the primary cause behind the amazing growth of an application's code when a framework of some kind is used. Most application frameworks on the market have tighter, and more detrimental, forms of coupling than are really necessary to accomplish their task. This requires that more of the framework is used than is needed. I have seen some third-party frameworks where the coupling is so bad, and so unnecessary, that it completely negates the benefit of using the framework in the first place. I'll get off my soapbox, now; this is a pet peeve of mine with regard to object-oriented tools available today.

Thus, there is strong motivation to limit any form of coupling to the extent possible. We cannot eliminate all forms of coupling, nor do we want to. A collection of completely uncoupled components cannot work together to accomplish anything. Instead, limit coupling to two kinds: that which is inherent in the problem domain and about which we can do nothing, and that which limits the types and scope of changes to as small a portion of the design as possible. In order to understand what this really means, we have to explore the many forms of coupling that can exist in an application.

EMPIRICAL VIEWS

Berard (1993) defines two broad classes of coupling: necessary and unnecessary. Necessary coupling is that which is inherent in the problem domain, along with the coupling required to support interaction among components of the design.

Unnecessary coupling is everything else. Every problem domain implies a certain amount of coupling between elements of that domain. Certain components have to communicate with other components and certain components are structurally related to other components. Necessary coupling, in all of its variety of forms, cannot be avoided. It can be mitigated, but not avoided.

Unnecessary coupling is the result of bad or lazy design. The only reason such coupling exists is because the designer didn't take the time and effort to remove it, or did not have the technical knowledge or experience to figure out how to remove it. Unnecessary coupling is sinister in that it can look and feel just like necessary coupling; it has many of the same forms as necessary coupling. It is also sinister in that it can look innocuous in a design, but can create many difficult problems when it comes time to modify the design. I have learned first hand the kinds of problems unnecessary coupling can cause when a design needs changing. It is especially annoying when the design has already been coded, and I have to recode half of my design, which used to be working code. I've had to do this more than twice, but on my third project, I had learned my lesson.

Several classifications for coupling have been proposed over the years. The first was presented by Myers (1976) and includes six types of coupling between modules in a system. They are, from better to worse, making this an ordinal scale measure:

1. *No coupling*: Two modules have no communication, visible or otherwise.
2. *Data coupling*: Two modules communicate via parameters in function calls or via a homogeneous set of data elements (e.g., an array), which do not include any control elements.
3. *Stamp coupling*: Two modules accept the same record type or structure; this structure may contain a heterogeneous set of elements. This type of coupling may create an interdependence between two otherwise unrelated modules (and can be hard to find, too).
4. *Control coupling*: Two modules communicate through parameters which have the intent and effect of controlling the receiving module's behavior (e.g., one of the parameters is a control flag or operation code).
5. *Common coupling*: Two modules refer to the same global data; this type of coupling is worse than stamp coupling because the two modules are not only coupled by the structure of the global data, but also by the value of the global data.
6. *Content coupling*: One module refers to the inside of another: It branches into it or alters a statement.

Several authors have proposed forms of coupling that are (purported to be) unique to objects. Coad and Yourdon (1991) define interaction coupling and inheritance coupling. Interaction coupling is the complexity of the connection between two objects or classes, or the degree to which information in a message is used by the receiving object rather than passed along. Inheritance coupling is the degree to which a derived class uses inherited attributes and methods.

Wild (1991) defines three broad classes of object coupling:

1. *Interface coupling*: One object refers to another specific object and makes references to one or more items in the public interface of the referred object; Berard claims that almost all forms of module coupling are included in the class of interface coupling types.

2. *Inside internal coupling*: Describes the forms of coupling which occur between the components of an object or class; it comes in two forms:
   - The methods of an object are coupled to the state information for the object; that is, the methods are coupled to an object's attributes.
   - The component objects that make up a composite object are coupled to each other and with the composite class itself.

3. *Outside internal coupling*: Describes the forms of coupling which occur between two classes, other than through their public interfaces, and represents the knowledge that one class has of the internals of another; it comes in two forms:
   - From the side: One of a pair of otherwise unrelated objects is aware of the internal structure of the other; it may access internal, and even private, attributes or functions of the other object.
   - From underneath: A specialization accesses attributes and methods of its generalization in a way other than through the generalization's public interface.

Wild's framework is depicted graphically in Figure 9.1.

Gamma and colleagues (1995), sometimes referred to as the "Gang of Four" in the patterns literature, describe a form of coupling they call abstract coupling. A class participates in an abstract coupling if it is coupled to an abstract class. In this form of coupling, the class is dependent only on the type or interface of the abstract class, not on the implementation of its properties (attributes or behaviors). I have made good use of this form of coupling to avoid compile-time dependencies between classes in a design.

In the course of my work, I have happened upon another form of coupling which amazingly has not been discussed in the literature. I call it value coupling. It occurs when one object's value, or the value of one of its attributes, depends upon the value of another object, or upon the value of an attribute of another object, and there are no other forms of dependence. This is a variant of Myers's common coupling, but it is not common coupling in that the dependence exists only in the problem domain and is not a physical property of the design. As an example, consider the case where the domain-level identifier for an object is composed of (parts of) two or more attributes and the combination is required to be unique. If another object comes along with the same combination, both this new object and the original must have their identifiers modified with a tie-breaker of some kind. If either of these objects is subsequently deleted, the tie-breaker must be removed from the other. This form of coupling is not limited to just pairs of objects. I have seen whole chains of objects coupled in this way. I inherited an

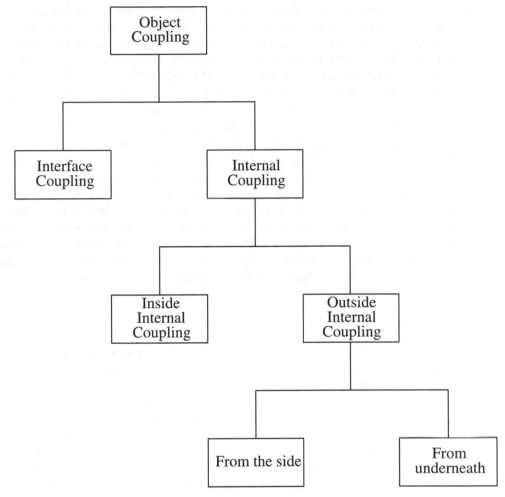

Figure 9.1 *Wild's taxonomy of coupling.*

application that suffered from this form of coupling. It caused the majority of my effort whenever I changed the application; the entities coupled in this way were the two primary components in the application and were involved in nearly every change.

Moving to a different view of coupling, let's examine it on two levels: within the design and within a class. Design coupling is manifested in the physical connections between classes. The only connections which may exist between classes are instances of the four relationship types defined in Chapter 6: inheritance, association, aggregation, and message links. Inheritance coupling can be mitigated by using delegation rather than inheritance, without reducing the cohesion of the combined structure. Message coupling can take any of the forms of module coupling and can thus be classified by the type of connection.

The coupling within a class is manifested by the connections between the methods of the class and its state information. The public methods of a class may, for example, access directly the attributes of the class. If this is the case, they are coupled. If the type of any attribute changes, the public method must also be changed. Wirfs-Brock, Wilkerson, and Wiener (1990) recommend using private selectors and modifiers to decouple the public methods from the attributes. This design technique has merits, but can also create other problems. I have used it in some cases, but not in others. The decision to use this technique is based on the effect it has on the rest of the design, including the dynamic performance of the design, and the risk or likelihood that a change to an attribute's type will occur, or if it does, will require substantial revision to a public method.

The methods of a class may also be coupled to each other in ways that do not involve the attributes directly. Any time one method in a class calls another method in the class, the two methods are coupled. Interestingly, this form of coupling is often a tradeoff with coupling between methods and attributes. You cannot eliminate both forms of coupling; you can only trade instances of one for instances of the other. How you make that trade depends upon your design circumstances.

FORMAL PROPERTIES

Briand, Morasca, and Basili (1996) define five properties which they believe should be met by all measures of coupling. Like other measures, these properties may be in addition to, or follow from, the properties imposed by any representation we might try to construct. The model underlying this notion of coupling is the directed graph, where nodes represent design components and edges represent the connections between them. Briand and colleagues discuss coupling only at the design level and do not consider in any way the coupling within a class. In these properties, denote the coupling of a design component C by $cu(C)$. The graph is denoted by $G = \langle V, E \rangle$ where V is the set of design components and E is the set of edges. A component x may be an entire graph or any connected component in a graph.

Property CU1: Coupling is nonnegative:

$$cu(C) \geqslant 0 \qquad (9.1)$$

Property CU2: Coupling can be null

$$\{e \in E \mid e = xRa \lor e = aRx\} = \varnothing \Rightarrow cu(x) = 0 \qquad (9.2)$$

where a is some other design component.

Property CU3: Adding an intercomponent relationship does not decrease coupling:

$$G_1 = \langle V, E_1 \rangle \land G_2 = \langle V, E_2 \rangle \land xRb \notin E_1 \land E_2$$

$$= E_1 \cup \{xRb\} \Rightarrow cu(G_2) \geqslant cu(G_1) \qquad (9.3)$$

Property CU4: Merging two components does not increase coupling

$$G_1 = \langle V, E_1 \rangle \wedge G_2 = \langle V, E_2 \rangle \wedge G_3$$

$$= G_1 \cup G_2 \Rightarrow \mathrm{cu}(G_1 \circ G_2) \leqslant \mathrm{cu}(G_3) \tag{9.4}$$

where the operation $\circ$ may be addition, as Briand and colleagues maintain, or some other numeric relationship.

Property CU5: Merging two unconnected components does not change coupling:

$$G_1 = \langle V, E_1 \rangle \wedge G_2 = \langle V, E_2 \rangle \wedge E_1 \cap E_2 = \varnothing \wedge G_3$$

$$= G_1 \cup G_2 \Rightarrow \mathrm{cu}(G_1 \circ G_2) = \mathrm{cu}(G_3) \tag{9.5}$$

To this set, I add the following property:

Property CU6: Coupling forms a weak order; design components and whole designs can be ordered in terms of the level of coupling they contain.

EMPIRICAL RELATIONAL STRUCTURES

It is time to relate our intuitive notions of coupling to the formal model developed in Chapter 6. All of the presented views of coupling are expressed in terms of connections between design components. This naturally leads us to focus on the arrows in our categorical representations of designs and classes. In the category **DesignState**, we surmise that coupling will be measured in terms of the number of relationship arrows, by type, between the classes in the design. For message links, look further at the preconditions and postconditions to see what changes are made by a method. The type of message coupling will be determined by the types of changes caused by the method.

In the category **Class**, we focus on the attribute arrows, including those representing aggregations of classes, and the operation arrows. Interestingly, the arrows in this category do not tell us much about the coupling within a class. The preconditions and postconditions for an operation tell us which attributes it depends on, accesses, or modifies.

From a category standpoint, this may require a new view of a class, with attributes and operations as objects, and arrows which indicate the relationships between these as indicated in the preconditions and postconditions for the operations. We can represent this as a category for each operation. Such a category will have one operation object and some number of attribute objects. The arrows are labeled with the predicate in the precondition or postcondition which indicates the relationship. We can build such a category without permanently modifying the formal model in Chapter 6. This is an example of modifying the model to fit the need, which is part of the process for developing a measure in Chapter 3. As long as the modification is built from, and consistent with, the permanent model, we are fine. Our new category might look like the example in Figure 9.2. In this

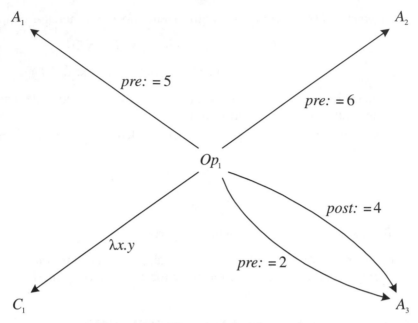

Figure 9.2 *The category Operation.*

category, the coupling for the operation Op_1 would be the count of arrows by type (*pre*, *post*, and λ).

This additional category has an interesting property. The union of the λ-arrows taken over all of the operation categories for a class should match exactly to the set of message link arrows for the class in the **DesignState** category. If these two sets do not match exactly, the design is inconsistent: One of the two sets of arrows is wrong.

Given this view of coupling, there are several possible empirical relational structures from which to choose. Most obvious is a four-factor conjoint structure for the coupling of classes in a design and a three-factor conjoint structure for the coupling among the components of a class. In both cases, there is one factor for each type of arrow, assuming that each type contributes in a different way to the overall level of coupling.

We could settle for four and three element vectors, and use vector addition and subtraction to compare designs and classes, respectively. We could also try to build metric spaces out of the vectors. At first blush, we can't see why metric spaces would not be attainable. So, let's aim for one of these representations in the next section. If we can achieve one of them, we get both of them, since they contain the same kinds of empirical elements and relations.

POTENTIAL MEASURES

Let's construct a representation for the coupling of classes within a design. With four dimensions, it is the more interesting of the two problems. It is also the most familiar to most of you. The attempt is to create a four-dimensional metric space to measure the total coupling of a class within a design. All four of the dimensions are based upon absolute scales of counts of arrows, so no difficulties are anticipated.

The requirements for an additive-difference metric structure, given in Chapter 5, look formidable. If you look closely, you can see they form five steps. The first two steps form ordinal scale representations, and the third and fourth form interval scale representations. The fifth step achieves the ratio scale. If, for some reason, you fail to achieve a particular step, you can always fall back on the previous step and have an ordinal or interval scale measure for the coupling of classes in a design. As an aside, if the arguments in this section remind you of the previous chapter, you are very observant: They are the same arguments with the appropriate adjustments for the number of dimensions and the dimension names. The results will be different, however, as you will see.

The first step requires that the structure form a factorial proximity structure. The logic here is that unless you can form a proximity structure which is factorial, you have no hope of measuring coupling as a four-dimensional metric space.

For the remainder of this section, denote the structure as $A = A_g \times A_s \times A_a \times A_m$, where A_g is the set of generalization arrows for which the class is the (categorical) domain, A_s is the set of association arrows for which the class is either the domain or the codomain, A_a is the set of aggregation arrows for which the class is the domain, and A_m is the set of message link arrows for which the class is the domain. These definitions imply that all forms of coupling, except association, are unidirectional. This is an intuitive result, since the direction of each type of arrow, except for association, also indicates the sole direction for the class dependencies that result from the relationship.

The magnitude in each dimension is represented by the cardinality of the arrow set for the dimension. Thus $a_g = |\{aRb \in \textbf{DesignState} \mid R$ is a generalization arrow and $a = \text{dom}(R)\}|$. A class is thus characterized, for the purposes of this chapter, by the cardinalities of each of its arrows sets, denoted by the 4-tuple $a = \langle a_g, a_s, a_a, a_m \rangle$. Denote intervals between classes by the absolute differences of their cardinalities, taken one pair at a time: $(a, b) = \langle |a_g - b_g|, |a_s - b_s|, |a_a - b_a|, |a_m - b_m| \rangle$.

A factorial proximity structure $\langle A \times A, \succeq \rangle$ is one for which:

1. $\langle A \times A, \succeq \rangle$ is a weak order.
2. $(a, b) > (a, a)$ whenever $a \neq b$.
3. $(a, a) \sim (b, b)$ (minimality).
4. $(a, b) \sim (b, a)$ (symmetry).
5. $A = \times_{i=1}^{n} A_i$.

To build a weak order on $\langle A \times A, \succeq \rangle$, the classes must be ordered in all four dimensions. To do this, compare one dimension at a time while holding the others constant. You can't do much more until you can show that you actually have a multidimensional spatial proximity structure of some kind. Suppose you define four relations $\succeq_g$, $\succeq_s$, $\succeq_a$, and $\succeq_m$, which are the induced orderings on each dimension separately. You can easily define the four relations $\sim_g$, $\sim_s$, $\sim_a$, $\sim_m$ in terms of these. Given two points in the four-dimensional space, a and b, you can say that:

$$a_g \succeq_g b_g \wedge a_s \sim_s b_s \wedge a_a \sim_a b_a \wedge a_m \sim_m b_m \Rightarrow a \succeq b \qquad (9.6b)$$

$$a_s \succeq_s b_s \wedge a_g \sim_g b_g \wedge a_a \sim_a b_a \wedge a_m \sim_m b_m \Rightarrow a \succeq b \qquad (9.6b)$$

$$a_a \succeq_a b_a \wedge a_g \sim_g b_g \wedge a_s \sim_s b_s \wedge a_m \sim_m b_m \Rightarrow a \succeq b \qquad (9.6c)$$

and

$$a_m \succeq_m b_m \wedge a_g \sim_g b_g \wedge a_s \sim_s b_s \wedge a_a \sim_a b_a \Rightarrow a \succeq b \qquad (9.6d)$$

Using these results, you can show that the ordering $\succeq$ is both transitive and connected.

The second condition requires that any interval between two objects which occupy different points in space is greater than any interval between two objects which occupy the same point in space. Here, and throughout this section, $a = b$ does *not* mean that a and b are the *same object*, only that they have the same representation in the structure, or occupy the same point in space. The fact that two distinct objects can have the same representation is a problem, but one that will be discussed as part of the fifth layer of conditions. In the representation, the interval $(a, a) = \langle |a_g - a_g|, |a_s - a_s|, |a_a - a_a|, |a_m - a_m| \rangle = \langle 0, 0, 0, 0 \rangle$. Any interval between two objects in different points, (a, b) where $a \neq b$, will have some $|a_i - b_i| > 0$, $i = \{g, s, a, m\}$. Thus, this condition is satisfied.

The third condition requires that the intervals between all pairs of objects, all of which compare objects at the same point, are equivalent. This is obvious for the representation, both intuitively, and from the discussion about the second condition.

The fourth condition requires that the interval between a pair of objects is the same regardless of the direction from which the interval is measured. The use of absolute differences meets this condition very easily.

The fifth condition requires that the composite structure is formed from the cross product of each of the component sets. To meet this condition, simply define the structure to be constructed this way. Doing so imposes constraints down the line, but they constrain you in the direction you are already going. You have a factorial proximity structure.

The second step is to show that the structure is decomposable. To be decomposable, a factorial proximity structure must be one-factor independent. This means that for all a, b, c, d, a', b', c', and $d' \in A$, if the two elements in each of the pairs (a, a'), (b, b'), (c, c') and (d, d') differ in at most one factor, and the two elements in each of the pairs (a, c), (a', c'), (b, d), and (b', d') have identical components on that factor, then $(a, b) \succeq (a', b') \Leftrightarrow (c, d) \succeq (c', d')$. To see if the structure meets this condition, look at the set of generalization arrows, the 'g' dimension, first. Any results for this dimension can be applied to the other three without further work.

Select points a, b, c, d, a', b', c', and d' so that each of the pairs (a, a'), (b, b'), (c, c') and (d, d') differ in only the g dimension; they are identical in the s, a, and m dimensions. Further, each of the pairs (a, c), (a', c'), (b, d), and (b', d') must be identical in the g dimension; it is not important whether they vary in any of the other three. Then, try to show that $(a, b) \succeq (a', b') \Leftrightarrow (c, d) \succeq (c', d')$; that is, that the interval between a and b is at least as large as the interval between a' and b' if and only if the same is true for (c, d) and (c', d'). The strategy is to assume that $(a, b) \succeq (a', b')$ is true and show that $(c, d) \succeq (c', d')$ must be true as well. Then, reverse the process and show that if you assume the second, the first must also be true.

Suppose $(a, b) \succeq (a', b')$. You know that $a_s \sim_s a'_s$, $a_a \sim_a a'_a$, $a_m \sim_m a'_m$, $b_s \sim_s b'_s$, $b_a \sim_a b'_a$, and $b_m \sim_m b'_m$. This means that $(a_g, b_g) \succeq_g (a'_g, b'_g)$ by equations (9.6a–d). Since $a_g \sim_g c_g$, $a'_g \sim_g c'_g$, $b_g \sim_g d_g$, and $b'_g \sim_g d'_g$, you can thus infer that $(c_g, d_g) \succeq_g (c'_g, d'_g)$. Since $c_s \sim_s c'_s$, $c_a \sim_a c'_a$, $c_m \sim_m c'_m$, $d_s \sim_s d'_s$, $d_a \sim_a d'_a$, and $d_m \sim_m d'_m$, it must be the case that $(c, d) \succeq (c', d')$, giving half the desired result. The other half is easy to show by swapping c with a, c' with a', d with b, and d' with b' and $\succeq$ with $\preceq$ in all cases. By extension, you can apply the same logic to the s, a, and m dimensions. You have a factorial proximity structure with one-factor independence, which provides at least an ordinal scale representation.

The next step is to test whether you have an intradimensional difference structure, which is the first structure that can provide an interval scale representation. To do this, you must show that the empirical model satisfies the betweenness axioms, restricted solvability, and the Archimedean axiom.

Given a factorial proximity structure $\langle A, \succeq \rangle$ that satisfies one-factor independence, let $\succeq_i$ denote ordering in each of the four dimensions. We say that b is between a and c, denoted by $a \mid b \mid c$, if and only if $(a_i, c_i) \succeq_i (a_i, b_i)$ and (b_i, c_i) for each $i \in \{g, s, a, m\}$. For $\langle A, \succeq \rangle$ to satisfy the betweenness axioms, the following must hold for all $a, b, c, d, a', b', c' \in A$:

1. If a, b, c, d differ in at most one factor, and $b \neq c$, then:
   - $a \mid b \mid c \wedge b \mid c \mid d \Rightarrow a \mid b \mid d \wedge a \mid c \mid d$
   - $a \mid b \mid c \wedge a \mid c \mid d \Rightarrow a \mid b \mid d \wedge b \mid c \mid d$

2. If a, b, c, a', b', c' differ in at most one factor, $a \mid b \mid c$, $a' \mid b' \mid c'$, and $(b, c) \sim (b', c')$, then $(a, b) \succeq (a', b') \Leftrightarrow (a, c) \succeq (a', c')$.

A factorial proximity structure $\langle A, \succeq \rangle$ satisfies restricted solvability if and only if, for all $e, f, d, a, c \in A$, if $(d, a) \succeq (e, f) \succeq (d, c)$, then there exists $b \in A$ such that $a \mid b \mid c$ and $(d, b) \sim (e, f)$. A factorial proximity structure $\langle A, \succeq \rangle$ satisfies the Archimedean axiom if and only if, for all $a, b, c, d \in A$, with $a \neq b$, any sequence $e_k \in A$, $k = 0, 1,...$, such that $e_0 = c$, $(e_k, e_{k+1}) > (a, b)$ and $(c, d) > (c, e_{k+1}) > (c, e_k)$ for all k is finite.

Let's tackle the betweenness axioms first. Since both of these conditions contain the phrase ". . . differ in at most one factor . . . ," examine them for the g dimension, holding the other dimensions constant, and assume that the objects are all equivalent in the s, a, and m dimensions. This means that, given three classes

a, b, and c, you can say that $a \mid b \mid c$ if $a_g \mid b_g \mid c_g$ since they are equivalent in the other dimensions. According to the previous definition of betweenness, $a_g \mid b_g \mid c_g$ if $(a_g, c_g) \succeq_g (a_g, b_g)$ and (b_g, c_g). In other words, b_g is between a_g and c_g if the interval from a_g to c_g is at least as great as the interval from a_g to b_g and the interval from b_g to c_g. Note that b_g could be either a_g or c_g and the conditions will still be met. Since $a_s \sim_s b_s \sim_s c_s$, $a_a \sim_a b_a \sim_a c_a$ and $a_m \sim_m b_m \sim_m c_m$, the definition holds for those dimensions and you can thus apply betweenness to a, b, and c.

The first betweenness axiom assumes you can find four classes, a, b, c, and d, which differ in at most one factor, and for which $b \neq c$, which means that b and c are not the same class and do not occupy the same point in space. The first part of the axiom requires that if $a \mid b \mid c$ and $b \mid c \mid d$, then $a \mid b \mid d$ and $a \mid c \mid d$; that is, if b is between a and c, and c is between b and d, then b and c must both be between a and d. If you place four marbles along a line, this condition is obvious, in the sense that it is easy to see how it is met. This is illustrated in Figure 9.3. The second part of the axiom requires that if $a \mid b \mid c$ and $a \mid c \mid d$, then $a \mid b \mid d$, and $b \mid c \mid d$; that is, if b is between a and c, and c is between a and d, then b must be between a and d, and c must be between b and d. Again, if you place four marbles along a line, as in Figure 9.3, this condition is obvious.

Working with cardinalities of sets, we say that $x \succeq y$ if $|x| \geq |y|$. With this in mind, it is easy to show that the g dimension satisfies the first of the betweenness axioms, and likewise for the s, a and m dimensions, because you can replace our marbles in Figure 9.3 with set cardinalities and see that the conditions all hold.

The second of the betweenness axioms assumes six classes, a, b, c, a', b', and c', that differ in only one factor. Again, use the g dimension and assume the six classes are equivalent in the s, a and m dimensions. The axiom requires that if $a \mid b \mid c$, $a' \mid b' \mid c'$, and $(b, c) \sim (b', c')$, then $(a, b) \succeq (a', b') \Leftrightarrow (a, c) \succeq (a', c')$; that is, if b is between a and c, and b' is between a' and c', and the intervals between b and c and b' and c' are the same, then the interval between a and b is at least as great as the interval between a' and b' only when the intervals between a and c, and a' and c' share the same relationship.

You already know how to represent betweenness with set cardinalities and that you can represent intervals between set cardinalities by taking the absolute value of their difference. Thus, for $(b_g, c_g) \sim_g (b'_g, c'_g)$, it must be the case that $\||b_g| - |c_g|\| = \||b'_g| - |c'_g|\|$. In other words, b_g and c_g, and b'_g and c'_g must be the same distance apart, but not necessarily in the same direction; the first two assumptions

Figure 9.3 *The first betweenness axiom, illustrated.*

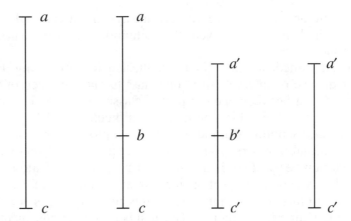

Figure 9.4 *The second betweenness axiom, illustrated.*

handle this for you. With this information, you can take the interval between b_g and c_g and map it onto the interval between b'_g and c'_g, and get a perfect match.

For b to be between a and c, $\|a_g| - |c_g\| \geq \|b_g| - |c_g\|$. Likewise for a'_g, b'_g, and c'_g. So, if all of these conditions are met, you need to show that $\|a_g| - |b_g\| \geq \|a'_g| - |b'_g\|$ only when $\|a_g| - |c_g\| \geq \|a'_g| - |c'_g\|$. To do this, imagine a pair of two-part line segments, shown in Figure 9.4, for which the second segments match exactly in terms of length. You are trying to show that the first part of the first line segment can be longer than the first part of the second line segment only when the first segment as a whole is longer than the second segment as a whole. Looking at the figure, the intent of the requirement is obvious. It is also easy to see that the chosen representation meets this requirement.

Restricted solvability requires that if you have classes a, c, d, e, and f, such that the intervals between d and a, e and f, and d and c are given in decreasing order, you must be able to find a class b between a and c and such that the interval between d and b matches the interval between e and f. This situation is illustrated in Figure 9.5. Note these conditions place c between d and a.

Basically, restricted solvability requires that given any two classes, you can always find a third class which is between them. This does not mean that you must actually *have* a class that lies between them, but only that it is possible to *construct* such a class. Betweenness allows the middle class to be one of the end classes, so this is not a difficult requirement. Since set cardinalities map to the

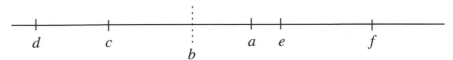

Figure 9.5 *An illustration of restricted solvability.*

cardinal numbers, and since you can always find a cardinal number between any two cardinal numbers, given the definition of betweenness, you meet this requirement.

The Archimedean axiom is a complicated way of saying that any nonoverlapping sequence of intervals from one class to another, each of which is equivalent to the interval between another pair of classes, is finite. This requirement is illustrated in Figure 9.6. This axiom can be difficult to satisfy. You can weasel out of it, however, by noting that the Archimedean property of real numbers also applies to the cardinal numbers. The Archimedean property of real numbers says that for any real number y, there is a real number x and an a finite integer n such that $nx > y$. This is another way of saying that any sequence of intervals between x and y that is n units long is finite. Since this property holds for the real numbers, it holds for your representation. The number of intervals in the sequence can be very, very large, but even very, very large is finite.

Now you have an intradimensional subtractive structure, and thus a representation that is at least an interval scale.

In general, two additional requirements must be satisfied in order to achieve an additive-difference structure, which combines an intradimensional subtractive structure with an interdimensional additive structure: the Thomsen condition and independence. Since you are working with four dimensions, the Thomsen condition is not required. Independence requires swapping the requirements for one-factor independence and still being able to show the same results. The addition of the interdimensional additive structure allows the model to account for different contributions of each component (see Chapter 5).

A factorial proximity structure $\langle A, \succeq \rangle$ satisfies independence if for all a, a', b, b', c, c', d, $d' \in A$, if the two elements of each of the pairs (a, a'), (b, b'), (c, c'), and (d, d') have identical components on one factor, and the two elements of each of the pairs (a, c), (a', c'), (b, d), and (b', d') have identical components on all of the remaining factors, then $(a, b) \succeq (a', b') \Leftrightarrow (c, d) \succeq (c', d')$. Thus, if $a_i \sim a_i'$ and $b_i \sim b_i'$, then for $(a, b) \succeq (a', b')$ to hold, the ordering of a and b must be independent of the ith factor. You should be able to change the common value of a and a', and b and b', and still have $(a, b) \succeq (a', b')$ hold.

In the model, this means that if you have four classes a, b, a', and b', and assume $a_g \sim_g a_g'$ and $b_g \sim_g b_g'$, then the ordering of a and b must be based on the s, a and m dimensions in order for $(a, b) \succeq (a', b')$. Further, you should be able to substitute any other value for a_g and b_g, and achieve the same ordering. Intuitively, our empirical model based on set cardinalities meets this requirement. All four dimensions depend on populations of arrows and are independent of each

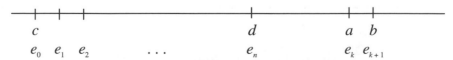

Figure 9.6 *A strictly bounded standard sequence.*

other. To show this, select the points a, b, c, d, a', b', c', and d' so that each of the pairs (a, a'), (b, b'), (c, c') and (d, d') are identical in the g dimension; it is unimportant whether they vary in either of the other three. Further, each of the pairs (a, c), (a', c'), (b, d), and (b', d') must differ in only the g dimension; they must be identical in the s, a and m dimensions. Then, try to show that $(a, b) \succeq (a', b') \Leftrightarrow (c, d) \succeq (c', d')$. As before, assume that $(a, b) \succeq (a', b')$ is true and show that $(c, d) \succeq (c', d')$ must be true as well. Then you can reverse the process and show that if you assume the second, the first must also be true.

Suppose $(a, b) \succeq (a', b')$. You know that $a_g \sim_g a'_g$, $b_g \sim_g b'_g$, $c_g \sim_g c'_g$, and $d_g \sim_g d'_g$. This means that $(a_g, b_g) \sim_g (a'_g, b'_g)$ and $(c_g, d_g) \sim_g (c'_g, d'_g)$. Since $a_s \sim_s c_s$, $a_a \sim_a c_a$, $a_m \sim_m c_m$, $a'_s \sim_s c'_s$, $a'_a \sim_a c'_a$, $a'_m \sim_m c'_m$, $b_s \sim_s d_s$, $b_a \sim_a d_a$, $b_m \sim_m d_m$, $b'_s \sim_s d'_s$, $b'_a \sim_a d'_a$, and $b'_m \sim_m d'_m$, you can thus infer that $(c, d) \succeq (c', d')$, giving half the desired result. The other half is easy to show by swapping c with a, c' with a', d with b, and d' with b' and $\succeq$ with $\preceq$ in all cases. By extension, you can apply the same logic to the s, a, and m dimensions. You have an additive-difference structure, which provides a representation on the interval scale, but which also allows for differing contributions by the elements of each dimension to the overall value.

The final step is to see if you can achieve an additive-difference metric structure, which gives a power metric log-interval scale for $r > 1$, and a ratio scale for $r = 1$. For all intents and purposes, a log-interval scale can be used whenever a ratio scale is required.

The only additional requirements for the additive-difference structure to be a metric is that it be complete and segmentally additive. A proximity structure is complete and segmentally additive if and only if the following hold for all $a, c, e, f \in A$ (Krantz et al. 1989):

1. If $(a, c) \succeq (e, f)$, then there exists $b \in A$ such that $(a, b) \sim (e, f)$ and for all $a', b', c' \in A$, both of the following hold:
   - $(a, b) \succeq (a', b') \wedge (a', c') \succeq (a, c) \Rightarrow (b', c') \succeq (b, c)$
   - $(c, b) \succeq (c', b') \wedge (c', a') \succeq (c, a) \Rightarrow (b', a') \succeq (b, a)$
2. If $e \neq f$, then there exist $b_0,..., b_n \in A$ such that $b_0 = a$, $b_n = c$, and $(e, f) \succeq (b_{i-1}, b_i)$, $i = 1,..., n$.
3. If $e \neq f$, then there exist $b, d \in A$, with $b \neq d$, such that $(e, f) > (b, d)$.
4. Let $a_1,..., a_n,...$ be a sequence of elements of A such that for all $e, f \in A$, if $e \neq f$, then $(e, f) \succeq (a_i, a_j)$ for all but finitely many pairs $\langle i, j \rangle$. Then there exists $b \in A$ such that for all $e, f \in A$, if $e \neq f$, then $(e, f) \succeq (a_i, b)$ for all but finitely many i.

Intuition leads to the belief that you should be able to easily construct a segmentally additive metric structure. As usual, the mathematics appears more complex than it is when you tackle one requirement at a time. The first condition is called the segmental solvability axiom. Its purpose is to ensure that spacing within the structure is independent of direction and the location of the starting point. For set cardinalities, this means that you measure distances in terms of absolute values of the differences, and that it does not matter which point you choose as the starting point. An interval of length (e, f) will always have a length (e, f), no matter what point you choose as e, nor which direction you go from there.

The main clause of the first condition states that given two intervals, the first of which is at least as great as the second, you can always find a point within the first interval, and the length of this new interval is equivalent to the length of the second.

The first part of the first condition is illustrated by the line segments in Figure 9.7a. Looking at points on a line, the condition given by this part is obvious.

The second part of the first condition is illustrated by the line segments in Figure 9.7b. Since the first condition requires that both parts must hold, you need to find a situation where this works. If you make $a \sim a'$, $b \sim b'$, and $c \sim c'$, as shown in Figure 9.7c, both parts hold, and you are still dealing with the relation $\succeq$.

The second condition, as complex as it looks, is really rather intuitive. All it requires is that you can construct a sequence of intervals, all of which are the same length and positive (their endpoints are distinct), that begin at one point and end at another, these two points forming a larger segment. This condition allows you to mark centimeters on a meterstick. To show this condition holds for set cardinalities, pick two distinct values. Since cardinal numbers are real numbers, you know you can always find a number between them. Thus, you can always construct a sequence of equally spaced intervals which together coincide exactly with larger interval in question.

The third condition says that if you have an interval with distinct endpoints, you can always find another pair of distinct points, the interval between which is

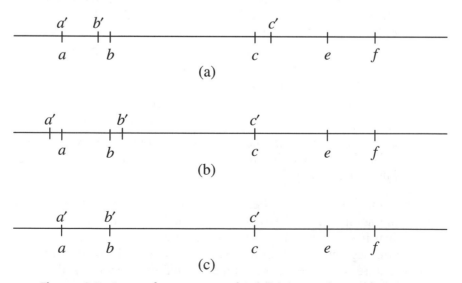

Figure 9.7 *A test for segmental additivity and completeness.*

smaller than the first. Assume that the first pair of points differs by only one arrow in the same dimension and they have the same number of arrows in all other dimensions. This is the most degenerate case. You cannot find another pair of points for which the interval is strictly smaller than this first pair. Thus, you fail to meet this condition and cannot achieve an additive-difference metric.

You are thus "stuck" with an additive-difference structure, which is not a metric, giving an interval scale representation for class coupling. You will find the same results apply to the model of coupling within a class.

SUMMARY

Coupling was defined in terms of the physical connections between elements of a design. Like complexity, the model of coupling is limited to a single layer of the design. An empirical view of coupling was developed based on the formal model in Chapter 6. To represent the coupling within a class, a new category was created, which was not named, to model the relationships between an operation and the attributes of the class. Three types of arrows were identified for this new category: preconditions, postconditions, and message sends. The union of the sets of message send arrows, taken across all operations for a class, will match exactly the set of message link arrows for which the class is the domain in the category **DesginState**.

A four-dimensional additive-difference representation was developed for the coupling of a class within a design. This representation lies on the interval scale. However, we could not reach an additive-difference metric representation, which would have given us a ratio scale. It was noted that the same representation, in three dimensions, can be constructed for the coupling of class components within the category **Class** and our new category model for an operation.

10

SUFFICIENCY

The primary purpose of object-oriented analysis is to discover the essential abstractions in the problem domain. The primary purpose of object-oriented design is to implement these essential abstractions correctly and efficiently. An abstraction is an element in the domain model which represents all or part of a concrete or conceptual object in the domain (see Bunge 1977). Many object-oriented design methods represent abstractions initially as single classes (see, for example, Booch 1994; Embley, Kurtz, and Woodfield 1992; Rumbaugh et al. 1991; and Jacobson et al. 1992). Doing so is confusing, at best, and technically incorrect, at worst. An abstraction is nothing more than a collection of properties—attributes and behaviors—possessed by the domain object it represents. Abstractions exist in the domain and are implemented by design components, which may be individual classes, or whole frameworks of classes. This is the most difficult and most important step in object-oriented development. Start with the wrong set of abstractions and you will never get the design right. I've been there.

Abstractions also arise in the design itself. For example, a list is an abstraction. There are many ways to implement a list, but as an abstraction, it only matters that the list provides the behaviors expected of a list, and no additional behaviors. Likewise, any other form of collection, typically called a collection class, is an abstraction. The use of the term "collection class" is a misnomer, because none of the collection abstractions I use in my programming consist of a single class—not a one. The model/view/controller design pattern also creates design-level abstractions, in this case, at least three of them. Typically, an instance of the pattern will contain one model and one controller, which may very well be individual classes, and multiple views, each of which may involve whole frameworks of classes. Still, each view can be treated at some level as a single abstraction with a defined set of expected properties.

A key characteristic of a set of abstractions is that together they possess at least those properties of the domain object which allow them to serve as a surrogate for the domain object in a given context. A key characteristic of a set of design components is that together they implement all of the properties possessed by the abstraction they implement in the design.

When we analyze a problem domain, we approach it from one or more points of view. In most projects, we limit our view to only that of the application we are constructing. In such a case, we identify only those abstractions and properties necessary to fulfill the obligations of our application. When we assume multiple points of view, we may discover that we require a larger subset of the properties of the domain objects. At the extreme, we include essentially all of the properties of the domain objects, in effect replicating the domain itself.

Comparing sets of properties—those of an abstraction to a domain object and those of a design component to an abstraction—assesses a characteristic I call *quality of abstraction*. Quality of abstraction consists of three components: *sufficiency*, *completeness*, and *cohesion*. Sufficiency is the degree to which a set of abstractions possess the properties of a domain object such that they can be a surrogate for the object in a single point of view. Completeness is the degree to which a set of abstractions possess the properties of a domain object such that they can be a surrogate for the object in all points of view relevant to the enterprise. Cohesion is the degree to which a set of abstractions possess the properties of one and only one domain object.

Applied to a design component, sufficiency is the degree to which a set of design components implement an abstraction which is sufficient from a single point of view. Completeness is the degree to which a set of design components implement a complete abstraction. Cohesion is the degree to which a set of design components implement one and only one abstraction.

Sufficiency is explored in this chapter. Completeness is explored in Chapter 11. Cohesion is covered in Chapter 12.

MOTIVATION AND ORIGINS

Booch and Berard are the only authors I have found to write on the subject of sufficiency. Booch (1994, p. 137) gives a single sentence on the subject. He defines it as the degree to which "a class or module captures enough characteristics of the abstraction to permit meaningful and efficient interaction." Berard (1993) defines it as the degree to which a minimum number of characteristics of the problem domain are included in the design to make it useful to clients of the design. Both definitions compare the properties of a design component to the properties of an abstraction.

We often use container objects of various kinds to maintain collections of objects. Common examples include lists, stacks, queues, and arrays. Each of these containers is an abstract data type with an underlying data structure and operations which are characteristic of its type. The behaviors for a list include Add, Remove, and Locate. The behaviors for a stack include Push and Pop. In addition, all types of containers must be able to create empty instances of themselves, and to enforce the constraints imposed by their type. Any design component representing a list, whether a single class or a set of classes, must faithfully represent the behaviors of a list in order to be a sufficient list representation—likewise for stack, queue, and array.

Both definitions can also be applied to the problem domain. Suppose we are trying to represent an automobile for a registration application. The relevant characteristics of an automobile, for this application, include its type, its legal and registered owners, its identification number, and its license number. Other characteristics may be required, but these suffice for now. It is pretty easy to determine whether the Auto component in our design contains a sufficient set of features. Now, suppose that our particular design requires that we store this information in a relational database. The Auto component needs the ability to store and retrieve itself from the database. This may or may not involve other design components; I've implemented it both ways. To be sufficient for this application, the Auto component must contain not only those attributes and behaviors required by our problem domain, but also those attributes and behaviors which make it work in our design.

We measure sufficiency because we want to make sure that our abstractions and design components can actually be used as they are intended to be used. An abstraction or design component which is insufficient is simply not useful for our purposes. This is a roundabout way of saying that we want to make sure our abstractions and design components meet their requirements, at least for our particular application.

During the early design stages, we identify necessary design components and allocate the application's requirements among them. This very important activity generates only part of the requirements for an individual component, however. Other required behaviors and properties are generated as we define ways in which a design component is used by the other components in the design. Sufficiency is much more than just tracing application requirements into the design.

Thus, there are two primary sources for requirements: the problem domain and the solution domain. Both impose expectations and requirements on the behaviors and properties of a component. A sufficient component will satisfy both types of requirements by containing the minimum set of features needed to support them.

EMPIRICAL VIEWS

Throughout this discussion, we have implicitly compared two sets of features: those features actually possessed by an abstraction or design component and those features we require it to possess. The chief difficulty with comparing identified requirements to actual requirements is defining the set of actual requirements. Positively defining this set means that all the actual requirements have been identified, and what then is the point of the comparison? Rather than comparing intersections of sets of features, we are really looking for features that are not in the set of identified requirements. As these missing features are found, they become identified, and the set of identified features becomes more sufficient. Thus, we can measure the sufficiency of a set of identified features as a function of the difference between it and the required features. This suggests a form of the contrast model described in Chapter 5.

Alternatively, we can compare the two feature sets by taking the ratio of the size of the intersection of these two sets to the size of the set of required features. Thus, a feature set which contains none of the required features will be fully insufficient, and one which contains all of the required features will be fully sufficient. It is intuitive to map these two values to zero and one, respectively, which suggests a form of conditional or unconditional probability described in Chapter 5.

FORMAL PROPERTIES

To date, no one has identified a set of formal properties for a measure of sufficiency. One reason is that no one has yet described what such a measure might look like. A feature set can vary from being fully insufficient to being fully sufficient. A natural absolute minimum and absolute maximum is thus imposed on a sufficiency measure. Any representation we construct should reflect this.

The most obvious form of representation with this property is a percentage in which sufficiency varies from 0 percent to 100 percent. To build such a representation, we need to map our empirical view of sufficiency into the real interval $[0, 1]$. There are other structures which have essential limits as inherent properties, several of which will be explored in the next section.

For now, we need to define those properties we expect a measure of sufficiency to possess, regardless of the form it takes or the interval into which it is mapped. Two obvious properties come to mind. For this discussion, denote the sufficiency of a set of features x as compared with those of a set y by $\mathrm{suff}(x, y)$. All features are drawn from the set X which contains all possible features. All of our sets are thus elements of $\mathbb{P}X$. For convenience, give $\mathbb{P}X$ the name S, so $S = \mathbb{P}X$.

Property S1: Sufficiency has an essential minimum:

$$\exists a \in S \mid \forall b, x \in S \cdot \mathrm{suff}(a, x) \leqslant \mathrm{suff}(b, x) \tag{10.1}$$

Define the sufficiency of such a set a to be $\min(x)$.

Property S2: Sufficiency has an essential maximum:

$$\exists c \in S \mid \forall b, x \in S \cdot \mathrm{suff}(c, x) \geqslant \mathrm{suff}(b, x) \tag{10.2}$$

Define the sufficiency of such a set c to be $\max(x)$.

The next property is inspired by one of the properties for cohesion defined by Briand, Morasca, and Basili (1996).

Property S3: Sufficiency is independent of size:

$$\forall x, y \in S \cdot \mathrm{suff}(x, y) \rightarrow [\min(y), \max(y)] \tag{10.3}$$

Finally, we add the usual requirement that sufficiency form a weak order over our potential feature sets, all of which are compared to the same set x.

Property S4: Sufficiency forms a weak order:

$$\forall a, b, x \in S \cdot \mathrm{suff}(a, x) \geqslant \mathrm{suff}(b, x) \vee \mathrm{suff}(b, x) \geqslant \mathrm{suff}(a, x) \tag{10.4a}$$

and

$$\forall a, b, c, x \in S \cdot \mathrm{suff}(a, x)$$
$$\geqslant \mathrm{suff}(b, x) \geqslant \mathrm{suff}(c, x) \Rightarrow \mathrm{suff}(a, x) \geqslant \mathrm{suff}(c, x) \quad (10.4\mathrm{b})$$

EMPIRICAL RELATIONAL STRUCTURES

It seems natural to map our essential minimum sufficiency to the real number 0. We could map it to $-\infty$, but there doesn't seem to be much point, since nothing is gained by allowing negative sufficiency. So, map $\min(x) \to 0$, and any sufficiency measures $\mathrm{suff}(a, x) \to [0, \max(x)]$. The question of where to map $\max(x)$ is not so easily answered. We could map it to 1, but there are many naturally occurring systems which have an essential maximum which is definitely not 1. Relativistic velocity is perhaps the most familiar example of such a system.

If we chose to map $\min(x)$ to 0, and $\max(x)$ to 1, we can build a representation of the form

$$\mathrm{suff}(a, x) = |a \cap x|/|x| \quad (10.5)$$

which requires that x be nonempty. It is not yet clear whether this representation can be made into a probability structure and whether we can use it as a valid representation for sufficiency.

If we decide not to map $\max(x)$ to 1, we might be able to construct a representation using an extensive structure with an essential maximum. Constructing an extensive measure out of anything that involves set union is problematic at best. In addition, this structure requires that we can actually point to an essential maximum which is inherent in the problem domain. We cannot do so in our case; we have an essential maximum, but we do not yet know what it is.

There is another way of looking at things. The contrast model in the section on Feature Proximity Representations in Chapter 5 takes the form

$$\delta(a, b) = \alpha\varphi(a\backslash b) + \beta\varphi(b\backslash a) - \theta\varphi(a \cap b) \quad (10.6)$$

This model measures the dissimilarity of two sets of features as the distance between them. The more similar two sets are, the smaller the distance. The more dissimilar, the greater the distance. The contrast model does not naturally yield a measure in the interval [0, 1]. Rather, it forms a three-component additive conjoint structure in which each component is weighted by some real-value functions. As with all additive conjoint structures, the contrast model yields a measure on the interval scale.

This model contains only an essential maximum, and the closest you can be is perfect similarity, where $\delta(a, b) = 0$. If we adopted this view, we would map $\max(x)$ to 0, and map $\min(x)$ to some value greater than 0. This notion of distance is intuitively appealing, especially when we equate distance from our target as a lack of sufficiency. Adopting such a model may require that we modify or abandon our requirement that sufficiency has an essential minimum. It may be the case that this requirement does not add anything to our understanding of sufficiency. We can transform this model into one which is expressed in terms of similarity by setting $\alpha = \beta = \theta = -1$. Of course, there is no requirement that α, β, and θ have the same value; we require only that they all be less than 0. But, in doing so, we invert our intuition about distance; this can cause confusion.

We appear to be faced with a difficult decision: we have a choice of empirical relational structures, with no clear way to choose between them. If we choose a percentage structure, we are assuming that sufficiency is measured by the degree to which the set of required features is a subset of the set of actual features. That is, as the proportion of the required features contained in the intersection of that set with the set of actual features increases, the sufficiency of the actual feature set increases. This is a viable model and requires the constructing of a probability structure. Constructing the set of required features presents difficult practical issues.

On the other hand, the notion of decreasing sufficiency as increasing distance from a target point is appealing in its representational possibilities. This model also allows for differing contributions of the different types of differences and intersections.

I should make one other point. The contrast model includes three different comparisons, described in terms of our particular problem:

1. The set of features required but not included in the abstraction or design component.
2. The set of features in the abstraction or design component but not required (not in the set of required features).
3. The set of features in both sets (their intersection).

We are only interested in the relative sizes of sets 1 and 3 as compared to the set of required features. This implies that we need two of the components of the contrast model. However, as the abstraction or design component becomes more sufficient, features will be moved from set 1 to set 3. Full sufficiency is achieved when set 1 is empty and set 3 is wholly contained within the set of required features and contains all features of the design component. This leads us to lean toward a model similar to equation (10.5) for our empirical relational structure.

It is worth noting that the form of equation (10.5) looks a lot like the form of a conditional probability structure. Unfortunately, we cannot construct a representation based on conditional probability (we fail to meet at least one of the requirements). We can, however, construct a representation based on unconditional probability and lose nothing by doing so. With this in mind, we choose to represent sufficiency as the ratio of the size of the intersection of the set of required features and the set of actual features to the size of the set of required features, giving it the form of equation (10.5).

POTENTIAL MEASURES

When we measure sufficiency, we compare the sufficiency of an abstraction to a set of requirements, and the sufficiency of a design component or set of design components to an abstraction deemed to be (sufficiently) sufficient. This allows us to represent a single abstraction with a set of design components. When we do this, we compare the union of the feature sets for the design components to the feature set for the abstraction. We can thus use the same measure to assess the sufficiency of our chosen abstractions, compared to what is needed, and our designs, compared to our chosen abstractions.

We are trying to build a finitely additive probability space, as defined in the section "Probability Representations" in Chapter 5, for which the following is true:

1. $P(A) \geqslant 0$.
2. $P(X) = 1$.
3. $A \cap B = \varnothing \Rightarrow P(A \cup B) = P(A) + P(B)$.

where X is a nonempty set, E is an algebra of sets for which $E \subseteq \mathbb{P}X$ holds, and $A, B \in E$. Define X as the set of required features from only the points of view required by the current application and $E = \mathbb{P}X$. Define $A = a \cap x$, so that $P(A) = |A|/|X|$. $A \cap B$ will have its usual interpretation: $A \cap B = \varnothing$ if A and B have no features in common. $P(A \cup B)$ would then be $|A \cup B|/|X|$, which satisfies condition 3.

To build a finitely additive probability space, we must be able to show that our structure $\langle X, E, \succeq \rangle$ is an Archimedean structure of qualitative probability. Chapter 5 gives five requirements for such a structure. Given a nonempty set X, an algebra of sets on X E, and a binary relation $\succeq$ on E, the triple $\langle X, E, \succeq \rangle$ is an Archimedean structure of qualitative probability if and only if for every $A, B, C \in E$:

1. $\langle E, \succeq \rangle$ is a weak order.
2. $X \succ \varnothing$ and $A \succeq \varnothing$.
3. $A \cap B = A \cap C = \varnothing \Rightarrow (B \succeq C \Leftrightarrow A \cup B \succeq A \cup C)$.
4. For every $A \succ \varnothing$, any standard sequence relative to A is finite.
5. If $D \in E$, $A \cap B = \varnothing$, $A \succ C$ and $B \succeq D$, then there exists C', D', and $F \in E$ such that:
   - $F \sim A \cup B$
   - $C' \cap D' = \varnothing$
   - $F \supset C' \cup D'$
   - $C' \sim C$ and $D' \sim D$

First, define $\succeq$ so that $A \succeq B \Leftrightarrow P(A) \geqslant P(B)$, or $A \succeq B \Leftrightarrow |A|/|X| \geqslant |B|/|X|$. With this definition, we can easily show that $\langle E, \succeq \rangle$ forms a weak order: $\succeq$ orders E in terms of the ratio of the cardinality of a member set to the cardinality of X.

The second condition requires that $X \succ \varnothing$; no problem there, since $|X|/|X|$ is always nonzero. It also requires that $A \succeq \varnothing$. Again, given our definitions, we can easily satisfy this condition.

The third condition requires that, given two sets both disjoint from A, combining them with A does not change their relative ordering. In other words, adding A to both sides does not change the results. Our test is $|B|/|X| \geqslant |C|/|X| \Leftrightarrow (|A| + |B|)/|X| \geqslant (|A| + |C|)/|X|$, which is obviously true, since we know that A

is disjoint from both B and C, and since disjoint union is additive in terms of cardinalities.

The fourth condition is the Archimedean condition and requires some extra work. First, we need to define what a standard sequence relative to A would be like in our structure. Krantz and colleagues (1971) define such a sequence inductively. A sequence of one set consists of a set A_1, which is also B_1, and which is equivalent to A. To build A_2, find a set C_1, which is disjoint from B_1 and is equivalent to A, and take $A_2 = B_1 \cup C_1$. To build A_3, find a set B_2 which is equivalent to A_2, and may in fact be A_2, and a set C_2 which is equivalent to A and disjoint from B_2, and set $A_3 = B_2 \cup C_2$. We continue doing this until we run out of sets to add to our sequence. The requirement is that any such sequence is finite.

In our structure, $A \succeq B$ means that $|A|/|X| \geq |B|/|X|$, so we know that $|A| \geq |B|$. We also know that $A \sim B$ means that $|A| = |B|$. We start with A. To build A_1, we find some set B_1, disjoint from A, but with the same number of members. Then, set $A_1 = B_1$. To build A_2, find some set C_1 with the same number of members as A and disjoint from B_1, then set $A_2 = B_1 \cup C_1$. To build A_3, we find some set B_2 with the same number of members as A_2, and may use A_2 if that's all we can find. We then find some set C_2 with the same number of members as A but disjoint from B_2. If we use A_2 for B_2, we can't use C_1 again, because it is part of B_2. Then, we set $A_3 = B_2 \cup C_2$. We continue until we run out of sets.

It is very easy to show that such a structure is finite in our case. We defined our set E to be $\mathbb{P}X$. No matter how big X gets, the cardinality of $\mathbb{P}X$ is finite. Since we have only a finite number of sets from which to build our sequence, it follows that any sequence will also be finite.

The fifth condition requires that, given four events A, B, C, and D, if A and B are disjoint ($A \cap B = \varnothing$), A is more probable than C ($A \succ C$), and B is at least as probable as D ($B \succeq D$), then somewhere in E is an event F that is equally as probable as $A \cup B$. Furthermore, F includes events C' and D' which are disjoint, with C' equally as probable as C, and D' equally as probable as D.

For our structure, we look for two sets A and B which are disjoint. We must also find two sets C, which has fewer members than A, and D, which has the same number as or fewer members than B. Somewhere in E, we must be able to find a set F which has the same number of elements as $A \cup B$, and which includes a set C', with the same number of members as C, and a set D', with the same number of members as D, and which are disjoint from each other. The key to satisfying this requirement is noting that we only need to find one set of sets which meets this requirement.

Since X in our case is the set of properties in the domain object or abstraction, the size of E will usually be pretty small. Remember that x, $x \cap a$, and $x \backslash a$ are all in E, and so is every other combination of subsets of x. Define $A = x \cap a$, $B = x \backslash a$, $C \subset A$, and $D = B$. Then $P = A \cup B = x$. All we need to do is find a $C' \subset A$ for which $C \cap C' = \varnothing$, and define $D' = D = x \backslash a$. If $|A| \geq 2$, we can always meet this condition.

We have managed to construct a finitely additive probability space, which is an absolute scale. We represent the sufficiency of a set a, relative to a required set of features x, by the representation given in equation (10.5).

SUMMARY

Sufficiency was defined as the degree to which an abstraction possesses features required of it, or the degree to which a design component possesses features in its abstraction, from the point of view of the current application. The set of features required of an abstraction is subjective and very difficult to fully define. In practice, the set of features required of an abstraction can only be defined as they are identified and added to the abstraction. Thus, sufficiency is most useful when comparing a set of design components to an abstraction which has been deemed sufficient.

We discussed several possible approaches for constructing our representation, noting that there were no clear choices. In the end, the decision was based on convenience, using the structure with the fewest and least difficult set of requirements.

We represent sufficiency as the ratio of the cardinalities of an intersection between two sets to the cardinality of one of the sets, which maps our measure into the interval [0, 1]. We built our representation from a structure of qualitative probability in which the universe of events was the set of features we require in our abstraction or design component. By using such a structure, we created a measure on the absolute scale.

11

COMPLETENESS

Quality of abstraction was defined in Chapter 10 as the extent to which a set of abstractions in the domain model reflects the properties of the domain object they are to represent. For a set of design components, quality of abstraction is the extent to which they implement the properties of the abstraction they are to represent in the design. Quality of abstraction has three components: sufficiency, completeness, and cohesion.

Sufficiency was defined as the extent to which a set of abstractions possesses the properties of a domain object as identified from a single point of view. Likewise for a set of design components with respect to an abstraction. Completeness expands this concept to include all points of view relevant to the enterprise.

The difference between sufficiency and completeness is subtle, but important. Sufficiency measures the extent to which an abstraction contains the necessary properties for it to be useful in the current application. Applied to a design component, it measures the extent to which a design component contains the properties required by the abstraction, again from the point of view of the current application. Completeness measures the extent to which an abstraction captures all of the characteristics from multiple points of view. Applied to a design component, completeness measures the extent to which the component possesses all of the properties identified for the abstraction it represents, assuming the abstraction itself is (sufficiently) complete.

We defined a measure of sufficiency which compared the feature set of an abstraction with the set of features required, or the feature set of a design component—which may consist of more than one class—to the feature set of the abstraction the design component is to implement. Completeness is very similar. In fact, the only real difference is the feature set against which we compare our abstraction or design component. There is a philosophical difference as well. Sufficiency looks at an abstraction or design component from the view of the problem domain and asks: "What properties does this abstraction need to possess to be useful to me?" Completeness looks at a set of problem domains, or potential points of view, from the view of the abstraction and asks: "What properties do I need to possess to fully represent the thing I am intended to represent?"

These differences make themselves visible in the way we go about populating the required set of features. Once that set is defined, the mechanics of measuring completeness are identical to those for measuring sufficiency. Even our defined measures are identical.

MOTIVATION AND ORIGINS

Like sufficiency, Booch and Berard are the only authors to even mention completeness as a design characteristic. Again, Booch (1994, p.137) gives a single sentence on the subject. He defines completeness as the degree to which "the interface of a class or module captures all of the meaningful characteristics of the abstraction." Berard (1993, p.116) defines a complete set of methods as "that set of . . . methods that both allow us to easily work with the object, and fully captures the abstraction represented by the object." Both of these definitions compare the properties of a design component to the properties of an abstraction, which presumably has been previously defined.

An abstraction or design component with a complete set of properties is easier to reuse than one that is merely sufficient for a given application. In Chapter 10, we used the example of an auto abstraction for a vehicle registration application. We identified what could be a sufficient set of properties, relative to the particular application. But is the abstraction complete? If the application is being built for a licensing agency, then it may, in fact, be complete. If the owner of the application is a manufacturer, however, the abstraction as defined is far from complete.

For example, if the design for a model of automobile is contained within a computer-aided design package, the collection of data which represents the geometries and physical characteristics of the car's parts are also part of the abstraction. So are the behaviors which describe how the car reacts to turns, stopping forces, airflow, and many other behavioral aspects of a car. A complete abstraction for a car would also be able to present its bill of materials and to define the parts required to build it so that a manufacturing application could work from the data generated by the engineers. Thus, in a particular context, this case a manufacturer, "complete" takes on a very different meaning from that in the context of a licensing agency.

It is possible to imagine an enterprise which maintains a library of design components which completely represent the properties required from all of the points of view relevant to the enterprise. In this environment, application development means defining and creating the use cases which implement business-level operations on these various objects. The objects themselves would never have to be changed to reflect changes to the business, only the use cases would change. The objects would only require changing when the fundamental character of a particular object changed. As with sufficiency, requirements for completeness originate both in the problem domain and within the design itself.

EMPIRICAL VIEWS

Again like sufficiency, we can take two views of completeness: the degree to which an abstraction is complete relative to the domain and the degree to which a design component is complete relative to an abstraction. We are comparing the degree to which the one set of features, those we have defined for our abstraction or design component, contains elements of another set of features, those which we have identified as being required. We can make this comparison by taking the ratio of the size of the intersection of these two sets to the size of the set of required features. Thus, a feature set which contains none of the required features will be fully incomplete and one which possesses all of the required features will be fully complete.

It seems intuitive to map these two values to zero and one, respectively. This is the form our representation will take as we construct it in the following sections.

FORMAL PROPERTIES

Like sufficiency, no one has identified a set of formal properties for a measure of completeness. One reason is that no one has yet described what such a measure might look like. Intuitively, a feature set can vary from being fully incomplete to being fully complete. A natural absolute minimum and absolute maximum is imposed on a completeness measure. Any representation we construct should reflect this.

The most obvious form of representation with this property is a percentage in which completeness varies from 0 percent to 100 percent. To build such a representation, we need to map our empirical view of completeness into the real interval [0, 1].

For now, we define those properties we expect a measure of completeness to possess, regardless of the form it takes, or the interval into which it is mapped. Two obvious properties come to mind. For this discussion, denote the completeness of a set of features x as compared with those of a set y by $\mathrm{cmpl}(x, y)$. All features are drawn from the set X which contains all possible features. All of our sets are thus elements of $\mathbb{P}X$. For convenience, give $\mathbb{P}X$ the name S, so $S = \mathbb{P}X$.

Property CM1: Completeness has an essential minimum:

$$\exists a \in S \mid \forall b, x \in S \cdot \mathrm{cmpl}(a, x) \leqslant \mathrm{cmpl}(b, x) \qquad (11.1)$$

Define the completeness of such a set a to be $\min(x)$.

Property CM2: Completeness has an essential maximum:

$$\exists c \in S \mid \forall b, x \in S \cdot \mathrm{cmpl}(c, x) \geqslant \mathrm{cmpl}(b, x) \qquad (11.2)$$

Define the completeness of such a set c to be $\max(x)$.

The next property is inspired by one of the properties for cohesion defined by Briand, Morasca, and Basili (1996).

Property CM3: Completeness is independent of size:

$$\forall x, y \in S \cdot \mathrm{cmpl}(x, y) \rightarrow [\min(y), \max(y)] \qquad (11.3)$$

Finally, we add the usual requirement that completeness form a weak order over our potential feature sets, all of which are compared to the same set x.

Property CM4: Completeness forms a weak order:

$$\forall a, b, x \in S \cdot \mathrm{cmpl}(a, x) \geqslant \mathrm{cmpl}(b, x) \vee \mathrm{cmpl}(b, x) \geqslant \mathrm{cmpl}(a, x) \qquad (11.4a)$$

and

$$\forall a, b, c, x \in S \cdot \mathrm{cmpl}(a, x) \geqslant \mathrm{cmpl}(b, x)$$

$$\geqslant \mathrm{cmpl}(c, x) \Rightarrow \mathrm{cmpl}(a, x) \geqslant \mathrm{cmpl}(c, x) \qquad (11.4b)$$

EMPIRICAL RELATIONAL STRUCTURES

The discussion in the section on empirical relational structures in Chapter 10 regarding the possible ways to represent sufficiency applies to completeness as well. There, several possible ways to describe sufficiency empirically were discussed. We settled on one requiring that we construct a probability structure, which we did in "Potential Measures" on page 373. We will apply those same arguments to completeness, both to avoid repeating ourselves and to foster a new kind of reuse.

If we chose to map $\min(x)$ to 0 and $\max(x)$ to 1, we can build a representation of the form

$$\mathrm{cmpl}(a, x) = |a \cap x| / |x| \qquad (11.5)$$

which requires that x be nonempty. This is not a problem, since our set of required features will never be empty. If it is, why are we building this abstraction in the first place?

Noting that the form of equation (11.5) looks a lot like the form of a conditional probability structure, and knowing that we cannot construct such a structure, we construct a representation based on unconditional probability. Thus, we will represent completeness as the ratio of the size of the intersection of the set of required features and the set of actual features to the size of the set of required features, where "required" in this case includes all relevant points of view.

POTENTIAL MEASURES

We are going to represent completeness using the form of equation (11.5), where a is the set of features contained by our abstraction or design component, and x is the set of features required by the abstraction or design component. When measuring completeness, we will compare the completeness of an abstraction to a set of requirements, and the completeness of a design component or set of design components to an abstraction deemed to be (sufficiently) complete. This allows us to represent a single abstraction with a set of design components. When we do this, we compare the union of the feature sets for the design components to the feature set for the abstraction. We can thus use the same measure to assess the completeness of our chosen abstractions, compared to what is needed, and our designs, compared to our chosen abstractions.

The logic in this section is largely repeated from Chapter 10. It helps to repeatedly use the technique by which we construct a representation from an empirical understanding of the attribute we are trying to measure. This is the third time in writing this book that I've applied the logic required to build a probability structure. This is the first time that I have not had to change my understanding of such a structure.

We are trying to build a finitely additive probability space, for which the following is true:

1. $P(A) \geqslant 0$.
2. $P(X) = 1$.
3. $A \cap B = \varnothing \Rightarrow P(A \cup B) = P(A) + P(B)$.

where X is a nonempty set, E is an algebra of sets for which $E \subseteq \mathbb{P}X$ holds, and $A, B \in E$. Define X as the set of required features from all points of view relevant to the whole enterprise and $E = \mathbb{P}X$. Define $A = a \cap x$, so that $P(A) = |A|/|X|$. $A \cap B$ will have its usual interpretation: $A \cap B = \varnothing$ if A and B have no features in common. $P(A \cup B)$ would then be $|A \cup B|/|X|$, which satisfies condition 3.

To build a finitely additive probability space, we must be able to show that our structure $\langle X, E, \succeq \rangle$ is an Archimedean structure of qualitative probability. Chapter 5 gives five requirements for such a structure. Given a nonempty set X, an algebra of sets on X E, and a binary relation $\succeq$ on E, the triple is an Archimedean structure of qualitative probability if and only if for every $A, B, C \in E$:

1. $\langle E, \succeq \rangle$ is a weak order.
2. $X \succ \varnothing$ and $A \succeq \varnothing$.
3. $A \cap B = A \cap C = \varnothing \Rightarrow (B \succeq C \Leftrightarrow A \cup B \succeq A \cup C)$.
4. For every $A \succ \varnothing$, any standard sequence relative to A is finite.
5. If $D \in E$, $A \cap B = \varnothing$, $A \succ C$ and $B \succeq D$, then there exists C', D', and $F \in E$ such that:
   - $F \sim A \cup B$
   - $C' \cap D' = \varnothing$
   - $F \supset C' \cup D'$
   - $C' \sim C$ and $D' \sim D$

First, define $\succeq$ so that $A \succeq B \Leftrightarrow P(A) \geqslant P(B)$, or $A \succeq B \Leftrightarrow |A|/|X| \geqslant |B|/|X|$. With this definition, we can easily show that $\langle E, \succeq \rangle$ forms a weak order: $\succeq$ orders E in terms of the ratio of the cardinality of a member set to the cardinality of X.

The second condition requires that $X \succ \varnothing$; no problem there, since $|X|/|X|$ is always nonzero. It also requires that $A \succeq \varnothing$. Again, given our definitions, we can easily satisfy this condition.

The third condition requires that, given two sets both disjoint from A, combining them with A does not change their relative ordering. In other words, adding A to both sides does not change the results. Our test is $|B|/|X| \geqslant |C|/|X| \Leftrightarrow (|A| + |B|)/|X| \geqslant (|A| + |C|)/|X|$, which is obviously true, since we know that A is disjoint from both B and C, and since disjoint union is additive in terms of cardinalities.

The fourth condition is the Archimedean condition and requires some extra work. First, we need to define what a standard sequence relative to A would be like in our structure. Krantz and colleagues (1971) define such a sequence inductively. A sequence of one set consists of a set A_1, which is also B_1, and which is equivalent to A. To build A_2, find a set C_1, which is disjoint from B_1 and is equivalent to A, and take $A_2 = B_1 \cup C_1$. To build A_3, find a set B_2 which is equivalent to A_2, and may in fact be A_2, and a set C_2 which is equivalent to A and disjoint from B_2, and set $A_3 = B_2 \cup C_2$. We continue doing this until we run out of sets to add to our sequence. The requirement is that any such sequence is finite.

In our structure, $A \succeq B$ means that $|A|/|X| \geqslant |B|/|X|$, so we know that $|A| \geqslant |B|$. We also know that $A \sim B$ means that $|A| = |B|$. We start with A. To build A_1, find some set B_1, disjoint from A, but with the same number of members. Then, set $A_1 = B_1$. To build A_2, find some set C_1 with the same number of members as A and disjoint from B_1, then set $A_2 = B_1 \cup C_1$. To build A_3, find some set B_2 with the same number of members as A_2, and may use A_2 if that's all we can find. We then find some set C_2 with the same number of members as A but disjoint from B_2. If we use A_2 for B_2, we can't use C_1 again, because it is part of B_2. Then, we set $A_3 = B_2 \cup C_2$. We continue until we run out of sets.

It is very easy to show that such a structure is finite in our case. We defined our set E to be $\mathbb{P}X$. No matter how big X gets, the cardinality of $\mathbb{P}X$ is finite. Since we have only a finite number of sets from which to build our sequence, it follows that any sequence will also be finite.

The fifth condition requires that, given four events A, B, C, and D, if A and B are disjoint ($A \cap B = \varnothing$), A is more probable than C ($A \succ C$), and B is at least as probable as D ($B \succeq D$), then somewhere in E is an event F that is equally as probable as $A \cup B$. Furthermore, F includes events C' and D' which are disjoint, with C' equally as probable as C, and D' equally as probable as D.

For our structure, we are looking for two sets A and B which are disjoint. We must also find two sets C, which has fewer members than A, and D, which has the same number as or fewer members than B. Somewhere in E, we must be able to find a set F which has the same number of elements as $A \cup B$, and which includes a set C', with the same number of members as C, and a set D', with the same number of members as D, and which are disjoint from each other. The key to satisfying this requirement is noting that we only need to find one set of sets which meets this requirement.

Since X in our case is the set of properties in the domain object or abstraction, the size of E will usually be pretty small. Remember that x, $x \cap a$, and $x \backslash a$ are all in E, and so is every other combination of subsets of x. Define $A = x \cap a$, $B = x \backslash a$, $C \subset A$, and $D = B$. Then $E = A \cup B = x$. All we need to do is find a $C' \subset A$ for which $C \cap C' = \emptyset$, and define $D' = D = x \backslash a$. If $|A| \geq 2$, we can always meet this condition.

We have managed to construct a finitely additive probability space, which is an absolute scale. We represent the completeness of a set a, relative to a required set of features x, by the representation given in equation (11.5).

SUMMARY

Completeness was defined as the degree to which an abstraction possesses features required of it, or the degree to which a design component possesses features in its abstraction, from all points of view relevant to the organization for which the abstraction is being built. The set of features required of an abstraction is subjective and very difficult to fully define. In practice, the set of features required of an abstraction can only be defined as they are identified and added to the abstraction. Thus, completeness is most easily measured when comparing a set of design components to an abstraction which has been deemed complete. However, there are ways to identify features required of an abstraction in order for it to be complete. One way is to view the organization or enterprise from the view of the abstraction, and ask: "What features do I need to get along in this environment?"

We represent completeness as the ratio of the cardinalities of an intersection between two sets to the cardinality of one of the sets, which maps our measure into the interval $[0, 1]$. We built our representation from a structure of qualitative probability in which the universe of events was the set of features we require in our abstraction or design component. By using such a structure, we created a measure on the absolute scale.

12

COHESION

Quality of abstraction was defined in Chapter 10 as the extent to which a set of abstractions in the domain model reflects the properties of the domain object they are to represent. For a set of design components, quality of abstraction is the extent to which they implement the properties of the abstraction they are to represent in the design. Quality of abstraction has three components: sufficiency, completeness, and cohesion.

Sufficiency considers the set of required properties from a single point of view. Completeness expands this notion to include the properties from all points of view relevant to the enterprise. Cohesion introduces the notion that a set of abstractions should represent one and only one domain object, and that a set of design components should implement one and only one abstraction.

Our use of cohesion as a characteristic of quality of abstraction requires a departure, to some extent, from the traditional view of cohesion. Unlike sufficiency and completeness, definitions of cohesion abound. Chidamber and Kemerer (1994) implicitly define cohesion in terms of the similarity among methods. They define similarity in terms of the intersections of instance variables used by the methods. "If an object class has different methods performing operations on the same set of instance variables, the class is cohesive" (Chidamber and Kemerer 1994, p. 479). The IEEE (1990) defines cohesion as "the manner and degree to which the tasks performed by a single software module are related to each other." Berard (1993) defines object cohesion as a measure of strength of the *logical* relationships among the components that comprise an object. Booch (1994) defines cohesion as the degree of connectedness or strength of relationship among the components of a class.

All of these definitions have one thing in common: They define cohesion in terms of the relationships or connections between components of a module or class. Invariably, measures developed using these definitions, including those of

Chidamber and Kemerer (1994), Briand, Morasca, and Basili (1996), and Ott and colleagues (1995) are actually measures of forms of coupling. It is not valid to measure logical connections in terms of physical connections: The two sets do not always match.

Others have taken a different view of cohesion. Coad and Yourdon (1991b, p. 134) define it as "the degree to which the elements of a portion of a design contribute to the carrying out of a single, well-defined purpose." Rumbaugh and colleagues (1991, p. 250) have slightly more to say: "An entity, such as a class, an operation, or a module, is coherent if it is organized on a consistent plan and all its parts fit together toward a common goal. An entity should have a single major theme; it should not be a collection of unrelated parts." Durnota and Mingins (1993) say this: "A class is coherent if the methods work together to carry out a single, identifiable purpose."

All of these latter definitions also have one thing in common: They define cohesion in terms of singleness of purpose (my *Thesaurus* lists cohesion and coherence as synonyms). This view of cohesion meets our needs better; we will concentrate on improving this view to the point where it can be used for measurement. These latter definitions are similar in another way: They all imply that cohesion may be judged by examining the public interface of an abstraction or design component. The implication is that an abstraction can present a cohesive interface to the world, but be chaotic internally. They imply that an abstraction can be cohesive, but the design components which implement it need not be cohesive (they should be, but nothing forces the matter). This is yet another example of the benefits of separating the interface of an abstraction from its implementation.

The biggest problem is formally defining the purpose of an abstraction. I hinted at a purpose earlier when I stated that a cohesive abstraction contains the properties of one, and only one, concrete or conceptual object in the domain. Thus, a common purpose for any abstraction can be stated as "to represent domain object *x*." This problem will be attacked as we develop a measure for cohesion in the following sections.

MOTIVATION AND ORIGINS

Cohesive components are easier to reuse than noncohesive components. A cohesive component contains no surprises. As Booch puts it: ". . . the class *Dog* is functionally cohesive if its semantics embrace the behavior of a dog, the whole dog, and nothing but the dog" (Booch 1994, p. 137). A class *Dog* that contains non-dog behavior would not be cohesive.

A component that is complete and cohesive can be used in any application which requires the abstraction the component implements. A library of complete and cohesive domain components would save somewhere around 80 percent of the effort required to develop a new application. This is a rough guess from my experience on my own projects. About 80 percent of the effort on these projects went to defining, designing, and implementing domain-level components. If these had been part of a library, all we would have had to do was identify which components were required, then write the code that implemented the use case logic. Since the components are complete, they already contain all of the behavior expected of the domain objects they implement. Think of the value of such a library to any internal development shop. Of course, now that we have measures for completeness and cohesion, we can conduct empirical studies to determine the actual effect completeness and cohesion have on reusability and on actual reuse.

Many design characteristics such as size, complexity, and even coupling originate in the problem domain, and are things the designer must deal with. On the other hand, design characteristics such as sufficiency, completeness, and especially cohesion are things to which the designer aspires. They do not exist as inherent properties of domain objects, although all domain objects can be said to be sufficient, complete, and cohesive, since they are the standard against which all of our efforts as designers are compared.

EMPIRICAL VIEWS

Two basic views of cohesion are identified. The first, call it structural cohesion, deals with the physical connections between elements of a design component. Berard (1993) correctly identifies this as internal coupling, not cohesion. Some authors implicitly acknowledge this and define coupling within a component to be cohesion (see, for example, Heyliger 1994).

The second view, call it logical or semantic cohesion, deals with the strength of the logical connections between elements of a component, or between the elements of the component and a single, well-defined purpose. We can also assess semantic cohesion in terms of the relationship between the elements of a component and a single, overall abstraction.

Let's focus on the semantic form of cohesion. To develop a measure, we need to define empirically what we mean by "purpose," and we need to develop an empirical model of our intuitive understanding of cohesion in terms of our formal object model. We can identify two forms of semantic cohesion: The strength of relationship between the external properties of a component and the external properties of the abstraction it implements, or the contribution of the internal elements of a component to providing the external properties.

We can measure the first of these forms by comparing the set of properties evident in the external interface of a design component to the set of properties identified for the abstraction it implements. We can use this method to also measure the degree of cohesion in the abstraction by comparing its set of properties to those we require of it, or to those we would normally expect to be evident in an object of this kind. Such a measure might take the form of a feature proximity structure (see Chapter 5), or even an unconditional probability structure.

We can measure the second of these forms of cohesion using the more traditional approaches to measuring the cohesion of modules. Stevens, Myers, and Constantine (1974) defined a nominal scale classification for different types of cohesion. The classes of cohesion form an ordering in terms of preference, but do not qualify as an ordinal scale. The types of cohesion are, in order of increasing preference:

1. *Coincidental*: A module performs more than one unrelated function.
2. *Logical*: A module performs more than one function; these functions are only logically related.
3. *Temporal*: A module performs more than one function; these functions are related only in that they must be performed in the same time span.
4. *Communicational*: A module performs more than one function; these functions are related only in that they operate on the same body of data.
5. *Sequential*: A module performs more than one function but these functions must occur in a specified order.
6. *Functional*: A module performs a single, well-defined function.

Fenton (1991) adds a class, *procedural* cohesion, between communicational and temporal. He defines it as a module that performs more than one function; these functions are related only in that they collaborate to implement a general procedure in the application. He made these seven classes of cohesion into an ordinal scale by assigning the value 0 to coincidental cohesion and the value 6 to functional cohesion (Fenton 1991).

Fenton notes that these classes of cohesion seem to cause problems when applied to modules which implement an abstract data type. They also seem to present problems when applied to classes or abstractions. It appears, judging from this list, that any module which fully implements an abstract data type, or contains a complete class, can have only communicational cohesion. Yet, we consider such a module to be at least functionally cohesive. Macro and Buxton (1987) define a new type of cohesion, which they call abstract cohesion, as the degree to which a module implements an abstract data type. They place this class of cohesion above functional cohesion. Fenton claims that abstract cohesion is the strongest form of another scale of cohesion, a separate set of classes, which he calls data cohesion (Fenton 1991).

Ott and colleagues (1995), working with objects and classes, identified the need for a new type of cohesion they call data cohesion. They define it as the extent to which the methods of a class deal with the class's instance variables. This is similar to the implicit definition of class cohesion in Chidamber and Kemerer (1994).

We have not yet accomplished either of the tasks identified at the beginning of this section. The first of those is to define what we mean by purpose, and do so in such a way that we can compare the properties of an abstraction or design component to this purpose and tell whether more than one purpose is served. The purpose of any abstraction can be stated in terms of representing a single concrete or conceptual domain object. Thus, we can define the extent to which an abstraction is cohesive by comparing the properties we have defined for it to the set of properties possessed by the domain object. We can do the same for a design component by comparing the properties implemented by the component to those identified for an abstraction already determined to be cohesive to some extent, or directly to the properties of the domain object. We will develop such a measure later in this chapter.

FORMAL PROPERTIES

Despite misgivings about the measure for cohesion proposed by Briand, Morasca, and Basili (1996), some of the properties they propose for measures of cohesion make sense. In these properties, denote the cohesion of an abstraction or design component x relative to a domain object or abstraction a, respectively, by $\mathrm{coh}(x, a)$.

Property O1: Cohesion is nonnegative (Briand, Morasca, and Basili 1996):

$$\forall x \cdot \mathrm{coh}(x, a) \geqslant 0. \tag{12.1}$$

Property O2: Cohesion is independent of size (Briand, Morasca, and Basili 1996):

$$\forall x \cdot \mathrm{coh}(x, a): x \rightarrow [0, max] \tag{12.2}$$

Property O3: Cohesion can be null (Briand, Morasca, and Basili 1996)—this property follows from property O1:

$$\exists x \cdot \mathrm{coh}(x, a) = 0 \tag{12.3}$$

The remaining properties in Briand, Morasca, and Basili (1996) rely on their directed graph model of cohesion, which actually represents forms of coupling. Berard (1993) claims that it is desirable for the elements of a design component, including those of a class, to be highly cohesive, yet loosely coupled.

It seems the case that a class, for example, may contain behaviors expected of a thing of its kind, but which have no other relationship with each other. For example, the behavior of a dog wagging its tail when happy has no relationship to the behavior of a dog chewing on the furniture when left alone. The only possible connection between these two behaviors, other than they are both expected (if unwanted) behaviors of a dog, is that they share access to the emotion store (presumably a data structure of some kind). From this, we develop another property of cohesion:

Property O4: The cohesion of a collection of elements or properties is independent of the internal structure of the collection or its components. We cannot examine the internal of a collection and determine its cohesion. Put another way, cohesion is an external characteristic of a collection of properties and can only be viewed externally to the collection.

EMPIRICAL RELATIONAL STRUCTURES

It seems logical to compare the size of the intersection of our two sets of properties to the size of the set of properties for the domain object. This would give us a probability structure and a measure in the interval [0, 1]. But we are not interested in the properties contained in both sets. Of far more interest, in terms of measuring cohesion, are the properties included in the abstraction or design component that are *not* included in the domain object. This is one of the three components of the contrast model (Tversky 1977). The intersection of these two sets is one of the others. The third component of the contrast model, those properties in the domain object which are not in the abstraction or design component, is of no interest to us for measuring cohesion.

The contrast model of feature proximity does not naturally yield a measure in the interval [0, 1]. It actually forms a three-component additive conjoint structure in which each component is weighted by some real-valued function. As with all additive conjoint structures, the contrast model yields a measure on the interval scale. The contrast model does allow for one or more of the weights to be zero, thus rendering one or more components ineffectual. It also allows for reversing the signs on the weights, thus giving a similarity model. However, the failure of any of these forms to provide a measure guaranteed to be in the interval [0, 1] causes us to look to another form of empirical relational structure.

We know we need a probability structure of some kind, and we know that a structure for unconditional probability is the easiest to construct. Several such structures have been constructed so far in this book. All of these structures were built from ratios of set cardinalities. We are thus required to identify two sets for which the sizes are compared as a ratio. We have one such set for cohesion, which is defined as the set of properties in an abstraction or design component x that are not in the domain object a, denoted by $x \backslash a$. The size of this set is its cardinality, denoted by $|x \backslash a|$. If x is a design component, we can make a the set of properties in the abstraction x implements. This measures the cohesion of a design component relative to the domain model.

We now must define the other set for this comparison. We have two choices: the set of properties in the abstraction or design component (x) resulting in a measure of the form

$$\phi(x, a) = |x \backslash a| / |x| \tag{12.4}$$

or the set of properties in the domain object or abstraction (a) resulting in a measure of the form

$$\phi(x, a) = |x \backslash a| / |a| \tag{12.5}$$

In both of these cases, we get the ratio of the set of properties in x but not in a to the other set of properties. This results in a measure which is actually the inverse of cohesion, since it increases as $|x \backslash a|$ increases. To get our measure of cohesion, we need to subtract this value from one, which results in measures of the form:

$$coh(x, a) = 1 - (|x \backslash a| / |x|) \tag{12.6}$$

and

$$coh(x, a) = 1 - (|x \backslash a| / |a|) \tag{12.7}$$

Each of these measures has merit, and problems, but we need to pick one or the other.

Equation (12.6) will always be defined since x must be nonempty; otherwise, it is not a design component or an abstraction. The form in equation (12.6) results in some interesting situations, especially in the degenerate cases of null cohesion and full cohesion. Equation (12.6) will be zero, indicating null cohesion, precisely when none of the properties in x are in a; that is $|x \backslash a| = |x|$. Surprisingly, this matches our intuitive notion of null cohesion. Equation (12.6) will be one, indicating full cohesion, precisely when all of the properties in x are in a. This matches our intuitive notion of full cohesion. Equation (12.6) expresses the ratio in terms of the cardinality of our design component and seems to allow for a single design component to implement only part of an abstraction or domain object, or for a single abstraction to represent part of a domain object. So far, this is a good candidate for our measure.

Equation (12.7) will always be defined since a must be nonempty; there are no domain objects which possess no properties (see Bunge 1977). Equation (12.7) achieves null cohesion precisely when none of the properties in x are in a. This is the same as equation (12.6). Equation (12.7) achieves full cohesion precisely when all of the properties in x are in a and when $|x| = |a|$. Thus, equation (12.7) can be one only when a design component, or abstraction, is both fully cohesive and fully complete. This does not allow for a design component to partially implement an abstraction or domain object, nor does it allow for an abstraction to represent only part of a domain object. For this reason, equation (12.7) is dropped from further consideration.

Thus, we have settled on equation (12.6) as our target measure. We must now show that it indeed forms an unconditional probability structure.

POTENTIAL MEASURES

We are trying to build a finitely additive probability space, defined in Chapter 5, for which the following is true:

1. $P(A) \geqslant 0$.
2. $P(X) = 1$.
3. $A \cap B = \varnothing \Rightarrow P(A \cup B) = P(A) + P(B)$.

where X is a nonempty set, E is an algebra of sets for which $E \subseteq \mathbb{P}X$ holds, and $A, B \in E$. Define $E = \mathbb{P}X$ and $X = x$, then $x \in E$, $x \backslash a \in E$, and $x \cap a \in E$. Define $A = x \backslash a$, so that $P(A) = |A|/|X|$. $A \cap B$ will have its usual interpretation: $A \cap B = \varnothing$ if A and B have no features in common. $P(A \cup B)$ would then be $|A \cup B|/|X|$, which satisfies condition 3.

To build a finitely additive probability space, we must be able to show that our structure $\langle X, E, \succeq \rangle$ is an Archimedean structure of qualitative probability. Chapter 5 gives five requirements for such a structure. Given a nonempty set X, an algebra of sets on $X E$, and a binary relation $\succeq$ on E, the triple is a Archimedean structure of qualitative probability if and only if for every A, B, $C \in E$:

1. *$\langle E, \succeq \rangle$ is a weak order.*
2. *$X \succ \varnothing$ and $A \succeq \varnothing$.*
3. *$A \cap B = A C = \varnothing \Rightarrow (B \succeq C \Leftrightarrow A \cup B \succeq A \cup C)$.*
4. *For every $A \succ \varnothing$, any standard sequence relative to A is finite.*
5. *If $D \in E$, $A \cap B = \varnothing$, $A \succ C$ and $B \succeq D$, then there exists C', D', and $F \in E$ such that:*
   - *$F \sim A \cup B$*
   - *$C' \cap D' = \varnothing$*
   - *$F \supset C' \cup D'$*
   - *$C' \sim C$ and $D' \sim D$*

First, define $\succeq$ so that $A \succeq B \Leftrightarrow P(A) \geqslant P(B)$, or $A \succeq B \Leftrightarrow |A|/|X| \geqslant |B|/|X|$. With this definition, we can easily show that $\langle E, \succeq \rangle$ forms a weak order: $\succeq$ orders E in terms of the ratio of the cardinality of a member set to the cardinality of X.

The second condition requires that $X \succ \varnothing$; there is no problem here, since $|X|/|X|$ is always nonzero. It also requires that $A \succeq \varnothing$. Again, given our definitions, we can easily satisfy this condition.

The third condition requires that, given two sets both disjoint from A, combining them with A does not change their relative ordering. In other words, adding A to both sides does not change the results. The test is $|B|/|X| \geqslant |C|/|X| \Leftrightarrow (|A| + |B|)/|X| \geqslant (|A| + |C|)/|X|$, which is obviously true, since we know that A is disjoint from both B and C, and since disjoint union is additive in terms of cardinalities.

The fourth condition is the Archimedean condition and requires some extra work. First, we need to define what a standard sequence relative to A would be like in our structure. Krantz and colleagues (1971) define such a sequence inductively. A sequence of one set consists of a set A_1, which is also B_1, and which is equivalent to A. To build A_2, we find a set C_1, which is disjoint from B_1 and is equivalent to A, and take $A_2 = B_1 \cup C_1$. To build A_3, we find a set B_2 which is equivalent to A_2, and may in fact be A_2, and a set C_2 which is equivalent to A and disjoint from B_2, and set $A_3 = B_2 \cup C_2$. We continue doing this until we run out of sets to add to our sequence. The requirement is that any such sequence is finite.

In our structure, $A \succeq B$ means that $|A|/|X| \geqslant |B|/|X|$, so we know that $|A| \geqslant |B|$. We also know that $A \sim B$ means that $|A| = |B|$. We start with A. To build A_1, find some set B_1, disjoint from A, but with the same number of members. Then, set $A_1 = B_1$. To build A_2, find some set C_1 with the same number of members as A and disjoint from B_1, then set $A_2 = B_1 \cup C_1$. To build A_3, find some set B_2 with the same number of members as A_2, and may use A_2 if that's all we can find. We then find some set C_2 with the same number of members as A but disjoint from B_2. If we use A_2 for B_2, we can't use C_1 again, because it is part of B_2. Then, set $A_3 = B_2 \cup C_2$. We continue until we run out of sets.

It is very easy to show that such a structure is finite in our case. We defined our set E to be $\mathbb{P}X$. No matter how big X gets, the cardinality of $\mathbb{P}X$ is finite. Since we have only a finite number of sets from which to build our sequence, it follows that any sequence will also be finite.

The fifth condition requires that, given four events A, B, C, and D, if A and B are disjoint ($A \cap B = \varnothing$), A is more probable than C ($A \succ C$), and B is at least as probable as D ($B \succeq D$), then somewhere in E is an event F that is equally as probable as $A \cup B$. Furthermore, F includes events C' and D' which are disjoint, with C' equally as probable as C, and D' equally as probable as D.

For our structure, we are looking for two sets A and B which are disjoint. We must also find two sets C, which has fewer members than A, and D, which has the same number as or fewer members than B. Somewhere in E, we must be able to find a set F which has the same number of elements as $A \cup B$, and which includes a set C', with the same number of members as C, and a set D', with the same number of members as D, and which are disjoint from each other. The key to satisfying this requirement is noting that only one set of sets which meets this requirement needs to be found.

Since X in our case is the set of properties in the abstraction or design component, the size of E will usually be pretty small. Remember that x, $x \cap a$, and $x \backslash a$ are all in E, and so is every other combination of subsets of x. Define $A = x \cap a$, $B = x \backslash a$, $C \subset A$, and $D = B$. Then $F = A \cup B = x$. All we need to do is find a $C' \subset A$ for which $C \cap C' = \varnothing$, and define $D' = D = x \backslash a$. If $|A| \geq 2$, then we know we can meet this condition. Thus, whenever a design component contains at least two properties which are in the abstraction or domain object, or when an abstraction contains at least two properties which are in the domain object, we know we can meet this condition.

We have managed to construct a finitely additive probability space, which is an absolute scale. Our measure is of the form in equation (12.6).

SUMMARY

The definition of cohesion used in this chapter focuses on the extent to which an abstraction or design component fulfills a single, well-defined purpose. The purpose of an abstraction was defined as the representation of all or part of a single concrete or conceptual object in the problem or design domains. The purpose of a design component was defined as the implementation of all or part of a single abstraction.

The cohesion of an abstraction is measured by comparing the set of properties it possesses which are not part of the domain object it is supposed to represent to its full set of properties. An abstraction is not cohesive when none of its properties are in the domain object. An abstraction is fully cohesive when all of its properties are in the domain object.

An absolute scale measure for cohesion of a design component was developed by comparing the set of properties it possesses which are not part of the abstraction or domain object it is supposed to implement to its full set of properties. A design component is not cohesive when none of its properties are in the abstraction or domain object. A design component is fully cohesive when all of its properties are in the abstraction or domain object.

Both of these measures allow fully cohesive design components to be partial implementations of abstractions or domain objects, or fully cohesive abstractions to be partial representations of domain objects. These results fit well with our intuition of cohesion, sense of purpose, and the need to represent single domain objects as collections of abstractions, or to implement single abstractions as collections of design components.

13

PRIMITIVENESS

Primitiveness is the degree to which a method cannot be implemented without intimate knowledge of, and access to, the internals of a class (Booch 1994; Berard 1993). A primitive method is one which cannot be constructed out of sequences of other methods of the same class. Because primitiveness is relatively new to designers as a property, some extra effort will be spent in understanding what it means for a method to be primitive and how we can tell, from the design, without the source code, whether a method is primitive.

We also wish to assess the primitiveness of a class and to have classes which are as primitive as possible. In this sense, primitiveness equates with simplicity, and we follow Einstein's advice to keep things "as simple as possible, but no simpler." We will make use of our measure of the primitiveness of a method to assess the overall primitiveness of its class.

MOTIVATION AND ORIGINS

According to Berard (1993), primitive methods are functionally cohesive, short, and easier to extract and reuse than nonprimitive methods. The overall primitiveness of the methods of a class also indicates the completeness of the class design. Primitiveness and elegance go together. A class for which a majority of its operations are primitive indicates that the designer was able to identify and capture the essential capabilities of objects of the class. A class for which the majority of its operations are not primitive indicates that either the class design needs more work or the class deserves special attention for some other reason. Classes whose objects direct the operation of an application, or direct other objects through messages may be nonprimitive, but may also be as primitive as their roles allow.

Like cohesion, primitiveness does not originate in the problem domain. Primitiveness is a quality to which a designer aspires. Attaining a class of primitive methods begins in the analysis activities: If you can't find the essential operations of a domain-level abstraction, you cannot make primitive methods in the class or classes that implement it.

It's strange: As useful as this property is for assessing the quality of a method or class design, this chapter is the most that has been written about the subject in the software engineering literature.

EMPIRICAL VIEWS

Primitiveness can be viewed at two levels: the class and the individual method. The two levels are related. Let's start by examining individual methods.

What does it mean to say that a method is primitive? The definition given in this Chapter's introduction provides an appealing and intuitive understanding of the notion of primitiveness, but offers little in the way of determining whether a particular method is primitive. Without such a process, we cannot hope to measure the primitiveness of a method, or a class, for that matter.

Berard contrasts a composite method against his notion of a primitive method (Berard 1993). A composite method is one which is, or can be, constructed from one or more primitive methods. By looking at a method, we can tell whether it *was* constructed from one or more primitive methods, or whether it *looks* primitive. But, given an apparently primitive method, we cannot tell whether it *could have been* constructed from other primitive methods. Furthermore, since we are dealing with the design, none of the methods have actually been constructed, so looking at the implementation won't help. All we have at the moment is a description of the effects of the method. It is to these descriptions that we now turn.

We can determine the effects of a method by comparing the state of the object described in the preconditions with the state described in the postconditions. Intuition tells us that a primitive method is one which causes a minimal change to the state of an object; a change which cannot be decomposed further. The smallest possible change to the state of an object is to modify the value of a single attribute. A state change in which the value of more than one attribute is modified can be decomposed into a sequence of one-attribute modifications. We must also allow for the case in which the state of the object does not change.

So far, a primitive method has been defined as one which modifies zero or one attribute values of an object. Booch (1994) and Berard (1993) identify five types of primitive methods:

1. *Modifiers*: An operation which changes the state of an object.
2. *Selectors*: An operation which accesses but does not change the state of an object.
3. *Iterators*: An operation that permits all parts of an object to be accessed in some well-defined order.
4. *Constructors*: An operation which creates and initializes the state of an object.

5. *Destructors*: An operation which frees the state and destroys the object itself.

An iterator allows its user to access all of the parts of an object. The iterator may not modify the state of the object. Iterators are commonly found in collection objects, what Berard calls homogeneous composite objects (Berard 1993).

Berard stipulates further that any method which sends a message to another object of the same or a different class is not primitive. This implies that any method which requires the services of another object cannot be made primitive. This doesn't feel right to me, as it may be the case that the function implemented by the method cannot be implemented without full knowledge of and access to the internals of its class, plus the services of one or more other objects. We should be able to distinguish such a method from one which requires the services of one or more other classes, but which can be constructed from a sequence of more primitive methods of its own class.

Wirfs-Brock, Wilkersen, and Wiener (1990) suggest that class operations can be decoupled from the attributes of the class by accessing them only through private selector and modifier methods. This approach to class design can insulate the class operations from the types and internal structures of the attributes. It seems undesirable to declare a method nonprimitive just because we choose to replace direct attribute accesses with access through selectors and modifiers. An otherwise primitive method still cannot be implemented without detailed knowledge of the structure of the object, even if it must use gatekeeping functions to access that structure. We need to allow the use of selectors and modifiers in primitive operations. In keeping with the notion that a primitive method may cause at most one attribute to change its value, we limit a primitive method's use of modifiers to no more than one and allow the use of any number of selectors.

We will still declare as nonprimitive any method which uses an iterator, constructor, or destructor. Such methods do not require direct access to the internal structure of the object, so are not primitive. Further, any method which has direct access and performs an operation performed by, or which would be performed by, an iterator, constructor, or destructor is also nonprimitive.

To sum up, a method is primitive if it is one of the five types identified by Booch and Berard, or uses some number of selectors and no more than one modifier. A method is not primitive if it can be designed in such a way as to make use of one or more primitive methods. We identify primitive methods in the design by the fact that the state changes defined in the comparisons between their preconditions and postconditions cannot be decomposed into a sequence of smaller changes. Any method in which the state changes can be decomposed is nonprimitive.

It appears that a method is either primitive or not, with nothing in between. We can live with that. Now, let's move up to the class level and see how we can make use of method primitiveness in assessing the primitiveness of a class.

It is reasonable to declare a class to be primitive if all of its methods are primitive. It also seems reasonable to call a class primitive if at least a majority of its methods are primitive. In fact, it seems that a class can have degrees of primitiveness, from not primitive at all to completely primitive. This smacks of a percentage-based measure.

If we take the set of methods for a class as our universe, we can compare the set of classes which are primitive to this universe to find the degree of primitiveness for the class. A class in which no methods are primitive is not primitive at all. A class in which all methods are primitive is completely primitive. This suggests that we assess the primitiveness of a class in terms of the ratio of the set of primitive methods to the set of all methods. We can indeed order our classes in terms of this ratio, and so we empirically define primitiveness for a class to be, given two classes a and b:

$$a \succeq b \Leftrightarrow \mathrm{prim}(a) \geqslant \mathrm{prim}(b)$$
$$\Leftrightarrow |\text{primitive methods of } a|/|\text{methods of } a|$$
$$\geqslant |\text{primitive methods of } b|/|\text{methods of } b| \qquad (13.1)$$

FORMAL PROPERTIES

The discussion reveals four desired properties of a measure of primitiveness for classes. Three of these properties either apply or can be made to apply to methods as well.

First, it seems reasonable to restrict the value of our primitiveness measure to the positive numbers. I can see no benefit from negative primitiveness. What would that mean empirically?

Property P1: Primitiveness is nonnegative:

$$\mathrm{prim}(x) \geqslant 0 \qquad (13.2)$$

It also seems reasonable to allow the value of the primitiveness measure to be null. Our empirical understanding of class primitiveness indicates that null primitiveness is an intuitive result when none of the methods of the class are primitive. This would also be the value for primitiveness of a class which contains no methods.

Property P2: Primitiveness can be null:

$$\{m \in x \mid m \text{ is primitive}\} = \varnothing \Rightarrow \mathrm{prim}(x) = 0. \qquad (13.3)$$

If we are to use primitiveness to order our classes, any measure for primitiveness must allow us to construct such an order.

Property P3: Primitiveness forms a weak order:

$$x \succeq y \Leftrightarrow \mathrm{prim}(x) \geqslant \mathrm{prim}(y) \wedge (x \succeq y \vee y \succeq x) \wedge (x \succeq y \succeq z \Rightarrow x \succeq z)$$
$$(13.4)$$

This property cannot be applied to the primitiveness of a method, since our measure partitions the set of methods into two equivalence classes; every method belongs to one class or the other, but not both.

Finally, the primitiveness of a class should be independent of the number of methods in the class. This implies that our measure must map a class into the interval [0, *max*]. We use 0 as the lower bound because this follows from properties *P1* and *P2*. Intuition tells us that 1 is a reasonable upper bound, indicating a fully primitive class.

Property P4: Primitiveness is independent of the population of methods:

$$\text{prim}(x): x \rightarrow [0, 1] \tag{13.5}$$

EMPIRICAL RELATIONAL STRUCTURES

A method is either primitive or not. Thus, primitiveness at the method level is a binary nominal scale measure. It allows us to group methods into one of two equivalence classes. At the class level, we can assess the primitiveness of a class by determining the portion of the methods of that equivalence class which contains the primitive methods. The greater the portion, the more primitive the class. The primitiveness of a class looks much like an unconditional probability structure.

POTENTIAL MEASURES

Our measure of the primitiveness of a class, prim(x), is defined by the ratio of the number of methods in the class which are primitive to the total number of methods in the class. Formally, this is defined by:

$$\text{prim}(x) = |m \in x \wedge m \text{ is primitive}|/|m \in x| \tag{13.6}$$

We are trying to build a finitely additive probability space, defined in Chapter 5, for which the following is true:

1. $P(A) \geqslant 0$.
2. $P(X) = 1$.
3. $A \cap B = \varnothing \Rightarrow P(A \cup B) = P(A) + P(B)$.

where X is a nonempty set, E is an algebra of sets for which $E \subseteq \mathbb{P}X$ holds, and $A, B \in E$. Define X as the set of methods in the class and let $E \subseteq \mathbb{P}X$, rather than require that $E = \mathbb{P}X$. The members of E are defined as the various combinations of methods, all of which are primitive. In other words, E contains the possible sets of primitive methods for the class. Given a set $A \in E$, define $P(A) = |A|/|X|$. $P(A \cup B)$ would then be $|A \cup B|/|X|$, which satisfies condition 3. $A \cap B$ will have its usual interpretation: $A \cap B = \varnothing$ if A and B have no methods in common.

To build a finitely additive probability space, we must be able to show that our structure $\langle X, E, \succeq \rangle$ is an Archimedean structure of qualitative probability. Chapter 5 gives five requirements for such a structure. Given a nonempty set X, an algebra of sets on X E, and a binary relation $\succeq$ on E, the triple is an Archimedean structure of qualitative probability if and only if for every A, B, $C \in E$:

1. $\langle E, \succeq \rangle$ is a weak order.
2. $X \succ \varnothing$ and $A \succeq \varnothing$.
3. $A \cap B = A \cap C = \varnothing \Rightarrow (B \succeq C \Leftrightarrow A \cup B \succeq A \cup C)$.
4. For every $A \succ \varnothing$, any standard sequence relative to A is finite.
5. If $D \in E$, $A \cap B = \varnothing$, $A \succ C$ and $B \succeq D$, then there exists C', D', and $F \in E$ such that:
   - $F \sim A \cup B$
   - $C' \cap D' = \varnothing$
   - $F \supset C' \cup D'$
   - $C' \sim C$ and $D' \sim D$

First, define $\succeq$ so that $A \succeq B \Leftrightarrow P(A) \geqslant P(B)$, or $A \succeq B \Leftrightarrow |A|/|X| \geqslant |B|/|X|$. With this definition, we can easily show that $\langle E, \succeq \rangle$ forms a weak order: $\succeq$ orders E in terms of the ratio of the cardinality of a member set to the cardinality of X.

The second condition requires that $X \succ \varnothing$; there is no problem here, since $|X|/|X|$ is always nonzero. It also requires that $A \succeq \varnothing$. Again, given our definitions, we can easily satisfy this condition.

The third condition requires that, given two sets both disjoint from A, combining them with A does not change their relative ordering. In other words, adding A to both sides does not change the results. The test is $|B|/|X| \geqslant |C|/|X| \Leftrightarrow (|A| + |B|)/|X| \geqslant (|A| + |C|)/|X|$, which is obviously true, since we know that A is disjoint from both B and C, and since disjoint union is additive in terms of cardinalities.

The fourth condition is the Archimedean condition and requires some extra work. First, we need to define what a standard sequence relative to A would be like in our structure. Krantz and colleagues (1971) define such a sequence inductively. A sequence of one set consists of a set A_1, which is also B_1, and which is equivalent to A. To build A_2, find a set C_1, which is disjoint from B_1 and is equivalent to A, and take $A_2 = B_1 \cup C_1$. To build A_3, find a set B_2 which is equivalent to A_2, and may in fact be A_2, and a set C_2 which is equivalent to A and disjoint from B_2, and set $A_3 = B_2 \cup C_2$. We continue doing this until we run out of sets to add to our sequence. The requirement is that any such sequence is finite.

In our structure, $A \succeq B$ means that $|A|/|X| \geqslant |B|/|X|$, so we know that $|A| \geqslant |B|$. We also know that $A \sim B$ means that $|A| = |B|$. We start with A. To build A_1, find some set B_1, disjoint from A, but with the same number of members. Then, set $A_1 = B_1$. To build A_2, find some set C_1 with the same number of members as A and disjoint from B_1, then we set $A_2 = B_1 \cup C_1$. To build A_3, find some set B_2 with the same number of members as A_2, and may use A_2 if that's all we can find. We then find some set C_2 with the same number of members as A but disjoint from B_2. If we use A_2 for B_2, we can't use C_1 again, because it is part of B_2. Then, we set $A_3 = B_2 \cup C_2$. We continue until we run out of sets.

It is very easy to show that such a structure is finite in our case. Our set E was defined as a subset of $\mathbb{P}X$. No matter how big X gets, the cardinality of $\mathbb{P}X$ is finite and so is the cardinality of E. Since we have only a finite number of sets from which to build our sequence, it follows that any sequence will also be finite.

The fifth condition requires that, given four events A, B, C, and D, if A and B are disjoint ($A \cap B = \varnothing$), A is more probable than C ($A \succ C$), and B is at least as probable as D ($B \succ D$), then somewhere in E is an event F that is equally as probable as $A \cup B$. Furthermore, F includes events C' and D' which are disjoint, with C' equally as probable as C, and D' equally as probable as D.

For our structure, we are looking for two sets A and B which are disjoint. We must also find two sets C, which has fewer members than A, and D, which has the same number as or fewer members than B. Somewhere in E, we must be able to find a set F which has the same number of elements as $A \cup B$, and which includes a set C', with the same number of members as C, and a set D', with the same number of members as D, and which are disjoint from each other. The key to satisfying this requirement is noting that we only need to find one set of sets which meets this requirement.

Since X is the set of methods in a class, the size of E will usually be pretty small. We define A and B so that $A \cap B = \varnothing$, $C \subset A$, and $D = B$. Then $F = A \cup B$. All we need to do is find a $C' \subset A$ for which $C \cap C' = \varnothing$, and define $D' = D = B$. If $|A| \geq 2$, then we know we can meet this condition. Thus, we can satisfy this condition whenever our class contains at least two methods.

We have managed to construct a finitely additive probability space, which is an absolute scale. Our measure of class primitiveness is of the form in equation (13.6).

SUMMARY

Primitiveness is a useful property for assessing the quality of the design of a class and it exists on two levels: individual methods and classes. A binary, nominal scale measure for the primitiveness of a method was defined and considerable effort was spent defining the conditions under which a method can be considered primitive.

Using our measure of method primitiveness, we partition the set of methods for a class into those which are primitive and those which are not. Our measure of class primitiveness is the ratio of the size of the set of methods which are primitive to the size of the set of methods for the class. Our measure thus maps a class into the interval [0, 1], giving us an absolute scale measure of the primitiveness of a class. We then showed that this measure does indeed meet the conditions of a finitely additive probability space.

14

SIMILARITY

As a design property, similarity is new. To my knowledge, this is the first attempt to define and measure similarity. Similarity is the degree to which two design components or domain-level abstractions match in terms of structure, function, behavior, or purpose. Immediately, we see that we have four different views of similarity; all four will be defined in the chapter. A measure will be developed for one of these views in the last two sections. The structure used can be extended to any of the other four views.

MOTIVATION AND ORIGINS

I have often faced the situation in which two classes look a lot alike, but not exactly alike. The methods or attributes in one class may be named differently than in the other. The method signatures (number and types of parameters) may be slightly different. In many of these situations, I have found common features that could be extracted into a common base class. Many of these pairs of classes were true subtypes of a common supertype I had not identified. Other pairs simply had common features; factoring out a common base class cut down on the amount of work. I have long wanted a way to measure the similarity, or the dissimilarity, between two classes. This is an example of using similarity of structure to make design decisions.

Similarity of purpose can be used to determine the best way to allocate responsibilities among the abstractions in a domain model. There have been a few instances where I combined domain abstractions because, although they were structurally different, they served the same purpose. I was able to adjust the structures to allow the physical combination.

Similarity of function, defined in terms of the operations performed, can help you identify some types of classes in the domain. For example, in a fixed asset management application, any of four or five depreciation methods can be used to determine the annual depreciation, or the current book value, for an asset. Each of these depreciation methods involves very different calculations, but all perform basically the same function: They transform asset cost, previous depreciation, and the age of the asset into a depreciation amount for the current period and a new asset book value. Noting the similarities can help you factor the design so that the assets and the depreciation method are physically separated, resulting in a more flexible application.

Similarity of behavior can be used to identify the cases where common control mechanisms can be used by otherwise dissimilar components. For example, data structures such as queues and stacks all have uses in control applications such as process or thread scheduling in an operating system. The behavior exhibited by objects in the problem domain can be compared to the general pattern of stack behavior or queue behavior, and the closest match can then be used to implement the domain.

EMPIRICAL VIEWS

Four different views of similarity or, conversely, dissimilarity have been identified: structural, functional, behavioral, and purpose. Each of these views will be explored in terms of our formal model in Chapter 6 and developed to the extent that we can define empirically when two objects are similar from each view.

Structural Similarity

Two objects are structurally similar when they have similar structures. This statement is not always as obvious as it looks. There are two classes of structural similarity: internal and external. Internal structural similarity can take three forms: The attributes can be similar and the operations different; the operations can be similar and the attributes different; and both the attributes and operations can be similar. To further complicate things, each of these forms can have three forms: The names are similar and the types are different; the names are different and the types are similar; or the names and types are both similar. For operations, define type similarity to mean that the number and types of the operation parameters are similar. If the parameters are presented in a different order in two operations, but the parameters are otherwise similar, the operations can be made similar by adjusting one or both parameter lists.

First, look at attributes. In terms of our model, the name of an attribute is the label placed on the attribute's domain projection arrow in the category **Class**. If attribute arrows for two different classes have the same label, they share name similarity. If attribute arrows for two different classes have the same codomain—they terminate at the same attribute domain—they share type similarity. If two attributes share type similarity, they are considered similar, whether they share name similarity. If two attributes share both name and type similarity, they are, for all intents and purposes, not just similar, they are the same attribute.

When two attributes, each from a different class, share only type similarity, you need to look at their respective purposes to see if they are really the same attribute. The extent to which two attributes need to be similar to consider them interchangeable will be defined later in this section.

For operations, use the category **Method** from our formal model. Two operations, two instances of this category, share name similarity if the central category object—the domain for all of the arrows—carries the same label. Two operations share type similarity if there is an isomorphism from one set of arrows to the other, including their codomains and excluding their labels. This isomorphism ensures that both the number and types of the attributes are the same, but does not consider the order in which the arrows appear in the category. There is an isomorphism between two method categories if you can take one, overlay it on the other, and arrange it so that you can only see one set of arrows. The arrows may carry one or two labels; it doesn't matter which. The codomains for an arrow from each category, the attribute domains at which they terminate, must match exactly in order to combine the arrows.

When two operations share type similarity, they are structurally similar. Two objects can be similar in the structure of their attributes, their operations, or both. Which type of similarity you measure depends on the design decision you are trying to make. If two objects are similar in the structure of a substantial portion of their attributes, it may be a good idea to factor these similar attributes into a common abstract or concrete base class. If you use selector and modifier methods to control access to your attributes, these will be factored into the common base class as well. If two objects are similar in their operations, but not in their attributes (this doesn't happen very often), it may be possible to combine the classes into a single class with both sets of attributes and a common set of operations. Remember, the public interface, those operations exposed to the outside, determine the "type" for an object. Two objects with similar external interfaces are considered similar by their respective clients regardless of hidden internal differences.

Two objects are externally similar when they participate in the same number and types of relationships, with the same set of classes. That is, two classes—objects in the category **DesginState**—are structurally similar when there exists an isomorphism from one class to the other for which the remote ends of the arrows coincide. The two classes can be either the domain or codomain for a relationship arrow. It doesn't matter which condition is the case, as long as both classes are either the domain or codomain. If two classes are externally similar structurally, you can overlay the relationship arrows for one of the classes onto the other class and arrange them so that the arrows and the classes to which they connect coincide. It does not matter whether the combined arrows carry one or two labels.

In the case of associations, the further restriction that the anchor sets for the relationship also match must be imposed. See the section "The Category **DesignState**" in Chapter 6 for an explanation of anchor sets and the role they play in an association.

I have not seen a case in which two classes participate in a similar set of relationships where they did not also serve the same purpose and were not also internally structurally similar. So, similarity of relationship for two classes is a clue to look further into the internal similarity of the classes. It seems unlikely that two classes which participate in a similar set of relationships are legitimately different classes.

Functional Similarity

Functional similarity deals with the transformations performed by an operation. Functional similarity can take two forms: physical or logical. To compare the physical transformations of two operations, compare the changes between their preconditions and postconditions. Two operations which cause the same changes are functionally similar in the physical sense; it does not matter what mathematics they apply to transform the precondition into the postcondition. Two functions are logically similar if they apply the same mathematics, regardless of the physical changes between their preconditions and postconditions.

In an earlier example of the depreciation method, the operations which implement each method are physically but not logically similar. Likewise, two operations which sort, say, an array of objects, one of which uses a quicksort and the other of which uses a heapsort, are physically but not logically similar. On the other hand, two sort operations, both of which use a heapsort, but which operate on different types of structures, such as an array and a list, are logically but not physically similar.

Physical functional similarity is determined by mapping the deltas between preconditions and postconditions for two operations. If we can find an isomorphism for the predicates in one delta to the predicates in the other, the two operations are physically similar. We determine logical similarity by comparing the mathematics applied by two operations. If we can find an isomorphism from one set of mathematical operations to the other, in terms of the mathematics of the problem domain, the two operations are logically similar.

I have found that in most cases, two operations which are logically similar are also very similar physically, with some notable and predictable exceptions, one of which I already mentioned. When two functions are logically similar, it may be possible to place them in a parameterized class, such as a C++ template, which can then deal with any physical dissimilarities, such as different data structure types.

Behavioral Similarity

Two classes are behaviorally similar if they have similar sets of states, similar sets of transitions, respond to a similar set of events, or have similar responses to their events. State similarity follows from attribute type similarity: Similar sets of attributes which share type similarity will necessarily share similar sets of states. Transition similarity is the natural consequence of both attribute and operation type similarity. Since these two forms of behavioral similarity are caused by forms of structural similarity, we will not deal with them any further.

Two classes share event similarity if they respond to similar sets of events. A form of event similarity will be defined in later sections. Two classes share event response similarity if they have similar responses to a similar set of events. Event response similarity implies event similarity, which makes event similarity a precondition for event response similarity.

In our formal model, an event is indicated in the trigger for an operation in the category **Class**. Events are not explicitly indicated in this category; they are embedded in the labels for the operation arrows. To determine whether two classes share event similarity, it is necessary to extract the set of events to which each class responds. In most of my projects, this event list is one of the inputs into the development of the class state model, so no extraction is required. If you must extract the event list from the state model, you either failed to perform an important analysis activity or you are missing valuable documentation. Once you have the two sets of events, you simply compare them.

The response to an event is defined by the changes caused in the state of the application by the action taken in response to the event trigger. In our model, these changes are described in the differences between the domain and codomain of each operation arrow in the category **Class** for which a particular event is a trigger. This amounts to comparing the physical similarity between the operations which these arrows represent.

We cannot simply dismiss event response similarity as a consequence of event and physical operations similarity. It is possible, even probable, that the response to the same event by two classes occurs from different states. Thus, the domains for the operation arrows must also be similar. In other words, the preconditions for the operations in each class which serve as the response to the same event must be similar in both classes. This is an additional constraint to both event similarity and physical similarity.

Similarity of Purpose

Two components, whether they are classes, class categories, subsystems, or domain-level abstractions, share similarity of purpose if they exist for the same reason. While accurate, this description doesn't help identify when similarity of purpose occurs. In Chapter 13, the purpose of a domain-level abstraction was defined as representing all or part of a single concrete or conceptual domain object. Likewise, the purpose of a design component was defined as implementing all or part of an abstraction. Working these definitions into a view of similarity, it is said that two abstractions share similarity of purpose when they represent the same part of the same domain object. Likewise, two design components share similarity of purpose when they implement the same part of the same abstraction.

It may seem redundant to have two abstractions or two design components share similarity of purpose. There are cases where either or both are legitimate. For example, in a particular domain, it is possible to have two abstractions represent the same domain object, yet not be the same abstraction. If neither of the abstractions is complete, and each is sufficient from a different point of view, one cannot take the place of the other—both must exist. It is often desirable to implement the same part of an abstraction in more than one way, resulting in two design components which share similarity of purpose, but no other form of similarity.

Of course, it is possible for two abstractions or design components which share similarity of purpose to be truly redundant. The point is, simply sharing similarity of purpose is insufficient for indicating such redundancy.

When confronted with two abstractions, or two design components, it is often difficult to determine if they share similarity of purpose simply by looking at them. As has been seen, similarity of purpose does not imply any other form of similarity. Likewise, structural, functional, or behavioral similarity, alone or in combination, does not imply similarity of purpose.

Unfortunately, the only way to judge similarity of purpose is to determine the existence of a property I call substitutability or satisfaction. Two components have this property if the user of one would be satisfied to receive the other; that is, if one component can be substituted for the other. Some structural modifications may be required to make this substitution possible. Measuring substitutability or satisfaction from this point of view is similar to measuring customer satisfaction: The only way to measure it is to ask the users of a component if they would be willing to use the other. Consequently, similarity of purpose is in the eye of the beholder and remains a subjective measure.

As we develop our properties and measures for similarity, we will work with the general notion of the similarity of sets, since all of the forms of similarity, except for similarity of purpose, have this same basic structure. The only real difference between them is the membership of the two sets being compared.

FORMAL PROPERTIES

The discussion about the various forms of similarity reveals a small set of properties for any measure of similarity we might develop. In this section, we denote the similarity, of some unspecified kind, between two objects x and y by $sim(x, y)$. Two candidate properties seem obvious, or at least intuitive:

Property SM1: Similarity is nonnegative:

$$\forall x,.y \cdot sim(x, y) \geqslant 0 \qquad (14.1)$$

Property SM2: Similarity can be null:

$$\exists x, y \cdot sim(x, y) = 0 \qquad (14.2)$$

To hint at what's to come, these two properties will become a hindrance and will be dropped.

It may seem tempting to impose a maximum value on similarity, effectively limiting the value of some similarity measure to a specific interval. I refrain from doing so for two reasons. First, I'm not totally convinced there is an essential maximum to similarity. As two objects become more and more similar, they become the same object, or perhaps two identical objects in every way, but with separate identities. I see the concept as analogous to points in three-dimensional space. It is possible for two objects to occupy the same point in this space—to have the same values for each of the three dimensions—but not be the same object. In some other systems, two objects which occupy the same point in space are necessarily the same object. It is not clear to me which of these views applies to similarity.

The second reason for my hesitation to impose an upper limit on similarity is that doing so often requires the use of a ratio of some kind. In other chapters, measures have been built from the ratio of the sizes of two sets. Here, we are comparing two separate sets. It is not clear which of these should be used as the basis for a ratio, if indeed either of them can be used as such a basis.

A third property which we can justify is that similarity form a weak order:

Property SM3: Similarity forms a weak order:

$$[(a, b) \succeq (c, d) \Leftrightarrow \text{sim}(a, b) \geqslant \text{sim}(c, d)]$$

$$\Leftrightarrow [(a, b) \succeq (c, d) \vee (c, d) \succeq (a, b) \wedge (a, b)$$

$$\succeq (c, d) \succeq (e, f) \Rightarrow (a, b) \succeq (e, f)] \tag{14.3}$$

EMPIRICAL RELATIONAL STRUCTURES

The most obvious choice for comparing the similarity of two sets is a proximity feature-structure defined in the section "Feature Proximity Representations" in Chapter 5. We can build one such structure for each of the seven types of similarity identified earlier (attribute, operation, external structure, physical function, logical function, event, and event response—exclude similarity of purpose because it is not based on the membership of two sets). All seven of these structures use the same construction technique, which I provide in the next section.

We can in turn view each of these seven types of similarity as one dimension in a seven-dimensional space of some kind. It is not clear, until we test it, whether we can build a seven-dimensional metric space or must be satisfied with a seven-dimensional additive-difference structure. In either case, it is possible to measure the similarity of two objects (classes, abstractions, class categories, subsystems, or whatever) by comparing their proximity in this seven-dimensional space. Interestingly, we cannot place individual objects in this space because the values in each dimension are comparing pairs of objects. Thus, we can determine how far apart two objects are in this space, but not where either object is located. Nevertheless, it is possible that we can construct a ratio scale measure of similarity.

POTENTIAL MEASURES

Chapter 5 defines a model for assessing the dissimilarity between two sets of features. The contrast model (Tversky 1977) has the general form

$$\delta(a, b) = \alpha\varphi(a\backslash b) + \beta\varphi(b\backslash a) - \theta\varphi(a \cap b) \tag{14.4}$$

where $\delta(a, b)$ denotes the distance between sets a and b, and $(a\backslash b)$ denotes the usual set difference operation. This model can handle cases in which the contribution of $(a \backslash b)$ differs from $(b \backslash a)$; they are the same, or in which any term has no contribution at all, all by adjusting the value and/or the sign of the coefficient. The fact that all three components have the same function φ is deliberate.

Chapter 5 provides the conditions for several forms of this model, each with increasing constraints, but providing more accurate measures. We will test these conditions, from weakest to strongest, stopping when we either satisfy them all or fail to satisfy one of them. The measure we have built up to but not including the stopping point will be our measure of similarity, with the scale type we have achieved at that point.

We are defining a single measure which can be used for any of the seven types of similarity. All of them are simple set comparisons and differ only in the members of the sets they compare.

Several terms, defined in the section entitled "Feature Proximity Representations" in Chapter 5, are restated here. The set S is the set of all possible relevant features. The set A is a family of subsets of S which contains every non-empty subset of S, so $A \subseteq \mathbb{P}S$. Each element $a \in A$ is an object and a subset of S. We limit the features in S to those that are relevant for the type of similarity which we are measuring. From these definitions, we can construct the ordered pair $(a, b) \in A \times A$, and the sets $a \backslash b$, $b \backslash a$, and $a \cap b$. In Chapter 5, two additional families of sets are also defined: $S_D = \{a \backslash b \mid a, b \in A\}$ and $S_C = \{a \cap b \mid a, b \in A\}$. We define the relation $\succeq$ on $A \times A$ as the ordering of pairs of objects in terms of their dissimilarity (we'll turn this into similarity later). We also define the relations $\succeq_1$ and $\succeq_2$ on S_D and $\succeq_3$ on S_C as the contributions of each component to the overall ordering $\succeq$.

We will construct $\succeq$ from some combination of $\succeq_1$, $\succeq_2$, and $\succeq_3$. We choose to base the orderings $\succeq_1$ and $\succeq_2$ on S_D, and $\succeq_3$ on S_C in terms of the cardinalities of the sets $a \backslash b$, $b \backslash a$, and $a \cap b$, respectively. Thus, we can be sure that $\succeq_1$, $\succeq_2$, and $\succeq_3$ are weak orders on their respective sets. Since our three component orderings are based on cardinalities of sets, $\succeq$ will be based on the combination of cardinalities of sets. We assume that the combination is additive in nature, since that is the general form of the contrast model. Additive combinations of cardinal numbers all form weak orders, so we have met the first two of our conditions for a proximity feature-structure.

The third condition requires that each $\succeq_i$ is an extension of the partial order by set inclusion on S_D or S_C. This means that when $a \backslash b$, $b \backslash a$, and $a \cap b$ are ordered in terms of set inclusion, then the respective $\succeq_i$ holds. This can be stated formally as, for example, $a \backslash b \supseteq c \backslash d \Rightarrow a \backslash b \succeq_1 c \backslash d$. Ordering by numbers of elements meets this condition, since $x \supseteq y \Rightarrow |x| \geqslant |y|$.

The fourth condition requires that each $\succeq_i$ form at least two equivalence classes. That is, we must be able to find at least two pairs (a, b) and (c, d) for which $a \backslash b \sim_1 c \backslash d$, or $|a \backslash b| = |c \backslash d|$, and two other pairs (e, f) and (g, h) for which $|e \backslash f| = |g \backslash h|$, but $|e \backslash f| \neq |a \backslash b|$. Likewise for $b \backslash a$ and $\sim_2$, and $a \cap b$ and $\sim_3$. This condition really requires that we be able to construct such pairs from our family of objects A. It does not necessarily require that our sample of objects contain four such pairs.

The fifth condition requires that the notion of dominance holds. Dominance is defined in Chapter 5. In our case, if $|a\backslash b| \geq |c\backslash d|$, $|b\backslash a| \geq |d\backslash c|$, and $|a \cap b| \geq |c \cap d|$ then it is obvious that $(a, b) \succeq (c, d)$ (if we choose our coefficients α, β, and θ carefully, say, for example, setting them all to one).

We have successfully constructed a proximity feature-structure, which is the basic building block for our subsequent representations. If $\langle A \times A, \succeq \rangle$ has an order dense subset (ours does), we can obtain an ordinal scale measure of the form

$$\delta(a, b) = F[\varphi_1(a\backslash b), \varphi_2(b\backslash a), \varphi_3(a \cap b)] \qquad (14.5)$$

where F is strictly increasing in its first two components and strictly decreasing in its third component.

The next several conditions allow us to build an additive conjoint structure where $F(\varphi_1, \varphi_2, \varphi_3) = \varphi_1 + \varphi_2 + \varphi_3$. The first of these requires that our structure be partially factorial, which in turn requires that for any $a, b, c, d, e, f, g, h \in A$ such that

1. $|a\backslash b| \geq |c\backslash d|$.
2. $|b\backslash a| \geq |f\backslash e|$.
3. $|a \cap b| \geq |g \cap h|$.

we can find a' and b' such that

4. $|a'\backslash b'| = |c\backslash d|$.
5. $|b'\backslash a'| = |f\backslash e|$.
6. $|a' \cap b'| = |g \cap h|$.

It is sufficient that we can construct our a' and b'. Since A contains every non-empty subset of S, we can always find elements $a', b' \in A$ that meet these six conditions.

Factorial connectedness, the next requirement, requires that any two pairs of objects are connected by a finite order-preserving chain in which successive pairs are factorially comparable. Two pairs (c, d) and (e, f) are factorially comparable if their components lie in a Cartesian product bounded by some pair (a, b), that is:

1. $|a\backslash b| \geq |c\backslash d|, |e\backslash f|$.
2. $|b\backslash a| \geq |d\backslash c|, |f\backslash e|$.
3. $|a \cap b| \geq |c \cap d|, |e \cap f|$.

Given the definitions of our ordering relations, every pair in A is factorially comparable with every other pair in A.

Given two pairs $(c, d) \succeq (e, f)$, we construct our sequence $(a_0, b_0), ..., (a_n, b_n)$, for which $(a_0, b_0) = (c, d)$ (a_0 and c, and b_0 and d are the same objects, respectively), $(a_n, b_n) = (e, f)$, and each $(a_{i-1}, b_{i-1}) \succeq (a_i, b_i)$, $i = 1, ..., n$, are factorially comparable. We can use (e, f) to bound this sequence and be certain that each adjacent pair is factorially comparable. If $(c, d) \sim (e, f)$, and we set $(a_0, b_0) =$

(c, d) and $(a_n, b_n) = (a_1, b_1) = (e, f)$, it is obvious that (c, d) and (e, f) are factorially connected. We can extend this sequence one element in one factor at a time, rotating through each factor each time, taking (c, d) and (e, f) as far apart as we can, and still be able to construct our sequence. Our structure, as we have defined it, is factorially connected.

Independence requires that if two pairs (a, b) and (c, d) agree on two components (see Chapter 5 for the definition of agreement), (a', b') and (c', d') agree on the same two components, and (a, b) and (a', b'), and (c, d) and (c', d') agree on the third component, then $(a, b) \succeq (a', b') \Leftrightarrow (c, d) \succeq (c', d')$. Suppose that $|a \backslash b| = |c \backslash d|$, $|b \backslash a| = |d \backslash c|$, $|a' \backslash b'| = |c' \backslash d'|$, and $|b' \backslash a'| = |d' \backslash c'|$. Suppose further that $|a \cap b| = |a' \cap b'|$ and $|c \cap d| = |c' \cap d'|$. For $(a, b) \succeq (a', b')$, it must be the case that *one* of the following conditions holds:

1. $|a \backslash b| > |a' \backslash b'|$ and $|b \backslash a| = |b' \backslash a'|$.
2. $|a \backslash b| = |a' \backslash b'|$ and $|b \backslash a| > |b' \backslash a'|$.
3. $|a \backslash b| > |a' \backslash b'|$ and $|b \backslash a| > |b' \backslash a'|$.

If condition 1 holds, since $|a \backslash b| = |c \backslash d|$ and $|a' \backslash b'| = |c' \backslash d'|$, then $|c \backslash d| > |c' \backslash d'|$. Since $|b \backslash a| = |d \backslash c|$ and $|b' \backslash a'| = |d' \backslash c'|$, then $|d \backslash c| = |d' \backslash c'|$. Putting these results together, we get $(a, b) \succeq (a', b') \Leftrightarrow (c, d) \succeq (c', d')$. We can show the same if conditions 2 or 3 are met. If we swap (a, b) with (c, d) and (a', b') with (c', d'), we can show the same results given each of the three conditions in turn. We can thus conclude that our structure is independent.

Restricted solvability requires that if $(a, b) \succeq (c, d) \succeq (e, f)$, we can find a $(p, q) \in A \times A$ such that $(p, q) \sim (c, d)$ and agrees with (a, b) and (e, f) on every component for which they agree with each other. Suppose that $|a \backslash b| = |e \backslash f|$ and $|b \backslash a| = |f \backslash e|$ [(a, b) and (e, f) agree on components one and two]. We need to find a $(p, q) \sim (c, d)$ for which $|p \backslash q| = |a \backslash b|$ and $|q \backslash p| = |b \backslash a|$. Equivalence overall does not imply equivalence on every component, only that $\delta(p, q) = \delta(c, d)$.

So, if (a, b) and (e, f) agree on components one and two, then it must be the case that $|a \cap b| > |p \cap q| > |e \cap f|$ in order for the initial and final conditions to hold. Since our structure adds the components together, and for the time being has assigned all three coefficients the value of one, one of the following three conditions must hold:

1. $|p \cap q| = |c \cap d|$ and either $|p \backslash q| > |c \backslash d|$ and $|q \backslash p| < |d \backslash c|$ by the same amount or $|p \backslash q| < |c \backslash d|$ and $|q \backslash p| > |d \backslash c|$ by the same amount.
2. $|p \cap q| < |c \cap d|$ and either $|p \backslash q| > |c \backslash d|$ by the same amount and $|q \backslash p| = |d \backslash c|$, $|q \backslash p| > |d \backslash c|$ by the same amount and $|p \backslash q| = |c \backslash d|$, or $|p \backslash q| - |c \backslash d|$ and $|q \backslash p| - |d \backslash c|$ combine to offset $|c \cap d| - |p \cap q|$.
3. $|p \cap q| > |c \cap d|$ and either $|p \backslash q| < |c \backslash d|$ by the same amount and $|q \backslash p| = |d \backslash c|$, $|q \backslash p| < |d \backslash c|$ by the same amount and $|p \backslash q| = |c \backslash d|$, or $|p \backslash q| - |c \backslash d|$ and $|q \backslash p| - |d \backslash c|$ combine to offset $|p \cap q| - |c \cap d|$.

Again, given the fact that A contains all nonempty subsets of S, we can construct a $(p, q) \in A \times A$ that meets these conditions. Thus, we conclude that our structure satisfies restricted solvability.

The next condition is the Archimedean condition which requires that any sequence of nested intervals with a common first object c, all of which are contained within the interval (c, d), and where the difference between adjacent intervals in the sequence is larger than the interval between some reference pair (a, b), is finite. This situation is illustrated in Figure 14.1. This is very similar to marking off equivalent intervals on the line between objects c and d.

To show that our structure is Archimedean, let's build the required sequence backwards. Suppose that $a = b$, which means that $|a \cap b| = a = b$ and $|a \backslash b| = |b \backslash a| = 0$. This is as small an interval as we can get (remember, $\delta(a, b)$ is a *dis*similarity measure at the moment). The sets in our sequence interval (e_k, e_{k+1}) must differ by at least one element, which means $|e_k \cap e_{k+1}| = |e_k| - 1$, and either $|e_k \backslash e_{k+1}| = 1$ and $|e_{k+1} \backslash e_k| = 0$ or $|e_k \backslash e_{k+1}| = 0$ and $|e_{k+1} \backslash e_k| = 1$. Thus, (c, e_k) must differ by only one element. We build the sequence by making each subsequent e_k differ by one additional element, continuing to do so until some $e_k = d$. Since S in any real-life situation will be finite, all members of A are finite, which means that c is finite (has a finite number of features). If we change one element at a time, there will be only finite changes until we change c enough to turn it into d. In fact, we will only fail the Archimedean condition when c is infinite, which raises the possibility of an infinite number of changes to make c into d.

Given that our proximity feature-structure is partially factorial, factorially connected, and satisfies independence, restricted solvability, and the Archimedean condition, we can construct a measure of the form

$$\delta(a, b) = \varphi_1(a \backslash b) + \varphi_2(b \backslash a) - \varphi_3(a \cap b) \qquad (14.6)$$

in which φ_1, φ_2, and φ_3 are all interval scales with a common unit, and δ is also an interval scale (it is also an additive conjoint structure). In our case, φ_1, φ_2, and φ_3 are identical in that $\varphi_1(x) = \varphi_2(x) = \varphi_3(x) = |x|$.

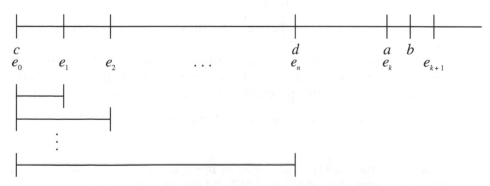

Figure 14.1 *A strictly bounded standard sequence.*

To make $\delta(a, b)$ into a ratio scale, we can ensure that it is either invariant or extensive. We cannot show that our particular structure is invariant since it fails uniformity (see Chapter 5). Our only option therefore, is, to attempt to show that our structure is extensive.

Extensivity is surprisingly easy to establish in our case. The lone requirement, other than that we have a proximity feature-structure, is that whenever $x \subseteq S$ is disjoint from $a \cup b \cup c \cup d$ and the required unions with x are in A, then:

$$(a, b) \succeq (c, d) \Leftrightarrow (a \cup x, b) \succeq (c \cup x, d)$$

$$\Leftrightarrow (a, b \cup x) \succeq (c, d \cup x) \qquad (14.7)$$

$$\Leftrightarrow (a \cup x, b \cup x) \succeq (c \cup x, d \cup x)$$

Since we defined A to contain all nonempty subsets of S, A must be closed under the union operation as long as all elements are taken from A. This means that all of the unions with x in equation (14.7) are indeed in A.

Given that x is disjoint from $a \cup b \cup c \cup d$, and thus from each separately, the addition of the elements of x in the combinations given in equation (14.7) do not affect the relationship on any component and has no effect on the overall relationship. For example, if $|a\backslash b| \geq |c\backslash d|$, then $|(a \cup x)\backslash b| \geq |(c \cup x)\backslash d|$ since $|a \cup x| = |a| + |x|$ (they are disjoint, remember) and $|c \cup x| = |c| + |x|$. In effect, taking the unions of a and c with x is like adding $|x|$ to both sides, which never changes an inequality or equality. We can show the same for each of the other components in the first condition and for each of the other conditions in equation (14.7)

Thus, we can conclude that our dissimilarity structure is extensive, which makes $\delta(a, b)$ a metric in three dimensions and a ratio scale.

There are two last pieces of business. Our metric, $\delta(a, b)$, is a *dis*similarity metric which, in effect, measures the distance between a and b. $\delta(a, b)$ increases as a and b become less similar. We need a metric $\delta^{-1}(a, b)$ which decreases as $\delta(a, b)$ increases. The simplest transformation from δ to δ^{-1} would be to reverse the signs for all of our coefficients. This would make our similarity metric take the form:

$$\delta^{-1}(a, b) = |a \cap b| - |a\backslash b| - |b\backslash a| \qquad (14.8)$$

It is not difficult to show that δ^{-1} satisfies the same conditions δ and is also a metric.

The last problem is that δ^{-1} as defined in equation (14.8) fails to satisfy both our properties *SM1* and *SM2*, in that it can be both negative and the smallest value is nonnull. To solve this problem, we can perform a linear transformation

$$\text{sim}(a, b) = \delta^{-1}(a, b) + |a| + |b| = |a \cap b| - |a\backslash b| - |b\backslash a| + |a| + |b|$$

$$(14.9)$$

which is unfortunately once again an interval scale. Rather than suffer this indignity, drop properties *SM1* and *SM2* and define $\text{sim}(a, b)$ as

$$\text{sim}(a, b) = \delta^{-1}(a, b) = |a \cap b| - |a\backslash b| - |b\backslash a| \qquad (14.10)$$

This means that our measure of similarity will fall into the interval $[-(|a| + |b|), |a|]$.

SUMMARY

Four different ways to empirically assess similarity as a design property were identified. One of these views can be assessed only subjectively. The other three views can be objectively measured by comparing the cardinalities of various sets. Seven distinct comparisons were identified. The membership of the sets we use will be determined by the view of similarity we are trying to measure.

A true metric was developed, which lies on the ratio scale, to measure the dissimilarity between two sets, based on their cardinalities and the cardinalities of sets resulting from various operations on the initial sets. We then transformed this metric into a similarity metric, also a ratio scale, but which mapped pairs of objects (a, b) into the interval $[-(|a| + |b|), |a|]$. Noting that this violated two intuitive properties of a similarity measure, we applied a linear transformation to meet our properties. This resulted in a similarity measure on the interval scale. We then decided to drop the properties in favor of a ratio scale representation for similarity.

15

VOLATILITY

Volatility is the likelihood or probability that a change will occur. It is an important characteristic of applications, domains, and design components and must be watched—carefully.

In this chapter, volatility is explored as a characteristic, including its origins and why we should care about it. From our new understanding, we look for ways to spot volatility in an application domain. This is followed by the development of ways to measure its impact on components which would be affected directly by these changes and components which will be affected by changes to other components. Then, a measure of volatility is developed. Ways to combat volatility are not explored, since that is the subject of a book on software design and this is a book on software measurement.

MOTIVATION AND ORIGINS

Conventional wisdom says that maintenance effort is a function of size. Another large group of people claim that complexity is a better predictor of maintenance effort. Well, they are both wrong, and both right, at least in part. Both the size and the complexity of a chunk of software are big factors in the amount of effort that will be required to maintain it. But, if the software never changes, then it doesn't matter how big or complex the chunk of software is: The maintenance effort will be zero. This implies that a true predictor of software maintenance effort will be a function of size, complexity, perhaps some other attributes, and the likelihood that the software will have to be changed at all.

I call the likelihood of change volatility. A highly volatile chunk of software will be under constant modification and will require the complete attention of some number of maintainers. These people, if measured by size per person, will show very low productivity. In fact, these people are constantly working and are probably much more productive than other folks (you change a particular piece of software often enough, you get very good at it).

Volatility plays an important role in the design of software, starting with the architecture. I like to know which parts of an application are volatile before I begin work on the architecture. If none of the application is volatile, adaptability and flexibility are less important than getting the job done. If major parts of the application are highly volatile, I have to make sure the architecture can handle the adaptation and change requirements. During the detail design activities, I try to isolate the volatile parts of the application from the rest of the application. In particular, I try to insulate the nonvolatile parts of the application from the changes that will inevitably affect the more volatile parts.

Volatility has two sources: changes directly due to changes in the problem domain and changes due to changes in other parts of the application. Volatility does not include any change that results from fixing defects. Software that requires constant work to fix defects is just bad software and should be discarded.

When analyzing a problem domain, you get clues as to which areas are likely to change most often. In a typical business application, the business rules and policies change most often, while the properties of the business domain objects change least often. This truism led to the rise of data model-based software development techniques. In scientific and engineering software, the algorithms and calculations will change more often than the properties of the objects to which they are being applied. On the other hand, the same set of calculations may be applied to multiple types of objects, each with a different set of properties, in which case it may appear that the properties change frequently. In real-time software, the environment is changing constantly. Any change to the environment of a real-time application can send ripples of change through the software. Real-time software especially must be designed to limit these ripples to as small a part of the application as possible.

Coupling between components can create volatility where none naturally exists. Any component that is tightly coupled to a highly volatile component is itself highly volatile. At the very least, you will have to open the component up to see if changes are required whenever the other component is modified. This means that the scope of change for the highly volatile component has just widened to include less volatile components, and only because the designer didn't take the time and effort to provide the proper insulation from change.

My experience suggests that volatility, from both of these sources, affects maintenance effort, at least in the form of the scope of a change, more than any other factor. Its influence on the scope of change makes size a factor that depends on volatility. If volatility causes external components to fall under the scope of a change, it also has a material effect on the complexity of the software to be examined.

Thus, volatility is something to be tightly controlled. Highly volatile aspects of an application are to be isolated as much as possible from the rest of the application. They should be isolated from each other, as well. Ideally, highly volatile aspects of the application will be contained within single classes or small groups of classes, scattered throughout the application.

EMPIRICAL VIEWS

Two primary sources of volatility have been identified: the problem domain itself and other components. The objective is to be able to identify and measure each source separately. In that vein, let's explore the various forms of volatility from an empirical perspective.

Volatility which originates in the domain manifests itself as a high rate of requirements changes. Caution is due here: A high rate of requirements change does not necessarily indicate a highly volatile domain; it could mean a defective requirements gathering process or an incomplete understanding of the business on the part of the customer. In a volatile domain, the domain itself undergoes frequent change. As a developer, this means the business of your customer is changing, and not just your customer's view of that business. If the low level of understanding of the business of software development among developers is any indication, the level of understanding that most software users have of their own business is also very low.

To identify volatile parts of the problem domain, you need to look at the history and future of that domain, not just its current state. Tell me, have you ever consciously looked into the historical and future trends of your customer's business? I thought not. Most software analysts have a difficult enough time understanding the business as it exists today. That's not as insulting as it sounds: In order to effectively develop an application, an analyst must understand the business at least as well as the customer. In my experience, most business people have only a rudimentary understanding of their own business. Those people who truly understand the business they are in are few and far between. This is not an indictment, just a fact of life. It makes our job as software developers more difficult and is probably the chief cause behind requirements creep.

So, volatility in the problem domain has two aspects: changes to the basic nature of the business and changes to our customer's understanding of that business. The effects of change from either source are the same, as far as the software is concerned. They are identified as separate sources because each requires a different set of skills, and a different level of understanding of the domain, to identify and predict each type's respective effect on the software.

Volatility also comes from other components in the design. I have found two primary types of intercomponent volatility: dependence and exposure. An aggregate is dependent on its component objects. A subclass is dependent on its superclasses. Any class that sends a message to another class is dependent on that other class.

Dependence can increase a component's exposure, but does not necessarily do so. Dependence is a necessary characteristic of the design. Exposure is the result of sloppy design. A designer can (almost) always insulate components from certain types of changes to the components on which they depend. For example, a class which sends a message to another class is dependent on the external interface of the other class. The dependent class will only require modification if the message format of the other class changes. There are design techniques that can isolate a message sender from all types of changes made to the receiver, except for changes to the actual external interface. John Lakos (1992) has been working in this area for a long time and has some very good techniques.

Exposure is the likelihood that a component will have to be changed because of a change in some other component. Exposure typically follows lines of coupling, but a coupling relationship does not inherently increase the exposure. A class tightly coupled to a nonvolatile class is not exposed to change from that other class.

Exposure can be viewed from both logical and physical viewpoints. Logical exposure resides in the design. Changes to a component which require changes to other components are examples of logical exposure. The effects of these changes can range from having to modify the design to modifying the source code, to recompile, relink, or no change at all. A design objective should be to limit the types of changes to those which are the least painful, and preferably no change at all.

Physical exposure has many of the same characteristics and effects as logical exposure but results from physical links between the components in an application. Physical exposure is often not considered by the designer. Problems caused by physical exposure led me to create a whole class of design activities. Chapter 2 discusses physical design, a set of activities the whole purpose of which is to locate and mitigate the effects of physical exposure.

So far, volatility has been discussed in a qualitative sense and two sources of volatility have been identified: changes in the problem domain which directly cause changes to a component, called likelihood of change; and changes to other components which cause changes to a component, called exposure. I am personally looking forward to the day when the acronym LOC generally means likelihood of change, rather than lines of code; I find the former a much more important and useful characteristic.

A quantitative form of our understanding of volatility has not been discussed. My instincts tell me that volatility is a probability of some kind. The likelihood of change is the probability that a change to the domain will require a change to a component. As yet, I have no way to objectively determine this probability and must rely on intuition and experience.

Exposure is also a probability, but is a combination of the likelihood of change to a component to which my component is exposed and the type of change that is likely to be required. Intuitively, a change to a remote component that requires my component to be relinked or recompiled is not as much exposure as a change that requires modifying the source code or design of my component. I'm not sure how much of an effect the type of exposure should have on the value of volatility; that will have to be empirically determined through observation or experiment.

FORMAL PROPERTIES

Given that volatility is at its core a probability, there are some obvious properties of a volatility measure. Denote the likelihood of change of a component x by $loc(x)$, and the exposure of x to a change in component y by $exp(x, y)$. Volatility is some combination of these, the nature of which will be determined in the following sections. For now, denote the volatility of an object x as $vlt(x) = f[loc(x), exp(x, y)]$.

Property VL1: Volatility is nonnegative:

$$loc(x) \geq 0; \qquad exp(x, y) \geq 0; \qquad vlt(x) \geq 0 \qquad (15.1)$$

Property VL2: Volatility can be null:

$$\exists x \cdot loc(x) = 0; \qquad \exists x, y \cdot exp(x, y) = 0; \qquad \exists x \cdot vlt(x) = 0 \quad (15.2)$$

Property VL3: Volatility is null precisely when both the likelihood of change and the exposure to the change of any component is null:

$$loc(x) = 0 \wedge \forall y \cdot exp(x, y) = 0 \Leftrightarrow vlt(x) = 0 \qquad (15.4)$$

Property VL4: Volatility maps an object into the interval [0, 1]:

$$loc(x): x \rightarrow [0, 1]; exp(x, y): x \rightarrow [0, 1]; vlt(x): x \rightarrow [0, 1] \qquad (15.4)$$

Property VL5: Volatility forms a weak order:

$$[x \succeq y \Leftrightarrow vlt(x) \geq vlt(y)] \Leftrightarrow [(x \succeq y \vee y \succeq x) \wedge (x \succeq y \succeq z \Rightarrow x \succeq z)] \qquad (15.5)$$

EMPIRICAL RELATIONAL STRUCTURES

There is only one obvious choice for empirically representing the likelihood of change for a component: an Archimedean structure of qualitative probability based on unconditional probability. The next section will formally develop $loc(x)$ using such a structure. The only weakness of this measure is that the probability must be subjectively assigned. There is no objective way to assess the probability of change to a domain at this point, in general. However, there may be specific cases where such probability can be assigned objectively.

One possibility is to look at the historical churn rate for a component. I define churn rate as the number of changes per year applied to a single component, averaged over the life of the component. A high churn rate indicates a high likelihood of change. One caveat: Be sure to remove changes to fix defects and those due to changes to other components from your calculation of churn rate. You want to include only those changes due to changes in that part of the domain implemented by the component. Even with this data, the assignment of an actual probability is only made easier; it remains subjective. The likelihood of change, as defined in this chapter, should be a good predictor of churn rate; that is, a high likelihood of change should be followed by a high, or higher than normal, actual churn rate.

Exposure is a knottier problem. The exposure of component x to a change in component y is influenced by the type of coupling between x and y. It is also possible for component x to be coupled to y in more than one way. Further, it is possible for component x to be coupled to more than one other component, in more than one way, of course. Furthermore, it appears that exposure is a form of conditional probability, which complicates matters on its own. You should be getting a headache about now.

You can view an instance of coupling between component x and component y by noting that component x is really coupled to a feature of y, which we denote y_i. This implies that the exposure of x is limited to the likelihood that feature i of component y will be changed, which makes sense. From the viewpoint of component x, you can assume that the likelihood of a change to feature i of component y is independent of a change to feature j of component y. This may not actually be the case, but that can only be determined when you peer inside component y. From outside the component, you expect that a change to one feature does not require a change to another, a perfectly reasonable expectation for a client to hold.

Suppose x is coupled to features i and j of component y. Given that you view these features as independent of each other, the exposure of x to any change in component y is $\exp(x, y) = \exp(x, y_i) + \exp(x, y_j)$. In general, this becomes:

$$\exp(x, y) = \sum_{i=1}^{n} \exp(x, y_i) \tag{15.6}$$

If the value of n grows too great, or the values of $\exp(x, y_i)$ have the right combinations, it is possible for the value of $\exp(x, y)$ as defined in equation (15.6) to exceed one.

Leaving that problem for a moment, suppose that component x is coupled to one feature each in components y and z. You can view the exposure of x to changes in y as independent of the exposure of x to changes in z (again, this may not actually be the case, but it appears to be the case from the view of component x). Thus, the total exposure of x becomes $\exp(x) = \exp(x, y) + \exp(x, z)$, where $\exp(x)$ denotes the exposure of component x to all components to which it is coupled in some way. In general, this becomes

$$\exp(x) = \sum_{k \in A} \exp(x, k) \tag{15.7}$$

where A is the set of components in the design. Like before, if the size of the set A is too large, or the values of $\exp(x, k)$ have the right combinations, it is possible for the value of $\exp(x)$ to exceed one.

It is entirely possible for component x to be coupled to multiple features in multiple components. You can combine equations (15.6) and (15.7) to get a more general form of $\exp(x)$:

$$\exp(x) = \sum_{k \in A} \sum_{i=1}^{n} \exp(x, k_i) \qquad (15.8)$$

It is very easy to see that the value of $\exp(x)$ can exceed one in many cases. The easiest way to handle this problem is simply to cut $\exp(x)$ off at one. If this occurs in a real situation, the object x is simply too exposed to change and the design should be altered to alleviate the problem.

POTENTIAL MEASURES

Since $\mathrm{loc}(x)$ is a standard representation of unconditional probability, the requirements for the representation are the same as those for a probability structure. In this case, rather than being a set of requirements, view these conditions as a set of blueprints. From another view, you can always find events, objects, which have the desired properties. Given both of these circumstances, we short-circuit the proof process and claim, rather, that since you are building a probability structure out of probabilities, and not something else, you meet all of the requirements. Simply declare $\mathrm{loc}(x)$ to be an Archimedean structure of qualitative probability.

At first glance, $\exp(x)$ would appear to be a classic case of conditional probability. Conditional probability, denoted $P(x \mid y)$, measures the probability of x given the information that y has already occurred. When the probability of an event y is 0, $P(y) = 0$, y cannot be used as the conditioning event. This will not do for our purposes. Being able to compute $\exp(x, y)$ when $\mathrm{vlt}(y) = 0$ is very important. It is very likely that you want to assign $\exp(x, y) = 0$ whenever $\mathrm{vlt}(y) = 0$, but even this modification violates conditional probability.

Assume, rather, that x is certain when y occurs: If a change occurs to y, the object x must at least be examined. Thus, you are more interested in the volatility of y. More specifically, you are interested in the volatility of the features of y to which x is coupled. This is definitely *not* conditional probability. It is, however, unconditional probability based on the volatility (likelihood of change plus the exposure) of the object y.

You are actually assessing the volatility of one or more features of y, and modifying that probability by the type of coupling between x and each feature of y. The volatility of the features of y must be subjectively assessed by the designer. These modifiers must be empirically defined. The best that can be done at the moment is to define $\exp(x, y_i)$ by

$$\exp(x, y_i) = \alpha \, \mathrm{vlt}(y_i) \qquad (15.9)$$

where α is the modifying factor for the type of coupling. Assume that all modifying factors will be ≤ 1, since any form of coupling can only reduce the exposure of x to changes in y_i, not increase it. So, for the time being, you can conservatively estimate $\alpha = 1$, and thus use

$$\exp(x, y_i) = \mathrm{vlt}(y_i) \qquad (15.10)$$

for the measure of exposure. Generalizing to the form in equation (15.8), you get

$$\exp(x) = \sum_{k \in A} \sum_{i=1}^{n} \text{vlt}(k_i) \qquad (15.11)$$

where $\text{vlt}(k_i)$ is the volatility for each feature i of each object k to which x is coupled in some way.

This meets the conditions for an Archimedean structure of qualitative probability, since it was built from a set of independent structures, each of which met the conditions.

Combining $\text{loc}(x)$ and $\exp(x)$, you get the measure of volatility:

$$\text{vlt}(x) = \text{loc}(x) + \exp(x) \qquad (15.12)$$

Note that both $\text{loc}(x)$ and $\exp(x)$ are independent of each other and are both probabilities, so adding them in this way is a valid operation. It is possible for $\text{vlt}(x)$ to exceed one, which violates the properties of a probability measure. However, any object for which $\text{vlt}(x)$ exceeds .6 or so, especially if most of that is contributed by $\exp(x)$, should be redesigned.

SUMMARY

A notion of volatility was defined that depends on the likelihood of changes to an object due to changes in the domain and the exposure of an object to changes in objects to which it is coupled. A probability measure was developed in which the underlying probabilities must be subjectively assigned, by either the designer or the customer. As yet, there is no way to objectively assess the probability of a change being required.

The likelihood of change to an object due to a change in the domain was defined as a simple unconditional probability value. The exposure of an object to changes in other objects was defined as the volatility of the specific features of the objects to which our object is coupled, modified by the type of coupling between them. The modifying factor for each type of coupling will have to be empirically determined. However, they are all bounded on the high end by the value of one, so we use, for the moment, a modifier of one, which will increase our calculated exposure above what we expect the actual exposure to be. This gives us a more conservative estimate of volatility, which is good, at least in the short run.

EPILOGUE

Measurement requires knowledge, skill, experience, and understanding. Measurement of software also requires a certain creativity. Rather than provide you with a set of half-baked measures, existing or new, I provide you with the tools to develop technically sound, empirically valid measures from scratch. The section "Scales" in Chapter 5, in particular, provides the necessary theory for extending measurement to structures that haven't even been dreamed of. In short, I have taught you how to fish.

Now, these tools are not reserved for those who develop measures as a career, the metrologists among us. These tools are intended to help you, the designer, with specific measurement techniques to solve specific design problems, the nature of which can't even begin to be predicted. You can now make measures to suit your needs as you need them. There is no need to go looking through the literature, hunting for a measure that just doesn't quite fit your particular problem and has a questionable basis. If you can describe your problem, you can measure. It's that simple.

I have tried to convince you that measurement is not only a useful but also an essential tool in the design of quality software. I provide a framework you can use to build measurement programs, not just for measuring design characteristics. I describe for you my own software development process, through the design activities, to give you ideas about how measurement can fit into the design process and provide the raw technical information to assist you as you learn, really learn, how to measure.

Along the way, I managed to discover a formal technique for analyzing the static and dynamic behavior of a design, something I've wanted since the very first days of my software career. I also discovered (invented requires too much credit on my part) a technique for constructing measures that leads you from initial understanding of a characteristic to validation of a new measure against theoretical requirements. The technique is surprisingly simple and is more tedious than difficult. I used this technique to develop the measures introduced in this book, so it has been tried and tested.

I hope you will begin to see measurement as a tool, an ally, and a friend. I know I have. I have enjoyed working on this book, have learned much in the process, and have become a better developer because of it. I can only hope you get as much benefit out of using this book as I did writing it.

If you have any comments, questions, or complaints about the book, please contact me via e-mail at scottw@advsysres.com. I try to answer my mail quickly. Thank you, and good luck!

REFERENCES

Aczél, J. 1996. *Lectures on Functional Equations and Their Applications*. New York: Academic Press.

Albrecht, A. 1979. Measuring Application Development Productivity. *Proceedings of IBM Application Development Symposium*, GUIDE International and Share, Inc., IBM.

Albrecht, A. 1984. AD/M Productivity Measurement and Estimate Validation. *IBM CIS&A Guideline 313*. IBM.

Alencar, A. J., and J. A. Gognen. 1992. OOZE. In *Object-Orientation in Z*, ed. S. Stepney, R. Barden, and D. Cooper, 79–94. London: Springer-Verlag.

Alper, T. M. 1985. A Note on Real Measurement Structures of Scale Type $(m, m + 1)$. *Journal of Mathematical Psychology*. 29:73–81.

Alper, T. M. 1987. A Classification of all Order-Preserving Homeomorphism Groups of the Reals that Satisfy Finite Uniqueness. *Journal of Mathematical Psychology*. 31:135–154.

Arora, V., K. Kalaichelvan, N. Goel, and R. Mumkoti. 1995. Measuring High-Level Design Complexity of Real-Time Object-Oriented Systems. *Proceedings of the Annual Oregon Workshop on Software Metrics*.

Bailin, S. 1994. Object-Oriented Requirements Analysis. In *Encyclopedia of Software Engineering*, ed. J. Marciniak, 740–756. New York: John Wiley & Sons.

Barr, M., and C. Wells. 1995. *Category Theory for Computing Science*. Englewood Cliffs, NJ: Prentice-Hall.

Bartlett, M. S. 1950. Tests of Significance in Factor Analysis. In *British Journal of Psychology, Statistical Section*, 3:77–85.

Basili, V. R. 1980. Qualitative Software Complexity Models: A Summary. In *Tutorial on Models and Methods for Software Management and Engineering*. Piscataway, NJ: IEEE Computer Society Press.

Basili, V. R., G. Caldiera, and H. D. Rombach. 1994a. Goal Question Metric Paradigm. In *Encyclopedia of Software Engineering*, ed. J. Marciniak, 528–532. New York: John Wiley & Sons.

Basili, V. R., G. Caldiera, and H. D. Rombach, 1994b. Measurement. In *Encyclopedia of Software Engineering*, ed. J. Marciniak, 646–661. New York: John Wiley & Sons.

Basili, V. R., L. C. Briand, and W. L. Melo. 1995. Measuring the Impact of Reuse on Quality and Productivity in Object-Oriented Systems. University of Maryland Dept. of Computer Science Technical Report, CS-TR-3395.

Basili, V. R., L. C. Briand, and W. L. Melo. 1996. A Validation of Object-Oriented Design Metrics. *IEEE Transactions on Software Engineering*, SE-22(10), (October):751–761.

Berard, E. V. 1993. *Essays on Object-Oriented Software Engineering. Vol. 1.* Englewood Cliffs, NJ: Prentice-Hall.

Berard, E. V. 1994. Object-Oriented Design. In *Encyclopedia of Software Engineering*, ed. J. Marciniak, 721–729. New York: John Wiley & Sons.

Beiman, J., and L. Ott. 1994. Measuring Functional Cohesion. *IEEE Transactions on Software Engineering*, SE-20(8). (August):644–657.

Biggs, N. 1985. *Discrete Mathematics*. Oxford: Clarendon Press.

Biggs, N. 1993. *Algebraic Graph Theory, 2E* Cambridge: Cambridge University Press.

Blair, G., J. Gallagher, D. Hutchinson, and D. Sheperd. 1991. *Object-Oriented Languages, Systems, and Applications*. New York: Halsted Press.

Boehm, B. W. 1981. *Software Engineering Economics*. Englewood Cliffs, NJ: Prentice-Hall.

Boehm, B. W., J. R. Brown, and M. Lipkov. 1976. Quantitative Evaluation of Software Quality. *Proceedings of International Conference on Software Engineering*:592–605.

Booch, Grady. 1994. *Object-Oriented Analysis and Design with Applications*. Redwood City, CA: Benjamin/Cummings.

Booch, G., and J. Rumbaugh. 1995. *Unified Method for Object-Oriented Development*. Santa Clara, CA: Rational Software Corporation.

Bowles, A. 1993. A Foundation for Quality: Process, Products, and People. *Object Magazine* 3, no. 1 (June).

Boyd, N. 1993. Building Object-Oriented Frameworks. *The Smalltalk Report* 3, no. 1 (September):1–6, 14–16.

Briand, L., S. Morasca, and V. R. Basili. 1994a. Goal-Driven Definition of Product Metrics Based on Properties. University of Maryland Dept. of Computer Sciences Technical Report, CS-TR-3346.

Briand, L., S. Morasca, and V. R. Basili. 1994b. Defining and Validating High Level Design Metrics. University of Maryland Dept. of Computer Sciences Technical Report, CS-TR-3301.

Briand, L., K. El Emam, and S. Morasca. 1995. On the Application of Measurement Theory in Software Engineering. International Software Engineering Research Network Technical Report #ISERN-95-04.

Briand, L., S. Morasca, and V. R. Basili. 1996. Property Based Software Engineering Measurement. *IEEE Transactions on Software Engineering*, SE-22 1 (January):68–85.

Brien, S., and N. John, eds. 1992. *Z Base Standard, Version 1.0*. Oxford: Oxford University Press.

Brooks, F. 1975. *The Mythical Man Month*. Reading, MA: Addison-Wesley.

Budge, T., and G. Hambrick. 1994. A Tutorial on Transcript and Converging. *IBM 7th OO Conference* (July).

Bunge, M. 1977. *Treatise on Basic Philosophy I: The Furniture of the World*. Dordrecht, Holland: Riedel.

Bunge, M. 1979. *Treatise on Basic Philosophy II: The World of Systems*. Dordrecht, Holland: Riedel.

Campbell, N. R. 1957. *Physics: The Elements*. Cambridge University Press, 1920. Reprinted as *Foundation of Science: The Philosophy of Theory and Experimentation*. New York: Dover Publications, 1957.

Card, D., and R. Glass. 1990. *Measuring Software Design Quality*. Englewood Cliffs, NJ: Prentice-Hall.

Chidamber, S. R., and C. F. Kemerer. 1994. A Metrics Suite for Object-Oriented Design. *IEEE Transactions on Software Engineering*, SE-20 6 (June):476–492.

Chonoles, M. J., and C. C. Gilliam. 1995. Real-Time Object-Oriented System Design Using the Object Modeling Technique (OMT). *Journal of Object-Oriented Programming* 8, no. 3 (June):16–24.

Churcher, N. I., and M. J. Shepperd. 1995a. Comments on A Metrics Suite for Object-Oriented Software. *IEEE Transactions on Software Engineering*, SE-21 3 (March): 263–265.

Churcher, N. I., and M. J. Shepperd. 1995b. Towards a Conceptual Framework for Object-Oriented Software Metrics. *ACM SIGSOFT Software Engineering Notes* 20, no. 2 (April): 69–76.

Carnegie Mellon University/Software Engineering Institute (CMU/SEI). *The Capability Maturity Model: Guidelines for Improving the Software Process*. Reading, MA: Addison-Wesley.

Coad, P., and E. Yourdon. 1991a. *Object-Oriented Analysis, 2nd ed*. Englewood Cliffs, NJ: Yourdon Press/Prentice-Hall.

Coad, P., and E. Yourdon. 1991b. *Object-Oriented Design*. Englewood Cliffs, NJ: Yourdon Press/Prentice-Hall.

Cohen, M. A., and L. Narens. 1979. Fundamental Unit Structures: A Theory of Ratio Scalability. *Journal of Mathematical Psychology* 20:193–232.

Conte, S. D., H. E. Dunsmore, and V. Y. Shen. 1986. *Software Engineering Metrics and Models*. Reading, MA: Benjamin/Cummings.

Curtis, B. 1980a. In Search of Software Complexity. *Proceedings of the IEEE Workshop on Quantitative Software Models for Reliability, Complexity, and Cost*: 95–106.

Curtis, B. 1980b. Measurement and Experimentation in Software Engineering. *Proceedings of the IEEE* 68, no. 9 (September):1144–1147.

Cusack, E., and G. H. B. Rafsanjani. 1992. ZEST, *Object-Orientation in Z*, ed. S. Stepney, R. Barden, and D. Cooper, 113–126. London: Springer-Verlag.

Davis, A. M. 1990. *Software Requirements Analysis and Specification*. Englewood Cliffs, NJ: Prentice-Hall.

DeMarco, T. 1978. *Structured Analysis and System Specification*. Englewood Cliffs, NJ: Yourdon Press.

DeMarco, T. 1982. *Controlling Software Projects*. Englewood Cliffs, NJ: Yourdon Press.

Duke, R., P. King, G. Rose, and G. Smith. 1991. The Object-Z Specification Language Version 1. *Technical Report 91-1*, Software Verification Research Centre, Dept. of Computer Science, University of Queensland, Australia (May).

Durnota, B., and C. Mingins. 1993. Tree-based Coherence Metrics in Object-Oriented Design. In *TOOLS 12 & 9*, ed. C. Mingins, B. Habich, J. Potter, and B. Meyer, 489–504. Englewood Cliffs, NJ: Prentice-Hall.

Dye, D. 1994. Abstraction. In *Encyclopedia of Software Engineering*, ed. J. Marciniak, 1–3. New York: John Wiley & Sons.

Ellis, B. 1966. *Basic Concepts of Measurement*. Cambridge: Cambridge University Press.

Embley, D. W., B. D. Kurtz, and S. N. Woodfield. 1992. *Object-Oriented Systems Analysis: A Model Driven Approach*. Englewood Cliffs, NJ: Yourdon Press/Prentice-Hall.

Fenton, N. 1991. *Software Metrics: A Rigorous Approach*. London: Chapman-Hall.

Fenton, N., and A. A. Kaposi. 1987. Metrics and Software Structure. *Journal of Information and Software Technology* 29 (July):301–320.

Finklestein, L. 1984. A Review of the Fundamental Concepts of Measurement. *Measurement* 2, no. 1:25–34.

Foldes, S. 1994. *Fundamental Structures of Algebra and Discrete Mathematics*. New York: John Wiley & Sons.

Fountain, R., T. Hastings, and M. Schoonveldt. 1994. *Sizing in Object-Oriented Environments*. Australian Software Metrics Association, Release 1 (October).

Gamma, E., R. Helm, R. Johnson, and J. Vlissides. 1995. *Design Patterns: Elements of Reusable Object-Oriented Software*. Reading, MA: Addison-Wesley.

Gause, D., and G. Weinberg. 1989. *Exploring Requirements: Quality BEFORE Design*. New York: Dorset House.

Gödel, K. 1940. The Consistency of the Continuum Hypothesis. *Studies, Annals of Mathematics*. Princeton, NJ: Princeton University.

Grady, R. 1992. *Practical Software Metrics for Project Management and Process Improvement*. Englewood Cliffs, NJ: Prentice-Hall.

Grady, R., and D. Caswell. 1987. *Software Metrics: Establishing a Companywide Program*. Englewood Cliffs, NJ: Prentice-Hall.

Graham, I. 1996. Making Progress in Metrics. *Object Magazine* 6, no. 8 (October).

Gray, C. 1981. *Essentials of Project Management*. Princeton, NJ: Petrocelli Books.

Gries, D. 1981. *The Science of Programming*. New York: Springer-Verlag.

Grogono, P., and M. Gargul. 1994. A Graph Model for Object-Oriented Programming. *ACM SIGPLAN Notices* 29, no. 7 (July).

Halsted, M. 1977. *Elements of Software Science*. Holland: Elsevier North-Holland.

Harrison, W., K. Magel, R. Kluczny, and A. DeKock. 1982. Applying Software Complexity Metrics to Program Maintenance. *Computer* 15, no. 9:65–79.

Henderson-Sellers, B. 1996. *Object-Oriented Metrics: Measures of Complexity*. Englewood Cliffs, NJ: Prentice-Hall.

Henderson-Sellers, B., and J. Edwards. 1994. *The Working Object*. Englewood Cliffs, NJ: Prentice-Hall.

Heyliger, G. 1994. Coupling. In *Encyclopedia of Software Engineering*. ed. J. Marciniak, 220–228. New York: John Wiley & Sons.

Hölder, O. 1901. Die Axiome der Quantität und die Lehre vom Mass. *Ber. Verh. Kgl. Sächsis. Ges. Wiss. Leipzig, Math.-Phys., Classe* 53:1–64.

Humphrey, W. 1990. *Managing the Software Process*. Reading, MA: Addison-Wesley.

Institute of Electrical and Electronic Engineers. 1990. Standard Glossary of Software Engineering Terminology. IEEE Std 610.12.

International Function Point Users Group. 1994. *Function Point Counting Practices Manual*, Release 4.0.

Jackson, M. 1975. *Principles of Program Design*. London: Academic Press.

Jacobson, I., M. Christerson, P. Jonsson, and G. Övergaard. 1992. *Object-Oriented Software Engineering: A Use-Case Approach*. Reading, MA: Addison-Wesley.

Jacobson, N., 1980. *Basic Algebra II*. New York: W. H. Freeman.

John, R., Z. Chen, and P. Oman. 1995. Static Techniques for Measuring Code Reusability. *Proceedings of the Annual Oregon Workshop on Software Metrics*.

Jones, T. C. 1988. *A Short History of Function Points and Feature Points*, Cambridge, Mass.: Software Productivity Research, Inc.

Khoshgoftaar, T., and D. Lanning. 1995. Improving Development Process Feedback by Considering Software Product Similarity. *Proceedings of the Annual Oregon Workshop on Software Metrics*.

Kitchenhann, B., S. L. Pfleeger, and N. Fenton. 1995. Towards a Framework for Software Measurement Validation. *IEEE Transactions on Software Engineering*, SE-21(12) (December).

Kolewe, R. 1993. Metrics in Object-Oriented Design and Programming. *Software Development* (October).

Kolmogorov, A. N. 1956. *Grundbergriffe der Wahrscheinlichkeitsrechnung*. Springer, 1933. Trans. N. Morrison (*Foundations of the Theory of Probability*). Chelsea.

Koqure, and Y. Akao. 1993. Quality Function Deployment and CWQC in Japan. *Quality Progress* (October).

Krantz, D. H., R. D. Luce, P. Suppes, and A. Tversky. 1971. *Foundations of Measurement; Volume I: Additive and Polynomial Representations*. New York: Academic Press.

Krantz, D. H., R. D. Luce, P. Suppes, and A. Tversky. 1989. *Foundations of Measurement; Volume II: Geometrical, Threshold, and Probabilistic Representations*. New York: Academic Press.

Krantz, D. H., R. D. Luce, P. Suppes, and A. Tversky. 1990. *Foundations of Measurement; Volume III: Representation, Axiomatization, and Invariance*. New York: Academic Press.

Kriz, J. 1988. *Facts and Artifacts in Social Science: An Epistemiological and Methodological Analysis of Empirical Social Science Research Techniques*. New York: McGraw-Hill Research.

Krzanowski, W. H., and F. H. C. Marriott. 1994. *Multivariate Analysis, Part I: Distributions, Ordination, and Inference*. Part of *Kendall's Library of Statistics*. New York: Halsted Press.

Kyburg, H. E. 1984. *Theory and Measurement*. Cambridge: Cambridge University Press.

Lakos, J. 1992. Designing-In Quality for Large Scale C++ Projects. *Proceedings of Pacific Northwest Software Quality Conference*: 275–294.

Lakshmanan, K. B., S. Jayaprakash, and P. K. Sinha. 1991. Properties of Control Flow Complexity Measures. *IEEE Transactions on Software Engineering* 17, no. 12 (December): 1289–1295.

Lang, S. 1971. *Algebra*. Reading, MA: Addison-Wesley.

Li, W., and S. Henry. 1993. Object-Oriented Metrics that Predict Maintainability. *Journal of Systems and Software* 23:111–122.

Lieberherr, K. J., I. Holland, and A. Riel. 1988. Object-Oriented Programming: An Objective Sense of Style. *Proceedings of ACM Conference on Object-Oriented Programming, Systems, Languages, and Applications (OOPSLA)*: 323–334.

Liskov, B. 1987. Data Abstraction and Hierarchy. *Addendum to Proceedings of OOPSLA*.

Liskov, B., and J. Wing. 1993. Family Values: A Behavioral Notion of Stereotyping. CMU-CS-93-187 (July). Pittsburgh, PA: Carnegie Mellon University.

Littlewood, B. 1988. Forecasting Software Reliability. *Software Reliability, Modeling and Identification*. In Lecture Notes in Computer Science 341. ed. S. Bittanti, 141–209. London: Springer-Verlag.

Lorenz, M., and J. Kidd. 1994. *Object-Oriented Software Metrics*. Englewood Cliffs, NJ: Prentice-Hall.

Luce, R. D. 1986. Uniqueness and Homogeneity of Ordered Relational Structures. *Journal of Mathematical Psychology* 30:391–415.

Luce, R. D. 1987. Measurement Structures with Archimedean Ordered Translation Groups. *Order* 4:165–189.

Luce, R. D., and L. Narens. 1983. Symmetry, Scale Types, and Generalizations of Classical Physical Measurement. *Journal of Mathematical Psychology* 27:44–85.

Luce, R. D., and L. Narens. 1985. Classification of Concatenation Structures by Scale Type. *Journal of Mathematical Psychology* 29:1–72.

Mac Lane, S. 1971. *Categories for the Working Mathematician*. (Corrected 1994.) New York: Springer-Verlag.

Macro, A., and J. Buxton. 1987. *The Craft of Software Engineering*. Reading, MA: Addison-Wesley.

McCabe, T. J. 1976. A Complexity Measure. *IEEE Transactions on Software Engineering*. SE-2(4), (April):308–320.

McKim, J. C., and D. A. Mondon. 1993. Class Interface Design: Designing for Correctness. *Journal of Systems and Software* 23:85–94.

McMenamin, S. M., and J. F. Palmer. 1992. *Essential Systems Analysis*. Englewood Cliffs, NJ: Yourdon Press.

Martin, R. 1994. Object-Oriented Design Quality Metrics: An Analysis of Dependencies. Unpublished white paper (August).

Mellichamp, D. A. 1983. *Real-Time Computing with Applications to Data Acquisition and Control*. New York: Van Nostrand Reinhold.

Mens, T., K. Mens, and P. Steyaert. 1994a. OPUS: A Formal Approach to Object-Orientation. Dept. of Mathematics and Computer Sciences, Brussels Free University. Tech. Report vub-tinf-tr-94-02.

Mens, T., K. Mens, and P. Steyaert. 1994b. OPUS: A Calculus for Modeling Object-Oriented Concepts. Dept. of Computer Sciences, Brussels Free University. Tech. Report vub-tinf-tr-94-04.

Moreau, D. R., and W. D. Dominick. 1989. Object-Oriented Graphical Information Systems: Research Plan and Evaluation Metrics. *Journal of Systems and Software*: 23–28.

Morris, K. 1988. *Metrics for Object-Oriented Software Development*. MIT Sloan School Masters Thesis.

Mostow, J. 1985. Toward Better Models of the Design Process. *AI Magazine* 6, no. 1 (Spring).

Munson, J., and G. Hall. 1995. Software Measurement Based Statistical Testing. *Proceedings of the Annual Oregon Workshop on Software Metrics*.

Myers, G. 1976. *Software Reliability—Principles and Practices*. New York: John Wiley & Sons.

Myers, R. H. 1990. *Classical and Modern Regression with Applications*. Duxbury Press.

Narens, L. 1981a. A General Theory of Ratio Scalability with Remarks about the Measurement-Theoretic Concept of Meaningfulness. *Theory and Decision* 13:1–70.

Narens, L. 1981b. On the Scales of Measurement. *Journal of Mathematical Psychology* 24:249–275.

Narens, L. 1985. *Abstract Measurement Theory*. Cambridge, MA: MIT Press.

Nielsen, K., and K. Shumate. 1988. *Designing Large Real-Time Systems with Ada*. New York: McGraw-Hill.

Opdyke, W., and R. Johnson. 1993. Creating Abstract Superclasses by Refactoring. *Proceedings of the 21st Annual Computer Science Conference (ACM CSC)*: 66–73.

Ott, L., J. Bieman, B. K. Kang, and B. Mehra. 1995. Developing Measures of Class Cohesion for Object-Oriented Software. *Proceedings of the Annual Oregon Workshop on Software Metrics*.

Page-Jones, M. 1980. *The Practical Guide to Structured Systems Design*. Englewood Cliffs, NJ: Yourdon Press/Prentice-Hall.

Page-Jones, M., and S. Wiess. 1992. Object-Oriented Analysis and Design: The Synthesis Model. *Proceedings of Software Development Conference*.

Perlis, A., F. Sayward, and M. Shaw. 1981. *Software Metrics: An Analysis and Evaluation*. Cambridge, MA: MIT Press.

Petroski, H. 1985. *To Engineer Is Human*. New York: St. Martin's Press.

Pfleeger, S. L., and J. D. Palmer. 1990. Software Estimation for Object-Oriented Software. *Proceedings of IFPUG Fall Conference*, 181–196.

Pierce, B. 1991. *Basic Category Theory for Computer Scientists*. Cambridge, MA: MIT Press.

Reynolds, R., and E. Zannoni. 1994. Metrics. In *Encyclopedia of Software Engineering*, ed. J. Marciniak, 676–685. New York: John Wiley & Sons.

Roberts, F. 1979. Measurement Theory with Applications to Decision Making, Utility, and the Social Sciences. In *Encyclopedia of Mathematics and its Applications*. Reading, MA: Addison-Wesley.

Roberts, T. 1992. Workshop on Metrics for Object-Oriented Software Development. OOPSLA Report (unpublished).

Rose, G. 1992. Object-Z. In *Object-Orientation in Z*, ed. S. Stepney, R. Barden, and D. Cooper, 59–77. London: Springer-Verlag.

Roskies, R. 1965. A Measurement Axiomatization for an Essentially Multiplicative Representation of Two Factors. *Journal of Mathematical Psychology* 2:266–276.

Rumbaugh, J., M. Blaha, W. Premerlani, F. Eddy, and E. Lorensen. 1991. *Object-Oriented Modeling and Design*. Englewood Cliffs, NJ: Prentice-Hall.

Savage, L. J. 1954. *The Foundations of Statistics*. New York: John Wiley & Sons.

Scheffé, H. 1959. *The Analysis of Variance*. New York: John Wiley & Sons.

Schneidewind, N. 1994. Methodology for Validating Software Metrics. In *Encyclopedia of Software Engineering*, ed. J. Marciniak, 666–676. New York: John Wiley & Sons.

Scott, W. R. 1987. *Group Theory*. New York: Dover Publications.

Scott, D., and P. Suppes. 1958. Foundational Aspects of Theories of Measurement. *Journal of Symbolic Logic* 23:113–128.

Sharble, R. C., and S. S. Cohen. 1993. The Object-Oriented Brewery: A Comparison of Two Object-Oriented Development Methods. *ACM SIGSOFT Software Engineering Notes* 18, no. 2 (April):60–73.

Shaw, M. 1995. Comparing Architectural Design Styles. *IEEE Software* 12, no. 6 (November).

Sheetz, S. D., et al. 1992. Measuring Object-Oriented System Complexity. *University of Colorado Working Paper*.

Shlaer, S., and S. Mellor. 1988. *Object-Oriented Systems Analysis: Modeling the World in Data*. Englewood Cliffs, NJ: Yourdon Press/Prentice-Hall.

Shlaer, S., and S. Mellor. 1992. *Object Lifecycles: Modeling the World in States*. Englewood Cliffs, NJ: Yourdon Press/Prentice-Hall.

Siegel, S., and N. J. Castellan. 1988. *Nonparametric Statistics for the Behavioral Sciences, 2E*. New York: McGraw-Hill.

Simon, H. A., and A. Ando. 1961. Aggregation of Variables in Dynamic Structures. *Econometrics* 29 (April):111–138.

Sommerville, I. 1989. *Software Engineering, 3E*. Reading, MA: Addison-Wesley.

Spivey, J. M. 1992. *The Z Notation Reference Manual, 2E*. Englewood Cliffs, NJ: Prentice-Hall.

Sprent, P. 1993. *Applied Nonparametric Statistical Methods, 2E*. London: Chapman and Hall.

Stepney, S., R. Barden, and R. Cooper, eds. 1992. *Object-Orientation in Z*. London: Springer-Verlag.

Stevens, S. S. 1946. On the Theory of Scales of Measurement. *Science* 103:677–680.

Stevens, S. S. 1951. Mathematics, Measurement, and Psychophysics. In *Handbook of Experimental Psychology*, ed. S. S. Stevens, 1–49. New York: John Wilcy & Sons.

Stevens, W., G. Myers, and L. Constantine. 1974. Structural Designs. *IBM Systems Journal* 13, no. 2:115–139.

Szabo, R. and T. Khoshgoftaar. 1995. Modeling Software Quality in an Object-Oriented Software System. *Proceedings of the Annual Oregon Workshop on Software Metrics*.

Thramponlidis, K., and K. Agavankis. 1995. Object Interaction Diagram: A New Technique in Object-Oriented Analysis and Design. *Journal of Object-Oriented Programming* 8, no. 3 (June):25–32, 39.

Tian, J., and M. V. Zelkowitz. 1992. A Formal Program Complexity Model and its Application. Journal of Systems and Software 17:253–266.

Tuijn, C., and M. Gyssens. 1996. CGOOD, A Categorical Graph-Oriented Object Data Model. *Theoretical Computer Science* 160:217–239.

Tversky, A. 1977. Features of Similarity. *Psychological Review* 84:327–352.

Ullman, J. D. 1988. *Principles of Database and Knowledge-Base Systems*, Vol. I. Rockville, MD: Computer Science Press.

Van der Linden, F. 1994. Formal Methods: From Object-Based to Object-Oriented. *ACM SIGPLAN Notices* 29, no. 7 (July).

Wand, Y. A. 1989. A Proposal for a Formal Model of Objects. In *Object-Oriented Concepts, Databases and Applications*, ed. W. Kim and F. H. Lochovsky. Reading, MA: ACM Press/Addison-Wesley.

Wegner, P. 1989. Capital Intensive Software Technology. *Software Reusability*, Vol. 1: *Concepts and Models*. ACM Press.

Weyuker, E. 1988. Evaluating Software Complexity Measures. *IEEE Transactions on Software Engineering*, SE-14(9) (September):1357–1365.

Whitmire, S. A. 1992a. 3D Function Points: Scientific and Real-Time Extensions to Function Points. *Boeing Technical Report BCS-G3252*, The Boeing Company. Published in *Proceedngs of Pacific Northwest Software Quality Conference*.

Whitmire, S. A. 1992b. Measuring Complexity in Object-Oriented Software. *Proceedings of Applications of Software Measurement Conference*.

Whitmire, S. A. 1993. Applying Function Points to Object-Oriented Software. In *Software Engineering Productivity Handbook*, ed. J. Keyes. New York: McGraw-Hill.

Whitmire, S. A. 1994. Object-Oriented Measurement of Software. In *Encyclopedia of Software Engineering*, ed. J. Marciniak, 737–739. New York: John Wiley & Sons.

Whitmire, S. A. 1995. An Introduction to 3D Function Points. *Software Development* 3, no. 4 (April).

Whitmire, S. A. 1996. A Theory of Objects. *Proceedings of Object-Oriented Product Metrics Workshop*, OOPSLA.

Whysall, P. J. 1992. Z Expression of Refinable Objects. In *Object-Orientation in Z*, ed. S. Stepney, R. Barden, and D. Cooper, 29–35. London: Springer-Verlag.

Wienberg, G. M., and E. L. Shulman. 1974. Goals and Performance in Computer Programming. *Human Factors* 16, no. 1 (February):70–77.

Wild, F. III. 1991. Managing Class Coupling: Applying the Principles of Structured Design to Object-Oriented Programming. *UNIX Review* 9, no. 10 (October):44–47.

Wirfs-Brock, R., and B. Wilkerson. 1989. Variables Limit Reusability. *Journal of Object-Oriented Programming* 2, no. 1 (May/June):34–42.

Wirfs-Brock, R., B. Wilkerson, and L. Wiener. 1990. *Designing Object-Oriented Software*. Englewood Cliffs, NJ: Prentice-Hall.

Woodcock, J., and M. Loomes. 1989. *Software Engineering Mathematics*. Reading, MA: Addison-Wesley.

Yourdon, E., and L. L. Constantine. 1979. *Structured Design*. Englewood Cliffs, NJ: Prentice-Hall.

Yuan, G. 1995. A Depth-First Process Model for Object-Oriented Development with Improved OOA/OOD Notations. *Report on Object-Oriented Analysis and Design* 2, no. 1 (May/June):23–37.

Zachman, J. A. 1987. A Framework for Information Systems Architecture. *IBM Systems Journal* 26, no. 3.

Zuse, H. 1991. *Software Complexity: Measures and Methods*. Berlin: De-Gruyter.

Zuse, H. 1994. Complexity Metrics/Analysis. In *Encyclopedia of Software Engineering*, ed. J. Marciniak, 131–165. New York: John Wiley & Sons.

Zuse, H., and T. Fetcke. 1995. Properties of Object-Oriented Software Measures. *Proceedings of the Annual Oregon Workshop on Software Metrics*.

INDEX

AUTHOR INDEX